INTRODUCTION
TO THE BIBLE

INTRODUCTION TO THE BIBLE

by
JOHN H. HAYES

THE WESTMINSTER PRESS
Philadelphia

Scripture quotations from the Revised Standard Version of the Bible are copyright, 1946 and 1952, by the Division of Christian Education of the National Council of Churches, and are used by permission.

ISBN 0-664-20885-1 (cloth)
ISBN 0-664-24883-7 (paper)

LIBRARY OF CONGRESS CATALOG CARD No. 76-105395

Book Design by Dorothy Alden Smith

Third printing, 1976
Published by The Westminster Press ®
Philadelphia, Pennsylvania

PRINTED IN THE UNITED STATES OF AMERICA

To Heather Ruth

and John Alexander

CONTENTS

PART ONE

A GENERAL INTRODUCTION
TO THE STUDY OF THE BIBLE

PART TWO

THE LIFE AND LITERATURE OF ANCIENT ISRAEL

PART THREE

THE LIFE AND LITERATURE OF POSTEXILIC JUDAISM

PART FOUR

THE LIFE AND LITERATURE OF EARLY CHRISTIANITY

LIST OF CHARTS
AND ILLUSTRATIONS

CHARTS

ILLUSTRATIONS

FOREWORD

This work has arisen out of the need for a substantial volume that would introduce the reader to both the Biblical literature and the life and faith of ancient Israel, early Judaism, and early Christianity. The book is therefore primarily an introduction to the Bible, although it discusses historical and theological as well as literary concerns. Non-Biblical texts and documents have been used where they have a direct or significant relationship to the Biblical writings or to the communities that produced them.

An introduction to the Bible must be more than a discussion of the contents of the Bible. It cannot be simply a summary of the present status of Biblical studies. It must, in a way, be both of these. An introduction must be a discussion of the Biblical materials in the light of the present status of literary, historical, theological, and archaeological research on the Bible and its environment.

A historical-chronological framework has been used throughout the book. Such a scheme seems to present fewer problems than alternate possibilities that make use of thematic approaches or discuss the traditions in the order of the Biblical books. Such a historical framework presupposes the general results of a critical literary-historical approach to Biblical studies.

Any work of this kind which attempts to encompass the whole of the Old and New Testaments must necessarily be selective or rather superficial; otherwise the book could easily become unwieldy. Not every Biblical writing is discussed in the present volume. The choice was made to discuss the most significant writings in depth rather than try to cover all the material. The standard Biblical introductions generally provide an inclusive treatment of every book in the Bible and can be used if desired to supplement the present approach.

The text of the Revised Standard Version has been used throughout, with one modification. This translation, following ancient Jewish practice, uses "the LORD" in place of the personal name of the Hebrew deity, generally assumed to have been "Yahweh." The personal name of the deity has been reintroduced where it appears in the Hebrew text.

Bibliographical references have been limited to works available in English or in English translation. References in the text to maps refer to the Westminster Historical Maps of Bible Lands, which are included at the back of this volume.

I am indebted to my colleagues in the department of religion at Trinity Uni-

versity who have used some of this material in an earlier form in classroom instruction and offered many valuable comments. A special thanks in this regard
is due to William O. Walker, Jr., who prepared the New Testament portion of
a syllabus that has been used at Trinity in a one-semester course on the Bible
and that has been a great help in the preparation of Part Four of the present
volume. A grant from the Faculty Research and Development Council at
Trinity has provided assistance in the completion of the manuscript.

My wife, Sarah, has worked on the manuscript at all stages of its production.
I am greatly indebted to her for aid in the correction of style and grammatical
form. A special word of thanks is due to my student assistant, Karen Keilers,
who, with her usual skill and competence, has transformed the manuscript
from its original "hieroglyphic" state to a finished product.

J. H. H.

Trinity University

PART ONE

A GENERAL INTRODUCTION
TO THE STUDY OF THE BIBLE

1 | AN APPROACH
TO THE STUDY OF THE BIBLE

The influence of the Bible permeates almost every aspect of life in the twentieth-century Western world—laws, literature, art, music, architecture, morals, and of course religion. Many of the Bible's words and phrases are a part of our current speech, and allusions to its stories are widely understood. It is a vital part of our total cultural heritage; indeed, many people would claim that it is, for a variety of reasons, the most important and influential collection of writings ever brought together and bound in a single volume. The Bible is a perennial best seller and has been translated into more than a thousand different languages and dialects.

THE TERM "BIBLE"

The word "Bible," derived from the Greek *biblia,* which means simply "books," refers in a general sense to a collection of writings regarded as possessing special religious sanctity and authority. It is important to note, however, that the term is not always applied to exactly the same collection of writings. When Jews speak of the "Bible," they mean only those ancient Hebrew and Aramaic writings which Christians refer to as the "Old Testament." A distinctively Jewish term for these writings, which are arranged in such a way as to form twenty-four books, is "Tanak," a word formed from the first letters of the names of the three divisions of the Hebrew Bible: *torah* ("law" or "instruction"), *neviim* ("prophets"), and *kethuvim* ("writings"). Christians, on the other hand, use the term "Bible" to refer to a much more extensive collection. They include not only the twenty-four books of the Hebrew Bible, which they arrange so as to form thirty-nine books and call the "Old Testament," but also twenty-seven early Christian writings known as the "New Testament." The word "testament" means "covenant" or "agreement" and refers to the Biblical concept of an "agreement" between God and man. Moreover, many Christians —Roman Catholics, Eastern Orthodox Catholics, and some Protestants—include in the Old Testament an additional six or seven books as well as certain supplements to the books of Esther and Daniel and refer to these materials as "deuterocanonical" (meaning that these were accepted as authoritative later than the other books, after the matter had been debated by the early church

3

fathers and churches). Most Protestants relegate these "deuterocanonical" materials to what is commonly known as the "Apocrypha." This latter term refers to books that are not a part of the Hebrew Bible and whose authority is rejected by many Christians.

Thus, the word "Bible" can refer to the twenty-four books of the Jewish Scriptures, the sixty-six books accepted by Protestants, or the seventy-two or seventy-

Chart 1: THE BOOKS OF THE OLD TESTAMENT

JEWISH BIBLE (TANAK)	ROMAN CATHOLIC AND EASTERN ORTHODOX OLD TESTAMENT	PROTESTANT OLD TESTAMENT
Torah (Law)	Pentateuch	Pentateuch
* Bereshith (Genesis)	Genesis	Genesis
Shemoth (Exodus)	Exodus	Exodus
Wayiqra (Leviticus)	Leviticus	Leviticus
Bemidbar (Numbers)	Numbers	Numbers
Debarim (Deuteronomy)	Deuteronomy	Deuteronomy
Neviim (Prophets)		
Former Prophets	Historical Books	Historical Books
Yehoshua (Joshua)	Josue (Joshua)	Joshua
Shofetim (Judges)	Judges	Judges
**	Ruth	Ruth
Shemuel (I–II Samuel)	I and II Kings (I and II Samuel)	I and II Samuel
Melakim (I–II Kings)	III and IV Kings (I and II Kings)	I and II Kings
**	I and II Paralipomenon (I and II Chronicles)	I and II Chronicles
**	I and II Esdras (Ezra and Nehemiah)	Ezra and Nehemiah
	*** Tobias (Tobit)	
	*** Judith	
**	Esther (with additions)	Esther
	Poetry and Wisdom	Poetry and Wisdom
**	Job	Job
**	Psalms	Psalms
**	Proverbs	Proverbs
**	Ecclesiastes	Ecclesiastes
**	Canticle of Canticles (Song of Solomon)	Song of Solomon
	*** Wisdom of Solomon	
	*** Ecclesiasticus (Wisdom of Jesus the Son of Sirach)	

Latter Prophets	Prophetical Writings	Prophetical Writings
Yeshayahu (Isaiah)	Isaias (Isaiah)	Isaiah
Yirmeyahu (Jeremiah)	Jeremias (Jeremiah)	Jeremiah
**	Lamentations	Lamentations
	**** Baruch (including the Epistle of Jeremias)	
Yehezqel (Ezekiel)	Ezechiel (Ezekiel)	Ezekiel
**	Daniel (with Supplements: Prayer of Azariah and Song of the Three Young Men; Susanna; Bel and the Dragon)	Daniel
Tere Asar (Book of the Twelve)	Osee (Hosea)	Hosea
	Joel	Joel
	Amos	Amos
	Abdias (Obadiah)	Obadiah
	Jonas (Jonah)	Jonah
	Micheas (Micah)	Micah
	Nahum	Nahum
	Habucuc (Habakkuk)	Habakkuk
	Sophonias (Zephaniah)	Zephaniah
	Aggeus (Haggai)	Haggai
	Zacharias (Zechariah)	Zechariah
	Malachias (Malachi)	Malachi

Historical Books

*** I and II Maccabees

Kethuvim (Writings)

Tehillim (Psalms)
Iyyob (Job)
Mishle (Proverbs)
Ruth
Shir Hashirim (Song of Solomon)
Qoheleth (Ecclesiastes)
Ekah (Lamentations)
Ester (Esther)
Daniel
Ezra-Nehemyah (Ezra-Nehemiah)
Libre Hayamim (I–II Chronicles)

* In the Jewish Bible, the opening word or a key word is often used as the title of a book.
** The Jewish Bible has these books later in the Kethuvim.
*** These books are found only in the Roman Catholic and Eastern Orthodox Bibles. They are labeled "deuterocanonical books" by Catholic scholars and are relegated to the Apocrypha by Protestants. They are not in the Jewish Bible.
**** This book is not in the Jewish or Eastern Orthodox Bibles and is relegated to the Apocrypha by Protestants. Catholics include it among the deuterocanonical books.

three books accepted by the Roman Catholic and Orthodox Churches. Since some decision regarding terminology is necessary for the sake of clarity, the Protestant designations will be employed in this volume. Some of the books and content of the Apocrypha will be discussed and no significant distinction in principle will be made between "canonical" and "apocryphal" writings. Both will be used as sources for understanding the life of ancient Israel and postexilic Judaism. In addition, the Christian practice of referring to the ancient Hebrew and Aramaic writings in the Bible as the "Old Testament" and the early Christian documents as the "New Testament" will be followed.

Differences in content and arrangement between the Jewish Bible, the Roman Catholic and Eastern Orthodox Old Testament, and the Protestant Old Testament can be seen in the lists in Chart 1.

THE SIGNIFICANCE OF THE BIBLE

The Bible is a diverse and complex collection of writings that were composed many centuries ago by persons whose problems and interests were often much different from our own. It is extremely difficult to understand in places and occasionally quite tedious to read. What, then, is so important about the Bible? Why should twentieth-century man bother to study it? These are surely legitimate questions, particularly at a time when the explosion of knowledge forces people to neglect many areas of intellectual inquiry that were once considered absolutely essential to an adequate education. It is our conviction, however, that the Bible is a tremendously important collection of writings even today and that no citizen of the Western world can claim to be even moderately well educated without some familiarity with its contents and history.

First of all, the Bible possesses a profound religious importance. The first part of the Bible (known as the Old Testament by Christians and the Tanak by Jews) has for many centuries been regarded as sacred Scripture by Judaism. That is to say, devout Jews have looked to these writings for authority in matters of faith, worship, and conduct and have found them a primary source of inspiration and comfort for daily life. Christians have regarded the entire Bible as the "Word of God" in much the same way. Furthermore, Islam, though it has its own holy book, known as the "Koran," has been influenced by the Old Testament and to some extent by the New. Thus, the Bible is significant from a religious point of view because of its role in the history and life of the three great monotheistic religions of the modern world. Moreover, the religious background of most twentieth-century Westerners lies directly or indirectly in either Christianity or Judaism, and so, quite apart from one's personal attitude toward religion, a knowledge of the Bible is necessary for an understanding and appreciation of our own religious heritage.

The Bible is also important because of its cultural influence. It contains some of the world's great literature and thus constitutes an important part of the Western literary tradition. In addition, the pervasive influence and extensive use of Biblical themes and imagery can be seen in the writings of many of the major literary figures of the Western world.[1] The Bible has inspired much of the painting, sculpture, architecture, and music of Western civilization, and many of our legal and social traditions are heavily dependent upon Biblical ideas and practices.[2] The Bible is a significant part of our total cultural heritage, and no one can understand or appreciate that heritage without some knowledge of the Biblical writings.

Furthermore, the Bible is an important collection of source materials for the historian, for without it his knowledge of ancient Near Eastern history is seriously limited, and he can say virtually nothing about the life and history of ancient Israel and the early Christian movement. The Biblical writers were not primarily historians; they were essentially theologians and "evangelists," but their conviction that God makes known his purpose and will through the actual events of human history guaranteed that the Biblical documents would preserve valuable historical material. Thus, if we are to understand not only the history of the ancient Near East in general but also the origins and early development of Judaism and Christianity, we are dependent upon a knowledge of the contents of the Bible.

Finally, one can speak of the "existential" significance of the Bible. The Bible is not one book, but many, and it reflects many different and sometimes conflicting ideas and viewpoints, but over and over again it raises many of the crucial questions of human existence and suggests solutions to many of the problems that confront men everywhere and at all times. Who is man? What are his origins? Why is he here? What is his destiny? Does *my* personal existence really matter in the total scheme of things? Such questions can often be focused and clarified through a study of the Biblical writings. No modern Westerner will find all the Biblical answers satisfying or meaningful, but it is quite possible that he will come to a fuller understanding of himself and his world as he attempts to understand and appreciate the thoughts of the ancient "prophets and apostles."

Because of its religious importance, cultural influence, historical value, and existential significance, a study of the Bible can be extremely meaningful and helpful to modern man as he attempts to grapple with the problems of his own life in the world.

DIFFICULTIES IN THE STUDY OF THE BIBLE

Many obstacles confront the student of the Bible, and it is well to recognize some of these at the very outset. First of all, there is the sheer bulk and diversity

---

[1] Numerous examples could be cited of writers who have employed Biblical themes and imagery in their works. John Milton's *Paradise Lost* is a classic treatment of the problem of evil in the world in terms of the Biblical story of the fall of man; in the twentieth century, Archibald MacLeish has written a play entitled *J.B.* (Houghton Mifflin Company, Sentry Editions, 1961), which is based upon the Biblical book of Job.

[2] For discussions of the cultural influence of the Bible in the Western world, see, for example: Edwyn R. Bevan and Charles Singer, eds., *The Legacy of Israel* (Oxford: Clarendon Press, 1927); and Ernst von Dobschütz, *The Influence of the Bible on Civilization* (Charles Scribner's Sons, 1914).

of the Biblical materials. Most editions of the Bible contain more than one thousand pages of tightly packed print. The Bible reflects the faith and life of two distinct communities—ancient Israel and primitive Christianity—and for this reason is divided into two major collections of documents. These various documents were produced by numerous authors, spanning a period of more than a thousand years, in at least three different languages (Hebrew, Aramaic, and Greek). They represent a variety of literary forms—legend, history, fiction, law codes, poetry, sermons, letters, and the like. And they exhibit a bewildering diversity, and often conflict, of perspectives, viewpoints, and ideas. To read the Bible is in many ways like studying a large selection of representative British and American literature since *Beowulf*, assuming that the student's native language is not English and he must read these works in translation.

Then, too, the historical and geographical remoteness of the Biblical world makes for great difficulty in the study of the Bible, particularly since many of the Biblical writings place so much emphasis on persons, places, and events. The time span encompassed by the Biblical materials is separated from the present by from two to three millennia, and the events of the Biblical narrative, the participants in those events, and the composition of the Biblical documents are set within the context of cultures far removed in space and time from the twentieth-century Western world. In order to understand the Bible, we must somehow put ourselves back into historical periods and geographical regions that are strange and unfamiliar to most of us.

Closely related to the historical and geographical remoteness of the Biblical world is the fact that the thought world of the Bible is in many respects quite foreign to contemporary Western man. The Biblical view of the origin and structure of the universe, for example, differs radically from modern scientific views, and many Biblical presuppositions and concepts are unfamiliar and even unacceptable to modern minds. Not only the Biblical languages (Hebrew, Aramaic, and Greek) but also much of the Biblical terminology and many of the Biblical concepts require extensive translation and interpretation if they are to be comprehensible today. For many people, the thought world of the Bible is indeed a "strange new world."

Finally, most of us have certain preconceived ideas about the Bible which can make a realistic and objective study of it exceedingly difficult. These include presuppositions about the nature and origin of the Bible, about its contents, and about the correct method of interpreting it. Somehow, these preconceived ideas about the Bible, whether sympathetic or hostile, must be recognized and surmounted if we are truly to understand what the Biblical writers were attempting to say in their own day.

VARIOUS VIEWS ON THE NATURE OF THE BIBLE

There are many different viewpoints about just what the Bible is and thus many different approaches to the study of the Bible. Within the Jewish and Christian communities, the Bible has traditionally been regarded as a depository of divine revelation. Some have insisted that it is the infallible Word of God as dictated to human writers, while others have understood it as the final and authoritative basis for man's knowledge of God and his will, without insisting upon its verbal dictation and absolute inerrancy.[3] In either case, Jews and Christians have for centuries looked to some or all of the writings of the Bible as God's revelation to man.

During the nineteenth and early twentieth centuries, as scholars increasingly recognized differences of viewpoint and belief within the Bible, it became customary in many circles to apply an evolutionary philosophy of history to Biblical study and to view the Bible as the reflection both of God's progressive self-revelation and of man's ever increasing understanding of that revelation. This approach assumes that the unique and enduring content of the Biblical writings is to be found in their developing ideas about God, man, good and evil, and the like, and that the central themes and concepts of the Bible, if understood in this evolutionary perspective, can be made meaningful and productive in the life of modern man.[4]

More recently, a renewed interest in "Biblical theology" has led many to view the Bible as the human record and interpretation of God's activity in history and of man's response to that activity. Basic to this view is the conviction that God has revealed his purpose and will primarily through the series of crucial historical events which comprise the Biblical narrative and that these events demand an appropriate response of faith and obedience. This understanding of the nature of the Bible seems to be close in many ways to the view of some of the Biblical writers themselves.[5]

It is also possible, of course, to view the Bible strictly in terms of its historical and sociological significance. It is a human representation of the origins and early life of two ancient communities: Israel and the early Christian church. This approach assumes that these two communities came into being and developed in ways analogous to other ancient groups and emphasizes the total cultural situation of the people, including their modes of thinking and the ways in which they structured their personal and social existence.[6]

---

[3] A good recent treatment of the Bible as the unique Word of God, which does not insist upon a doctrine of verbal dictation, is A. Berkeley Mickelsen, *Interpreting the Bible* (Wm. B. Eerdmans Publishing Company, 1963).

[4] The best-known representative of this approach is Harry Emerson Fosdick; see his *The Modern Use of the Bible* (The Macmillan Company, Macmillan Paperbacks, 1961) and *A Guide to Understanding the Bible: The Development of Ideas Within the Old and New Testaments* (Harper Chapel Books, 1956).

[5] This approach is often labeled the "salvation history" or "history of salvation" (German, *Heilsgeschichte*) approach. It is ably set forth in G. Ernest Wright, *God Who Acts: Biblical Theology as Recital* (London: SCM Press, Ltd., 1952); see also Oscar Cullmann, *Salvation in History*, tr. by Sidney G. Sowers (Harper & Row, Publishers, Inc., 1967).

[6] The best-known and most influential treatment of the Old Testament from this perspective is Julius Wellhausen, *Prolegomena to the History of Ancient Israel*, tr. by J. Sutherland Black and Allan Menzies (Meridian Books, Meridian Library, 1957); this is a reprint of a work which first appeared in German in 1885. For more recent cultural and anthropological emphases, see Johannes Pederson, *Israel: Its Life and Culture*, tr. by Annie I. Fausbøll, 4 vols. (London: Oxford University Press, 1926–1940). For a somewhat similar approach to the New Testament, see Shirley Jackson Case, *The Social Origins of Christianity* (The University of Chicago Press, 1923).

Or, again, the Bible can be understood primarily as an anthology of the literature produced by ancient Israel and primitive Christianity, with particular reference to the aesthetic value, artistic excellence, and ideational content of the various documents.[7]

A good case can be made supporting each of these views about the nature of the Bible, but for purposes of general education the Bible can perhaps best be understood simply as a collection of historical, theological, and instructional materials produced, utilized, preserved, and eventually "canonized" (declared authoritative) by ancient Israel and the early Christian church. Such an approach attempts to relate the historical, literary, and theological aspects of the Biblical materials to the context in which they developed, without thereby making judgments about the possible contemporary relevance or value of the materials.

METHOD IN THE STUDY OF THE BIBLE

In order to understand the Bible, it is necessary to develop an approach that recognizes and attempts to deal realistically with both the difficulties inherent in Biblical study and the nature of the Biblical materials. Through the centuries, various approaches have been utilized by both Jewish and Christian scholars, as well as by those whose interests have been primarily historical or literary rather than religious. Particular approaches have been dependent to a large extent upon each scholar's presuppositions regarding the essential nature of the Biblical writings.[8]

Until modern times, the popular belief was that, whoever may have written the actual words, the real author of the Bible was the Spirit of God, who had spoken through the various authors. This doctrine of divine inspiration implied infallibility, and so the Bible was regarded as in a very literal sense the Word of God. Beginning with the Renaissance, however, and particularly during the Enlightenment, men began to question many things, including the idea of a divinely dictated sacred book, and scholars called attention to two significant facts about the Bible. First, they pointed out that there are differing and often conflicting perspectives and viewpoints within the Bible itself and that these differences extend not only to literary and historical matters but also to points of theology. Second, as knowledge of ancient history in general and of other ancient Near Eastern cultures and religions in particular increased, striking parallels and similarities were noted between the Biblical materials and other writings from antiquity. As a result, there was developed during the eighteenth and nineteenth centuries an approach to the Bible known generally as "Biblical

---

[7] For treatments of the Bible as literature, see, for example: Mary Ellen Chase, *The Bible and the Common Reader*, rev. ed. (The Macmillan Company, 1952); Charles Allen Dinsmore, *The English Bible as Literature* (Houghton Mifflin Company, 1931); Richard G. Moulton, *The Literary Study of the Bible*, rev. ed. (D. C. Heath and Company, 1899); and Laura H. Wild, *A Literary Guide to the Bible* (George H. Doran Company, 1922).

[8] See, for example, Robert M. Grant, *A Short History of the Interpretation of the Bible*, rev. ed. (The Macmillan Company, Macmillan Paperbacks, 1963).

criticism," which sought to understand the Biblical writings within the context of the original communities that preserved and used them and within the broader social, cultural, and religious context of Near Eastern life and history. This approach has now gained widespread acceptance, at least in principle, in scholarly circles.[9] The term "criticism" here does not imply faultfinding or a disapproving judgment; rather, it refers to a careful, systematic, open-minded examination of the documents in an attempt to learn all that can be learned about and from them.

The basic presupposition of Biblical criticism is that the Bible, whatever else it may be, is a collection of human documents written by human authors in human language and therefore subject to the same canons of historical and literary investigation as all other books. In other words, the Bible is to be read and studied in exactly the same way as any other collection of ancient documents. This means that one should not approach the Bible with any preconceived ideas about its origin, nature, content, meaning, or relevance for today, but rather should form opinions on these matters only after a careful study of the Biblical materials themselves.

A second presupposition of Biblical criticism is that the initial concern of the student must be to understand the Biblical materials not in terms of their possible relevance or value for today but rather in their original historical and cultural context. What did these materials mean at the time they were composed? What were the writers attempting to say? Did any of the materials circulate within the ancient communities before being reduced to writing and included in the books that now make up the Bible, and, if so, how were they used and understood in their preliterary form? The primary question, then, is not, What do they mean now? but rather, What did they mean then?

The first step in Biblical criticism is called "lower criticism" (sometimes known as "textual criticism"). It has as its goal the recovery of the actual words written by the various authors. This kind of study is necessary because the original copies of the Biblical books have all been lost, and, for many centuries before the invention of printing, the documents were copied by hand. Inevitably, many variations appeared in the texts, most of them relatively insignificant, but some affecting extensive passages or important matters of history or theology. Textual criticism attempts, through a careful comparison of the thousands of extant manuscripts, to determine what the author originally wrote. It is not an exact science, but in a great many cases it can achieve a high degree of probability. Where considerable question remains as to the original wording in a particular passage, modern translations of the Bible such as the Revised Standard Version indicate this through the use of footnotes. Obviously, the average student cannot concern himself with the details of textual criticism, since he lacks the necessary linguistic tools (knowledge of Hebrew, Aramaic, Greek, Syriac, Coptic, Latin, and other ancient languages). Furthermore, it is a very complex

---

[9] For a good discussion of modern study of the Old Testament, see Herbert F. Hahn, *The Old Testament in Modern Research*, expanded ed., with a Survey of Recent Literature by Horace D. Hummel (Fortress Press, 1966); the best history of modern study of the New Testament is Stephen Neill, *The Interpretation of the New Testament, 1861–1961* (Oxford University Press, Galaxy Books, 1966).

and highly tedious type of study which does not appeal to many people. Nevertheless, modern study of the Bible has profited greatly from the painstaking labors of the textual critics.[10] One might also include under "lower criticism" the translation of the Bible from its original Hebrew, Aramaic, and Greek into the languages of today. This, too, must be the work of the scholar. Translation inevitably involves interpretation, and scholars will often disagree as to how a particular word, phrase, or idea in the Bible can best be expressed in English.

The second step in Biblical criticism is "higher criticism" (also known as "historical criticism" or "literary-historical criticism"), which deals with questions about the origin and history of the Biblical materials. These questions include the following: Who wrote a given document? When, where, in what language, why, and for whom did he write it? Did he use sources, and, if so, what were they? Did the original author write the book essentially as we now have it, or were additions, deletions, and/or alterations made later, and, if so, when and for what purpose? What do we know about the historical and cultural matrix out of which the Biblical materials emerged which might help in determining the meaning of the writings? Oftentimes, these questions cannot be answered with any real assurance; for example, we cannot be certain who wrote any book of the Old Testament. Nevertheless, every bit of information that can be gained about the origin and history of the Biblical materials is potentially valuable as we attempt to understand these writings.[11]

Higher criticism originally dealt almost exclusively with the final literary form of the Biblical materials. As it became apparent, however, that in many cases a long process of oral tradition lay behind the written documents, scholars grew increasingly interested in the preliterary or oral form of these materials. Thus was born a kind of study known as "form criticism" (German, *Formgeschichte*) which attempts to trace the history and development of the Biblical traditions before they were reduced to writing. Such study has been extremely fruitful in illuminating the various facets of the communal life of ancient Israel and the early Christian church, for it has often been able to show how the separate traditions were used and understood within the communities. This, in turn, has helped scholars in their attempt to understand the meaning of the materials as they were eventually incorporated into the writings that now make up the Bible.[12]

The overall goal of Biblical criticism, in short, is to place the various parts of the Bible in their concrete historical and cultural setting and to allow these writings to speak for themselves within their own context. Or, to put it some-

---

[10] For a brief discussion of textual criticism as it applies to the Old Testament, see D. R. Ap-Thomas, A *Primer of Old Testament Text Criticism*, 2d ed. (Fortress Press, 1964). A comparable treatment of New Testament textual criticism is Vincent Taylor, *The Text of the New Testament: A Short Introduction* (St. Martin's Press, Inc., 1961).

[11] A classic example of the historical-critical method as applied to the Old Testament is Samuel R. Driver, An *Introduction to the Literature of the Old Testament*, 9th ed. (Charles Scribner's Sons, 1913); a similar treatment of the New Testament is James Moffatt, An *Introduction to the Literature of the New Testament*, 3d ed. (Charles Scribner's Sons, 1918).

[12] A good recent discussion of form criticism is Klaus Koch, *The Growth of the Biblical Tradition: The Form-Critical Method*, tr. by S. M. Cupitt (Charles Scribner's Sons, 1969).

what differently, the goal of Biblical criticism is to help the modern reader of the Bible to put himself back in the position of the ancient communities that produced and used the Biblical materials and thus to determine what these materials meant to those communities. The critical study of the Bible is no different in principle, therefore, from the critical study of other ancient documents. This approach can set the stage, of course, for asking questions about the possible contemporary relevance and value of the Bible, but does not itself deal with such questions.

A final word should be added here about the enormous value of certain related disciplines, such as history of religions, linguistic study, and especially archaeology as aids to the historical-critical study of the Bible. The discipline known as history of religions (or comparative religions, as it is often somewhat misleadingly called) not only reveals many significant parallels between Biblical concepts and practices and those of other ancient cultures and religions, but in many instances helps us to understand the Biblical phenomena by revealing how they developed historically and by disclosing how similar phenomena functioned and were understood in these other cultures and religions. In some cases, but certainly not always, such study emphasizes the distinctiveness of the Biblical perspectives and practices. Linguistic study often illuminates the meaning of Biblical words and idioms by showing how the same or related terminology was used in non-Biblical materials written in the same or kindred languages. Archaeology seeks to recover the material remains, including literature, of past human cultures and events and to examine these remains in such a way as to shed light upon those cultures and events. When used by the Biblical scholar, its purpose is neither to confirm nor to contradict statements in the Bible, but rather to illuminate in whatever way possible the total historical background and cultural context of the Biblical writings, and in this respect it has been extremely valuable. It is important to keep in mind, of course, that the "facts" of archaeology, like all facts, must be interpreted, and different scholars will often arrive at widely divergent conclusions after a careful examination of the relevant evidence.[13]

---

[13] Most books on Biblical archaeology also deal to some extent with history of religions and linguistic study; good treatments can be found in the following works: John Gray, *Archaeology and the Old Testament World* (Harper Torchbooks, 1964); Roland K. Harrison, *The Archaeology of the Old Testament* (Harper Chapel Books, 1967); Roland K. Harrison, *Archaeology of the New Testament* (Association Press, 1964); G. Ernest Wright, *Biblical Archaeology*, abridged ed. (The Westminster Press, 1961).

2 | THE FORMATION
AND TRANSMISSION OF THE BIBLE

In the preceding chapter it was noted that the Biblical documents in the form in which we now possess them are a compilation of diverse types of literary materials produced over a period spanning perhaps a millennium. They are then, at the least, the end product of a long and complex process that began with their original composition and ended with their acceptance as authoritative Scripture. Much of this material, however, was utilized within the life of the Hebrew and Christian communities in an unwritten predocumentary form or written in a form different from the present documents. In addition, most people today read the Bible in translation, that is, in a language different from that of the original documents.

The purpose of this chapter is to outline briefly the formation, transmission, and translation of the Biblical traditions. How did these materials originate? How were they transmitted and preserved? Why and how did this particular body of documents come to be accepted as authoritative? What is the history of the Bible in English?

THE ORIGIN OF THE BIBLICAL MATERIALS

The order of the Biblical writings in the Christian tradition recognizes the existence of several literary types. The Old Testament is divided into the broad categories of law, history, poetry and wisdom, and prophecy, while the New Testament contains gospels, history, and letters. Some of these writings or books probably came into existence in exactly the form in which we now possess them and show little sign whatever of being compilations or of having existed in a nonwritten form. An example of this type of book is Paul's letter to Philemon composed on the occasion of a runaway slave's return to his master after having been imprisoned, perhaps with Paul. This book conforms to the basic pattern in which letters were written at the time of Paul. With the exception of vs. 3 and 25, which may be quotations from widely used Christian greetings and benedictions, the content of the letter to Philemon follows a single form and was composed by the apostle for a very particular situation.

Others of the Biblical books, perhaps the majority, show signs of being compilations of materials from diverse "sources" and reflect numerous literary forms.

14

In many cases, then, the final author was more of an editor than a writer. Even within the books that were produced in their present form by an author, the writer may quote material with which he was familiar but which he did not compose. For example, Paul, in one of his letters, may quote a passage of widely known poetry or a confessional summary of the "gospel." Or, in the Old Testament, a historical book may incorporate a psalm or song written in a poetical fashion.

All of this suggests that if one wishes to study the origin of the Biblical materials, one must in many cases go behind the final written forms of the books and ask questions about the form and use of the traditions in their unwritten phase or about their written form prior to their incorporation into the present documents. The method of approach that attempts to deal with the origin, use, and development of these traditions is called form criticism and/or tradition history.[1] Although this method has been introduced in the previous chapter, it is necessary at this point to discuss the approach further and to illustrate its employment.

The Form Critical Approach. The form critical method rests on three foundational assumptions. The first is the thesis that various situations in the everyday life of ancient communities produced and utilized various structural forms through which they gave expression to their folklore, history, faith, and beliefs. Such everyday situations as funerals, weddings, court hearings, worship and liturgical acts, teaching, celebration of military victories and defeats, and so on, followed basic formed patterns. Part of these behavior patterns involved not only prescribed actions but also spoken elements and oral components. Much of the Biblical material had its original usage within these behavior patterns, and thus a proper understanding of the material must attempt to relate it to its original situation in life.

A second assumption of this method of approach argues that different situations in the community's life would produce different verbal elements with differing forms of expression and content. A song sung in conjunction with a funeral would be entirely different in content and form from that sung at a wedding. The components in the celebration of a military victory would differ considerably from those associated with a military defeat. The function of the occasion determined both the pattern of action and the form of the verbal components. To use an analogy in the field of architecture, one can see that the function which a building has determines its structure and furnishing. At the same time, from the structure and furnishing, one can determine the function of the building and thus distinguish between a residence, a railway station, a factory, and so on, provided of course that one is familiar with the overall culture in which the architectural features are found. In Biblical study it is often necessary to deduce from the content and form of a song, saying, story, or psalm the original function it served and the context within which it was used. The study of the institutions, everyday life, and literature of other Near Eastern cultures often aids in such attempts to reconstruct the original situation in life out of which the Biblical traditions came.

---

[1] On form critical methodology, see Koch, *The Growth of the Biblical Tradition.*

A third presupposition of the form critical method is the assumption that many of the Biblical traditions circulated and were transmitted in oral form before being written down.[2] Although writing was widely used in the ancient world, even in the earliest days of Israel, traditions were often passed down from generation to generation in an unwritten form, since writing required a specialized knowledge and training as well as a specific purpose.[3] The bearers of these oral traditions were the institutions and persons concerned with the life and interests reflected in the traditions. For example, legal material had its origin and employment within the institutions responsible for the administration of justice, and it was these institutions which handed on legal rulings, precedent cases, and standards of justice. Material related to the cult and worship, such as psalms, confessions, laws governing ritual and sacrifice, and so on, were preserved and passed on within the life of the religious institutions. The use of material in an oral form allowed for the expansion, reinterpretation, and adaptation of traditions to meet new needs and circumstances within community life. The traditions in an oral form were, therefore, a living and growing part of communal life and faith.

In summary, form criticism assumes that behind the written Biblical documents lie stages of development in the use of the Biblical materials. Particular circumstances and needs within the total life of the communities led to the formation of definite types of tradition with particular form and content intended for specific usage within definite life situations. As situations and needs changed, so did the form and content of the traditions.

Any attempt to discover the origin, use, and development of the preliterary forms of the Biblical traditions works under certain limiting factors. In the first place, some of the material in the Biblical documents had no preliterary history. It came into existence as written literature from the very beginning. Secondly, our knowledge of the everyday and institutional life of ancient Israel and early Christianity is far from complete. We are not sufficiently acquainted with the life of these communities to be able to reconstruct all the actual situations in which the preliterary traditions were used. Nonetheless, attempts must be made to do this wherever possible. Thirdly, some of the preliterary traditions may not have been bound to particular institutional usage. One must take into consideration the creative ability of a people or persons to transcend their institutional structures and assimilate in new ways the older traditional materials.

Some Examples. A few illustrations will show how the form critical approach has helped in understanding the origin and use of the Biblical traditions. Most of the Old Testament psalms, for example, are today rightly understood as having their origin and use within services of worship. Some of their introductions make reference to this fact. Psalm 92 is "a song for the Sabbath." Psalm 61 contains a notation for the choirmaster: the psalm is to be sung accompanied "with stringed instruments." Psalm 57 was to be sung "according to Do Not Destroy," no doubt a popular tune in ancient Israel. The employment of Psalm

[2] See Eduard Nielsen, *Oral Tradition* (SCM Press, Ltd., 1954).
[3] On the history of writing, see Godfrey R. Driver, *Semitic Writing: From Pictograph to Alphabet,* 2d ed. (London: Oxford University Press, 1954).

24, which has no notations about its usage, can be determined from a form critical analysis which shows the following structure:

HYMN OF PRAISE: The earth is the LORD's and the fulness
    thereof,
    the world and those who dwell therein;
for he has founded it upon the seas,
    and established it upon the rivers.
(Ps. 24:1–2.)

QUESTION: Who shall ascend the hill of the LORD?
    And who shall stand in his holy place?
(V. 3.)

ANSWER: He who has clean hands and a pure heart,
    who does not lift up his soul to
        what is false,
    and does not swear deceitfully.
He will receive blessing from the LORD,
    and vindication from the God of his
        salvation.
(Vs. 4–5.)

RESPONSE: Such is the generation of those who seek
    him,
    who seek the face of the God of Jacob.
(V. 6.)

CHORUS: Lift up your heads, O gates!
    and be lifted up, O ancient doors!
    that the King of glory may come in.
Who is the King of glory?
    The LORD, strong and mighty,
    the LORD, mighty in battle!
Lift up your heads, O gates!
    and be lifted up, O ancient doors!
    that the King of glory may come in.
Who is this King of glory?
    The LORD of hosts,
    he is the King of glory!
(Vs. 7–10.)

What form does this passage take? What situation of usage does it presuppose? The passage is obviously a liturgy. Its structure reflects its association with an entrance ritual to a temple in which the pilgrims request the qualifications for those entering. The priests enumerate these from within the sanctuary area. The pilgrims respond by saying that they are that type of people. There is then sung a chorus, perhaps by priests and pilgrims, at the opening of the gates signifying the entrance of the pilgrims into the precincts accompanied by the Lord.

In Deut. 26:1–11 is given part of the ritual to be used in conjunction with a person's offering to the Lord the first of his crops to ripen. As the basket was set before the altar, the worshiper responds:

A wandering Aramean was my father; and he went down into Egypt and sojourned there, few in number; and there he became a nation, great, mighty, and populous. And the Egyptians treated us harshly, and afflicted us, and laid upon us hard bondage. Then we cried to the LORD the God of our fathers, and the LORD heard our voice, and saw our affliction, our toil, and our oppression; and the LORD brought us out of Egypt with a mighty hand and an outstretched arm, with great terror, with signs and wonders; and he brought us into this place and gave us this land, a land flowing with milk and honey. (Deut. 26:5–9.)

This passage is a confession of faith which had its situation in life within a sacrificial ritual. The person offering the confession makes reference to his patriarchal ancestor, the descent into and exodus from Egypt, and the settlement in the Land of Promise. This confession is then a skeleton outline of the first six books (the Hexateuch) of the Old Testament. Or to put it more accurately, the Hexateuch represents the most expanded form of this type of confession. This small confession of faith is a summary of the people's sacred national history and illustrates how the Israelites utilized many of their historical traditions.

Within the New Testament one can see a similar use of traditions about Jesus that were employed to meet the needs and practices of the early church. In writing to the church at Corinth, Paul quotes from the living traditions of the church that he had received and passed on and refers to the use of these traditions within the worship of the church.

The Lord Jesus on the night when he was betrayed took bread, and when he had given thanks, he broke it, and said, "This is my body which is for you. Do this in remembrance of me." In the same way also the cup, after supper, saying, "This cup is the new covenant in my blood. Do this, as often as you drink it, in remembrance of me." (I Cor. 11:23–25.)

He then adds that as often as they (the Corinthian Christians) did this, they proclaimed "the Lord's death until he comes" (I Cor. 11:26). These sayings of Jesus were preserved in the church in conjunction with their usage in the Eucharist, or Lord's Supper, celebration. The writers of the Gospels about Jesus (especially Matthew, Mark, and Luke) have recorded these eucharistic words of Jesus in almost identical form. This suggests that Paul and the Gospel writers drew upon the oral traditions of the church as these were used in their services of worship.

A further reference to important early church traditions is found in I Cor. 15:3–7. Again Paul makes reference to what he had received and delivered. The first part of this passage is a creedal statement about Jesus' death and resurrection:

Christ died
   for our sins
      in accordance with the scriptures;

> he was buried;
> he was raised
>> on the third day
>>> in accordance with the scriptures.
>>>> (I Cor. 15:3–4.)

The circumstances in which this summary was used in the early church are not given by Paul, but it is obviously a Christian confession which combines statements about Jesus with interpretations and explanations about their significance.

In this same context, Paul refers to another tradition about the appearances of the resurrected Jesus. He speaks of the appearances to Cephas (Peter), the twelve, five hundred, James, all the apostles, and lastly to himself. Paul uses this tradition to argue for the actuality of the resurrection and for his own inclusion among the select group that witnessed the appearances. Paul is here obviously dependent upon the oral traditions of the early church, but it is interesting to note that the Gospel writers emphasized the appearances to the women, which Paul omits, and made no reference to any appearance to James. Two conclusions related to the use of oral tradition may be drawn from this. In the first place, the early Christians used the stories of the appearances to authenticate their preaching of the resurrection. Secondly, the traditions about the resurrection appearances were known and used in more than one form by the early Christians.

Acts, ch. 2, is a narrative about the first public preaching of the Christian faith which contains a sermon purported to have been preached by Peter. In this sermon, reference is made to the fulfillment of Old Testament prophecies, to the mighty works and signs done by Jesus, to the death of Jesus, to his resurrection and ascension to the heavens. If this represents, as is likely, an outline of a typical early Christian sermon, then one can see from this the features emphasized about Jesus by the early church. The outline of this sermon is almost identical to the outlines of the Gospels about Jesus, which suggests that the traditions about Jesus were at home in the preaching of the early church. It also suggests that the Gospels were the outgrowth of the early church's preaching about Jesus.

The above examples show that much of the Biblical material had its origin and usage within the actual life of the communities. The traditions were used to meet the needs of the community, to give expression to its faith and beliefs.

FROM WRITINGS TO SACRED SCRIPTURE

The process that produced the Biblical documents was not a unitary and evolutionary process.[4] One must not assume that the various stages in the development of the Biblical traditions unfolded in a sequential manner so that one can speak of the origin of the material, a period of use in oral form, a time

---

[4] See Edgar J. Goodspeed, *How Came the Bible?* (Abingdon Press, Apex Books, 1940) and H. G. G. Herklots, *How Our Bible Came to Us* (Oxford University Press, Galaxy Books, 1957).

when the material was written down, and finally a time when the material was declared authoritative and unchangeable. Portions of the Bible came into existence in a written literary form and perhaps never passed through any oral stage of development. Other traditions may have been used and transmitted in oral form for years, or in the case of the Old Testament for centuries, before being finally committed to written form.

As is obvious, all the material that we now designate as the Bible came to exist in written form. The writing down and editing of the oral traditions as well as the editing of the written materials was probably dependent upon a number of considerations. Sometimes this may have been done because of the desire of some groups within the communities to present the material in a particular perspective so as to advocate a new or different viewpoint or to preserve an older interpretation from some new challenge. Critical circumstances that threatened to break off the living traditions or that confronted the community with possible extinction led to intense literary and editing activity. This happened in Judah with the fall of the state and the temple and the subsequent deportation of the leading families. In the early church this occurred with the passing of the first generation of Christians and with the developing conflict between the church and the Roman Empire.

Both Judaism and Christianity eventually selected a body of documents that they regarded as sacred and authoritative. Such a collection of writings is referred to as a "canon," a Semitic word in origin which originally meant "reed" and which in Greek came to mean "measuring rod," "rule," or "norm." The idea of a canon of Scripture has both positive and negative connotations. Positively, it is the recognition that certain writings are understood as the authentic voice of religious authority. Negatively, a canon excludes writings that the community does not accept as bearing authority. The development of a canon, like the writing down, collecting, and editing of traditions, was the response of the communities to internal needs or crises such as theological disputes and to external pressures such as the threat of annihilation or absorption by alien cultures.

The development of a canon within both Judaism and Christianity was a process of growth, and in neither was there a definite meeting of religious authorities and a deliberate decree declaring certain writings as "canonical." The development of an authoritative body of writings occurred in the two communities over a long period of time and in several stages. Inclusion of specific documents within this body was based upon the assumption that these writings expressed the true faith and practice of the communities, their veneration as documents of antiquity, and their association with or supposed authorship by revered early leaders of the communities.

The earliest group of writings to be granted an authoritative status within Judaism was, as one would expect, the Torah (Pentateuch). Scholars assume that this had occurred by ca. 400 B.C. There is, however, evidence in the Old Testament which shows that even at an earlier date books of law had been given an authoritative status. II Kings 22:3 to 23:3 tells how, in the eighteenth year of King Josiah (621 B.C.), Hilkiah the high priest in Jerusalem discovered a book of the law which was accepted as authoritative by the king and the people and was used in instituting wide reforms. After the Judean exile, Ezra returned to Jerusalem (in the fifth century B.C.) with the law of God in his hands (Ezra 7:14), which was accepted by the people as an authoritative rule for community life. The texts, however, do not tell us the content and the extent of this law.

A second group of documents, known as the Neviim (Prophets), seems to have achieved its final form by about 200 B.C. In the introduction to the Greek translation of Ecclesiasticus (made about 130 B.C.), the translator, who was a grandson of the author, Jesus ben Sirach, makes reference to "the law and the prophets and the other books of our fathers." This shows that collections of writings were regarded with reverence and attributed to the fathers. This division possesses the same three groups of writings as the final Hebrew Bible. In Ecclesiasticus itself, the author, writing about 180 B.C., makes reference to Isaiah, Jeremiah, Ezekiel, and the Twelve, the so-called Latter Prophets, which suggests that he was familiar with the documents that now make up the second division of the Hebrew Bible.

The references in Ecclesiasticus should not be taken, however, as evidence of the existence of a fixed canon of Scripture in which nothing could be changed, added to, or taken away. This type of authority was originally granted only to the first five books of the Old Testament. This is shown by the fact that among the Jews in the late pre-Christian era there was a wide variety in the usage of sacred books with agreement being limited to the Torah. The Samaritans, a Jewish group living in Samaria that was descended from the northern Israelites, accepted only the Torah as authoritative and this they wrote in their own and special script. The Qumran community, another Jewish group which we know about from the Dead Sea Scrolls, used a body of sacred literature that was much broader in scope than even that referred to in Ecclesiasticus. The Sadducees, a major party in Judaism at the time of Jesus, accepted only the Torah as canonical, although the other books were prized and read as edifying works. The Greek-speaking Jews who lived in Alexandria in Egypt accepted the Torah as canonical, revered the books in the Prophets and Writings but ordered them differently from the Palestinian Jews, and accepted books on a par with the Prophets and Writings which were never included in the Hebrew canon. The Alexandrian Jews had begun the translation of the Torah into Greek during the third century B.C. and later translated the remainder of the Hebrew books into Greek.

The final Hebrew canon was the work of Palestinian Jews, primarily the party of the Pharisees which survived the fall of Jerusalem in A.D. 70. The Pharisaic Jewish historian Josephus (ca. A.D. 37–100), who wrote several apologetic works in Rome, gives the first definite picture of an Old Testament canon identical in content to the present Hebrew Bible. In a work, *Against Apion* (I. 38–40), written at Rome between A.D. 94 and 96, he says:

> Among us there are not countless discordant and conflicting books, but only twenty-two, containing the account of all history and rightly given credence. Five of these books are by Moses; they contain the laws and the tradition from the creation of mankind up to his death (a period of about 3,000 years). From

the death of Moses to [the time of] Artaxerxes king of the Persians, the prophets after Moses composed the history of their times in thirteen books. The remaining four contain hymns to God and moral precepts for men.[5]

His statements here and elsewhere show the assumptions made by him and his Jewish contemporaries concerning the nature of these sacred writings. These were: (1) they were written by inspired men in the period from Moses to Artaxerxes; (2) they were distinguished from other works written after this period by their holiness, since the succession of prophets ended in the Persian period; (3) they were limited in number, namely, twenty-two[6] (which equaled the number of letters in the Hebrew alphabet); and (4) their wording was sacrosanct.

The references by Josephus illustrate that the Jewish canon had reached a definite form in Palestinian Judaism by A.D. 100 although there continued to be some objection to the authoritative status of Ezekiel, Song of Songs, Ecclesiastes, and Esther. The canon was discussed by a council of Jewish leaders held at Jamnia (Jabneh) in Palestine (A.D. 85–90), but there is insufficient evidence concerning its conclusions.[7] This Pharisaic canon was later accepted throughout the Jewish world. Pharisaic Judaism, however, continued to accept as valid and binding oral traditions that were associated with or interpretations of the canonical writings.

The books that had been widely used in some Jewish circles but that were not included in the Hebrew canon seem to have been excluded for a number of reasons. Some of these had been written after the Persian period and thus did not fall within the "age of inspiration and revelation." Some had been originally composed in Greek and thus represented a compromise with heathen culture. Others were written under the name of some pre-Mosaic person and thus seemed to claim an authority above the law. Many of these contained teachings that were not in line with true faith and practices. The fact that Christians and other sectarian Jewish groups made use of some of these writings may have also been a prominent factor.

The early Christians used and quoted as sacred Scriptures those books used by their Jewish contemporaries.[8] One finds references in the New Testament to "the law and the prophets" (Matt. 5:17; Acts 28:23) or to the "holy writings" (Rom. 1:2; II Tim. 3:15). Luke 24:44 speaks of "the law of Moses and the prophets and the psalms." This shows that the early Christians were familiar with the Palestinian collection in which the third division of the canon had not reached a final canonical status. Within the New Testament there are quotations from or reminiscences of books that were excluded from the Hebrew canon

---

[5] Translation from Robert M. Grant, *The Formation of the New Testament* (Harper & Row, Publishers, Inc., 1965), p. 34.
[6] The number reflects the association of Lamentations with Jeremiah and of Ruth with Judges and, of course, reckons the Twelve Prophets as one book.
[7] See J. P. Lewis, "What Do We Mean by Jabneh?" *Journal of Bible and Religion*, XXXII (1964), pp. 125–132.
[8] See Albert C. Sundberg, Jr., *The Old Testament of the Early Church* (Harvard University Press, 1964) and his "The 'Old Testament': A Christian Canon," in *The Catholic Biblical Quarterly*, XXX (1968), pp. 143–155.

(I Maccabees, Enoch, Wisdom of Solomon, and so on). Early Christianity was thus acquainted with a broad collection of sacred books that could be quoted as Scripture, but they did not inherit from Judaism a closed canon of Scripture. As Christianity moved into the larger Greek-speaking world, it tended to take over and use the Greek translations of the sacred writings and in time created its own canonical but more inclusive collection of Old Testament traditions (the so-called Septuagint). This remained the case until the time of the Protestant Reformation in the sixteenth century when many Protestants adopted as canonical only those writings found in the Hebrew canon (see Chart 1).

The Bible of the early Christians was the sacred writings of the Jewish people. The teaching and the preaching of Jesus and of the early apostles, however, were taken as the "key" for understanding these writings which of course provided an interpretation which differed from that of non-Christian Judaism.

The "sayings and teachings of Jesus" came to have an authoritative status at an early stage in the life of the early church. This is supported by references within the New Testament itself. Paul, while discussing questions of marriage and divorce, says:

> To the married I give charge, not I but the Lord, that the wife should not separate from her husband (but if she does, let her remain single or else be reconciled to her husband)—and that the husband should not divorce his wife. (I Cor. 7:10–11.)

Here Paul is referring to a saying of Jesus concerning separation and divorce which was also preserved in the Gospels (see Mark 10:11–12). In a sermon contained in Acts, ch. 20, reference is made to "remembering the words of the Lord Jesus, how he said, 'It is more blessed to give than to receive' " (v. 35). Here is preserved a quotation of Jesus that was not included in the Gospels but that was used for authoritatively clinching an argument.

The sayings of Jesus and narratives about him were widely used in the early church, originally in an oral form. These were employed in worship, instruction, evangelism, and controversy. The collecting, editing, and writing of these traditions will be further discussed in conjunction with the treatment of "the historical Jesus" in Chapter 17.

Several gospels or collections of the sayings and acts of Jesus circulated in the early church. The four Gospels (Matthew, Mark, Luke, and John) were most widely used, although other gospels such as the recently discovered Gospel of Thomas were used by fringe groups of Christians. Even after the gospels were written, many in the early church continued to value and utilize oral traditions. Papias of Hierapolis (ca. A.D. 130–140) is reported to have written: "I did not suppose that the things from the books would aid me so much as the things from the living and continuing voice."

The teaching, preaching, and writings of the early church leaders came to have a normative authority. Paul presupposed and referred to the public reading of his letters to the various churches (I Thess. 5:27), and the exchange of letters between churches no doubt took place (Col. 4:16). In his writings, Paul often claimed an authoritative status for "his gospel," which he set over against any other gospel (Gal. 1:6–9). This authority of the apostle was based on a claim to a divine commission from the risen Lord (Gal. 1:1) or possession of the Spirit of God (I Cor. 7:40).

Toward the end of the first century A.D., a norm of Christian teaching and life developed around the authoritative voice of the Lord and the apostles.[9] This led to the collection and veneration of writings containing the words of the Lord and the teaching of the apostles during the early part of the second century. It is entirely possible that a collection of Paul's writings was already in existence before A.D. 100. By the end of the second century, the four Gospels and the thirteen letters attributed to Paul along with other writings ascribed to the apostles were regarded, by the majority of the churches, as inspired Scripture, were placed on a par with the authority of the Christian Old Testament, and were read in public worship. Other writings (Hebrews, II and III John, II Peter, James, Jude, and Revelation) were debated and their apostolic origin challenged. In addition, other writings (such as the Gospel of Thomas, the Shepherd of Hermas, I Clement, and the Didache) were used as authoritative in many early churches. Various minority Christian groups worked out authoritative collections of their own, some excluding the writings of Paul, others excluding the writings, such as the Gospel of Matthew, which continued strong Jewish influence, and some excluding the Old Testament as Christian scripture.

The canon of the New Testament in the form that we now possess was almost universally accepted by the end of the fourth century. Bishop Athanasius, in a Festal Letter written in A.D. 367 and widely circulated, gave a listing of the New Testament writings and declared them canonical. This helped settle matters in the Western church, although there continued to be some discussion of certain books, the most controversial being Revelation.

ANCIENT MANUSCRIPTS AND TRANSLATIONS

None of the original copies of any of the Biblical books has survived. The oldest forms of these books in existence today are manuscript (= hand-written) copies which possess varying relationships to the supposed originals. It was not until the invention of the printing press with movable type in the fifteenth century that copies could be produced without laboriously copying letter by letter. Of the several thousand manuscript copies and fragments of the various writings that exist today, no two are identical.[10]

The two most common writing materials in use at the time when the Biblical books were being reproduced were papyrus and parchment. Papyrus, from which our word "paper" comes, was primarily a product of ancient Egypt. Papyrus was made by cutting the stem of the papyrus plant into sections, removing the pith, which was cut into thin strips, and pressing two or more strips together so that the fibers ran in opposite directions. Parchment was made from the skins of such animals as cattle, goats, sheep, and antelopes. The skins were treated with a lime bath, scraped to remove the hair, then dried, stretched, and rubbed

---

[9] On the origin of the New Testament canon, see Robert M. Grant, *The Formation of the New Testament.*

[10] On the text, manuscripts, and translations of the Bible, see B. J. Roberts, *The Old Testament Text and Versions* (Cardiff: University of Wales Press, 1961), and Bruce M. Metzger, *The Text of the New Testament*, 2d ed. (Oxford University Press, 1968).

smooth with some substance such as chalk or pumice. Sheets of papyrus or parchment were sewn or glued together to produce scrolls. These were divided into columns and the texts written on them in ink. The scrolls were then wound on two sticks. Scrolls intended for frequent usage seldom exceeded thirty feet in length. This was of sufficient length to contain any one of the Biblical books. The main Isaiah Scroll from the Dead Sea library, for example, is about 24 feet in length and contains 54 columns, while the newly discovered Temple Scroll (a non-Biblical text) is 28 feet in length and contains 66 columns.

The scroll form was relatively inconvenient to use. One had to employ both hands, unrolling the scroll with one hand and rolling it up with the other. Finding specific passages in a scroll was a difficult and laborious task. The codex, or leaf form of book, came into extensive use in the church during the second and third centuries, although Judaism tended to adhere to the use of the scroll. A codex was made by folding sheets in the middle and sewing them together. The codex permitted greater facility in usage and carriage and allowed for writing on both sides of the sheets.

The hand copying of texts allowed numerous errors and scribal mistakes to creep into the text. Deliberate alterations of the texts were sometimes made in the interest of theology. It has been estimated that there are over 300,000 known variations in extant manuscripts of the New Testament, but most of these are slight and insignificant.

Prior to the discovery of the famous Dead Sea Scrolls,[11] beginning in 1947, the oldest complete copies of books of the Hebrew Bible dated from the late ninth and tenth centuries. The finds of scrolls since 1947 in caves in the Qumran area and the wilderness of Judah contain portions of every Old Testament book, with the exception of The Book of Esther, but the vast majority of these are extremely fragmentary and only The Book of Isaiah has been found in its entirety. Some of these manuscript fragments may date from as early as the second century B.C.

The oldest fragmentary manuscripts of the New Testament date from the second century A.D. Complete copies of the entire New Testament date from the fourth century.

The text of the Old and New Testaments was originally written without punctuation marks and in the latter without word division. The Old Hebrew script was purely consonantal, with some consonants occasionally used to represent vowel sounds. This sufficed as long as the language was in common usage. Gradually, a system for representing the vowels had to be worked out. This was done by the Masoretes (from an Aramaic word meaning "to hand down"), who were the scribal transmitters of the Hebrew text. They devised a system of points to represent the vowel sounds and added these above and below the consonantal text. The division of the Hebrew text into sections was already evident in the Dead Sea Scrolls and by the second century A.D. the text had been divided into verses (without numbering). Subsequently, the material was divided (with the exception of the Psalms) into sense paragraphs, which were noted by blank spaces in the text. The New Testament was often provided with notations placed in the margins which divided the texts into sections and

---

[11] These will be discussed further in Chapter 17.

EARLY BIBLICAL MANUSCRIPTS AND THE FIRST
PRINTED EDITION OF THE BIBLE

[1]

JOHN TREVER

[2]   THE UNIVERSITY OF MICHIGAN LIBRARY

[3]

[4]

[1] The Isaiah Scroll (1 Q Isa^a), discovered in Cave I at Qumran, is the most complete of all the Dead Sea Scrolls. Scribal additions and corrections were written in the margins and between the lines. [2] A leaf from the Michigan Papyrus (papyrus 46), which gives the opening line from the letter to the Ephesians, dates from the early third century A.D. [3] A leaf from the Codex Sinaiticus, a manuscript from the early fourth century which once contained the entire Old and New Testaments as well as several apocryphal writings. Notice the scribal notations and the absence of word division. [4] The Gutenberg Bible was the first edition of the Scriptures printed with movable type. This work was produced in Mainz in 1456.

sometimes noted the content of the section. The division into chapters to which we are accustomed today dates from about A.D. 1200 and was first used in the New Testament. Tradition traces this division to Stephen Langton, archbishop of Canterbury (d. 1228). This chapter division was taken over into the Hebrew texts in the fourteenth century. The present-day verse division and numbering date from the printed editions of the sixteenth century (N.T., 1551; O.T., 1571).

The spread of Judaism and Christianity into new language areas and the widespread use of such international languages as Aramaic, Greek, and Latin led to the translation of the Bible from the original languages (Hebrew and some Aramaic for the Old Testament; Greek for the New Testament) into the vernacular tongues. Some of these translations, technically called versions, had been made or at least parts of the Bible translated before the establishment of closed Hebrew and Christian canons.

One of the earliest translations was of some of the Old Testament into Greek. In his prologue to Ecclesiasticus, Ben Sirach's grandson, writing in Egypt about 130 B.C., tells us that "the law and the prophets and the others that followed them" had been translated into Greek at that time. From the third century B.C., there was a large Jewish population in Egypt, especially at Alexandria, and such a translation was a necessity. Other translations of the Old Testament into Greek were later made by Jewish scholars, often attempting to produce a very literal rendering to offset and combat the rather loose translations favored by the Christians. The main language in common use among the Hebrews at the beginning of the Christian era was Aramaic, which had functioned as an international language in the Near East from the sixth century. In the synagogue, the reading of the Scriptures was often followed by translation into Aramaic. These translations were called Targums, which actually means "interpretations." These extempore renderings gradually attained fixed written form, for most of the Hebrew Scriptures and various Targums for most of the Old Testament still exist.

The Christian canon was also translated into several of the ancient languages such as Syriac and Coptic. The most important was the Latin translation made by Jerome in the late fourth century. This translation had been ordered by the Roman pontiff Damasus (A.D. 366-384) to bring order into the numerous Latin texts that then existed. This new text, after some alterations and changes, became the official text of the Western church. Jerome's translation has been known as the "Vulgate" since the thirteenth century.

THE HISTORY OF THE BIBLE IN ENGLISH [12]

The first English translation of the entire Bible from the Latin Vulgate was

---

[12] A history of the English Bible in its various translations is given in Geddes MacGregor, A *Literary History of the Bible: From the Middle Ages to the Present Day* (Abingdon Press, 1968). A broader perspective can be found in *The Cambridge History of the Bible*, Vols. II and III (Cambridge: Cambridge University Press, 1963, 1969). The third projected volume (Vol. I) in this series will deal with the origin of the Biblical writings and the development of the Old and New Testament canons.

completed under the leadership of John Wycliffe in 1382 or soon thereafter, although parts of the Bible had been translated or paraphrased earlier. William Tyndale produced the first translation of the New Testament based on the Greek text in 1525 and began a translation of the Old Testament from Hebrew but was executed as a heretic before the task was completed. His translation greatly influenced most subsequent versions.

Miles Coverdale issued a Bible in 1535 which was not actually a translation from the Hebrew and the Greek, but rather a compilation based on various Latin, German, and English versions. Matthew's Bible, printed in 1537 probably by John Rogers, an associate of Tyndale, included portions of Tyndale's and Coverdale's versions, and it was followed in 1539 by a revision at the hands of Richard Taverner. The Great Bible of 1539 was Coverdale's version of the Matthew's Bible, and its second edition of 1540, known as Cranmer's Bible, was designated the official Bible for the English church.

In 1560, the Geneva Bible, a scholarly revision of Tyndale and the Great Bible, was completed by a group of English refugees in Geneva and soon gained wide acceptance. The Bishops' Bible, issued in 1568 in an attempt to supplant the Geneva Bible, became the authorized version in the English church. An English translation of the Latin Vulgate for Roman Catholics, known as the Rheims-Douay Bible, was completed in 1610.

The Authorized Version of 1611, better known as the King James Version, was essentially a revision of the Bishops' Bible carried out by a group of scholars appointed by King James I. This version became so popular that for more than two centuries it remained the most widely used Bible in the English-speaking world. Toward the end of the nineteenth century, progress in the study of Hebrew and Greek, as well as the discovery of many ancient manuscripts, made it obvious that there were many defects in the King James Version and a group of scholars began a thorough revision. This was completed in 1885 and published in England as the Revised Version, and, in 1901, an American committee issued the American Standard Version, which differed only slightly from its British counterpart. A further revision was completed in 1952 and published as the Revised Standard Version, which has subsequently gained widespread acceptance. Thus, the main line in the history of the English Bible runs from Tyndale through the Revised Standard Version, and most of the versions that have appeared have been essentially revisions of earlier translations.

Beginning in 1947, a panel of British scholars set out to produce a completely new translation of the entire Bible into contemporary English. The New Testament portion of this version, known as the New English Bible, appeared in 1961; the Old Testament and Apocrypha were published in 1970. A new Jewish translation is in preparation, of which the Torah has appeared (1962).

From time to time, certain individuals or groups have issued independent translations. These include translation of all or part of the Bible. The most widely circulated and used of these have been the translations by Weymouth (1903), Moffatt (1924–1926), Edgar Goodspeed and others (1923–1927), Knox (1944–1954), J. B. Phillips (1958), the Jerusalem Bible (1966), and American Bible Society (1966).

3 | THE BIBLICAL WORLD

Any attempt to understand the life and thought of a people must take into consideration the physical environmental conditions in which the people lived. Geographical and climatic factors have a formative and significant influence on a community's and nation's history, customs, and beliefs. Geography is the cradle out of which history and culture develop. If this is true of any people, it was especially true of ancient Israel and the two religious communities of Judaism and Christianity. Not only were their history and fate determined in no small measure by their geographical setting but also their expressions of faith and existential concerns were formulated in symbols and imagery often dependent upon geographical considerations.

PALESTINE AND THE NEAR EAST
(See map II)

In its broadest scope, the world of the Bible includes the lands located in an area extending from Egypt in the south to Asia Minor in the north and from Persia in the east to Italy in the west. This, however, represents the focus of the Biblical traditions in their widest range of vision. In a narrower perspective, the world of the Bible refers to what has been piously termed "the holy land," a small sliver of the earth's surface abutting the Mediterranean Sea at the southwestern tip of the continent of Asia.[1]

The Names of the Land. There was no single ancient geographical term originally used to refer to the whole of the region which we know today as the Holy Land. One of the most frequently occurring designations for part of this region between Syria and Egypt, in both Biblical and non-Biblical texts, was Canaan. The origin and the meaning of this name are not certain. It has generally been associated with a term meaning "purple," just as the coastal region of the eastern Mediterranean was later known by the Greeks as Phoenicia (*phoinix*, "purple"). One of the industries of this region was the production of purple dye from the

---

[1] A good summary of the geographical, linguistic, and cultural background to Biblical history is E. A. Speiser, ed., *At the Dawn of Civilization* (Rutgers University Press, 1965), which is Vol. I of the first series of *World History of the Jewish People.*

Murex shellfish which was used for coloring wool and the name may derive from the product although the product could have been named from the region. It has been suggested that the name Canaan may have originally meant something like "Westland" or "the Land of the Sunset." [2]

The "land of Israel" is used in the Biblical text in a number of ways and is not as inclusive a designation as Canaan. The term originally referred to that northern portion of Canaan populated by Israelites as distinct from the surrounding land controlled by the Canaanites and the Philistines (I Sam. 13:19). As a rule, "Israel" was used to denote the group of tribes settled north of Jerusalem, while those settled in the south were known as Judah. For a time, under the United Kingdom, the term was extended to include both of these areas, but with the division of the state after the death of Solomon, the name Israel was used again in a restricted sense. The name ceased to be used in reference to a political entity after the fall of the northern state to the Assyrians, although the Judeans did subsequently utilize the name for themselves in a nonpolitical sense.

The name Judah was originally applied to the tribal territory and state in the south, and after the fall of Jerusalem, in the postexilic period, it was the official name of the Persian province with its center at Jerusalem. At the time of the Jewish independent state in the second and first centuries B.C., the name Judah was applied to the whole of the Land of Canaan and was retained by the Romans in the title *Provincia Judaea.*

The name Palestine, which is of course widely used today, was one of the last designations to be applied to the Holy Land. This term is derived from "Philistia," which referred to the "land of the Philistines" along the southwest coast of Canaan. The name was Hellenized to *Palaestina* and was used by several Greek writers (Herodotus, Josephus, and Philo of Alexandria) with reference to the general east Mediterranean coast. After the second unsuccessful Jewish revolt against Rome (A.D. 132–135), the Roman emperor Hadrian expunged the name Judah from the political nomenclature and designated the land *Provincia Syria Palaestina,* which became Palestine in later usage.

The Fertile Crescent. The geographical locale of the Holy Land can be understood in a number of perspectives. One such concept is that of "the Fertile Crescent," a designation first used by the Egyptologist James H. Breasted. This term refers to the vast sickle of cultivable land that extends from the Persian Gulf northward up the valleys of the Tigris and Euphrates rivers and then arches southward down the eastern Mediterranean seaboard toward Egypt. This great curve of arable land was the cradle of some of the earliest developments leading to urban civilization. The Fertile Crescent was enclosed by three great barriers to movement: the mountains to the north in Asia Minor (modern Turkey) and to the east in Persia (modern Iran), the arid Arabian Desert to the south, and the Mediterranean Sea to the west. The ancient Israelite homeland was located at the southwestern end of the crescent.

---

[2] See Michael C. Astour, "The Origins of the Terms 'Canaan,' 'Phoenician,' and 'Purple,' " *Journal of Near Eastern Studies,* XXIV (1965), pp. 346–350.

The Semitic Quadrangle. Another concept of Near Eastern geography that is helpful in elucidating the geographical environment of the Holy Land, especially for the history of ancient Israel, is the so-called Semitic Quadrangle. This term refers to a hypothetical uneven rectangular area bounded on the southwest by the Red Sea, on the southeast by the Indian Ocean, on the northeast by the Persian Gulf and the Iranian Plateau, and on the northwest by the Taurus Mountains and the Mediterranean Sea. This area incorporates the Fertile Crescent and also includes the great land mass of the Arabian Peninsula. It is within this zone that the Semitic peoples lived and their civilizations flourished.[3]

The term "Semitic," of course, does not refer to an ethnic group or race but is a linguistic designation applied to peoples who spoke one of a number of kindred languages belonging to a common linguistic family and included among others Akkadian, Arabic, Aramaic, Hebrew, and Syriac. This use of the term "Semitic" is dependent upon the Biblical tradition concerning the sons of Noah, among whom was Shem (Gen. 5:32) whose descendants, according to the Biblical genealogy (Gen. 10:21–31), occupied the primary area which has been referred to as the Semitic Quadrangle.

The original home of the Semites appears to have been the Arabian Peninsula, which has been occupied throughout history by more or less nomadic groups. Much of the peninsula is desert land, that is, land which, because of its aridity, will not support a permanently settled population. Although the region possesses numerous oases, the larger percentage of the land area is usable only during the winter months when the limited rainfall produces enough vegetation to sustain the flocks of pastoral nomads. During the summer months, these pastoral groups withdraw to the oases or else move with their flocks along the fringes of the Fertile Crescent using the recently harvested croplands as grazing areas.

These pastoralists tended to encroach upon the more settled districts of the cultivated lands creating what has been called "the conflict between the desert and the sown." Throughout history, shepherding desert groups have exerted pressure upon the agricultural or sown lands seeking opportunity to acquire more than merely grazing rights from the indigenous peoples. As opportunity presented itself, many of the pastoral population chose to settle down in the cultivated lands and adopt an agriculturally oriented culture. This pressure of the desert upon the sown seems to have been rather constant, and only periodically was it able to translate itself into massive migration, invasion, and conquest and only then during times of political weakness and instability within the civilizations of the Fertile Crescent. Three such major migrations are fairly well known: the Amorite, near the end of the third millennium and the beginning of the second; the Aramaean, during the last half of the second millennium; and the Arab under the influence of Islamic faith in the sixth and seventh centuries of the present era. During these migrations, new Semitic groups poured into the Fertile Crescent, founded states of their own, and in

---

[3] On the Semitic peoples and their relationships to other non-Semitic peoples of the Near East, see Sabatino Moscati, *The Face of the Ancient Orient* (Quadrangle Books, Inc., 1960).

turn were forced to defend themselves against the pressure of the more marginal and desert, but nonetheless kindred, populations.

The land of the Hebrews was part of the western portion of the Semitic Quadrangle and thus it shared in the common Near Eastern Semitic heritage. The Hebrews traced their origin to a movement of their ancestors along the fringes of the Fertile Crescent which eventually led to their occupation of territory. The Hebrews, after their settlement in the Holy Land, were faced with the unrelenting task of protecting their homeland and defending their security against would-be conquerors and settlers from the desert.

The Coastal Corridor. The Hebrew homeland was part of a narrow strip of land lying between the Arabian Desert and the Mediterranean Sea which served as a corridor joining the continents of Asia and Africa. In the fertile lands to the north and east lay the great civilization center called Mesopotamia (meaning "between the rivers," i.e., the Tigris and Euphrates).[4] The southern part of this region, below present-day Baghdad, was the land of Babylonia. The northern part of Mesopotamia was Assyria. At various times in ancient history these two peoples, the Babylonians and the Assyrians, were able to centralize their control over the entire Mesopotamian area and to incorporate surrounding peoples into their far-flung empires. During much of the Biblical period, Palestine was under the control of these two mighty imperial powers.

To the south of Palestine and beyond the desert stretches of the Sinai Peninsula was another major civilization center located along the Nile River— the land of Egypt.[5] Egypt, like the Mesopotamian region, developed an irrigation economy, but unlike Mesopotamia where the two rivers were dependent upon a somewhat unpredictable rainfall pattern that occasionally produced massive flooding, Egypt's irrigation system was governed by the almost changeless routine of the annual Nile inundation. The Nile River, which flows northward through a narrow trough carved from desert sandstone and limestone, is fed by the tropical rains of equatorial Africa and begins its flood of lower Egypt (north) in late June with the waters reaching their peak in September followed by gradual subsiding. This river-dominated culture was totally free of any reliance upon rainfall, and in fact most of the Nile Valley receives little or no rainfall per year. Because of this climatic peculiarity, Egypt was often a refuge for the drifting populations of the Arabian Peninsula during times of drought in the areas to the north which were dependent upon rainfall. Throughout much of the second millennium, Egypt and its rulers claimed Canaan as a province and exercised varying degrees of control over the area, and even after Egypt lost direct authority in the region, it actively intervened in the life of the states of Israel and Judah.

---

[4] On Mesopotamian cultures, see A. Leo Oppenheim, *Ancient Mesopotamia: Portrait of a Dead Civilization* (The University of Chicago Press, 1964); and H. W. F. Saggs, *The Greatness That Was Babylon* (Hawthorn Books, Inc., 1962) and his *Everyday Life in Babylonia and Assyria* (G. P. Putnam's Sons, 1965).

[5] On Egypt, see Alan Gardiner, *Egypt of the Pharaohs* (Oxford University Press, Galaxy Books, 1961); and John A. Wilson, *The Culture of Ancient Egypt* (The University of Chicago Press, Phoenix Books, 1956).

Palestine, with its eastern boundary facing the inhospitable desert lands of the Arabian Peninsula and its western reaches washed by the waters of the Mediterranean, lay astride the communication route between Mesopotamia and Egypt. Through this artery passed traders bearing their merchandise and armies

The cedars of Lebanon were once sought by Mesopotamian kings to the east and Egyptian pharaohs to the south. Nestled in the Lebanon Mountains, groves of these trees grew at altitudes over a mile above sea level. Only about 400 trees remain from the great forests that once attracted traders and conquerors and supplied wood for Solomon's Temple in Jerusalem.

ARAB INFORMATION CENTER, N.Y.

in pursuit of conquest. In this maelstrom of competing and conflicting Near Eastern cultures, the inhabitants of the land struggled and fought to preserve their traditions and security, being as often the victim as the object of hostilities. From a cultural perspective, this meant that Palestine was open to multiple and diverse cultural and religious influences imported by foreigners who made use of its territory. The Hebrew people had therefore to hammer out their own religious thought, morals, and way of life in the midst of these influences, often in direct conflict with them but sometimes borrowing and utilizing. Involved in almost constant struggles between the great powers of antiquity, the inhabitants of the land found it difficult to establish and maintain political independence. Yet alliances with either of the major power centers invoked hostility from the other.

It was perhaps not only in spite of but because of this strategic economic and military position of the land which thrust it into the midst of the ancient world's commerce and war that ancient Israel developed distinctive religious, moral, and political beliefs, forms, and hopes and passed these on as a legacy to Judaism and Christianity and subsequently to the world.

THE GEOGRAPHY OF PALESTINE
(See map I)

The importance of Palestine's geographical setting within its Near Eastern context should not overshadow the importance which the size and character of Palestinian terrain had on its people's history and culture. Palestine is small in size but a land of multiple contrasts.[6]

The Size of the Land. The Biblical writers generally fixed the north-south limits of the land by reference to the town of Dan in the north and Beer-sheba in the south, a distance of about 150 miles. The east-west boundaries were set by the desert and the sea which are separated by varying distances but by an average of approximately 60 miles. The size and shape of this territory is roughly comparable to that of Vermont. Located between 31° and 33°20' north latitude, Palestine is on a parallel with a band that cuts across the United States from south Georgia to southern California. During the course of history, the territory claimed and controlled by the Israelites varied, being sometimes larger and sometimes smaller than the general description given above.

The Palestinian landscape is dominated by two mountain ranges running parallel to the coast, with an extremely deep depression between them. This factor divides the land into four main elongated regions with a north-south orientation which is only occasionally broken by valleys cutting diagonally through the mountains in a generally east-west direction. These four regions are the coastal plain, the central highlands, the Jordan rift, and the Transjordanian highlands.

The Coastal Plain. The coastal plain, along the shore of the Mediterranean, is a narrow band extending southward from the neighborhood of the Phoenician city of Tyre. The strip broadens in the south because of the westward bend in the coastline. The shoreline is broken by Mt. Carmel, which juts out into the

---

[6] There are a number of good geographies of Palestine available. See the beautifully written and long-used classic by George Adam Smith, *The Historical Geography of the Holy Land,* rev. ed. (Harper Torchbooks, 1966); and Denis Baly, *The Geography of the Bible* (Harper & Brothers, 1957) and his *Geographical Companion to the Bible* (McGraw-Hill Book Company, Inc., 1963).

sea. The coastal plain north of Carmel is rather narrow; however, it broadens at the point where it joins the Jezreel Valley, which is the largest east-west rift in Palestine and the only valley that completely bisects the central highlands and thus connects the coast with the Jordan Valley. The Jezreel Valley is a

The Valley of Jezreel separates the district of Galilee to the north from Samaria to the south. From the Carmel range, the plain stretches east-ward toward Mt. Tabor to the north and to the city of Megiddo to the south. Covered with a good alluvium and blessed with an abundance of rain, the plain is one of the most fertile areas in Palestine.

ROBERT B. WRIGHT

large, fertile, triangular-shaped plain later known as Esdraelon through which flowed the Kishon River in a westerly direction. This plain was heavily populated and well traveled. The cities of Megiddo and Taanach guarded the valley which was the scene of many crucial, international battles in antiquity.

South of Carmel lies the section of the coastal zone known as the Plain of Sharon which in ancient times was partially covered by dense oak forests which escaped deforestation since much of the plain is a poor red sand unsuited for agriculture. At the northern and southern extremities of this plain were the harbors of Dor and Joppa, the latter serving as the port for the city of Jerusalem. In the Roman period, Herod the Great converted a small seaport town (Strato's Tower) into the large port city of Caesarea which later became the official center and virtual capital of the country during the rule of the Roman procurators over the province of Judea.

The southernmost region of the coastal strip was called after its inhabitants —the Philistine Plain. Much of the northern part of this district is covered with sand dunes, but in the south where the plain widens to a breadth of over twenty miles, the area possesses good farmland and the five main cities of the Philistines (Gaza, Ashdod, Ashkelon, Gath, and Ekron) were located in this district.

Between the southern coastal plain and the central highlands is a range of low foothills, called the Shephelah, famous for its olive and sycamore trees. Through the Shephelah run a number of valleys leading into the heartland of Judah and because of this the area was densely populated and heavily fortified. In the region were such important Judean towns as Lachish, Beth-shemesh, Gezer, and Beth-horon.

Through the coastal plain ran one of the most important international highways in antiquity. Called "the way of the land of the Philistines" or "the way of the sea" (later, Via Maris), this was the primary commercial and military route between Egypt and Mesopotamia and a major military objective of Palestinian conquerors.

The Central Highlands. This central mountain range forms the backbone of Palestine west of the Jordan and is the continuation of the Lebanon mountain system to the north. This range extends the entire length of Palestine, being broken only by the great plain of the Jezreel Valley.

The northernmost and highest of the central mountain regions is Galilee, where several peaks have a height of over 3,300 feet, although the elevation of the region decreases toward the south. In Old Testament times, Galilee was somewhat sparsely settled, characterized by numerous small villages, some thickly forested areas, productive fruit and olive groves, and isolation from the main communication routes. Few of its towns played any important role in Hebrew history partly because of the difficulty of north-south travel in the area. Nazareth, Jesus' hometown, lay in the foothills of lower Galilee.

South of the Jezreel Valley was the district of Mt. Ephraim, later known as Samaria, which is a broad limestone upland spotted with fertile valleys and small plains. This area was one of the most important political and population regions of ancient Israel. Travel and communication were much easier here than in Galilee, and numerous urban areas existed at the junctions of principal roads. Among these were Shechem, Tirzah, Dothan, and, after the ninth century, Samaria.

The hill country of Judah begins north of Jerusalem without any drastic change in the terrain, the division being more a result of history than of nature. Known in early Biblical times as Mt. Judah (see Josh. 21:11, where RSV reads "hill country of Judah"), this region possesses steep slopes to the east and west, stony outcrops, a forbidding appearance and much land suitable only for pasturage. Areas of fertile soil produced good crops, but the terrain required extensive terracing to preserve moisture and prevent erosion. The eastern slope is excessively steep and dry, plummeting downward to the Dead Sea basin. This eastern region was called "desert" or "wilderness" (in Hebrew *midhbar,* which designated land suitable only for pasturage). This desert area

*The Shechem pass was an important geographical point in ancient
Canaan, for here east-west and north-south commerce routes converged.
Mt. Gerizim, shown slightly bald from recent archaeological excavations, and Mt. Ebal dominate the pass. The city of Shechem, visible
just above the end of the row of trees, was an important political and
religious center. The modern village of Balata surrounds the mound of
the ancient city.*

ROBERT B. WRIGHT

is dotted with caverns and chasms which have offered refuge for outlaws and
rebels, Jewish sectaries, and Christian recluses and which, in recent years, have
yielded scrolls and manuscripts. Judah was far more isolated than Mt. Ephraim
to the north because of the greater difficulty of east-west travel and the fact
that the major international highways bypassed the district. This isolation was
in many ways a plus value for Judah, contributing to its political independence.

Judah was traversed by a major road that ran along the eastern edge of the
tableland and served as a major unifying element. Along this road were located
the main and important Judean cities of Hebron, Bethlehem, and Jerusalem.

The mountain range of central Palestine continues south of Judah into what
is called the Negeb[7] (in Hebrew this means "dry land" but was also used to
designate the "south"). The determinative factor in this area is not the terrain
but the climate, that is, the lack of sufficient rainfall. Most of the Negeb was
wilderness, usable on a seasonal basis by shepherding groups who utilized the
occasional springs in the area. Permanent settlement was primarily along the
main wadies (wadi = stream bed) through which water flowed on rainy days.
Only during times of a strong Judean state did the Negeb possess any extensive

---

[7] See Nelson Glueck, *Rivers in the Desert: A History of the Negev*, rev. ed. (W. W. Norton
& Company, Inc., Norton Library, 1968).

population; although the later Nabateans,[8] who were hydraulic specialists, developed numerous settlements in the area through skillful water conservation. The primary city in the Negeb for Biblical history was Beer-sheba, the town that marked the traditional southern limit of the Holy Land.

The Jordan Rift. The third strip in the successive zones paralleling the coast is the deep depression of the Jordan and Arabah valleys, a massive geological fault bounded on the east and west by mountain ranges rising over 3,000 feet. It is this massive fissure, once a great inland arm of the sea, which has contributed most to the shaping of the Palestinian landscape. The Jordan River,[9] which flows through about one half of this rift, has its origin in several rivulets near the foot of snow-covered Mt. Hermon (elevation 9,232 feet), and its name, if Semitic in origin, means "the descender," which aptly describes its movement. Just south of the Israelite city of Dan and the New Testament town of Caesarea Philippi, both on tributaries of the Jordan, the stream flows into the

---

[8] The Nabateans, with their capital at Petra, played an important role in the history of Palestine, especially during the last century B.C. and the first century A.D. See Nelson Glueck, *Deities and Dolphins: The Story of the Nabataeans* (Farrar, Straus and Giroux, 1965).
[9] See Nelson Glueck, *The River Jordan*, rev. ed. (McGraw-Hill Book Company, Inc., 1968).

The Wilderness of Judah is a barren, mountainous region primarily suitable for only seasonal pasturage.

ROBERT B. WRIGHT

swampland of the Huleh basin which was formed by the damming action of volcanically produced basalt. To the southeast of Lake Huleh (known in New Testament times as Semechonitis) was the important town of Hazor which, during the second millennium, covered an area of 183 acres and had a population of several thousands.

On leaving Lake Huleh, the Jordan flows for ten miles, emptying into the Sea of Chinnereth (also known as the Sea of Tiberias or Sea of Galilee), descending from an elevation of 230 feet above sea level to 695 feet below sea level. The Sea of Galilee, heart-shaped and covering about 66 square miles, is surrounded by a narrow beach and steep hills, the latter being a contributing factor to the sudden storms which agitate its waters. Along the shores of this beautiful lake, with its abundant fish supply and adjacent lush vegetation, were such important New Testament towns as Capernaum and Tiberias.

The Jordan Valley proper, between the Sea of Galilee and the Dead Sea, is a deep gorge about seventy miles in length which broadens in places to almost seven miles in width. Through this valley, the river meanders, its length being almost two and one half times the air mileage. Along the immediate banks of

The Sea of Galilee is a large inland lake formed by the Jordan River. This photograph shows the southern end of the sea, with the Transjordan mountains in the background.

the stream is a dense, entangled growth of bushes, trees, and wild grasses which was inhabited in Biblical times by lions and other predatory animals.

The Jordan empties into the Dead Sea (known in Old Testament times as the Salt Sea or Sea of the Arabah and in the Roman period as Lake Asphaltitis) whose surface is almost 1,300 feet below sea level, the lowest point on the earth's surface, and whose bottom is another 1,300 feet deeper. The sea has no outlet and is thus a natural evaporation basin with water composed of better than twenty-five percent mineral salts, which precludes any marine life whatsoever. In Biblical times, the salt in the vicinity and the bitumen which occasionally rises to its surface were important trade commodities. The most important towns in the fairly heavily populated Jordan Valley were Beth-shan (known as Scythopolis in Hellenistic times and later), where the Jezreel Plain joins the valley, and Jericho, seven miles north of the Dead Sea, where there existed the earliest known Palestinian town with massive defenses and a large population by 7000 B.C.

The Jordan Rift continues south of the Dead Sea, rising again above sea level, and is known as the Arabah. The rift extends, in fact, across the Red Sea, forming the Gulf of Aqabah and picks up as the Great Rift in Africa. The Arabah, about one hundred miles in length, ended at the seaport of Elath (Ezion-geber) from which profitable sea trade with South Arabia and the East African coast was conducted. Copper mines existed in the eastern mountains of the Arabah and their economic importance led to fierce rivalry between the Israelites and peoples to the east over their control and use.

The Transjordanian Highlands. The fourth major natural region of Palestine is the pastoral plateau district east of the Jordan (whence the name Transjordan). Much of this area is true tableland, although there are numerous mountains over three thousand feet in elevation. Four perennial streams flowing into the Jordan Rift (Yarmuk, Jabbok, Arnon, and Zered) drain the plateau land and help divide the land into four districts (Bashan, Gilead, Moab, and Edom).

A major international trade route, the so-called King's Highway, ran the entire length of Transjordan, connecting Elath on the Gulf of Aqabah with the Syrian capital of Damascus in the north. Because of the highway the area was constantly open to invasion from the north, and the proximity of Transjordan to the desert opened the region to nomadic incursions. These two factors contributed to the political insecurity of the area and made Israelite control sporadic and difficult.

CLIMATE AND AGRICULTURE

Two factors have combined to give Palestine a greater diversity of climatic conditions than is to be found on any similar-sized region on the face of the earth. These are the close proximity of desert and sea and the tremendous variations in elevation.

Located in a subtropical zone, Palestine has primarily two seasons in the year, a rainy season during the winter and a rainless season during the summer. The westerly winds, which blow in from the sea, produce the wet storms during the winter, often falling with extreme ferocity. The easterly winds from the desert are hot and dry in the summer and moistureless and cool during the winter. The rainy season begins in late October or early November ("the early rains") and ends in late March ("the latter rains"). Fall cereal planting took place after the beginning of the early rains, and harvesting after the latter rains in the spring. Lack of rain in the fall or rain too late in the spring could wreak havoc with the harvest. Even the winter rains varied greatly from year to year. During a dry year, large areas of agricultural land would revert to partial desert, while during an extremely wet year large areas of even the Arabah and Negeb blossomed with flowers and offered the shepherd lush winter pastureland.

The particular locale of a district determines the average amount of rainfall received, and a matter of miles can make a significant difference. The rainfall diminishes according to the degree that a region is lower in elevation, southerly in direction, and removed in distance from the sea. The two areas receiving the highest amount of rainfall are therefore the Mediterranean coast and the northern mountains in the central highlands and Transjordan. Some examples of rainfall averages illustrate the extreme diversity. Gaza, on the southern coast, receives 16 inches per year; Beer-sheba, thirty miles inland, gets 8 inches; while the southern Dead Sea area, thirty miles farther inland, receives 1.6 inches. Jerusalem receives an average of about 25 inches per year, while the annual rainfall in Upper Galilee averages almost 40 inches. The clouds blowing in from the sea lose their moisture in rising over the central highlands, so that, for example, the western face of the mountains in Judah receives better than 20 inches per year, whereas on the east face (the Desert of Judah), the rainfall is negligible. The absence of rainfall throughout Palestine during the period from April to October is offset to a degree by heavy dews which form, especially in late summer, and help carry vegetable crops to fruition.

The temperature range in the country varies considerably, again because of the special topographical conditions. The Jordan Valley, the Arabah, and the Negeb have extremely hot summers. The higher elevations to the west and the coastal region pick up a cooling breeze from the sea during the afternoon. The length of the cloudless summer days and the elevation of the sun (81.7° above the horizon on the longest day) mean that the land receives as high an amount of solar radiation as any place on the globe. The hot desert winds (the sirocco or khamsin) that blow across the land for days late in the spring and early in the fall have a devastating effect on the vegetation and a demoralizing effect on the people.

The winter temperatures are not excessively severe. Short-lived snowfalls occur annually in the higher elevations as well as do subfreezing temperatures. However, in such places as the Jordan Valley, below-freezing temperatures are very rare.

Palestinian economy has, throughout history, been based primarily on agriculture and shepherding. The latter was centered on sheep and goats, as most of the land is not conducive to the raising of large cattle. The main agricultural products of the land are reflected in various places throughout the Old Testament.

> For the LORD your God is bringing you into a good land, a land of brooks of water, of fountains and springs, flowing forth in valleys and hills, a land of wheat and barley, of vines and fig trees and pomegranates, a land of olive trees and honey. (Deut. 8:7–8.)

Agriculture was dependent upon rainfall, since the land was one that "drinks water by the rain from heaven" (Deut. 11:11) and unsuited to and incapable of irrigation on any large scale. The basic crops of ancient Palestine were wheat and barley, grapes, and olives, from which came the staples of bread, wine, and oil.

HISTORICAL OVERVIEW

The geographical location of Palestine and the military and political significance of this location meant that the land was involved in all the major international struggles of the Near East. The following paragraphs will offer a skeletal summary of the history and politics of the Biblical period in order to provide the reader with a general perspective.[10]

For several centuries, the ancestors of the Israelites lived under tribal conditions within Palestine and along the fringes of the land. The Israelite state, governed by a monarchy, emerged around the end of the second millennium B.C. For almost a century, the tribes were allied as a common nation. During this period of the United Kingdom under the reigns of Saul, David, and Solomon, the Israelites were in control of practically the entire Holy Land with the exception of the southwestern and northwestern coastal zone, where there existed, respectively, the Philistine and Phoenician powers.

Following the death of Solomon in the latter part of the tenth century, the United Kingdom split into the two states of Israel (Ephraim) in the north and Judah in the south. Neither of these two small states was able ultimately to withstand the tide of invaders from Mesopotamia. Assyria threatened Palestine as early as the ninth century and, in the late eighth century, overran the northern Israelite kingdom, incorporated the area into its provincial system, and carried much of its population away into political exile. Judah was seriously weakened by Assyria nearer the end of the same century and forced into a vassal relationship to the stronger Mesopotamian power.

With the fall of the Assyrian empire in the late seventh century, Judean independence was able to reassert itself for a short time. Her freedom was short-lived, however, for Judah was caught in a vise during the struggles between Egypt and Babylonia to fill the political vacuum created by the demise of Assyrian hegemony. For a time, Egypt controlled Palestine only to give way to the Babylonians, who eventually destroyed Jerusalem in the second decade of

---

[10] An excellent summary of Palestinian history from the earliest days of the Hebrews until the First Revolt is given in Ernst Ludwig Ehrlich, A Concise History of Israel, tr. by James Barr (Harper Torchbooks, 1965).

the sixth century and brought the Judean state to an end. The capture of
Jerusalem by the Babylonians was followed by the deportation of leading Jewish
families into exile in Babylonia.

This scattering of the Jews[11] was the beginning of what was called the
Diaspora (dispersion), which led to the establishment of Jewish communities
outside of Palestine. The dispersion was not due entirely to the practice of
exiling captured people followed by the Assyrians and Babylonians since some
Jews seem to have voluntarily fled Palestine, especially to Egypt. The deportation by the Babylonians was of great import for the subsequent history of the
Jews both in and out of Palestine. Most of the Israelites deported by the
Assyrians lost their identity because of assimilation to and absorption by the
populations among which they were settled, a factor that led to the creation of
legends about "the ten lost tribes of Israel."

The Persian empire, which succeeded that of the Babylonian in 539 B.C.,
ruled over Palestine for two centuries. Persia's policy toward captured peoples
was much more lenient than that of its forerunners, and the Jews were given
the opportunity to return to Palestine from their exile and to reinstitute their
life as a religious community.

Palestine was drawn into the orbit of western and European control when the
Macedonian Alexander (the Great) gained possession of the land in 333 B.C.
in the early years of his invasion of the Persian empire. This was of course not
the first time that Palestine had had contact with the western Mediterranean
world. Imported pottery, discovered on an extensive scale and dated prior to
1200 B.C., shows that Palestine was involved in trade with Mycenean and
Cypriote centers, and in later history Cretan and Greek mercenaries served in
Judean armies. But with the advent of Alexander, Palestinian history entered
a new phase and its future faced westward.

With the death of Alexander, Palestine became a pawn in the military
struggles between the Egyptian Ptolemies and the Mesopotamian Seleucids. The
former dominated Palestine for a century and during this period numerous
Jews either voluntarily immigrated to Egypt or were deported. Eventually the
Ptolemies lost control of Palestine to the Seleucids (198 B.C.), whose policies
soon ignited into revolt the flame of Jewish hopes for religious freedom and
political independence. This Maccabean revolt, after numerous military victories and internal Seleucid squabbles, led to the establishment of an independent Jewish state which lasted until the Romans took over Palestine in 63
B.C.

Throughout the New Testament period, Palestine and Jews and Christians
alike were under the control of Rome. Before the middle of the second
century A.D., two unsuccessful revolts by the Palestinian Jews were attempted
against the Romans. The first (A.D. 66–73) resulted in the destruction of the city
of Jerusalem and the Herodian temple; the second produced a humiliating defeat, the end of any realistic hopes for Jewish independence in the Roman Empire, the rebuilding of Jerusalem as a pagan city called Aelia Capitolina, and the
removal of the name Judea from the annals of Roman geography.

[11] Our English word "Jew" comes from the Old French term *giu*, derived from the Latin
judaeus, which in turn ultimately comes from the Hebrew word for "Judean."

PART TWO

THE LIFE AND LITERATURE
OF ANCIENT ISRAEL

4 | THE EARLY HISTORY
OF THE HEBREW PEOPLE

The early history of any ancient people is extremely difficult to reconstruct with any degree of clarity. The beginnings of the great civilizations of the Sumerians, Egyptians, Babylonians, and Assyrians are still shrouded in uncertainty in spite of the diligent efforts of historians and archaeologists to reconstruct their origins. Although it is possible to ascertain some of the factors and general lines of development involved in their prehistory, it is impossible to delineate these in detail and with certainty. What is true about the prehistory of other Near Eastern civilizations is also true about ancient Israel.

There are several reasons why the reconstruction of an ancient people's early history is so difficult. Written documents discussing historical events are not produced in a civilization until the culture has reached an advanced state of sophistication and the people have developed an awareness of their historical existence.[1] Thus contemporary documents from the formative early years do not exist and the historian is forced to work with materials written many decades and often centuries after the events. In addition, materials written at a later time often present a highly idealized or legendary version of the preceding periods, sometimes with an overt desire to make the "past" relevant to later situations. Thus ancient documents, because of the writers' lack of full and accurate historical data or because of the influence of later beliefs and viewpoints, often present the present-day historian with an account of what was believed to have happened or what ideally should have happened. Ancient source material on a people's prehistory, therefore, must be used by the historian in a discriminating and critical fashion in his attempt to reconstruct a hypothetical and approximate picture of the actual course of events. Fortunately, ancient

---

Biblical readings: The basic Biblical materials discussed in this chapter are the patriarchal narratives (Gen., chs. 12 to 35), the story of the exodus (Ex., chs. 1 to 4; 12 to 14), and the making of the Sinai covenant (Ex., chs. 19 and 24). See maps II and III.

[1] On the writing of history in the Near East, see Robert C. Dentan, ed., *The Idea of History in the Ancient Near East* (Yale University Press, 1955), especially the first four chapters; and Hartmut Gese, "The Idea of History in the Ancient Near East and the Old Testament," in James M. Robinson *et al.*, eds., *The Bultmann School of Biblical Interpretation: New Direction* (Vol. I of *Journal for Theology and the Church* [Harper Torchbooks, 1965]), pp. 49–64.

Israel provided a fuller documentation of its early history than did any other Near Eastern civilization.

Archaeology has made tremendous contributions to our knowledge of the early history of Near Eastern civilizations, including that of the Israelites.[2] This is especially the case regarding the material culture where archaeological excavations have elucidated the military, domestic, and urban conditions of the times. However, archaeology does not provide sufficient data to reconstruct in detail the early history and chronology of a people. Its findings are most useful as a supplement to and a check on the written documents themselves.

Any attempt at writing a portrayal of the early history of the Hebrew people must be based therefore on a critical use of the available documents supplemented whenever possible with archaeological data.

THE NATURE OF THE SOURCE MATERIALS

The traditions about the early ancestors of Israel are found in the first five books of the Hebrew Scriptures, the so-called Pentateuch. The chronological perspective of this material covers a time span extending from the creation of the world to the death of Moses. Gen., chs. 1 to 11, presents the Israelite version of creation's beginning and the origin of human history and disobedience. Beginning with Gen., ch. 12, the material focuses upon the figure of Abram (Abraham), with whom ancient Israel began the narrative of her own prehistory. The story is continued with episodes about the ancestors Isaac and Jacob and the fate that befell Jacob's offspring. The book of Genesis closes with the descendants of Jacob living in Egypt and mourning the death of Jacob and his favorite son Joseph.

In the remainder of the Pentateuch, the central human character is Moses. It is he who leads the Hebrews in the exodus from Egypt (Ex., chs. 1 to 13) and guides them to the sacred mountain where the divine laws are spoken (Ex., chs. 14 to 40; Leviticus; Num. 1:1 to 10:10). After a lengthy stay at the sacred mountain, the people depart and spend several years wandering in the desert wilderness, in abortive attempts to enter the country west of the Jordan River, and in warfare conquering the territory of the Transjordanian Plateau (Num. 10:11 to 36:13). The final book of the Pentateuch (Deuteronomy) contains major speeches by Moses surveying the historical events from the time of the people's encampment at the sacred mountain and reiterating the sacred laws to his followers assembled in the conquered land of Moab prior to their crossing of the Jordan River into the Land of Promise. With the narrative of Moses' death, the Pentateuch comes to a close.

With a cursory reading, the narratives of the Pentateuch appear to present a unified story of the history of the Hebrew people prior to their final settlement in the Land of Canaan. A detailed study of these traditions, however, leads to the conclusion that the Pentateuch in its final form is actually a compilation of

---

[2] An excellent introduction to Palestinian archaeology is Kathleen M. Kenyon, *Archaeology in the Holy Land*, 2d ed. (Frederick A. Praeger, Inc., Publisher, 1965).

several collections and literary complexes derived from various authors and periods of Israelite history.[3] Such a conclusion is supported by the fact that the material contains numerous historical and factual inconsistencies, legal traditions with contradictory regulations, differences in literary style, and a variety of theological perspectives.

Some examples chosen from the traditions can illustrate their diversity and multifarious nature. In Gen., ch. 37, for example, there is the story of Joseph's being sold into Egyptian slavery. One group of passages in this chapter has Joseph's brothers selling him to the Ishmaelites, who then sold him to an Egyptian (vs. 25–27; see also ch. 39:1). Another passage has Midianites kidnapping Joseph from the pit into which he had been thrown, without the knowledge of his brothers, and later selling him to an Egyptian officer named Potiphar (ch. 37:28–36). The reference to the fact that the Midianites sold him to the Ishmaelites, in v. 28, suggests that the two variant stories were edited with additions, at a later time when they were combined, in order to provide a more harmonious account. Thus this episode shows evidence of two diverging accounts of the same incident plus the addition made at the editing stage.

The Biblical accounts contain two narratives about the changing of Jacob's name to Israel. In Gen. 32:28, the name change occurs after Jacob has wrestled during the night with a heavenly being at a place called Peniel in Transjordan. However, according to Gen. 35:10, Jacob's name was changed to Israel at Bethel after he had dedicated an altar there. Perhaps these two narratives reflect the influence of different geographical considerations with each of the stories told so as to associate the name change with a particular locale.

Within the laws of the Pentateuch there are diverging legal stipulations at times directly contradictory. In the laws related to Hebrew slaves, Ex. 21:2–11 stipulates that a male slave should be released after six years of servitude but notes that such a regulation does not apply to females (v. 7), whereas in Deut. 15:12 the same requirement of release is extended to both male and female slaves. Altars to the deity, according to Ex. 20:24, could be constructed in numerous places, but in Deut. 12:14 the offering of sacrifice is restricted to a single sanctuary. The regulation concerning the cooking of the passover lamb in Ex. 12:8 requires that it be roasted, whereas similar requirements in Deut. 16:7 demand that it be boiled. Such diversity within Israel's legal traditions suggest that more than one set of laws was in use among the ancient Israelites and that these have been combined in the final form of the Pentateuch.

Perhaps the most prominent disagreement within the Pentateuchal traditions concerns the names used for the deity. Within the Hebrew Scriptures, the Israelite deity is referred to under a number of names and honorific titles. The distinctive name used for this deity was Yahweh,[4] but the traditions differ as to

---

[3] On the criteria used in distinguishing the various sources in the Pentateuch, see H. H. Rowley, *The Growth of the Old Testament* (Harper Torchbooks, 1963), pp. 15–37; and Otto Eissfeldt, *The Old Testament: An Introduction*, tr. by Peter R. Ackroyd (Harper & Row, Publishers, Inc., 1965), pp. 182–188.

[4] It is generally assumed by scholars, on the basis of references by Greek writers, that the original pronunciation of the name of the Israelite deity was "Yahweh." The Hebrew consonantal text gives the name as YHWH. Because of its sacred character, the name ceased

when this name was first used. Exodus 6:2 assumes a revelation of the name for the first time during Moses' early career:

> God said to Moses, "I am Yahweh. I appeared to Abraham, to Isaac, and to Jacob, as El Shaddai, but by my name Yahweh I did not make myself known to them."

Another point of view is represented in the Scriptures, since there are numerous passages in Genesis which declare that the deity was known to the patriarchs by his name Yahweh. In fact, one tradition assumes that Yahweh was worshiped by this name from the beginning of human history. Genesis 4:26 places the beginning of Yahweh worship among the immediate descendants of Adam and Eve when "at that time men began to call upon the name of Yahweh." In many passages the name Yahweh is used without hesitation; in other passages it is rigorously avoided until after the narrative reaches the Mosaic period. These facts suggest the existence of two different theological perspectives concerning the revelation of the deity's sacred name.

Another example of the diverse theological perspectives in the Pentateuch is the two accounts of creation found in Gen., chs. 1 and 2. In the first account (Gen. 1:1 to 2:4a), the created orders are formed out of a watery chaos, in a seven-day scheme, with man and woman created together as the climax of the divine creative activity. In this account the deity is simply referred to as God (Elohim), with no reference to Yahweh. In the second account (Gen. 2:4b–25), the chaos is that of a waterless waste, the acts of creation do not follow a daily scheme, the human male is created before the animals, woman is made after the animals prove to be less than satisfactory as man's companions, and the deity is referred to as Yahweh. These diverse accounts are obviously not from the same stratum of tradition nor by the same author but have been preserved as two accounts supplementing each other.

How are these variations and contradictions in the Pentateuch to be explained? During the past two centuries, since the birth of the historical-critical study of the Bible, scholars have sought to explain these differences along geographical, chronological, and theological lines. Variations in the tradition may reflect contemporary accounts which originated and were utilized in different geographical areas, giving, for example, southern and northern versions. Diverging materials may have developed in one locale over a long period of time and thus reflect an evolutionary process which incorporated interpretations and additions which grew with usage. Theological differences may be explained as the result of contemporary divergent viewpoints with differing localities of usage or as the result of changing theological perspectives and interests which adjusted to new historical and chronological situations. The historical books, the so-called former prophets in the Hebrew canon, provide scholars with, al-

---

to be pronounced in later Judaism, and in the public reading of the Bible, either Adonai ("Lord") or Shema ("the Name") was substituted. When vowels were added to the consonantal text through the use of a system of points, the so-called tetragrammaton (YHWH) was pointed with the vowels of the substituted word to be pronounced. "Jehovah" is an erroneous composite based on the consonants YHWH plus the vowels of "Adonai." In the RSV, YHWH is translated as "the LORD."

though to a limited extent, an account of the historical and theological developments in Israel which may be reflected in the various traditions of the Pentateuch. The content of these historical books makes it possible to outline in broad terms the historical and theological developments within Israel and thus allows for tentative dating of the Pentateuchal materials.

Today, scholars are practically unanimously agreed that the Pentateuch in its final form is a work composed and edited from at least three, perhaps four, literary complexes.[5] The oldest of these is the Yahwistic source often designated by the letter J since it consistently uses the name Yahweh (spelled Jahweh by the Germans, who pioneered in source criticism work) and because of its special interest in places located in the southern state of Judah. This source probably dates from the tenth century.[6] The Elohistic source, or E, so named because of its use of the term "Elohim" for the deity and its interests in the northern tribes, of which Ephraim was the most important, presents material parallel and supplementary to that found in J. Since this source is less prominent than any of the others, is often difficult to distinguish from J, and because it has survived in fragmentary form, it is more difficult to place chronologically. Many scholars argue that E never represented an independent source but was merely additions to and re-editing of the basic material which formed the nucleus of J. A third source is the Deuteronomic material, designated D and found almost exclusively in the book of Deuteronomy. This material, it is widely assumed, provided the legal stipulations for the religious reformation carried out in Jerusalem in the late seventh century. For this reason, D in its literary form is dated to the seventh century B.C.[7] A final complex is the Priestly source, or P, which is particularly oriented to priestly interests and cultic regulations and was probably given its final edited form after the fall of Jerusalem to the Babylonians in 586 B.C.[8] These four main sources or strands of tradition were combined in various stages, probably reaching their final and present form about 400 B.C.[9]

All these sources, without doubt, incorporate material much older than the time of composition. The date at which a tradition was written down or given final shape in oral form may have little to say about the antiquity and historicity of the tradition itself. The writing down of traditional material must be considered as more of an end event in a long process than as the creative act of the writer. Study of individual traditions will generally show the marks of a long period of transmission, usage, and modification.

What implications does this composite nature of the Pentateuchal tradi-

---

[5] Scholars are not unanimous in their division of the sources or in the terminology used; see the summary of Pentateuchal studies in Otto Eissfeldt, *The Old Testament*, pp. 158–182.

[6] Further discussion of J will be given in Chapter 8.

[7] The Deuteronomic material will be treated in Chapter 11.

[8] A discussion of P will be given in Chapter 13. For a position challenging the late dating of P, see Yehezkel Kaufmann, *The Religion of Israel*, tr. by Moshe Greenberg (The University of Chicago Press, 1960), pp. 153–211.

[9] Many scholars choose to speak of "strata" rather than documents in regard to these Pentateuchal sources. See Aage Bentzen, *Introduction to the Old Testament*, Vol. II, 4th ed. (Copenhagen: G. E. C. Gad, 1958), pp. 24–71; and C. R. North, "Pentateuchal Criticism," in H. H. Rowley, ed., *The Old Testament and Modern Study* (London: Oxford University Press, 1951), pp. 48–83.

tions have for the historian who would attempt a reconstruction of early Israel's prehistory? It means, first of all, that there is not one but several Biblical versions of this prehistory which must be evaluated in the light of one another. The existence of duplications and divergencies forces the conscientious reader to make choices about historical probability. Secondly, there are no written documents contemporary with the events narrated, and this means that the historian must always be alert to the interpretations which later generations read into the traditions in order to make them meaningful and relevant to their own times.[10] Thirdly, the primary interests of those who transmitted and edited the traditions about Israel's prehistory were more concerned with religious and theological matters than with reporting the bare facts of history. Thus the layers of tradition in the Pentateuch are often of more aid in illuminating the religious pilgrimage of Israel than in reconstructing the course of Israel's prehistory.

THE ISRAELITE USE OF THE PATRIARCHAL NARRATIVES

Quite early in the history of the Israelite community in the Land of Canaan, the people gave confessional expression to their faith by enumerating and interpreting several decisive events of the past. The elements most emphasized were the activity and faith of the patriarchs, the deliverance from slavery in Egypt, the divine guidance in the wilderness, the giving of the law at the sacred mountain, and the settlement in the Land of Promise. One can immediately recognize in this scheme the skeleton, the cohesive outline, of the Pentateuch. Through the recital of these "redemptive events," the people affirmed its faith in the nation's historical uniqueness and offered its praise to Yahweh.[11]

In the nation's liturgies of thanksgiving (see Deut. 26:1–11) and psalms of worship (see Ps. 105), Israel traced her origins back to the patriarchal period, to the time when her future was destined in the election of the fathers to whom was granted the promise of the Land of Canaan. The following quotation from a hymn of thanksgiving illustrates this perspective:

> Remember the wonderful works that he has done,
>   his miracles, and the judgments he uttered,
> O offspring of Abraham his servant,
>   sons of Jacob, his chosen ones!
> He is Yahweh our God;
>   his judgments are in all the earth.
> He is mindful of his covenant for ever,
>   of the word he commanded for a thousand generations,

---

[10] The question of the use of the Pentateuchal traditions in order to make them relevant to later Israelite generations has been debated by G. Ernest Wright and Gerhard von Rad in articles on "History and the Patriarchs," *Expository Times*, LXXI (1960), pp. 292–296, and LXXII (1961), pp. 213–216.

[11] On the confessional nature of the Pentateuchal traditions, see Gerhard von Rad, *The Problem of the Hexateuch and Other Essays*, tr. by E. W. Trueman Dicken (McGraw-Hill Book Company, Inc., 1966), pp. 1–78.

the covenant which he made with Abraham,
   his sworn promise to Isaac,
which he confirmed to Jacob as a statute,
   to Israel as an everlasting covenant,
saying, "To you I will give the land of Canaan
   as your portion for an inheritance."
(Ps. 105:5–11.)

The narratives about the Israelite ancestors, now found in Gen., chs. 12 to 50,[12] served as instruments and conveyors of the nation's theological beliefs and cultural customs. Many of these stories served an etiological function in order to explain the existence of customs, religious practices, sacred sites, natural phenomena, and ethnic relationships which were a part of Israelite society. This etiological interest is apparent in a number of the Genesis narratives. Two examples will suffice as illustrations. The nineteenth chapter of Genesis contains the story of the destruction of the cities of Sodom and Gomorrah, places understood as the epitome of human corruption with their male citizens guilty of inhospitality and dominated by homosexual lust. The destruction of the area by brimstone and fire is used to explain the desolate terrain around the Dead Sea, which, so it was believed, had once been well-watered land (see Gen. 13:8–13). Lot, Abraham's nephew, escaped with little more than his life to a nearby village, small in comparison to Sodom, and thus the town received its name— Zoar—which means "little" in Hebrew. The existence of a figurelike salt pillar in the vicinity could be explained as a moralistic part of the story—Lot's wife should never have looked back! The story continues in etiological fashion to explain the origin of two tribal groups, the Moabites and the Ammonites (Ben-Ammi). The names of these people were etymologically explained, with Moab understood as meaning "from father" and Ben-Ammi as "son of my kinsman," [13] since the Israelites suggested that their birth was due to drunken, incestuous relationships between Lot and his two daughters. No doubt the Israelites appreciated this bawdy story about the origins of two of their neighbors and sometimes enemies in spite of their distant kinship, and without doubt the Moabites and the Ammonites had different accounts of their ancestry!

In Gen. 32:22–32 there is a narrative which contains a cluster of etiological motifs. In the story, Jacob is returning to Canaan from northern Mesopotamia after an absence of twenty years. Spending the night alone at the ford of the Jabbok River, Jacob wrestles with a nocturnal being, and in spite of an injury inflicted on his thigh he prevails and forces the "heavenly man" to bless him before the coming dawn. The significance of this episode is found in the three, perhaps four, etiologies which it incorporates. The origin of the name Israel is

---

[12] The best commentary on Genesis is Gerhard von Rad, *Genesis, A Commentary*, tr. by John H. Marks (The Westminster Press, 1961). For a different treatment of the traditions see E. A. Speiser, *Genesis* (The Anchor Bible [Doubleday & Company, Inc., 1964]).

[13] In Hebrew, *'ab* means "father" and *mo* could be understood as a contraction of the preposition *min*, "from." *Ben* means "son" and *'am* means "people" or "kinsman." Most of the Biblical play on words is based on the similarity of sounds rather than scientific etymologies.

traced to this "event," since Jacob is blessed with a new name, "Israel," which is taken to mean "he strives with God" (or "God strives"). The name of the town Peniel near the Jabbok is traced to Jacob's comment, "I have seen God (*el*) face (*pan*) to face." The wounding of Jacob's thigh is understood as the origin of the Israelite prohibition against eating the sciatic muscle of sacrificed animals. It may be that Jacob's limping once formed part of an etiology for a cultic limping dance (see I Kings 18:26).

Other of the patriarchal narratives served as patterns in an exemplary or typical manner, illustrating to the Israelite community the nature of the deity's demands and the character of the required human responses. A passage representative of this perspective is Gen., ch. 22. In this episode, Abraham was commanded by God to sacrifice his beloved son Isaac in the land of Moriah. Abraham submitted willingly to this demand even to the point of binding his son to the wood and lifting the knife for the slaughter. But the patriarch did not execute the act, being told that his obedience had been demonstrated. A ram was sacrificed instead of the lad. Perhaps one of the earliest functions of this story was to legitimize the redeeming of children from the necessity of being sacrificed and the substituting of animals as victims. But the story, in its present form, shows the extreme limits to which radical faith and obedience may lead. Abraham's future was embodied in Isaac, the child of promise. With obedience, the future led into darkness. The reader can easily sense the extreme call to obedience that such a story made upon those who told it and those to whom it was addressed.

A third usage of the patriarchal narratives within the life of ancient Israel was much more theological in emphasis and served to bind the whole of the traditions into a structural unity. The material that reflects this purpose concentrates upon the divine promise of the Land of Canaan, showing the tortuous tension which existed between the promise and its fulfillment, the human actions which constantly threatened the possibility of fulfillment, and the divine direction which led toward the final accomplishment often in spite of the human recipients. Without doubt, the promise of the land was already a constituent feature in the narratives during the process of oral transmission before the Yahwist made this theme the unifying thread for the entire presettlement period.

Genesis 12:10–19 relates an account of Abraham's migration to Egypt during a time of famine in Canaan. In the story, Abraham fears for his life during this sojourn in a foreign land and so recommends that his wife Sarah (Sarai) pretend to be only his sister (see Gen. 20:12), supposing that the husband of so beautiful a woman would be in greater danger than her brother.[14] (One must assume that Sarah was still young in this account which circulated as an independent tale unconnected with any chronological data but which after being added to the other narratives made Sarah about sixty-five years old in this episode.) As a result of this ruse, Sarah became an addition to the pharaoh's harem, with

---

[14] Sarah's beauty was a common theme in Jewish folklore. One of the non-Biblical Dead Sea Scrolls, The Genesis Apocryphon, extols her beauty. For a translation and study of this document, see Joseph A. Fitzmyer, S.J., *The Genesis Apocryphon of Qumran Cave I* (Rome: Pontifical Biblical Institute, 1966).

Abraham shown apparently profiting from the transaction. At this point in the story, the hearer would have become aware of the jeopardy in which the promise had been placed. How could the promise, "To your descendants I will give the land," reach fulfillment in the light of such conditions? Would not a child that might be born to Sarah be the pharaoh's rather than the patriarch's? But the thrust of the story was intent on demonstrating that God protects his promise and directs it toward its goal, even overcoming the actions of the one to whom the promise was made. Yahweh afflicts the pharaoh and his house, the truth is discovered, and Abraham sent on his way. If Yahweh guided the course of his promise, was not his word always to be believed?

THE PATRIARCHAL PERIOD

In view of the fact that the Pentateuch represents a composite of four major and diverse literary collections and in the light of the multiple uses that ancient Israel made of the patriarchal traditions, is it still possible to discover within these traditions something of the chronology, the historical background, and the religion of these ancestors of Israel? In spite of the fact that "not a single document in the Pentateuch was written simply to narrate history," [15] the above question must be answered in the affirmative. And it is to this question we now turn.

The Date of the Patriarchal Age. Chronological references within the Bible seem to provide adequate data for placing the ancestors of Israel within a defined time span. According to I Kings 6:1, the exodus from Egypt occurred four hundred and eighty years before construction was begun on the Jerusalem temple in the fourth year of Solomon's rule. If Solomon began his rule about 960 B.C., then the exodus could be dated about 1436 B.C. Exodus 12:40 states that the people dwelt in Egypt for four hundred and thirty years prior to the exodus, which would date the descent into Egypt about 1866 B.C. According to the statistics in Genesis, Abraham would have migrated to Canaan some two centuries earlier, or in the twenty-first century.[16]

There are a number of indications, however, which suggest that the patriarchal period should be placed much later in history.[17] In the first place, scholars,

[15] Samuel Sandmel, *The Hebrew Scriptures* (Alfred A. Knopf, Inc., 1963), p. 337.
[16] For an attempt to date Abraham in the twenty-first to the nineteenth centuries, see Glueck, *Rivers in the Desert*, pp. 60–84. The whole problem of the patriarchs and history has been discussed by Roland de Vaux, O.P., "The Hebrew Patriarchs and History," *Theology Digest*, XII (1964), pp. 227–240, and his "Method in the Study of Early Hebrew History," in J. Philip Hyatt, ed., *The Bible in Modern Scholarship* (Abingdon Press, 1965), pp. 15–29.
[17] W. F. Albright and his students place the patriarchal period between the twentieth and sixteenth centuries. See W. F. Albright, *The Biblical Period from Abraham to Ezra* (Harper Torchbooks, 1963), pp. 1–9, and his "Abram the Hebrew: A New Archaeological Interpretation," *Bulletin of the American Schools of Oriental Research*, CLXIII (Oct., 1961), pp. 36–54; and John Bright, *A History of Israel* (The Westminster Press, 1959), pp. 60–93.

for reasons to be discussed below, are practically unanimously agreed that the exodus events took place in the first half of the thirteenth century and not in the fifteenth. Secondly, the ancient Greek and Samaritan versions of Ex. 12:40 assign only two hundred and fifteen years to the sojourn in Egypt (see also Gal. 3:15–18). This suggests that the references to four hundred and eighty years and four hundred and thirty years may be late and artificial formulations[18] (see Gen. 15:16, which reckons with four generations from the descent to the settlement, whereas in Gen. 15:13 there is reference to a four-hundred-year sojourn in Egypt). Thirdly, Biblical genealogies claim that Moses was a fourth-generation descendant of Jacob. The lineage is Jacob, Levi, Kohath, Amram, Moses (see Gen. 46:8–11; Ex. 6:18–20; note Gen. 15:16). Allowing twenty-five to forty years for a generation, this would place the patriarchal age in the late fifteenth and early fourteenth centuries. Fourthly, many of the age spans of the ancestors appear as artificial creations used to heighten the miraculous in the stories. This would appear to be the case with such stories as Sarah's giving birth at the age of ninety. According to the Biblical figures, Jacob was about one hundred years old when he was sent away to the old homeland to seek a wife. At such an age he could hardly be accused of making a hasty, immature decision about matrimony! Finally, the patriarchal figures are closely associated with the forefathers of the Moabite, Edomite, Ammonite, and Aramean civilizations, which, according to archaeological evidence and non-Biblical texts, came into existence only in the thirteenth and twelfth centuries.[19] All the above arguments converge to suggest that the patriarchal age is to be fitted into the late fifteenth century and afterward.[20]

A further question arises: Is the historical substratum that is reflected in the stories of Abraham, Isaac, and Jacob and his twelve sons to be related to specific historical personages, or are these *primarily* eponyms representing early tribes and clans? It is obvious that the references to the twelve sons of Jacob do not refer to individuals but represent the personification of tribes. The very old songs about the sons of Jacob now contained in the "blessings of Jacob and Moses" (Gen., ch. 49, and Deut., ch. 33) clearly reflect tribal history, and Gen. 49:28 explicitly states that these blessings refer to tribal units.

An analysis of the stories about the patriarchs leads to a similar conclusion. These narratives fall into three major complexes: an Abraham cycle (Gen., chs. 12 to 23), a truncated Isaac cycle (Gen., chs. 24 to 26), and a Jacob cycle (Gen., chs. 27 to 35). Interest in the eponymous ancestors of non-Israelite but related groups and a close association with particular geographical areas are characteristic of the three cycles of tradition. Abraham migrated from Haran in northern

---

[18] On the Old Testament interest in schematic chronology, see Godfrey R. Driver, "Sacred Numbers and Round Figures," in F. F. Bruce, ed., *Promise and Fulfilment* (Edinburgh: T. & T. Clark, 1963), pp. 62–90.

[19] See Nelson Glueck, "Transjordan," in D. Winton Thomas, ed., *Archaeology and Old Testament Study* (Oxford University Press, 1967), pp. 429–453. Current archaeological work in Transjordan may necessitate a reevaluation of the Late Bronze Age in this area.

[20] A fifteenth-century or later date for the patriarchal age is advocated by Cyrus H. Gordon, *The Ancient Near East*, 3d ed. (W. W. Norton & Company, Inc., 1965); and Otto Eissfeldt, "Palestine in the Time of the Nineteenth Dynasty," *The Cambridge Ancient History*, Vol. II, 2d ed. (Cambridge: Cambridge University Press, 1965), Ch. XXVI (a).

Mesopotamia[21] in conjunction with Lot, the representative of the Moabites and Ammonites. Abraham is brought into relationship with the Ishmaelites and other Arabian tribes (Gen., chs. 16 and 25:1–18). Many of the Abrahamic traditions were closely associated with the southern area around Hebron and especially with the tree sanctuary at Mamre. Isaac was connected in the traditions with Ishmael his half-brother and Esau his son, the latter clearly being an eponym for Edom (see Gen. 36:1). The sanctuaries associated with Isaac, Beer-sheba and Beer-lahai-roi, were located in the far south. The Jacob cycle emphasizes the relationship between Jacob and the Aramean Laban and their contact in northwest Transjordan and to a lesser degree the relationship of Jacob and Esau. The stories about Jacob are primarily concerned with the sanctuary centers of Bethel and Shechem in central Palestine and Peniel east of the Jordan.

If some of the stories about Abraham, Isaac, and Jacob reflect the historical fortunes of early tribal and clan groups, some of which later became Israelite, then the geographical locales referred to in the stories show the areas used by these proto-Israelites. The emphasis on the kinship groups shows that these ancestral migrations were part of a larger movement of peoples with connections in both northern Mesopotamia and the Arabian Peninsula. The patriarchal ancestors of Israel may have been originally much more loosely associated with one another than the present structure of the stories suggests. The geographical references in the various cycles might suggest that these traditions once existed independently of each other. Some of the older confessional statements such as Deut. 26:5 mention only one patriarch, in this case probably Jacob, without any reference to the other ancestral heroes. The traditions about the three patriarchs, originally unassociated and unrelated, may have been unified through the use of an artificial lineage of family relationships which pictured the ancestors as father, son, and grandson.[22]

The Amarna Age. In the Biblical traditions, Abraham is designated "Abraham the Hebrew" (Gen. 14:13), while Jacob is spoken of as "a wandering Aramean" (Deut. 26:5). These two terms provide clues for a possible elucidation of the patriarchal age.[23]

The first certain historical reference to Arameans is in an inscription from the reign of the Assyrian king Tiglath-pileser I (ca. 1115–1077 B.C.).[24] In this text they are living along the fringes of the Syrian Desert and appear as bedouin

[21] Abraham is also connected with "Ur of the Chaldeans" (Gen. 11:31; 15:7) in southern Mesopotamia, but the Greek texts read "land" instead of "Ur." Chaldeans do not appear in Near Eastern history until the end of the second millennium. Cyrus H. Gordon, "Abraham and the Merchants of Ura," *Journal of Near Eastern Studies*, XVII (1958), pp. 28–31, has attempted to locate Abraham's Ur in northern Mesopotamia.

[22] On the artificiality of this genealogy and Abraham as a strictly Judean figure, see the comments of John L. McKenzie, S.J., *The World of the Judges* (Prentice-Hall, Inc., 1966), p. 83.

[23] The most ambitious treatments of the patriarchal world are John Marshall Holt, *The Patriarchs of Israel* (Vanderbilt University Press, 1964); and Ignatius Hunt, O.S.B., *The World of the Patriarchs* (Prentice-Hall, Inc., 1967). Both follow Albright's chronology.

[24] Translated in James B. Pritchard, ed., *Ancient Near Eastern Texts*, 3d ed. (Princeton University Press, 1969), pp. 274–275.

groups. Later, a strong Aramean state was established in Syria with its capital in Damascus and several smaller Aramean states were founded in adjacent areas. It must, however, be assumed that Aramean groups moved into Syro-Palestine before the twelfth century. The distinguished archaeologist W. F. Albright has concluded that "the original speakers of Aramaic were nomads of mixed origin, who began settling down on the fringes of the Syrian Desert in the third quarter of the second millennium." [25] From their base in the Syrian Desert, some of the Arameans pushed their way eastward into lower Babylonia, northward into the provinces of western Assyria, and even as far south as Egypt. If the Jacob group was part of this Aramean migration, then Aramaic was probably the original language of the Israelite ancestors who later adopted the Canaanite dialect of the land in which they settled.

According to the Biblical traditions, Jacob married two daughters of Laban the Aramean (Gen., ch. 29), who is portrayed as an owner of herds of sheep and goats, the primary animals of a seminomadic culture. Jacob's wives, Leah and Rachel, as the "mothers" of the primary Israelite tribes emphasize the Aramean background of the later Israel. It must be remembered that Laban is described as Jacob's uncle. The Biblical tradition, therefore, which calls Jacob an Aramean would place some of the Israelite ancestors within the context of the great Aramean movements of the Late Bronze Age (1500–1200 B.C.) which resulted eventually in the creation of a number of Syro-Palestinian states.

Frequently within the Pentateuch, the Israelite ancestors are referred to as Hebrews (Gen. 14:13; Ex. 1:15, 19; etc.). The term "Hebrew" ('ibri) appears to be etymologically related to the term "Habiru" (or 'Apiru) which occurs in numerous Near Eastern documents during the second millennium.[26] The Habiru were not an ethnic, racial, or linguistic group but were a heterogeneous people who were "wanderers" or "aliens" within the established cultures enjoying very limited civic rights. The Habiru were basically social "outcasts" of very inferior status who subsisted by hiring out themselves and their services to individuals, cities, and states. They frequently appear as mercenary soldiers or as bandits.

One of the first references to Habiru in Palestine is found in a victory inscription of Pharaoh Amenophis II (1450–1425 B.C.).[27] Among a list of his captives, 3,600 'Apiru are noted and this group comprised about six and one half percent of the prisoners taken in his military campaign in Syro-Palestine. This percentage suggests that the Habiru groups were fairly numerous but by no means the dominant element in Canaan.

Our primary knowledge of the Habiru in Palestine comes from the so-called Amarna Letters.[28] The first collection of these texts, written in Akkadian

---

[25] W. F. Albright, "Syria, the Philistines, and Phoenicia," *The Cambridge Ancient History*, Vol. II, 2d ed., Ch. XXXII, Sec. iv.

[26] The majority of the texts related to the Habiru question and an analysis of the problems can be found in Moshe Greenberg, *The Hab/piru* (The American Oriental Society, 1955).

[27] A translation of the inscription is given in Pritchard, ed., *Ancient Near Eastern Texts*, pp. 245–247.

[28] On the Amarna Letters, see Edward F. Campbell, Jr., *The Chronology of the Amarna Letters* (The Johns Hopkins Press, 1964); and W. F. Albright, "The Amarna Letters from Palestine," *The Cambridge Ancient History*, Vol. II, 2d ed., Ch. XX.

cuneiform, was accidentally discovered by an Egyptian peasant woman at el-
Amarna in Middle Egypt in 1887. Almost half of the more than 350 letters
eventually excavated were written from Canaanite kings who were nominally
under the suzerainty of the Egyptian pharaoh. The letters were addressed to

*Pharaoh Akhenaton and his queen
Nefertiti stand with raised offering
before the sun-god Aton, represented
by the solar disk. Akhenaton's cultural
and religious revolution was characterized by the first known movement toward an absolute monotheism. This
limestone relief from el-Amarna is now
in the Cairo Museum.*

THE METROPOLITAN MUSEUM OF ART

Amenophis III (1417–1379 B.C.) and Amenophis IV (1379–1362 B.C.), the
latter being better known under the name Akhenaton, which he assumed in conjunction with his religious reform undertaken to establish Aton as the supreme
Egyptian deity. The extreme disarray that had overtaken the Canaanite city-
states during this period is reflected in the letters as well as in the inability
of the Egyptian authority to keep firm control over the area.

In the Amarna tablets one of the basic foes of the native rulers and Egyptian
authorities is the Habiru, who, operating in bands, infringe upon the territories
of the city-states. The Habiru appear not only to have been intruders in
Canaanite culture but also to have been part of a lower-class social revolt
against the Canaanite city-state culture.[29] Several of the letters from local rulers

---

[29] George E. Mendenhall has argued, perhaps with some overstatement, that the Habiru in
Palestine were not immigrants or invaders but rebellious groups drawn from the native

accuse their counterparts of being in league with the Habiru, offering them aid and encouragement. The ruler of Shechem, Labaya, apparently operated in association with the Habiru in his attempt to extend his territorial control. This is of particular importance, since Gen., ch. 34, speaks of the privileges granted to the Israelite ancestors in the vicinity of Shechem although the friendly relationships were broken by the Hebrews (see Gen. 48:22). Later in history, the Shechem area is shown under Israelite control without any reference made to subsequent military action being carried out in the postpatriarchal age.

The overall picture of the Habiru gained from the Amarna correspondence shows numerous similarities to the portrayal of Israelite ancestors. Both groups moved on the fringes of the established Canaanite culture. Like the Habiru, Abraham is described as an "alien" (ger) or "sojourner" without full rights. The patriarchs are generally pictured as much more peaceful than the Habiru; however, Gen., ch. 14,[30] in which Abraham is termed "the Hebrew" presents him as the chief of a band of 318 fighters who acts in consort with local powers to expel invaders. Likewise Gen., ch. 34, illustrates the warlike actions in which the ancestors could participate. The Amarna Letters make no reference to the Habiru's living as pastoral seminomads, but this may simply be the result of the character of the correspondence which was concerned basically with the question of military security.

Without doubt, the ancestors of the later Israelites are to be closely associated with the Palestinian Habiru. This does not mean that the Habiru and the later Israelites are to be identified. Even as late as the tenth century, there were still Hebrews (Habiru?) functioning as mercenary soldiers in Palestine but who were not part of the Israelite state (I Sam. 14:21–22).[31] Some of the Israelite ancestors were simply part of the Aramean migrations and Habiru class associated with Palestine in the third quarter of the second millennium.

It is possible, then, to speak of the patriarchal period as the earliest phase of the settlement in the Land of Canaan by the Israelite ancestors. The Biblical traditions present this settlement in terms of seminomadic shepherds with their donkeys, sheep, and goats seeking out new pasturelands. Since ancient times and even under present-day conditions, Palestine has been used by such shepherding groups during the summer months when the sparse vegetation of the fringe areas proves insufficient for the needs of the flocks. Special agreements or treaty arrangements between the local inhabitants and the seminomadic groups were necessary for peaceful relations. The patriarchs are shown entering into such treaty arrangements with Melchizedek of Salem

population. See his "The Hebrew Conquest of Palestine," *The Biblical Archaeologist*, XXV (1962), pp. 66–87.

[30] Gen., ch. 14, would appear to provide the historian with excellent references to the political rulers at the time of Abraham, but all attempts at identification have proved unsatisfactory, as well as the efforts to assign this chapter to a Pentateuchal source. See the explanation offered by Michael C. Astour, "Political and Cosmic Symbolism in Gen. 14 and in Its Babylonian Sources," in Alexander Altmann, ed., *Biblical Motifs* (Harvard University Press, 1966), pp. 65–112.

[31] See Julius Lewy, "Origin and Signification of the Biblical Term 'Hebrew,' " *Hebrew Union College Annual*, XXVIII (1957), pp. 1–13.

(Gen. 14:18–20), Abimelech of Gerar (Gen. 26:26–33), and Hamor of Shechem (Gen. 34:1–12).

This type of social structure was always open to the development of disputes between different groups of those seeking grazing privileges and between the seminomads and the settled population. The first is illustrated by the dispute between the shepherds of Abraham and Lot (Gen., ch. 13) over rights to pasture and the watering places. The second is illustrated by the conflict between the shepherds of Abimelech and those of Abraham and Isaac over the use of wells (Gen. 21:22–34 and ch. 26:12–32).

One of the basic needs of the seminomads was a burial place for their dead. Such burial grounds are often located in districts visited only periodically but near inhabited areas to prevent desecration and looting. Genesis, ch. 23, recounts the story of Abraham's purchase of the cave of Machpelah from the Hittites in the vicinity of Hebron to be used as a burial area. Tradition asserts that Sarah, Abraham, Isaac, Rebekah, Leah, and Jacob were later buried in this cave. There is, however, a second tradition, probably of northern origin, which postulated a sacred burial area for the Jacob group in the vicinity of Shechem (Gen. 33:19; 47:29–31; 50:4–11; Acts 7:15–16).

The transition from a seminomadic form of life to a more sedentary existence had perhaps already begun among the Israelite ancestors during the Amarna age. Such a transition often involves more than a generation or so, depending upon the circumstances. The patriarchal traditions are almost unanimous in their depiction of the Hebrews as "tent dwellers." Jacob, however, is said to have built a house at Succoth in the Jordan Valley (Gen. 33:17).

The Religion of the Patriarchs. According to two of the primary Pentateuchal traditions—the Elohistic and the Priestly—the patriarchal ancestors were not worshipers of the national Israelite god Yahweh.[32] This probably preserves an accurate historical memory. Patriarchal religion seems to have centered on the worship of a personal god associated with the particular group or clan. Biblical passages frequently refer simply to "the god of Abraham, the god of Isaac, and the god of Jacob." As the personal god of the clan, it was this deity who was understood as the protector and director of the life of the group, the one who guided the fate and fortune of the clan. Occasionally these clan deities are referred to by name. "The Fear [or "Kinsman"] of Isaac" (Gen. 31:42, 53) and "the Mighty One [or "Bull"] of Jacob" (Gen. 49:24) appear in association with these patriarchs.

It is to be assumed that a close bond or covenant was thought to exist between the clan or patriarch and the deity. Genesis 15:7–21 seems to preserve the remnants of a very old covenant-making ceremony although the present Yahwistic text has made Yahweh into the covenanting deity. In the account,

---

[32] The basic study on the patriarchal religion is Albrecht Alt, "The God of the Fathers," now translated in his *Essays on Old Testament History and Religion,* tr. by R. A. Wilson (Doubleday & Company, Inc., 1967), pp. 1–100. A reassessment of Alt's theory is made by Frank M. Cross, Jr., "Yahweh and the God of the Patriarchs," *Harvard Theological Review,* LV (1962), pp. 225–259.

Abraham takes several animals—a heifer, a she-goat, and a ram—and cuts them in half, separating the pieces of the carcasses. Just after sunset, a ritual was enacted in which the participant or the deity passed between the sundered parts of the animals. In the present text, the deity, represented as a smoking

A circular altar at Megiddo which dates from the twenty-fifth century B.C. represents a type of altar in use into the patriarchal age. Six steps lead up to the six-foot-high oval platform which is twenty-nine feet in diameter. Animal bones and other debris discovered at the base show that the altar was used for animal sacrifice.

THEODORE A. ROSEN

pot and a flaming torch, passes through the parts, assuring the patriarch of the eventual fulfillment of the promise of the land. Through such ritual as this, a covenant (berit)[33] was established between the parties invoking the commitment of both. Since such a covenant-making ritual was already present

---

[33] This term for covenant appears to go back to a Semitic word, biritum in Akkadian, meaning "space between." It is possible that it may be related to beritu in Akkadian, meaning "fetter, binder," or perhaps derived from the Hebrew barah, "eat."

in the culture of Mari in the eighteenth century B.C., where the slaughtered animal was a donkey, there is no reason to doubt the historicity of such a ceremony.[34] This covenant of the patriarchal god must have focused on the promise of the land.

In addition to the "Gods of the Fathers," the patriarchs are shown worshiping the god El particularly in their relationship to Canaanite peoples and places. Abraham worships El Elyon ("God Most High," or "El, the Most High") at Salem (Gen. 14:17–21), El Shaddai ("God Almighty," or "El, the One of the Mountains") at Hebron (Gen. 17:1), and El Olam ("God Everlasting," or "El, the Eternal") at Beer-sheba (Gen. 21:33). Isaac worships El Roi ("God of Seeing," or "El, the Seeing One") at Beer-lahai-roi (Gen. 16:14; 24:62) and Jacob is associated with El Bethel ("God of Bethel," or "El of Bethel") at Bethel (Gen. 35:6–7) and erects an altar to El, god of Israel, at Shechem (Gen. 33:20).[35] All these are references to various forms of the great Canaanite high-god El. Since the discoveries of the Ugaritic texts beginning in 1929, the world of Canaanite religion has become better known and correspondingly our knowledge of the role and nature of El in this religion.[36] El was the senior deity or father-god in the Ugaritic divine hierarchy. In the texts, he is designated as "king," "the creator of creatures," and "the father of mankind." His judgment was sought by the other deities as the final word in matters affecting the cosmic order.

The participation of the ancestors in the El cult at various Canaanite sanctuaries was part of their association with Canaanite culture and urban markets. In their exchange of products such as cattle, cheese, and wool for articles manufactured by Canaanite craftsmen, in their treaties over pastoral grazing rights, and in their agreements to allow intermarriage (see Gen. 34:8–12), the semi-nomads shared in the life and religion of the settled population. Some of the ritual requirements made upon the worshipers of the patriarchal deities is reflected in an episode recorded in Gen. 35:1–4. Jacob and his family are required to leave their garments and amulets associated with these "foreign gods" in order to be purified for admission to the El cult at Bethel. Such practices as these are still observed in present-day Arabic pilgrimages to Mecca, where only "holy" garments are worn within the sacred precinct. II Kings 10:20–23 indicates that the worshipers of a particular deity wore special garments in the sanctuary area during the festivals associated with that deity.

The religion of the patriarchs was, therefore, a blend of elements from the worship of the ancestral gods of the fathers and the El cult of ancient Canaan.[37]

---

[34] See Martin Noth, "Old Testament Covenant-Making in Light of a Text from Mari," in his The Laws in the Pentateuch, and Other Studies, tr. by D. R. Ap-Thomas (Fortress Press, 1967), pp. 108–117.

[35] On the nature of El worship and its possible influence on Yahwism, see Otto Eissfeldt, "El and Yahweh," Journal of Semitic Studies, I (1955), pp. 25–37.

[36] For a general discussion of the Ugarit discoveries and texts, see Arvid S. Kapelrud, The Ras Shamra Discoveries and the Old Testament, tr. by G. W. Anderson (Oxford: Basil Blackwell, 1965). On El in the texts, see Marvin H. Pope, El in the Ugaritic Texts (Leiden: E. J. Brill, 1955).

[37] In the patriarchal narratives, there is no concern with the Canaanite god Baal who played such an important role in the agricultural religion. This absence may be due to the lack of

The amalgamation of these diverse traditions no doubt began in the initial stages of contact between the migrating fathers and the indigenous population of Canaan.

THE HEBREWS IN EGYPT

The most frequently occurring confessional statement in the Hebrew Scriptures affirms: "We were Pharaoh's slaves in Egypt; and Yahweh brought us out of Egypt with a mighty hand" (Deut. 6:21). This act of deliverance from slavery to a hostile power represented for the ancient Israelite the primary example of divine redemption. This deliverance was understood as no ordinary event but as a miraculous act accomplished by Yahweh.

The Descent Into Egypt. The Biblical traditions present the migration of the Israelite ancestors to Egypt as the result of a severe famine in the Land of Canaan. The absence of vegetation for their flocks forced the shepherding groups to seek pasture outside Palestine (Gen. 47:4). Such migrations of small groups of seminomadic Asiatics into Egypt, which was not dependent upon rainfall for its water, was a common occurrence in antiquity (Gen. 12:10; 26:1). The report of an Egyptian frontier official to the pharaoh which is dated to the late thirteenth century illustrates this type of migration:

> Another communication to my lord, to wit: We have finished letting the bedouin tribes of Edom pass the fortress . . . to the pools of Per-Atum (Pithom?) . . . to keep them alive and to keep their cattle alive . . . [38]

The size of the group going into Egypt cannot be historically determined, since the editors of Israel's historical traditions later assumed that all the ancestors (i.e., "all Israel") had participated in the descent into and the exodus from Egypt. The introduction to the book of Exodus places the number at seventy (Ex. 1:5), but this may not be a reliable figure, since the passage takes it for granted that this was the total number of Israel's ancestors in existence at the time. The importance of the part played by Joseph, the eponymous hero of the tribe of the same name, would suggest that at least some, if not all, of the members of the house of Joseph migrated to Egypt to find grazing lands for their flocks in the Nile Delta. The presence of such Egyptian personal names as Hophni, Phinehas, and Merari among members of the house of Levi would argue for the assumption that members of this group were also in Egypt. Moses, also a Levite, bore an Egyptian name (from a verb meaning "to beget") which appears as an element in such Egyptian names as Thutmosis and Ramesses.[39]

---

agricultural concerns among the patriarchal ancestors or it may suggest that Baal had not supplanted El as the primary god at this time. For a discussion of Baalism, see Chapter 5.

[38] Translated in Pritchard, ed., *Ancient Near Eastern Texts*, p. 259.

[39] The play on the origin of Moses' name in Exodus is based on the similarity of sounds between Moses' name (*mosheh*) and the verb "to draw out" (*mashah*). *Mosheh* is an active participle form and if dependent on *mashah* would mean "the one who draws out."

The Work of Moses. The stay of the Israelite ancestors in Egypt eventually resulted in their being subjected to forced labor and conscripted for Egyptian construction projects. There is no direct evidence outside the Biblical traditions to support the fact that the Hebrews were compelled to suffer the rigors of state slavery, but it is inconceivable that a people would have created these stories about such dishonorable bondage. Their subjection to forced labor was closely associated with the rise of a new pharaoh who reversed the favorable treatment given the ancestors (Ex. 1:8) and with the construction of the cities of Pithom and Rameses in the Nile Delta (Ex. 1:11). Renovations and constructions at these two cities were carried out during the Nineteenth Dynasty in Egypt especially during the reigns of Sethos I (1318–1304 B.C.) and Ramesses II (1304–1237 B.C.). From the reign of these two monarchs, there are references in Egyptian sources to 'Apiru people who hauled stone and labored on the construction of royal cities. Such references tend to substantiate the Biblical narratives and suggest that the enslavement of the Israelite ancestors in Egypt occurred during the reign of these two pharaohs. If this be the case, the exodus from Egypt should be dated sometime in the thirteenth century.

The central character in the story of the enslavement and exodus is Moses. The account of Moses' birth, his rescue from the Nile by the pharaoh's daughter, and his upbringing at the royal court (Ex., ch. 2) reflect many elements common to a type of folklore tradition widespread in the Near East.[40] The emphasis on the abandonment, the miraculous deliverance, and the rise to rulership of a child are common motifs in the Near Eastern version of the "from log cabin to the White House" tradition. For example, the Akkadian ruler Sargon (twenty-fourth century B.C.) told of his being born in secret as an illegitimate child, then placed in a basket of rushes sealed with bitumen and set afloat in the river to be discovered by Akki the drawer of water by whom he was reared. From such an assumed, inauspicious beginning, Sargon rose to kingship.[41] In the Moses story, the reference to the Egyptian desire to slaughter the male Hebrew children (Ex. 1:15–16) served to provide an acceptable reason for the child's being placed in the river without the suggestion of abandonment. Moses' connection with the Egyptian court may represent an authentic historical tradition.

After killing an Egyptian and hiding his body in the sand, Moses fled to the land of Midian, fearing the wrath of Egyptian authority. The traditional location of Midian places it in northwest Arabia on the east shore of the Gulf of Aqabah, but since the Midianites were nomadic shepherds, the exact area meant is difficult to determine and may refer to the eastern Sinai Peninsula. In exile, Moses married the daughter of a priest who in certain passages is called Jethro (Ex. 3:1) but elsewhere called Reuel (Ex. 2:18; Num. 10:29). Sometimes this priest is designated a Midianite (Ex. 3:1) and at other times a Kenite (Judg. 1:16). These variations are perhaps no more than the reflections of different literary traditions.

---

[40] On the Moses' birth tradition, see Brevard S. Childs, "The Birth of Moses," *Journal of Biblical Literature*, LXXXIV (1965), pp. 109–122.

[41] A translation of this legend is given in Pritchard, ed., *Ancient Near Eastern Texts*, p. 119.

According to the Biblical traditions of Ex., chs. 3 and 4, the revelation of the personal name of "the God of Israel" and the commission to lead the Hebrews out of Egypt came to Moses while he was shepherding his father-in-law's flocks in the land of Midian. Moses is shown astonished at the presence of a burning bush that was not consumed by the flame, and turning aside to observe the phenomenon hears a divine voice. The speaker identifies himself as "the God of your father, the God of Abraham, the God of Isaac, and the God of Jacob" (Ex. 3:6). Moses appears discontent with such a title, since he could not exhort his fellow Hebrews to leave Egypt without the knowledge of the exact name of the God (Ex. 3:13). The following passage (Ex. 3:14–15) is the only text in the Biblical traditions that offers an explanation of the divine name Yahweh.[42] The narrator explains the name by connecting it with the Hebrew verbal root *hyh*, which means "to happen, to become, to be," and by having the deity reply in the first person, "I am [or "I will be"] who I am [or "I will be"]." The writer no doubt associated the sound and consonants of the first person singular verb "I am" (*'eyeh*) with the consonants and sound of the noun Yahweh. If Yahweh was originally a verbal form, it would be third person singular. Probably, the narrator also had in mind the previous reference in the promise, "I will be (*'eyeh*) with you" (Ex. 3:12) and thus sought to emphasize Yahweh's "being present." This emphasis on the name must be understood in the light of the fact that in Near Eastern thought a name could be understood as a statement about the nature of the one so named. Without a knowledge of the divine name, the possibility of a relationship between men and the deity was considered almost nonexistent; without possession of the name, man lacked the basic means to influence the deity.

Whatever the original meaning of the name Yahweh may have been, and this may continue to remain an unknown, the material in Ex., chs. 3 and 4, embodies several historical reflections and points toward answers for the questions that automatically arise from a study of the passages. When did the worship of Yahweh become an important element in the ancestral religion? According to these traditions, Yahwism was introduced to those Israelite ancestors who had gone to Egypt only during the Mosaic era. Who were the original worshipers of Yahweh? The so-called Kenite hypothesis,[43] which is based on an interpretation of this material, supposes that the Kenites (Midianites?) were already familiar with Yahweh worship and that the Hebrews were introduced to this cult through Moses' contact with this clan. This is perhaps an oversimplification, since the seminomadic ancestors of Israel, particularly those in the south, no doubt were in contact with the Kenite groups and Yahwism before the Mosaic era. This latter fact could explain why the southern tradition in the Yahwistic document assumes that Yahweh had always been known and worshiped. The Biblical traditions, at any rate, do not hesitate to show the Kenites as Yahwists, and in the depiction of a later encounter between Moses and his father-in-law, it is Jethro who acts as the superior and as

---

[42] The literature on the origin of the name of Yahweh is enormous. Most Bible dictionaries provide a summary of the various theories.

[43] On the Kenite theory, see H. H. Rowley, *From Joseph to Joshua* (London: Oxford University Press, 1950), pp. 148–163.

the Yahwistic priest (see Ex., ch. 18). Where was the original site sacred to Yahweh? Exodus 3:1 and ch. 3:12 point to a mountain in northwest Arabia or at least to a sacred mountain east of the Jordan Rift. Such a conclusion is supported by other Biblical references that mention Yahweh's coming from this region (Deut. 33:2; Judg. 5:4–5; Hab. 3:3).

THE EXODUS

Upon Moses' return to Egypt, he confronted the pharaoh with the demands of Yahweh, "Let my people go!" In explicating the meaning of this demand, words are placed on the lips of Moses which suggest that "the land of promise" was not the original goal of the exodus-seeking Hebrews:

> The God of the Hebrews has met with us; let us go, we pray, a three days' journey into the wilderness, and sacrifice to Yahweh our God. (Ex. 5:3.)

A three days' journey into the wilderness implies that the Hebrew desire was to travel on a holy pilgrimage perhaps to celebrate some Yahwistic festival in the desert (see Ex. 7:16). Or was Moses being intentionally deceptive about the ultimate aims and goal of the Hebrew desire to get out of Egypt?

In the stories of the subsequent encounters between Moses and the pharaoh, the narrator shows the pharaoh as a man difficult to convince. The scheme of ten plagues which is incorporated into the narrative of the exodus (Ex., chs. 7 to 10) and which builds to a crescendo in the slaughter of the firstborn among the Egyptians (Ex., chs. 11 and 12) is not primarily intended, however, to serve as an illustration of the pharaoh's stubbornness but rather to emphasize the Israelite belief that Yahweh, even in a land so alien as Egypt, could act in a miraculous way to deliver his people.

The immediate events of the Hebrew exodus from Egypt are preserved in two versions. In one tradition, the Hebrews fled from Egypt without the pharaoh's knowledge (Ex. 14:5a), in great haste without preparation (Ex. 12:39). In another tradition, the departure is very deliberate and the Hebrews leave as an armed military columr carrying the bones of Joseph (Ex. 13:18b–19) but only after relieving the Egyptians of much of their wealth (Ex. 11:1–2; 12:35–36). The references to a nocturnal flight appear to be more germane to the accounts than the references to the despoiling of the Egyptians.

The number of Hebrews leaving Egypt is placed at 600,000 men along with their wives and children plus a mixed multitude that accompanied them (Ex. 12:37–38).[44] Such a figure envisions about two and a half million people or a number almost equal to the population of the modern State of Israel. Enough to reach in single file from Cairo to Jerusalem and back again! Such a number must surely incorporate legendary elements. One must think in terms of a

---

[44] It has been suggested that 600,000 is not the best translation of the Hebrew and that the word for thousand should be translated "family group"; see George E. Mendenhall, "The Census Lists in Numbers 1 and 26," *Journal of Biblical Literature*, LXXVII (1958), pp. 52–66. Others have seen the number as a census list from the time of David.

relatively small group, especially if two midwives were sufficient to handle the birth of Hebrew children (Ex. 1:15).

THE WILDERNESS PERIOD

In ancient Israel's theological recital of the significant episodes of her past through which her life and faith were nourished, no cycle of traditions offered greater possibilities for reflection and interpretation than those which sought to recount the events associated with the time from the departure from Egypt to the entrance into the Land of Canaan. The primary incidents expounded in this body of materials are the miraculous crossing of the sea, the stay at Kadesh, the pilgrimage to Mt. Sinai, and the movement into Transjordan.[45] The massive amount of material that became associated with these themes now occupies the bulk of the Pentateuch (Ex., ch. 13, through Deut., ch. 34). The sheer extent of this material immediately raises a question: Why did the collectors of the traditions of ancient Israel assign such an importance to this phase of history? The time in the wilderness between the Exodus and the Entrance was considered that decisive interim in which the people were molded into being "the people of Yahweh" and Yahweh became and showed himself in a unique way "the God of Israel." Exactly when and why the Israelites began to ascribe such significance to the wilderness period cannot be historically determined. Some of the earliest confessions of Israel make little or no reference to the wilderness period (see Deut. 6:21–25; 26:5–11; Josh. 24:1–13), whereas elsewhere, as in the Pentateuch, it is the dominant element (see Ps. 78:17–53; 106:13–39).

The extent and the treatment of the wilderness traditions are due to what might be termed Israel's theological employment of this period as a "type-time." By the use of this term, it is being suggested that the regulations, relationships, and actions *ascribed* to a particular period are often considered in religion and politics as normative and authoritative for subsequent generations. As such, a particular period serves as a pattern or paradigm. In the culture of the United States, the colonial period and the days of the Revolutionary War often tend to function in this capacity. In ancient Israel, there were not only "type-times" but also individuals who functioned for later generations as "type-persons." Moses was of course one who functioned in this capacity as the only valid proclaimer of the divine commandments. Thus all the evolving and developing laws of Israel were given their sanction by being associated with Moses and incorporated into the traditions of the wilderness period. Interestingly enough, the wilderness period as a type-time could be explained in contradictory categories: as either a time of the people's obedience when the Hebrews were divinely protected and kept alive not even suffering the rigors of travel (Jer. 2:1–3; Deut. 8:2–4; 11:1–7) or as a period of absolute infidelity when Yahweh destroyed his own people (Ps. 78:17–53; Deut. 2:14–15). It should also be

---

[45] See Eissfeldt, "Palestine in the Time of the Nineteenth Dynasty," *The Cambridge Ancient History*, Vol. II, 2d ed., Ch. XXVI (a); and George W. Coats, *Rebellion in the Wilderness* (Abingdon Press, 1968).

noted that even Moses, the mediator of the law, according to one tradition, was denied admission to the Land of Promise for failure to keep a divine commandment (Num. 20:2–13).

The Miraculous Crossing of the Sea. The Pentateuchal sources refer to a miraculous event executed by Yahweh at "the sea" to save the departing Hebrews from the pursuing Egyptian army.[46] The basic account of this episode in Ex., ch. 14, does not identify "the sea," though other passages (see Ex. 15:4) call it the *yam suph*, which the Greek versions translated as "Red Sea." The term perhaps means "Reed Sea" or "Papyrus Lake," since *yam* is the Hebrew word for "sea" and *suph* for "papyrus" or "reed." The sea referred to may have been a body of water somewhere in the vicinity of the present-day Suez Canal, although in unambiguous Biblical passages the *yam suph* refers to what is today the Gulf of Aqabah (see I Kings 9:26).

The present form of the narrative of the crossing of the sea is a composite account. One tradition, perhaps the oldest, told of Yahweh's driving "the sea back by an east wind all night" (Ex. 14:21b) allowing the Hebrews to cross on dry land, while the Egyptian army in pursuit drove blindly into the sea after it had returned to its normal flow the following morning (Ex. 14:27). A more miraculous account speaks of the parting of the waters which stood like great walls on either side through which the Hebrews passed, with the Egyptians drowning in the returning flood. Both versions of this episode proclaimed and celebrated Yahweh's intervention in rescuing the fleeing Hebrews and annihilating the Egyptian troops.[47]

This miraculous rescue of the Hebrews at the sea was understood by ancient Israel as the great saving act of Yahweh. As such it was commemorated in song, hymn, and confession as the redemptive work by which Yahweh victoriously intervened to deliver his people. Israelite faith and hope gave expression to its confidence in Yahweh through retelling and reliving the experience of the exodus. Miriam, the sister of Moses, is said to have led the Hebrews in a song of praise after the deliverance:

> Sing to Yahweh, for he has triumphed gloriously;
> the horse and his rider he has thrown into the sea.
>   (Ex. 15:21.)

Israelite parents taught their children that obedience to the will of Yahweh was based on the fact that "Yahweh brought us out of Egypt with a mighty hand" (see Deut. 6:20–25).

---

[46] On the connection of the crossing of "the sea" with the guidance in the wilderness theme, see George W. Coats, "The Traditio-Historical Character of the Reed Sea Motif," *Vetus Testamentum*, XVII (1967), pp. 253–265.

[47] The heightening of the miraculous in the story may be the reflection of influence from the Canaanite myth about Baal's defeat of Yam (sea), which will be discussed in Chapter 5. See Norman H. Snaith, "Yam Suph: The Sea of Reeds: The Red Sea," *Vetus Testamentum*, XV (1965), pp. 395–398; and Frank M. Cross, Jr., "The Song of the Sea and Canaanite Myth," in H. Braun *et al.*, eds., *God and Christ: Existence and Province* (Vol. V of *Journal for Theology and the Church*, Harper Torchbooks, 1968), pp. 1–25.

The Stay of Kadesh. The actual itinerary of the Hebrews' movement through the wilderness cannot be reconstructed with any exactitude. Two places— Kadesh and Sinai—figure most prominently in the traditions. Remnants of an old tradition that understood Kadesh as the destination of the Hebrews' "three day march" (see Ex. 5:3; 15:22b) out of Egypt are preserved in Ex. 15:22 to 18:27.[48] Kadesh, whose name in Hebrew means "sacred," was an oasis area in the northeastern part of the Sinai Peninsula.[49] Indications suggest that the horde which left Egypt conquered the territory around Kadesh (Ex. 17:8–13) where they encamped for a lengthy period .(Deut. 1:46). Contact between the new arrivals and the tribal groups that used southern Palestine as pastureland or that had settled permanently in the southern area could have occurred during this sojourn. The connection of Levi (Deut. 33:8–11) and certain clans associated with the tribe of Judah, especially Caleb, with Kadesh is affirmed from several passages. Apparently, there was once a tradition that spoke of the giving of the law at Kadesh:[50]

> There he [Moses? Yahweh?] made for them a statute and an ordinance and there he proved them. (Ex. 15:25b.)

The Kenites, who were worshipers of Yahweh, appear in texts that belong to the Kadesh cycle (Ex., ch. 18). All these lines of evidence suggest that Kadesh was a sanctuary area sacred to Yahweh and used by several tribal groups, some of which later became part of the Israelite state.[51] The movement to Kadesh of the Hebrews coming out of Egypt would have served to reestablish relationships between this group and other Semitic seminomads who had not gone into Egypt. The bond between some of the later tribes no doubt had its origin in the shared religious life at Kadesh.

The Pilgrimage to Sinai. The immense quantity of the Sinai traditions sits like a granite block within the Pentateuch. The people are pictured as arriving at Sinai in the third month after the exodus from Egypt (Ex. 19:1) and not departing for almost a year (Num. 10:11–13). All the material intervening—the second half of the book of Exodus, the entire book of Leviticus, and the first ten chapters of Numbers—purports to contain incidents and laws that had their setting at Sinai. Most scholars believe, however, that practically all of this

---

[48] The similarity of the narratives in Ex., chs. 16 and 17 with Num., chs. 11 ff., with references in both to the contention and strife, water from the rock, quail for food, and manna from heaven, suggests that these are parallel Kadesh traditions. On the nature of the manna and its connection with Arabic *man*, a sticky substance produced by insects, see F. S. Bodenheimer, "The Manna of Sinai," *The Biblical Archaeologist*, X (1947), pp. 2–6; reprinted in *The Biblical Archaeologist Reader*, I, ed. by David N. Freedman and G. Ernest Wright (Doubleday & Company, Inc., 1961), pp. 76–80.

[49] On the location and tradition of Kadesh, see Murray Newman, *The People of the Covenant* (Abingdon Press, 1962), pp. 72–101.

[50] On the inclusion of the Sinai traditions and Sinai as the place of the giving of the law within the Pentateuchal scheme, see von Rad, *The Problem of the Hexateuch*, pp. 13–20.

[51] The use of a sacred area by different clan groups lacking political unity is illustrated in the pre-Islamic tribal use of Mecca. See E. C. Wolf, "The Social Organization of Mecca and the Origins of Islam," *Southwestern Journal of Anthropology*, VII (1951), pp. 329–356.

material in its present form comes from a time later than the wilderness period, since it reflects a highly sophisticated cultic system and presupposes an agricultural and sedentary background.

The Sinai traditions, nonetheless, embody three primary perspectives which are undoubtedly based upon authentic and historical recollections. There is, first of all, the close association between Yahweh and the holy mountain. Sinai was in a unique way the abode of Yahweh. Israel's songs of military victory celebrated the coming of Yahweh from Sinai to aid his people in distress (Judg. 5:4–5). Secondly, Sinai was the object of sacred pilgrimages. Even as late as the ninth century, the prophet Elijah is shown going in pilgrimage to Horeb (Sinai) to rejuvenate his faith in Yahweh (I Kings 19:8). There is no reason to doubt the tradition that narrates the visit to Sinai of the escaping Hebrews from Egypt during the course of their stay in the wilderness. This sacred area must have been periodically visited by the Yahweh worshipers in the south, among whom were some of the neighbors of the later Israel. Thirdly, Sinai was a place of covenant-making. Chapters 19 and 24 of Exodus record the succinct features of the covenant-making festival perhaps as it was originally celebrated at Sinai and later reenacted at sanctuaries in the Land of Canaan.[52] The festival appears to have been a three-day affair[53] in which two days were spent in purification and consecration, including the washing of one's garments, the strict observances of certain taboos, and perhaps fasting (Ex. 19:10–16). The third day was characterized by the actual ceremony of covenant-making and the subsequent celebration (Ex., ch. 24). The basic element in the covenant ceremony involved the proclamation of the divine demands and commandments, the commitment of the people to obedience, and a ritual act in which Yahweh and the people shared, thus sealing the bond between worshipers and deity. This act binding together Yahweh and the people is reflected in the sacrifice and blood ritual (Ex. 24:4–8) and in the eating and drinking associated with the covenant sacrifice (Ex. 24:9–11).

---

[52] The nature and content of this covenant will be further discussed in Chapter 5.
[53] In early Israel, the day was reckoned from sunrise to sunrise. See Jack Finegan, *Handbook of Biblical Chronology* (Princeton University Press, 1964), pp. 7–15.

5 | THE HEBREW TRIBES
IN THE LAND OF CANAAN

Throughout the years, a consistent feature of Near Eastern culture has been the perpetual struggle between "the Desert and the Sown." The nomads of the desert and the seminomads and socially dispossessed on the fringes of civilization tend to encroach upon the settled and agriculturally rich lands of the "Fertile Crescent." The description of Canaan as a "land flowing with milk and honey" (Deut. 26:9) expresses the sentiment of groups living on the borders of the cultivated areas. Every stratum of the early historical traditions of ancient Israel affirms that the nation's ancestors had moved into Canaan and occupied the land. In Joshua, with Yahweh as the alleged speaker, this opinion is clearly expressed:

> I gave you a land on which you had not labored, and cities which you had not built, and you dwell therein; you eat the fruit of vineyards and olive-yards which you did not plant. (Josh. 24:13.)

How did the Hebrew tribes eventually come to possess the Land of Canaan? Was the land subdued in one massive onslaught? What forms of government and association found expression among the tribes in the early days of Israelite occupation of "the promised land"? It is to these questions that we now turn our discussion.

THE SETTLEMENT AND CONQUEST TRADITIONS

The Biblical traditions contain two major presentations of the occupation of Canaan.[1] One account is preserved in the first twelve chapters of The Book of Joshua. In this narrative, the settlement is pictured as a swift and destructive conquest from across the Jordan River in which all the tribes participate under the single leadership of Joshua. In a grand strategy with three attacks on the center, south, and north, the people are shown taking complete possession of

---

Biblical readings: The basic Biblical materials discussed in this chapter are Josh., chs. 1 to 11; 24; Judg., chs. 1 to 5; 17 to 18. Important texts are also found in Gen. 49:1–27 and Deut., ch. 33.

[1] See G. Ernest Wright, "The Literary and Historical Problem of Joshua 10 and Judges 1," *Journal of Near Eastern Studies,* V (1946), pp. 105–114.

the land and annihilating all the population, with the exception of those groups which aided the invaders (Josh. 6:22–25) or else made treaties of peace with the newcomers (Josh., ch. 9). The outlook of this material is reflected in the following summary:

> So Joshua took all that land, the hill country and all the Negeb and all the land of Goshen and the lowland and the Arabah and the hill country. . . . There was not a city that made peace with the people of Israel, except the Hivites, the inhabitants of Gibeon; they took all in battle. For it was Yahweh's doing to harden their hearts that they should come against Israel in battle, in order that they should be utterly destroyed, and should receive no mercy but be exterminated, as Yahweh commanded Moses. (Josh. 11:16–20.)

A different version of the conquest is found in the opening chapter of The Book of Judges. In this account, there is no single leader, the tribes operate individually, groups participate that were only loosely related to the later Israelite tribes, much of the invasion takes place from the south, it is primarily the hill country that is occupied, and the Canaanites are not slaughtered. Embodied in this chapter, there is also the so-called "negative conquest tradition" which enumerates the districts not conquered by the invaders (see esp. Judg. 1:27–33). The perspective of this collection with its interest in the tribe of Judah is represented by the following summary verse:

> Yahweh was with Judah, and he took possession of the hill country, but he could not drive out the inhabitants of the plain, because they had chariots of iron. (Judg. 1:19.)

It is obvious that these two accounts do not describe two sets of events that happened in historical succession, although they have been edited within the Bible in a chronological sequence. If the job of conquering Canaan had been carried out as is described in Josh., chs. 1 to 12, then the events in Judg., ch. 1, defy understanding! If the narrated form of Josh., chs. 1 to 12, was in existence before Judg., ch. 1, it is impossible to explain why and how Judg., ch. 1, came into existence. So it must be assumed that the latter version is older and more authentic than the former. However, even the account in Judg., ch. 1, contains episodes of a legendary nature (ch. 1:5–7) whose interests are not strictly historical as well as direct contradictions (compare Judg. 1:8 with 1:21).

Both of these accounts already show the tendency to consolidate traditions and to ascribe to the larger and better-known groups (such as Judah and Israel) events that originally involved smaller and less-important groups. This can be illustrated by an example: Who originally took over the city of Hebron, a large and important town twenty miles south of Jerusalem? According to Josh. 15:13–14, the city was taken by Caleb, the eponymous hero of a tribe by the same name. However, in Judg. 1:9–10, it is Judah who takes Hebron, defeating the same persons as Caleb. In Josh. 10:36–37, it is all Israel under Joshua who is portrayed as the conqueror. Undoubtedly, the original version told of the capture of Hebron by the Calebites, with the episode being ascribed to Judah at a later time when the Caleb clan became a part of Judah. The conquest by all Israel represents a third, later, and more idealized account.

ARCHAEOLOGICAL CONSIDERATIONS

In attempting to interpret properly the divergent portraits of the conquest depicted in Josh., chs. 1 to 12, and Judg., ch. 1, the historian would be greatly assisted if some external evidence outside the Bible could be used as a guide and check on the Biblical traditions. The most obvious possible source of such evidence is archaeological excavations, since a number of the sites referred to in the accounts of the conquest have been explored by archaeologists. The capture of the cities of Jericho and Ai is discussed in some detail in Josh., chs. 6 to 8. Without doubt the most dramatic narration concerns the taking of Jericho, where the followers of Joshua circumambulated the city for seven days, after which the massive walls "came tumbling down." Excavations at Tell es-Sultan,[2] the site of ancient Jericho, have shown, however, that Jericho was uninhabited in the thirteenth century when the Hebrews were supposed to have entered Canaan after leaving Egypt. During the preceding century the only settlement on the site was small and unfortified. Archaeological excavations at Ai,[3] whose capture as the result of an ambush is told in Josh., chs. 7 and 8, have shown that this city was unoccupied from about 2000 B.C. until 1200 B.C. So there would have been no major city on the site when the Hebrews moved into Canaan!

Archaeological evidence suggests that the Jericho and Ai stories cannot be taken as historical. They must be simply etiologies told to explain the existence of impressive ruins (Ai in Hebrew means "the ruin") and to ascribe the destruction to the Israelite ancestors. The Jericho story appears to be patterned after some cultic celebration, judging from the role played by the priests, the use of shouts and trumpets, and the sevenfold sacred circling of the site.

Other excavated sites, such as Lachish (Josh. 10:31–32), Hazor (Josh., ch. 11), and Bethel (Judg. 1:22–26), do show a major destruction phase which can be dated to the late thirteenth and early twelfth centuries.[4] Some of these could have been destroyed by the invading Hebrews, although it is difficult to be certain since a destruction level does not necessarily have to be the result of a military attack. It should also be noted that military destruction of some of these cities could have been the result of warfare between rival city-states, the work of the "Sea Peoples" some of whom were invading Palestine from the west during this period, or the consequence of the Egyptian expeditions into Palestine conducted by the pharaohs Ramesses II (1304–1237 B.C.) and Merneptah (1236–1223 B.C.).

---

[2] See Kathleen M. Kenyon, *Digging Up Jericho* (Frederick A. Praeger, Inc., Publisher, 1957), pp. 256–265.

[3] It is assumed that the site of Ai is at et-Tell. On the most recent excavations there, see Joseph A. Callaway, "The 1964 Ai (et Tell) Excavations," *Bulletin of the American Schools of Oriental Research*, CLXXVIII (April, 1965), pp. 13–40, and his "New Evidence on the Conquest of 'Ai," *Journal of Biblical Literature*, LXXXVII (1968), pp. 312–320.

[4] On the excavations at Lachish, see the summary by G. Ernest Wright, "Judean Lachish," in *The Biblical Archaeologist Reader*, II, ed. by Edward F. Campbell, Jr., and David N. Freedman (Doubleday & Company, Inc., 1964), pp. 301–309; on Hazor, the article by Yigael Yadin, in the same volume, pp. 191–224; and on Bethel, James L. Kelso, *et al.*, *The Excavation of Bethel* (1934–1960) (American Schools of Oriental Research, 1969).

One can only conclude that the archaeological evidence relative to the thirteenth-century invasion by the Hebrews is about as ambiguous as the literary traditions.[5] The best that the historian can hope for is the establishment of a hypothetical reconstruction of the final settlement which takes full account of both the archaeological evidence and the literary accounts. Any such presentation, however, must be understood as tentative and lacking the type of data which makes a hypothesis conclusive.

RECONSTRUCTION OF THE SETTLEMENT

In Israel's final portrayal of the settlement in the land of Palestine, the twelve tribes—Reuben, Simeon, Gad, Judah, Issachar, Zebulun, Manasseh, Ephraim, Benjamin, Dan, Asher, and Naphtali (see Num., ch. 26)—act together in simultaneous assault to conquer the Promised Land (Josh., chs. 1 to 12) which was then divided among the tribes by lot (Josh., chs. 13 to 19). This version certainly represents a romanticized and idealized account which is clearly unhistorical and is even contradicted by other Biblical texts. Even though this is not the way things actually happened, it is still possible to utilize the traditions unencumbered by this perspective and arrive at some of the major outlines of the actual course of events.[6]

As was suggested in the preceding chapter, the earliest phase of the Hebrew settlement in Palestine is reflected in the patriarchal narratives. This initial penetration of the Israelite ancestors no doubt occurred in the course of seasonal migration by seminomads in search of pasturage for their flocks. During the summer months, when foliage deteriorated in sparsely watered areas, the hill country with its forests and the recently harvested grain lands would have been sought out by the shepherding groups. In the course of time, the transition to a more sedentary way of life would have taken place, with settlement being limited to the less-populated hill districts. Such a transition would perhaps have been possible under fairly peaceful conditions so long as the settling groups were not very numerous. As a whole, the patriarchal narratives show the incomers living as "guests" and primarily in peaceful relationships with the Canaanite inhabitants.

Which of the tribal groups were the first to move into Canaan and consolidate is difficult to tell. It may be that the folklore stories about the birth of the tribal ancestors (Gen. 29:1 to 30:24; 35:16–21) contain some hints in their division of the "sons of Jacob" among two wives and two concubines.[7] The oldest sons of the oldest wife, Leah, were Reuben, Simeon, Levi, and Judah (Gen. 29:31–35), while the primary but late-born son of the younger but favored wife, Rachel, was Joseph (Gen. 30:22–24). By Rachel's female servant, Jacob

---

[5] See McKenzie, *The World of the Judges*, pp. 45–75.

[6] In this and following sections, the discussion is indebted to Alt, *Essays on Old Testament History and Religion*, pp. 173–221; and Yohanan Aharoni, *The Land of the Bible*, tr. by A. F. Rainey (The Westminster Press, 1967), pp. 174–253.

[7] On the Leah-Rachel tribes, see Otto Eissfeldt, "The Hebrew Kingdom," *The Cambridge Ancient History*, Vol. II, 2d ed., Ch. XXXIV, Sec. iv.

became the father of Dan and Naphtali (Gen. 30:1–8) and by Leah's servant, the father of Gad and Asher (Gen. 30:9–13). Leah later gave birth to Issachar and Zebulun (Gen. 30:14–24), and, lastly, Benjamin was born to Rachel within the Land of Canaan (Gen. 35:16–21).[8] If there is any historical information reflected in this narrative, the stories would suggest that there were two basic Jacob groups: the older Leah-tribes (Reuben, Simeon, Levi, Judah, Issachar, and Zebulun) and the young Rachel-tribe of Joseph. The concubine tribes probably had a more indirect historical and ethnic relationship to the primary groups.

The Leah-tribes were perhaps the oldest tribal groups and were among the first to have entered Canaan, maybe as early as the fourteenth century. It is conceivable that Judg. 1:3–20 preserves the remnants of an account about the Leah-tribes' entrance into Canaan from the south. At any rate, the oldest independent tribal narratives in Genesis concern three of these tribes. In Gen., ch. 34, Simeon and Levi[9] are shown attacking Shechem in central Palestine, but apparently they suffered severely and were forced back southward (see Gen. 49:5–7). In Gen., ch. 38, Judah is shown peacefully intermarrying with the local southern Canaanite population and thus acquiring settlement rights and territory. Issachar, and probably Zebulun, was able to settle in northern Palestine only when "he bowed his shoulder to bear and became a slave at forced labor" (Gen. 49:14–15; see also Deut. 33:18–19). Issachar in Hebrew means "hired man," "hireling," and suggests that the tribe was named after the status.[10] Very little is known about Reuben except that the tribe became decimated (Deut. 33:6) and was forced out of southern Canaan and had to resettle in Transjordan.[11]

Very little is known about the concubine tribes. Asher is referred to in an Egyptian document dating from the reign of Ramesses II.[12] Apparently the tribe was already settled in Galilee by the thirteenth century. The tribe of Dan was one of the last tribes to settle permanently. The tribe originally settled in southwest Canaan (Judg. 1:34–35) but was unable to hold its territory and most of its members were forced to migrate and resettle in the far north (Judg., ch. 18).[13] The narrative of the Danite migration graphically illustrates the way in which the tribes acted in independent fashion to secure territory. The movement of the tribe of Naphtali into the hill country of northern Galilee may be referred to in an inscription set up in the city of Beth-shan by the Egyptian pharaoh Sethos I (1318–1304 B.C.).[14] The stele refers to 'Apiru who were moving

---

[8] See James Muilenburg, "The Birth of Benjamin," *Journal of Biblical Literature*, LXXV (1956), pp. 194–201.

[9] Outside of the narrative in Gen., ch. 34, and the reference in Gen. 49:5–7, Levi does not appear as a secular tribe. The Levites were a religious order and though classed as a tribe, they did not possess a territory.

[10] The settlement of Issachar is probably related to the use of laborers by the king of Megiddo after a war with Labaya. See Aharoni, *The Land of the Bible*, p. 175.

[11] Reuben's settlement west of the Jordan is inferred from place names: see Martin Noth, *The History of Israel*, 2d ed., tr. rev. by Peter R. Ackroyd (Harper & Brothers, 1960), pp. 63–65.

[12] See the reference in Pritchard, ed., *Ancient Near Eastern Texts*, p. 477.

[13] See Martin Noth, "The Background of Judges 17–18," in Bernhard W. Anderson and Walter Harrelson, eds., *Israel's Prophetic Heritage* (Harper & Brothers, 1962), pp. 68–85.

[14] For a translation of this text, see Pritchard, ed., *Ancient Near Eastern Texts*, p. 255.

into the area and causing trouble for the local Asiatics. The tribe of Gad, which moved into southern and central Transjordan (Gilead), appears to have belonged to the earliest phase of Hebrew penetration, but the tribe appears to have remained nomadic for some time (Gen. 49:19). Judges 11:26 with its reference to three hundred years of Hebrew occupation in Gilead suggests a fourteenth-century date for Gad's movement into Transjordan.

The Rachel-tribes were the last wave to move into the land and it was certainly this group, or a part of it, which went into Egypt and experienced the events of the exodus and wilderness wanderings. It was this group which invaded Palestine in the second half of the thirteenth century. The Rachel-tribes, which were originally designated the "house of Joseph," split into three tribal groupings, Ephraim, Manasseh, and Benjamin, after entering the Land of Canaan. The Ephraim tribe acquired its name from the geographical expression "Mount Ephraim," which was the name of the central mountain region (see Josh. 17:15; I Sam. 1:1; I Kings 4:8). "Benjamin" is a geographical term meaning "son of the south" and expresses the relationship of this group to the other members of the house of Joseph. The tradition about Benjamin's birth (Gen. 35:16-21) preserves the recollection of the formation of the Benjamin tribe within the Land of Canaan.[15]

The movement of the house of Joseph into central Canaan was much more of a military invasion than was the penetration of the other and older tribal groups. Joshua was apparently the "commander" of this group and an Ephraimite (see Josh. 24:29-30, which gives the tradition of Joshua's burial). After leaving Kadesh, the house of Joseph seems to have attempted an invasion of Palestine from the south (Num. 14:44-45), but its efforts were frustrated by the local inhabitants. The house of Joseph eventually secured a foothold and corridor in Transjordan by overcoming Sihon the king of the city-state of Heshbon (Num. 21:21-26).[16] With control of this territory, their movement across the Jordan followed and this no doubt involved military struggles, as the story of the capture of Bethel (Judg. 1:22-26) indicates. This invasion of the house of Joseph may have served as a catalyst to spur other of the tribes to take military action against the Canaanite city-states. If so, the destruction levels excavated at several Palestinian sites may be the result of this and subsequent action.

In summary, the following can be said about the settlement in the Land of Canaan: The process was a gradual one extending over several centuries and reaching its final stages only in the time of Saul and David at the beginning of the tenth century. Much of the occupation was the result of peaceful infiltration. Most of the tribes came into existence in Palestine after various clan groups settled in geographical proximity and consolidated and amalgamated. Many of these tribal elements may have been indigenous to Canaan, local peasant groups that allied themselves with the new arrivals.[17] As a rule, the tribes

---

[15] On the geographical factors involved in the settlement and naming of the tribes, see Noth, *The History of Israel*, pp. 53–68.

[16] On the Transjordanian conquest, see Aharoni, *The Land of the Bible*, pp. 184–192.

[17] On this indigenous population, see Mendenhall, "The Hebrew Conquest of Palestine," *The Biblical Archaeologist*, XXV (1962), pp. 66–87.

operated independently in their acquisition of territory. The entry of the house of Joseph under Joshua in the thirteenth century was the most militant phase of the settlement. It was this phase which later popular tradition, for nationalistic and military reasons, turned into the story of a devastating military onslaught by "all Israel" under the direction of Joshua.

CHART 2: THE LATE BRONZE AGE (1500–1200 B.C.)

B.C.	EGYPT	PALESTINE	SYRIA-MESOPOTAMIA
1500	The New Kingdom Tuthmosis III (1504–1450)* Strong Egyptian state	City-states under Egyptian control	Hittite and Mitanni states
		Beginning of migration of Israelite ancestors into Palestine	
	Amenophis II (1450–1425) Tuthmosis IV (1425–1417)	Patriarchal Age	
	Amarna Age Amenophis III (1417–1379)	Weakening of Egyptian authority	Strong Hittite empire
1400		Armana Letters showing city-state warfare and activity of Habiru	
	Amenophis IV (1379–1362)	Aramean migrations	
		Continued migration of Israelite ancestors into the land	Old Assyrian kingdom
		Leah-tribes	
	Strong Nineteenth Egyptian Dynasty (1320–1200)	Migration to Egypt by some Israelite ancestors	
	Sethos I (1318–1304)		
1300	Ramesses II (1304–1237)		
	Merneptah (1236–1223)	Exodus from Egypt	Fall of Ugarit
		Invasion of house of Joseph	End of Hittite empire
	Weakening of Egyptian empire	Invasion of "Sea Peoples"	
1200	Twentieth Dynasty (1200–1085)	Warfare of city-states against "Sea Peoples" (Philistines) and Israelite ancestors	Assyrian decline
	Ramesses III (1198–1166) Wars with invading "Sea Peoples"		

* Dates of Egyptian rulers are from the 2d ed. of *The Cambridge Ancient History*, Vols. I and II.

ISRAEL AND JUDAH

In the years following the settlement of the tribes in the Land of Canaan, the tribal groups allied themselves into two major tribal federations.[18] This later organization of the tribes into northern and southern alliances is reflected in the designations Israel and Judah. In Josh., ch. 24, Joshua is shown officiating at a major ceremony in which the leaders of the tribes of Israel bound themselves together in a covenant agreement swearing their allegiance to Yahweh.[19] This ritual is associated with the ancient town of Shechem in central Palestine, a town that had been a major political and religious center throughout the Middle and Late Bronze Age periods. In the convocation, a predominant role is played by Joshua and emphasis is placed on the Yahweh worship of "his house."

Who was the Israel that swore its allegiance to Yahweh in this ritual? The text does not tell us, and in the final editing of the traditions it was assumed that the Israel referred to was the classical twelve tribe group. If the origin of the name Israel were known for certain, this might aid in reaching a conclusion, but the origin is unknown. The term was used occasionally as a concept of political geography to refer to a territorial area (see I Sam. 13:19 and II Sam. 2:8–9). The term also seems to have been used to designate a pre-Yahweh group in Canaan centered around the city of Shechem, since Jacob is shown erecting an altar in Shechem and calling it "El, the God of Israel" (Gen. 33:18–20).[20] The fact that the name is formed through the use of the name of the Canaanite god El suggests that it was employed by a group before the association of the name with Yahweh worshiping tribes. The earliest non-Biblical reference to Israel is found on a commemorative victory stele set up by Pharaoh Merneptah in the fifth year of his reign (ca. 1230 B.C.). Part of the inscription reads:

> The princes are prostrate, saying: "Peace!"
>   Not one raises his head among the Nine Bows (i.e.,
>   Egypt's enemies).
> Desolation is for Tehenu; Hatti is pacified;
>   Plundered is the Canaan with every evil;
> Carried off is Ashkelon; seized upon is Gezer;
>   Yanoam is made as that which does not exist;
> Israel is laid waste, his seed is not;
>   Hurru is become a widow for Egypt.[21]

---

[18] The most ambitious exposition of the two-tribal federations theory is that of Newman, *The People of the Covenant*, pp. 39–71.

[19] Martin Noth's theory of a twelve-tribe amphictyony formed in the early period of the Judges, accepted by most German, British, and American Old Testament scholars, goes beyond the evidence. See his *The History of Israel*, pp. 85–108; and the criticism of this theory by Harry M. Orlinsky, "The Tribal System of Israel and Related Groups in the Period of the Judges," *Oriens Antiquus*, I (1962), pp. 11–20.

[20] On the basis of Ugaritic studies, it is possible to translate Gen. 33:20: "There he erected an altar and called out 'Truly, El is the God of Israel.' "

[21] The name Israel is written in this inscription with an Egyptian determinative that suggests a people rather than a land. Translation is from Pritchard, ed., *Ancient Near Eastern Texts*, p. 378.

Whether the Israel mentioned by Merneptah is to be identified with the pre-Yahwistic group or with the Yahwistic Israel that came into existence after the invasion of those Hebrews who had experienced the exodus from Egypt is uncertain. Perhaps a dichotomy between the two groups never existed. Hebrews who had been in Palestine all along may have been part of a tribal group called Israel. With the arrival of the members of the house of Joseph, one of the new elements introduced into central Palestine was Yahwism, with which the tribes had come into contact in the Sinai and Kadesh areas. The emphasis in Josh., ch. 24, is not so much, even in its present form, concerned with the formation of a new tribal league as with the introduction of Yahwism and the challenge to faithful decision and obedience.

The Yahwistic tribal league "Israel" has been profitably compared with similar tribal leagues or amphictyonies which are known to have existed among the ancient Greeks and Arabs.[22] In such an amphictyony, the tribes were loosely bound together by treaty and shared common religious and military obligations. Generally, such tribal confederacies made use of a central sanctuary in their observance of special religious festivals. The laws that stipulated the responsibilities and obligations of the tribes were administered in conjunction with the primary sanctuary. Care of the central sanctuary seems to have been delegated to the tribes in rotation, and for this reason six or twelve was a favored number of tribes making the yearly share of responsibility easily ascertainable. In times of major military crisis, the tribes were expected to rally to one another's aid.

A number of Biblical passages suggest that the tribal federation of Israel was composed of the six major tribes settled in central and northern Palestine west of the Jordan River. These tribes were Benjamin, Ephraim, Manasseh, Zebulun, Asher, and Naphtali.[23] The Transjordanian tribes appear not to have been part of this "Israel" in the earliest days of its existence. This last statement is illustrated by an episode narrated in Josh., ch. 22. In this account, the Transjordanian tribes had "built an altar at the frontier land of Canaan, in the region about the Jordan, on the side that belongs to the people of Israel" (Josh. 22:11). The altar had been built west of the Jordan by these eastern tribes in order to establish their right to participation in the Israelite Yahweh cult and as a memorial to this right lest there be future misunderstanding on this point (Josh. 22:26–28). The subsequent negotiations were carried on with "the people of Israel" who had their sanctuary center at Shiloh. The date of this episode cannot be determined, though Shiloh was the primary Israelite sanctuary in the middle of the eleventh century, but how much before this time is uncertain.

The six-tribe nature of the Israel federation is further substantiated by passages that describe the tribal holdings.[24] The "negative conquest tradition" in Judg. 1:21, 27–33, which enumerated the cities not taken by the invading Hebrews, refers to Benjamin, Manasseh, Ephraim, Zebulun, Asher, and Naphtali. In Josh., chs. 13 to 19, there is preserved a complex of geographical descrip-

---

[22] On the structure of the amphictyony, see Bruce D. Rahtjen, "Philistine and Hebrew Amphictyonies," *Journal of Near Eastern Studies*, XXIV (1965), pp. 100–104.
[23] The absence of Issachar from the early six-tribe Israel may have been due to its subservient status.
[24] On the tribal holdings, see Aharoni, *The Land of the Bible*, pp. 227–239.

tions concerning the traditional tribal holdings and inheritances. These chapters utilized various types of sources from different periods of Israelite history. One set of these traditions provides boundary descriptions that defined the exact boundaries between the various tribes. The boundary delineation lists are limited to a description of the territory claimed by the six tribes that we have designated above as "Israel." These lists are somewhat idealistic in that they claim all the territory as Israelite which fell within the boundaries. At this stage in history, most of the cities within the territory were not held by Israel. The listing of cities as border points in these descriptions rather than as tribal centers supports what has been previously said—namely, that the conquest did not begin with Canaanite cities but focused rather on the less-populated areas around the Canaanite cities. The boundary lists of the six Israelite tribes can be accepted as an accurate reflection of the boundaries existing between the tribes and recognized in the tribal covenant.

The southern tribal alliance, designated the house of Judah (see II Sam. 2:1–4a), apparently had its tribal center at Hebron.[25] Although very little can be said in detail and with certainty about the existence of this southern association, the assumption that it existed helps to explain many facets of later history. The six tribes most likely to have shared in the life of this federation were Judah, Simeon, Caleb, Kenaz, the Kenites (on these, see Judg. 1:3–20), and Jerahmeel (see I Sam. 27:10; 30:29). It is entirely possible that the Danite tribe before its migration to the north was a participating member of this league. The predominance of Judah with its tribal center at Bethlehem eventually led to the absorption of most of the other tribal elements, so much so that later tradition simply considered these tribes as Judean clans.

IN THE DAYS WHEN THE JUDGES RULED

The editor of The Book of Judges summed up his evaluation of the life of the tribes during the two centuries between the entrance and the founding of the monarchy with a rather disdainful comment:

> In those days there was no king in Israel; every man did what was right in his own eyes. (Judg. 21:25.)

Such a verdict reveals not only the editor's favorable appraisal of the monarchy but echoes the turbulent and trying times which he considered characteristic of the period of the Judges (ca. 1200–1020 B.C.). The major traditions that Israel preserved from this period (Judg. 3:7 to 21:25; I Sam., chs. 1 to 7) are all characterized by a military orientation. (One should note that a different type of interest in the period of the Judges is reflected in The Book of Ruth with its absence of any reference to military undertakings.)

During this era, the tribes struggled on two fronts to preserve and enlarge their territorial integrity and independence. On the one hand, there were external threats: invasions and attacks from neighboring states, marauding raids

---

[25] On the importance of Hebron, see Newman, *The People of the Covenant*, pp. 136–140.

by the bedouin from the eastern desert, and the movement of the Philistines into Canaan from the west. On the other hand, the surviving Canaanite city-states and enclaves posed an internal threat to the life and stability of the tribes and sought to stifle their further territorial acquisition.

Before this period is examined in any more detail, it is necessary to comment on the historical and theological framework within which the stories of the tribal struggles have been incorporated. The theological editor has utilized the individual narratives to illustrate the historical themes of fidelity, apostasy, oppression, and deliverance. This basic theology of history is represented in the discussion of Judg. 2:6 to 3:6 which proclaims that fidelity to Yahweh brings good times and peace while lack of fidelity to Yahweh brings hard times, defeat, and oppression. Seven examples illustrating this cycle of obedience and peace, disobedience and oppression, are given in the following pattern:

1. As long as the divinely ordained ruler was alive, the people were faithful in their worship of Yahweh.
2. With the death of the ruler, "the people of Israel did what was evil in the eyes of Yahweh" by forsaking him and serving the other gods of the surrounding people.
3. The anger of Yahweh was kindled against the people and he gave them over to their enemies, who oppressed them.
4. When the people cried to Yahweh in penitence, Yahweh raised up for them a deliverer and rescued them from their enemies.
5. As long as the deliverer was alive, the people served Yahweh but with his death, the cycle was repeated.

In addition, the editor has cast the traditions that once concerned individual tribes and episodes into an "all Israel" mold and arranged them in chronological sequence. The various wars described were local affairs which seldom involved more than one tribe or particular region. The local heroes of the stories have been made into leaders of "all Israel" and placed in a chronological scheme, although some of these may have been contemporary with one another. There were, no doubt, many more leaders and conflicts for which no traditions have been preserved. The individual narratives that were collected, however, are of extreme historical value and are unquestionably derived from very old traditions.

The military leaders of the tribes during this period were charismatic personalities who rose to meet a particular threat and possessed the ability to rally followers to the cause. The personal power of the individual was attributed to the fact that "the spirit of Yahweh came upon him." These leaders in times of crisis were called "judges." In Hebrew, the term "to judge" (*shaphaṭ*) is not so limited to legal connotations as is the case in English and can be translated either "to rule" or "to judge." It is entirely possible that these judges performed both military and legal functions and served as tribal authorities after the cessation of military troubles.[26]

---

[26] On the judges as legal authorities, see McKenzie, *The World of the Judges*, pp. 114–118. Noth's original theory about this function of the judges rested on the assumption that the "minor judges," about whom very little information was given (see Judg. 10:1–5; 12:8–15), were amphictyonic custodians of the law. But the editor of Judges probably included these

Most of the battles fought by the tribes were efforts to repel would-be invaders. Othni-el of Kenaz is said to have defeated Cushan-rishathaim of Mesopotamia (Judg. 3:7–11), but historically nothing is known of this figure.[27] A Moabite king, after encroaching upon Jericho, was killed by Ehud of Benjamin (Judg. 3:12–30). Shamgar Ben-Anath fought against the Philistines and killed, we are told, six hundred with an oxgoad (Judg. 3:31). Samson, who is better known for his other deeds of physical strength and romantic weakness (Judg., chs. 13 to 16), on one occasion, it is said, slew a thousand Philistines with the jawbone of an ass (Judg. 15:14–17). The camel-riding nomads from Midian who came swarming into the agriculturally rich valley of Jezreel in search of plunder were routed by Gideon of Manasseh (Judg., chs. 6 to 8), aided by the tribes of Asher, Zebulun, and Naphtali (Judg. 6:35). Hostilities between Transjordanian tribes and the Ammonites over territorial rights flared into warfare. The Ammonites were defeated in battle by the tribes of Gilead led by Jephthah, whose sacrifice of his daughter to Yahweh in fulfillment of a vow made before battle was commemorated by an annual celebration in which Israelite maidens wept over her fate (Judg. 10:6 to 11:40).[28]

The most consequential battle engaged in by the Israelite tribes during this era was the struggle against a coalition of Canaanite forces under Sisera for control of the Valley of Jezreel which is celebrated in the Biblical traditions in both a prose (Judg., ch. 4) and a poetical version (Judg., ch. 5). Through this valley ran the main commercial route between Egypt and Mesopotamia. Two large fortified Canaanite cities—Megiddo and Taanach—guarded the eastern pass into the valley.[29] The time of warfare had been preceded by a period of oppression when the Canaanites sought to impose their authority upon the Israelite tribes of Galilee.

> In the days of Shamgar, son of Anath,
>   in the days of Jael, caravans ceased
>   and travelers kept to the byways.
> The peasantry ceased in Israel, they ceased
>   until you arose, Deborah,
>   arose as a mother in Israel.

(Judg. 5:6–7.)

The Israelite leaders in the battle were the prophetess Deborah and Barak.

---

minor judges to support his twelve-tribe concept by reference to twelve judges: Othni-el and Ibzan from the two Judean tribes; Ehud, Shamgar, Barak, Gideon, Tola, Elon, Abdon, and Samson from the eight northern tribes; and Jair and Jephthah from the two Transjordanian tribes.

[27] Cushan-rishathaim ("Cushan of Double Wickedness") may have been simply invented, but see Abraham Malamat, "Cushan Rishathaim and the Decline of the Near East Around 1200 B.C.," *Journal of Near Eastern Studies*, XIII (1954), pp. 231–242.

[28] The story of Jephthah's daughter represents an Israelite attempt to historicize a cultic ritual of weeping for a fertility goddess. See Flemming F. Hvidberg, *Weeping and Laughter in the Old Testament* (Leiden: E. J. Brill, 1962), pp. 103–105.

[29] On archaeological excavations at Megiddo, see the summary by G. Ernest Wright, "The Discoveries at Megiddo, 1935–1939," *The Biblical Archaeologist Reader*, II, pp. 225–239; on Taanach, see Paul W. Lapp, "Taanach by the Waters of Megiddo," *The Biblical Archaeologist*, XXX (1967), pp. 2–27.

According to the prose account, the basic tribes involved were Zebulun and Naphtali (Judg. 4:10), although the poetical version (the so-called Song of Deborah, which is one of the oldest passages of poetry in the Bible, if not the oldest passage)[30] also affirms the participation of Ephraim, Benjamin, Machir (Manasseh), and Issachar (Judg. 5:14–18). There is no reason to doubt the poetical version's portrayal of the battle as involving much more than a local conflict. The Israelite tribes gathered at Kadesh near the sacred Mount of Tabor and were roused into battle spirit by Deborah (Judg. 4:12–14). The triumph over the Canaanites with their nine hundred chariots of iron was accomplished when a massive rainstorm swelled the waters of the brook Kishon, which flowed through the Jezreel Valley, and the ensuing muddy fields put the charioteers out of operation. The excited exuberance of the victorious Israelites can still be felt reverberating through the stanzas of the song of triumph:

> The kings came, they fought;
>   then fought the kings of Canaan,
> at Taanach, by the waters of Megiddo;
>   they got no spoils of silver.
> From heaven fought the stars,
>   from their courses they fought against Sisera.
> The torrent Kishon swept them away,
>   the onrushing torrent, the torrent Kishon.
>
> .   .   .   .
>
> Then loud beat the horses' hoofs
>   with the galloping, galloping of his steeds.
>   (Judg. 5:19–22.)

THE INSTITUTIONS OF THE TRIBES

Before beginning a discussion of the subsequent historical developments that eventuated in the establishment of a monarchical Israelite state, we would do well to look at the fabric of ancient Israelite tribal life and society in a somewhat systematic fashion. The social, cultic, military, and legal activities of the tribal groups are fairly well documented in the Biblical traditions and can be reconstructed with some precision, though there are frequent gaps in our knowledge.[31]

The structures of Israelite society that developed during the period of the Judges were a blend of two cultural traditions. On the one hand, there were

---

[30] On the antiquity of the Song of Deborah, see W. F. Albright, "The Song of Deborah in the Light of Archaeology," *Bulletin of the American Schools of Oriental Research*, LXII (1936), pp. 26–31.

[31] On the institutions of the Israelites, see Max Weber, *Ancient Judaism*, tr. and ed. by Hans H. Gerth and Don Martindale (The Free Press of Glencoe, 1952); Julian Morgenstern, *Rites of Birth, Marriage, Death and Kindred Occasions Among the Semites* (Quadrangle Books, Inc., 1966); and the comprehensive and excellent handbook by Roland de Vaux, O.P., *Ancient Israel: Its Life and Institutions*, tr. by John McHugh (McGraw-Hill Book Company, Inc., 1961).

elements inherited from a seminomadic background with its very strong tribal and rural orientations and with an economy based on shepherding. On the other hand, there were elements taken over from the indigenous population of Canaan with its city-state and semifeudalistic culture with an agrarian and limited manufacturing and trade orientation. The arts and crafts were, as one would expect, much more highly developed among the Canaanites than among the early Israelites. Archaeological excavations have demonstrated the high level of material culture that existed in these city-states. It must be remembered that the alphabet was a Canaanite invention.[32]

The transition to a more agricultural economy must have taken place rather rapidly after the settlement. In the very old tribal songs (Gen., ch. 49, and Deut., ch. 33), the tribes are frequently described in imagery drawn from farming. Of Judah it was said:

> Binding his foal to the vine
>   and his ass's colt to the choice vine,
> he washes his garments in wine
>   and his vesture in the blood of grapes;
> his eyes shall be red with wine,
>   and his teeth white with milk.
>   (Gen. 49:11–12.)

Two of the tribes are even associated with ships and the sea.[33] Zebulun and Issachar were said to "suck the affluence of the seas and the hidden treasures of the sand" (Deut. 33:18–19).

> Zebulun shall dwell at the shore of the sea;
>   he shall become a haven for ships,
>   and his border shall be at Sidon.
>   (Gen. 49:13.)

The Family Institutions. Among the early Israelites, the tribal structures of society predominated for generations and were the determinative elements even after the formation of a national state. The basic unit in the tribe was of course the family—"the house of the father"—which comprised not only the father, his wife or wives, and their unmarried children but also the married sons and their wives and children along with the servants and slaves. Several such families constituted a clan, which was bound together by ties of real or supposed blood relationship and geographical proximity. A number of clans went to make up a tribe. This type of tribal structure is reflected in the ordeal described in Josh. 7:10–21.

---

[32] On the Canaanites and their culture, see John Gray, *The Canaanites* (Frederick A. Praeger, Inc., Publisher, 1964); and W. F. Albright, "The Role of the Canaanites in the History of Civilization," in G. Ernest Wright, ed., *The Bible and the Ancient Near East* (Doubleday & Company, Inc., 1961), pp. 328–362.

[33] On the basis of such references as these, it is possible to assume that generally the Mediterranean world was an influence in Israelite culture in the period of the Judges. For some bold suggestions in this regard, see Cyrus H. Gordon, *Before the Bible* (Harper & Row, Publishers, Inc., 1963).

In the household unit, the final authority rested with the patriarch of the family, whose word and wisdom were equated with "law." Final authority in the clan and tribe seems to have rested with a council of elders—"heads of their fathers' houses, the leaders of the tribes" (Num. 7:2), as is the case among modern-day Arabic bedouin tribes. As was suggested above, the "judges" may have functioned as final authorities in matters of major dispute because of their charismatic qualities and have been responsible for the knowledge and enforcement of tribal law.

The extended family unit and the clan supplied the context and participants for the significant human events of birth, circumcision, marriage, and death. Such events have been aptly termed "rites of passage" by the French anthropologist van Gennep,[34] since these are rituals and celebrations which mark the transition from one phase of human experience to another.

The desire for a large number of children, especially sons to perpetuate the name and fortune of the family, was a characteristic of Israelite society and was given expression in every type of its literary tradition.

> Sons are a heritage from Yahweh,
>> the fruit of the womb a reward.
> Like arrows in the hand of a warrior
>> are the sons of one's youth.
> Happy is the man who has
>> his quiver full of them!
>>> (Ps. 127:3–5a.)

A woman's inability to have children was considered a grievous trial or a direct chastisement from God (I Sam. 1:3–11).

Immediately after birth, the child was washed, rubbed with salt (Ezek. 16:4), and named. The naming of the child was usually done by the mother (see the naming episodes in Gen. 29:31 to 30:24). The mother was ritually impure for a period after giving birth (according to Lev., ch. 12, for forty days if the child was a male, for eighty days if a female). The child was weaned at the age of two or three years and the event was probably celebrated as a festive occasion (Gen. 21:8).

The male child was circumcised; according to the Priestly tradition this occurred on the eighth day (Lev. 12:3; Gen. 17:12). Circumcision is a very old custom and was practiced by most of the Semitic peoples.[35] Scholars differ on their explanation of the original meaning of circumcision, though most agree that hygienic concerns were not involved. Two theories about the origin of circumcision are most widely held. One theory argues that circumcision was originally an initiation rite associated with puberty which initiated the person

---

[34] Arnold van Gennep, *The Rites of Passage*, tr. by M. B. Vizedom and G. L. Caffee (The University of Chicago Press, 1960).

[35] On the antiquity of circumcision, see Jack M. Sasson, "Circumcision in the Ancient Near East," *Journal of Biblical Literature*, LXXXV (1966), pp. 473–476. On rites of initiation, see Mircea Eliade, *Rites and Symbols of Initiation*, tr. by W. R. Trask (Harper Torchbooks, 1965).

into manhood with its accompanying duty and privilege of marriage. This explanation is supported by the following Biblical evidence: In Ex. 4:24–26, Moses is circumcised in a context referring to marriage and in Gen., ch. 34, the circumcision of the Shechemites is an essential prerequisite to marriage with the Hebrews. In Hebrew, the words for "bridegroom," "son-in-law," and "father-in-law" are derived from the same verb (*hatan*) which in Arabic means "to circumcise" but which does not, however, appear in Biblical Hebrew with this meaning. Another theory assumes that circumcision was a redemption ritual in which a part of the victim was sacrificed in place of the taking of the life of the person. Ex. 22:29b required that the firstborn child be given to the deity in sacrifice as were the firstborn of the domestic animals (Ex. 22:30; Lev. 22:26–30). Circumcision as an act of redemption served to remove this taboo requirement. In time, the substitution of an animal for the firstborn son developed (Ex. 34:20) but with circumcision being retained. It should be noted that child sacrifice was practiced on occasion in Israel (II Kings 21:6; compare Gen., ch. 22) but was repudiated in Yahwistic circles.

Israelite youths seemed to have married at an early age, probably in the early teens, although this is simply a calculation made on the basis of the ages given for the kings at their accession and the ages of their sons at their accession. There is no legal stipulation on the subject in the Biblical traditions, though later rabbinical rulings fixed the minimum age at twelve for girls and thirteen for boys. The bridegroom or his family was required to pay a bridal price to the family of the bride. The amount probably varied depending on the social standing of the families. In the case of a compulsory marriage as the result of the rape of a virgin, the payment was fifty shekels of silver (Deut. 22:28–29), but this may have included a penalty along with the marriage payment. Betrothal or the promise of marriage apparently had binding legal power. There were no special religious rites associated with the ceremony of marriage, though acts were probably performed to ward off evil spirits and bad luck. The primary element associated with the marriage celebration was a period of feasting (Judg. 14:10) and the basic ceremony was the entry of the bride into the house of the bridegroom. A man was allowed to have more than one wife and concubines as well (Deut. 21:15–17; Ex. 21:7–11). Although polygamy was sanctioned and practiced, economic factors no doubt encouraged monogamy. Marriage between first cousins was commonly practiced, and marriage with one's half-sister (with a different mother) was allowed as late as the time of David (see II Sam. 13:7–14) but later prohibited (Lev. 18:11).

The wife was classified as the possession of her husband (Ex. 20:17) and the verb "to marry a wife" literally means "to become master of." A husband could divorce his wife (Deut. 24:1), but the wife did not possess this right. A wife could not, however, be sold into slavery (Deut. 21:14), a protection that did not extend to the daughter (Ex. 21:7). The widow did not possess the right of inheritance. This privilege was held by the sons, or in the case of a man without children the property passed to the man's nearest male kinsmen. In ancient Israel, if a man died without offspring, it was the responsibility of his nearest of kin to marry his widow (Deut. 25:5–10 and see the narrative of Gen., ch. 38) and the firstborn of this new marriage was regarded as the son of the deceased.[36] The woman possessed fewer rights and privileges in Israelite society than was the case in most Near Eastern cultures.

The ancient Israelites seemed to have taken a very realistic attitude toward death and accepted it as the natural termination of a man's life. Unlike Egyptian culture, there was no preoccupation with death and no developed theory of an afterlife. The meaning of life was fulfilled in the person's accomplishments, in his participation in the life of the community, and in his name and memory preserved by his offspring. But for the ancient Israelite, death was not annihilation: a shadowy existence in the subterranean abode of Sheol was taken as man's fate. In Yahwistic religion, there were apparently no special cultic or religious services associated with burial. Mourning rites, such as the tearing of one's clothes, the wearing of sackcloth and veils, and putting dirt on one's head, as well as fasting were observed by family and friends (Gen. 37:33–35; II Sam. 1:11–12), but these were also customary during other periods of calamity and sorrow. Burial was considered a necessity, and to be left unburied was considered a terrible fate (I Kings 14:11). Cremation was not practiced and the burning of a body was inflicted only on persons guilty of notorious crimes (Gen. 38:24; Lev. 20:14). The archaeological excavations of Israelite tombs show that burial was primarily in tomb chambers, dug out of soft rock or in natural caves. A single tomb area was used by a family or group over a long period with the bones of preceding burials being moved aside for subsequent burials. Personal belongings and pottery containers were often put beside the corpse and these may have been funeral offerings for use by the deceased.[37] The primary funeral ceremony was the lamentation for the dead with cries of mourning and poetic funeral hymns (II Sam. 1:17–27) often no doubt performed by "professionals." The Biblical prohibition against self-mutilation and shaving of the head on account of the dead (Deut. 26:14) suggest that remnants of a cult to the dead survived in Israelite society. According to Priestly tradition, the corpse, the tomb, and the house of the deceased were considered unclean, and contact with these rendered a person unclean, necessitating purification rituals (Lev. 21:1–4; Num. 19:11–22).

The Cultic Institutions. The cultic institutions and practices of the tribes were dependent upon the ancient ancestral cults, the Canaanite religious observances, and Yahwism.[38] The worship of the people focused upon both historical and fertility elements. The historical elements in Israelite religion celebrated Yahweh's election of his people, the deliverance from bondage in Egypt, the miraculous rescue at the sea, and the covenant with his worshipers.

---

[36] This is the so-called levirate marriage; see H. H. Rowley, "The Marriage of Ruth," in his *The Servant of the Lord*, 2d ed. (Oxford: Basil Blackwell, 1965), pp. 169–194.

[37] Deductions about a people's beliefs based on burial remains are very tenuous. How, for example, might future archaeologists describe American beliefs after excavating Grant's Tomb and a rural cemetery?

[38] On the cult, see M. J. Buss, "The Meaning of 'Cult' and the Interpretation of the Old Testament," *Journal of Bible and Religion*, XXXII (1964), pp. 317–325; Hans-Joachim Kraus, *Worship in Israel*, tr. by Geoffrey Buswell (John Knox Press, 1966); and H. H. Rowley, *Worship in Ancient Israel* (Fortress Press, 1967).

Yahwism was strengthened and nurtured by the military successes of the tribes, since Yahweh was in a special way "a man of war" (Ex. 15:3) who struck "terror and dread" in the hearts of the opponents (Ex. 15:13–18).[39] The victory songs sung by the warriors celebrated Yahweh's intervention on behalf of his people.

> Yahweh, when thou didst go forth from Seir,
>   when thou didst march from the region of Edom,
> the earth trembled,
>   and the heavens dropped,
>   yea, the clouds dropped water.
> The mountains quaked before Yahweh,
>   yon Sinai before Yahweh, the God of Israel.
>   (Judg. 5:4–5.)

The jealousy and intolerance of Yahweh and the militant nature of Yahwism stem without doubt from the function of Yahweh as a god of war in the tribal battles for the land.

Much of Israel's ritual centered upon man's everyday needs and anxieties, seeking to ensure the stability of the world, fecundity for flocks, fields, and people, and prosperity and health. In many ways this emphasis was due to the direct influence of Canaanite religion, especially Baalism, on the tribal faith. In order to elucidate this statement, we must discuss in some detail the nature of Canaanite Baalism as this is known from the epic and ritual texts from Ugarit.[40]

The dominant god in the Canaanite pantheon was Baal, whose name means "lord" or "owner." Baal was a male god of fertility whose power was reflected in the seasonal patterns of the Canaanite year. The female consort (and sister) of Baal was the warrior goddess Anat, though by the period of the Judges and in the Biblical traditions Baal seems to have taken over the high god El's consort Asherah[41] or else he is associated with the goddess Ashtart (mentioned in the Bible in the plural form Ashtaroth, see Judg. 2:13; 10:6; etc.). As the representative of the cosmic male principle, Baal was the lord of the winter rains and storms and lord of heaven; his consort as the embodiment of the female principle was what we might call "mother nature." The fate of Baal in the Canaanite myth which was given expression in the cultic ritual mirrored the agricultural year with its winter rains and growing season, spring harvest, and hot, dry summer. Baal was therefore a dying and rising deity whose death coincided with the end of the rains and whose resurrection in the fall brought renewed vegetation.

In the mythological texts, Baal struggles with two other powers—Yam and Mot—in order to assert his authority as king and to function as the bringer of

---

[39] See Frank M. Cross, Jr., "The Divine Warrior in Israel's Early Cult," in Altmann, ed., *Biblical Motifs,* pp. 11–30.

[40] On Canaanite religion, see John Gray, *The Legacy of Canaan,* 2d ed. (Leiden: E. J. Brill, 1965).

[41] On Asherah in the religion of Israel, see Raphael Patai, "The Goddess Asherah," *Journal of Near Eastern Studies,* XXIV (1965), pp. 37–52.

The "Baal of the Lightning" stela from the ancient site of Ugarit shows the god standing on top of the mountains brandishing a club in his right hand. His left hand holds a lance in the form of a stylized tree or perhaps a representation of lightning.

THE LOUVRE AND C. F. A. SCHAEFFER

fertility. Yam, whose name means "sea," was the personification of the primordial waters of the deep. Using weapons forged by the artisans of the gods, Baal slew Yam. As a consequence, Baal was acclaimed as king and a palace (temple) was constructed for him on Mount Zaphon, the Olympus of Canaanite mythology. Baal's troubles were not ended, however, for he had to fight Mot ("death"), the power of summer drought and sterility. Mot was victorious and the death of Baal was greeted in the council of the gods with mourning, self-mutilation, and lamentation. The consort of Baal searched for the body of the deceased god; finding it, she buried it on Mount Zaphon, and weeping prepared a funeral feast for the departed. The resurrection of the dead god took place after Mot was slaughtered by Baal's consort and his resurrection and the ensuing fertility were hailed in the assembly of the gods.

> In a dream of El the Kindly One, the Merciful,
> In a vision of the Creator of Creatures,
> The skies rain oil,
> The wadis flow with honey.
> He raises his voice and cries:
> "I shall sit and take my ease,
> And the soul shall repose in my breast,
> For Baal the Mighty is alive,
> For the Prince, Lord of the earth, exists!"

The Canaanite ritual which enacted and participated in the Baal myth gave expression to the tensions and uncertainties of the seasonal cycle in the polarities of mourning–lamentation and rejoicing–celebration.[42] Mourning for the departed god and lamentation for the drought-stricken land were followed by rejoicing at his resurrection and celebration in anticipation of the new season's productivity. Associated with the ritual were sexual acts and sacred prostitution which imitated the fertility-producing sexual relations presumed to have taken place between the god and the goddess. By imitating the deities, it was assumed that the worshipers stimulated and shared in the life of the cosmic sexual acts and thus aided in the fertility-producing process.

Baalistic religion held a strong attraction for an agriculturally oriented society. It offered an interpretation of life in terms that the farmer could understand and appreciate and provided him with a sense of meaningful participation in the cosmic order. The Israelites no doubt shared and joined in this Baalistic religion and cult. In the popular religion, there may have been very little awareness of the vast cleavage separating Baalism with its nature and fertility orientation from Yahwism with its exclusive character, its emphasis on historical events as the arena of divine action, and its affirmation that Yahweh was no victim of the natural forces but one whose purposes the storm and stars could be made to serve. Among the militant Yahwists and in times of military strife, Yahweh was proclaimed as a zealous god who demanded uncompromising allegiance.

In the period of the Judges, worship was conducted in numerous places and

---

[42] On this cycle of worship, see T. H. Gaster, *Thespis: Ritual, Myth, and Drama in the Ancient Near East* (Harper Torchbooks, 1967).

Figurines of nude females and goddesses have been found in Palestine from the third to the first millennium. Female deities were an important part of the Canaanite pantheon, and ritual prostitution was an element in the cultic practices.

J. B. PRITCHARD AND THE UNIVERSITY MUSEUM

not confined to a single sanctuary. The choice of sites for public worship was not made arbitrarily but was based upon the belief that a manifestation or activity of the divine was associated with the place. Many of these places had no doubt been holy spots for many years before the settlement and were accepted as such along with the mythology associated with the site. Many of the places of worship were connected with sacred waters, springs, trees, or heights, each with its special religious significance. Important families possessed individual shrines and supervised the priesthood and the use of the cultic furniture, as is evidenced by the story of a certain Micah's establishment of a cult (see Judg., ch. 17) and such references as the yearly sacrifice held by the family of David at the time of the new moon (I Sam. 20:6). Every city and major village would have possessed its sacred area, or "high place," where religious observances were held (I Sam. 9:11–14). Tribal units no doubt possessed cultic places for the common use of the entire tribe, as is illustrated in the story of the founding of the Mosaic cult by the tribe of Dan (Judg., ch. 18). Because of the special sanctity of a cultic place, it could function as a place of worship for several groups living in the vicinity. Mount Tabor with its cult place of Kadesh seems to have been sacred to the tribes of Zebulun, Issachar, and Naphtali (Deut. 33:18–19; Judg. 4:4–14).

The Yahwistic faith was given expression in major shrines. Shechem and Shiloh were the most important sanctuaries for this "national" religion of the Israelites, while Hebron, with its sacred oak at Mamre, and Beer-sheba were the most important for the Judeans. Two special cult objects played central roles in the people's worship; these were the Tent of Meeting and the Ark of Yahweh.[43] Except in the Pentateuch, the Tent of Meeting is hardly referred to in the Biblical traditions. It appears to have been a movable sanctuary used in securing oracles which was set up apart from the community dwellings (see Ex. 33:7–11). The Tent of Meeting was probably a cult object connected with the southern tribal groups, since most of the Biblical passages locate it in the south. The Ark was a cultic symbol perhaps understood as a throne on which the deity sat (I Sam. 4:4; Num. 10:35) or as a container for the tablets of the sacred covenant (Deut. 10:1–5). In either or both of these usages, it symbolized the presence of Yahweh among his people. The Ark seems to have been stationed at the primary sanctuary of the Israelite confederacy. At Shiloh, the Ark was housed in a temple (I Sam. 1:9) probably of a kind usual among the Canaanites for many centuries. A permanent hereditary priesthood at the central sanctuaries and other major shrines is presupposed by the Biblical traditions.

The cultic observances of the people centered around four annual festivals. The Feast of Passover, Pesach,[44] was a home celebration observed on the night of the full moon nearest to the spring equinox. The basic ritual of this festival

---

[43] On these two religious objects, see von Rad, *The Problem of the Hexateuch*, pp. 103–124; and Ronald E. Clements, *God and Temple* (Fortress Press, 1965), pp. 28–39.

[44] This nomadic Passover celebration was probably the festival referred to in Ex. 5:3 in Moses' demand that the Hebrews be allowed to serve Yahweh in the wilderness. On the festival, see Roland de Vaux, O.P., *Studies in Old Testament Sacrifice* (Cardiff: University of Wales Press, 1964), pp. 1–26.

consisted in the slaughter and eating of a lamb, with the victim's blood being smeared on the doorposts and lintels. The celebration seems to have originally been an apotropaic ceremony performed by shepherds to protect the flocks and ensure their fertility, and as such it must have been a primary festival for the seminomads of the desert. In the course of time, the ritual was historicized and connected with the exodus from Egypt (Ex. 12:21–27; note the retention of the reference to the nocturnal destroyer in v. 23).

The three other annual festivals were pilgrimage festivals requiring an appearance at the sanctuary. "Three times in the year shall all your males appear before Yahweh" (Ex. 23:17). One of the oldest festal calendars enumerated these festivals in the following terms:

> Three times in the year you shall keep a feast to me. You shall keep the feast of unleavened bread . . . at the appointed time in the month of Abib. . . . You shall keep the feast of harvest, of the first fruits of your labor, of what you sow in the field. You shall keep the feast of ingathering at the end of the year, when you gather in from the field the fruit of your labor. (Ex. 23:14–16.)

All these festivals were agricultural in nature, being oriented to the cycle of the harvest seasons, and thus in their origin they belonged to the Land of Canaan. The adoption of these celebrations went hand in hand with the development of an agricultural economy.

The Feast of Unleavened Bread, Matzoth, was held at the time of the barley harvest (the name of the month Abib means "ripe barley"). To mark the transition to a new harvest year, the first sheaf was offered to the deity, and bread baked from the new crop was made without yeast, since the use of a "starter" would have contaminated the produce of the new crop with that of the old. The offering of the first of the harvested crop redeemed the remainder or "desacralized" it for common usage. The Feast of Harvest, also called the Feast of Weeks, Shevuoth, coincided with the wheat harvest and was celebrated some seven weeks after the beginning of the spring harvest season. The Feast of Ingathering, or Feast of Booths, Sukkoth, was observed in the autumn at the completion of the agricultural year (grapes and olives were gathered in the fall). It was also a New Year celebration, marking the end of one full season and the commencement of a new agricultural year. It was apparently an occasion of great celebration, a vintage festival, with a carnival-like atmosphere, when sacrifices were made, accompanied by the eating of meat and the drinking of wine. Something of the character of this festival's celebration at Shiloh has been preserved. The sacrifice and eating and drinking are reflected in I Sam., ch. 1, and Judg. 21:19–23 refers to the dancing of the maidens among the vineyards, followed by their "ritual" stealing by the men of Benjamin.

It is a widely accepted assumption among present-day Old Testament scholars that the covenant between Yahweh and the tribes was periodically renewed in a special covenant festival. The idea of a covenant as an agreement between two parties in which each pledged loyalty to the other had a history of usage in both the ancestral and the Canaanite cults.[45] In the vicinity of Shechem,

---

[45] On the covenant form in the Old Testament and Near Eastern treaties, see D. J. McCarthy, S.J., *Treaty and Covenant* (Rome: Pontifical Biblical Institute, 1963), and his

Baal-Berit ("Lord of the Covenant") was worshiped (Judg. 8:33; 9:4) as well as El-Berit ("El of the Covenant," Judg. 9:46). It is not surprising, then, to find that the clearest expression of Israel's covenant ceremony has its location at Shechem.[46] As was suggested in the previous chapter, Sinai too was remembered as a place of covenant-making (Ex., ch. 24),[47] although the narrative of the Sinai covenant tends probably to reproduce the elements of the covenant festival at Shechem. On the basis of Ex., ch. 24 (the Sinai covenant), Josh., ch. 24 (the Shechem covenant), and Deut., ch. 27 (a cursing ritual at Shechem), it is possible to reconstruct the primary elements in the covenant festival as follows:

1. The assembly of the tribal leaders (Ex. 24:1; Josh. 24:1)
2. Confessional preaching affirming Yahweh's past deeds on behalf of the people (Josh. 24:2–13)
3. Call to commitment (Josh. 24:14–15)
4. Recital of the covenant stipulations (Ex. 24:3a; Josh. 24:25)
5. Pledge to observe the stipulations (Ex. 24:3b; Josh. 24:16–18, 21–22)
6. Pronouncement of curses and blessings (Josh. 24:19–20; Deut. 27:14–26)
7. Setting up of a commemorative pillar (Ex. 24:4; Josh. 24:26b)
8. The covenant sacrifice and feast (Ex. 24:5–11)
9. The dismissal of the people (Josh. 24:28)

In the renewal of the covenant, the anointing of the existing pillar would have filled the function of the pillar's original erection. No doubt in the renewal services, judgment preaching played a role in which the people were reminded of their transgressions against previous stipulations and their apostasy from Yahweh. Penitential rituals and confessions of sin would have also been a part of the renewal festival, replacing the mourning rituals of the Baal cult.

It is uncertain how frequently the covenant festival was observed or on what occasions. Deuteronomy 31:9–13 suggests a special ceremony every seven years, though the ceremony may have been held in the premonarchical period with no scheduled regularity but with observance based upon community and especially military needs.

The Legal Institutions. The responsibility for the administration of justice in early Israelite culture was in the hands of the family, the tribal leaders, and the elders of the towns. The extended family seems not only to have functioned as the primary unit in the socialization process but also to have borne the basic responsibility for social morality and the preservation of law and order. Commandments concerning conduct, warnings about wrongdoing, exhortations to

---

"Covenant in the Old Testament: The Present State of Inquiry," *The Catholic Biblical Quarterly*, XXVII (1965), pp. 217–240.

[46] On the excavations at Shechem and its Canaanite temples, see G. Ernest Wright, *Shechem: The Biography of a Biblical City* (McGraw-Hill Book Company, Inc., 1965).

[47] The association of Yahweh and Sinai was preserved after the covenant festival became a part of the religion in the land; see Clements, *God and Temple*, pp. 17–27.

the good and industrious life, and even instructions in the faith were part of the family teaching and discipline. Punishment of crimes and disobedience within the family were the family's responsibility (Deut. 21:18–21; II Sam. 14:4–7). Respect for family authority was demanded (Ex. 20:12; 21:15, 17). Remnants of tribal justice are found in the Biblical traditions. For example, the tribe had the duty of punishing criminal acts performed by members of the tribe, and failure to do so could bring amphictyonic action against the tribe, as is illustrated in the famous story of the Levite whose concubine was raped to

The "high place" at Gezer consisted of ten massive monoliths and a stone "basin" or "socket." The exact purpose of such pillars is not completely certain, though they may have served some commemorative purpose such as is referred to in Josh. 4:1–10. The Gezer "high place" dates from the middle of the second millennium.

THEODORE A. ROSEN

death by the men of Gibeah in Benjamin (Judg., chs. 19 and 20). The right to avenge murder was a tribal as well as a family duty and privilege (Ex. 21:12–14; Deut. 19:1–10).

Justice was administered publicly, usually in the courtyard adjoining the main city gate where court proceedings were held and cases heard. Actions were brought by persons who "cried out" the wrong done to them and then functioned as the accuser or adversary. Each party pressed or defended his own case. Witnesses were called and accepted responsibility for the sentence, apparently being required to cast the first stones if the condemned party were put to death (Deut. 17:7). According to the Deuteronomic traditions, two witnesses were required to convict, and false witnesses (see Ex. 20:16) could be subjected to the punishment that would have befallen the condemned (Deut. 19:15–20). The elders of the community served as judges and declared the parties guilty or innocent, i.e., righteous or unrighteous. The court imposed punishments dependent upon the nature of the crime and the guilt involved. Fines and punishments were prescribed on the principle of proportionate compensation, and although the law of retaliation—"an eye for an eye, a tooth for a tooth"—is affirmed in the Biblical traditions (Ex. 21:23–25), it was applied only in the case of murder. Bodily mutilation, required by the *lex talionis*, was apparently not administered as punishment except in one very special circumstance (Deut. 25:11–12). The decisions of the court produced statutes of "civil law" which became precedents for later cases. Such statutes were referred to as *mishpatim* ("judgments" or "rulings") and generally took the form of hypothetical cases ("If a man does so and so, . . . then such and such shall be the consequences"). This process of court or "justice in the gate" [48] was the source of much of the legal material in the Old Testament. The oldest collection of such judgments, probably from the time before the formation of the state, is found in Ex. 21:1 to 22:17.

The priests also played a certain role in judicial affairs. If no decision could be reached by the court or if there was an absence of witnesses, recourse could be made to "the judgment of God" at the sanctuary, where the accused subjected himself to an ordeal swearing an oath in the name of the deity (Num. 5:11–31; Deut. 17:8–13). In addition to administering the ordeal, the priests gave instruction (*torah*) and decisions in the name of Yahweh concerning the sacred and the profane, the clean and the unclean. The proclamation of the will of the deity in terms of absolute demands ("You shall do so and so") or prohibitions ("You shall not do so and so")[49] in the context of worship as well as the pronouncement of blessings and curses was a priestly function.

The Military Institutions. Warfare in ancient Israel was both a military and a religious endeavor and could thus be described as "holy war" or "Yahweh's war." The early tribes possessed no standing army nor stable military organization but depended upon the call up of men of military age during times of need or crisis. Much of the tribal strategy depended upon surprise attack and the choice of the opportune moment. For example, Gideon fought at night (Judg. 7:19–20), Sisera was defeated in a rainstorm (Judg. 5:20–21), and Joshua

---

[48] On "justice in the gate," see Ludwig Koehler, *Hebrew Man*, tr. by Peter R. Ackroyd (Abingdon Press, 1957), pp. 127–150. Israelite law was given authority in that practically all legal regulations and requirements were considered to have been spoken by Yahweh or his representative and thus all laws were "religious" through this type of association. (The wisdom traditions do contain some legal-type material unassociated with this religious orientation.) On Israelite law, see Noth, *The Laws in the Pentateuch*, pp. 1–107. A summary of Israelite laws, excluding the cultic regulations, is given in Ze'ev W. Falk, *Hebrew Law in Biblical Times* (Jerusalem: Wahrmann, 1964).

[49] On the forms of Israelite laws, see Alt, *Essays on Old Testament History and Religion*, pp. 101–171. In a limited way Alt's arguments have to be modified, but in spite of this his is the best introductory essay on the subject.

fought in the predawn (Josh. 10:12–14).[50] Before battle, efforts were made to consecrate the troops and allow Yahweh to direct the battle. Sacrifice was offered and Yahweh consulted by means of the sacred lots ("the Urim and Thummim"), so that he decided when and under what conditions the battle should be fought. Abstinence from sexual relations and cleanliness of the camp were demanded. The Ark could be taken into battle as a visible symbol of Yahweh's presence. Troops went into battle with the certainty of victory, being assured that already Yahweh had given the enemy into their hands. Faith in the assurance of victory and single-mindedness were presumably conditions for participation (see Deut. 20:1–9). Curses and oracles against the enemy before battle may have been used to aid in his defeat and to rally the troops. After a victory, the spoils of battle were often consecrated to Yahweh as herem, which sometimes involved the holy massacre of all the living both animal and human. The primary human leaders in Yahweh's wars were the charismatic judges. (Most of the elements in early Israelite warfare can be seen in the narratives of Judg. 4:4–22 and I Sam. 15:1–33.)

---

[50] This last passage is the famous episode about Joshua's making the sun stand still. The poetical section (vs. 12b–13a), quoted from The Book of Jashar, implies a predawn fight, since Gibeon was to the east and the valley of Aijalon was to the west. The editor of the material (vs. 13b–14) misunderstood and assumed that the sun was halted overhead.

6 | SAUL AND DAVID

In the middle of the eleventh century (ca. 1050 B.C.), an external threat confronted the Israelite and Judean tribes with the possibility of a complete loss of freedom. The threat was posed by the expansion policy of the Philistines, who moved to take over control of the entire land of Palestine. In their reaction to this major threat, the tribes were welded together in common action, advanced from tribalism to statehood, adopted a monarchical form of government, and entered their greatest hour of glory. These changes brought about radical transformations in the entire political, cultural, and theological fabric of their society.

THE PHILISTINE MENACE

The Philistines had settled in Canaan early in the twelfth century B.C.[1] In origin, they were one element in the massive migration of "Sea Peoples" from the islands and coastlands of the northern Mediterranean during the Late Bronze Age (1500–1200 B.C.), a migration possibly triggered by the Dorian invasion of the Greek mainland. The first appearance of the Sea Peoples in Egypt and Palestine was in conjunction with their service as mercenaries. But by 1200 B.C., they had launched a momentous movement of conquest which threatened many major Middle Eastern powers and threw western Asia into a state of political chaos.

The Philistines were first mentioned by name as part of an invasion force that attacked Egypt in the eighth year of Ramesses III (ca. 1198–1166 B.C.). This invasion was repulsed by the Egyptians, at the price of military exhaustion, and part of the defeated force conquered and settled southwest Palestine, perhaps at the beginning as garrison troops with the consent and nominal control of Egypt.

Biblical readings: The basic Biblical materials discussed in this chapter are I Sam., ch. 4 (the Philistine menace), I Sam., chs. 9 to 15; 28; 31 (the Saul narratives), and I Sam., chs. 16 to 18; 25; II Sam., chs. 1 to 8 (portions of the narratives about David). See map V.

[1] See the summary of available Near Eastern material related to the Philistines in Albright, "Syria, the Philistines, and Phoenicia," *The Cambridge Ancient History*, Vol. II, 2d ed., Ch. XXXIII, Sec. i.

The Philistines were later politically organized in a confederation of five city-states (Ashdod, Askelon, Gaza, Gath, and Ekron) under the control of military rulers backed by well-armed troops and charioteers. Sometime about the middle of the eleventh century, the Philistines undertook a large-scale movement to take over all of Palestine, perhaps beginning their advance by dominating the trade routes along the coast and in the Jezreel and Jordan valleys.[2] The pressure of the Philistines had already been felt by the southern tribes. In the Samson legends, the hero is warned by the men of Judah about causing trouble, since "the Philistines are rulers over us" (Judg. 15:11).

United action by the Israelite tribes was no match for the well-armed Philistine soldiers who routed the poorly armed Israelite militia in battle between Aphek and Ebenezer (I Sam., ch. 4). During the clash, the Israelite Ark was taken captive and several members of the priesthood at Shiloh were slain. The Israelites may have earlier been forced to move the center of their tribal league from Shechem to Shiloh because of the vulnerability of the former.

The Biblical traditions and archaeological evidence suggest that the Philistine domination eventually included practically all the land west of the Jordan and possibly the Transjordanian trade routes. The Philistines stationed garrisons in

Characteristic Philistine pottery from the early Iron Age has been found at many Palestinian sites, which suggests a widespread control of the area by the Philistines. Shown here are typical amphorae and stirrup-jars.
ISRAEL DEPARTMENT OF ANTIQUITIES
AND MUSEUMS

various strategic places in the land (I Sam. 10:5; II Sam. 23:14), carried out punitive raids perhaps for the collection of tribute (I Sam. 13:16–18; 23:1–5),

---

[2] On the expansion of the Philistines, see G. Ernest Wright, "Philistine Coffins and Mercenaries," *The Biblical Archaeologist*, XXII (1959), pp. 53–66, reprinted in *The Biblical Archaeologist Reader*, II, pp. 59–68, and his "Fresh Evidence for the Philistine Story," *The Biblical Archaeologist*, XXIX (1966), pp. 70–85.

and curtailed weapon production and increased their industrial profits through their monopoly on the iron industry (I Sam. 13:19–22). The process of smelting iron was developed by the Hittites in Asia Minor about the fourteenth century B.C., and it was from them that the Sea Peoples apparently learned the art.

The Biblical traditions suggest that the Israelites were on occasion able to mount offensive action against the Philistines. I Samuel 7:14 points out that under the leadership of Samuel,[3] cities taken away from Israel were recaptured from Ekron and Gath, but this probably is merely a reflection of the ongoing warfare between the two which lasted for several years. This verse, however, does point to a fact that should not be overlooked when it states that "there was peace between Israel and the Amorites." (In addition to the term Canaanites, Amorites is used in the Bible to refer to the indigenous non-Israelite population of Canaan.) This passage shows the cooperation which existed between Israel and the Amorites in their opposition to a common enemy, a factor that no doubt furthered the amalgamation of the two groups and cultures.

THE BEGINNING OF THE MONARCHY

The Philistine threat paved the way for a new chapter in Israelite history. Out of this challenge to their independence, the tribes responded by adopting, for them, a new form of political structure, the monarchy. The decentralized and charismatic structures had proved incapable of meeting the needs of an hour of real crisis.

Saul's Rise to Kingship. The present edited form of the Biblical traditions does not present a unified narrative of the way in which Saul came to be the first king of the nation Israel. Scholars point out the apparent existence of three different accounts of the beginning of the monarchy.

In one account (I Sam. 9:1 to 10:16), Saul is pictured as a young, tall, and handsome lad in search of his wealthy father's lost asses. In his pursuit, Saul came to "the land of Zuph," where he met the seer Samuel, who presided over the sacrificial meal at a local sanctuary. The visit of Saul had been revealed to Samuel by Yahweh on the previous day and Samuel had been told to anoint the youth as prince[4] over Israel. So at the instigation of Yahweh, Samuel secretly took a vial of oil and poured it on Saul's head and designated him to save Israel from the hand of the Philistines. This narrative emphasizes the participation of Yahweh and Samuel in the choice of Saul and the latter's designation as a young lad.

Another account (I Sam. 10:17–27) attributes the impetus for the selection of a king to the people of Israel (see I Sam., ch. 8) against the wishes of Samuel

---

[3] The historical figure of Samuel is difficult to discover, since four offices (priest, prophet, seer, and judge) were ascribed to him in popular tradition. See McKenzie, *The World of the Judges*, pp. 169–175, and his "The Four Samuels," *Biblical Research*, VII (1962), pp. 1–16.

[4] The Hebrew word translated "prince" is *nagid*, which should be rendered "military commander."

B.C.	EGYPT	PALESTINE	SYRIA-MESOPOTAMIA
1200	Twentieth Dynasty (1200–1085) Egypt generally quite weak after massive invasion by "Sea Peoples"	Period of the Judges (1200–1020) Consolidation of tribal holdings Final settlement of Philistines Establishment of Israel and Judah as united tribal leagues Major battles between Canaanites and Hebrews Deborah, ca. 1125 Battles against Moabites, Midianites, and others before and after Deborah	No major power
			Brief revival of Assyria under Tiglath-pileser I
1100	Twenty-first Dynasty (1084–935) Continued Egyptian weakness	Philistine control over Judah Major Philistine invasion of Israelite territory Samuel Battle of Aphek Philistine domination Saul anointed as ruler (ca. 1020) * Union of Israel, Judah, and Transjordanian tribes Saul wars with Philistines Saul dies in battle (ca. 1000)	Phoenician development of sea trade
1000		David king over Judah Ishbaal king over Israel David king over Israel and Judah Capture of Jerusalem Israelite domination over all of Canaan Expansion of Davidic empire Revolt of Absalom Revolt of Adonijah Death of David (ca. 961) Reign of Solomon (ca. 961–922)	
	Twenty-second Dynasty (935–725) Revival of Egyptian power		Recovery of Assyrian power begins
		Division of United Kingdom	Aramean independence

* Dates for Israelite and Judean kings are based on the chronology of W. F. Albright.

and Yahweh. In this narrative, Saul was chosen as king by lot at the sanctuary of Mizpah in a ceremony presided over by Samuel. Saul is shown in this account as a shy, unassuming person discovered hiding among the baggage at the time of his selection.

A further representation of Saul's rise to kingship is found in I Sam., ch. 11. Here Saul is pictured as an adult farmer working his land at Gibeah when the Transjordanian town of Jabesh-gilead was threatened by the Ammonites. Saul responded to the call for assistance, rallied Israelite and Judean support, won a victory over the Ammonites, and was crowned king at the sanctuary in Gilgal. This narrative portrays Saul as a charismatic leader, similar to the earlier judges, but one who was designated by the people as king.

How can one explain the existence of these diverse perspectives on the origin of kingship in ancient Israel? Several things should be noted about these narratives. In the first place, they are frequently infused with material of a legendary nature reflecting the art of the storyteller. (This is especially the case with I Sam. 9:1 to 10:16.) Secondly, much of the material incorporates an anti-monarchic and anti-Saul sentiment. There were no doubt in early Israel many who opposed the institution of kingship, and in later history Saul was seldom looked upon in a favorable light. Thirdly, the stories are associated with two main sanctuaries, Mizpah and Gilgal, which would suggest that early forms of these stories were told at these centers.

In spite of the fact that these stories have been told and edited to reflect a bias in favor of or against the monarchy in general and Saul in particular, it is possible to construct a hypothesis that would explain their existence.[5] Saul was probably first of all designated as a leader in Israel's struggles by Samuel and his prophetic circle[6] in a fashion similar to the designation of Barak by the prophetess Deborah (Judg. 4:6) and the later designation of Jehu by Elisha and "the sons of the prophets" (II Kings 9:1–10). The Mizpah narrative may reflect the recognition of Saul as king over the combined leagues of Israel and Judah. It was probably only during the Philistine crisis that Israel and Judah united in a common bond. The Gilgal narrative and the story of the triumph over the Ammonites reflect a major victory won by Saul and his Israelite and Judean followers in Transjordan. It was probably as a result of this victory that the Transjordanian tribes were incorporated into the broadened Israelite state. The ceremony at Gilgal with its acclamation of Saul as king could have been the occasion for this union.

The Reign of Saul. The course of events in the reign of Saul and the nature of his rule are difficult to determine, since the traditions have been collected and edited with a bias in favor of Saul's successor, David. The collectors of Israelite

---

[5] For some suggestions in this direction, see C. E. Hauer, Jr., "Does I Samuel 9:1–11:15 Reflect the Extension of Saul's Dominions?" *Journal of Biblical Literature*, LXXXVI (1967), pp. 306–310.

[6] On the prophetic circle associated with Samuel, see the works by McKenzie cited in footnote 3 of this chapter and W. F. Albright, *Samuel and the Beginnings of the Prophetic Movement* (Hebrew Union College Press, 1961), reprinted in Harry M. Orlinsky, ed., *Interpreting the Prophetic Tradition* (KTAV Publishing House, Inc., 1968).

traditions chose to picture Saul as the man forsaken by Yahweh, the antitype of David the man after God's heart, and his reign as a political interlude before the coming of the true kingdom of David. In Israel's later "roll call" of its heroes, Saul does not appear (see Ecclus., chs. 44 to 50; Heb., ch. 11). Even the length of Saul's reign cannot be determined, since the only chronological reference states that "Saul was a year old when he began to reign and he reigned two years over Israel" (I Sam. 13:1), which is absurd. Later Jewish tradition and modern scholars assume that his reign was much longer than two years (Acts 13:21 assigns forty years to Saul).

Saul was from a landowning family whose hometown was Gibeah, a place located on the highroad joining Judah and Israel and thus centrally located between the two tribal leagues. The site seems to have been unoccupied prior to the Israelite settlement, and excavations there have exposed part of a small but well-fortified citadel which probably served as Saul's "palace." [7]

What prerogatives were granted Saul as king are not stated, though reference is made to "the rights and duties of the kingship" (I Sam. 10:25) agreed to by the people and Saul and laid before Yahweh. He was certainly granted the right to function as military commander-in-chief and to call out the militia, i.e., the men of military age, and it was this which was the source of his power and authority. The major associate of Saul was his cousin Abner, who functioned as commander of the militia. The use of professional soldiers and mercenaries was begun by him, and this too must have been a privilege granted him by the tribes as well as the right to raise the finances to support them probably through feudal-type land grants as well as taxation.[8] This first Israelite draft into a standing army is referred to in the fact that "when Saul saw any strong man, or any valiant man, he attached him to himself" (I Sam. 14:52).

In a number of points, the Biblical materials suggest that Saul's reign was surprisingly successful. I Samuel 14:47–48 gives a summary of his military exploits. In his struggle against the Philistines, he was at least partially successful (I Sam., ch. 14) perhaps breaking their control over the central highlands. Also, he is said to have fought against enemies to the south, east, and north of Canaan. In addition, Saul was able to incorporate into his state some of the non-Israelite elements living in Canaan. I Samuel 14:21 notes that the still existent non-Israelite Hebrews joined Saul and his forces after a victory over the Philistines. The autonomy of some of the Canaanite city-states was apparently taken away by Saul. This is especially noted in the case of Gibeon (II Sam. 21:1–3), with whom the earlier Israelites had entered into an alliance. In matters of religion, Saul suppressed the practices of "the mediums and the wizards" (I Sam. 28:3) associated with the veneration and consultation of the dead.

All of this suggests that Saul was the major unsung hero of Israelite history.

---

[7] See L. A. Sinclair, "An Archaeological Study of Gibeah (Tell el-Ful)," *Annual of the American Schools of Oriental Research for 1954–56* (American Schools of Oriental Research, 1960), pp. 5–52; summarized in *The Biblical Archaeologist*, XXVII (1964), pp. 52–64.

[8] See I Sam. 22:6–8; and John Gray, "Feudalism in Ugarit and Early Israel," *Zeitschrift für die alttestamentliche Wissenschaft*, LXIV (1952), pp. 49–55.

The union and cooperation of the several tribes, the establishment of central political structures, the defense of Israelite freedom, and the welding together of the diverse groups and cultures in Canaan reached a new phase during the time of Saul, although it was David who really reaped the benefits and praise.

In spite of the many benefits to his people which can be attributed to Saul, his career was clouded by tragedy and disaster. This was partially due, on the one hand, to his split with the ambitious David, the rising star of Judah, and, on the other hand, to his conflicts with Samuel, who sought to regulate and condemn the activity of the king in terms of the older tribal customs and perhaps in line with the thought and actions of Samuel's prophetic circle. But, undoubtedly, some lamentable change came over Saul himself and made him subject to fits of suspicion and depression and to irrational acts of violence.

Saul and three of his sons died on the battlefield fighting the Philistines (I Sam., ch. 31), struggling to protect the freedom and territory of his people. The scene of the battle, the Valley of Jezreel and Mt. Gilboa, suggests that Saul had begun to break the Philistine control over the Palestinian trade routes. Saul was buried in Jabesh-gilead after some of its citizens had snatched away his body from the wall of a Beth-shan temple where it had been exposed by the Philistines.[9] This act reflected the honor in which these Transjordanians held Saul, who had earlier been their savior.

THE CAREER OF DAVID

The years of David's rule over Israel were the days of the nation's greatest success and glory. So outstanding was David as a warrior, political administrator, and ruler that his name was recalled in Israelite faith and history "like the name of the great ones of the earth" (II Sam. 7:9). But behind David and his glory, the nation's theologians saw the hand and will of Yahweh.

> He [Yahweh] chose David his servant,
> and took him from the sheepfolds;
> from tending the ewes that had young he brought him
> to be the shepherd of Jacob his people,
> of Israel his inheritance.
> With upright heart he tended them,
> and guided them with skilful hand.
> (Ps. 78:70–72.)

David's Rise to Prominence. The Biblical traditions contain three independent narrative accounts of David's rise to prominence. Each of these glorifies David and emphasizes the theological and legendary characteristics ascribed to him in the Jerusalemite royal ideology.

I Samuel 16:1–13 tells of David's anointment by the prophet Samuel as the replacement for Saul while the latter was still alive and reigning. In the story,

---

[9] David had the bones of Saul and Jonathan reinterred in Saul's homeland of Benjamin (II Sam. 21:11–14).

David is pictured as the eighth and youngest son of Jesse of Bethlehem. The older sons were bypassed by Yahweh and his choice fell on the shepherd lad who "was ruddy, and had beautiful eyes, and was handsome" (I Sam. 16:12; compare with v. 7). The emphasis of this story falls on David as the chosen of Yahweh, selected and designated at a young and innocent age, untarnished by political ambition.

In another account (I Sam. 16:14–23), David was said to have been brought to the court of Saul because he was "skilful in playing the lyre" in the hopes of soothing the king "whenever the evil spirit from God was upon Saul." The theme of David as the great musician and the founder of Israelite music played a prominent role in later Israelite tradition, and it is this theme which dominates this narrative.

The story of David's slaying of Goliath (I Sam., ch. 17) presupposes that David and Saul are unknown to each other (note vs. 38, 55–58) and have their first encounter on the field of battle. This well-known story portrays David as the courageous and ideal man of faith who fights his battles and wins his victories through the power of Yahweh. II Samuel 21:19, which ascribes the killing of Goliath to a certain Elhanan from Bethlehem, suggests that this story of David "the giant killer" has been secondarily applied to David and is therefore unhistorical.

Incidental references within the Biblical traditions suggest that David originally came to the court of Saul as an experienced and professional soldier. I Samuel 16:18 describes David as a "man of war" who entered Saul's service and became his armor-bearer, thus becoming a personal attendant to the king perhaps in both a military and an advisory capacity. Other texts (I Sam. 22:14; 18:5) refer to the fact that David became captain over the king's bodyguard. This group was no doubt the mercenary troops, a military element and royal police guard independent of the national militia. As the head of this fighting unit, David distinguished himself in battles with the Philistines and was held in high esteem by the common populace who sang its praises of his military exploits (I Sam. 18:5–9, 30).

> Saul has slain his thousands,
> and David his ten thousands.
> (I Sam. 18:7.)

David was a favorite at the royal court and enjoyed the close friendship and personal devotion of Saul's son Jonathan, who "loved him as his own soul." Eventually, David married Saul's daughter Michal (I Sam. 18:20–27), thus acquiring further status at the royal court as the king's son-in-law.

David as a Refugee. Saul's personal jealousy of his younger and more popular officer, together perhaps with David's ambitions, led to a deterioration in the two men's relationship. David was eventually forced to flee from the court after attempts were made on his life. He first sought shelter with Samuel and his prophetic circle (I Sam. 19:18–24) and afterward left his parents for safety's sake in the care of the king of the Moabites, a people with whom David had blood relation through his grandmother Ruth (see Ruth 4:18–22).

As a fugitive from the court, David spent some time in the eastern Judean Desert, where he gathered around himself a personal army of four hundred men composed of "every one who was in distress [i.e., criminals], and every one who was in debt, and every one who was discontented" (I Sam. 22:2). David and his band of outlaws partially supported themselves through the operation of a "protection racket" which is admirably illustrated in I Sam., ch. 25. In this story, David wished to collect from a wealthy sheep and goat breeder for protection he and his gang had offered ostensibly without the need or knowledge of the owner. The demands and threats of David led to the heart-attack death of the herds' owner who left behind a beautiful widow and three thousand sheep and one thousand goats. In order to alleviate this dire situation, David "agreed" to marry the widow and assume responsibility for the management of the departed's estate.

Saul continued his pursuit of David, which may have contributed to the weakening of the Israelite defense against the Philistines, although nothing like a civil war between David and Saul developed since the latter seems to have held the support of the majority of the Judeans. David finally sought security by becoming a mercenary-vassal to Achish, the Philistine king of Gath. For this service, David and his army, now numbering six hundred men, were granted as a fief the city of Ziklag in the Judean Shephelah (I Sam. 27:1–7). From this base, David carried out raids against the nomadic and caravan groups in the southern Negeb, being careful to annihilate all the living so that the Philistines would not discover that he wasn't raiding Judean towns (I Sam. 27:8–12) with whose elders he actually shared his booty in order to win Judean support (I Sam. 30:26–31). David did not participate in the major Philistine attack on Israel which resulted in the death of Saul. He was spared this fate, not because of his own scruples, but because of the mistrust of some of the Philistine leaders.

David Becomes King. With the death of Saul, David immediately took action which revived the ancient tribal animosity and led to the division of the Israelite kingdom into the two states of Israel and Judah. In agreement with the Philistines, or at least with their permission, he transferred his residence to the Judean center of Hebron and had himself anointed as king over the house of Judah (II Sam. 2:1–4).

In the north, Abner placed Ish-baal,[10] the son of Saul, on the throne, moving the capital to the safer Transjordanian town of Mahanaim. Here he ruled "over Gilead and the Asherites [correcting the Hebrew term Ashurites, i.e., Assyrians] and Jezreel and Ephraim and Benjamin" (II Sam. 2:8–11). These five areas no doubt reflect the administrative districts of Saul's kingdom minus Judah.

Warfare between Israel and Judah prevailed for some time during which "David grew stronger and stronger, while the house of Saul became weaker and weaker" (II Sam. 3:1). Abner, reading the signs of the time and because of a personal grievance with Ish-baal, chose to throw in his lot with David and went

---

[10] The editors of the Hebrew text of Samuel altered Ish-baal's name, which means "man of Baal," to Ish-bosheth ("man of shame") because of the former name's reference to the Canaanite god. The correct form appears in I Chron. 8:33; 9:39.

to Hebron to work out the final negotiations but was murdered by Joab, David's chief commander (II Sam. 3:26–27). Finally, with the murder of Ish-baal after a two-year reign (II Sam. 4:5–12), the way for David to rule over "all Israel" was completely clear. The northern tribes offered the throne to David

The pool at Gibeon was apparently the scene of a battle between the forces of David and those of Ish-baal (see II Sam. 2:12–17). This pool, which required the removal of almost 3,000 tons of limestone for its construction, was part of the water supply system at Gibeon. Thirty-seven feet in diameter and thirty-five feet deep, the pool is extended downward by another forty-five feet to the water level by a tunnel.

J. B. PRITCHARD AND THE UNIVERSITY MUSEUM

and after the conclusion of a covenant and anointment, David became ruler over the reunited kingdom of Israel and Judah.

THE ESTABLISHMENT OF AN EMPIRE

Internal Developments. David ruled in Hebron for seven and a half years (II Sam. 5:5). He was able to solidify his rule over Israel and Judah and to centralize his government over the tribes after his capture of the independent city-state of Jerusalem.[11] Prior to its capture, the city had been a Jebusite strong-hold. The town was taken by David's personal army which apparently gained access to the town through its subterranean water channel (II Sam. 5:6–8). No reference is made in the texts to the city's destruction nor to the annihilation of its population. The town was not incorporated into the territorial holdings of the tribes but was retained as a private possession of David and his successors just as was done with David's old Philistine fief of Ziklag (I Sam. 27:6). It was this fact which is reflected in the description of Jerusalem as "the city of David" (II Sam. 5:9).

The Philistines didn't take action against their former vassal until David had established himself in Jerusalem (II Sam. 5:17). Perhaps prior to this time he had given them no cause to doubt his old allegiance. David's former masters made two attempts to bring him back under control, but both attacks ended in decisive victories for the Israelites (II Sam. 5:18–25), after which the Philistines were no longer a major threat.

The central location of Jerusalem and its lack of connection with tribal his-tory made it an excellent neutral capital. David sought to turn Jerusalem into the religious center as well as the political capital of the state. He did this by bringing the Ark of Yahweh to Jerusalem (II Sam., ch. 6). This sacred re-ligious object had played a significant role in Israelite religion and history. Its presence at a sanctuary or in the midst of warfare represented the presence of Yahweh among his followers. The Ark had been earlier captured by the Philistines, who, according to I Sam., chs. 5 and 6, had returned it to Israelite territory after suffering from a plague which they associated with the Ark. The story of David's transference of the Ark illustrates the sacredness of the occa-sion with its references to sacrifices, shouting, blowing of the horn, the blessings, and David's performance of a ritual dance as well as his distribution of food. With the Ark in Jerusalem, the Israelite traditions, priesthood, and beliefs as-sociated with it were transferred to a new setting which became the object of religious pilgrimage. David did not construct any elaborate temple to house the Ark, although he did secure the land on which a temple was subsequently built by his son when he purchased the threshing floor of Araunah in order to build an altar to Yahweh (II Sam. 24:15–25).

In order to stifle any possibility that the house of Saul might seek to retake the monarchy, David participated in and encouraged the killing of two of Saul's sons and five of his grandsons in a fertility ritual performed to alleviate a drought (II Sam. 21:1–9). This left alive only one male member of Saul's im-mediate family, a crippled son of Jonathan.

All the independent Canaanite enclaves were annexed by David and in-corporated into the Israelite state. The native population of these city-states was not destroyed but merely absorbed. This brought into Israelite society another infusion of culture and customs as well as a higher material civilization and industrial development.

The first census taken in Israel was carried out by David. The description of

---

[11] On the excavations in Jerusalem, see Kathleen M. Kenyon, *Jerusalem: Excavating 3000 Years of History* (McGraw-Hill Book Company, Inc., 1967).

The Davidic city of Jerusalem lay outside the walls of what is now called the Old City of Jerusalem. The walls of the Old City were completed by Suleiman the Magnificent in A.D. *1535. Jerusalem in the time of David was located on what is today called Ophel, shown in the center and dotted with modern houses. The Old City and the Temple area are to the upper left, and the Brook Kidron, Gethsemane, and the Mount of Olives are at the upper right.*

ROBERT B. WRIGHT

the boundaries covered (II Sam. 24:1–9) shows that Israel, Judah, Transjordan, and the Canaanite cities were now integral parts of the United Kingdom. The purpose of this census was undoubtedly related to the military draft and taxation. This census-taking provoked opposition among the people, reflecting the ancient taboo against "counting heads."

International Developments. The status of international politics was extremely favorable to David's development of a major empire. Egypt to the south and Assyria to the north were both in a state of political weakness and much of the Near East was still recovering from the effects of the invasion of the Sea Peoples. The major record we possess of David's foreign campaigns is found in II Sam., ch. 8. In extending his rule, David subdued Philistia and conquered the Transjordanian states of Moab, Ammon, and Edom. His most formidable foes were the several Aramean (Syrian) states to the north, but these were defeated and Israelite troops were even stationed in Damascus. States farther to the north, such as Hamath, chose to establish good relations with David. The Phoenicians along the northern coast entered into a treaty relationship with Israel which restricted the former's territory but encouraged their further involvement in the lucrative sea trade in the Mediterranean.

These territorial conquests under David gave Israel control over a major network of international trade routes. Thus Israel was able to dominate the land commerce between Egypt and Mesopotamia as well as the overland trade with the kingdoms of South Arabia.

The states conquered by David were forced to pay tribute into the Israelite treasury. This, coupled with the control of the international trade routes, produced a rapid increase in Israel's prosperity especially among the social class involved in military leadership, commerce, and administration. The greatest benefactors from this prosperity were of course the members of the royal court.

The Administration of the Empire. The organization and government of the large and complex empire that had fallen into David's hands required the talents and skills of an educated and cultured ruling class as well as an elaborate and developed bureaucracy. The Biblical traditions preserve two lists of David's ministers of state (II Sam. 8:16–18; 20:23–26). Under Saul, there had been no more than three major officers (see I Sam. 20:25): Abner, commander of the militia; David, the captain of the professional and mercenary troops; and Jonathan, the king's adviser. How different were the needs of David's empire! The lists mentioned above show that David possessed a bureaucracy encompassing political, military, and religious divisions. There was a general of the regular Israelite army, a chief of the mercenary troops among whom were foreigners such as Cretans and Hittites, a recorder whose task was probably that of state herald and foreign minister, a secretary of state or state scribe, a person in charge of the forced labor or "minister of public works," and a personal royal priest as well as two chief priests. Under many of these heads of state there were no doubt large and well-trained staffs.

The art of international diplomacy and commerce and the administration of a far-flung empire required a well-educated, trained, and cultured class of officials. The Israelites had had no previous experience or even need for much of this administrative machinery and officialdom. What, then, were the sources upon which David drew for his pattern and personnel in such administration? One obvious source was the court circles of Jerusalem and the other Canaanite city-states. These had, for a long time, been involved in international negotiation and diplomacy especially during their state of vassalage to the Egyptians. Another source, no doubt drawn upon by David, was the Egyptian administrative system itself, either directly from the Egyptians or through the Phoenicians. Many of the nonmilitary officers in David's cabinet had their almost exact counterparts at the Egyptian court. Foreigners were probably hired to fill many of the lower echelon posts and some of the names of major ministers of state under David and his successor appear to be non-Hebraic.[12]

---

[12] Adoram, Abda, Shisha, and Elihoreph fall into this category.

Education and training were the basic requirements for building an administrative system. What the international language was at the time of David is uncertain; it may have still been Akkadian, as it was in the Amarna Age, but at any rate it probably wasn't the Hebrew dialect of Canaan. If it were the nonalphabetic scripts of either Egyptian hieroglyphics or Akkadian cuneiform, learning to write and employ such a language was an arduous task requiring competent instruction. It can be assumed that this required the establishment of an educational system—schools—at the royal court in Jerusalem and perhaps in other towns as well. Foreign and/or Canaanite scribes would have been a necessity. The texts used in such schools would have included the "classic texts" in the language involved. In other words, the concepts, ideas, and world views of other cultures would have become an important element in the upper and official levels of Israelite society.

The expansion of the Israelite state into a major empire thrust the nation into the mainstream of Near Eastern affairs. It opened Israelite life and culture to the thought, the products, and the prosperity of other cultures and in turn altered the entire fabric of Israelite life. The importance and influence of this fact will be further discussed in the next chapter.

DAVID'S DOMESTIC TROUBLES

In spite of the fact that David was in many ways a masterful ruler under whom the Israelite state reached its pinnacle of political greatness, his reign was not completely free from internal domestic and political problems. These were caused by internal struggles within his family, political discontent with the demands of David's policies of aggression, and the old north-south (Israel-Judah) tensions.

The Old Testament has preserved the names of nineteen of David's sons but notes that this is an incomplete list (I Chron. 3:1–9).[13] The existence of a number of male offspring created a situation filled with the possibility of internal rivalry and harem intrigue. David's ineptitude in handling family matters and his indecisiveness concerning the succession did not aid matters. In addition, David's tremendous ambitions and sometimes ruthless acts may have served as patterns for his sons' imitation.

David's adulterous affair with Bathsheba and his subsequent orders to have her husband Uriah the Hittite killed in battle were used by the Biblical narrator to set the stage for David's family problems (II Sam., chs. 11 and 12). In the story, David, walking on the palace roof, spied the bathing Bathsheba and was overcome by lust for her and had her brought into the palace. Biblical commentators have consistently laid all the blame on David for this affair, but it is obvious that Bathsheba was an ambitious lady herself who probably knew when and where to bathe in order to attract the king's attention. When Bathsheba became pregnant, David tried to extricate himself by bringing Uriah

---

[13] David's second-born son, Chileab (II Sam. 3:3), played no role in the stories concerning the succession. Apparently he died as a youngster.

"home on furlough" so that the child would be considered his. Uriah, however, was faithful to the sacred demands of warfare which required sexual continence (see I Sam. 21:1–6) and neither winsome persuasion nor royal wine could entice him home to his wife. His well-laid plans frustrated, David, probably in anger, sent Uriah back to the battlefield bearing a letter sketching the plot for his own demise. This story's themes of lust, conspiracy, and murder are then carried over into the narrator's accounts of David's children.

Amnon, the king's oldest son, was overcome by lust for his half-sister Tamar and devised a plan to get her into seclusion and there raped her (II Sam., ch. 13). After two years, Tamar's brother Absalom avenged his sister's rape by having his servants kill Amnon at a sheepshearing festival, being aware no doubt that this would leave him as the oldest of the king's sons and thus the most likely to succeed to the throne.

It was almost a decade after the death of Amnon before the ambitious Absalom was able to ride a general discontent with David into open rebellion against his father (II Sam., chs. 15 to 18). The disaffection of the people with the king was perhaps due to his pursuit of international and military policies which placed heavy burdens on the population and led to neglect of some domestic matters (see II Sam. 15:1–6). Absalom formed a conspiracy and had himself acclaimed king in Hebron, the city of his birth and David's first capital. David was forced to flee from Jerusalem to Transjordan, and Absalom reigned in his father's place for a few days. Absalom died at the hands of David's troops after having entangled his head in the limb of an oak tree while riding his mule underneath.

David was confronted with at least one other major challenge to his rule. The motives behind this revolt were the old rivalry between the north and south and the Benjaminites' dislike for David because of his treatment of the house of Saul (see II Sam. 16:5–8). After Absalom's death, a dispute broke out between the leaders of Israel and those of Judah over escorting the king back to Jerusalem and David's obvious favoritism toward Judah. Both groups were anxious to show their loyalty to the king and to purge themselves of any responsibility in the Absalom conspiracy.

Sheba, from the tribe of Benjamin, sounded the trumpet of revolt and raised the cry of rebellion:

> We have no portion in David,
> and we have no inheritance in the son of Jesse;
> every man to his tents, O Israel!
>
> (II Sam. 20:1.)

The Israelite uprising was a spontaneous and short-lived movement that ended with a siege and the leader's decapitation (II Sam. 20:1–22).

Behind the facade of unity in the Davidic kingdom, there lay deep feelings of resentment and discontent and forces for which the new orders in the new state held no attraction, forces which could be held in check only through a powerful, personal leadership willing to employ strong and sometimes oppressive policies.

7 | THE SOLOMONIC ERA

An aged and decrepit David presided over the transference of his throne to a successor, but not before the royal court and the city of Jerusalem were seething with intrigue and divisive political coalitions. David's eldest surviving son, Adonijah, assuming that he would succeed his father, had, like Absalom before him (II Sam. 15:1), chosen to act as heir apparent and had not been reprimanded by David (I Kings 1:5–6). The failure of the king to make a public declaration concerning the succession, however, had left matters uncertain.

With David incapacitated, Adonijah moved to claim the throne. He was supported by Joab, a kinsman of David and commander of the Israelite militia, by Abiathar, the priest who had been David's companion and consultant from the time of the latter's break with Saul, and by numerous royal officials of Judah (I Kings 1:7, 9–10). In opposition to the move of Adonijah, another coalition supporting David's younger son Solomon sprang into action and used Adonijah's self-proclamation as king to force David into a decision. Solomon's cause was championed by his mother, Bathsheba, and the court prophet, Nathan, who were aided by the priest Zadok and Benaiah, the commander of the professional and mercenary troops (I Kings 1:8).

Nathan and Bathsheba succeeded in convincing the king in his dotage that he had made her a promise that Solomon would rule after him (I Kings 1:11–31). The entire story and the absence of any previous reference to such a promise suggests that it was an invention that mainly owed its success to David's favoritism for Bathsheba. Such "harem intrigues" on behalf of a favorite son were not unknown in Near Eastern history.

The orders of David to his personal retainers initiated the process that led to the anointing and enthronement of Solomon and aborted the efforts of Adonijah. The latter sought asylum by clinging to the horns of the altar, which placed one under the special protection of the divine. Adonijah, perhaps knowing that he would have killed Solomon had his attempt been successful, feared for his life and left the sanctuary of the altar only after being assured that

---

Biblical readings: The primary Biblical materials discussed in this chapter are the Throne Succession Story (II Sam., chs. 9 to 20; I Kings, chs. 1 and 2), the traditions of Solomon's rule (I Kings, chs. 3 to 11), the royal psalms (Ps. 2, 21, 45, 72, 89, and 110), and the Zion psalms (Ps. 46–48, 76). See map V.

Solomon would not kill him if he proved himself worthy (I Kings 1:49–53). With the capitulation of Adonijah, "Solomon sat upon the throne of David his father; and his kingdom was firmly established" (I Kings 2:12).

THE THRONE SUCCESSION STORY

The Biblical narrative of Solomon's rise to power is part of a large complex of traditions that focus upon the internal problems of David's household and the struggle over the succession (II Sam., chs. 9 to 20, and I Kings, chs. 1 and 2). This narrative is often, though inaptly, referred to as the Court History of David. Although the theme of this writing is historical and its episodes concern the Davidic court, it does not attempt to present a history of the rule of David. The interest of the writing is much narrower than this and centers almost solely on the question of the succession to the throne. For this reason, the narrative can be best designated the Throne Succession Story.[1]

Since this document was separated from its context and studied apart from its present setting in the Biblical text, scholars have been almost unanimous in their praise of the author as a literary genius. The work has been described as "a masterpiece, unsurpassed in historicity, psychological insight, literary style, and dramatic power."[2]

The Throne Succession Story is a historical novel written to demonstrate how Solomon came to sit on the throne of his father. Every incident in the writing is an integral part of the whole, showing how alternative possibilities to succeed David were eliminated. The writer reminds the reader of the still-existing house of Saul, which represented an actual but remote possibility of reestablishing itself in the persons of Saul's grandson, Merib-baal[3] (II Sam., chs. 9; 16:1–4; 19:24–30) or his more distant kinsman, Shemei (II Sam. 16:5–14; 19:16–23; I Kings 2:8–9). II Samuel, chs. 10 to 12, shows the origins of the one who was eventually to reign in his father's place. This episode with its narration of David's adultery with Bathsheba prepares the reader for David's subsequent ineptitude in dealing with his family affairs. Then, one by one, the writer introduces the rival candidates for the throne. Amnon, overcome by lust as was his father, raped his half-sister and was murdered by her brother Absalom (II Sam., ch. 13). Absalom, the next oldest son, overcome by desire for power, sought to usurp the throne from his father and died in battle (II Sam. 14:1 to 19:8). The aftermath of Absalom's attempted coup provoked the northern tribes, especially Benjamin, into rebellion against David, and the author shows how this movement was squelched (II Sam. 19:9 to 20:22). The final act in the drama deals with the unsuccessful attempt by Adonijah to secure power and Solomon's eventual triumph (I Kings, chs. 1 and 2).

---

[1] See Roger N. Whybray, *The Succession Narrative* (London: SCM Press, Ltd., 1968).
[2] Robert H. Pfeiffer, *Introduction to the Old Testament*, rev. ed. (Harper & Brothers, 1948), p. 357.
[3] The name Mephibosheth is a late scribal change to remove the reference to the god Baal in the name Merib-baal (see I Chron. 8:34).

The Throne Succession Story is one of the major literary masterpieces in the Hebrew Scriptures. In its psychological analysis of human character and activity and in its objective description of significant events, it stands alone among the historical writings of ancient Near Eastern cultures. A comparison of its portrayal of David with that found in later Hebrew tradition (for example, in I Chron., chs. 11 to 29) illustrates how willing and able the author was to picture the king in all his strength and weakness and to expose even the seamy side of his life. The multiple characterizations in the story present the reader with realistic persons and not impersonal stereotypes. His understanding of historical events as the results of human actions is evident in each episode. Only occasionally does the writer pause in his description to express a theological judgment concerning Yahweh and his relationship to the events at hand (see II Sam. 11:27; 12:24–25; 17:14).

When and why was such a work as this written? The intimate detail and the familiarity with the events narrated as well as the lack of any mention of the final disruption of the kingdom suggest that the Throne Succession Story was written during the lifetime of Solomon. Undoubtedly the author was a contemporary who lived through the experiences depicted and perhaps witnessed them from a position within the royal court itself. Interest in the question of dynastic succession and the right of Solomon to rule must be seen as the motive behind the composition of the narrative. In this regard, it is a novel of political propaganda.[4] The advocacy of Solomon's divine right to rule is anticipated already in the story of Solomon's birth (II Sam. 12:24–25), where it is said that "Yahweh loved him, and sent a message by Nathan the prophet; so he called his name Jedidiah [i.e., "beloved of Yahweh"]." Solomon as Yahweh's elected successor to David is emphasized in the speeches of David (I Kings 1:29–30, 33–35) and Benaiah (I Kings 1:36–37) in conjunction with the account of Solomon's enthronement. The most probable time for the writing of such a political document intent on justifying the regime of Solomon as the rightful successor in the Davidic dynasty was during the early years of his rule soon after the events described in I Kings, chs. 1 and 2, when the disaffected sentiments concerning the succession were still alive.

THE RULE OF SOLOMON

In order to ensure the stability of his throne, Solomon acted swiftly to remove the court officials who had opposed his rise to power. Adonijah was put to death when he requested a former concubine of David for his wife (I Kings 2:13–25). Solomon, who was no doubt waiting for a pretense to act, took this request as an indirect move to lay claim to the throne. The appropriation of a late king's harem was one of the signs used by the new king to affirm his rule (see II Sam. 16:21–22), and it may have been that Adonijah made his request hoping to keep alive his aspirations for the throne. The priest Abiathar was

---

[4] On Egyptian novels of political propaganda, see Whybray, *The Succession Narrative*, pp. 96–116.

banished to the town of Anathoth and his office taken over by Zadok (I Kings 2:26–27). Joab was killed while hanging to the altar pleading for sanctuary, and Benaiah the commander of the mercenaries took over his position as head of the Israelite army (I Kings 2:28–35). The purge of Solomon eventually included Shemei, a member of the Benjaminite house of Saul, whom the king had forced to settle in the crown property of Jerusalem where the traditional Israelite social conventions based on ancestral land and kinship ties were not so binding (I Kings 2:36–46). In all these cases, Solomon could claim a legitimate reason for his purge, and the author of the Throne Succession Story shows Solomon as simply carrying out the orders of the dying David; but it was no longer the tribal or village community that executed vengeance and justice, it was a despotic monarch and his mercenary henchmen. A new day had indeed dawned in ancient Israel!

The narratives that we possess concerning the subsequent rule of Solomon in I Kings, chs. 3 to 11, are of a diverse nature amassed from various sources dependent upon popular saga, royal annals, and public archives and are without the overall chronological and historical structure and value of the Throne Succession Story. In spite of this, the Biblical traditions provide sufficient material to elucidate various aspects of his reign.

Military Organization. The long years of Solomon's reign were almost completely free from warfare with any foreign power. Unlike the time of David, it was a period of Israelite military consolidation and defensive preparation. Solomon introduced a new force into Israel's military organization. This was the employment of chariots which, although previously known and used in the Near East, had not been extensively adopted by David (see II Sam. 8:4). Chariotry required a highly professional military elite and extensive facilities for training and upkeep. Although the Biblical evidence is not completely clear (compare I Kings 4:26 with ch. 10:26), it has been estimated that his force averaged fourteen hundred chariots and four thousand horses. To house and supply this chariot force, Solomon constructed several "chariot cities" containing barracks for his charioteers, supply depots, and stables for his horses. One such area has been excavated at the site of ancient Megiddo.

In addition to the chariot cities, numerous Israelite towns, located at strategic and defensive military positions, were rebuilt and refortified (I Kings 9:15–22). Excavations at Gezer, Hazor, and Megiddo[5] have unearthed city walls with casemate construction (parallel walls with intermittent cross walls) in association with a special type of city gate with four buttresses flanking the entryway. These defensive moves on Solomon's part were no doubt influenced by the reassertion of political independence by the Arameans in the Damascus area

---

[5] On the excavations at these sites, see H. Darrell Lance, "Gezer in the Land and in History," and William G. Dever, "Excavations at Gezer," *The Biblical Archaeologist*, XXX (1967), pp. 34–47 and 47–62; and Yigael Yadin, "Hazor," and J. N. Schofield, "Megiddo," in Thomas, ed., *Archaeology and Old Testament Study*, pp. 245–263 and 309–328; and Yigael Yadin, "Solomon's City Wall and Gate at Gezer," *Israel Exploration Journal*, VIII (1958), pp. 80–86.

(I Kings 11:23–25) and by the renewed intervention of Egypt in Palestinian affairs after two centuries (I Kings 9:16).

Two factors were of import insofar as the ordinary Israelite militia was concerned. Solomon's appointment of Benaiah to replace Joab as the commander of the (nonprofessional) army (I Kings 2:35) suggests that he combined the militia and mercenary forces under one commander, which would have greatly altered the previous military structure. In addition, the military reliance on chariotry and the rather peaceful international relations meant that the Israelite levy could be and was conscripted for use in the construction of general public works (I Kings 5:13–18).

Internal Administration. Solomon ruled over a state which was, in principle and practice, a bipartite kingdom composed of Israel and Judah. I Kings 4:7–19 provides a list of the administrative districts in Israel. These were twelve in number and each was governed by a high official. This list dates not from the beginning of Solomon's reign but from sometime later in his rule, since two of the district commissioners were his sons-in-law. The text is not explicit concerning the administration of Judah except to refer to the fact that "there was one officer in the land of Judah" (I Kings 4:19b). Since the time of Absalom's rebellion and the ensuing revolt of Sheba, David may also have employed two separate administrative systems in ruling over Israel and Judah.

These administrative districts were set up for the purpose of governmental efficiency especially in regard to the draft, taxation, and the collection of revenue to provide for the needs of the royal court and the military. The administrators may have been responsible also for the labor levy in use on public works projects (see I Kings 11:28, where the "house of Joseph" may be equivalent to the district of Ephraim in I Kings 4:8). Special favoritism seems to have been shown to Judah in this administrative organization, as the ratio of twelve districts to one would suggest. The extra taxation burden on Israel foreshadowed troublesome days for the state, and the separate administration shows that the union of Israel and Judah was the exception rather than the rule.

Trade and Commerce. During Solomon's reign, foreign trade flourished through caravan commerce between Israel and Asia Minor and Mesopotamia to the north and Egypt and Arabia to the south. Solomon obtained horses from Cilicia and chariots from Egypt and resold these to neighboring states (I Kings 10:28–29).[6] In a joint enterprise with Hiram, king of the Phoenician city of Tyre, Solomon engaged in sea trade, constructing a fleet of ships and a seaport at Ezion-geber on the Gulf of Aqabah (I Kings 9:26–28; 10:11, 22). The subsequent commerce with the African and Arabian cities along the Red Sea was based on Solomon's exploitation of the copper and iron deposits in the Arabah that provided him with raw materials for use in trade exchange (see Deut. 8:9).[7] The legends of King Solomon's Mines are of course based on this mining

---

[6] In I Kings 10:28, "Egypt and Kue" in the RSV should be read "Musri and Kue," both provinces in Asia Minor. On the foreign relations of Solomon, see Abraham Malamat, "Aspects of the Foreign Policies of David and Solomon," *Journal of Near Eastern Studies*, XXII (1963), pp. 1–17.

[7] See Nelson Glueck, "Ezion-Geber," *The Biblical Archaeologist*, XXVIII (1965), pp. 70–87.

activity in the Arabah. The story of the Queen of Sheba's visit to Jerusalem (I Kings 10:1–10) may reflect trade negotiations between the Israelites and southwestern Arabia, which was a source of luxury commodities such as incense and spices.

Tradition has, with some justification, considered Solomon an enthroned merchant. It should be noted that the commercial enterprises presided over by Solomon were a royal monopoly. The influx of wealth from his trading activities contributed greatly to the opulence of the royal court which, according to the description of one day's needs found in I Kings 4:22–23, was extravagant. The king was said to have "made silver as common in Jerusalem as stone, and . . . cedar as plentiful as the sycamore of the Shephelah" (I Kings 10:27), though one must allow perhaps for some slight exaggeration. The increased wealth and luxury were no doubt enjoyed by only a small percentage of the population, namely, the members of the royal family, officials, and merchants,

Solomon seems to have retained control of the major trade routes between the Euphrates and the Nile. This gave him the right to levy taxes on commerce passing along the trade routes. In one instance, Israelite territory had to be (I Kings 9:10–14).
transferred to Hiram, apparently because of a deficit in the balance of trade

Palace and Temple. Tradition and legend remembered Solomon not only as an enthroned merchant but also as a master builder. Solomon's building activity, which has already been referred to in connection with the chariot cities, military depots, and city refortifications, reached its most glorious and monumental stage in his constructions in the capital city of Jerusalem. Although he

The site of Solomon's Temple is today the location of the Haram esh-Sherif with its major mosque, the Dome of the Rock. The Solomonic Temple was built north of the City of David. The large platform of the present Temple area dates from the time of King Herod. The later temples of Zerubbabel and Herod were also built on this site.

ROBERT B. WRIGHT

is said to have reconstructed the walls of Jerusalem and undertaken various works (I Kings 9:15, 24; 11:27), the Biblical texts focus attention only on the building of the royal palace complex and the associated temple of Yahweh.

In addition to his palace, the royal buildings (I Kings 7:1–8) included the House of the Forest of Lebanon, used as an arsenal for weapons and as a treasury; the Hall of Pillars, which probably served as a receiving area; and the Hall of the Throne, which was the royal audience chamber containing the highly decorated gold and ivory throne (I Kings 10:18–20).

The building of the Temple took seven years and was constructed, as were the other buildings, with the aid of Phoenician craftsmen and artisans (I Kings 6:37–38).[8] It followed the pattern of temple architecture common to the Canaanite-Phoenician area and may have drawn upon the plans of the old Israelite temple at Shiloh (see I Sam. 3:3). The building was oriented to face the east and was divided into three main units (I Kings 6:2–6). At the front was the vestibule or portico (10 by 20 cubits) which led into the main hall or

---

[8] Recent archaeological discoveries suggest that Solomon built more than one temple. Israelite temples from the time of the united monarchy have been recovered at Arad and Lachish. See Yohanan Aharoni, "Arad: Its Inscriptions and Temple," *The Biblical Archaeologist,* XXXI (1968), pp. 2–32. The Lachish finds are as yet unpublished.

The Howland-Garber reconstruction of Solomon's Temple shows the interior furnishings of the sanctuary as well as some of the assumed methods of construction. The cherubim and the Ark of the Covenant were kept in the Holy of Holies. An incense altar and lampstands can be seen in the main hall.

PAUL L. GARBER

nave (40 by 20 cubits). To the rear was the inner sanctuary (20 by 20 cubits), later called the Holy of Holies. The height of the building was 30 cubits, with the exception of the inner sanctuary which was 20 cubits high and thus a perfect cube. The floor of the inner sanctuary was elevated, apparently being constructed over the sacred rock that had served as the threshing floor for the Jebusite Araunah and had been purchased by David for the construction of an altar to Yahweh (II Sam. 24:18–25). The present-day Muslim "Dome of the Rock" is built over the same massive stone.

The overall size of the Temple is a little uncertain, since the dimensions given are probably inside measurements and the exact length of the cubit employed is in doubt. The ordinary cubit was about 18 inches, but there was also a royal cubit of about 21 inches. Using the former, the building was 105' × 30' × 45', which certainly does not represent a structure to be used for large crowds or even a sizable congregation. The size suggests that the building itself was constructed primarily for use by the royal family and the officiating priests.

The entrance to the Temple was flanked by two free-standing bronze pillars called Jachin and Boaz which were 18 cubits high and crowned by decorated capitals 5 cubits in height (I Kings 7:15–22). These served no structural function but may have been understood as the traditional pillars associated with

The Mesopotamian winged, man-headed bull closely resembles the description of the Biblical cherubim. Such composite figures, as this one from the ninth-century palace of the Assyrian king Ashurnasirpal, were guardian beings. Similar figures appear in Egypt and in Phoenician art.

THE BRITISH MUSEUM

the "high places" or perhaps as representations of the mythological cosmic pillars that supported the eastern sky and between which the sun rose.

The Temple proper was surrounded by a large open-air courtyard where most of the religious activities took place. The altar of sacrifice stood in the courtyard in front of the entryway (I Kings 9:25). Also in the courtyard was the "molten sea," a colossal water holder resting upon twelve bronze bulls facing in the four directions of the compass (I Kings 7:23–26). This molten sea has its parallels in the sacred lake of Egyptian temples and the reservoirs of some Mesopotamian temples that represented the cosmic sea and also provided water for priestly purification and cleaning purposes.

INTERNATIONALISM AND ENLIGHTENMENT

The transformation of the old tribal state into a major Near Eastern empire had occurred in Israelite culture within a comparatively brief span of time, within the period from Saul to Solomon. The accompanying changes that occurred within Israel during these years, however, were radical and far-reaching.

The Israelites were thrust into the mainstream of international life and culture and thus were exposed to diverse foreign influences.[9] This internationalism of the Davidic-Solomonic era can best be seen at the royal court. Solomon is said to have had seven hundred wives and three hundred concubines (I Kings 11:1–3), among whom were Moabite, Ammonite, Edomite, Phoenician, and Hittite (= North Syrian) women as well as an Egyptian princess (I Kings 9:24). Although one might suspect the number as something of an exaggeration, the cosmopolitan character of the royal harem can hardly be doubted. Along with these ladies of the royal court, many of whom were probably "gifts" from foreign rulers, would have come the thought, habits, and culture as well as the religious practices (I Kings 11:4–8) of other lands. The international influence at the royal court was not limited to the royal harem. The Israelite administrative bureaucracy was highly influenced by, if not patterned after, its Egyptian counterpart. The architecture of the Solomonic building program was dependent upon and executed by the Phoenicians. Foreign mercenaries, aliens to Israelite culture but with an unfailing devotion to the ruler, served to back up the monarch. Administrative officials and assistants versed in the international language, the affairs of diplomacy, and the intricacies of commerce and trade operated at the center of governmental authority.

The new status in which Israel found herself led to a certain secularization of her life and orders. This is nowhere more obvious than in the function of the military. In the premonarchical period war was conducted as a religious undertaking in the name of Yahweh and understood as a defensive maneuver on behalf of the general population. Beginning with David, warfare was conducted for the purpose of territorial conquest and economic advantage and was no longer basically a sacral undertaking. Under Solomon, the development of

---

[9] See Gerhard von Rad, *Old Testament Theology*, Vol. I (Harper & Brothers, 1962), pp. 36–68.

chariotry further de-emphasized and demilitarized the agriculturally oriented peasants and shepherding pastoralists. Israel had become a major state, and policy and political decisions were primarily determined and executed on the basis of expediency and sagacity.

This economic prosperity and political bureaucracy created new bases of power in Israelite society. In premonarchical times, social power was primarily based on such things as land ownership, patriarchal standing, charismatic possession, and religious office. One new basis for power that developed under Solomon was the more extensive use of wealth calculated not in foodstuffs, land, or slaves but wealth founded upon a "money" economy which utilized precious metals that could be exchanged for consumer goods, commodities, and services. The frequent references to gold and silver in the narratives about Solomon suggest a widespread use of these as a medium of exchange. The use of a money economy allowed the amassing of more wealth in the hands of fewer people, especially the members of the royal house and the bureaucratic administrators and merchants. Concurrent with this development would have been a shift of the economic power and importance away from the rural areas to the major towns, particularly to those cities with governmental installations. The peasant class and small farmers must have begun to feel the squeeze of this economic centralization which further eroded the importance of the clans and the social orders built upon them.

A further new basis for power lay in the area of education. The task of administering an empire required an educated elite that could not only govern effectively but also participate in the finesse associated with international diplomacy. The type of discretion and polish required of the court attendants and servants is aptly illustrated in the story of the visit of the Queen of Sheba (I Kings 10:1–10). A description of the ideal David in one of the stories of his coming to the court of Saul reflects the qualities of the good royal servant: "skilful in playing [musical instruments], a man of valor, a man of war, prudent in speech, and a man of good presence" (I Sam. 16:18). Such cultural and educational requirements naturally excluded great segments of the Israelite population and gave power to those qualified to advise, serve, and execute the orders and wishes of the king.

The presence of new intellectual forces in Israel fostered the cultivation of an educated taste and an interest in the intellectual traditions of other countries. The wider contacts of the time coupled with the existence of an educated, rather leisured class at the royal court brought Israel into touch with a form of intellectual tradition that was widespread in the Near East and international in its appeal. This is a tradition that is commonly referred to in Biblical studies as "wisdom." [10] In its most elemental form, wisdom gives expression to human insights into life through the use of proverbial sayings and through stories intent on illustrating the values of a given moral system. As such, wisdom is one of the oldest intellectual activities of man. In the tribal and family life situations the

---

[10] Wisdom will be further discussed below in Chapter 14. On international wisdom, see the introduction to R. B. Y. Scott, *Proverbs and Ecclesiastes* (The Anchor Bible [Doubleday & Company, 1965]), pp. xv–liii.

Israelites were quite familiar with this form of folk wisdom, and no doubt the elders sought to pass on to the new generation the insights gained from practical experience and observation and to lay down rules for proper behavior required by the community and necessary for social success. But with the establishment of the Davidic-Solomonic court, there developed an interest in a type of wisdom that was associated with literacy, with an ideal of culture, with the totality of human experience, with what we might call a "liberal arts" education. This type of wisdom had a long prehistory of usage in Mesopotamia and Egypt, where it was cultivated at the royal court and in the scribal schools. No doubt, the necessity to train scribes for the court led to the establishment of scribal schools in Jerusalem, perhaps originally being partially staffed by non-Israelite educators. Wisdom texts from other cultures may have made their way into Israel through these schools where they served as models and textbooks. It has long been recognized that part of the book of The Proverbs is an adaptation of an Egyptian text called the Instruction of Amenemope. This introduction of foreign wisdom allowed Israelite culture to share more fully in the general reservoir of human experience.

Solomon was understood as the patron of the wisdom movement. He was said to have possessed wisdom surpassing that of Egypt and the people of the East. Three thousand proverbs and a thousand and five songs were ascribed to him. In addition, he is said to have spoken of trees, beasts, birds, reptiles, and fish (I Kings 4:29-34). The botanical and zoological phenomena mentioned remind one of the primitive encyclopedic works known in Egyptian and Babylonian wordlists and onamastica that sought to order the natural phenomena into classified groupings.[11] This portrayal of Solomon as patron and author of wisdom traditions reflects the intense wisdom activity current at the court during his reign.

It is even possible to speak of a humanism or enlightenment that characterized the Davidic and especially the Solomonic era. Such was a result of the secularization and education of the time. This humanistic intellectualism reflected a keen interest and curiosity about the natural world, human life, and man's psychological self-consciousness. This humanistic spirit can be illustrated in several ways in addition to those mentioned above. I Kings 10:22 notes that Solomon's ships brought back to Israel not only gold, silver, and ivory but also apes and peacocks. The first three items one could anticipate from export trade, but the last two, far from being necessities or usable commodities, illustrate a curiosity concerning the exotic elements of the natural order and presuppose a cultural sophistication with leisure time to study the unusual. Could one conclude that these animals were destined for some royal zoological gardens in Jerusalem?

The general tone and the psychological interests of the Throne Succession Story display a humanistic orientation.[12] The cult and the sacral orders are

---

[11] See Gerhard von Rad, "Job XXXVIII and Ancient Egyptian Wisdom," in his *The Problem of the Hexateuch*, pp. 281–291.

[12] See John F. Priest, "Humanism, Skepticism, and Pessimism in Israel," *Journal of the American Academy of Religion*, XXXVI (1968), pp. 311–326.

pushed into the background. The story contains no account of any miraculous interventions of Yahweh into the arena of history. The writer is primarily interested in the human side of events and their results. His analysis of Amnon's lust for his half-sister shows a penetrating psychological interest in human behavior. The statement that Amnon, after his rape of Tamar, "hated her with very great hatred; so that the hatred with which he hated her was greater than the love with which he had loved her" (II Sam. 13:15) reveals a deep awareness of the psychological factors involved in human sexuality.

It would be entirely false to assume that this secularized, humanistic spirit came to dominate Israelite culture during the Solomonic era. On the contrary, its influence was probably limited to the circles at the royal court, that is, the upper levels of Israelite society. Its lasting influence in Israelite culture, however, was great, and in the history of the Hebrew Scriptures it was decisive, since most of the Biblical writings were produced by this educated upper class. It would also be wrong to assume that this new spirit was anti-Yahwistic. In one respect the educated class at the court was dealing with areas of human life and experience that previously had not been associated with Yahwism at all. At the same time, even in the Throne Succession Story there is no denial of the fact that Yahweh governs history. The emphasis is shifted to portray Yahweh as working not through charismatic characters or miraculous interventions but through the natural course of events.

THE THEOLOGY OF THE DAVIDIC DYNASTY

The practical political needs of the tribes led to the adoption of a monarchical rule. The adoption of the monarchy led in turn to the formulation of a theology of kingship. A brief description of the Near Eastern ideologies concerning kingship will aid in an appreciation of the Israelite understanding of the king and his function.[13]

In Egyptian culture, the king, or pharaoh, was considered a god. He ruled therefore in the strictest sense by divine right. The divinity of the pharaoh was the link between the cosmic and human orders. He ruled as an absolute despot, and was obeyed and served as an act of devotion offered to a deity. The ruler was identified with the god Horus in this life; at death he became the god Osiris. Periodic festivals celebrated the deity of the pharaoh, and the rituals associated with his death, mummification, and burial were to ensure his proper transmigration into the order of the cosmic powers.

Deity was not ordinarily ascribed to the king by the Babylonians and the Assyrians, although kingship was regarded as an essential institution in human and cosmic affairs. Kingship was understood as one of the primeval gifts of the gods to mankind. As one of the ancient texts put it, kingship was "lowered from heaven." The king in Mesopotamian culture was considered the chief servant of the primary god (Marduk in Babylon and Asshur in Assyria) and the special object of the deity's love and concern.

---

[13] A good description of Egyptian and Mesopotamian kingship is given in Henri Frankfort, *Kingship and the Gods* (The University of Chicago Press, 1948).

We are less informed concerning the conception of kingship current among the Canaanite and Phoenician city-states. From some of the Ugaritic texts it can be concluded that kingship probably operated on the assumption of dynastic succession and that the king was considered a son of the deity (El), and thus kingship was given a divine sanction. The order and well-being of the community were dependent upon the king, who embodied a sacramental union between the people and their god.[14]

The most radical political innovation in early Israelite history was the movement to a monarchical form of government. The idea of an absolute ruler was alien to the patriarchal, charismatic, and rather democratic structures of the old tribal society. In order to support and justify the idea of kingship, it had to be buttressed by a royal ideology. How much of this was developed under Saul is uncertain. The right of dynastic succession was certainly assumed by his family upon his death. It remained, however, for the Davidic house and the Jerusalemite court to formulate a substantial theology of kingship.

The Davidic theology finds expression in numerous Biblical passages but especially in the oracle of the court prophet Nathan in II Sam., ch. 7, and in the royal psalms of the Psalter (especially, Ps. 2; 21; 45; 72; 89; and 110), which were employed in cultic services in which the king was the center of attention.[15] All

The Israelite temple at Arad, discovered during recent excavations, dates from the Solomonic period and continued in use for about two centuries. The existence of this building suggests that Solomon constructed more than one temple to Yahweh. Three steps lead up from the main hall into the inner shrine here flanked by incense altars.

YOHANAN AHARONI AND THE ARAD
ARCHAEOLOGICAL EXPEDITION

this material probably doesn't date from the reigns of David and Solomon, but the primary outlines of the royal theology were already established during this

---

[14] See Gray, *The Legacy of Canaan*, pp. 218–230.

[15] See Aubrey R. Johnson, *Sacral Kingship in Ancient Israel*, 2d ed. (Cardiff: University of Wales Press, 1967).

period. For its expression, this theology drew upon the concept of a covenant relationship to Yahweh that was basic to Israelite religion, the ritual and ideas of kingship found in the royal courts of neighboring empire states, and the royal concepts of Canaanite culture, perhaps especially that of pre-Israelite Jerusalem. Numerous occasions at the royal court, such as coronations, enthronement anniversaries, and times of national crisis and triumph, offered opportunity for the usage of this theology.

The cornerstone of the Jerusalemite royal theology is found in the oracle of Nathan, addressed to David as a word of Yahweh, giving divine assurance and justification for the perpetual rule of the house of David. This oracle is set within the context of David's desire to build Yahweh a house (temple) in Jerusalem. Nathan assures David that "Yahweh declares to you that Yahweh will make you a house [dynasty]. . . . And your house and your kingdom shall be made sure forever before me; your throne shall be established forever" (II Sam. 7:11b, 16).[16] This divine right of the Davidic family to rule in perpetuity was never really challenged from within the Jerusalem court, and when its rule was ended by outside forces the right was caught up in the anticipation and hopes for the future which looked forward to the restoration of Davidic rule.

The royal theology was given its fullest expression in the ritual of enthronement, a description of which is recorded in two Biblical narratives (I Kings 1:32–48 and II Kings, ch. 11). In neither of these accounts is there an attempt to detail the elements in the coronation ritual; they are both intended to narrate the activity associated with two extenuating circumstances that required special precautions. The first is the story of Solomon's hasty accession to abort the moves of Adonijah; the second tells of the assassination of the usurper queen Athaliah and her replacement with the young lad Joash.

In the sanctuary, or in the case of Solomon at the sacred spring Gihon, the future king was anointed with holy oil, thus making him the messiah. (The term "messiah" simply means "anointed.") He was then presented with the crown and the testimony and joyously acclaimed as king. Conducted to his palace, the king ascended the throne and began his rule, receiving the homage of his officials and subjects.

Many of the royal psalms (such as Ps. 2 and 110) were utilized within the context of the coronation and gave expression to the Jerusalemite beliefs about the king. These psalms may be understood as containing the verbal accompaniment to the ritual of the coronation. In the enthronement ritual the king became associated in a special way with Yahweh and was elevated to a unique position. It can be assumed that the testimony presented to the new ruler was a written document containing the actual commission to rule granted by Yahweh which was based on the divine promises to the monarch and perhaps incorporated a statement of the king's obligation to Yahweh and his people. Psalm 2 appears to contain quotations made from such a royal testimony. Part of this psalm represents statements made by some cultic functionary, perhaps a court prophet (see vs. 1–6, 10–12) and also the king's recitation of the divine decree.

---

[16] For a discussion of this significant chapter, see Martin Noth, "David and Israel in II Samuel VII," in his *The Laws in the Pentateuch*, pp. 250–259.

> I will tell of the decree of Yahweh:
> He said to me, "You are my son,
>   today I have begotten you."
>   (Ps. 2:7.)

The king was thus considered the divine son of Yahweh through his adoption into a filial relationship with the deity. The day of his coronation was the day of his rebirth. There is no real evidence to suggest that this idea was understood mythologically in the sense that the king was actually and physically begotten by the deity.[17]

The king was also promised a universal dominion and rulership over the nations of the earth. The decree of the king in Ps. 2 continues:

> [Yahweh said to me:]
> "Ask of me, and I will make the nations your heritage,
>   and the ends of the earth your possession."
>   (Ps. 2:8.)

Psalm 72, a prayer on behalf of the king, expresses a similar sentiment:

> May he [the king] have dominion from sea to sea,
>   and from the River to the ends of the earth!
> May his foes bow down before him,
>   and his enemies lick the dust!
> May the kings of Tarshish and of the isles
>   render him tribute,
> may the kings of Sheba and Seba bring gifts!
> May all kings fall down before him,
>   all nations serve him!
>   (Ps. 72:8–11.)

This concept of the king as the universal ruler was proclaimed as a part of the court theology in both the Egyptian and the Mesopotamian cultures and might be the source for this aspect of the Davidic theology.

It is possible that this universal rulership over the nations of the world was acted out symbolically in the context of the coronation. Psalm 2:9 refers to the fact that the Davidic king would break the nations "with a rod of iron, and dash them in pieces like a potter's vessel." Psalm 110:1 quotes Yahweh as saying to the king: "Sit at my right hand, till I make your enemies your footstool." In the Egyptian royal festivities the universal rule of the pharaoh was acted out by such feats as the releasing of pigeons toward the four corners of the earth, the pacing off of a rectangular field representing the earth, and the smashing of pottery vessels and figurines representative of the Egyptian enemies. Among the finds in the tomb of Tutankhamen were two footstools with stylized representations of the traditional enemies of Egypt. Thus when the pharaoh sat on his throne, his enemies were his footstool! Similar actions no doubt formed part of

---

[17] See Gerald Cooke, "The Israelite King as Son of God," *Zeitschrift für die alttestamentliche Wissenschaft*, LXXIII (1961), pp. 202–225.

the Israelite ritual, with quotations such as Ps. 2:8–12 and 110:1 being the spoken accompaniment. The reference in Ps. 110:1 to the king's sitting "at the right hand of Yahweh" refers of course to the fact that the king's throne room was to the right of the temple in which Yahweh was enthroned over the Ark.

The Davidic rulers in Jerusalem were not only king over the states of Israel and Judah but also ruler over the city-state of Jerusalem. It is in this light that the following verse is to be understood:

> Yahweh has sworn
>   and will not change his mind,
> "You are a priest for ever
>   after the order of Melchizedek."
>   (Ps. 110:4.)

Melchizedek is mentioned in one other place in the Old Testament. This is in Gen. 14:18–20, where he is described as the priest-king of the god El-Elyon (God Most High) in Salem. In Ps. 76, Salem and Zion are identified, so that one can conclude that Melchizedek was the legendary king of Jerusalem. As king of the royal property of Jerusalem, the Davidic kings were considered the successors in the old order of the Jebusite priest-kings.

The new status of the king as ruler and son of Yahweh was probably recognized by his being given a new name and/or a set of titles. Several kings are known by two names in the Bible. Solomon was also known as Jedidiah, "beloved of Yahweh" (II Sam. 12:25), and such passages as II Kings 23:34 refer to the name change that occurred at the king's coronation. In the Egyptian ritual, the pharaoh was generally given five new name-titles. There is one passage in Isaiah which suggests that new Davidic kings were also given new titles at their coronation. The verse in question states that "a child is born, to us a son is given; and the government shall be upon his shoulder," which clearly refers to a ruler and the birth perhaps means the king's "birth" as the son of Yahweh in the royal ritual. The passage continues:

> His name will be called
> "Wonderful Counselor, Mighty God,
> Everlasting Father, Prince of Peace."
>   (Isa. 9:6.)

The accession of the new king in Jerusalem was heralded as the announcement of a new order in human life and even in the world of nature.

> May he live while the sun endures,
>   and as long as the moon, throughout all generations!
> May he be like rain that falls on the mown grass,
>   like showers that water the earth!
> In his days may righteousness flourish,
>   and peace abound, till the moon be no more!
>
>   .   .   .
>
> May there be abundance of grain in the land;
>   on the tops of the mountains may it wave;
>   may its fruit be like Lebanon;

and may men blossom forth from the cities
like the grass of the field!

(Ps. 72:5–7, 16.)

The king was the special instrument and defender of justice among his people
and the guardian of the law:

Give the king thy justice, O God,
and thy righteousness to the royal son!
May he judge thy people with righteousness,
and thy poor with justice!

May he defend the cause of the poor of the people,
give deliverance to the needy,
and crush the oppressor!

(Ps. 72:1–2, 4.)

This idea of the king as the source of justice and the special protector of the
poor was a widespread Near Eastern concept. Hammurabi in his law code declares that the gods established him in rulership

to promote the welfare of the people,
to cause justice to prevail in the land,
to destroy the wicked and the evil
that the strong may not oppress the weak.[18]

The Davidic theology was certainly not given universal acceptance in ancient
Israel. It seems to have had its strongest appeal to the citizens of Jerusalem,
where the court was located, and to the Judeans from whose midst David had
come. The northern tribes of the old confederacy of Israel seemed to have preferred a less autocratic and more charismatic form of kingship and saw in the
emphasis on the house of David a further corrosion of the tribal and patriarchal
authority and independence. Coupled with this was always the fact that an absolute kingship carried with it many royal prerogatives which could express
themselves in the form of oppressive policies and unfair feudalistic demands.
Such a sentiment against this aspect of kingship is found in Samuel's speech
denouncing kingship at the time of Saul's rise to power:

These will be the ways of the king who will reign over you: he will take your
sons and appoint them to his chariots and to be his horsemen, and to run
before his chariots; and he will appoint for himself commanders of thousands and commanders of fifties, and some to plow his ground and to reap his
harvest, and to make his implements of war and the equipment of his chariots.
He will take your daughters to be perfumers and cooks and bakers. He will
take the best of your fields and vineyards and olive orchards and give them to
his servants. He will take the tenth of your grain and of your vineyards and
give it to his officers and to his servants. He will take your menservants and
maidservants, and the best of your cattle and your asses, and put them to his
work. He will take the tenth of your flocks, and you shall be his slaves. (I Sam.
8:11–17.)

---

[18] Translation is from Pritchard, ed., *Ancient Near Eastern Texts*, p. 164.

THE ZION THEOLOGY

The city-state of Jerusalem (Zion was the fortified acropolis) became an Is-raelite possession and a place sacred to Yahweh only at the time of David and thus at a fairly late stage in Hebrew history. By bringing the Ark to Jerusalem, David made the city the primary religious center of the Israelite nation. Along with the Ark, there came some of the old Yahwistic tribal traditions and senti-ments. The building of the Temple by Solomon greatly enhanced the signifi-cance of Zion and provided the state cult and its god with an adequate and mag-nificent edifice.

The importance of Zion in both the religious and the political spheres was given expression in a definite theology of the Holy City which seems to have been a combination of elements taken partially from the older Yahwism and par-tially from the pre-Israelite Jerusalem cult. It should be recalled that David had two major priests—Abiathar, from the Israelite priesthood; and Zadok, who was first mentioned in the texts after the capture of Jerusalem and was in all prob-ability a representative of the pre-Israelite Jerusalem cult. This special Zion theology found expression in numerous places throughout the Psalter but espe-cially in such Zion psalms or songs (see Ps. 137:3) as Ps. 46; 48; and 76.

Zion was considered the dwelling place of Yahweh where he sat enthroned in the temple and it was claimed that he had founded the city just as he had created the earth.

> In Judah God is known,
>   his name is great in Israel.
> His abode has been established in Salem,
>   his dwelling place in Zion.
>   (Ps. 76:1–2.)

> He chose the tribe of Judah,
>   Mount Zion, which he loves,
> He built his sanctuary like the high heavens,
>   like the earth, which he has founded for ever.
>   (Ps. 78:68–69.)

Zion was identified with the cosmic "mountain of god" which was a common phenomenon of faith in the Near East, as is evidenced by the artificial moun-tains (ziggurats) associated with Mesopotamian religion and the mountain abodes of the Canaanite deities.[19] In giving expression to this aspect of the sacred city and mountain cosmology, the Jerusalem circles seem to have borrowed from the mythologies associated with the two major Canaanite gods, El and Baal. Psalm 46:4 speaks of "a river whose streams make glad the city of God, the holy habitation of the Most High [Elyon]." The psalm goes on to identify Elyon with Yahweh, and the holy habitation is clearly understood as Zion. There was of course no river in Zion, but in the El mythology of the Canaanites, El dwelt "at the source of the two streams, in the midst of the source of the deeps."

---

[19] See Clements, *God and Temple*, pp. 40–62.

Here one sees the idea of a cosmic dwelling of the god at the source of the cosmic streams (note the rivers that flowed out of the Garden of Eden according to Gen. 2:10–14) which became associated in the Zion theology with Yahweh. The Psalms contain the following affirmation:

> Great is Yahweh and greatly to be praised
> in the city of our God!
> His holy mountain, beautiful in elevation,
> is the joy of all the earth,
> Mount Zion, in the far north [or in the recesses of Zaphon],
> the city of the great King.
> Within her citadels God
> has shown himself a sure defense.
>
> (Ps. 48:1–3.)

Here the Zion tradition has taken over mythology associated with Baal, who, following his defeat of Yam, was acclaimed as king of the gods, and subsequently had a temple on Mount Zaphon constructed for him. It should be noted in this connection that Yahweh had been understood from earliest times to be closely associated with a sacred mountain, namely, Mt. Sinai.

A constant theme in Ps. 46; 48; and 76 is the stability and security of Zion. Though the nations rage, armies assault, the mountains quake, and the earth melt, Zion is to stand firm and witness the destruction of her enemies.

There are a number of factors which suggest that this Zion theology was given expression in an annual celebration commemorating the founding of the city and the beginning of Yahweh's kingship in Zion over the nations of the world.[20] This celebration was probably part of the autumn festival, which also included the New Year celebration. The New Year was the time of the coronation of the Davidic rulers and the subsequent anniversary celebrations as well as the time of the initial dedication of the Temple (I Kings 8:2). Such a festival commemorating Yahweh's kingship in Zion would have been a reenactment of that primordial time when David first brought the Ark to Jerusalem (II Sam., ch. 6) and when Solomon later placed it in the Temple (I Kings 8:1–11). Both of these events were accompanied by solemn assemblies of the people, sacrifices, processions, and royal dispensations of blessings. It is entirely possible that the Ark was removed from the Temple in conjunction with the festival and "ritually" lost just as it had once been captured by the Philistines (see Ps. 132).[21] Without the Ark and Yahweh in Zion, nature and men were placed in a state of suspended animation awaiting the reestablishment of Yahweh's rule. In the course of the festival, the Ark would have been refound and accompanied to Jerusalem by pilgrims going to the Holy City for the celebration of Yahweh's kingship. Perhaps to this part of the ceremony belong many of the "Psalms of Ascent" or

---

[20] See Sigmund Mowinckel, *The Psalms in Israel's Worship,* Vol. I, tr. by D. R. Ap-Thomas (Abingdon Press, 1962), pp. 106–192.

[21] See T. E. Fretheim, "Psalm 132: A Form-Critical Study," *Journal of Biblical Literature,* LXXXVI (1967), pp. 289–300.

"Psalms of Going-Up" (Ps. 120 to 134) sung as the pilgrims and the Ark neared Jerusalem. The greatness of Zion was extolled:

> Walk about Zion, go round about her,
>   number her towers,
> consider well her ramparts,
>   go through her citadels;
> that you may tell the next generation . . .
>   (Ps. 48:12–13.)

The entrance ritual reflected in Ps. 24, discussed above, was probably enacted at the outer gate of the Temple and the entry of the Ark through the gates so timed as to coincide with the rising sun of the autumnal equinox whose morning rays blazed through the pylons, Jachin and Boaz, into the heart of the sacred sanctuary.

> Lift up your heads, O gates!
>   and be lifted up, O ancient doors!
>   that the King of glory may come in.
> Who is this King of glory?
>   Yahweh of hosts,
>   he is the King of glory!
>   (Ps. 24:9–10.)

With the reinstatement of the Ark in the Temple, Yahweh again reasserted his rule over Israel and the nations.

> Yahweh reigns [or has become king];
>   let the peoples tremble!
> He sits enthroned upon the cherubim;
>   let the earth quake!
> Yahweh is great in Zion;
>   he is exalted over all the peoples.
>   (Ps. 99:1–2.)

> Clap your hands, all peoples!
>   Shout to God with loud songs of joy!
> For Yahweh, the Most High [Elyon], is terrible,
>   a great king over all the earth.
> He subdued peoples under us,
>   and nations under our feet.
> He chose our heritage for us,
>   the pride of Jacob whom he loves.
> God has gone up with a shout,
>   Yahweh with the sound of a trumpet.
>   (Ps. 47:1–5.)

This rule extended not only over Israel and the nations but included the world of creation and the gods.

Yahweh is a great God,
   and a great King above all gods.
In his hand are the depths of the earth;
   the heights of the mountains are his also.
The sea is his, for he made it;
   for his hands formed the dry land.
(Ps. 95:3–5.)

8 | THE YAHWISTIC HISTORY
OF ISRAEL

As we have already seen, the beginnings of an Israelite literature, in the strict sense of the term, do not predate the period of the united monarchy. Prior to that time there may have been epic or poetic works in existence in some form which told of the heroic exploits and feats of tribal leaders and warriors. An epic work referred to as the Book of the Upright (Jashar) is said to have contained Joshua's command to the sun at the battle of Gibeon (Josh. 10:12–13) as well as David's lament over the death of Saul and Jonathan (II Sam. 1:17–18). A passing reference is made to a work called the Book of the Wars of Yahweh in Num. 21:14 and a short excerpt from it is quoted. Neither of these two works has survived, and therefore practically nothing can be said about their origin, nature, and content.

THE BEGINNINGS OF NATIONAL HISTORIOGRAPHY

Several factors are necessary to support the perspective of an intellectual plateau from which a people writes its history.[1] Among these are national self-consciousness, cultural achievement, educational attainment, and political needs. During the Davidic-Solomonic era, the educational and humanistic spirit, which was discussed in the last chapter, joined with certain distinctive theological and political needs and led to a phenomenal outpouring of historical writings.

The learned scribes at the royal court were familiar with and perhaps were influenced by the literature of other countries and no doubt possessed their own translations and imitations of this foreign literature. I Kings 11:41 speaks of the Book of the Acts of Solomon, which was probably the official annals of his reign, and perhaps the same type of record had been kept under David's rule. This annalistic record-keeping may have been the forerunner to the production of extended historical works.

Biblical readings: The primary Biblical materials discussed in this chapter are the Yahwistic passages in the opening chapters of the Bible (Gen. 2:4b to ch. 4; 6:1–4; 6:5 to ch. 8; 9:18–27; 11:1–9; 12:1–3).

[1] See Sigmund Mowinckel, "Israelite Historiography," *Annual of the Swedish Theological Institute*, II (1963), pp. 4–26; and Gerhard von Rad, "The Beginnings of Historical Writing in Ancient Israel," in his *The Problem of the Hexateuch*, pp. 166–204.

Scholars generally assume that at least two major histories were written during this Davidic-Solomonic era. These were the Throne Succession Story (II Sam., chs. 9 to 20; I Kings, chs. 1 and 2) and the Yahwistic history of Israel (now one of the strands of the Pentateuch but found primarily in Genesis, Exodus, and Numbers). Perhaps a finished form of the account of David's rise to power (I Sam. 16:14 to II Sam. 5:12) may also have been committed to writing during this time. It is the Yahwistic history that is our immediate concern in this chapter, but before discussing this, we might ask why such extensive writing of a historical form developed in Israel and is without parallel in the ancient Near East.

The fact that much of Israel's literature took the form of historical narrative was not due to some belief wholly unique to the Hebrews about the ability of their god to act in history.[2] Most Near Eastern deities were considered capable of intervening and were believed to have intervened in the affairs of history on behalf of their devotees. Marduk of the Babylonians and Chemosh of the Moabites were, like Yahweh, gods who acted in history. But we possess no extensive historical narratives from the Babylonians or Moabites comparable to Israel's histories of herself. In the case of the Moabites, this may be due to their failure to develop a relatively free and sophisticated material culture over a long period of time, but this was not so with the Babylonians.

A number of reasons probably contributed to Israel's extensive use of historical narrative as a literary form. In the first place, Israel was a rather late comer on the stage of history. She became a state only at the beginning of the first millennium B.C., at a time when other major states had existed for many hundreds of years. For this reason she could not trace her unique political beginnings back to that mythological time when all things began. Secondly, the Hebrews traced their origins to a place outside their occupied Land of Canaan and thus they understood themselves as immigrants and conquerors who held their land as a special favor of the deity. In such thought, the significant events in a people's life are those important times and points of departure and arrival. For these reasons, Israel took a rather ambivalent attitude toward the settled agrarian culture. Thus the people, for example, historicized the agricultural festivals of Canaan while simultaneously preserving much of their older form. Festivals originally associated solely with the cycles of nature were interpreted in relation to the Israelites' knowledge of their past. Thirdly, Israel understood Yahweh from the earliest times as a "folk god" whose primary relationship and concern were with a people and not with the world of nature or the cosmos. To this extent, the work of the deity was seen in the history of the group. Finally, Yahweh was initially understood as a militant war god, jealous of his worshipers. By nature, war gods are intolerant and unaccommodating to other deities. As such an intolerant deity, Yahweh was not associated with a female cosmic principle or a part of a pantheon in strict Yahwism, factors so necessary if people are to understand their world in terms of a cosmological mythology rather than in a historicized mythology.

---

[2] On the relationship between the gods and history, see Bertil Albrektson, *History and the Gods* (Lund: C. W. K. Gleerup, Publishers, 1967).

SOURCE MATERIALS USED BY THE YAHWISTIC HISTORIAN

The artistic Yahwistic historian attempted to produce a history of his people covering a time span that extended from the creation of the world until the time of the Hebrew conquest of Canaan.[3] The writer assumes that the deity had been known and worshiped as Yahweh throughout human history and this has led scholars to designate the work "Yahwistic." Sometimes this epic is referred to as the J source of the Pentateuch. Such a designation is based on the fact that the Germans, who pioneered in source criticism of the Pentateuch, spell the name of the deity "Jahweh." Most scholars assume that the history was written in the southern part of the United Kingdom, or Judah.

Various traditions and sources were available to and utilized by the author or authors of the Yahwistic narrative. No doubt the vast majority of these were in oral form, a living part of the people's heritage kept alive in the memory which we must realize was far more highly developed in a culture that was not accustomed to seeing everything "written down."

One of the most important sources for the Yahwist was the historical summaries that the Israelites had used in confessing their faith in Yahweh and in affirming the nation's election as Yahweh's people. These confessions gave expression to the people's belief as to how they had come to be Yahweh's chosen people in the Land of Promise. Examples of such summary credos can be found in Deut. 26:5–11; Josh. 24:1–13; Ps. 78; 105; 106; and so on. These examples illustrate the diverse ways in which these summaries could be used: in preaching, hymnic praise, hymnic confession, and instruction. All these examples focus primarily on four themes: the Patriarchs, the exodus from Egypt, the sojourn in the wilderness, and the occupation of the Land of Canaan. The manner in which and the extent to which these themes were developed seemed to have depended on the situation within which they were used. Deuteronomy 26:5–11 is a confession of faith and confidence in Yahweh without any effort to create among the people a sense of guilt. It makes no mention of the wilderness period. Psalms 105 and 106 focus on the theme of the wilderness period, but the former does so in such a way as to glorify the mighty works of Yahweh, while the latter aims at creating a sense of sin and disobedience. The skeletal structure of these summaries suggests that there had developed a sort of canonical pattern in which the Hebrews had come to express their "sacred history" but which could be elaborated and expanded to suit the needs of the situation.[4]

Also available to the Yahwist were tribal and ancestor sagas. Some of these were ethnological in nature, explaining the kinship between Israelites and neighboring groups, oftentimes deprecating the origin of other peoples (as in Gen. 19:24–38). Many sagas were etiological in nature, intent on explaining the existence of some custom, belief, or name, a type of tradition and folk story that is universal in its appeal and employment. Ancient tribal songs and poems sum-

---

[3] See Peter Ellis, C.Ss.R., *The Yahwist: The Bible's First Theologian* (Fides Publishers, 1968).
[4] See Gerhard von Rad, "The Form-Critical Problem of the Hexateuch," in his *The Problem of the Hexateuch*, pp. 1–78.

marizing and characterizing tribal history and behavior seem to have been in widespread usage among the Israelites, as they are today among bedouin Arabs. The Yahwist also found ready at hand a number of stories concerning the founding of cultic places of worship in which the local sanctuary or altar was associated with some patriarchal hero (for example, Gen. 28:10–22). These foundation legends were closely bound to the cult places which they served to justify and sanctify.

The Yahwist was most certainly familiar with the concept of the covenant which the Israelites used to express their relationship to Yahweh and their deity's gracious relationships toward them. The covenant-renewal festival, with its proclamation of the demands of Yahweh and the people's oath of allegiance as a reenactment of the Sinai covenant, was clearly known to the Yahwist and incorporated into his presentation of Israelite faith.

Common Near Eastern legends and mythology about the creation of the world, primeval history, and the origins of the human predicament were also drawn upon by the Yahwist. Many of these legends and myths had their earliest known existence already in the ancient cultures of the fourth and third millennia B.C. and often dealt with themes and patterns common to man's universal existential situation. Tracing the exact source of some of this mythology is almost impossible, since some of it may have reached the Israelites from Egypt and Mesopotamia via the Phoenicians and the Canaanites, whereas some of these mythological motifs may have had their origin in the common northwest Semitic culture to which the Israelite ancestors belonged.[5]

THE PURPOSES OF THE YAHWISTIC HISTORY

It is possible to discern a number of purposes interwoven into the Yahwistic narrative. Some of these are the special emphases of the Yahwistic author(s), whereas others were already embodied in the traditions taken over into the epic and incorporated into the general narrative structure. In order to understand the purposes behind the Yahwistic history, it is necessary to examine the structure and scaffolding that sustain the work. The fulcrum on which the entire Yahwist history balances is found in the call of Abraham and the divine promise made to him:

> Now Yahweh said to Abram, "Go from your country and your kindred and your father's house to the land I will show you. And I will make of you a great nation, and I will bless you, and make your name great, so that you will be a blessing. I will bless those who bless you, and him who curses you I will curse; and by you all the families of the earth shall bless themselves." (Gen. 12:1–3.)

This threefold promise emphasized Abraham's becoming "a great people," possessing "a great name," and his being a source of blessing for "all the families of the earth." What precedes the call of Abraham in the epic is the prologue depict-

---

[5] S. H. Hooke, *Middle Eastern Mythology* (Penguin Books, 1963), supplies a good survey of Near Eastern mythology and Biblical parallels.

ing the human situation and world history within which the promise is made. What follows the giving of the promise is the epilogue showing how Yahweh guided the promise through history toward its fulfillment. It is this covenant promise to Abraham which sustains the entire structure of the Yahwistic work.

For the author, the existence of the United Kingdom and the Israelite occupation of the Land of Canaan were part and parcel of Yahweh's plan for human history. Behind the Yahwistic historian's picture of the Abraham promise there stand the figure of David and the Davidic covenant.[6] It was in the Davidic state that the Yahwist saw the first realization of the promises to Abraham: a mighty nation with an international reputation and the means to be a blessing to all mankind. Expressions of the Davidic theology in the book of The Psalms are often almost identical to the call of Abraham:

> May his name endure for ever,
>   his fame continue as long as the sun!
> May men bless themselves by him,
>   all nations call him blessed!
>
> (Ps. 72:17.)

The author, then, not only drew upon the Davidic covenant for his portrayal of Abraham but overtly related the promises to Abraham to the accomplishments of the Davidic-Solomonic empire in such a way as to emphasize the sacredness and authority of the empire as the fulfillment of the promise. To this extent, then, the Yahwistic history was nationalistic and evangelistic in intent. It sought to give a theologically sound rationale for the state and its existence by ascribing to it a sacred hallowness, the realization of an ancient promise.

The concept of a unified prehistory of the diverse Israelite ancestors also dominates the perspective of the Yahwist. Already with Abraham, the Israel of the United Kingdom is present in germ and promise. Abraham is the father of all Israel; what happens to one of the sons of Jacob is shared in by the whole. Events, then, that were originally associated with smaller groups are displayed as the acts of all Israel. The reason for this emphasis on "all Israel" is obvious, since a constant plague of the Hebrews in Canaan was their disunity and divisions which at times threatened to tear the Davidic state apart and eventually succeeded in doing so. By concentrating on the theme of a common prehistory, the Yahwist was a spokesman for the unity of the state.

The United Kingdom, for the Yahwist, was much more than the theological and political union of the twelve tribes of all Israel. It was also the state which incorporated within its political boundaries the Canaanite cities absorbed into Israel and within its theological limits the perspectives and content of an agricultural and sedentary life and thought. The ancestral gods of the fathers and the Canaanite gods of the land are identified with Yahweh by the historian. Cultic practices and places of diverse origin are amalgamated into Yahwism. Yahweh, the militant god of Sinai, had taken over, especially from El, the characteristics of creatorship and universality. The primary attributes of the Canaanite gods El and Baal were associated with Yahweh in the Zion theology (see above, pp.

---

[6] See Ronald E. Clements, *Abraham and David* (London: SCM Press, Ltd., 1967).

131–134) and were given expression in historical narrative: Yahweh was the high god, the ruler of men and history. So a rather positive attitude is taken by the Yahwist in regard to the culture and institutions of the Israelites which had developed in the Land of Canaan. All in all, there is little anti-Canaanite bias in the material.

THE PRIMEVAL PERIOD

The first eleven chapters of Genesis are often referred to as primeval history, since they attempt to set forth the prehistorical ages prior to the entry of Yahweh's chosen people into the arena of history.[7] The ancients seem to have understood the events associated with this period to have, in a real way, "happened" as they are depicted, since they are incorporated into their chronological and genealogical reckonings. At the same time, they seem to have understood some of these stories as depicting not only "once upon a time" events but also as embodying "everytime" perspectives. That is, the stories not only may refer to what happened at the beginning but also may contain an analysis of the human factors that led to similar recurrences in the contemporary.

Human history as described in the opening chapters of the Bible, and almost universally throughout Near Eastern thought, is conceived of in terms different from that common to modern man. For the ancients, history began not in an evolutionary tooth-and-claw condition which gradually developed toward more improved conditions but in a paradise situation which rapidly deteriorated to produce life as the author knew it with all its problems, hardships, and heartaches. For the Yahwist, human life began under ideal conditions on a paradisical plateau, but, through man's efforts and acts, human history lost this tranquil and ideal state and, as a result, moved downward in decline and depravity.

The basic material in the primeval history which is generally assigned to the Yahwistic history is Gen. 2:4b to 4:26; 6:1–4; one of the accounts in the composite story of the Flood in chs. 6:5 to 8:22; 9:18–27; and 11:1–9. All these narrative sections seem to have originally existed as independent units which the Yahwist found in his nation's folk tradition. What the Yahwist did was to bring these together to form a connected narrative. At points many of the details in the stories are not fully integrated. The stories are like pearls which the Yahwist has strung together but without destroying their individuality.

The material in the primeval history serves as an introductory prologue to the call of Abraham in Gen. 12:1–3 and shows the predicament of mankind which had resulted from human disobedience and the subsequent curses of Yahweh on man and the world. These opening chapters of Genesis present the disintegrating and accursed history of humanity which is the background for the redemptive and redeemed history of Israel foreshadowed in the election of Abraham.

Creation and Paradise. Both Biblical accounts of the creation of man and the world in the opening chapters of Genesis are basically narratives not about

---

[7] On the questions involved in the primeval materials, see Alan Richardson, *Genesis I–XI* (London: SCM Press, Ltd., 1953).

the "divine creation" of the world but about the "divine formation" of the world and its orders.[8] Neither account presupposes a state of nothingness out of which something or the existence of matter and the world developed. The emphasis is, rather, on the formation of a formless waste, the formation of order out of disorder, of cosmos out of chaos.

The Yahwistic sketch of creation (Gen. 2:4b–25) might be called the dry account of creation, since it assumes that the earth originally existed as a waterless waste without rainfall to produce vegetation and without man to care for the land. The first act of Yahweh was the formation of man (*'adam*) from the dust of the ground (*'adamah*), as a potter shapes a vessel. Man's vitality and motility—his life—comes when Yahweh breathes into his nostrils and man becomes a "living being." One could describe the Yahwistic view of the world's orders as a series of concentric circles with man at the center—the firstborn of creation—and the rest of the created orders brought into being around him. Man is placed in an ideal state, the Garden of Eden, and the flora and fauna are created around him for his usage and enjoyment.

The idea of primeval man's living in an ideal or paradise state was widespread among the Near Eastern cultures. One version pictured this ideal state as an island free from sickness, old age, or any of the problems that beset mankind.[9] Another form of this story, in the so-called Gilgamesh epic,[10] depicts a uniquely created man named Enkidu who lived on the steppe in peaceful contentment with the animals, who befriended him and roamed the land beside him until he sexually associated with a human female, an act that brought to an end his idyllic existence in the animal kingdom. There is another picture of this ideal state reflected in Ezek. 28:13–14 in which the Garden of Eden was located on a holy mountain. All these versions of man's original idyllic state were intent to show how man once lived free from trouble, and they embody the symbolic projections of man's psychological longings for the perfect and the content in the midst of a life with problems and imperfections.

The Yahwist version of the Garden of Eden envisions man as a primordial worker: he is to till and keep the garden (Gen. 2:15). According to the story, man's freedom was hedged in by only one restraint: a command of Yahweh that he not eat from the tree in the midst of the garden. Should he eat, death would be his destiny (Gen. 2:16–17). The episode of the creation of woman appears in the story as something of an afterthought, perhaps the writer's way of emphasizing woman's complementary and assumed derivative nature. It is only after the animals prove not to be proper companions for man that woman is made from the man's rib. The fact that woman is made from part of man once formed

[8] S. G. F. Brandon, *Creation Legends of the Ancient Near East* (London: Hodder and Stoughton, 1963), provides a good survey of the various Near Eastern creation legends, including the Biblical materials. See also Bernhard W. Anderson, *Creation Versus Chaos* (Association Press, 1967).

[9] A good discussion of the earliest known mythology and the idea of paradise is found in Samuel N. Kramer, *The Sumerians* (The University of Chicago Press, 1963), pp. 112–164.

[10] See Alexander Heidel, *The Gilgamesh Epic and Old Testament Parallels*, 2d ed. (The University of Chicago Press, Phoenix Books, 1949). A translation of the epic is given in Pritchard, ed., *Ancient Near Eastern Texts*, pp. 72–99. This document also contains the Babylonian account of the great flood.

the basic stratum of an independent etiological story: the sexes have an irresistible urge for each other and can become one flesh in sexual union and in the infant offspring because they were originally one. Upon seeing the female whom Yahweh has built for him, man breaks out into poetry:

> This at last is bone of my bones
>   and flesh of my flesh;
> she shall be called Woman (*'ishshah*),
>   because she was taken out of Man (*'ish*).
>   (Gen. 2.23.)

Man and woman, in their naïveté, were naked but unashamed.

Disobedience and Curse. In Gen., ch. 3, the writer returns to the prohibition against the eating of the fruit from the tree in the midst of the garden in order to explain the existence of man in a world that was far from paradise. Insofar as the tree is concerned, the Yahwist appears to have borrowed an ancient piece of folklore concerning man's quest for immortality in which the tree of life played the central role and man's hope to be like the gods was his desire to secure the secret of perpetual youth. This is a central theme in the Gilgamesh epic, which depicts the hero seeking, finding, and then losing to the snake (whose annual shedding of its skin prefigured rebirth) the branch from "the tree that makes one young in his old age." The Yahwist has introduced into the story the second tree, that of the knowledge of good and evil, thus making man's acquisition of knowledge his fatal attainment. Exactly what the Yahwist understood by "the tree of knowledge of good and evil" remains a mystery. Is the knowledge related to intellectual familiarity with mysteries that lie beyond man? Or to any knowledge whatever? Or to the discovery of the power of discrimination and discernment? Or to the consciousness of sex? Perhaps the tree serves only to show how man failed when confronted with the necessity of decision in the light of a divine command.

The nature of temptation seems to have been a vital concern of the writer, who, in common with practically all Near Eastern traditions, associated the occasion for disobedience with the female. The serpent in the story was not understood as any power of evil but was simply a necessary, crafty character in the drama already found in its pre-Yahwistic form. Temptation is portrayed as an enticement to attain what has been denied blended with overstatements of the divine command. (Note that the serpent extends the prohibition to every tree; and woman, defending the command, makes it include not touching as well as not eating.) The immediate results of eating the forbidden fruit[11] were man's and woman's loss of their naïveté—they now knew they were naked and in shame sought to hide their bodies, and fear became man's uncanny companion.

After the disobedience, man and woman refused to accept the responsibility for their guilt and engaged in a primordial game of "passing the buck," arguing "If it had not been for . . ." As a result of the disobedience, Yahweh pro-

---

[11] The idea that the forbidden fruit was the apple dates from Latin Christianity and developed because of the similarity of the Latin words for "apple" (*malum*) and "evil" (*malus*).

nounces a series of curses upon the participants. The curses (Gen. 3:14–19) are highly etiological in nature, explaining why the snake is bound to the dust and universally despised, why woman experiences such pain in childbearing and is subordinate to man in society, and why man's labors are so unproductive and why his end is death and dissolution, a return to the dust whence he came. Although these etiologies may have been understood as describing the situation of humanity at large, the Yahwist clearly understood them as pertaining in a special way to the original human couple, Adam and Eve (Gen. 3:20–21). The curse, however, is not Yahweh's final act. The original threat of immediate death is not executed, although the pair are prevented from securing immortality by eating from the tree of life (Gen. 3:24). The two are not banished from the garden until Yahweh has graciously clothed them, providing some relief from their shame and preparing them for life outside paradisical conditions. In spite of man's disobedience and revolt against Yahweh, life and its orders, although somewhat askew, continue.

Cain and Abel. This episode (Gen. 4:1–16) and the following Cainite genealogy (Gen. 4:17–22) illustrate the manner in which independent narratives were incorporated into the Yahwist's traditions. The reader is left to wonder at many questions. Why are the ground and man again cursed to unproductivity (Gen. 4:11–12)? Who could be expected to take Cain's life at the first opportunity (Gen. 4:14b)? Where did Cain get his wife (G. 4:17)? Such questions only illustrate the independence of this tradition, originally perhaps unconnected with the Adam-Eve stories.

A number of interests are reflected in the Cain narratives, such as occupational conflict and cooperation (the shepherd versus the farmer), cultural and sociological conditions (such as the origin of cities and music), and the origin of the nomadic kinsmen of the Hebrews, the Kenites who were probably a tinkering and blacksmithing tribe. The Yahwist has used the story to show the development of human evil which in jealousy leads man to fratricide. As a result of having killed his brother, Cain is refused the possibility of a fruitful and settled life and is forced into a wandering existence, haunted by a tormenting fear of death. Again, Yahweh doesn't leave the victim to his fate but in a gracious act places a mark upon Cain, perhaps understood as a tribal tattoo or sign, which grants him immunity. In this section, Gen. 4:26 should be noted, since it takes the worship of Yahweh back to the immediate offspring of Adam.

The Flood. At this point in his narrative, the Yahwist incorporated the story of the great deluge. The story serves to mark a radical break in human history leading almost to a new beginning, a new creation. The account of the Flood is preceded by a fragment (Gen. 6:1–4) of what must have once been a much larger mythological work telling of the origin of a superhuman race produced through the marriage of the "sons of god" (divine beings) to the "daughters of men." The Yahwist seems to have included this enigmatic passage to emphasize the "demonic" quality of human evil plagued by even an intrusion from the divine world, a breakdown between the separate divine and human worlds. Or was he merely familiar with the story of giants in the world in bygone ages and wished to note that they lived before and not after the Flood and therefore no longer existed?

The Yahwist took this narrative as the occasion to comment on the shortening of human life as a judgment of Yahweh: man's life-span is reduced to a limit of 120 years. This number may sound extremely large but it pales in significance when one compares 120 years with the ages of the heroes in Gen., ch. 5, who lived up to 969 years. Why was such a venerable longevity assigned to these pre-Flood heroes? Even more monumental figures are found in the Sumerian king list, where some of the pre-Flood rulers reign up to thirty thousand years.[12] Apparently the ancients sought to do two things in ascribing long life to the antediluvians. In the first place, they were expressing a belief in a golden age at the beginning, with the extraordinary as the rule. Secondly, assigning long lives to these heroes was a way of expressing a belief in the antiquity of the world. Stretching the time, rather than cramming the name lists, gave expression to the sense of the world's ancient age.

The story of the Flood in Gen. 6:5 to 8:22 is a composite account of the Yahwistic version interlaced with a later-developed Israelite narrative, the so-called Priestly source. The tale of a universal flood was widespread in Near Eastern cultures from the time of the Sumerians on. Perhaps belief in such a world-wide catastrophe was the ancients' way of demarcating world ages, and a flood was one way to allow for both destruction and germinal preservation. The accompanying chart presents the various features of the Flood story in one of its non-Biblical and in both Biblical forms.

In the Biblical tradition, the Flood is understood in a monotheistic and ethical context. Only Yahweh, not a plurality of gods, is involved, and it is not the divine caprice but judgment that brings on the deluge. In the Yahwistic writer's reflections on the Flood (Gen. 6:5–8; 8:21–22) which encase the traditional story, there reappear the double motifs of punishment and providence. In spite of man's radical propensity to evil, Yahweh promises the continuation and stability of the natural orders and vows never again to execute so great a judgment.

Noah's Curse and Blessing. With this episode (Gen. 9:18–27), the Yahwist no longer focuses his attention on humanity in general but on the immediate peoples of the Palestinian scene: Shem (Israelites and their kinsmen), Canaan, and Japheth (Philistines). This material possesses its difficulties, since the common geographical and linguistic division of the world of the nations in the Bible worked with Shem, Ham, and Japheth (as in Gen., ch. 10), and understood these in broader categories than do the curse and blessings in this passage. Noah was understood as the first practitioner of viniculture and, as such, provided man with "relief from our work and from the toil of our hands" (Gen. 5:29). What is condemned in the story is not Noah nor his use of wine (see Ps. 104:14–15) but the act of Ham, and one suspects that the original version spoke of a more

---

[12] See Thorkild Jacobsen, *The Sumerian King List* (The University of Chicago Press, 1939). A translation of the Sumerian text is given in Pritchard, ed., *Ancient Near Eastern Texts*, pp. 265–266.

repulsive deed than merely seeing the nakedness of his father. When the reader moves to the curse pronounced by Noah, it is no longer Ham who figures in the picture but Canaan, which suggests that the beginning of one story has been combined with the conclusion of another. The blessing of Shem and Japheth at

Chart 4: VARIOUS ACCOUNTS OF THE FLOOD

BABYLONIAN	YAHWIST	PRIESTLY
Gods decree flood.	Yahweh decrees destruction of man for his wickedness (Gen. 6:5–7).	God decrees destruction of all flesh for its corruption (Gen. 6:11–12).
Goddess Ishtar protests. Utnapishtim, hero of Deluge.	Noah, hero of Deluge. Noah finds favor with Yahweh (6:8).	Noah, hero of Deluge. Noah the only righteous man (6:9–10). Noah warned by God (6:13).
Utnapishtim warned by Ea in dream. Ship: 120 × 120 × 120 7 stories 9 divisions		Ark: 300 x 50 x 30 3 stories (6:14–18).
	Instructions to enter the ark (7:1).	
All kinds of animals.	7 pairs of clean; 2 of unclean animals (7:2–5, 7–8). Yahweh shuts Noah in (7:16b).	2 of all animals (6:19–22; 7:9).
Flood from heavy rain and storm.	Flood from rain (7:10, 12, 17b, 22–23).	Fountains of great deep broken up, and windows of heaven opened. Exact date of beginning and end of Flood given (7:6, 11, 13–16a, 17a, 18–21).
Gods cowered like dogs in fear. Flood lasts 6 days.	Flood lasts 40 days, retires after 2 (3?) periods of 7 days (8:2b, 3a, 6).	Flood lasts 150 days, retires in 150 days (7:24; 8:1–2a, 3b).
Ship grounds on Mt. Nisir.		Ark grounds on Mt. Ararat (8:4–5, 13a, 15–19).
Utnapishtim sends out dove, swallow, and raven. Utnapishtim offers sacrifice on Mt. Nisir. Gods gather like flies to the sacrifice. Immortality and deification for Utnapishtim and his wife.	Noah sends out raven and dove (8:7–12). Noah offers sacrifices on altar (8:13b, 20). Yahweh smells the sweet savor (8:21a). Yahweh resolves not to curse the ground again for man's sake (8:21b–22).	God makes a covenant with Noah not to destroy the earth again by flood (9:1–11). God gives rainbow as a sign of covenant (9:12–17).
Ishtar's necklace of lapis lazuli given as a sign of remembrance.		

the expense of Canaan may have originated in some rallying cry during the twelfth century when the Hebrews and Philistines were taking over territory at the expense of the Canaanites.

The Tower of Babel. This episode (Gen. 11:1–9) was included in his work by the Yahwist because he could use it as the capstone of his presentation of primeval history. It does not completely fit into the context, since the Noah stories and the table of nations in Gen., ch. 10 (which in part is Yahwistic material), had already spoken of the division of mankind into groups. The original story was an etiology to explain the existence of multiple language groups with its play on the words *Babel* (Babylon) and *babal* ("confuse"). The actual model for this make-believe tower of Babel was the ancient artificial terraced mountains with temples and stairways built for communication with the deities in Mesopotamian culture and called ziggurats. The story is used by the writer to show how arrogance ("Let us make a name for ourselves") and anxiety ("lest we be scattered abroad") lead to the inability of peoples to understand one another and to act in concert.

Summary. The opening episodes in the Yahwistic work sketch the downward course of human history. In acts of ever-increasing severity and degeneration, man is shown forfeiting and jeopardizing his place in the created order and disrupting his relationship with the deity. Although the writer never speaks theologically or theoretically about "sin," one could say that he shows, through narrative presentations, the eruption and spread of sin in human life and culture. Depicting man's failures is not the only interest of these stories. They portray man's condition and status as the result of divine reaction to human action; man's life is life under the curse, life burdened by the judgment and punishment of Yahweh. Emphasis is placed, however, not only on Yahweh's punishment but also on the divine preservation of man in spite of the latter's disobedience. Human life and the created orders are allowed to continue. Yahweh's acts of preservation (the clothing of Adam and Eve, the mark on Cain, the continuation of human and animal life after the Flood) do not rescind the curses, they are not "blessings." Only the tower of Babel incident closes without reference to any special act on behalf of Yahweh to alleviate the "international disorder," but this is followed so closely by the call of Abraham that one must see the reference in Gen. 12:3b ("By you all the families of the earth shall bless themselves") as the hopeful antithesis to the general disarray of humanity at large. It is in the election promises to Abraham that the writer displays the deity once again taking the initiative and speaking for the first time of the positive promise of blessings. The preceding chapters had spoken of the curse; the election of Abraham speaks of the blessing. It is here that we see the writer's great affirmation: the hope of salvation for humanity lies in Abraham and his descendants; the hope of blessing for primeval and universal history lies in the sacred history of Abraham and his offspring.[13]

---

[13] See Hans Walter Wolff, "The Kerygma of the Yahwist," *Interpretation*, XX (1966), pp. 131–158. I am indebted to this article for some of the ideas in the following paragraphs.

FROM THE PATRIARCHS TO THE SETTLEMENT
IN THE LAND

It is impossible to discuss at length the additional material in the Yahwistic history, and to some extent it is unnecessary, since much of this has been covered in earlier chapters. In the subsequent narratives, the Yahwist primarily worked with traditional material but always with the promises to Abraham in view. The history sought to show how these promises had been jeopardized, renewed, hindered, but divinely led on toward fulfillment: Abraham's name did become great, and his offspring a great nation.

In the Yahwistic history's emphasis on Israel as the source and mediator of Yahweh's blessing to the nations (Gen. 12:3b), a new theme was introduced into the confessional traditions of Israel which had already spoken of the promise of the land and its fulfillment. Over and over again, the Yahwist took up the theme of Abraham and his descendants as a source of blessing to the nations or their failure to be this because of their lack of faith or uncooperative spirit. Abraham's deceit in passing off Sarah as his sister threatens the Egyptian pharaoh (Gen. 12:17). On the other hand, Abraham's intercession on behalf of Sodom and Gomorrah aided Lot, the father of Moab and Ammon (see Gen. 18:16–33; esp. vs. 17–19). Abraham's obedience to Yahweh ensures the promise of Yahweh to bless all nations (Gen. 22:15–18). Isaac's willingness to cooperate with the Philistines, and their recognition of him as the blessed of Yahweh, produced peaceful relations between these would-be antagonists (Gen., ch. 26). Through Jacob, Yahweh blesses Laban the Aramean (Gen. 30:27–30), and Joseph is shown as Yahweh's blessing on Egypt (Gen. 39:1–6). This reiteration of the blessing to the nations theme (see further Ex. 10:16–19; 12:31–32; Num. 24: 1–9) focuses on those nations which were the immediate concern of the Davidic state. Was the Yahwist attempting to challenge the Solomonic empire to its task of being a blessing to all mankind through these narrative examples from the past? To be a blessing through intercession with Yahweh, through peaceful agreements and community of life with other powers, and through economic assistance and material life? This emphasis of the Yahwist was certainly not alien to the Davidic-Jerusalemite cult which saw the nations of the earth as "the people of the God of Abraham" (Ps. 47:8–9) and the Davidic king as the blessed of the nations (Ps. 72:17).

9 | ISRAELITE HISTORY AND PROPHECY

Following the death of Solomon, pent-up pressures within the state and centrifugal forces within the empire exploded, rending the Israelite kingdom. Internally, the Solomonic realm separated into two small and mutually hostile states, Judah in the south and Israel in the north. Externally, much of the territory outside the Land of Canaan that David had incorporated into his holdings was lost irretrievably. Israel and Judah became two among several second-rate states in the Syria-Palestine area.

THE DIVISION OF THE KINGDOM

The Reasons for the Schism. A number of factors contributed to the division of the United Kingdom. In the first place, the Israelite monarchs had never really succeeded in welding into one union the older pre-Saul tribal groupings of Israel and Judah. Solomon had ruled over the two in the form of a dual kingdom. The original union of the two tribal leagues had been something of an artificial creation necessitated by historical circumstances (the Philistine menace) and was held together by David and Solomon, who were strong personalities but who often had to resort to the forceful suppression of divisive and popular elements. Historically and geographically, the two areas lacked many of the necessary components of unity.

Secondly, the widespread Israelite discontent with Solomon's reign, especially his labor and taxation programs which seem to have favored Judah, had brought the kingdom to the breaking point even prior to his death. In the third place, the older Israelite elements probably objected to the new theological and political trends with their emphasis on the house of David and Jerusalem and the centralization of power which was further corroding the tribal and patriarchal authority and independence. Insofar as tribal history was concerned, Jerusalem had risen to prominence late in tribal history and, at any rate, was crown property, an independent entity separate from tribal authority. Cities

---

Biblical readings: The history of the states of Israel and Judah, until the collapse of the former, is given in I Kings, chs. 12 to 16; II Kings 9:1 to 17:6. The prophetic books of Amos and Hosea are also discussed in this chapter. See map VI.

and sanctuaries such as Shechem in the north and Hebron in the south had far more authentic claims to Hebrew sanctity than had Jerusalem. The Zion and Davidic theologies no doubt sounded to many like an Israelite sellout to Canaanite and foreign thought and culture. In this regard, the jealousy and political ambitions of northern elements must also have played a significant role.

The incompetent handling of the succession situation by Solomon's son Rehoboam proved to be the immediate catalyst that precipitated the division (I Kings 12:1–20). Rehoboam, apparently the eldest of Solomon's sons, had no trouble in succeeding his father as king over the city-state of Jerusalem and the state of Judah. Assembling in Shechem, the representatives of the tribes of the people Israel met with Rehoboam to negotiate the question of rulership with a plea that the oppressive policies of Solomon be lightened. The new king's older advisers, carry-overs from the Solomonic era, counseled him to give in to the demands of the Israelites. Rehoboam, however, sought advice from a group designated "the young men who had grown up with him" (I Kings 12:10), who advocated a stricter and more tyrannical policy.[1] Among these advocates of a more repressive administration were no doubt numerous sons of Solomon, brothers of Rehoboam, who feared that a change in policy would mean a reduction in royal income and state labor and thus a reduction in their standard of living.

Rehoboam's negative reaction to the Israelite request led to the failure of the northern tribes to accept him as king. With their separation came a revival of the old rallying cry of Israel: "What portion have we in David? We have no inheritance in the son of Jesse. To your tents, O Israel" (I Kings 12:16; see II Sam. 20:1)! The king's inept handling of the situation is nowhere more evident than in his sending Adoram, the state "taskmaster over the forced labor," to negotiate with or try to force into line the dissident elements. Adoram was stoned to death, and the king forced to flee ignominiously to Jerusalem.

The Results of the Schism. Following the division of the United Kingdom, Israel possessed the larger share of territory, which included the best agricultural land, the larger population, and greater access to the major communication lines passing through Canaan. The latter offered opportunity for commerce and taxation but at the same time could turn Israel into a desirable ally or a tempting prey when more powerful nations sought control over commercial activities and military routes. Domination over the trade routes between the Euphrates and the Nile, which Solomon had enjoyed, was no longer the privilege of either Israel or Judah. Vassal states, such as Ammon and some of the Arameans, asserted their independence, and their tribute no longer flowed into Israelite coffers. Judah was left far the poorer of the two states, but the importance of the Davidic dynasty and the significance of Zion produced a stability in politics and religion that was unknown in Israel, and her isolated geographical

---

[1] See Abraham Malamat, "Kingship and Council in Israel and Sumer: A Parallel," *Journal of Near Eastern Studies,* XXII (1963), pp. 247–253; and D. G. Evans, "Rehoboam's Advisers at Shechem, and Political Institutions in Israel and Sumer," in the same journal, XXV (1966), pp. 273–279.

position allowed her to escape some of the international political entangle-
ments. The geographical concentration of Judah allowed for a more efficient
administration and tended to eliminate regional conflicts.

The northern leaders chose to continue the monarchical form of government.
Their first king was Jeroboam, a man who had served as a labor officer under
Solomon. After attempting a revolt against Solomon while still in service to
the king, Jeroboam had been a wanted man and escaped with his life only
by seeking asylum in Egypt (I Kings 11:26–40). How much of a role Jeroboam
played in Israel's secession from the kingdom is unknown. I Kings 11:29–39
contains a story about Jeroboam's designation as future king by the prophet
Ahijah from Shiloh at the time of his attempted rebellion against Solomon.
If this story has any historical value, it suggests that prophetic circles may
have been influential in the division of the state, just as they had aided earlier
in the rise of Saul and had sheltered David for a time. Thus the future king
had been first proclaimed by a prophet and then later acclaimed in the Shechem
assembly. The dynastic principle never firmly established itself in Israel as it did
in Judah, and thus the former was to be plagued constantly by political rivalry,
revolution, and competition for the throne. This type of leadership, which
certainly allowed for the political intervention of the people and prophets,
was similar to the premonarchical system of charismatic leaders.

Jeroboam acted quickly to give his new kingdom a political center and official
state cult. For his capital, he selected the ancient Israelite tribal center of
Shechem, a town laden with tradition and importance from the premonarchical
era (I Kings 12:25). Such a move was no doubt proclaimed as a return to
"the good old days." Two major state sanctuaries were established at the ancient
cultic centers of Bethel and Dan in order to prevent his subjects from going
on pilgrimages to Jerusalem. Two golden calves were made and set up in these
places of worship (I Kings 12:26–29). The existence of these calves does not
mean that Jeroboam instituted a state cult that was non-Yahwistic, although
the southern historian who edited the books of Kings seems to have wanted
to give this impression. The function of the bulls or calves was apparently
rather similar to the function of the Ark in Jerusalem: they were understood
as the pedestal or platform on which the deity stood. The association of bulls
with deities was very old and widespread in the Near East, and one should
note that a very old Biblical text makes reference to a deity called the "Bull
of Jacob" (Gen. 49:24, translated as "the Mighty One of Jacob" in RSV).
Jeroboam's reference to the exodus from Egypt implies that the state religion
harkened back to the Mosaic traditions and to the Sinai covenant. In addition,
the king set aside a special festival period in the eighth month to celebrate
the autumn harvest and to compete with the major Festival of Tabernacles
(or New Year festival) celebrated in Jerusalem in the seventh month (I Kings
12:32–33).

A state of hostility and at times open civil war between Israel and Judah
followed the separation of the Solomonic kingdom. Rehoboam sought to take
over the Israelite throne by force, but this effort was soon abandoned, due,
according to the Biblical text (I Kings 12:21–24), to the intervention of
Shemaiah, a man of God, who declared the plans contrary to the will of

The storm god riding a bull is depicted on a stela from Arslan Tash in upper Mesopotamia. The deity, known as Hadad in northern Mesopotamia and as Baal in Canaan, is clothed in a robe, wears a special headdress, and carries in each hand a double three-pronged fork, representing lightning. The golden calves set up by Jeroboam must have been understood as a pedestal for Yahweh similar to the bull in this relief.

J. B. PRITCHARD AND THE UNIVERSITY MUSEUM

Yahweh. Much of the fighting between the two states was in an effort to define a common frontier.

ISRAEL AND JUDAH: A HISTORICAL SYNOPSIS

The political fortunes of Israel and Judah following the division of the Solomonic kingdom were dependent to no small degree on the political capabilities and ambitions of other Near Eastern powers. The Israelite state survived for some two centuries after the death of Solomon, and Judah was to endure as a continuing political entity for another 135 years. In this section, we shall out-line briefly the political fortune of the two states until 750 B.C.

The Nature of the Source Material. The primary historical traditions in the Biblical text relating the history of Israel and Judah are to be found in I and II Kings, which covers the period from the death of David until the time just after the fall of Jerusalem in 586 B.C. This material was edited by an author or circle who was attempting to explain the reasons behind the fall of the two states.[2] His basic premise was the conclusion that Yahweh brings blessings and prosperity to those who obey his will and punishment to those who disobey his commands. The work is sympathetic to the interests of Judah and Jerusalem. Not a single Israelite king is praised; all are condemned for following in the footsteps of Jeroboam by supporting shrines outside Jerusalem and contributing to the infidelity of the people by causing them to worship and serve gods other than Yahweh. Only two Judean kings, besides David and Solomon, are offered outright laurels of glory.

As a rule, the historical material is edited in a rather stereotyped form that correlates the reigns of Israelite and Judean kings. The work first discusses the reign of an Israelite king, dating him by cross-references to the Judean, and then picks up a Judean king and traces his reign. This cross-referencing pro-vided a chronological tie-in between the two states and is sometimes helpful in dating, which is always rather complicated, since the ancients did not work with a calendar that had an absolute date from which reckonings could be made.[3] The following represents the general scheme used to present the his-torical material:

JUDAH	ISRAEL
1. In such and such a year of so-and-so, king of Israel, began so-and-so to reign over Judah.	1. In such and such a year of so-and-so, king of Judah, began so-and-so to reign over Israel.
2. Facts about his age, length of reign, and the queen mother.	2. Statements about the length and place of his reign.
3. Evaluation of his reign in compari-son with David.	3. Condemnation of the ruler for his doing evil and walking in the way of Jeroboam and his sin.
4. Events during his reign.	4. Events during his reign.
5. Reference to further material related to the reign in the Book of Chron-icles of the Kings of Judah.	5. Reference to further material re-lated to the reign in the Book of Chronicles of the Kings of Israel.
6. Concluding statement about his death and successor.	6. Concluding statement about his death and successor.

---

[2] A discussion of this historian is given in Chapter 13.

[3] The problems of chronology for the period of the monarchy are legion; see Edwin R. Thiele, *The Mysterious Numbers of the Hebrew Kings*, rev. ed. (Wm. B. Eerdmans Publishing Company, 1965). One absolute date in Near Eastern chronology is fixed by an Akkadian reference to a total eclipse of the sun which can be dated from astronomical computation to June 15, 763 B.C.

In places, this scheme is expanded, often with the insertion of extended material about various prophets or with narration about events of consequence to the Judean ruler and Jerusalem. References to the Book of Chronicles of the Kings of Israel and Judah point to the existence of royal annals detailing the major events in the reigns of the various kings which apparently were still available for use at the time the books of Kings were written. Unfortunately these sources have not survived. The work tends to be selective in the material it incorporated, utilizing that which supported its particular points of view. For many of the kings, especially the Israelites, who we know from archaeology or extra-Biblical texts were outstanding leaders, the text is almost silent, leaving gaping holes in the history of the times.

HISTORICAL DEVELOPMENTS

The petty border rivalry between Judah and Israel was brought to a temporary halt in the fifth year of Rehoboam's reign when Palestine was invaded by Pharaoh Shishak (I Kings 14:25–28). The renewed Egyptian intervention into Palestinian affairs had already begun during the time of Solomon when such fugitives as Jeroboam and Hadad of Edom were granted Egyptian asylum. Shishak's campaign was a major invasion of plunder and conquest.[4] The Biblical account merely emphasizes the tribute paid from the Jerusalem treasures, but the pharaoh's inscription shows that he devastated much of Israel's territory, even in Transjordan, and regained control over the Arabian trade routes passing to the south of the Negeb.

Hostilities between Israel and Judah resumed upon the withdrawal of Egyptian forces and continued intermittently for several decades. Egypt did not meddle significantly in Palestinian affairs again for about three centuries. The nations' major enemies were to come from the north rather than the south. The Aramean (Syrian) state, with its capital at Damascus, in alliance with other Aramean states in the area proved to be the major rival to Israel for control of Transjordan and the northernmost areas of the Holy Land.[5] Damascus first intervened in Israelite affairs when it was paid by Asa, a Judean king, to invade Israel and force the Israelites to withdraw troops from their southern border (I Kings 15:16–24). This invasion was a herald of troubles to come because, for almost three fourths of a century, Israel and Damascus were to be the bitterest of enemies.

The economic and political fortunes of Israel took a drastic turn for the better after an Israelite military commander named Omri was raised to power during a period characterized by a coup, countercoup, assassinations, political suicide, and open civil war. His family was to bring stability to Israel for over three decades. The accomplishments of Omri were numerous. He negotiated a treaty with the Phoenicians of Tyre, ended the state of hostility with Judah, which recognized Israel as the dominant power in Palestine, and brought much

---

[4] See Aharoni, The Land of the Bible, pp. 283–290.

[5] See Benjamin Mazar, "The Aramean Empire and Its Relations with Israel," The Biblical Archaeologist, XXV (1962), pp. 97–120, reprinted in The Biblical Archaeologist Reader, Vol. II, pp. 127–151.

of Transjordan back under Israelite control. The reconquest of Transjordan and the alliance with Phoenicia, the dominant Mediterranean sea power, allowed Israel to share significantly again in Near Eastern trade.

The relations with Tyre and Judah were sealed through the marriage of Omri's son Ahab to the Phoenician Jezebel and Omri's granddaughter Athaliah to Jehoram of Judah—marriages fraught with dire consequences for both states. Utilizing a strategic location, Omri built a totally new capital at Samaria, turning it into the most powerful and prominent Israelite town.[6]

CHART 5: FROM THE DEATH OF SOLOMON TO THE FALL OF ISRAEL (922–722 B.C.)

B.C.	PALESTINE		SYRIA-MESOPOTAMIA
	JUDAH	ISRAEL	
922	Rehoboam (922–915)	Jeroboam I (922–901)	Recovery of Assyrian
	War between the states		power
	Invasion of Shishak		Aramean states strong
900			
	Jehoshaphat (873–849)	Omri (876–869)	Assyrian expansion
		Samaria built	
	Peaceful relations		
		Ahab (869–850)	Battle of Qarqar (853)
	Jehoram (849–842)	Elijah the prophet	
		Elisha the prophet	
	General coup		
	Queen Athaliah (842–837)	Jehu (842–815)	Tribute to Assyria paid by Jehu (842)
	Joash (837–800)		
		Jehoahaz (815–801)	Aramean power broken by Assyrians
800			
	Uzziah (783–742)	Jeroboam II (786–746)	Assyrian weakness
	General prosperity		
		Amos	
		Hosea	
		Zechariah (746–745)	Tiglath-pileser III (745–727)
	Isaiah begins career	Shallum (one month)	
	Jotham (742–735)	Menahem (745–736)	Tribute to Assyria by Menahem
		Pekahiah (736–735)	
	Ahaz (735–715)	Pekah (735–732)	
	Aramean Israelite coalition against Assyria		Fall of Damascus (732)
	Appeal to Assyria	Israel defeated	
		Hoshea (732–724)	Shalmaneser V king of Assyria (727–722)
		Fall of Samaria (722)	Sargon II (722–705)

---

[6] See Peter R. Ackroyd, "Samaria," in Thomas, ed., *Archaeology and Old Testament Study,* pp. 343–354.

The policies of Omri were continued by his son Ahab with apparent economic and military success. The Bible speaks of the "ivory house" and the cities that he built, and this is substantiated by archaeological excavations at Megiddo, Samaria, and Hazor. The Biblical traditions refer to several military encounters

The excavations at Hazor have revealed impressive ruins from the time of King Ahab. The remains of a large colonnaded hall and public building complex dated to his reign can be seen in the upper portion of the photograph. The four-entryway gate and casemate wall in the immediate foreground are from the Solomonic city.

YIGAEL YADIN, THE HAZOR EXPEDITION, HEBREW UNIVERSITY

between Israel and Aram which cost Israel greatly and weakened her control over Transjordan. This interregional warfare was temporarily halted with the appearance of the Assyrian war machine rolling westward. A coalition of twelve kings, including Hadadezer of Damascus and Ahab of Israel, met the Assyrian king Shalmaneser III in battle at Qarqar (853 B.C.). This battle goes unmentioned in the Biblical text, but it was noted by the Assyrian king, who made dubious claims about an outright victory.[7] Israel contributed the largest contingent of chariots to the league, and the large number (2,000) illustrates the basic strength of Ahab's military force. The Assyrian threat to the west was halted temporarily, and with its partial demise the old animosities among several members of the league revived.

[7] A translation of Akkadian texts discussing this battle is given in Pritchard, ed., *Ancient Near Eastern Texts*, pp. 276–281.

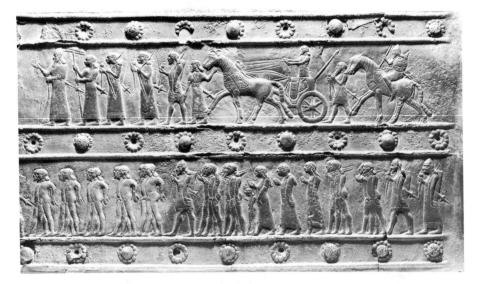

Shalmaneser III is shown in this bronze Assyrian gate relief being followed by his attendants and chariot. The lower register depicts bound prisoners being led away from the captured city of Hazazu. Ahab and a coalition of Syro-Palestinian rulers fought Shalmaneser at the battle of Qarqar in 853 B.C.

THE BRITISH MUSEUM

Although economic and military matters under Omri and Ahab were far more stable than they had been since the disruption of the Solomonic state, religious conflict tore at the fabric of the state. This was primarily due, according to the Biblical text, to the Baalistic crusading carried on by Jezebel, who obviously was an overpowering person and did not hesitate to offer her advice on how to "govern Israel" (I Kings 21:7). Jezebel brought with her the worship of the Tyrian god Baal-Melkart, for whom there was a temple constructed in Samaria with an altar and a statue of Asherah, the goddess (I Kings 16:31–33). With an evangelistic zeal, Jezebel propagated her faith and worship, imported Baalistic prophets, persecuted the Israelite prophetic groups, and forced Yahwistic loyalists underground (I Kings 18:3–4).[8]

The Omrid family was toppled from leadership by a revolutionary and bloody purge. The support for the coup came from the military and from conservative Yahwistic groups, especially the prophetic circles. The revolt was sparked by the prophet Elisha, who sent one of his subordinates to the battlefield to anoint Jehu, one of the Israelite commanders, as king (II Kings 9:1–13). The failure of

[8] The open and hostile contest between Baalism and Yahwism in Israel first developed during the Omrid period and not, as some of the Biblical traditions suggest, in the period immediately following the settlement. See F. E. Eakin, Jr., "Yahwism and Baalism Before the Exile," *Journal of Biblical Literature*, LXXXIV (1965), pp. 407–414.

the northern state to develop a dynastic ideology of kingship and the tenacity of the older, more democratic charismatic ideal provided the opportunity for prophetic interventions into state politics, especially after a time when the freedom of the prophetic circles had been severely curtailed. Another strong supporter of Jehu's take-over was Jehonadab, the head of a Yahwistic sectarian group that opposed a settled agricultural culture, idealizing a pastoral existence and passionate devotion to Yahweh, and that refused to live in houses, till the soil, or drink wine (II Kings 10:15–17; see Jer., ch. 35). The existence of such groups shows the variety of ways in which Yahwism was understood and practiced.

Jehu's slaughter of the Omrid family was as merciless as it was complete. The reigning king was killed at Jezreel, where he was recovering from wounds received in battle (II Kings 9:14–28). Jezebel was thrown from an upper window and died in the fall (II Kings 9:30–37). The Judean king and members of his family, visiting their sick relative, were likewise annihilated (II Kings 10:12–14). In the meanwhile Athaliah, the Omrid queen in Jerusalem, usurped the throne and liquidated all the remaining male members of the Davidic house, with one exception (II Kings 11:1–3). For seven years, the Davidic rule was interrupted and a queen sat upon Solomon's throne in Jerusalem. Jehu's gory rampage culminated in the decapitation of seventy male members of the Omrid house, which eliminated all claimants to the throne (II Kings 10:1–11), and in the slaughter of the Baal worshipers in Samaria, who had been craftily assembled under the pretense of having a "sacrifice" to Baal (II Kings 10:18–27).

Jehu's revolt and reign proved to be a temporary political disaster for Israel that thwarted the Yahwistic reforms. The killing of Jezebel and the Omrids ended the treaty and trade alliance with Phoenicia. During Queen Athaliah's seven-year reign in Judah, friendly relations between these two states ended. To compound his problems, Jehu was immediately faced by the marauding Assyrian army which forced him to capitulate. This humiliation of Jehu and his payment of tribute were recorded on the Black Obelisk inscription of Shalmaneser III but were not mentioned in the Biblical text.[9] The Assyrian pressure on Israel was temporary, for shortly this distant enemy was entangled in struggles far from Palestine. Near the end of Jehu's reign and during the ensuing years, the Arameans of Damascus reduced Israel to a vassal state, took over much of her territory, and eventually even forced Judah to pay a heavy tribute (II Kings 10:32–33; 12:17–18).

The family of Jehu, which ruled over Israel for more than a century, was to see far better days in the first half of the eighth century than it had experienced in the latter half of the ninth. The circumstances that produced this radical change in fortune were described by the Biblical writer as due to the fact that "Yahweh gave Israel a savior" (II Kings 13:5). This savior was none other than the Assyrian monarch. Near the end of the ninth century, the Assyrians renewed their westward movement and brought the Aramean state to its knees from which it never fully recovered, and thus was broken the Aramean yoke on Israel's neck. Shortly thereafter, because of wars with powers to their north the

---

[9] For a translation of this text, see Pritchard, ed., *Ancient Near Eastern Texts*, p. 281.

Jehu offering tribute to the Assyrian ruler is depicted in one of the panels of the Black Obelisk of Shalmaneser III. Jehu is shown bowing in submission at the feet of the Assyrian monarch. Attendants of the Israelite king carry part of the tribute gifts.

Assyrians were forced to surrender their hold on Syria-Palestine and for over half a century did not march their armies westward.

Israel and Judah enjoyed economic prosperity, military prowess, and political conquest during the first half of the eighth century such as they had not had since the days of Solomon. The states reached their peak during the reigns of Uzziah of Judah and Jeroboam II in Israel, both of whom were competent leaders greatly aided by the weakness of the Assyrian and Aramean states. The borders of the states were extended almost to the old limits of the Davidic empire at its height of power (II Kings 14:28). Once again, the international trade routes in the area were ruled over by Israel and Judah. It was during this zenith of political power and economic well-being that the prophets Amos and Hosea put in their appearance in Israel.

THE BACKGROUND TO CLASSICAL PROPHECY

The Development of Israelite Prophecy. The age of classical prophecy in ancient Israel began about the middle of the eighth century (750 B.C.). The earliest of the so-called writing prophets, that is, prophets whose preaching has been preserved in book form, dates from this time.

When modern man hears the word "prophet" or "prophecy," he is apt to think immediately and almost solely in terms of soothsayers and prognostications about the future. Such a definition is far too narrow to encompass the

The Moabite Stone, a black basalt stela measuring three feet ten inches high, two feet wide, and fourteen inches thick, contains an inscription of the Moabite king Mesha. This ruler, who reigned about the middle of the ninth century B.C., successfully rebelled against Israelite authority in Transjordan. The thirty-four lines of the inscription written in Moabite, a dialect closely resembling Hebrew, narrate his exploits.

ISRAEL DEPARTMENT OF ANTIQUITIES AND
MUSEUMS

phenomenon of Israelite prophecy. The prophets were certainly concerned about the future—especially the immediate future—but they were also concerned with the whole fabric of their contemporary culture. They were more than predictors; they were preachers and spokesmen who addressed their contemporaries with their understanding of Yahweh's will and word. The Hebrew word for prophet, navi, comes from a term meaning "to call," so one could say that the prophet was "one who is called" or "the one who calls."

Prophecy was not a late innovation in Israelite society, nor was it a homogeneous phenomenon. Older forms of prophecy had existed from premonarchical times, and certain types of prophets were not uncommon in non-Israelite cultures being found at ancient Mari (c. 1800 B.C.), among the Hittites in Asia Minor (fourteenth century B.C.), and among the Arameans and the Canaanites. These early prophetical types, sometimes called "seers" (see I Sam. 9:9), were a means of receiving revelation from the deity in addition to dreams, omens, and decisions from the sacred lots. They functioned in a number of contexts and quite frequently employed music and dance to induce possession by the "spirit of Yahweh" and the prophetic mood (sometimes suggesting a trance).[10]

Some early prophets were closely associated with the cult, perhaps being present on special days for consultation (II Kings 4:18–25) or to preside at religious functions.[11] Samuel was pictured as a seer presiding over sacrificial meals (I Sam. 9:11–14), and I Sam. 10:5–8 mentions prophets coming from a "high place with harp, tambourine, flute, and lyre before them, prophesying." In the sanctuary, they perhaps acted as intercessors between Yahweh and the people and on festival occasions may have preached Yahweh's word and law to the pilgrims.

Court prophets were common in the Near East and in Israel where they functioned as court advisers, assisted in determining the will of the deity, and gave divine sanction to the policies of state. The most famous Israelite court prophet was Nathan, whose oracle from Yahweh sanctioned the rule of the Davidic dynasty but who was also capable of censuring the king, as he did in the Bathsheba affair. In the days of Ahab, there were said to be four hundred prophets at the Israelite court (I Kings 22:5–6).

Some prophets served as functionaries in warfare, rallying the troops to battle (Judg. 4:4–9), assuring the participants of victory, planning strategy (I Kings 20:13–15), symbolically or orally announcing the defeat of the enemy (I Kings 22:10–12), and pronouncing curses and judgment upon the opponents (I Kings 20:28).

These early prophets often operated in bands or groups (I Sam. 10:5–8), which were frequently referred to as the "sons of the prophets." The famous prophets, Elijah and Elisha, are shown as leaders ("fathers") of such prophetic guilds (II Kings 2:3; 4:38; 6:1–2).[12] Such groups tended to live a communal existence, at least part of the time, on the outskirts of society. Special marks or clothing may have been used to designate membership in such a company (I Kings 20:35–43; the bandage in the story seems to have covered some tattoo or mark worn on the forehead). These circles were strongly pro-Yahwistic, often exerting powerful political strength capable of precipitating revolution in Israel's more charismatic form of monarchy (I Kings 11:29–33; II Kings 9:1–10).

During the ninth and eighth centuries, several prophets appeared in Israelite society, pronouncing judgment upon practically every facet of Israel's public life and worship and claiming a divine authority for their proclamations, an authority exceeding that of the established religious orders. Among such prophets were Elijah and Elisha in the ninth century and Amos and Hosea in the eighth. A number of factors contributed to the rise of these radical prophets. In the first

---

[10] For the early history of Israelite prophecy, see Johannes Lindblom, *Prophecy in Ancient Israel* (Fortress Press, 1963), pp. 47–104. The closest Near Eastern parallel to Israelite prophecy is found in the documents from ancient Mari; see H. B. Huffmon, "Prophecy in the Mari Letters," *The Biblical Archaeologist*, XXXI (1968), pp. 101–124.

[11] On the possible relationship between the prophet and the cult, see Aubrey R. Johnson, *The Cultic Prophet in Ancient Israel*, 2d ed. (Cardiff: University of Wales Press, 1962); and H. H. Rowley, "Ritual and the Hebrew Prophets," in his *From Moses to Qumran* (London: Lutterworth Press, 1963), pp. 111–138.

[12] See Anthony Phillips, "The Ecstatics' Father," in Peter R. Ackroyd and Barnabas Lindars, eds., *Words and Meaning* (Cambridge: Cambridge University Press, 1968), pp. 183–194.

place, the religious threats to Yahwism had become acute during the ninth-century reign of Ahab and Jezebel. To a large extent, the Baalistic worship prior to this period had been amalgamated into Yahwism or practiced alongside Yahwism, but Jezebel sought to suppress Yahwistic worship, going so far as to exterminate Yahwistic elements (I Kings 18:4) in her advocacy of the Tyrian god, Baal-Melkart. The royal capital at Samaria possessed a temple dedicated to Baal, but there is never any reference to a Yahweh sanctuary in the city. This emphasis on Baalism and the suppression of Yahwism produced a militant Yahwistic reaction among the prophetic circles and triggered the rise of some outstanding individual prophets.

A further cause for the development of this radical prophetism is to be found in economic and social developments. From the time of the development of the monarchical state, the dominant economic power was in the hands of the patricians of the towns, that is, the merchants, officials of state, military leaders, and persons with feudal grants from the royalty. The taxation and exploitation of the peasants and wage earners by the state and the wealthy produced an oppressed lower-class population who struggled to exist as free men under the burden of numerous social grievances. As a rule, the prophets sided with the oppressed of Israelite society and attacked, in the name and word of Yahweh, the social structures that produced such social and economic inequities.

A third influential factor in the rise of classical prophetism was the major shift of power in international affairs represented by the resurgence of Assyria. This rise and imperial expansion of a militaristic power threw the small nations of the Near East into a state of anxious and uncertain existence and posed questions concerning the future of the states of Israel and Judah. Simultaneously, it raised the problem of interpreting and integrating the existence of a powerful foreign aggressor and the possible extinction of the Israelite state into an understanding of history based on Yahwism. The prophets spoke out on the political and religious circumstances with analysis, evaluation, and recommendations.

Prophetical Traditions and the Prophetical Books. Amos and Hosea are the earliest prophets for whom there are books named in the Hebrew Scriptures. Before discussing these prophets, we need to say a word about the origin and the nature of the prophetical books. Most of the books of prophecy contain three types of material—namely, biographical material about the prophet, written in the third person; autobiographical, or first-person, material; and finally, sermonic or oracular material, generally in poetic form given as the spoken words of the prophet. This diversity of material reflects that the material in the prophetical books came from various sources and that the final product was an edited work. One should not think of the prophets as sitting down and writing out their books in the forms that we now possess. The autobiographical and sermonic portions may have derived from the prophet, whereas the biographical material reflects stories and sayings told about the prophet.[13]

Jeremiah, ch. 36, serves as a good example to illustrate how on occasion the

---

[13] See Lindblom, *Prophecy in Ancient Israel*, pp. 220–291, which provides a discussion of the formation of the various prophetic books.

prophets aided in the process of transcribing oral preaching into written form. Jeremiah, under house arrest, could not at the time deliver his sermons orally. In order to provide for the circulation of his words, the prophet dictated his earlier preaching to his scribe, who wrote the material on a scroll which eventually was read to the king. The king subsequently burned it because of his displeasure with Jeremiah's preaching. The prophet proceeded then to redictate the sermons, which the scribe wrote on a second scroll. This particular scroll cannot be identified with any certainty within the present book of Jeremiah. Without doubt, many of the oracles contained in that scroll have been edited into the Biblical traditions associated with Jeremiah. This episode shows that the prophets could assist in the collection of their words, that followers and friends of the prophet shared in the transmission of the material, that prophetical books could go through several "editions," and that the biographical material probably originated among the prophet's followers.

The collecting and editing of the prophetical traditions was often a long process. Collections and oral traditions were often supplemented over the years by the prophet's disciples and sympathizers in order to make the words applicable to a new situation or to make them reflect a different emphasis. Since the prophetical books did not require an authoritative status until quite late in Jewish history, this supplementation continued in some cases for many years. Because the books were edited in the southern religious community, practically all of them have a Judean emphasis.

The prophetical traditions weren't always collected and edited according to either a chronological or a topical arrangement, which often makes their content appear very disorganized and difficult to grasp and understand. Most of the books were edited so as to end on a note of hope which was preceded by oracles of doom on both Israel and the nations of the world. Several of the prophetical books are actually compilations of numerous smaller collections of traditions.

AMOS [14]

The prophet Amos was a southerner from the Judean town of Tekoa, about a two hours' walk south of Bethlehem. One should not suppose, however, that Tekoa was a remote, isolated village nestled in the Judean mountains. From the time of Rehoboam it had been a garrisoned military fortress (II Chron. 11:6), and when Joab sought a woman of wisdom to influence a decision of King David, he turned to Tekoa (II Sam. 14:1–2), which must have had a reputation for its wisdom circles.

Amos was not a professional prophet. He disclaimed any connection with the prophetic circles, basing his authority instead on an immediate commissioning by Yahweh.

---

[14] See James L. Mays, *Amos, A Commentary* (The Westminster Press, 1969); Arvid S. Kapelrud, *Central Ideas in Amos* (Oslo: Oslo University Press, 1961); and James M. Ward, *Amos and Isaiah* (Abingdon Press, 1969), pp. 17–140.

I am [or was] no prophet,[15] nor one of the sons of the prophets; but . . .
Yahweh said to me, "Go, prophesy to my people Israel." (Amos 7:14–15.)

Amos must not be understood as if he were merely an uncultured and poor
shepherd who vented his social frustrations in a tirade against the upper classes
of Israelite society. He is described as being from "among the shepherds (noqe-
dim) of Tekoa" (Amos 1:1) and as "a herdsman [or cattleman] and a dresser
of sycamore trees" (Amos 7:14). The only other person described as a noqed
in the Bible was King Mesha of Moab, who was said to pay to Israel an annual
tribute of "a hundred thousand lambs and the wool of a hundred thousand
rams" (II Kings 3:4); this clearly suggests that a noqed was a sheep breeder
rather than a shepherd. Since neither cattle nor sycamore trees were native to
Tekoa, Amos may have been involved in economic pursuits outside his home
area. The prophet is better understood as a man of means and reputation than
as an itinerant laborer or a wage-earning shepherd.

Amos carried out his ministry in the northern state of Israel, shattering the
calm of the royal sanctuary of Bethel. The question of why he should have left
his native Judah and have ventured into the north can be answered only by
pointing to the prophet's belief that Yahweh had sent him. In all probability,
Amos' prophetical career was short-lived. The introduction to the book dates
his ministry to a period "two years before the earthquake" (Amos 1:1). His
one encounter with the priest Amaziah (Amos 7:10–15), who scolded and
charged him with subversive activity, also suggests that he may have preached
only one extended sermon, perhaps intruding into the celebration rituals of the
New Year festival.[16]

Visions of the Coming Judgment. The final three chapters of The Book of
Amos contain, along with other material, the accounts of five visions experienced
by the prophet. These were used as a part of his preaching in order to illustrate
the certainty of judgment that Yahweh had revealed to him. The experience
of these must have taken place over a period of time prior to his appearance at
Bethel and perhaps may have been a major contributing factor to his becoming
a prophet. The visions weren't included in the book to provide autobiographical
material but rather to proclaim the inevitability of judgment. In the first two
visions (Amos 7:1–6), the prophet sees the land being consumed by locusts
and fire, and his plea on behalf of Israel intercedes to avert Yahweh's intent.
The prophet could certainly claim that he had sought not the destruction but
the preservation of Israel. In the final three visions, Amos no longer intervenes;
the decision of judgment is given as irretrievable. Israel has been measured with
a plumb line and does not measure up (Amos 7:7–9); she is like a basket of
summer fruit (qayits) whose end (qets) has come (Amos 8:1–3). In the last
vision, Amos sees Yahweh standing upon the altar decimating the land, in terms

---

[15] The difficulty in translating this verse is due to the fact that the Hebrew has no verb here
but merely reads, "No prophet I no son of a prophet I."

[16] For this idea and a study of Amos' one sermon, see Julian Morgenstern, "Amos Studies:
Part Four," *Hebrew Union College Annual,* XXXII (1961), pp. 295–350.

of an earthquake, allowing no one to escape the calamity (Amos 9:1–4; see also ch. 3:13–15). The imagery of the prophet moves from the fields and locusts and summer fruit to the city and the altar at the heart of the sanctuary.

Yahweh: Guardian of International Relations. Amos' sermon opens with denunciations of several international powers for atrocities committed against one another (Amos 1:3 to 2:3): Damascus, Edom, and Ammon are condemned for brutality in warfare; Gaza and Tyre, for participation in the slave trade; and Moab, for the desecration of a royal tomb. The arrangement of these nations in the sermon moves from the northeast to the southwest to the northwest to the southeast—thus touching on the four geographical points of the compass in order to emphasize universality (on this phenomenon in the royal ritual, see pp. 128–129). The prophet thus presupposes the existence of an international code of conduct, perhaps developed over the years in treaty agreements. He envisions Yahweh as the protector of these laws of international relations and the one who punishes the culprits when the laws are broken. Yahweh watches over not only Israel's doings but those of other nations as well.

Social Injustice and Luxurious Living. Amos' meteoric ministry fell sometime near the end of the prosperous and peaceful reign of Jeroboam II when Israel was enjoying one of her finest hours of economic glory. But Israel's society was cleft in two. On the one hand there was an extravagant luxury and on the other hand an oppressed poor, the pawns of the wealthy deprived of their rights. Amos lashed out at the self-indulgent lovers of luxury:

> Woe to those who lie upon beds of ivory,
>   and stretch themselves upon their couches,
> and eat lambs from the flock,
>   and calves from the midst of the stall;
> who sing idle songs to the sound of the harp,
>   and like David invent for themselves instruments of music;
> who drink wine in bowls,
>   and anoint themselves with the finest oils,
>   but are not grieved over the ruin of Joseph!
>
> (Amos 6:4–6.)

He condemned the wives of Israel's wealthy, whom he compared to the fat cows of Bashan (Amos 4:1), and those who felt secure in their ease (Amos 6:1–3). Amos' denunciations fell heavily upon the wealthy because they misused the poor (Amos 4:1), perverted the justice of the courts (Amos 5:10–13), and dealt dishonestly in commerce:

> Hear this, you who trample upon the needy,
>   and bring the poor of the land to an end,
> saying, "When will the new moon be over,
>   that we may sell grain?
> And the sabbath,
>   that we may offer wheat for sale,

that we may make the ephah small and the shekel great,
>   and deal deceitfully with false balances,
that we may buy the poor for silver
>   and the needy for a pair of sandals,
>   and sell the refuse of the wheat?"

(Amos 8:4–6.)

Over against the greed, bribery, and intemperance of the times, Amos declared the demands of Yahweh:

>   Seek good, and not evil,
>   that you may live; . . .
>   Hate evil, and love good,
>   and establish justice in the gate.
>   (Amos 5:14–15.)

Amos seems to have completely turned the tables on Israelite ethical theory. For him, the righteous were the poor, the oppressed.[17] For Israelite society, righteousness and a man's fortune supposedly went hand in hand. The righteous were the prosperous, the leaders, those whom Yahweh presumably had exalted. Amos' challenge to this perspective was a radical challenge to the ethical beliefs of the upper class (see Amos 2:6; 5:7, 12).

Cultic Zeal and Religious Optimism. Amos did not preach to an irreligious audience, nor did he encourage the people to a greater piety and a fuller participation in the cult. Instead, the prophet spoke to a people who were, according to Amos' description, almost fanatical about religion. They went on pilgrimages to numerous shrines (Amos 4:4; 5:4–5) and offered sacrifices to the deity far beyond the ordinary requirements (Amos 4:4–5). The prophet has Yahweh express his disgust at the offering of sacrifices and the attendance at noisy festivals:

>   I hate, I despise your feasts,
>   and I take no delight in your solemn assemblies.
>   Even though you offer me your burnt offerings and cereal offerings,
>   I will not accept them,
>   and the peace offerings of your fatted beasts
>   I will not look upon.
>   Take away from me the noise of your songs;
>   to the melody of your harps I will not listen.
>   But let justice roll down like waters,
>   and righteousness like an ever-flowing stream.

(Amos 5:21–24.)

Along with this frenzied cultic activity there was a pervasive optimism current in Israelite culture. Integral to this confidence was the concept of the "day of

---

[17] See Arvid S. Kapelrud, "New Ideas in Amos," in *Volume du Congrès: Supplements to Vetus Testamentum*, XV (Leiden: E. J. Brill, 1966), pp. 193–206.

Yahweh." The exact origin of the idea of the day of Yahweh is not known.[18] It may have originated as a term to describe the times of military victory when the Israelite army secured victory over its enemies. Or it may have been a term used in the celebration of the New Year festival; the day of Yahweh was the time when the destiny of the coming year was decreed. The idea of a fate-determining day when the immediate future is decreed was widespread in the Near East and exists even today in our culture: resolutions are made for the coming year and certain foods are eaten to ensure a prosperous year. At any rate, the Israelites looked forward to the day of Yahweh with expectations and hope. The prophet completely reversed the concept of the day and declared it a time of Yahweh's judgment rather than a time of joy and light.

> Woe to you who desire the day of Yahweh!
>> Why would you have the day of Yahweh?
> It is darkness, and not light;
>> as if a man fled from a lion,
>> and a bear met him;
> or went into the house and leaned with his hand against the wall,
>> and a serpent bit him.
> Is not the day of Yahweh darkness, and not light,
>> and gloom with no brightness in it?
>
> (Amos 5:18–20.)

That Amos attacked and denied the value of the entire Israelite cultic ritual cannot be denied. Whether he would have been opposed to the ritual if it had been accompanied by social justice and fidelity is a matter for discussion but is ultimately unanswerable. The prophet doesn't condemn his audience for hypocrisy in cultic matters, that is, going through the ritual acts but not believing in their significance; he appears to have assumed that the people were serious in their worship. Amos seems to have opposed the sacrificial cult in principle (Amos 5:25).[19] With his special emphasis on the social nature of religion, one can easily see why he would oppose the cultic ritual if it were understood as the sole expression of obedience to Yahweh. This represented far too narrow an understanding of religion, far too limited an interpretation of obedience to Yahweh.

The Desacralization of Israel. Amos was quite familiar with the Israelite belief that Yahweh had chosen Israel as his unique possession and had guided the people's destiny in the sacred history of the past (Amos 2:9–11). Transposing this thought into a new key, Amos declared that Israel's special treatment as Yahweh's people was now the basis for Yahweh's special judgment (Amos 3:2). Israel was no longer to be coddled; she was no longer a sacral people; Israel had become like the nations and would be dealt with in like manner. The behavior

---

[18] See Gerhard von Rad, "The Origin of the Day of Yahweh," *Journal of Semitic Studies*, IV (1959), pp. 97–108; and M. Weiss, "The Origin of the 'Day of the Lord' Reconsidered," *Hebrew Union College Annual*, XXXVII (1966), pp. 29–60.

[19] See J. Philip Hyatt, *The Prophetic Criticism of Israelite Worship* (The Hebrew Union College Press, 1963), reprinted in Orlinsky, ed., *Interpreting the Prophetic Tradition.*

of the Israelite population had brought to an end the nation's sacral status, her elect position.

This desacralization of Israel finds expression in the fact that Amos can place Israel within the context of speeches on other nations in Amos, chs. 1 and 2. The clearest statement on this point is the following:

> "Are you not like the Ethiopians to me,
>> O people of Israel?" says Yahweh.
> "Did I not bring up Israel from the land of Egypt,
>> and the Philistines from Caphtor and the Syrians from Kir?
> Behold, the eyes of the Lord Yahweh are upon the sinful kingdom,
>> and I will destroy it from the surface of the ground."
>>> (Amos 9:7–8.)

This passage has often been understood as Amos' declaration of Yahweh's universal dominion. What the passage emphasizes is not Yahweh's universal nature, which is assumed, but rather Israel's desacralization. For Yahweh, Israel has now become like the Ethiopians, the Philistines, and the Syrians; just one more of the nations of the world. The curtain was closing on the sacred relation and the sacred history between Yahweh and his people.

Doom for the State. The prophet pronounced doom upon the nation as if its death penalty had already been decreed. In a profusion of images, he expounds on the judgment-laden events of the nation's immediate future in which Israel must prepare to meet her God (Amos 4:12), a God who had declared that "the end has come upon my people Israel" (Amos 8:2). In the wailing rhythm of a dirge, Amos sang Israel's funeral lament: "Fallen, no more to rise, is the virgin Israel" (Amos 5:2). The prophet saw the future of the state as a time of general destruction that would bring to an end the luxurious status of the wealthy and the service at the altar (Amos 3:13–15) producing widespread weeping and wailing in the streets and fields (Amos 5:16–17). How the prophet envisioned the occurrence of this destruction is in places expressed in terms of an earthquake (Amos 9:1) or in terms of a cosmic calamity (Amos 8:9–10). Most frequently, the imagery is in terms of a foreign aggressor who would devastate the land and carry the citizens into exile (Amos 3:9–11; 4:2–3; 5:27; 6:11–14). Although there is no clear statement of the fact, Amos must have seen in the slumbering Assyrian state the instrument of Yahweh's judgment, an instrument that was shortly to rise and engulf, like a tidal wave, one state after another.

The severity of Amos' denunciations and proclamations of judgment left little room for hope.[20] What, he said, would be left of Samaria would be only enough scraps to show the manner of her demise, just enough to affirm the death certificate (Amos 3:12; the passage should be compared with Ex. 22:10–13 which required a shepherd to show the scraps collected after an animal was killed to prove its actual death). Yahweh had repeatedly sought to bring Israel to repentance, but always unsuccessfully (Amos 4:6–11). All the prophet could

---

[20] The hopeful prophecies, with their Judean interests, in Amos 9:11–15 are apparently later additions.

hold out in hope was a whispered "perhaps," an "it may be" based on the condition of a wholesale change of goals and practices (Amos 5:14–15; see ch. 5:3).

HOSEA [21]

The prophetical career of Hosea spanned the most turbulent quarter century in the history of Israel, the last days of her existence as a nation. Unlike Amos, who may have spoken only on one occasion, Hosea's oracles belong to a lengthy period, perhaps from about 750 to 725 B.C.

The preaching of the prophet revolved around two central concerns. One was the Baalistic nature religion with its fertility rituals and sacred prostitution which had been such a major threat to Yahwism since the time of the Omrid rule. The second concern was the politics of the time: internal anarchy within Israel and power struggles within the international sphere. The total message of the prophet can be better understood by seeing it within the political context, since the prophets addressed themselves and were influenced by very specific situations.

The Political Turbulence. The second half of the eighth century saw the Assyrians rise to almost complete mastery over the Near East.[22] The architect of this imperial enterprise was the Assyrian ruler Tiglath-pileser III (745–727 B.C.), who is referred to in the Biblical text as Pul, a throne name he assumed when he became king of the city of Babylon. This ruler developed the practice of transplanting subjected populations, and this mixing of peoples from various territories suppressed local nationalism and taught the Israelites the horror and sadness of the word "exile." In addition, conquered territory was annexed to the Assyrian provincial system and governed by an Assyrian official. These factors, in association with Assyrian military might which was capable of ruthless suppression of revolts, made the Assyrians one of the most hated of Near Eastern powers.

Israelite political conditions became desperate after the death of Jeroboam II (ca. 746 B.C.). His son, Zechariah, succeeded him but ruled for only six months before being assassinated (II Kings 15:8–12). His assassin lasted for only one month before being killed by Menahem, who gained control of the state following a short-lived civil war (II Kings 15:13–16). He retained power by paying tribute to Tiglath-pileser (II Kings 15:17–22), which he exacted from the Israelite citizenry. Menahem ruled for about ten years and was succeeded by his son, who was slain after a two-year rule (II Kings 15:23–26). His assassin, Pekah, joined with the Arameans in a revolt against Assyria, which resulted in

---

[21] See James M. Ward, *Hosea* (Harper & Row, Publishers, Inc., 1966); and M. J. Buss, *The Prophetic Word of Hosea* (Berlin: Alfred Töpelmann, 1969).

[22] See W. W. Hallo, "From Qarqar to Carchemish: Assyria and Israel in the Light of New Discoveries," *The Biblical Archaeologist*, XXIII (1960), pp. 33–61, reprinted in *The Biblical Archaeologist Reader*, II, pp. 152–188.

Tiglath-pileser III is shown in this Assyrian relief from Nineveh. The king, accompanied by a driver and attendant, gestures from his chariot. This monarch, referred to in the Bible as Pul, was both competent and aggressive and his rule was marked by a rapid expansion of the Assyrian empire.

THE BRITISH MUSEUM

the loss of most of the Israelite territory, leaving Samaria as the capital of a truncated state composed of only the hill country of Ephraim (II Kings 15:27–29). Following this political fiasco, Pekah was killed and replaced by Hoshea (II Kings 15:30), Israel's last king, who held the remnant state together for a time and purchased his right to rule by paying tribute to the Assyrians. Eventually he was tempted to rebel, being enticed by Egyptian promises of aid and intervention. The Assyrians placed Samaria under siege, but its defensible position required three years to take (II Kings 17:1–6). With the fall of Samaria (in late 722 or early 721 B.C.), the Israelites were incorporated into the Assyrian empire. According to Assyrian records, over twenty-seven thousand persons were taken into exile and resettled elsewhere, and during the next few years diverse populations from other provinces were moved into Samaria (II Kings 17:24).

The Marriage of Hosea. The material in The Book of Hosea can be divided into two distinct parts. The first (Hos., chs. 1 to 3) deals with the marriage of Hosea and its symbolical enactment of the relationship between Yahweh and Israel. The second part contains sermons preached by the prophet.

The marriage of the prophet has given rise to numerous theories about Hosea's love life and how he came to be a prophet and even sparked attempts to subject him to psychoanalysis.[23] Part of the difficulty is due to the fact that ch. 1 contains a biographical narrative about Hosea and his marriage and ch. 3 contains an autobiographical narrative about Hosea's purchase of a woman. Are the two accounts different versions of the same episode? Do they involve two women? Are they different episodes in Hosea's relationship with one woman? The following discussion will attempt to construct a portrayal of his marriage, which takes into consideration all the data of the two chapters, assuming that only one woman was involved.

In order to illustrate Yahweh's relationship to Israel and Israel's status before Yahweh, Hosea at Yahweh's command married a prostitute who was probably a functionary in the Baalistic cult and therefore property of the religious institution (Hos. 1:2–3). The reference to the "children of harlotry" (Hos. 1:2), if this refers to the children subsequently born, suggests that Gomer continued to function as a cult prostitute even after her marriage. There are no Biblical texts that discuss such an arrangement as this, but frequent reference is made to cultic prostitutes in the Bible, both male and female, and even within the Jerusalem Temple itself. The sexual orientation of Baal religion would have necessitated cultic prostitutes, and the references in ch. 2 to the woman's lovers are associated with special festival and feast days of the Baals. In Mesopotamian religion, there were various kinds of cultic prostitutes, some of whom could

---

[23] For a survey of the various theories of Hosea's marriage, see H. H. Rowley, "The Marriage of Hosea," in his *Men of God* (Thomas Nelson & Sons, 1963), pp. 66–97. Ward, *Hosea,* p. 70, warns: "It is impossible to construct a romance of broken faith, wounded affection, wrathful indignation, and love-in-spite-of-everything out of these materials. The bittersweet story of Hosea's deathless love for a wayward wife and of his discovery of a parable of God and Israel in his own experience is the fabrication of sentimental critics."

marry and have children.[24] An old Akkadian proverb illustrates the possibility of marrying a cultic prostitute when it warns:

> Do not marry a harlot whose husbands are six thousand.
> An Ishtar-woman vowed to a god,
> A sacred prostitute whose favors are unlimited,
> Will not lift you out of your trouble.[25]

Hosea's wife, Gomer, had three children, although only the first was explicitly said to be the prophet's child. To these children, Hosea gave symbolical names expressive of Yahweh's relationship to Israel: "Jezreel," referring to the coming annihilation of the house of Jehu for its atrocious slaughter of the house of Omri at Jezreel (Hos. 1:4) and "Not Pitied" and "Not My People" to symbolize Yahweh's loss of his compassion and the rejection of his people (Hos. 1:6–9). These children were living embodiments in Israelite society of Hosea's prophetic interpretation of his people's condition before Yahweh.

Sometime after the birth of the third child, Hosea seems to have separated from or even divorced his wife for a time. (Hosea 2:1–13 is permeated with the terminology of divorce which could be applicable to both Gomer and Israel.) If the woman of Hos., ch. 3, is Gomer, then Hosea later reclaimed his wife from the cult. (Persons could become the property of the sanctuary by being given by their parents as an act of devotion in the fulfillment of a vow or by being sold into slavery.) Hosea purchased Gomer, paying "fifteen shekels of silver and a homer and lethech of barley," thus releasing all rights that the cult might have had on her (Hos. 3:1–2). He then isolated her for a time, refusing to have sexual relations with her to symbolize the days that Israel would live without political and religious institutions, "without king or prince, without sacrifice or pillar, without ephod or teraphim" (Hos. 3:4). In all of this, Hosea affirmed that he was acting out the concern and love that Yahweh had for his people but whom he must discipline in the crucible of history in order to educate her for the requirements of marital fidelity.

Religious Prostitution. Judging from The Book of Hosea, Israelite religion had become thoroughly saturated with the fertility cults originally at home in the nature religion of Baalism. The prophet is not explicit about whether this emphasis was due to the incursion of Baalistic practices into the Yahwistic cult or whether Baalism was practiced alongside or in place of Yahwism. Hosea was the first prophet to describe this submersion in Canaanite nature religion in terms of Israel's prostitution and adultery: the first expressing an abhorrence of the fertility cult and the second emphasizing the nation's disregard for the covenant relation between Yahweh and his people.

> They sacrifice on the tops of the mountains,
>   and make offerings upon the hills,
> under oak, poplar, and terebinth,
>   because their shade is good.

---

[24] See Michael C. Astour, "Tamar the Hierodule," *Journal of Biblical Literature*, LXXXV (1966), pp. 185–196.
[25] Translation is from Pritchard, ed., *Ancient Near Eastern Texts*, p. 427.

> Therefore your daughters play the harlot,
>> and your brides commit adultery.
> I will not punish your daughters when they play the harlot,
>> nor your brides when they commit adultery;
> for the men themselves go aside with harlots,
>> and sacrifice with cult prostitutes.
>
> (Hos. 4:13–14.)

Although the inventiveness of man in the area of sexual practices has seldom lacked for imagination (and note that Hosea blames the males and not the females for the emphasis on sacred prostitution: Hos. 4:14), one must assume that the people honestly, but according to the prophet mistakenly, believed that such sexual practices helped to ensure fertility of family, field, and flock. The real deception, according to the prophet, was the nation's failure to realize that it was Yahweh who gave her "the grain, the wine, and the oil" (Hos. 2:8). The prophet's association of Yahweh with the source of fertility is a basic emphasis in the book. Although Yahweh had been understood primarily as a god of war and history, he must certainly have already been portrayed as the source of fertility in northern Yahwistic circles in a fashion similar to that found in the Yahwistic account of creation. It must be recalled, however, that such strict Yahwists as the Rechabites refused to associate Yahweh in any way with agriculture. The use of the bull as a symbol of divine presence in Israelite religion certainly did not discourage the association of deity, sexuality, and fertility, and for this reason the prophet denounced the calf image (Hos. 8:5; 10:5–6). What Hosea sought to do was not to disassociate fertility and deity but to argue that Yahweh, not Baal, was its source and that what Yahweh wanted was not sexual rituals but absolute loyalty.

The Politics of Upheaval. Political affairs in Israel during her last gasps of independence and freedom were chaotic, turbulent, and violent. The prophet condemned, as a lack of faith and loyalty, the revolution, regicide, and recourse to foreign powers that characterized the frantic efforts which convulsed the state. The intrigue and plotting for political power were described by the prophet as a smoldering fire and the would-be rulers as an oven devouring their leaders (Hos. 7:1–7). Hosea repudiated the manner in which kings were chosen and destroyed and claimed that Yahweh had nothing to do with the enthronements. King-making and idol-making go hand in hand: both are the works of men (Hos. 8:1–5)! The prophet seems to have gone so far as to denounce the institution of kingship as such (Hos. 9:9, where Gibeah probably refers back to the origin of kingship with Saul).[26]

Israel's frantic efforts to stabilize her national life and improve her political status through dependence on the major foreign powers were sharply criticized by the prophet. The turning to Assyria and the payment of tribute were simply prostitution on an international scale, the hiring of lovers (Hos. 8:9), and thus infidelity to Yahweh. Falsehood and violence were interlaced in Israel's foreign

---

[26] See Ward, *Hosea*, pp. 179–183.

policy: "they make a bargain with Assyria, and oil is carried [as a sign of treaty relationship, see II Kings 17:4] to Egypt" (Hos. 12:1).

> Ephraim is like a dove,
> silly and without sense,
> calling to Egypt, going to Assyria.
>
> .   .   .   .
>
> Woe to them, for they have strayed from me!
> (Hos. 7:11–13.)

Knowledge of God. The opening passage in the second part of The Book of Hosea declares, in the terminology of a court case (see above, pp. 95–97), that Yahweh is bringing a legal charge against his people:

> Yahweh has a controversy with [or indictment of] the
> inhabitants of the land.
> There is no faithfulness or kindness,
> and no knowledge of God in the land.
> (Hos. 4:1.)

In his denunciation of the sacrificial cult in Israel, Hosea has Yahweh say, "I desire steadfast love and not sacrifice, the knowledge of God, rather than burnt offerings" (Hos. 6:6). What does the prophet mean by "the knowledge of God"? In Hos. 4:1–2, the lack of the knowledge of God is parallel to "swearing, lying, killing, stealing, and committing adultery," which suggests that one aspect of the knowledge of God was acquaintance with and obedience to the sacred legal traditions of Israel and in particular, in this case, some enumeration of these legal requirements similar to or identical with the Ten Commandments of Ex., ch. 20. In Hos. 6:6, knowledge of God is parallel to "steadfast love," which is an English translation of the Hebrew word *hesed*. The latter is used frequently in Biblical texts to describe the fidelity and loyalty of one party to another in a covenant relationship.[27] For the prophet, knowledge of God was also related to the remembrance of Yahweh's historical acts on behalf of his people, especially his deliverance of the people from Egypt and the divine guidance in the wilderness (Hos. 13:4–6). To know Yahweh was to preserve that relational fidelity which "harlotry" had destroyed (Hos. 5:4).

The failure of the nation to be acquainted with and responsive to the legal traditions and confessional history of her past was laid by the prophet at the feet of the religious and political leadership (Hos. 5:1–4). A primary responsibility of the priesthood was the teaching of the knowledge of God, but the priests had themselves forgotten the law and with them the people had stumbled (Hos. 4:4–9). Kings and state policy were no longer made through Yahweh in spite of the people's claim (Hos. 8:1–4). Neither the religious nor the political affairs were the expression of faith in Yahweh nor loyalty to the covenant relationship.

---

[27] See Nelson Glueck, *Hesed in the Bible* (KTAV Publishing House, Inc., 1968). A discussion of Hosea in terms of a covenant background is given by Walter Brueggemann, *Tradition for Crisis* (John Knox Press, 1968).

The Interlude of Judgment. Hosea argued that the people's deeds would "not permit them to return to their God" (Hos. 5:4); thus their doom was sealed. Like Gomer, Israel must be subjected to discipline; her religious and political institutions must be swept away (Hos. 3:4). The judgment to come could be described by the prophet as a return to Egypt (Hos. 8:13; 9:3, 6; 11:5), a return to that time when Israel did not exist as a people, when there were no alluring attractions of the land, no king, and no cult. The "return to Egypt" was used by the prophet as a symbol for the coming judgment, the oppressed future at the hands of Assyria (Hos. 10:6; 11:5) which would devastate Israel and destroy her people (Hos. 10:13–15; 13:15–16). Or the judgment could be portrayed in the terms of the nature cult. The future would bring not fertility but "no birth, no pregnancy, no conception," only "a miscarrying womb and dry breasts" (Hos. 9:11, 14). In the judgment, it is to be Yahweh himself who turns against his people, who is the cause of the nation's suffering, and who tears apart her society like a rampaging lion (Hos. 5:12–14; 8:13; 9:9).

After the Storm. The prophet did not end his message with the announcements of punishment. Like Hosea in his marriage, Yahweh suffers and agonizes over the condition of his people (Hos. 11:8–9). God is depicted struggling between his mercy and his wrath over this people whom he found "like grapes in the wilderness" (Hos. 9:10), whom he led out of Egypt like a child and taught to walk in gentleness and love (Hos. 11:1–4). Thus the prophet argues that beyond the storm and the future travail there lies a time of salvation and redemption. This optimism about the future beyond the interim seems to have been based on two factors. In the first place, Hosea understood the coming judgment as a time of re-education for Israel, when she would be trained in loyalty and fidelity through deprivation and suffering (Hos. 2:6–13). Israel, like Gomer, would live for many days deprived of those things which she deemed so important, after which "the children of Israel shall return and seek Yahweh their God, . . . and they shall come in fear to Yahweh and his goodness" (Hos. 3:4–5). Secondly, the prophet's optimism was anchored in his understanding of Yahweh's nature. Yahweh's love and loyalty could not destroy absolutely:

> How can I give you up, O Ephraim!
> How can I hand you over, O Israel! . . .
> My heart recoils within me,
> my compassion grows warm and tender.
> (Hos. 11:8.)

Hosea spoke of Yahweh's redoing the old deeds of Israel's salvation, alluring her again into the wilderness and, like a new lover, courting her afresh (Hos. 2:14–15). Yahweh will betroth Israel to himself again, love her as her husband, shower her with the blessings of heaven and earth, wiping from her memory the very name of Baal, and granting peace in the natural and international orders (Hos. 2:16–23). Such a portrayal depended heavily upon what Hosea had so strenuously opposed in its non-Yahwistic form—the understanding of the divine-human relationship in terms of sexuality. The book closes with a liturgy in which the people are called to repentance (Hos. 14:1–2a), to lament their sins (Hos. 14:2b–3), and in strongly mythological, almost Baalistic, terminology are assured of Yahweh's gifts of prosperity and fertility (Hos. 14:4–8).

10 | ISAIAH
AND THE ASSYRIAN CRISIS

During the ninth century, the Kingdom of Judah had been much more isolated from international events than the Kingdom of Israel. The swift conquests of the Assyrians begun by Tiglath-pileser, however, shattered this isolated position, and Judah found herself swept into the maelstrom of Near Eastern politics. For more than a century the ominous cloud of Assyria hovered over international life and thought, and its war machines rolled over one opponent after another.

The major prophetic spokesman during the early decades of these Judean-Assyrian relations was Isaiah, whose career was strongly oriented to the international politics of his day. The activity and preaching of Isaiah revolved around the maneuvers and revolts of Syro-Palestinian nations against the hegemony of Assyria.

A sketch of these troublesome times is necessary for a proper evaluation and understanding of Isaiah's preaching.[1] In 734–732 B.C., Aram and Israel formed an anti-Assyrian coalition along with other states and sought to force Judah's participation. The Judean king Ahaz refused to join the rebelling powers and chose instead to seek security under the wing of the Assyrian eagle. The Aramean capital at Damascus was seized, and most of Israel's territory was absorbed and incorporated into three Assyrian provinces. In 724–721 B.C., Samaria again sought to throw off the Assyrian yoke but was destroyed in the process. Thereafter, the Assyrian and Judean boundary met only a few short miles north of Jerusalem. A further rebellion broke out in 720 B.C. led by the Philistines but also again involving Samaria. A fourth revolt brought Assyrian armies into Palestine in 713–711 B.C. With the encouragement of Egypt and under the leadership of Ashdod, this revolt was temporarily joined by Judah, who seems, however, to have surrendered quickly to the enemy and thus was spared severe retaliation.

Biblical readings: The historical background to Isaiah's prophetic activity is given in II Kings, chs. 16; 18 to 20. The basic preaching of the prophet is found in Isa., chs. 1 to 11; 28 to 32. See maps VII and VIII.

[1] For a discussion of the international political situation and its reflection in Isaiah's preaching, see Norman K. Gottwald, *All the Kingdoms of the Earth* (Harper & Row, Publishers, Inc., 1964), pp. 147–203.

The closing years of the eighth century were the most consequential for Judah. The death of Sargon II in 705 provided the occasion for widespread revolt throughout the Assyrian empire. Palestine plunged into the midst of the general uprisings, and Hezekiah, the Judean king, was the chief of conspirators in the Syro-Palestinian area. It took three years for the new Assyrian ruler, Sennacherib, to squelch the revolting parties in the eastern part of the empire. In his third major campaign he marched against the small states along the eastern Mediterranean and triumphed over them and their Egyptian sympathizers. These efforts of Assyrian imperialism form the background against which Isaiah sought to interpret Judah's role in the international events of his time.

Before discussing the ministry and preaching of the prophet Isaiah, we shall need to comment briefly on the nature of The Book of Isaiah.

A COLLECTION OF PROPHETIC TRADITIONS

The Book of Isaiah is actually a library or anthology of prophetical traditions that scholars assume came from a period spanning over two hundred fifty years.[2] The present form of the book contains sixty-six chapters, but the differences between chs. 1 to 39 and 40 to 66 are quite noticeable. These differences are historical, literary, and theological. In the first part of the book, Assyria is the world power; in the second, it is Babylon, but a Babylon threatened by Persia under Cyrus. In chs. 1 to 39, the exile stands as a possible future threat; in chs. 40 to 66, the exile is an actuality or a thing of the recent past. In the first part, there is frequent reference to Isaiah; in the latter, he is not mentioned at all. Judgment is the primary theme of chs. 1 to 39, whereas redemption and consolation characterize chs. 40 to 66. The explicit formulation of a monotheistic outlook appears in the second half but not in the first half of the book. In the first part, biographical and autobiographical materials are intermixed; only oracles and sermons are found in the second part.

These differences have led scholars to make the following general division of the material: (1) chs. 1 to 39, generally from the ministry of the eighth century prophet; (2) chs. 40 to 55, from the time just prior to the fall of Babylon in 538 B.C., and authored by an anonymous prophet in the exile; (3) chs. 56 to 66, from the period following the return of the Jews of the exile to Judah following the take-over of Babylon by the Persians.

Insofar as the prophet Isaiah is concerned, only chs. 1 to 39 come into consideration. However, not all this material can be directly associated with Isaiah. Chapters 36 to 39 are historical narratives edited into The Book of Isaiah from II Kings 18:13 to 20:19. Isaiah, chs. 24 to 27, is characterized by an interest in the catastrophic end of the present world order, a type of thought and literature that was widespread in later Judaism. For this reason, this section is to be assigned to the period after the return from exile. Other parts of Isa., chs. 1 to 39,

---

[2] Some scholars still attribute all the material in The Book of Isaiah to the eighth-century prophet; see Edward J. Young, *Who Wrote Isaiah?* (Wm. B. Eerdmans Publishing Company, 1958).

especially in chs. 13 to 23, were probably edited into the book rather late in the course of the material's history.

Why these various traditions from different historical periods should have been edited to form one book remains a mystery. Were they associated because of similar interests, such as a consistent concern for Jerusalem? Did the later traditions originate among Jewish exiles who shared the original concerns of Isaiah? Was it merely the desire to produce a scroll of a length similar to that of Ezekiel, Jeremiah, and the Book of the Twelve? Was there an "Isaiah Party" or circle that continued to exist after the prophet's death and that preserved, revised, and supplemented his preaching?

Two passages in The Book of Isaiah show that small collections of Isaiah's words were produced while he was still alive. In Isa. 8:16–18, the prophet is said to have committed his words to his disciples who were to preserve them. These "words" were those spoken to King Ahaz in the crisis of 734–732 B.C. Again in Isa. 30:8, reference is made to the writing of the words to preserve them for a future time. Here the reference to the writing concerns Isaiah's preaching during the crisis of 705–701 B.C. If two collections of Isaiah's words were produced by his followers or under the prophet's direction, it is easier to see how these small collections would have been used, revised, and augmented with further small collections by those who preserved and cherished his words.

ISAIAH'S EARLY MINISTRY

Little biographical information is available on the prophet Isaiah. He was the son of Amoz (not to be confused with the prophet Amos), about whom nothing is known except his name. Isaiah was married and had at least two children, to whom he gave symbolic names (Isa. 7:3; 8:3). Apparently he was a citizen of Jerusalem, a townsman. His relationships with the king and the high court officials would suggest that he belonged to the higher circles of society in the city.[3] Unlike Hosea, who utilized the confessional traditions about Israel's early history, Isaiah made no mention of the exodus from Egypt and the associated traditions. Instead, Isaiah focused on the special concepts connected with the city of Jerusalem, those of David and Zion. Isaiah was the first of the writing prophets to function in the Kingdom of Judah. In an extraordinary way, his life and activity reflect an identification with Judah and her capital. Jewish legend told of his being sawn asunder during the reign of Manasseh (in the legendary work called *The Martyrdom of Isaiah*; see Heb. 11:37).

Isaiah began his ministry during the year of King Uzziah's (sometimes given as Azariah) death. This monarch had enjoyed a long and successful rule and was remembered for his territorial conquests, internal national strength, and economic prosperity, but he ended his life as a leper living in isolation (II Chron., ch. 26). With his demise, Judean political fortunes began a rapid decline.

---

[3] It has been suggested that Isaiah was a scribe at the royal court; see R. T. Anderson, "Was Isaiah a Scribe?" *Journal of Biblical Literature*, LXXIX (1960), pp. 57–58.

The Temple Vision. Isaiah's call to a prophetical career is given in an autobiographical form in Isa., ch. 6.[4] The reason the call narrative appears here rather than at the beginning of the book is probably due to the fact that chs. 6 to 8 composed the earliest collection of Isaiah's preaching even though chs. 1 to 5 contain some material from a time before the events in ch. 7.

The dating of the vision "in the year that King Uzziah died" (the exact year is uncertain; ca. 742 B.C.) suggests that Isaiah's call was associated with some event precipitated by the death of the king. The coronation of a new king was, of course, the significant event pursuant upon the death of a monarch. In all likelihood, the actual coronation of the new monarch took place in conjunction with or at least was celebrated at the time of the autumnal New Year festival.

In the context of the festival pageantry, Isaiah envisioned Yahweh exalted upon his throne with his train filling the temple. In association with Yahweh were the seraphim, each with six wings: two for flying, two for covering the eyes, and two for covering the feet (probably a euphemism for the genitals). This is the only passage in the Hebrew Scriptures in which there is a reference to six-winged seraph creatures. What were these guardian beings which stood watch over the deity's throne? The term *saraph* means "to burn." In all likelihood, the fiery serpents of Isaiah's vision are to be related to the "bronze serpent" that was used in Jerusalemite worship until removed from the Temple by King Hezekiah (II Kings 18:4).[5] The association of the snake with various, but especially fertility, aspects of the cult was widespread in the Near East. Near Jerusalem, there was the "Serpent's Stone" (I Kings 1:9) as well as "the spring of the serpent" (Neh. 2:13; translated as "Jackal's Well" in RSV) which shows that the Judean capital was familiar with serpent veneration. In Num., ch. 21, there is a story of Moses' construction of the bronze serpent in the wilderness, a story that no doubt served as the etiology to explain the serpent symbol used in the Jerusalem cult. The shape of the bronze serpent was probably similar to the erect cobra (or uraeus) which was used as a symbol of royalty in Egypt and was often depicted as winged. It has been suggested that part of the New Year ritual involved the opening of the Temple gates to allow the first rays of the rising sun to penetrate the Holy of Holies. If this were the case, then Isaiah's vision was probably dependent upon this tension-filled moment when the imagery of the Temple—Yahweh enthroned upon the Ark, the winged cherubim, the bronze serpent, and the rays of the rising sun—"came alive."

Isaiah heard the seraphim declaring the glory of Yahweh and proclaiming his holiness. Isaiah's reaction was the recognition of his unworthiness and that of his people and a fear for his life since he had beheld Yahweh, the King, in such a condition. Three elements are noteworthy in this reaction. First, the idea of the prophet seeing Yahweh upon his throne and standing in his presence during the prophetic vision had a history of usage in Israelite prophetism (see

---

[4] Some have considered this episode as a later rather than an initial experience of the prophet; see J. Milgrom, "Did Isaiah Prophesy During the Reign of Uzziah?" *Vetus Testamentum,* XIV (1964), pp. 164–182.

[5] See K. R. Joines, "Winged Serpents in Isaiah's Inaugural Vision," and his "The Bronze Serpent in the Israelite Cult," *Journal of Biblical Literature,* LXXXVI (1967), pp. 410–415, and LXXXVII (1968), pp. 245–256.

I Kings 22:13–23). Secondly, the emphasis on Yahweh as the king was an important element in the New Year ritual (see pp. 132–134) and Isaiah's vision emphasized that it was Yahweh, not the new monarch Jotham, who was understood as the real king in Jerusalem. Thirdly, Isaiah's sense of his unworthiness mirrored the status of the Judean population before Yahweh.

In his vision, Isaiah saw himself purged by a burning coal from the altar, which was taken by one of the seraphim and applied to his lips. Isaiah heard Yahweh speaking in the heavenly council [6] to the subordinate divine beings: "Whom shall I send, and who will go for us?" The prophet volunteered his services and was commissioned a spokesman of the deity to the people.

The content of Isaiah's commission is unlike that of any other prophet. The purpose of his preaching was to make it impossible for the people to repent and be healed! Instead, his work was to make their eyes droopy, their ears heavy, and their hearts fat (Isa. 6:9–10). In general Semitic thought the heart was considered the center not of the emotions but of the intellect and will. To his inquiry, "How long?", Isaiah was told that his activity must continue until cities lie waste and the land is utterly desolate (Isa. 6:11–13).

Yahweh's Vineyard. Chapters 1 to 5 of Isaiah undoubtedly contain material from the early years of the prophet's preaching, but unfortunately this is combined with material that obviously comes from late in Isaiah's career as well as with some non-Isaianic traditions. Much of the material in these opening chapters shows a strong kinship with the preaching of Amos in its emphasis on social righteousness and justice.[7]

Isaiah, perhaps in the form of a folk ballad, compared Yahweh and his people to a husbandman and a vineyard (Isa. 5:1–7). Like a conscientious farmer who prepared and watched over his field, so Yahweh had done for Jerusalem and Judah, only to discover that the vineyard yielded inedible wild grapes. Such a vineyard could only be treated as wild terrain unresponsive to agriculturalist care.

> He [Yahweh] looked for justice (*mishpaṭ*),
>   But behold, bloodshed (*mispaḥ*);
> for righteousness (*zedaqah*),
>   but behold, a cry (*ze 'aqah*)!
>
> (Isa. 5:7.)

Like Amos, Isaiah condemned the avarice of the affluent who sought to expand their holdings at the expense of the impoverished (Isa. 3:13–15; 5:8–10). According to the prophet, legal justice was perverted by bribes paid to secure acquittal in the court for the guilty or to convict the innocent (Isa. 1:23; 5:22–

---

[6] On the heavenly council, see H. W. Robinson, "The Council of Yahweh," *Journal of Theological Studies*, XLV (1944), pp. 151–157, Frank M. Cross, Jr., "The Council of Yahweh in Second Isaiah," *Journal of Near Eastern Studies*, XII (1953), pp. 274–277, and E. C. Kingsbury, "The Prophets and the Council of Yahweh," *Journal of Biblical Literature*, LXXXIII (1964), pp. 279–286.

[7] See Ward, *Amos and Isaiah*, esp. pp. 166–179.

23; see Ex. 23:6–8). Isaiah denounced the sacrificial cult with its burnt offerings, blood rituals, special days of assembly, and fervent prayers (Isa. 1:10–15), arguing that Yahweh's demands required instead that the people "cease to do evil, learn to do good; seek justice, correct oppression; defend the fatherless, plead for the widow" (Isa. 1:16–17). He compared Jerusalem to a rebellious child, more stupid than an ox (Isa. 1:2–3). For this waywardness, this disregard for justice, this religion without righteousness, Isaiah declared that Yahweh was entering into judgment with his people and would declare his case. And like the rebellious son delivered up to be stoned (see Deut. 21:18–21) or the guilty to be punished, so Yahweh would bring judgment that would force the high and the mighty to flee to the hills (Isa. 2:12–22) and thus would leave Jerusalem bereft of leaders (Isa. 3:1–12). Its women, who delighted in finery and walked to the jingle of jewelry, would be left to mourn and to live without men (Isa. 3:16 to 4:1).

THE ARAMEAN-ISRAELITE COALITION (734–732 B.C.)

Isaiah, chs. 7 and 8, provides a collection of traditions associated with the Aramean-Israelite (Syro-Ephraimitic) revolt against Assyria and the attempt to remove the Judean king, Ahaz, from the throne for lack of cooperation with the movement (Isa. 7:1–2; II Kings 16:5–9). This revolt led by Rezin, king of the Aramean state of Damascus, and Pekah, who had taken over as ruler in Samaria after assassinating his predecessor, was an attempt to unite all of Syro-Palestine in a common rebellion against Assyria. Ahaz was a pro-Assyrian ruler and thus represented a threat to the ambitions of his neighbors to the north.

Chapter 7 of Isaiah opens with a historical summary of the political state of affairs: Ahaz and Judah had been attacked from various directions (see II Kings 16:5–6; II Chron., ch. 28, provides a fuller description, but some of the details appear exaggerated) and the king was inspecting the defenses and water supply of Jerusalem anticipating siege conditions. Isaiah was commanded to encounter Ahaz, accompanied by his young son, Shear-jashub.[8] The latter's name means "a remnant shall return," obviously embodying a symbolic meaning. The term "remnant" was of military origin and referred to the persons who escaped with their lives in warfare which generally aimed at total annihilation. So the child's name could embody an optimistic prediction ("at least a remnant shall remain") or a pessimistic prediction ("only a remnant will survive"). If Shear-jashub were born shortly after Isaiah's call-experience, the latter meaning would seem the most appropriate and would have been intended by the prophet as a forecast of the havoc that would overtake Judah (see Isa. 6:11–13).

Ahaz was confronted with three alternatives. He could join the revolt, he could appeal to Assyria for military assistance, or he could remain neutral and

---

[8] See Sheldon H. Blank, *Prophetic Faith in Isaiah* (Wayne State University Press, 1967, paperback reprint of 1958 ed.), pp. 30–33, and his "The Current Misinterpretation of Isaiah's *She'ar Yashub*," *Journal of Biblical Literature*, LXVII (1948), pp. 211–215.

defend his city against attack. Isaiah was opposed to any policy other than one of neutrality and argued against any dependence upon or agreement with Assyria. An alliance with Assyria would have: forced Judah to become an Assyrian vassal, necessitated the paying of tribute, involved Judah in fighting against the Israelites in the north (a subsequent Judean invasion of Israelite territory is reflected in Hos. 5:8–12), and required political and religious concessions to Assyria. But most of all, reliance on Assyria meant trusting human power, human weapons, rather than trusting in Yahweh, the Holy One of Israel.

Isaiah, "at the end of the conduit of the upper pool on the highway to the Fuller's Field" (Isa. 7:3), appealed to Ahaz, personally assuring him that there was no reason to panic, that Yahweh had decreed the defeat of the plans of Rezin and Pekah, who were not flaming lights for freedom but rather two smoldering stumps, and that what Yahweh demanded was not alliances but confidence in the divine (Isa. 7:4–9). His admonition to Ahaz, "Be quiet, do not fear, and do not let your heart be faint," is reminiscent of the oracles of assurance addressed to the participants in the tribal holy wars. Isaiah concluded his speech to Ahaz with the demand that if Ahaz did not believe, he would not be established (Isa. 7:9). The demand is stated in the Hebrew by the use of two almost identical terms, a play on words that can be suggested by such a translation as, "If you are not steadfast, you shall not stand fast." The reference to Ahaz's believing should be seen against the background of the promises of Yahweh made to the ruler and the city in the Davidic and Zion theologies (see above, pp. 125–134). Apparently Isaiah made little progress in his efforts to convince Ahaz.

Failing in his appeal to Ahaz, Isaiah confronted the Davidic house and in the presence of the royal family challenged Ahaz to ask a sign of Yahweh if he wished for more assurance (Isa. 7:10–17). Ahaz responded in a pious fashion that one should not put Yahweh to a test. The prophet answered by saying that Yahweh would give a sign anyway. The sign is then described in the following manner:

> A young woman is with child and shall bear a son, and shall call his name God-with-us (Immanuel). . . . For before the child knows how to refuse the evil and choose the good, the land before whose two kings you are in dread will be deserted. (Isa. 7:14, 16, marginal readings.)

What was Isaiah referring to and what was the content of his promise? [9] In the first place, the oracle should not be understood as pronouncing doom or judgment upon Ahaz; it was a prediction that better days are ahead if Ahaz and

---

[9] This passage, partially because of its usage in the New Testament, has spawned a tremendous volume of literature. See most recently, William McKane, "The Interpretation of Isaiah VII. 14–25," *Vetus Testamentum*, XVII (1967), pp. 208–219; and J. J. Scullion, S.J., "An Approach to the Understanding of Isaiah 7:10–17," *Journal of Biblical Literature*, LXXXVII (1968), pp. 288–300. This passage in its Greek translation was accepted by the early church as a prediction of the virgin birth of Jesus. Such an interpretation was characteristic of Christianity for centuries. For a similar understanding by a contemporary scholar, see Edward J. Young, *The Book of Isaiah*, Vol. I (Wm. B. Eerdmans Publishing Company, 1965), pp. 277–295.

the royal family will have confidence in Yahweh to handle the political situation. Secondly, the sign must be related to the immediate crisis of the Aramean-Israelite war against Judah. The young woman (the Hebrew term used simply designated a person of sexual maturity without any reference to her sexual experience) must have been someone at the royal court who was obviously pregnant. Perhaps one should think in terms of a wife of Ahaz. When the child was born it would be named Immanuel, an expression at home in worship, where it was used like "Hosanna" and "Hallelujah" as a cultic shout, assurance, or prayer, but before the child knew "to refuse the evil and choose the good" (i.e., while still an infant; compare with Isa. 8:4), Aram and Israel would be overcome and prosperous times would follow for Judah (Isa. 7:17; "the king of Assyria" is probably a later addition). The child involved has often been assumed to be Hezekiah, the successor to Ahaz, but one cannot be this certain. Immanuel could have been a royal honorific name (see above, p. 129) given to a male member of the royalty. The idea of this royal birth and the naming of the child should be compared with the birth and the naming of Solomon by Nathan (II Sam. 12:24-25). Isaiah declared then that within a very short time Jerusalem's enemies would be devastated and the birth of a son within the royal family would be a sign of assurance if the royal house would wait in faith.

Abandoning his appeal to the royal house, which he seems not to have convinced of his policy of faith and nonalignment, Isaiah carried his case to the citizenry of Jerusalem (Isa. 8:1-4). In a symbolic act, Isaiah took a plaque or tablet and wrote upon it "belonging to Spoil-Speeds-Prey-Hastens" (Maher-shalal-hash-baz) in the common handwriting of the time and had this "notarized" by two witnesses. It is to be assumed that this was displayed in a public place with the prophet's explanation: the son he was to father by his wife would be given this name which expressed his belief that Damascus and Samaria would become spoil and prey for the Assyrians. Again, as in the Immanuel prophecy, this devastation of Judah's enemies was related to a time stipulation. Before the child could say the nonsense syllables, *abi* and *immi*, which, like "da-da" and "ma-ma" parents the world over have used to designate themselves, the danger to Jerusalem would be passed. In a way this symbolic act was intended to show to Jerusalem that Isaiah's understanding of the historical situation, which he identified with Yahweh's, was the best interpretation on which to base a course of action.

Ahaz chose an alliance with Assyria over reliance upon Isaiah's interpretation of Yahweh's demands. Sending his plea to Assyria for aid, Ahaz also sent his submission to vassalage and a present to seal the bargain (II Kings 16:7-9). This policy provoked Isaiah's harsh condemnation and the promise that the act would have far-reaching consequences. Isaiah saw this policy as a lack of faith in Yahweh, a refusal of "the waters of Shiloah that flow gently," and as confidence in the military might of Assyria, the land beyond the river Euphrates. As a warning, Isaiah declared that if Jerusalem wanted "the waters of the River," Yahweh would give it to them, but it would rush over Judah like a flood (Isa. 8:5-8).

ISAIAH'S LATER MINISTRY

Although there are scattered oracles in The Book of Isaiah that can be assigned to the years 732–715 B.C., we shall limit our further discussion to Isaiah's interpretation of the revolts of 713–711 and 705–701 B.C. Both of the latter belong to the rule of Hezekiah, who was a vigorous, reforming monarch with decidedly anti-Assyrian sentiments.

After the fall of Damascus (732 B.C.) and Samaria (722/721 B.C.), much of the plotting to throw off the Assyrian yoke was led by the Philistine city-states, which, because of geographical proximity, were greatly influenced by Egypt. One such revolt, led by the city of Ashdod, brought the Assyrians into Palestine and involved Judah and other states who probably offered only token participation. In an attempt to prevent Judah's participation and to symbolize the possible exile that would result from rebellion, Isaiah is said to have walked naked and barefoot around Jerusalem for three years (Isa., ch. 20). Such a demonstration was similar to the earlier symbolic acts of the prophet and was intended to draw attention in a graphic fashion that could not be easily ignored by the Jerusalem citizenry. When one recalls the Israelite taboo against public nudity, Isaiah's action becomes even more startling.

The death in battle of the Assyrian ruler Sargon II in 705 B.C. triggered massive uprisings throughout the empire. Judah was no longer a passive participant in the revolts, Hezekiah playing a leading role in the Palestinian area. Well-laid plans had been made far in advance of the rebellion, and adventurous effects were made in preparing to fight the inevitable conflict. The revolt in Palestine was synchronized with similar actions in the east. Messengers from the king of Babylon met in Jerusalem with Hezekiah in joint planning and strategy (II Kings 20:12–19). The staging of rebellions to coincide with the death of a monarch was, of course, in hopes that dynastic struggles might ensue or that an incompetent ruler might ascend the throne, which would allow moves for independence to succeed.

In preparation for the projected military encounter with the Assyrians, Hezekiah took a number of steps to strengthen his military position. A 1,777-foot water conduit was cut through solid rock to bring water from the spring of Gihon into the city of Jerusalem in order to withstand an extended siege. An inscription in this tunnel told how the workers had labored from opposite ends, eventually to join up in what was an extraordinary feat of engineering science.[10] The fortifications of Jerusalem were strengthened (Isa. 22:8–11) and apparently Hezekiah tried to gain the assistance and cooperation of the old northern Israelite population (II Chron. 30:1–12). It has been suggested that Hezekiah was aspiring to renew the Davidic rule over the whole of Palestine.

Isaiah was vehemently opposed to the revolt against the Assyrians and the Judean reliance upon Egypt for help. He saw this reliance upon Egypt and the hope for military solutions as a disregard of and lack of faith in Yahweh:

---

[10] A translation of the text is given in Pritchard, ed., *Ancient Near Eastern Texts*, p. 321.

The Pool of Siloam is at the southern end of Hezekiah's tunnel and is still used as a water source by the residents of Mt. Ophel. The construction of the pool was part of the king's ambitious efforts to ensure a supply of water for Jerusalem during siege. The pool area has been rebuilt several times, and the column bases were once part of a church built over the site.

ROBERT B. WRIGHT

"Woe to the rebellious children," says Yahweh,
 "who carry out a plan, but not mine;
and who make a league, but not of my spirit,
 that they may add sin to sin;
who set out to go down to Egypt,
 without asking for my counsel,
to take refuge in the protection of Pharaoh,
 and to seek shelter in the shadow of Egypt!"
         (Isa. 30:1–2.)

"Going down to Egypt" was to rely on horses and chariots and to turn away from the Yahweh, the Holy One of Israel (Isa. 31:1):

The Egyptians are men, and not God;
 and their horses flesh, and not spirit.
When Yahweh stretches out his hand,
 the helper will stumble, and he who is helped will fall,
 and they will all perish together.
         (Isa. 31:3.)

Egypt, so lavish in promises but so wanting in performance, was one that would bring "neither help nor profit, but shame and disgrace" (Isa. 30:4–5).

What the prophet recommended as a program for Judah and Hezekiah was a policy of pacifism and political nonalignment. Over against the efforts to throw off the Assyrian domination, Isaiah proposed a submission to the *status quo* based on faith in Yahweh to preserve and save his people. Not the frantic negotiations and frenzied military preparations but a quiet confidence was needed:

For thus said Yahweh God, the Holy One of Israel,
 "In returning and rest you shall be saved;
in quietness and in trust shall be your strength."
         (Isa. 30:15.)

With the eruption of the rebellion, Isaiah declared that the results would be a devastation of Judah. The coming fate of the people he described as a wall bulging to the point of collapse or the smashing of a clay pot until no fragmentary sherd would remain that was large enough to carry a burning coal or to dip water from a cistern (Isa. 30:12–14). Those who wished to hear only glowing prophecies about a rosy future would be greatly disappointed in the actual reality (Isa. 30:9–11).

Isaiah interpreted the coming disastrous situation as the work of Yahweh; in fact, in some passages it is said to be Yahweh who attacks and threatens Jerusalem (Isa. 29:1–4). Assyria was understood as an instrument that Yahweh used to carry out his work:

Ah, Assyria, the rod of my anger,
 the staff of my fury!

Against a godless nation I send him,
  and against the people of my wrath I command him,
to take spoil and seize plunder,
  and to tread them down like the mire of the streets.
          (Isa. 10:5–6; see ch. 5:26–30.)

The Assyrian ruler, Sennacherib (705–681 B.C.), marched against Palestine in 701 B.C. and defeated an Egyptian army and the Philistine city-states before

Sennacherib at the conquest of Lachish is shown sitting upon his royal throne being fanned by royal attendants. The inscription about the heads of the attendants facing the king is translated: "Sennacherib, King of the World, King of Assyria, sat upon a . . . throne and passed in review the booty (taken) at Lachish." *A huge panel in Sennacherib's palace at Nineveh portrayed the capture of the Judean city of Lachish.*
THE BRITISH MUSEUM

attacking Judah. He ravished "the fortified cities of Judah" (II Kings 18:13), claiming in his annals to have conquered forty-six strong cities and numerous villages and to have deported 200,150 people (this could be and probably is a scribal mistake for 2,150).[11] Hezekiah, the annals claimed, was "made a prisoner in Jerusalem, his royal residence, like a bird in a cage." Both the Old Testament and the Assyrian annals report a capitulation to Sennacherib by Hezekiah and the payment of tribute (II Kings 18:14–16). In neither account was Jerusalem said to have been taken.

At this point in an attempt to reconstruct the course of events associated with Sennacherib's conquest of Palestine, several problems arise.[12] II Kings 18:17 to 19:37 (with parallels in Isa., chs. 36 and 37) provides a narrative relating two accounts of negotiations between Hezekiah and an Assyrian commander over the surrender of Jerusalem. In both of these, Isaiah counsels Hezekiah not to surrender and promises deliverance. In his advice Isaiah is said to have promised that Sennacherib would "hear a rumor and return to his own land," perhaps a rumor of political dissension in his native country, and that he would "fall by the sword in his own land" (II Kings 19:7). Elsewhere the narrative states that "the angel of Yahweh went forth, and slew a hundred and eighty-five thousand in the camp of the Assyrians" (II Kings 19:35–37), after which Sennacherib returned to Nineveh and was murdered by his sons.

How can one reconcile accounts of a capitulation by Hezekiah, a return of the Assyrian ruler because of a political rumor, and the decimation of the invading army, all as part of one historical episode? Some have attempted to provide a solution by arguing for two invasions by Sennacherib (in 701 and again after 690 B.C.).[13] Others take everything except the narrative of the capitulation as later legend, attempting to portray Hezekiah and Isaiah in the best possible perspectives. It is possible to assume a capitulation by Hezekiah that was subsequently followed by negotiation over the surrender of Jerusalem, followed by a sudden withdrawal of the Assyrians due to an Egyptian threat, a threatened revolt in Nineveh, or a plague among the troops (see II Kings 19:1–7; 19:9; 19:35). As a rule, Assyrians did not display clemency toward the leaders of revolt such as Hezekiah; thus one can assume that Sennacherib withdrew under some form of duress. The fact that the Assyrian annals state that tribute was later sent to Nineveh suggests that the Assyrians withdrew before finally settling accounts with the rebel Judean. At present, our limited knowledge prohibits a final solution to the problem.

To return to Isaiah: What attitude did the prophet take concerning the siege of Jerusalem and the devastation of Judah? Although Isaiah had interpreted Assyria as a tool in the guiding hand of Yahweh, he seems to have understood the invader as overstepping the bounds of her allotted task and her extreme acts as manifestations of unwarranted ruthlessness and arrogance (Isa. 10:7–11; see Isa. 37:22–29). Isaiah predicted that Yahweh would deal with this haughty power and annihilate these invaders in the land of Judah.

---

[11] The text is translated in Pritchard, ed., *Ancient Near Eastern Texts*, pp. 287–288.
[12] A discussion of these is given in H. H. Rowley, "Hezekiah's Reform and Rebellion," in his *Men of God*, pp. 98–132; and in Brevard S. Childs, *Isaiah and the Assyrian Crisis* (London: SCM Press, Ltd., 1967).
[13] See Bright, *A History of Israel*, pp. 282–287.

"And the Assyrian shall fall by a sword, not of man;
and a sword, not of man, shall devour him;
and he shall flee from the sword,
and his young men shall be put to forced labor.
His rock shall pass away in terror,
and his officers desert the standard in panic,"
says Yahweh, whose fire is in Zion,
and whose furnace is in Jerusalem.

(Isa. 31:8–9.)

If Isa. 14:24–27 were uttered by the prophet, then he explicitly spoke of Yahweh's trampling of the Assyrian in "my land, and upon my mountains." (Such a prediction as this is perhaps part of the explanation for the legendary story of the slaughter of the Assyrians; an attempt to have the prophet's words completely fulfilled.)

Throughout the first part of The Book of Isaiah, there are numerous passages that refer to the inviolability of Zion, showing Jerusalem as a city divinely protected (see Isa. 29:5–8; 31:4–5). These ideas have been expanded in the narrative of Isa., chs. 36 and 37 in order to have the prophet predict that the Assyrians would never besiege Jerusalem (Isa. 37:33–35). It is difficult, if not impossible, to determine how much of this material comes from the historical Isaiah, or from the traditional Zion theology, or from the later traditionalists and editors of the book. Further discussion of these traditions will be considered in the next section in conjunction with the prophecies of Zion's future role.

THE ZION AND DAVIDIC TRADITIONS IN ISAIAH

The unique election traditions associated with the city of Jerusalem were the Zion and the Davidic traditions (see pp. 125–134). The historical Isaiah was strongly dependent upon both of these in his imagery, his criteria for judgment, and his proclamations of things to come. The prophet's concept of the people of Yahweh envisioned the community as a *polis*, a city of God. Needless to say, traditional material expounding the Zion and the Davidic thought was often attached to the original oracles of Isaiah, since there was a point of association in his preaching.

The Zion Theology. Isaiah never explicitly proclaimed the coming destruction of Jerusalem as did his contemporary, the prophet Micah (Micah 3:9–12). There is a certain paradoxical character, however, to the oracles about Jerusalem, constantly threatened, but finally delivered. Whether or not this goes back to the prophet cannot be determined. Some of the statements that obviously come from Isaiah do promise deliverance and redemption to Jerusalem, but it is a promise contingent upon faithful confidence in Yahweh (Isa. 30:15; 7:3–9). It is difficult to believe that Isaiah proclaimed the unconditional redemption and deliverance of Jerusalem as if Yahweh were no more than a patron god committed in advance to a course of action. His preaching, though dependent upon the traditions proclaiming the invulnerability of Zion, was a clear challenge to any overconfidence in inevitable protection.

Several passages in Isaiah speak of the coming role of Zion in the future life of the world of the nations. The most important and extensive of these is Isa. 2:2–4, a passage that also appears in almost identical form in Micah 4:1–3. This oracle predicts that at some time in the future Zion would be a place of pilgrimage for the nations of the world. Just as the people of Israel in the time of the United Kingdom went up to Jerusalem, so would the future nations of the world, in order to learn of the ways of the God of Jacob. The law and the word of Yahweh would go forth from Jerusalem to the world. On the basis of his word and law, Yahweh would judge the nations and adjudicate their claims. The result of this role of Jerusalem as a center for the nations of the world would be universal peace in which disputes would no longer be settled through armaments and warfare. Nations would then turn their military hardware into instruments of peaceful pursuits. The last part of this text assumes that warfare and conflict are unnatural states, the result of being learned.

The Davidic Traditions. The royal theology associated with the Davidic dynasty forms one of the basic concerns now represented in The Book of Isaiah. The concepts that were part of this royal theology provided the basis for a future-oriented messianism that spoke of the coming ideal ruler, the "new David." Isaiah 9:2–7 and ch. 11:1–9 are the clearest examples of this Davidic theology.[14] As has been argued above (see p. 129), the first of these passages did not speak of some future ruler but were part of the courtly ritual associated with the enthronement of a king. It has been argued that this passage was used at the coronation of Hezekiah in 715 B.C., at which time Isaiah functioned as the court prophet just as had Nathan at the coronation of Solomon. The form and content of this text made it possible for later interpreters to understand the references in terms of a future Davidic leader or an expected future messiah.

Isaiah 11:1–9 seems definitely to refer to a future ruler rather than to a person contemporary with Isaiah (or whoever wrote this passage) and thus represents an expression of messianic expectation. The expected ruler is said to be a "shoot from the stump of Jesse," suggesting the idea of Yahweh's making a new beginning from the ancestral family of David, whose father was Jesse. (The same sentiment appears in Micah 5:2–6 with its reference to Bethlehem.) The messianic figure is to be endowed with numerous charismas (Isa. 11:2) for the conduct of his office. The basic function of his rule is to serve as arbiter, to judge in righteousness and faithfulness, to aid the cause of the poor and meek (a task widely associated with the ideal of Near Eastern kingship), and to destroy the wicked (Isa. 11:3–5). The rule of this ideal king would result in the establishment of divine justice and a paradisaic peace in the world of nature that would eliminate all elements of conflict and danger (Isa. 11:6–8). The latter concept is clearly based on the assumption that at "the end time"

---

[14] Many scholars assign these passages to the postexilic period; but see Gerhard von Rad, *Old Testament Theology*, Vol. II (Harper & Row, Publishers, Inc., 1965), pp. 155–175.

there will be a return to the original harmony of the created order that existed at the beginning.

These expectations of the role of Zion in the future and of the ideal Davidic ruler to come are extremely utopian in their idealistic portrayals. It must be remembered that utopian thought not only served to kindle hope in an unborn future but also was a means of placing a present under judgment by a comparison of the actual with the ideal. No ruler on the Davidic throne could have doubted that the expectations of the ideal ruler in Isa. 11:1–9 were an indirect criticism of himself. If these passages come from Isaiah, their utopianism must be seen functioning in both perspectives.

11 | THE LAST DAYS
OF JUDEAN INDEPENDENCE

Jerusalem and Judah survived the catastrophic onslaught of the Assyrian army, emerging weakened and weary. The capital city was left, as Isaiah described it, "like a booth in a vineyard, like a lodge [i.e., "lean-to"] in a cucumber field" (Isa. 1:8). But Judah was far from finished. She was to survive for another century and to experience one of her finest hours of glory just prior to her loss of independence to the Babylonians.

THE REIGN OF MANASSEH

Peace with Assyria. With the end of Hezekiah's revolt and his submission to the Assyrians, Judah began a period of vassalage to the foreign power which was to endure for almost three quarters of a century. The territory under the control of Judah was severely curtailed and her military forces probably eliminated. This dominance by the hated Assyrians pervaded every aspect of Judean life. The waters of the River had overflowed its banks, swept on into Judah, and risen to their necks as Isaiah had predicted (Isa. 8:7–8).

When Hezekiah died (ca. 687 B.C.) he was succeeded by his son Manasseh, whose long reign (II Kings 21:1 says he ruled for fifty-five years, but this must include several years during which he was coruler with his ailing father) was dominantly pro-Assyrian. During these years Assyrian power was dominant in Near Eastern affairs, and Manasseh opted for political survival at the price of political expediency.

The Decline of Yahwism. During Manasseh's reign, Jerusalem was turned into a flourishing center of syncretistic and polytheistic religious practices. This was partially due to the influence of Assyrian religious practices that invaded subjected areas as part of the vassalage policy. Even during the days of Ahaz (735–715 B.C.), concession had already been made to Assyrian religion, and a special altar based on a foreign design had replaced the bronze altar to Yahweh in

---

Biblical readings: The historical background to the Yahwistic reformation and the last days of Judah is given in II Kings, chs. 21 to 25. The primary materials in Deuteronomy related to this reform are Deut., chs. 12; 16 to 18. The basic material in Jeremiah is Jer., chs. 1 to 7; 19:1 to 20:6; 24 to 29; 36 to 39; and in Ezekiel, Ezek., chs. 1 to 5; 8; 12; 16; 18; 23.

front of the Temple (II Kings 16:10–18). The reforming monarch, Hezekiah, had purged many foreign elements from the Jerusalem Temple and had destroyed the bronze serpent in conjunction with his anti-Assyrian revolt (II Kings 18:4–7). Manasseh seems to have deliberately set out to undo the influences of Hezekiah's religious reforms and to suppress any strong expressions of Yahwism (see II Kings 21:16), since Yahwistic religion and nationalism were so closely allied.

The account in II Kings 21:1–15 of the religious syncretism during Manasseh's rule attempts to show him as the archvillain of Judean history. He reconstructed the high places (local Yahweh shrines?) and reinstated official worship of the Canaanite god Baal and built images of the goddess Asherah, even putting these in the Jerusalem Temple. The worship of the host of heaven (the sun, moon, and stars) was fostered as well as various forms of astrology and divination, perhaps including necromancy, that is, consultation of the dead. In addition, child sacrifice was practiced and even the king is said to have burned his son as an offering.

No prophetical traditions dated to the reign of Manasseh are found in the Hebrew Scriptures (II Kings 21:10–15 is interpretation after the event). Probably no outspoken proclamation of Yahwism would have been tolerated. In the light of this, one can understand the later legendary tradition that told of Isaiah's being sawed in two during Manesseh's rule.

THE END OF ASSYRIAN HEGEMONY

The Assyrian empire reached its height in the first half of the seventh century. Esar-haddon (680–669 B.C.) subjected Egypt, which for generations had been a source of anti-Assyrianism in the west. For a time, Assyrian control extended over the entire Fertile Crescent, and powers from Upper Egypt to Elam were pawns in the hands of this massive giant.

From this apogee of political power and prestige, the Assyrian empire toppled quickly in the last three decades of the century. The cause for this sudden deterioration was probably due to six years of intensive civil war. Esar-haddon had drawn up an international treaty concerning the succession to the throne and had the vassal states ratify the agreement.[1] The agreement made his son Asshurbanipal king of the empire and another son king of Babylon, the traditional center of trouble in the east (recall Merodach-baladan's role in the general revolt upon the death of Sargon II in 705 B.C.). The subsequent civil war between the sons convulsed the empire (652–646 B.C.) and produced an apparent military exhaustion. (II Chronicles 33:11–17 records a forced visit of Manasseh to Babylon that might suggest Judean participation in the civil war.) The *Pax Assyriaca* was irreparably shattered, and the greatness that was Assyria was never to be again.

---

[1] The recently discovered text of this treaty has been published by Donald J. Wiseman, *The Vassal-Treaties of Esarhaddon* (London: British School of Archaeology in Iraq, 1958). A translation of this text is given in Pritchard, ed., *Ancient Near Eastern Texts*, pp. 534–541.

Esar-haddon's treaty with Ramataya committed the latter, who was king of Media, to support the Assyrian monarch's plans stipulating his son Asshurbanipal as his successor. This copy of the treaty, concluded in 672 B.C., was discovered in 1955. Being an Assyrian vassal, Manasseh may have concluded a similar treaty with Esar-haddon.

THE BRITISH MUSEUM

Asshurbanipal presided over the beginning of the disintegration of Assyrian power. As the only Assyrian ruler who prided himself on his literacy, he supervised the collection of a tremendous library of clay tablets at his capital at Nineveh. This library with its wide range of texts was first unearthed during the last century and constitutes a basic source for our knowledge of Assyrian life and culture. Asshurbanipal died in 627 B.C.,[2] and his successors were confronted with rebellions in the east (Babylon) and west (Judah) and invasions from the north and east (Media and diverse "barbarian" hordes). Egypt, who had gained her freedom from Assyria before the death of Asshurbanipal, proved to be Assyria's only ally, perhaps hoping to renew her claim to Palestine and Syria.[3] In 614 B.C., the Medes conquered the city of Asshur. Two years

---

[2] For years, the exact year of this king's death was uncertain. New texts discovered in 1956 make it possible to date his death to 627 B.C. The significance of this is the fact that we now know that the revolt of Judah was contemporary with Asshurbanipal's death. For a study of those texts, see C. J. Gadd, "The Haran Inscriptions of Nabonidus," *Anatolian Studies*, VIII (1958), pp. 35–92. A translation of this text is given in Pritchard, ed., *Ancient Near Eastern Texts*, pp. 560–562.

[3] Knowledge of the last days of Assyria has been greatly aided by the ·new discovery of Babylonian texts covering the years after 626 B.C. For a translation and study of these texts, see Donald J. Wiseman, *Chronicles of Chaldaean Kings* (London: The Trustees of the British Museum, 1956).

later, the capital city of Nineveh fell to a coalition of the Medes and Babylonians. Remnants of the Assyrian army held out in the northern part of Mesopotamia for a time, but even the aid of the Egyptians was of no avail.

NATIONALISTIC REVIVAL AND YAHWISTIC REFORM

The last flowering of Judean independence coincided with the years of Assyrian decline. Manasseh died in 642 B.C. and was succeeded by his son Amon, who ruled for only two years before being assassinated by his servants (II Kings 21:19–26). The reason for his murder is not given; it may have been due to the desire to start a rebellion against Assyria or the work of a strongly pro-Egyptian circle. The assassins, however, were not allowed to elevate their candidate to kingship. The "people of the land," that is, full Judean citizens[4] living outside Jerusalem, intervened to kill Amon's assassins and to place his son Josiah on the throne.

Josiah was only eight years of age at his accession, and thus the actual leadership must have come for some time from the forces that placed him in power. Josiah, however, was soon to exert a powerful and effective leadership coordinated with the shifting of political power in the Near East. According to II Chron. 34:3, Josiah inaugurated a reforming purge of Judean religion in the twelfth year of his reign, which would have been 628/627 B.C., or approximately the time of Asshurbanipal's death, which signaled a general outbreak of revolt throughout the empire. Religious reformation and political reforms—as in the time of Hezekiah—were inseparably bound, and although the Biblical traditions focus on the religious reforms, political actions and undercurrents were just as significant.

Josiah seems to have carried out his reform in various stages.[5] According to the Chronicles account, he began his reform by removing the Canaanite and Assyrian cults from Judah and Jerusalem. Then in the eighteenth year of his reign (622/621 B.C.), a law book was discovered in the Temple in the course of making repairs, no doubt as the result of the removal of images, altars, and other cultic paraphernalia of the non-Yahwistic cult (II Kings 22:1–8). The law book was read to the king by Hilkiah the high priest and Shaphan the royal secretary or scribe and authenticated by a prophetess (II Kings 22:9–20). Supported by these three authority groups—the priests, the prophets, and the scribes—the king led the people in a covenant-making ritual in which they bound themselves to obey the legal requirements of the law book (II Kings 23:1–3).

The account of Josiah's reformation in II Kings 23:4–27 has telescoped the various phases of the revolt and reform. The removal and destruction of the Baal and Asherah elements in the Jerusalem Temple, the deposition of idola-

---

[4] On the identity of the "people of the land," see Ernest W. Nicholson, "The Meaning of the Expression 'am ha'aretz in the Old Testament," *Journal of Semitic Studies*, X (1965), pp. 59–66. This term was later used in a pejorative sense to refer to the general population and was used by certain groups in Judaism to refer to "the sinners."

[5] See Ernest W. Nicholson, *Deuteronomy and Tradition* (Fortress Press, 1967), pp. 1–17.

trous priests, the destruction of the houses of the male prostitutes within the Temple, and the defiling of the place of child sacrifice in the Valley of Hinnom were probably part of the first phase (between 628 and 622 B.C.) when the reform was aimed at the non-Yahwistic elements in the capital and the area "from Geba to Beer-sheba," i.e., in Judah (II Kings 23:8). With the attempts to implement the stipulations of the recently discovered law book, interest focused on the destruction of the Yahwistic local shrines,[6] the centralization of worship in the Jerusalem Temple, the transformation of the family festival of Passover into a pilgrim festival restricting observance to the city of Jerusalem, and the extension of these reform measures to the old Israelite territory of the north (II Kings 23:15-25).

As was said earlier, the religious reforms of Josiah went hand in hand with political ambitions. As the power and authority of the Assyrians declined, Josiah sought to reestablish the boundaries of the earlier Davidic state by incorporating the old Israelite territory into the state of Judah. Many of the religious actions taken on the basis of the law book were directly related to these political goals. One of the political problems involved was the unification of the Judean and "Israelite" peoples and the creation of a loyalty to Jerusalem. The centralization of the religious cult and the destruction of local cult places (both Yahwistic and non-Yahwistic) were an attempt to increase the dependency of the general population upon the central sanctuary in Jerusalem and thus to provide a centralized religious authority and loyalty that carried with it a political commitment to Jerusalem and Josiah.[7] Hezekiah had apparently sought to do the same thing during the early days of his revolt against the Assyrians (see II Kings 18:22). The transformation of Passover into a pilgrim festival made it legally impossible to observe the major Yahwistic festivals outside Jerusalem. This emphasis on Passover stressed a festival of non-Canaanite and nonforeign origin and also played down the role of the New Year festival with its parallels in Assyrian culture and its solar emphasis (see II Kings 23:11, which refers to the destruction of the horses and chariots dedicated to the sun).

THE DEUTERONOMIC TRADITIONS

What was the law book found in the Temple on which Josiah carried out the second phase of his political and religious reformation? What relationship has it to the present form of the Hebrew Scriptures? What was its origin? How did it get into the Jerusalem Temple?

There are so many parallels between the reform measures taken by Josiah and the religious stipulations found *only* in the book of Deuteronomy that most scholars agree that the book of the law discovered in the Temple must have

---

[6] The recently discovered temple at Arad, constructed during the period of the united monarchy, was destroyed during the time of either Hezekiah's or Josiah's reform. See Aharoni, "Arad: Its Inscriptions and Temple," *The Biblical Archaeologist*, XXXI (1968), pp. 26–27.
[7] See Moshe Weinfeld, "Cult Centralization in Israel in the Light of a Neo-Babylonian Analogy," *Journal of Near Eastern Studies*, XXIII (1964), pp. 202–212.

been an early edition of Deuteronomy.[8] Nowhere else in the Torah (Pentateuch) are there the requirements for centralization of the cult (Deut. 12:13–15), for the right of the country priests to officiate at the central sanctuary (Deut. 18:6–8; but compare II Kings 23:9), and the observance of Passover as a pilgrim festival (Deut. 16:1–6). The primary legal traditions in chs. 12 to 26 of Deuteronomy are assumed, therefore, to have formed the original law book found in the Temple which may also have included the general introduction in chs. 5 to 11.

The Book of Deuteronomy.[9] The book found in the Temple was described as "the book of the covenant" (II Kings 23:2) or "the covenant document." If Deut., chs. 5 to 11, were an original part of the book, the elements of the covenant ritual are easily discernible in the book: the preaching and exhortation to fidelity on the basis of Yahweh's gracious deeds of the past (chs. 5 to 11), the legal stipulations (chs. 12:1 to 26:15), the acceptance of the covenant stipulations (ch. 26:16–19), and the recital of the blessings and curses as the possible rewards or punishments for obedience or infidelity (ch. 28). The book is composed in the form of a speech of Moses given to the people just prior to the conquest of the Promised Land. The writing then claims an authority going back to Moses and the wilderness period (on these as type-times and persons, see above, p. 68) and thus presents its legal stipulations as the law of the land. The covenant stipulations are therefore understood as the reiteration of the original will of Yahweh given to his people at Mt. Horeb (Sinai).

The theology of Deuteronomy[10] has been described in the catch phrase, "One God, One People, One Cult," and we can discuss the book's emphases around these rubrics. A number of ideas are emphasized in the book's statements about God. First, Yahweh is described as a unique deity: "Hear, O Israel: Yahweh our God, Yahweh is one" (Deut. 6:4; see RSV footnote) or better translated: "Hear, O Israel, Yahweh is our God, Yahweh alone!" Secondly, Yahweh is a God who in an act of election chose Israel as his people:

> For you are a people holy to Yahweh your God; Yahweh your God has chosen you to be a people for his own possession, out of all the peoples that are on the face of the earth. (Deut. 7:6; see ch. 14:2.)

This act of election was made real in Yahweh's deliverance of his people "out of the land of Egypt, out of the house of bondage," in his bringing of his people to the land promised to the patriarchs (Deut. 6:10–15; see ch. 9:1–5), and in his giving his commandments and ordinances in the covenant (Deut. 26:17–19). Thirdly, Yahweh is a God of love who rewards fidelity and punishes infidelity. Yahweh's choice of Israel was not based upon Israel's prior righteous-

---

[8] Some of the early church fathers (Chrysostom, Jerome, and Athanasius) were the first to identify Josiah's law book with Deuteronomy.

[9] See Nicholson, *Deuteronomy and Tradition*; and Moshe Weinfeld, "Deuteronomy—The Present State of Inquiry," *Journal of Biblical Literature*, LXXXVI (1967), pp. 249–262.

[10] See Ronald E. Clements, *God's Chosen People: A Theological Interpretation of the Book of Deuteronomy* (London: SCM Press, Ltd., 1968); and Gerhard von Rad, *Studies in Deuteronomy* (London: SCM Press, Ltd., 1953).

ness (Deut. 9:4) nor upon her notoriety or numerical superiority but "because Yahweh loves you" (Deut. 7:7–8). Yahweh is the God of steadfast love (ḥesed) who remains faithful to those loving and obeying him but who destroys those showing their "hatred" of him through disloyalty (Deut. 7:9–11).

Deuteronomy presents the people of Yahweh as a unique and chosen community, the elect people of God. As the elect of God, Israel was to be a unified nation, a theocratic community, a holy (separate) people. The ideal for the people of God in the Deuteronomic traditions appears to have been the tribal confederation of early Israelite history. The institution of kingship is considered a concession granted by Yahweh, but one hedged with restrictions (Deut. 17:14–20). The "Israel" of the book is the "all Israel" of the time before the creation of the two monarchical states after the death of Solomon. This ideal of Israel and Judah as one people, united, with a common history and a common future had survived the decades of divisiveness and reasserted itself in Josiah's reforms and the Judean revival.

The people of Yahweh in Deuteronomy is understood as a theocratic community ruled over by Yahweh and his law. The law, in addition to the Land of Canaan, was understood as the basic gift of Yahweh to his people, a gift providing guidance in the human-divine relationship and in human affairs, offering life to the faithful.

> Yahweh commanded us to do all these statutes, to fear Yahweh our God, for our good always, that he might preserve us alive, as at this day. (Deut. 6:24; see chs. 5:32–33; 12:28; 13:17–18.)

The law is not only to be obeyed, it asks for an inner assent, a commitment. Throughout the book, emphasis is placed on the assertion that Yahweh's covenant was not a matter of the past but was rather a reality of the present, addressed to the hearer (Deut. 5:2–3; 6:1). Loyalty to the commandments was to be based upon an assurance of Yahweh's redemption of his people from Egyptian slavery (Deut. 6:20–25). This inner assent to the law is synonymous with the Israelite's love of Yahweh. One should love Yahweh with "heart, soul, and might" and the words that Yahweh commands should be upon "the heart" (Deut. 6:5–6). To love Yahweh was to obey his commandments; to hate him was to disobey his statutes (Deut. 7:9–11). Because of this demand for assent, much of the Deuteronomic traditions were not so much legal stipulations as moral discourse intended to instill a humane pattern of behavior.[11] The admonition to generous lending and sharing, concern for the wage earner, and the reiterated phrase "remember you were a slave in Egypt" appealed to the conscience of the individual and could not be buttressed with the threat of legal punishment by the community (Deut. 15:7–11; 16:11–14; 24:14–22).

Israel was not only called to be a unified theocratic nation, it was also to be a holy, separated people. Or, to state it differently, Israel was "a people holy to Yahweh," which placed upon the nation a number of exclusivistic demands in their relationship to other people. The majority of these demands are

---

[11] See Moshe Weinfeld, "The Origin of the Humanism in Deuteronomy," *Journal of Biblical Literature*, LXXX (1961), pp. 241–247.

rooted in the ideology of the earlier tribal holy wars fought in the name of Yahweh. The traditions demanded the extermination of the inhabitants of the Land of Canaan. Israel was to show no mercy in dispossessing the population, nor was she to spare the sacred places and sanctuaries in the land (Deut. 6:18–19; 7:1–5; 7:16–26; 12:29–31; 19:1–2; 20:16–17). Intermarriage with the indigenous population was strictly forbidden, since this might turn the Israelites away from Yahweh (Deut. 7:3–4). Prophets, kinsmen, and cities that were guilty of apostasy from Yahwism were to be put to the sword without mercy (Deut. ch. 13). In the Deuteronomic traditions, the great national sin was the adoption of customs and worship from the Canaanite population. The vestiges of religious beliefs and practices of the pre-Israelite inhabitants aroused horror in the composers of the book.

In addition to an emphasis on "One God, One People," the Deuteronomic theology emphasized "One Cult":

> Take heed that you do not offer your burnt offerings at every place that you see; but at the place which Yahweh will choose in one of your tribes. (Deut. 12:13–14.)

The religion of earlier days had, of course, not required the exclusion of all Yahweh sanctuaries except one. (The prophet Elijah, for example, had condemned the Israelites for having torn down Yahweh's altars; see I Kings 19:10–14). The idea of the sinfulness of outlying Yahwistic sanctuaries cannot predate Hezekiah. The older law concerning the construction of altars promised that Yahweh would come and bless "in every place" where he was properly worshiped (see Ex. 20:21–26). The centralization of worship was a logical deduction from the Deuteronomic perspective and Jerusalem's needs. One God and one people should utilize one place of worship that would exclude pagan practices and the tendency to worship Yahweh the deity of specific shrines that could develop into Yahwistic pluralism. But primarily, one cult bound the people closer to Jerusalem.

The Deuteronomic reformers recognized that the restriction of sacrifice to one cult place would mean the loss of livelihood for numerous priests in the local and provincial sanctuaries. Thus the book stipulated that "country priests" shall have every right to officiate at the central shrine and to share in the benefits of this service (Deut. 18:6–8), a regulation that, however, was not followed (see II Kings 23:9).

The centralization of the cult carried with it the desacralization of much of Israelite life. In earlier times, every slaughter of an animal had been a sacrifice, a sacral undertaking; but with only one place of sacrifice in the land, the slaughter of animals in places far from Jerusalem became a secular or nonreligious event (Deut. 12:15–16, 20–24). Passover, which had previously been a home festival of an apotropaic character involving the slaughter of a lamb, the magical smearing of the blood, and the roasting of the whole animal without the breaking of a single bone (see Ex. 12:1–15), became a pilgrim festival and allowed the animal to be from the herd as well as from the flock, to be cooked as any other sacrifice and without any reference to the blood ritual (Deut. 16:1–

8). The tithe that had previously been offered in kind and in season at the local sanctuary could now be turned into money and periodically taken to the central sanctuary and used to purchase representative offerings there (Deut. 14:22–29).

The Origin of Deuteronomy. If an early form of Deuteronomy was the law book found in the Temple, how did it get there and who was responsible for the book's origin? [12] Unfortunately, no definitive answers can be given to these questions. In the broadest perspective, the Deuteronomic reformation carried out by Josiah can be seen as part of widespread seventh-century attempts to restore the past which involved many Near Eastern states.[13] Such attempts to revive the past and to return certain aspects of the culture to a previous stage were made in Egypt and Mesopotamia, where ancient rituals, writings, and ruins were rehabilitated. In the narrowest perspective, the book was utilized to support a nationalist move on the part of Josiah in an attempt to restore the grandeur of the Davidic state.

It is almost universally acknowledged that the vast majority of the legal traditions in Deuteronomy are older than 622 B.C. The parallels between Hosea and Deuteronomy suggest that these traditions may have originated in the north, were carried south after the fall of Samaria (722/721 B.C.), and were edited into book form during the reign of Manasseh, being influenced by or partially responsible for Hezekiah's attempts at reform. The rather severe restrictions placed on the king (Deut. 17:14–20) speak against any direct royal origin. The extremely militant character of much of the book which is interspersed with a holy war outlook could be traced back to circles such as the Levites and sons-of-the-prophets. Northern traditions at home in a Levitic or prophetic circle[14] probably were brought to Jerusalem, where they were edited to emphasize the centralization of the cult, but they argued that Yahweh himself did not dwell in the cult place but only his "name" (Deut. 12:1–14) and they stressed the election of the entire nation over against the Jerusalemite claim of Davidic election. The militant tone of the book, the emphasis on the holy war, and the stress on the total possession of the Promised Land may have been elements in the oldest of these traditions but they were certainly useful to Josiah in his territorial, anti-Assyrian struggles. The king was probably forced to resort to the ancient tribal military recruitment of troops, since it is doubtful if Judah had possessed any sizable standing army since the days of Hezekiah's revolt.

The Significance of the Deuteronomic Reformation. Without the Deuteronomic reformation, it is doubtful if the Judeans would have survived the overwhelming shock of the subsequent tragic events surrounding the fall of Jerusalem and the Babylonian exile. Deuteronomy provided Israel with a philosophy

---

[12] See Nicholson, *Deuteronomy and Tradition*, pp. 37–106.
[13] See W. F. Albright, *From the Stone Age to Christianity*, 2d ed. (Doubleday Anchor Books, 1957), pp. 314–321.
[14] On the prophetic and Levitic preservation of Yahwistic traditions, see N. W. Porteous, "The Prophets and the Problem of Continuity" and "Actualization and the Prophetic Criticism of the Cult," in his *Living the Mystery: Collected Essays* (Oxford: Basil Blackwell, 1967), pp. 113–125, 127–141.

of history which taught that historical success and fidelity to Yahweh go hand in hand and that historical calamity is due to infidelity and apostasy. This philosophy of history provided a perspective through which the past could be interpreted and tragedy endured.

The Deuteronomic reformation was the first time in Israelite and Judean history that a book, understood as the will of Yahweh, had been accepted and enforced as the religious and political law of the land. With the desacralization of much of the cult, religion tended to become more of a religion of the book and less a religion of the cult. Deuteronomy, as one of its requirements, stipulated that one should not "add to or take away from" its commandments (Deut. 12:32). This meant, of course, that the book required its own canonization; that it become the one Torah (law) for understanding the life and practices of the "One God, One People, One Cult." Deuteronomy proclaimed itself as what Yahweh had given once and for all, and thus it presented a norm by which to measure right practice and belief. This development opened the way for the formation of the institution of the synagogue with its emphasis on the reading and the exposition of the Torah. Simultaneously, Deuteronomy stressed the role of the family as a teaching unit in the life of the community, making the family responsible for instruction in "the testimonies, statutes, and ordinances" (Deut. 6:20–25). Finally, the Deuteronomic reformation firmly established Jerusalem as the center of cultic practices and pious affection and thus buttressed the claims of the city's uniqueness and thereby pervaded the Zion theology with Mosaic authority. Moses had spoken of the "place which Yahweh would choose," and in the light of the Deuteronomic reformation, that place was Jerusalem.

THE FALL OF JERUSALEM

Josiah met his death at the battle of Megiddo in 609 B.C. when he sought to halt the northward advance of the Egyptian army under Pharaoh Necho, who was marching to the aid of Asshur-uballit, the last Assyrian king, who was trying desperately to salvage a part of the former empire (II Kings 23:28–30). With Josiah's death, his kingdom disintegrated. Egypt took over the control of Palestine and asserted its authority by deposing Jehoahaz, who had been elevated to the kingship in Jerusalem, and by replacing him with his brother Eliakim (whose throne name was Jehoiakim) and subsequently by taking Jehoahaz into exile in Egypt, where he died (II Kings 23:31–35).

Judah was subjected to Egyptian vassalage for only a short time. In 605 B.C., Egyptian control over Palestine was broken when the Babylonian Nebuchadrezzar routed the Egyptian army at the battle of Carchemish and followed this victory by further successful military ventures in Syria-Palestine. Jehoiakim capitulated and was allowed to remain on the throne. For a time he was a loyal vassal to Babylon, but soon (in 598 B.C.) he refused to pay tribute. The reasons for Jehoiakim's revolt were probably numerous. One would have suspected adventurous programs from Josiah's sons, and Jehoiakim was certainly capable of daring ambitions. The extreme nationalism of the period of the Deuteronomic

CHART 6: FROM THE FALL OF SAMARIA TO THE
FALL OF JERUSALEM (722–586 B.C.)

B.C.	EGYPT	PALESTINE	SYRIA-MESOPOTAMIA
722	Egypt—reassertion of strength	Israel incorporated into Assyrian empire	Assyrian empire
	Twenty-fifth Dynasty	Hezekiah (715–687)	Sargon II (722–705)

Philistia, Edom, Moab, and Judah revolt against Assyrians under influence of
Egypt (714–711). Revolt suppressed

			Sargon murdered Sennacherib ruler (705–681)

General revolt throughout the empire, led in Palestine by Hezekiah, supported by
Egypt (705–701)

		Sennacherib invades Judah (701); Hezekiah pays tribute	
700			
		Manasseh (687–642) Subservience to Assyria	Sennacherib murdered Esarhaddon (680–669)
	Egypt invaded by Assyria Memphis taken (671)		Assyrian empire at its height
	Thebes sacked (663)		Asshurbanipal (669–627)
	Twenty-sixth Dynasty Egypt rebels against Assyria		
	Psammetichus I (663–609)	Amon (642–640) Josiah (640–609)	
		Beginning of Yahwistic reformation	Death of Asshurbanipal
			Nabopolassar king of Babylon (626–605)
		Discovery of law book (622/621)	rebels
			Invasion of Scythians and others
	Necho (609–593)	Death of Josiah at battle of Megiddo; Jehoahaz	Fall of Nineveh (612)
	Necho challenges Babylon	rules for three months	Assyria and Egypt join forces against Babylon
		Jehoiakim (609–598) Egyptian vassal (609–605)	
			Egypt defeated at battle of Carchemish (605);
		Babylonian vassal	Nebuchadrezzar king
600		Rebels against Babylon Jehoiakim dies (598)	(604–562)
		Jerusalem taken (March 16, 597)	
		Jehoiachin exiled after three months' reign	
	Psammetichus II (593–588)	Zedekiah (597–586)	
	Hophra (588–569)	Judah joins revolt against Babylon (588)	
		Jerusalem destroyed (586)	
		Judeans exiled; Judah incorporated into Babylonian empire	

reformation was still a vital factor in Judean life and was publicly preached by some prophetic circles. In 601 B.C., Egypt had fought Babylonian troops to a draw in the Palestine area, and no doubt Jehoiakim's pro-Egyptian tendencies saw in Egypt a means to escape Babylonian bondage. The Babylonian army laid siege to Jerusalem and seized the city on March 16, 597 B.C.[15] Jehoiakim had died before Jerusalem was taken and was succeeded by Jehoiachin. The latter was taken prisoner and carried along with the leading citizens and artisans into exile in Babylon (II Kings 24:1-16). The references in II Kings 24:14 and 16 mention deportations of ten thousand and eight thousand respectively, although Jer. 52:28 puts the total number at precisely 3,023, which may be only a reference to some special category of persons.

Nebuchadrezzar spared the city of Jerusalem and allowed the Davidic family to continue its rule by placing on the throne an uncle of Jehoiachin, whose

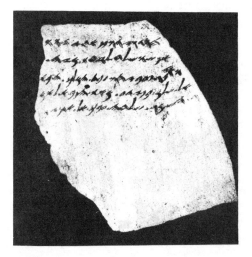

One of the Lachish Letters discovered in 1935 in the ruins of the Judean city of Lachish. These letters, written on pottery fragments, describe some of the efforts involved in trying to halt the advance of Nebuchadrezzar and also report some opposition to Judah's war against Babylonia.

AMERICAN SCHOOLS OF ORIENTAL
RESEARCH

throne name was Zedekiah. The latter soon succumbed to the enticements of Egypt and rebelled against Babylon. Jerusalem was again placed under siege, this time for a period of over two years. Zedekiah, who had been placed in a treaty relationship to Nebuchadrezzar (Ezek. 17:13), was thus guilty of covenant infidelity and after being captured was forced to watch the slaughter of his sons before being blinded (II Kings 25:1-7). Such punishment was no doubt an element in the international treaty agreement.[16] This time Jerusalem was treated without pity.[17] The temple and the town were looted and burned,

---

[15] The exact date is from the Babylonian annals; see Wiseman, *Chronicles of Chaldaean Kings*, pp. 32–37.

[16] The Assyrian treaty mentioned above in note 1 refers to such acts as the punishment for disobedience. See Matitahu Tsevat, "The Neo-Assyrian and Neo-Babylonian Vassal Oaths and the Prophet Ezekiel," *Journal of Biblical Literature*, LXXVIII (1959), pp. 199–204.

[17] On the last years and fall of Jerusalem, see Abraham Malamat, "The Last Kings of Judah and the Fall of Jerusalem," *Israel Exploration Journal*, XVIII (1968), pp. 137–156.

the walls of the city were pulled down, large elements of the population were exiled, and the state was incorporated into the Babylonian provincial system, with a governor appointed to administer the area (II Kings 25:8–22).

JEREMIAH

The prophetic career of Jeremiah spanned the years that saw the meteoric glory of the reign of Josiah followed by the political agitation and turmoil between Egypt and Babylon, whose desire for conquest ground Judah and Jerusalem into the dust. The beginning of Jeremiah's prophetic activity is dated to the thirteenth year of Josiah's reign (627 B.C.; Jer. 1:2), a time that closely coincided with the beginning of the Yahwistic reformation and the final collapse of Assyrian power.[18]

Because of the richness of the biographical material in The Book of Jeremiah, we know more about this prophet than any other in ancient Israel. For our knowledge of Jeremiah's origin and family background, we are dependent, however, on the few introductory comments of the book (Jer. 1:1–3) which say that he was from a priestly family that lived in the town of Anathoth. One is tempted to associate the prophet's priestly ancestry with Abiathar, who was David's priest during his days as an outlaw and who was banished by Solomon to his home in Anathoth for his support of Adonijah in the latter's struggle with Solomon for the throne. Conclusive evidence for such a genealogy is lacking, however.

Jeremiah's description of his call to prophecy (Jer. 1:4–19) stresses his sense of vocation, his predestination to a prophetical career.

> The word of Yahweh came to me saying,
> "Before I formed you in the womb I knew you,
> and before you were born I consecrated you;
> I appointed you a prophet to the nations."
>
> (Jer. 1:4–5.)

Jeremiah's protest to Yahweh that he was only a youth (Jer. 1:6) and the fact that he was active until at least about 580 B.C. suggest that Jeremiah, like Josiah, was an active Yahwist at a young age. Jeremiah states that Yahweh promised him a dual role—"to pluck up and to break down, to destroy and to overthrow, to build and to plant" (Jer. 1:10)—and one that would elicit the opposition of his contemporaries (Jer. 1:8, 17–19). Jeremiah told of two initial experiences through which Yahweh spoke to him. These were the intuitive experiences of the almond rod and the boiling pot (Jer. 1:11–16). In the former, Jeremiah saw a stick of almond wood (shaqed), and its name reminded him that Yahweh was watching (shoqed) over his word and would bring it to fulfillment. In the

---

[18] This date has been challenged by several scholars; see J. Philip Hyatt, "The Beginning of Jeremiah's Prophecy," *Zeitschrift für die alttestamentliche Wissenschaft*, LXXVIII (1966), pp. 204–214. For a defense of the traditional view, see H. H. Rowley, "The Early Prophecies of Jeremiah in Their Setting," in his *Men of God*, pp. 133–168. For the historical background to the prophet's oracles, see Gottwald, *All the Kingdoms of the Earth*, pp. 239–302.

latter, the prophet saw a boiling pot tipping over toward the south and about to spill its contents, symbolizing the coming destruction from the north that Yahweh would bring upon his people in executing his judgment upon them for their wickedness and apostasy.

During the early years of his ministry (reflected in Jer., chs. 2 to 6), Jeremiah's preaching revolved around two foci: the syncretistic religious practices of Judah and Jerusalem and the coming destruction by the enemy from the north. In his castigation of Judean Baalism, there are numerous parallels between Jeremiah and Hosea. The prophet condemned the nation for being an unfaithful bride who had lost her love for her husband and had become an international courtesan relying on Egypt and then Assyria (Jer. 2:1–19). The people were compared to a common prostitute who sought out lovers (foreign powers and other gods) like a young female animal in its breeding season. The nation had played the harlot "upon every high hill and under every green tree," and her gods were as numerous as her cities (Jer. 2:20–37). Such Baalism and sexually oriented religion were portrayed as symptomatic of the nation's desertion of Yahweh.

> I thought
>> how I would set you among my sons,
> and give you a pleasant land,
>> a heritage most beauteous of all nations.
> And I thought you would call me, My Father,
>> and would not turn from following me.
> Surely, as a faithless wife leaves her husband,
>> so have you been faithless to me, O house of Israel,
>>> says Yahweh.
>
> (Jer. 3:19–20.)

Jeremiah proclaimed the coming of disaster from the north which he envisioned as bringing total destruction upon the land, even accompanied by cosmic disturbances (Jer. 4:5–31).[19] Who this enemy was is not stated in the texts. Scholars have seen in "the enemy from the north" references to Assyria, Babylon, or nomadic invaders from what is today southern Russia, among whom were the Scythians. These latter nomadic, horse-riding groups were active in the Fertile Crescent at the time and aided in the downfall of the Assyrian state. However, it isn't really necessary to look for an actual historical reference, since the north was the main origin for Palestine's enemies and Jerusalem was most vulnerable from the north. In Canaanite mythology the gods dwelt in the north, so that the expression "the enemy from the north" could be used as a readily understood, though not necessarily specific, reference to God's avengers and executors of judgment.

Jeremiah's preaching against the current Baalistic and syncretistic religion must be seen in the light of the state of affairs under Manasseh and during the early days of Josiah's youthful rule. The prophet was certainly a spokesman for

---

[19] See Brevard S. Childs, "The Enemy from the North and the Chaos Tradition," *Journal of Biblical Literature*, LXXVIII (1959), pp. 187–198; and Victor Eppstein, "The Day of Yahweh in Jeremiah 4:23–28," *Journal of Biblical Literature*, LXXXVII (1968), pp. 93–97.

reform and a return to Yahwism. Similarly, the prophet Zephaniah, who preached during the reign of Josiah, called for a return to Yahwism and the elimination of foreign cults, promising the coming of the destructive "day of Yahweh" if this were not done. Zephaniah is said to have been a great-grandson of Hezekiah (Zeph. 1:1); if the latter were the reforming king, then Zephaniah was a prophetic spokesman for reform from within the royal family. There is no reason not to assume that the preaching of Jeremiah and Zephaniah helped to trigger some of the Yahwistic reforms. The Book of Jeremiah contains no explicit reference to the Deuteronomic reformation, unless Jer. 11:1–8 is an exception, which would suggest that Jeremiah was silent about or in favor of the movement.[20] Jeremiah certainly had a high opinion of Josiah (see Jer. 22: 15–16).

Following the death of Josiah, the prophet renewed his public proclamations with a sermon in the Temple courtyard, perhaps on the occasion of the new king's coronation at the New Year festival, and denounced the confidence of the Jerusalemites in their city and its Temple. The sermon and its aftermath are given in two accounts in the book (Jer., chs. 7 and 26). In his sermon Jeremiah denounced the constant and confident gibberish about the Temple and the security it offered (Jer. 7:2–4). He promised that Yahweh would destroy the Jerusalem Temple just as he had decimated the house of God at Shiloh (Jer. 7:12–15). The prophet argued that what Yahweh wanted was not fool-hardy confidence nor sacrifice but the obedience of Yahweh's commandments, social justice, and the elimination of foreign gods (Jer. 7:5–10). The people, led by the priests and the prophets, reacted quickly to Jeremiah's outburst and were at the point of killing him for his un-Israelite activity but were prevented from doing so when certain elders recalled that the prophet Micah had said similar things about Jerusalem and had not been put to death (Jer. 26:16–19). This precedent along with support from Ahikam of the influential family of Shaphan saved Jeremiah from the crowd and the king and the fate that befell the prophet Uriah (see Jer. 26:20–24).

Jeremiah and King Jehoiakim were never on friendly terms. Jehoiakim was an egotistical, adventurous, and tyrannical ruler who set about building himself a magnificent palace outside Jerusalem through the use of slave labor.[21] Jeremiah severely rebuked him for this, arguing that a palace does not a monarch make and predicting that the king's dead body would be dragged through Jerusalem like that of an ass and cast outside the city walls (Jer. 22:13–19). In 605 B.C., Jeremiah dictated his earlier sermons to his scribe Baruch in order to have them read publicly in the Temple precinct, where Jeremiah was forbidden to appear (see Jer., ch. 36). The contents of the scroll were so caustic that the officials at the public reading reported the matter to the king, who, after he had had the scroll confiscated and read aloud to him, proceeded to burn the writing by cutting off each column as it was read. Jeremiah subsequently redictated the sermons with harsh comments about the ultimate fate of Jehoiakim.

---

[20] See H. H. Rowley, "The Prophet Jeremiah and the Book of Deuteronomy," in his *From Moses to Qumran*, pp. 187–208.

[21] Remains of this palace have recently been excavated; see Yohanan Aharoni, "Beth-Hac-cherem," in Thomas, ed., *Archaeology and Old Testament Study*, pp. 171–184.

Jeremiah did not limit his prophetical activity to preaching in public or dictating scrolls in private. He also demonstrated and performed symbolic acts to illustrate his beliefs. On one occasion, Jeremiah purchased a pottery flask, gathered an audience of elders and priests, and acted out the coming destruction of Jerusalem (Jer. 19:1 to 20:6). Identifying the pottery vessel with the city, Jeremiah broke the flask, saying that in like manner Yahweh would destroy Jerusalem. It should be recalled that such symbolic rituals as this breaking of a vessel were employed in ancient cultures, and probably in Israel also, to destroy symbolically one's enemies. The symbolization was believed to aid in the actualization of the thing acted out. For this maneuver, Jeremiah was beaten and placed in stocks by the chief of the Temple police. Upon his release the next day the prophet had strong words for his fellow countryman.

After the capture of Jerusalem in 597 B.C., Jeremiah preached for an obedient submissiveness to the Babylonian ruler Nebuchadrezzar, whom the prophet proclaimed as the servant (in the sense of a vassal) of Yahweh and whose rule over the nations he announced as the divine will (Jer., ch. 27). Rebellion against this Babylonian sovereign he saw as tantamount to rebellion against Yahweh. To illustrate his belief, Jeremiah walked the streets of Jerusalem wearing an ox yoke strapped around his neck to focus attention upon his message. On one occasion, while he was walking in the Temple wearing his paraphernalia of protest against the prevailing public opinion, Jeremiah encountered the optimistic prophet Hananiah who was promising the immediate end of Babylonian power and the return of the exiles to Jerusalem (Jer., ch. 28). The confrontation that ensued resulted in the temporary humiliation of Jeremiah, whose sign of submission to Babylon was broken. Not to be daunted, Jeremiah reappeared proclaiming that Yahweh's yoke over the nations was one of iron and unbreakable. Presumably Jeremiah then wore around the city a yoke of iron. The text says that he promised Hananiah that he would die within the year, a prediction that was shortly realized.

Jeremiah's attitude toward the Babylonian exile of 597 B.C. differed widely from that held by the majority of the Jerusalem population. In the communications between the exiles and the Palestinian population, Jeremiah counseled against any expectations of a speedy return to the Promised Land and opposed any attempts of the exiles to rebel (Jer., ch. 29). Instead, Jeremiah advised the exiles to settle down, to go about the routines of life (building, planting, and marrying), and to seek the welfare, not the destruction, of Babylon. He spoke of seventy years before the exilic fate would be changed. Since seventy years was a life expectancy (see Ps. 90:10), Jeremiah was saying that those taken into captivity should entertain little hope that they themselves would ever make it home again. For the rabid nationalistic prophets, Jeremiah's words were treasonable, disheartening his countrymen and giving comfort to the enemy. Zedekiah and his contemporaries in Jerusalem were seen by Jeremiah as bad figs, "so bad that they could not be eaten," while the exiles represented the good figs of Judean society upon whom one could place some hope (Jer., ch. 24).

In many respects, Jeremiah was a singular individual.[22] His position on the

---

[22] See Sheldon H. Blank, *Jeremiah: Man and Prophet* (Hebrew Union College Press, 1961).

events of his day placed him in conflict with the political and religious policies and personalities of that time. He was severely opposed, publicly condemned, ridiculed by the priests and prophets in the religious establishment, and perhaps even threatened by his own family and villagers (see Jer. 11:21–23; 12:6). Much of his time was spent under "house arrest" with restricted privileges. He was imprisoned frequently and publicly beaten. For much of the population, he was a traitor to his nation, a spokesman for the Babylonians, and a prophet without honor. Anguish and suffering were a part of his everyday experience. The collectors and editors of the material associated with Jeremiah provided insight into this aspect of his life through the incorporation of biographical traditions and the so-called autobiographical "confessions of Jeremiah" (Jer. 11:18–23; 12:1–6; 15:10–21; 17:12–18; 18:18–23; 20:7–18). In the latter, Jeremiah laments his condition, appeals to Yahweh for solace, curses the day of his birth, and at times even blames Yahweh for his fate.

> I was like a gentle lamb
>   led to the slaughter.
> I did not know it was against me
>   they devised schemes, saying,
> "Let us destroy the tree with its fruit,
>   let us cut him off from the land of the living,
>   that his name be remembered no more."
>
> (Jer. 11:19.)

> O Yahweh, thou knowest;
>   remember me and visit me,
>   and take vengeance for me on my persecutors.
> In thy forbearance take me not away;
>   know that for thy sake I bear reproach.
>
> (Jer. 15:15.)

> Cursed be the day
>   on which I was born!
> The day when my mother bore me,
>   let it not be blessed!
> Cursed be the man
>   who brought the news to my father,
> "A son is born to you,"
>   making him very glad.
>
> (Jer. 20:14–15.)

> O Yahweh, thou hast deceived me,
>   and I was deceived;
> thou art stronger than I,
>   and thou hast prevailed.
> I have become a laughingstock all the day;
>   every one mocks me.
>
> (Jer. 20:7.)

During the days of the second rebellion against Nebuchadrezzar, Jeremiah advised Zedekiah to surrender, assuring him that this was the will of Yahweh and represented the only sensible course of action (Jer. 38:17–23). As long as he had the freedom of the city, Jeremiah preached that the people should desert to the enemy and surrender to the Babylonian army besieging Jerusalem (Jer. 38:1–3). For such action he was dubbed a traitor, one who sought not "the welfare of this people, but their harm." The prophet spent the last days just prior to the capture of the city as a prisoner, first in a mire-filled cistern and then in the court of the guard (Jer. 38:4–16).

When Jerusalem fell, Jeremiah was granted a number of privileges not accorded to the rest of the population (Jer. 40:1–6). He was granted the freedom to remain in Palestine or go to Babylon or wherever he might choose and was given an allowance of food and a present from the Babylonian commander, apparently at the orders of Nebuchadrezzar (see Jer. 39:11–14). Such special treatment was presumably based on the Babylonians' knowledge of Jeremiah's position in regard to the rebellion, but no doubt by many of his fellow Judeans it was seen as further confirmation of his disloyalty to his own people.

Jeremiah chose to remain in Judah, but he was eventually carried to Egypt by a group who had assassinated the governor appointed by the Babylonians (in 582 B.C.). The last sermons of the prophet were spoken in Egypt, where he declared that Yahweh had given Egypt and her ruler into the hand of Nebuchadrezzar (Jer. 44:30). Nothing is known of the end of Jeremiah's life; he no doubt died an unwilling exile in a foreign land.

EZEKIEL

Ezekiel was a younger contemporary of Jeremiah. He was one of the Judeans carried into exile by Nebuchadrezzar during the first deportation in 597 B.C. Although much of the material in Ezekiel would seem to make better sense if it were addressed directly to the Jerusalem population, the book assumes that Ezekiel's ministry was performed totally among the exiles and that he was only carried to Jerusalem "by the spirit, in visions." [23] The prophet's career, spanning the years from 593 to 570 B.C., was lived out among that group forced into exile in Babylon and settled by the river Chebar, a major canal near the city of Babylon.

The introduction to his book describes Ezekiel as a priest (Ezek. 1:1–3), and no other prophet shows a greater interest in cultic affairs and sacral orders than

---

[23] On the problems of the book, see H. H. Rowley, "The Book of Ezekiel in Modern Study," in his *Men of God*, pp. 169–210. On the historical background, see Gottwald, *All the Kingdoms of the Earth*, pp. 302–329. A good introduction to the prophet's preaching is given in a number of short writings by Walther Zimmerli: "The Special Form- and Traditio-Historical Character of Ezekiel's Prophecy," *Vetus Testamentum*, XV (1965), pp. 515–527; "The Word of God in the Book of Ezekiel," in Wolfhart Pannenberg *et al.*, eds. *History and Hermeneutic*, Vol. IV of *Journal for Theology and the Church* (Harper Torchbooks, 1967), pp. 1–13; and his "The Message of the Prophet Ezekiel," *Interpretation*, XXIII (1969), pp. 131–157.

he. The account of his call to prophesy (Ezek. 1:4 to 3:27) is filled with un-usual imagery and at times defies understanding. Ezekiel says that he saw a vision of God that came with a stormy wind out of the north accompanied by clouds and lightning (during a thunderstorm?). Associated with the wind were four creatures with composite features, partly human and partly animal, each possessing four wings and four faces (of a man, lion, ox, and eagle), perhaps in order to face all four directions at once. Accompanying the creatures were four wheels with unusual features, and above the heads of the four figures was a platform surmounted by a throne upon which Ezekiel saw the likeness of a man (the deity?) surrounded by fire and gleaming bronze and the colors of the rainbow. This psychedelic experience of the prophet appears to draw upon imagery such as the cherubim-borne throne (or Ark) of Yahweh, the protective deities or geniuses of the Babylonians which are shown in their art as possessing features of humans, birds, and animals, and the seraphim attendants of the deity in the Jerusalem Temple as well as upon the call-experiences of such prophets as Micaiah (I Kings, ch. 22) and Isaiah (Isa., ch. 6).

In the account of his call Ezekiel says that he was addressed out of the vision and commanded to go to the people of Israel, a rebellious nation, and to proclaim to them the words of Yahweh so that they would know a prophet had been among them (Ezek. 2:3–7). In preparation for his task Ezekiel was shown a scroll written upon on both sides and containing words of lamentation, mourn-ing, and woe. At the command of the deity, Ezekiel says he ate the scroll, which tasted sweet as honey (Ezek. 2:8 to 3:3). Ezekiel then described himself as being carried by the spirit to Telabib, where he sat overwhelmed for seven days after which he was to be bound by cords and was unable to speak for a time (Ezek. 3:4–27). The latter suggests that the effects of his vision were over-powering and that his contemporaries may have considered him temporarily and violently insane.

The bizarre character of Ezekiel's call-narrative may have been due to the special sensitivities of the prophet, but it also emphasized Ezekiel's belief that Yahweh had not deserted his people nor forsaken the exiles but could still be worshiped by them and was present in Babylon as in Jerusalem. In addition, the vision affirmed Ezekiel's claim that he spoke the word of Yahweh because he had eaten the written word and Yahweh's message had become a part of him to be proclaimed in word and deed to his fellow exiles. Behind the imagery of the written scroll there probably lies the Near Eastern idea of a heavenly book or tablet inscribed by the gods and containing the future destiny of people and world. By having eaten the scroll, Ezekiel could make known the days of woe and mourning that lay ahead.

The employment of symbolic acts and signs to dramatize a point of view and to assist, in a "magical" way, in the accomplishment of what was por-trayed was a characteristic of Israelite prophecy (recall Hosea's naming of the children and Isaiah's and Jeremiah's demonstrations in Jerusalem). For Ezekiel, it appears to have been an obsession. He carried out numerous acts to illustrate the coming destruction of Jerusalem and the horror and fear that would over-take the Judeans. The prophet drew the skyline of Jerusalem upon a large brick and attacked the brick with toy soldiers and siege weapons in order to show

Jerusalem under assault (Ezek. 4:1–3). The length of the Israelite and of the Judean punishment was acted out by the prophet, who lay on his left side for 390 days and on his right side for 40 days (Ezek. 4:4–8). The first symbolized Israel's 390 years of punishment and the latter, Judah's 40 years. Both of these periods of recline were understood by the prophet as his personal sharing in the punishment.

Ezekiel then acted out the conditions of the siege. He mixed food, weighed out scanty portions, measured his drink, and was told to cook his food by burning human excrement but was finally granted the privilege of using cow dung as fuel (Ezek. 4:9–17; see also ch. 12:17–20). The prophet's action elucidated Yahweh's word: "I will break the staff of bread in Jerusalem; they shall eat bread by weight and with fearfulness; and they shall drink water by measure and in dismay" (Ezek. 4:16).

The prophet proceeded to act out the fate of the people at the hands of their enemies (Ezek., ch. 5). Having cut his hair and his beard with a sword, he weighed it into three equal parts. One part he burned, another was cut with the sword, and the remainder was thrown into the air and scattered by the wind. Such was to be the fate of Jerusalem, said Ezekiel: A third of the population was to be consumed in the town, a third to die by the sword, and a third to be scattered among the nations in all directions.

On one occasion the prophet dramatized the coming trip of the Judeans into exile (Ezek. 12:1–16). Taking the meager baggage one would expect to be carried by a fugitive, Ezekiel dug a hole through the wall of his house and crawled through it to symbolize the coming flight of part of the Jerusalem populace.

The death of his wife was used by the prophet to express his belief about the fall of Jerusalem (Ezek., ch. 24). At the time of the siege of Jerusalem, Ezekiel's wife (the delight of his eyes) became ill, and Yahweh's word came to him that he should not mourn her demise nor weep over her death but instead should proceed with his normal affairs. Jerusalem, the delight of every Judean's eyes, was soon also to fall but only to receive her just treatment and thus should not be mourned (see Ezek. 24:6–14).

Why did Ezekiel perform such vivid and often rather bizarre symbolic acts? What did he hope to accomplish? Why did he deem Judah and Jerusalem so worthy of judgment and punishment at Yahweh's hand? It has been suggested that he executed these symbolic acts during the time immediately following his vision when he was incapable of speech (compare Ezek. 3:26–27 with ch. 24:25–27). However, many of his acts seem to have been accompanied by his oral interpretation. At the most elementary level, the prophet employed such acts as attention-attracting devices. One must recall that there were prophets aplenty both in Jerusalem and in the exile, and to attract a hearing was probably no easy matter. But obviously, Ezekiel used such acts as preaching and teaching devices to provide visual and parabolic illustrations to his prophetic commentary on the times. In addition, by acting out these symbols, the prophet saw himself as already sharing in and effecting the event symbolized. Just as a prophet might act out a victory promised by Yahweh (see I Kings 22:10–12), so Ezekiel acted out the coming doom of his people, assured that Yahweh had decreed the destruction. It had been written in the scroll, and Yahweh's word would march to fulfillment.

Much of the preaching of Ezekiel prior to the fall of Jerusalem in 586 B.C. was concerned with the question of the people's guilt and the necessity and purpose of the coming judgment. Ezekiel's predictions of judgment rested on the belief that Jerusalem and the Judeans were guilty of a radical departure from the proper observance of the sacred orders and that the history of Israel and Judah had been one of constant disobedience and religious adultery.

Chapter 8 of the prophet's book describes a visionary experience of Ezekiel in which he claims to have been carried to the sacred precincts of the Jerusalem Temple, where he witnessed the idolatry and debasement of the Jerusalem cult. At the entrance to the inner court stood the "image of jealousy" (Ezek. 8:5–6). Exactly what this was isn't stated, but the image could have been that of some Babylonian deity or perhaps that of a goddess. Within a secret room of the Temple, he saw seventy elders burning incense before beasts and reptiles portrayed upon the wall (Ezek. 8:7–13). At the entrance to the north gate, Ezekiel saw women weeping for the god Tammuz, a Mesopotamian dying and rising god parallel to the Canaanite Baal (Ezek. 8:14–15). In front of the Temple the prophet saw a group of men facing east offering worship to the sun (Ezek. 8:16–18), engaging in solar veneration, a practice widespread in the Near East.

If one assumes the integrity of Ezekiel's report, it appears obvious that there was a widespread proliferation of secret cults as well as general non-Yahwism in the days following the death of Josiah and the first capture of Jerusalem. Such cults probably represented a desperate effort to secure divine aid and response in a time when Judah's political fortunes were in a desperate state, a time when the leaders could say, "Yahweh does not see us, Yahweh has forsaken the land" (Ezek. 8:12). This outbreak of polytheistic cults was probably a response to the political failure of the monotheistic reforms under Josiah and the revolt against Babylon, an expression of religious frustration. It should be recalled that Josiah had begun his major reform under optimistic predictions spoken by prophets in the name of Yahweh (see II Kings 22:14–20 concerning the prediction that Josiah would die a peaceful death, as well as the promises of Deut. 28:1–14).[24] The reforms and political rejuvenation under Hezekiah, a century earlier, had ended in political failure and had been followed by a general period of religious polytheism and syncretism under Manasseh.

Ezekiel followed his description of the secret practices in the Temple precincts with severe denunciations of the Jerusalem community and the proclamation of the city's destruction (Ezek., chs. 9 to 11). The prophet described the actions of Jerusalem's executioners (Ezek. 9:1–11) and depicted Yahweh departing the city, forsaking it, leaving it to its fate (Ezek. 11:23–25).

Ezekiel offered his review of Israelite and Judean history and his portrayal of it as the basis for the judgment of Yahweh. In ch. 16, he described Jerusalem's life and history as that of an unwanted child, the offspring of an Amorite and a Hittite, who was abandoned without even having her umbilical cord cut or

---

[24] See S. B. Frost, "The Death of Josiah: A Conspiracy of Silence," *Journal of Biblical Literature*, LXXXVII (1968), pp. 369–382.

having been given a first bath. Yahweh rescued the forsaken child, guided her to maturity, wed her to himself, and clothed her with fine garments and jewelry. But the wife of Yahweh failed to remain faithful. She took her clothing and jewelry and made images and illegal shrines and offered her children as sacrifices to pagan deities. Jerusalem became an international harlot prostituting herself to the Egyptians, Assyrians, and Chaldeans (Babylonians) but not as an ordinary prostitute, for Jerusalem did not receive payments for her services but instead paid her lovers. Yahweh's verdict upon Jerusalem, according to Ezekiel, was to bring Jerusalem's lovers against her but this time as instruments of his judgment and punishment. (Verses 53–63 of this chapter appear to be hopeful passages later added to the prediction of judgment.)

In ch. 23, Ezekiel summarizes the ignoble history of Israel and Judah in some of the coarsest language found in the Old Testament. The two nations are portrayed as two sisters, the wives of Yahweh, to whom the prophet gave the names of Oholah (Israel) and Oholibah (Judah). The significance of these names is no longer known. The women are depicted, as was Jerusalem, as nymphomaniac harlots on an international scale. Oholah spent her passion on the Assyrians, but the one on whom she doted became her destroyer. Oholibah was more corrupt than her sister, loving Assyrians, Chaldeans, and Egyptians; and Ezekiel proclaimed her destruction:

> You shall drink your sister's cup
>   which is deep and large;
> you shall be laughed at and held in derision,
>   for it contains much;
> you will be filled with drunkenness and sorrow.
> A cup of horror and desolation,
>   is the cup of your sister Samaria;
> you shall drink it and drain it out,
>   and pluck out your hair,
>   and tear your breasts.
>
> (Ezek. 23:32–34.)

Ezekiel not only was concerned with analyzing the past historical guilt of Israel and Judah but also sought to expose the guilt of his contemporaries and to argue that each generation and each individual is judged by Yahweh and is declared guilty or innocent on the basis of its own righteousness. This is most clearly expounded in Ezek., ch. 18. In this chapter the prophet attacked a current interpretation that saw the predicament of the present as punishment for the past or the previous generation's guilt. This understanding of human guilt and divine punishment was summarized in a popular proverb: "The fathers have eaten sour grapes and the children's teeth are set on edge." (Exodus 20: 4–6 stipulates that the sins of the fathers would be visited upon the children to the third and fourth generations. The fall of Jerusalem was understood as the punishment brought on by Manasseh's evil; see II Kings 23:26–27.) Opposing this perspective, Ezekiel declared that if a man were righteous, and he summarizes the conduct of the righteous (Ezek. 18:5–9), he would be declared righteous by Yahweh. The father who has an evil son would not be punished for the acts of his offspring, nor should a son be blamed for the acts of his father:

> The soul that sins shall die. The son shall not suffer for the iniquity of the father, nor the father suffer for the iniquity of the son; the righteousness of the righteous shall be upon himself, and the wickedness of the wicked shall be upon himself. (Ezek. 18:20.)

Ezekiel proceeded to argue that it is not even the past in a man's own life that determines his righteousness or guilt (Ezek. 18:21–32). If the wicked changes and becomes righteous, none of his evil deeds shall be remembered; if a righteous man becomes wicked, none of his good deeds shall be remembered. What Ezekiel advocated was the idea that what determines whether man "shall live or die" is his condition at the moment of Yahweh's judgment; one could say his existential status at the time. For Ezekiel, Jerusalem and Judah's doom was Yahweh's judgment on the current unrighteousness and not the delayed punishment from some guilt of the past. Ezekiel's emphasis on individual responsibility constituted a polemic against a prevalent philosophy of historical judgment which argued that fate is determined by the acts of the past. It also helped to open further the door to an understanding of man's individualism before Yahweh, to a greater sense of guilt and responsibility for evil, and to a greater sense of the importance of personal devotion and repentance. "For I have no pleasure in the death of anyone, says Yahweh God; so turn, and live" (Ezek. 18:32).

12 | PROPHECIES OF A HOPEFUL FUTURE

The sixth century was a time of tragedy and sadness in Jewish history. The cherished symbols of Jewish faith and life—Jerusalem, the Temple, the Davidic dynasty, political independence—had been crushed beneath the heel of the Babylonian army. The people's choicest leaders and craftsmen had been taken into a Babylonian exile. Palestine had been incorporated into the enemy's provincial government.

The sixth century was more, however, than a time of heartrending desperation. It was also a creative epoch.[1] In world history, it was the century of the Ionian philosophers, Zoroaster, Buddha, and Confucius. In Jewish history, it was the century of Jeremiah, Ezekiel, the Isaiah of the exile, and numerous other knowns and unknowns who did so much in the collection and preservation of Israelite traditions. It was a time that saw the flowering of expectations about a renewed and hopeful future and a time that witnessed widespread reassessments and interpretations of the people's past.[2]

THE TRAUMA OF JERUSALEM'S CATASTROPHE

The fall of Jerusalem in 586 B.C. was only a small ripple on the contemporary sea of world history. But to the Judean population it was a shock of cataclysmic character with numerous repercussions in the Judean community.[3] The entire book of Lamentations gives vent and expression to the overriding sense of loss that accompanied the destruction of the city.[4] This book contains five poems

---

Biblical readings: The primary Biblical materials discussed in this chapter are Jer., chs. 30 to 32; Ezek., chs. 37; 47 to 48; and Isa., chs. 40 to 55.

[1] See D. Winton Thomas, "The Sixth Century B.C.: A Creative Epoch in the History of Israel," Journal of Semitic Studies, VI (1966), pp. 33–46.

[2] An excellent discussion of the history and literature of this period is given in Peter R. Ackroyd, Exile and Restoration: A Study of Hebrew Thought of the Sixth Century B.C. (The Westminster Press, 1968).

[3] See Martin Noth, "The Jerusalem Catastrophe of 587 B.C. and Its Significance for Israel," in his The Laws in the Pentateuch, pp. 260–280. The shock of the humiliation of the Davidic king is reflected in Ps. 89:38–52.

[4] On the book of Lamentations, see Norman K. Gottwald, Studies in the Book of Lamentations (London: SCM Press, Ltd., 1954). In later Jewish tradition the book was attributed to Jeremiah, perhaps on the basis of II Chron. 35:25, but without justification.

215

lamenting the fall and status of Jerusalem. Each poem is alphabetic in structure, so that all the lines in the first verse begin with the first letter of the Hebrew alphabet, the second verse with the second letter, and so on. This runs the gamut of the Hebrew alphabet of twenty-two letters (ch. 3 has 22 × 3) or laments the condition, as we would say, "from A to Z." This alphabetic structure was intended for the sake of memory and also to express the completeness of the disaster. Such psalms were perhaps used in regular rituals for mourning the destruction of the city (see Zech. 7:1-7). The pathos of the city is etched in every lament.

> How lonely sits the city
> that was full of people!
> How like a widow has she become,
> she that was great among the nations!
> She that was a princess among the cities
> has become a vassal.
> She weeps bitterly in the night,
> tears on her cheeks;
> among all her lovers
> she has none to comfort her;
> all her friends have dealt treacherously with her,
> they have become her enemies.
> (Lam. 1:1-2.)

The response to the fall of Jerusalem found expression not only in mourning the city's fate but also in animated expressions of hostility toward Judean enemies. Such sentiment is found in the following psalm reflecting the exilic condition:

> Remember, O Yahweh, against the Edomites
> the day of Jerusalem,
> how they said, "Rase it, rase it!
> Down to its foundations!"
> O daughter of Babylon, you devastator!
> Happy shall he be who requites you
> with what you have done to us!
> Happy shall he be who takes your little ones
> and dashes them against the rock!
> (Ps. 137:7-9.)

For many, the fall of Jerusalem led to a surrender of Yahwism and the acceptance of the worship of other gods and the service of other cults. For some, the historical realities must have meant that Yahweh had proved to be a weak god who had simply succumbed to the religion of the conquerors. Ezekiel, ch. 8, and Jer., ch. 44, reflect this return to older cults and the acceptance of the religion of the conquerors. The latter passage shows that the disaster could be interpreted as the failure to worship gods other than Yahweh. The women had complained to Jeremiah:

As for the word which you have spoken to us in the name of Yahweh, we will not listen to you. But we will do everything that we have vowed, burn incense to the queen of heaven and pour out libations to her, as we did, both we and our fathers, our kings and our princes, in the cities of Judah and in the streets of Jerusalem; for then we had plenty of food, and prospered, and saw no evil. But since we left off burning incense to the queen of heaven and pouring out libations to her, we have lacked everything and have been consumed by the sword and by famine. (Jer. 44:16–18; compare 7:16–20.)

The "queen of heaven" in this passage refers to a goddess of love and fertility, such as Astarte or Anat of the Canaanites or Ishtar the Mesopotamian goddess identified with the planet Venus. This argument used against Jeremiah assumed that the exclusive worship of Yahweh forced upon the people, probably in Josiah's reform, led to their ill fate.

The dominant interpretation of the fall of Jerusalem and the collapse of Judean independence saw these events as the deliberate work of Yahweh, as the action of the Judean God against his own people.

> Yahweh has destroyed without mercy
>   all the habitations of Jacob;
> in his wrath he has broken down
>   the strongholds of the daughter of Judah;
> he has brought down to the ground in dishonor
>   the kingdom and its rulers.
> He has cut down in fierce anger
>   all the might of Israel;
> he has withdrawn from them his right hand
>   in the face of the enemy;
> he has burned like a flaming fire in Jacob,
>   consuming all around.
> He has bent his bow like an enemy,
>   with his right hand set like a foe;
> and he has slain all the pride of our eyes
>   in the tent of the daughter of Zion;
> he has poured out his fury like fire.
>   (Lam. 2:2–4.)

The act of Yahweh in destroying his own people was not understood as divine whimsy; it was the just punishment of a righteous God upon his unrighteous followers for their sins and failures. In other words, the prophetical preaching of the coming judgment and the Deuteronomic emphasis on divine punishment provided the framework within which the calamity was understood.

> Yahweh has done what he purposed,
>   has carried out his threat;
> as he ordained long ago,
>   he has demolished without pity;
> he has made the enemy rejoice over you,
>   and exalted the might of your foes.
>   (Lam. 2:17.)

The fall of Jerusalem was associated with the prophetic predictions of the coming "day of Yahweh" (see Amos 5:18–20, which is discussed above, p. 166, and Zeph. 1:10–18). The prophets had spoken of this day as a day of judgment when Yahweh would act in opposition to his own people and annihilate his own followers. The following quotation from Lamentations shows this connection:

> Thou didst invite as to the day of an appointed feast
>   my terrors on every side;
> and on the day of the anger of Yahweh
>   none escaped or survived;
> those whom I dandled and reared
>   my enemy destroyed.
>
> (Lam. 2:22.)

Much of the language used in expressing the trauma of Jerusalem's fall drew from the terminology and ideas used in lamentation psalms which were employed in mourning rituals associated with such calamities as famine, military defeat, sickness of the king, and so on.[5] Such psalms generally gave a description of the distress, expressed confidence in the deity, prayed for deliverance from the disaster, and requested the defeat of the enemy. Psalm 79, which laments the destruction of the Temple, for example, provides a description of the sanctuary's defilement and ruin (Ps. 79:1–4), contains a plea for Yahweh to act and avenge the deed (Ps. 79:5–10), and pleads for the destruction of the enemy with a promise to offer thanksgiving (Ps. 79:11–13). Germane to the lamentation psalm and ritual was the expression of hope concerning the future and the alleviation of the distress.

Allied with the recognition of the fall of Jerusalem as the result of divine judgment was the hope of a promising future, the expectation of merciful and gracious acts of Yahweh that would reverse the status of his people.

> Yahweh will not
>   cast off for ever,
> but, though he cause grief, he will have compassion
>   according to the abundance of his steadfast love;
> for he does not willingly afflict
>   or grieve the sons of men.
>
> (Lam. 3:31–33.)

In the period following the collapse of the Judean state, the prophets turned their attention to the future and became the primary spokesmen of the new era awaiting Yahweh's people. They spoke of the new deeds that Yahweh would perform on behalf of his suffering people. Generally these prophecies focused on a number of the community's ancient concepts and symbols and promised that Yahweh would cause the old events of Israel's past to recur, he would redo them in a greater and more glorious way. The various prophets chose to express

---

[5] On the structure and usage of these psalms, see Claus Westermann, *The Praise of God in the Psalms*, tr. by Keith R. Crim (John Knox Press, 1965), pp. 52–81.

these hopes for the future in different ways, but they emphasized that the exiles would be led out of captivity as their ancestors had been led out of Egyptian slavery, the Land of Promise would be repossessed and allotted to the tribes anew, Mt. Zion and Jerusalem would be rebuilt, and Yahweh's united people would live in peace again. It is to these prophetic expectations and promises about the future that we now turn our attention.

JEREMIAH AND THE NEW COVENANT

Jeremiah's castigation and denunciation of Jerusalemite life would seem to have left open little room for the proclamation of a hopeful future. Yet the prophet, even before the final fall of Jerusalem, preached, like Hosea, that beyond the darkness of calamity there would break the dawn of a new day for Yahweh's people. Jeremiah's interest in this future was dependent, in the first place, on the promises that had been part of the "words of Yahweh" spoken in the deity's name to his worshiping community. Here one could think of the promises associated with the proclamation of the exodus faith as well as the promises of the Davidic and Zion theologies. The prophet was concerned not only with the Yahwistic promises but also with the human conditions that would be needed for Yahweh's people to live in obedience. Would not the recipients of the future and the fulfillments of the promises become, like the Israel of old, disobedient to the demands of Yahweh and recalcitrant in its service?

Three chapters of the prophet's book will allow us to examine his hope for the future. These are Jer., chs. 30–31 and 32, which the vast majority of scholars believes contain, at least in nucleus, authentic words of Jeremiah. In the latter chapter (Jer., ch. 32), dated to the year of the second capture of Jerusalem (587/586 B.C.), the prophet was imprisoned in the court of the guard in the royal palace. One of Jeremiah's kinsmen had taken refuge in Jerusalem and had decided to sell his landholding in Anathoth, possibly because part of the Babylonian army was bivouacked on the field. According to Israelite land laws, the next of kin possessed the first right of purchase, and so Jeremiah bought the land, had two deeds drawn up and witnessed, and had these placed in a pottery vessel for safekeeping "for a long time." Jeremiah interpreted his purchase as an acted parable to show that "houses and fields and vineyards shall again be bought in this land" (Jer. 32:15). The prophet has Yahweh promise a "return to normalcy":

> Just as I have brought this great evil upon this people, so will I bring upon them all the good that I promise them. Fields shall be bought in this land of which you are saying, It is a desolation, without man or beast; it is given into the hands of the Chaldeans. . . . For I will restore their fortunes, says Yahweh. (Jer. 32:42–44.)

In chs. 30 and 31, Jeremiah is much more explicit in regard to the restored fortunes of his people. The introduction to this section refers to it as a "booklet of comfort," perhaps understood as having been written after the beginning of the exile. In his predictions of the future, Jeremiah refers to the future fate of Israel and Judah. Although Israel had ceased to exist as a political entity almost 135 years earlier, the prophets continued to understand the two "states" as one people in their portrayals of the good time coming. Jeremiah refers to the gathering of the exiles from the land of captivity in a great return that would include even those slow in travel: the lame, the blind, and the pregnant, who would travel on a straight path (Jer. 30:10; 31:7–9). The cities of Palestine would be rebuilt, and once again there would be the sound and merriment of song and dance throughout the land (Jer. 30:18–20; 31:4, 13–14). Crops would be planted and vineyards worked and the grain, wine, and oil, and the young from flock and herd would bring sufficiency to meet the needs of the people (Jer. 31:5, 12). The city of Zion would be restored and would again be the center to which pilgrimages were made, so that there would be heard the call even "in the hill country of Ephraim [Israel]: 'Arise, and let us go down to Zion, to Yahweh our God'" (Jer. 31:6). The ruler over the restored community would be no foreigner, no conqueror, but a prince, one of Israel's own (Jer. 30:21) who should be understood as none other than a Davidic ruler.

In the passage concerning Yahweh's making of a new covenant sometime in the future (Jer. 31:31–34), the prophet emphasized what he considered to be the most radical difference between the present and the future.[6] Yahweh's people will themselves be different. This difference between the old and the new will be found in Yahweh's new covenant which will be unlike the covenant made with the fathers which was broken. The newness of the covenant will not be found in a different set of laws. The new covenant would still be centered in the law (torah) of Mt. Sinai, so in this regard there was to be no change, for the problem of the old covenant was not its inadequacy but the Israelites' inability to keep it and to obey its laws. The newness would be in the way in which the law was conveyed and the new people who would result. The old law had been engraved on stone tablets or written on scrolls which man had to be taught and which he sought to obey. In the new covenant, the law would be written on human hearts. Since the heart was understood as the seat of the intellect and the will, this meant that the law would be a part of man's being. Speaking and hearing of the law would be no longer necessary; no one would have to teach his neighbor or be taught, for each would know and obey the law from the least to the greatest. The law would be written into the nature of man and no longer would it be something encountering him from outside with its demands and threat of judgment. Under such conditions, disobedience would be inconceivable. The people of the new covenant would serve Yahweh, who would be their god, and they would be his people and never again would the tragedy of the past be repeated.

---

[6] See Bernhard W. Anderson, "The New Covenant and the Old," in *The Old Testament and Christian Faith*, ed. by him (Harper & Row, Publishers, Inc., 1963), pp. 225–242.

EZEKIEL AND THE NEW PEOPLE IN A RENEWED LAND

According to the present structure of The Book of Ezekiel, the prophet ceased his preaching of judgment upon Judah with the fall of the city of Jerusalem and began to speak instead of a promising future. Chapters 1 to 24 of the book are predominantly oracles of judgment against Judah, then follow chs. 25 to 32 with prophecies against foreign nations, and finally chs. 33 to 48 which are primarily prophecies about the future restoration of Yahweh's people. Examination of a few chapters from this final section will illustrate Ezekiel's perspectives on the coming acts of Yahweh and the resurrection, resettlement, and reorganization of the new people of Yahweh in the renewed Land of Canaan.

Ezekiel, ch. 37, is the well-known chapter about the prophet's vision of the valley of dry bones. Ezekiel was shown a valley filled with bones symbolic of the "death of the exiles," who complained: "Our bones are dried up, and our hope is lost; we are clean cut off" (Ezek. 37:11). The prophet was then asked, "Can these bones live?" or in other words, "Is there any hope for the re-creation of Israel and Judah from the graveyard of exile in a foreign land?" In his vision Ezekiel was told to prophesy over the bones and he did so. The bones rattled and began to join together, sinews and flesh covered the skeletons, and finally they were given breath and stood upon their feet. All of this Ezekiel preached to assure his hearers that Yahweh was to bring his people home to the ancestral land of Israel, put his spirit within them, and they should live. Ezekiel was not speaking of an actual resurrection from the dead, but the granting of a new life to his people. The idea of the granting of the new spirit is not fully developed in Ezek., ch. 37, but is expounded in some detail in Ezek. 36:22–32, where it is said that Yahweh would give a new heart and a new spirit. This is an idea very similar to the concept of the new covenant in Jeremiah's prophecies. This new heart would be a heart of flesh instead of the former heart of stone; that is, in the future Israel would be responsive to Yahweh and with the new spirit she would observe Yahweh's statutes and ordinances and obey the commandments perfectly. When the new Israel remembered her past, she would loathe herself because of her iniquities and abominable deeds.

The prophet says (Ezek. 37:15–23) that he was further commanded to take two sticks, one representing Judah and the other Israel, and to bind them together. Such a symbolic act was a promise that Yahweh would bring both the Israelite and the Judean exiles home from the nations among which they had gone and make them again into a single nation with a united political existence. The future of the Israelites in their ancestral land would involve the Davidic house and the ancient covenant (Ezek. 37:24–28). Ezekiel had Yahweh promise that his "servant David" would rule over the nation as their prince forever. This new life would be characterized by an everlasting covenant of peace and the eternal presence of Yahweh.

The final chapters (40 to 48) of The Book of Ezekiel contain a sketch of the restored community in the Land of Canaan and provide details of Ezekiel's vision of the reconstituted state. According to the prophet, the Land of Canaan in the restoration would be divided among the twelve tribes in equal measure with-

out regard to the previously held boundaries (Ezek. 47:13 to 48:35). This allotment was to be made by dividing the land into thirteen shares running east
to west. Such a distribution of the land suggests that the prophet envisioned
Yahweh's making a new beginning with Israel that would mark a radical break
with the past and no account would be given to any former greatness or significance. In addition, such a division would eliminate rival tribal claims and
equalize holdings and thus end tribal warfare and struggles over rights and territory. In addition to the twelve districts given to the tribes, there would be a
thirteenth area between the tribes of Judah and Benjamin that would be the
location of the ideal city and temple as well as provide property for the priests
and prince. The ideal city (one would assume that the city is the "New Jerusalem," although this identification is not made) would be laid out on a square
with three gates on each side, each gate named for a particular tribe. The name
of this city would be *Yahweh-shamma* ("Yahweh is there"). At the center of
this district was to be located the ideal temple (a description of the temple and
its furnishings as well as the cult and priesthood is given in Ezek., chs. 40 to 46).
The prophet saw in his vision the glory of Yahweh returning to take up residence in the reconstituted temple (the glory had left the Temple prior to the
fall of Jerusalem; see Ezek. 11:22–23). The layout of the temple, its furnishings,
and the orders of the priests are to be set up so as to preserve the purity of the
worship and service of Yahweh and to separate the holy from the profane.

The returned settlers in the land would rejoice, saying, "This land that was
desolate has become like the garden of Eden; and the waste and desolate and
ruined cities are now inhabited and fortified" (Ezek. 36:35). In many respects
the land described by Ezekiel was no longer the rugged hills and valleys of
Canaan but rather an idealistic land with paradise features, indeed, a Garden of
Eden. This is nowhere more evident than in Ezek. 47:1–12. In this passage,
Ezekiel sees a stream flowing from underneath the temple (on the background of
this idea in the Zion theology, see above, pp. 131–134) toward the east into the
Dead Sea region.[7] Ezekiel was led in the stream until it became too deep and
became, in fact, a river. The stream made the waters of the Dead Sea fresh, and
wherever the waters of the stream went, life abounded. Fish filled the waters,
and along the banks of the stream grew marvelous trees (like the tree of life?)
that bore fresh fruit every month and whose leaves possessed miraculous curative
and healing powers. Such a stream would indeed wash Canaan with a touch of
paradise.

Throughout Ezekiel's preaching, there is an emphasis on the actions of Yahweh as the self-vindication of Yahweh among his own people and in the midst
of the nations of the world. The exile was to teach his people to know "that I am
Yahweh God" (Ezek. 23:49) and so the nations of the world "shall know that
the house of Israel went into captivity for their iniquity" (Ezek. 39:23). With
the restoration of the people of Israel, Yahweh would have vindicated his holiness and made visible his honor "in the sight of many nations" (Ezek. 36:36;
39:25–29). This recognition of Yahweh's acts by the nations doesn't mean that

---

[7] See W. R. Farmer, "The Geography of Ezekiel's River of Life," *The Biblical Archaeologist*,
XIX (1956), pp. 17–22, reprinted in *The Biblical Archaeologist Reader*, I, pp. 284–289.

Ezekiel envisioned the conversion to Yahwism of the nations of the world. What it appears to mean is that the nations would recognize Yahweh as the God of Israel and Israel as the people of Yahweh and the nations would allow Israel to live out her obedience to Yahweh in peace. Yahweh's action "in the sight of many nations" made the nations witnesses to the divine activity. As witnesses, the nations could not be indifferent but were themselves involved in the action. For Ezekiel, what was at stake in the exile and in the restoration was none other than the honor of Yahweh himself. Only a restored Israel in the Land of Canaan could vindicate that honor and make the nations know "that I am Yahweh."

DEUTERO-ISAIAH AND THE NEW EXODUS

Another spokesman of an optimistic and promise-filled future was the anonymous prophet of the exile who is referred to as Deutero or Second Isaiah.[8] For a number of reasons, chs. 40 to 66 (and by some scholars, chs. 34 and 35 as well) of The Book of Isaiah are not considered to be directly related to the eighth-century prophet Isaiah and are seen as belonging to the exilic age (chs. 34; 35; 40 to 55) and afterward (chs. 56 to 66). The reasons for isolating this material and relating the central section of The Book of Isaiah to the exilic period have been discussed earlier (see above, p. 177), and may be only summarized here. Isaiah, chs. 40 to 55, presupposes the Jews in exile, Babylon as the world power, the destruction of Jerusalem and the Temple, and the rise of the Persian ruler Cyrus to international prominence and thus must be dated contemporary with these conditions.

The reason that this material was associated with that of Proto or First Isaiah can only be conjectured. Central to the varied collections is a concern with Zion. The Book of Isaiah seems to have grown through the bringing together of various smaller collections (such as Isa., chs. 1; 2 to 12; 13 to 23; 24 to 27; 28 to 31; 32 to 35; 36 to 39) which can actually be broken down into more minute groupings. The attachment of chs. 40 to 55 was simply a further stage in this process of growth of the traditions. Chapters 1 to 39 would not have produced a scroll of comparable length to Ezekiel and Jeremiah and thus would not have allowed for such further addition. The desire in editing some of the prophetical books was to make them end with promising prophecies, and this may have played a part in the editing of Isaiah. It has also been assumed that Isaiah had a number of disciples (see Isa. 8:16), one of whom may have been the anonymous prophet.

The political background to the prophecies of Deutero-Isaiah[9] was the meteoric rise of the Persian ruler Cyrus, who began his career in 559 B.C. as the king of Anshan, a Median vassal state. In 553 B.C. he rebelled and defeated the Median king and became master of his empire. Seven years later, he defeated Croesus, the powerful, wealthy, and legendary king of Lydia, with his capital at

---

[8] See H. E. von Waldow, "The Message of Deutero-Isaiah," *Interpretation*, XXII (1968), pp. 259–287.

[9] See Ackroyd, *Exile and Restoration*, pp. 17–38.

Sardis. People who had lived under the Babylonian yoke saw the rise of Cyrus as a blessed political omen, hailed him as a redeemer-savior, and attributed his rise to the intervention of their own particular deity.

Deutero-Isaiah saw Yahweh as the power behind the triumphs of Cyrus.

> Who stirred up one from the east
>   whom victory meets at every step?
> He gives up nations before him,
>   so that he tramples kings under foot;
> he makes them like dust with his sword,
>   like driven stubble with his bow.
> He pursues them and passes on safely,
>   by paths his feet have not trod.
> Who has performed and done this,
>   calling the generations from the beginning?
> I, Yahweh, the first,
>   and with the last; I am He.
>   (Isa. 41:2–4; see also 41:25–29.)

The prophet did not hesitate to apply to Cyrus all the honorific titles previously reserved in Israelite tradition for the Davidic rulers. Cyrus was designated as the shepherd of Yahweh who was to fulfill all his purposes (Isa. 44:28) and termed Yahweh's anointed (messiah), whose right hand had been grasped by the Israelite deity and whose name was called by Yahweh though Cyrus knew him not (Isa. 45:1–7).

Deutero-Isaiah saw in Cyrus' mushrooming domination of the Near East the dawning of a new day, the beginning of a new epoch for Yahweh's people. It meant the beginning of judgment and punishment for Babylon and the end of judgment and suffering for the exiles. For the prophet, the exile was no accidental event in a purposeless chain of history.

> Who gave up Jacob to the spoiler,
>   and Israel to the robbers?
> Was it not Yahweh, against whom we have sinned,
>   in whose ways they would not walk,
>   and whose law they would not obey?
>   (Isa. 42:24.)

> For your iniquities you were sold,
>   and for your transgressions your mother was put away.
>   (Isa. 50:1.)

The exile was Yahweh's punishment for his people, but now the prophet could proclaim that Israel's guilt had been paid for.

> Comfort, comfort my people,
>   says your God.
> Speak tenderly to Jerusalem,
>   and cry to her

> that her time of service is ended,
>   that her iniquity is pardoned,
> that she has received from Yahweh's hand
>   double [or the equivalent] for all her sins.
> (Isa. 40:12.)

The downfall and destruction of Babylon were proclaimed as imminent events by the prophet (Isa., ch. 47). Although Babylon had once been a pawn in the hand of Yahweh for the punishment of his people, she that was "mistress of kingdoms" had overstepped her mission in her treatment of the exiles, had boasted of her status, and was to become a widow and be forced into servitude and humility. For the prophet, the rise of Cyrus, the downfall of Babylon, and the release of the exiles were simply three aspects of one historical movement.

Deutero-Isaiah's preaching is filled with glowing prophecies concerning the future. Events are to be inaugurated that will dwarf the previous events in Israel's sacred history.

> Remember not the former things,
>   nor consider the things of old.
> Behold, I am doing a new thing;
>   now it springs forth, do you not perceive it?
> (Isa. 43:18–19.)

This new thing which Yahweh is to do may be summed up in the phrase "the new exodus." [10] The prophet depicts the return from exile in the category of a new exodus parallel to the original exodus out of Egypt but far more glorious and wonderful. A highway through the wilderness shall be made ready when the valleys are lifted up and the mountains are made low (Isa. 40:3–5) for the passage of Yahweh and his people. The desert wilderness will be transformed, watered, and will blossom with trees of all types (Isa. 41:17–20).

> I will make a way in the wilderness
>   and rivers in the desert.
> The wild beasts will honor me,
>   the jackals and the ostriches;
> for I give water in the wilderness,
>   rivers in the desert,
> to give drink to my chosen people,
>   the people whom I formed for myself
> that they might declare my praise.
> (Isa. 43:19–21.)

The summons to exit from Babylon (Isa. 48:20–21; 52:11–12) assures the hearers of Yahweh's power to intervene just as he did in the original exodus (Isa. 51:9–11). Those who go forth will not hunger or thirst, nor will the road be hard for them as in the days of the first exodus, and even the mountains shall

---

[10] See Bernhard W. Anderson, "Exodus Typology in Second Isaiah," in Anderson and Harrelson, eds., *Israel's Prophetic Heritage*, pp. 177–195.

break into song, the trees of the field shall clap their hands, and the whole world of nature shall join in the chorus (Isa. 49:9–13; 55:12–13).

According to the prophet, Zion would be remembered and restored, for the city was to Yahweh like a nursing child to its mother or graven upon his hand so that he could not fail to remember her (Isa. 49:14–18).

> How beautiful upon the mountains
>   are the feet of him who brings good tidings,
> who publishes peace, who brings good tidings of good,
>   who publishes salvation,
>   who says to Zion, "Your God reigns."
> Hark, your watchmen lift up their voice,
>   together they sing for joy;
> for eye to eye they see
>   the return of Yahweh to Zion.
>
> (Isa. 52:7–8.)

The prophet proclaimed the transformation of the ruined and desolate Jerusalem (see the descriptions in the book of Lamentations) into the Garden of Eden (Isa. 51:3) and promised that never again would her enemies, the uncircumcised and the unclean, enter her precincts to destroy (Isa. 52:1–2).

Deutero-Isaiah's preaching to his contemporaries often took the form of a disputation speech, that is, a dialogue or discourse with his hearers. Many of his fellow exiles had reached a state of despondency in which their faith had eroded and they no longer believed that Yahweh cared.

> Why do you say, O Jacob,
>   and speak, O Israel,
> "My way is hid from Yahweh,
>   and my right is disregarded by my God"?
> (Isa. 40:27.)

To many in Babylonian captivity, the worship of the native gods with its pageantry and self-assurance must have been an enticement too strong to resist.

Against this lack of confidence in Yahweh and the temptation of Babylonian cults, Deutero-Isaiah used rational arguments, assurances of redemption, emotional appeal, and satirical denunciations. To the argument that the exiles' condition was hid from and disregarded by Yahweh, Deutero-Isaiah reasoned that Yahweh was the creator of the world who did not grow faint and whose knowledge was unsearchable (Isa. 40:27–31). His people was to Yahweh like a sucking child, and could a mother ever finally forsake her own (Isa. 49:14–15)? Just as the priest in the cult or the military leader in the field had assured his listeners of divine concern, so Deutero-Isaiah assured his hearers: "Fear not, for I am with you, be not dismayed, for I am your God" (Isa. 41:10). No other God but Yahweh had predicted the future in the past and brought it to fulfillment. No other God but he could now declare what lay ahead (Isa. 42:9; 44:6–8; 45:20–21; 48:6–8). The prophet proclaimed the absolute uniqueness of Yahweh which led him to expound theoretical monotheism. This emphasis on the existence of one God and the denial of all other finds a clearer expression in Deutero-Isaiah than anywhere else in the Old Testament (Isa. 40:25–26; 45:4–7, 14, 22). Besides Yahweh, there was no other God, only man-made images! The prophet, on the basis of his monotheistic outlook, proceeded to satirize and caricature Babylonian deities and their associated images. The Babylonian gods were depicted as deities whose images were carried as a burden (Isa. 46:1–2), and as gods who must be carried they were one more of life's weights but no redeemer. According to the prophet, images are the products of human workmen (Isa. 40:19; 44: 9–20 which may be a later addition) and heathen gods are impotent, incapable of making known the future (Isa. 41:21–24). Unlike these powerless deities, burdens even to the animals that hauled their idols around (Isa. 46:1), Yahweh was the carrier of human history who had called and cared for Abraham (Isa. 51:1–2) and led Israel through the sea (Isa. 51:9–11) and who would make dawn the new day of redemption.

Deutero-Isaiah envisioned a coming "twilight of the gods." Yahweh's acts of deliverance and the redemption of his people would put to shame the heathen (Isa. 41:11–13; 42:14–17) who would recognize the sovereignty of Yahweh (Isa. 45:22–25). Kings and rulers would prostrate themselves, carry home the scattered people of Yahweh, and be forced to become subject to Israel (Isa. 49: 22–26; 45:14–17). This recognition of Yahweh and his acts by the nations of the world is sometimes expressed in Deutero-Isaiah in very nationalistic terms involving submission to Israel (for example, in Isa. 49:22–26), but often this is expressed in terms of Israel's being a "witness" to the nations (Isa. 43:10; 44:8; 55:4) and Yahweh is said to appeal to the nations to accept him and be saved (Isa. 45:22; 51:5), which implies a universalistic emphasis.

Special emphasis is given in Deutero-Isaiah to a figure called "the servant of Yahweh," and material relating to this figure is generally isolated and designated "the servant songs" (see Isa. 42:1–4; 49:1–6; 50:4–9; 52:13 to 53:12; but see also chs. 41:8–10; 42:18–19; 43:10).[11] These passages have much in common with the rest of the book insofar as general ideas and terminology are concerned. However, due to their particular interest in the servant figure, these songs are more similar to one another than to the rest of the book.[12]

In the first song (Isa. 42:1–4), the servant is spoken of in a divine speech framed as an introductory address. The servant is announced as the chosen of Yahweh, as one who possesses the divine spirit and as one who will bring forth justice (or truth) to the nations. The servant is depicted as a humble and quiet individual but as one who will not fail in his tasks.

In Isa. 49:1–6, the speaker is the servant who addresses the nations and affirms his call by Yahweh in a manner similar to the prophets' autobiographical com-

---

[11] On the problems of the servant's nature and identity, see C. R. North, *The Suffering Servant in Deutero-Isaiah*, 2d ed. (London: Oxford University Press, 1956); and Joachim Jeremias and Walther Zimmerli, *The Servant of God*, rev. ed. (London: SCM Press, Ltd., 1965), pp. 11–44.

[12] Harry M. Orlinsky, *Studies on the Second Part of the Book of Isaiah: The So-called "Servant of the Lord" and "Suffering Servant" in Second Isaiah* (Leiden: E. J. Brill, 1967), points out the overinterpretation, especially Christian, which has frequently characterized the studies on the servant of Yahweh.

ments on their designations (see Jer. 1:4–5). The figure complains of his lack of success, that he has spent his strength for nothing. This complaint, however, is transcended in a reaffirmation of his commitment and of Yahweh's commission. The servant's description of the task assigned him involves gathering and bringing Jacob (Israel) back to Yahweh, raising up the tribes of Israel, as well as being a light to the nations.

The third so-called servant song again appears as a speech of the servant. The primary emphases in this text center on the servant's divine endowments for his task and his commitment to that task in spite of suffering and opposition. Like a prophet, he was instructed and taught by Yahweh that he might comfort the weary. The servant, as in the psalms of lamentation, describes his condition: he has given his back to those who smote him, his cheeks to those who pulled out his beard, and his face has been subjected to shame and spitting. In spite of this condition and opposition, the passage expresses a confidence in Yahweh and an assurance that the adversaries will not triumph but instead shall be worn out like a garment.

The longest and most involved servant song is found in Isa. 52:13 to 53:12. In this passage the two spokesmen are the deity (Isa. 52:13–15; 53:11–12) and a chorus (Isa. 53:1–10) whose makeup (Israel? the nations? the servant's contemporaries?) assumed by Deutero-Isaiah is uncertain. The opening speech of Yahweh proclaims the coming exaltation of the servant. The glory of the servant shall astound the nations and their rulers just as the appearance of the servant— "marred beyond human semblance"—astonished those who saw him. In the choral section, tribute is paid to the servant by those who benefited from his function. The servant is here described as one without attractiveness and beauty, who was despised and unesteemed. The servant is then portrayed as one whose submissiveness is understood as the result of others' transgressions and iniquities but also as the will of Yahweh. Throughout, emphasis is laid on the figure's humility, his innocence, and his lack of rebellion. Isaiah 53:8–9 refers to the servant's being cut off from the land of the living and having made his grave with the wicked. The closing speech of Yahweh proclaims and promises the triumph of the servant and the rewards awaiting him.

How are these songs to be understood? "About whom does the prophet say this, about himself or about some one else?" (Acts 8:34). Our difficulties in understanding this material are due to a number of reasons. In the first place, no prophet in the Old Testament used more poetical imagery and more metaphorical language than Deutero-Isaiah. Many of his forms of speech and much of the content of his oracles are dependent upon the cultic use of the psalms which tended to employ stereotyped and typical terminology. The description of the servant's suffering, for example, is very similar to the psalms of lamentation which sought to depict one's condition in the boldest, most dramatic terms possible (see, for example, Ps. 22). In the second place, it is very difficult to tie in this material with the rest of the book. This may be due to the overall poetical character of the oracles, but such questions as how the servant figure fits into the context of oracles on Cyrus' rise to power, the downfall of Babylon, the new exodus from exile, and the resettlement in the land are left hanging. Thirdly, it is not certain whether the prophet is speaking about some actual entity such as

Israel, the exiles, the suffering Jews, or an actual person such as himself, a contemporary, or some future person, or whether he is speaking of an ideal entity or person.

Various attempts have been made to identify the servant referred to by Deutero-Isaiah. The first such effort is already found in the Biblical text where in Isa. 49:3 the servant is identified with Israel (see Isa. 41:8–10; 42:18–19; 43:10). The references have been seen as autobiographical, as reflective of some past individual such as Jeremiah, Josiah, or Jehoiachin, or as being purely predictive of some future person. No identification, however, is possible, but some of the influences on the prophet's preaching about the servant perhaps can be determined. There was, first, the influence of the cult and worship in which lamentation psalms portrayed the condition of king, community, and people in vivid terms stressing the actual and/or stereotyped suffering, humiliation, and contempt heaped upon the supplicant. This can be seen in a historical context in the so-called lamentations or confessions of Jeremiah. Integral to the lamentation ritual was the prayer for vindication and the hope of restoration beyond the distress. Secondly, the experience of the exile must have been a formative influence on Deutero-Isaiah's thought. Israel and her king had been humiliated, treated as the "laughing stock" of the nations, and subjected to Yahweh's punishment (see, for example, Ps. 89:38–52). This suffering of the exiles and of King Jehoiachin was considered a means of discipline for a purpose just as the earlier prophets had suggested. If so, then this suffering was in a way experienced by the exiles to a degree not shared by those Judeans who were not "cut off from the land." In this light, the prophet could understand suffering as serving a mediating, sacrificial role. Thirdly, the thought of the relationship between Israel and the nations was a specific problem of the exile. In the servant, Deutero-Isaiah sought to relate suffering and witnessing to the question of Israel's role in the world of the nations. Finally, the problem of the suffering of the innocent and the just seems to have been a special concern in the exilic period. The problem of punishment and guilt was dealt with in Ezekiel, and in the biographical material on Jeremiah the prophet's suffering was a paramount concern. In the Deuteronomic portrayal of Moses, the leader of Israel's first exodus is shown as a mediator between Israel and Yahweh, as one who suffered on behalf of Israel, and as the servant of God (Deut. 3:23–26; 4:21; 9:25–29; see also Ex. 32:32). This similar interest in the vicarious suffering on behalf of others is of course the hallmark of the servant songs.

13 | EXILIC INTERPRETATIONS
OF THE PAST

During the exilic period (586–538 B.C.), two major histories of Israel were completed which sought to provide interpretations of Israel's and Judah's past and to offer policies and programs of action for the reestablishment of community life. These two works were the Deuteronomic history and the Priestly history. The former surveyed the period of history extending from the time of Moses and the conquest of Canaan to the Babylonian exile. This extended work included the material now found in the books of Joshua, Judges, I and II Samuel, and I and II Kings. The Priestly history, now found almost exclusively in the Pentateuch, traced the development of Israel's sacral orders, practices, and institutions encompassing a time span from the creation of the world until the time of the conquest of Palestine. Both of these works represent a terminal stage in the collecting and editing of older traditions. In many ways, these histories are compilations of earlier historical and legal traditions organized to reflect particular viewpoints and perspectives and supplied with interpretative frameworks.

THE DEUTERONOMIC HISTORY

The title applied to this work stems from the close similarity of its primary emphases to those of the Deuteronomic traditions (on the latter, see above, pp. 196–201). The original book of Deuteronomy, which formed the law book of the Yahwistic reformation under Josiah, seems to have been incorporated into the Deuteronomic history and a general introduction, now found in Deut., chs. 1 to 4, was added as a prologue to the entire work. Thus the term "the Deuteronomic history" refers to Deuteronomy–Joshua–Judges–I and II Samuel–I and II Kings.[1]

Biblical readings: The structure and outlook of the Deuteronomic history can be seen in Deut., chs. 1 to 4; Josh., ch. 23; I Sam. 12:6–25; II Sam., ch. 7; I Kings 8:22–53; and II Kings 17:7–41. Material from the Priestly history discussed in this chapter is found in Gen., chs. 1:1 to 2:4a; 5; 6 to 8; 9:1–17; 17; and Ex., ch. 6.

[1] On the relationship between Deuteronomy and the Deuteronomic history, see Nicholson, *Deuteronomy and Tradition*, pp. 107–118. A full discussion and bibliography on the Deuteronomic history are given by Ackroyd, *Exile and Restoration*, pp. 62–83.

Whether the Deuteronomic history was produced by a single author-editor or by a group or circle can no longer be determined. Whether the work was written by exiles in Babylon or by Judeans who remained in Palestine is also an uncertainty. The similarity in outlook between the book of Deuteronomy and this history suggests that the circle responsible for and responsive to the Yahwistic reformation and Josiah's law book continued in existence after the death of Josiah and the fall of Jerusalem and that it was this group which interpreted the nation's history in terms of the Deuteronomic theology. The last event referred to in the book of II Kings (25:27–30) concerns the release of King Jehoiachin from Babylonian imprisonment in 561/560 B.C. The final form of the Deuteronomic history cannot therefore predate the thirty-seventh year of the exile. The history speaks out of and to Judeans under Babylonian rule, many of whom were aliens in a foreign land.

The Purposes of the Deuteronomic History. This history of Israel from the conquest to the exile was written in the shadows of the tragic events of 721 and 586 B.C. One might say that it was composed amid the ashes of the Holy City of Jerusalem. One obvious purpose of the Deuteronomic history was to explain why the destruction of Samaria and Jerusalem had taken place, why the cherished institutions of the sacred city, the chosen dynasty, and the holy cult had been obliterated with the destructive swipes of foreign swords. Such an explanation was made not on the assumption of Yahweh's arbitrariness but rather to show that the curtain had dropped because of the people's long history of unfaithfulness to Yahweh and disobedience to the Torah. The course of Israel's history had been the result of the covenant curse upon covenant disobedience.[2]

The Deuteronomic history was more than just a reprimand of a faithless people. It was also an exilic call to repentance and a return to the Torah of Yahweh. It was a call to the reaffirmation of faith, to a new expression of loyalty to Yahweh.

Another purpose was to proclaim hope, the promise of better days, to a shaken and disturbed people. The work holds out the assurance that Yahweh had punished but had not completely forsaken; he had rejected his people but had not abandoned them forever. Judgment, punishment, and hope were declared to be integral parts of Yahweh's word. Beyond the chasm created by the word of judgment lay the promise of the fulfillment of the word of hope.

A final purpose of the history was the presentation of the Deuteronomic Torah as the basis for a new community life. The program for reconstruction was to be founded on the stipulations and requirements of Deuteronomy. To this extent, the circle responsible for the Deuteronomic history advocated that the new Israel beyond the exile should be reconstructed along the lines of the Yahwistic reformation principles of Josiah's day. Josiah's reformation had not been too little but only too late. The Deuteronomic history proposed that the post-exilic community should anchor its foundations in the Deuteronomic Torah.

---

[2] See Walter Brueggemann, "The Kerygma of the Deuteronomic Historian," *Interpretation*, XXII (1968), pp. 387–402.

The Nature of the Deuteronomic History. The writer (or writers) of the Deuteronomic history was as much a compiler and editor as he was a creative author. Behind this theological history there are a number of earlier traditions, some probably already in literary form and others still oral. The Throne Succession Story in II Sam., chs. 9 to 20, and I Kings, chs. 1 and 2, prophetic legends such as the Elijah and Elisha traditions found in I Kings, ch. 17, to II Kings, ch. 13, and archival materials, such as Temple lists and court annals, were in fairly finished form at the time the work was produced and were utilized by the editor and often incorporated into his work with practically little or no comment. In addition, various forms of folk stories and legends, especially about premonarchical heroes, were available for usage by the author.

The particular emphases in the work led to the selection and use of materials that tended to support the writer's perspective. Frequent references are made to sources upon which the Deuteronomic historical traditions were dependent. Some of these were such works as the Book of the Acts of Solomon (I Kings 11:41), the Book of the Chronicles of the Kings of Judah, and the Book of the Chronicles of the Kings of Israel. These works must have been extensive historical, annalistic writings. Unfortunately, the Deuteronomic history included only the monarchical material that the writer viewed as pertinent to his purposes (although every king in Israel and Judah is discussed). Thus the book does not provide us with a thorough and complete history of Israel and Judah but with a theological version of the people's past.

The judgments and perspectives of the Deuteronomic history were expressed not only through the selection of the materials that were utilized but also in passages composed by the author that appear throughout the work. Some of the writer's reflections and theological emphases appear in the form of speeches that are placed in the mouths of the people's important leaders or are attributed to prophetical spokesmen. Other explanations and mediations are placed in the texts as summary statements and evaluations by the writer. It is in these speeches and summaries that one can most easily discover the primary theological emphases of the writer.

The Theological Emphases of the Deuteronomic History. According to the Deuteronomic historian, Yahweh's people were confronted at every important juncture in their history with the summons to obey the law and with the promise of blessing for obedience and with the threat of the curse for disobedience. In Deut., chs. 1 to 4, Moses, just prior to the conquest of Canaan, summarizes the people's past and explains how Yahweh had guided them through the wilderness and disciplined them in the desert and then he calls the people to an obedience to the statutes and ordinances of Yahweh.

> And now, O Israel, give heed to the statutes and the ordinances which I teach you, and do them; that you may live, and go in and take possession of the land which Yahweh, the God of your fathers, gives you. (Deut. 4:1.)

This summons to obedience with its assurance that "it may go well with you, and with your children after you, and that you may prolong your days in the land which Yahweh your God gives you for ever" (Deut. 4:40) is followed by a warning against disobedience to Yahweh's commands and especially the worship of the gods of the Land of Canaan (Deut. 4:9–24). The writer then has Moses, speaking to the assembled people viewing the Promised Land from the plains of Moab, issue a threat to the community which assures the hearers that if they act corruptly, then they will perish from the land and Yahweh will scatter them among the nations (Deut. 4:25–28).

In Josh., ch. 23, Moses' successor, Joshua, addresses the people after the conquest of the land and its allotment to the tribes but before the tribal settlements. The Deuteronomic historian has Joshua summon the people to an obedience to "do all that is written in the book of the law of Moses [Deuteronomy?], turning aside from it neither to the right hand nor to the left" (Josh. 23:6). He then warns the people that if they intermarry with the remaining Canaanite population and allow the nations and their gods to become a snare to them, then Yahweh's anger would be kindled against them and they would perish from off the good land that Yahweh had given them.

In I Sam., ch. 12, the Deuteronomic history has Samuel making a speech to Israel at the time of the founding of the monarchy. In this speech Samuel surveys the early sacred history of Israel to emphasize Yahweh's saving deeds (I Sam. 12:6–11). He then refers to the people's request for a king (see Deut. 17:14–20) and declares that if the king and people follow Yahweh faithfully, then things will go well, but if the people "rebel against the commandment of Yahweh, then the hand of Yahweh will be against you and your king" (I Sam. 12:15) and both people and king shall be swept away (I Sam. 12:25).

Another strategic period in Israelite history was the beginning of the rule of the Davidic dynasty in Jerusalem. For this period, the Deuteronomic historian added notations to the already existing material on the Davidic dynasty. The original Davidic theology had proclaimed the unconditional election of the Davidic house. For the Deuteronomic historian, writing after the promulgation of the book of Deuteronomy with its strictures on the king (Deut. 17:14–20) and after the Davidic king in Jerusalem had been exiled, the election of the Davidic dynasty was understood as conditional, dependent upon the obedience of the king to the law of Moses. II Samuel, ch. 7,[3] which contains Nathan's promise of an eternal rule to the house of David, now contains an element of judgment:

> When he [any successor to David] commits iniquity, I will chasten him with the rod of men, with the stripes of the sons of men; but I will not take my steadfast love from him, as I took it from Saul, whom I put away from before you. (II Sam. 7:14–15.)

This viewpoint of the Deuteronomic history has been made more explicit in a speech attributed to David in the final section of the Throne Succession Story. Here the dying David speaks to Solomon, his successor, and charges him to keep the whole law of Moses in order that he might prosper in whatever he does, and then David quotes the conditional promise attributed to Yahweh:

[3] See D. J. McCarthy, S.J., "II Samuel 7 and the Structure of the Deuteronomic History," *Journal of Biblical Literature*, LXXXIV (1965), pp. 131–138.

> If your sons take heed to their way, to walk before me in faithfulness with all their heart and with all their soul, there shall not fail you a man on the throne of Israel. (I Kings 2:4.)

Such a sweeping and total requirement of obedience as this which was placed upon Solomon and subsequent Davidic rulers is, of course, the editor's anticipation of the basis for the eventual disruption of the kingdom at the death of Solomon and the later deportation of the last Judean kings.

The dedication of the Temple in Jerusalem was another event of great significance in the life of Israel, and again at this point in the narrative there appears a passage, as a prayer of Solomon (I Kings 8:22–53), that emphasizes the obedience-blessing and disobedience-curse themes.

The Deuteronomic historian sought to show to his contemporaries that, at every critical point in her history, Israel and her rulers were presented with the Torah of Moses and were challenged to obedience to its commands, being warned of the consequences of disobedience. Moses before the conquest, Joshua at the settlement, Samuel at the beginning of the monarchy, Nathan at the time of David, and Solomon at the dedication of the Temple: all these venerable leaders at points burdened with significance for the future called the people to obedience or were called to obedience themselves, only to see the nation eventually lacking in its fidelity.

The Deuteronomic historian saw history not only in terms of disobedience and its consequences but also in terms of prophetic predictions and their corresponding fulfillments. This prophecy-fulfillment schema sees the "Word of Yahweh" as the controlling force in human history. Throughout the monarchical period, the writer introduces prophetic oracles and shows their subsequent fulfillment. Only the two major examples, namely, the fall of Samaria and of Jerusalem, need to be referred to here. The Deuteronomic historian's assessment of the fall of Samaria is given in II Kings 17:7–23, where the collapse of the state is seen in terms of prediction and fulfillment:

> Yahweh warned Israel and Judah by every prophet and every seer, saying, "Turn from your evil ways and keep my commandments and my statutes, in accordance with all the law which I commanded your fathers, and which I sent to you by my servants the prophets." . . . Until Yahweh removed Israel out of his sight, as he had spoken by all his servants the prophets. (II Kings 17:13, 23.)

The capture of Jerusalem, too, was seen as the result of "the word of Yahweh which he spoke by his servants the prophets" (II Kings 24:2; compare ch. 21: 10–15 with ch. 24:2–4).

In many respects, the Deuteronomic history is one long confession of guilt, a statement of the nation's disobedience and the correctness of Yahweh's judgment. The historian assessed the guilt of the people and their rulers on the basis of two standards: the requirements of the Deuteronomic law and David as the ideal ruler. David had walked after the way of Yahweh "with integrity of heart and uprightness," he pleased Yahweh with his heart wholly true to his God, and he kept his statutes and commandments (see I Kings 9:4; 11:4, 6, 38; 14:8;

15:5). David was the perfect anointed ruler who measured up to the ideal of the Deuteronomic king (Deut. 17:14–20). Of all the other kings, only Hezekiah (II Kings 18:5–7) and Josiah (II Kings 23:25) are commended without qualification. All of the Israelite kings are without exception condemned, for they had, among other things, forsaken the Davidic dynasty to whom Yahweh's promise had been given. Hezekiah and Josiah were favorably appraised because they "kept the commandments which Yahweh commanded Moses" (II Kings 18:6; 23:25). This latter phrase can only refer to the stipulations of the Deuteronomic code which required the absolute and exclusive worship of Yahweh, the destruction of foreign cults, and the centralization of worship. Israelite kings and most Judean kings were guilty of allowing or encouraging the worship of other deities (even Solomon, I Kings 11:1–8) and allowing worship outside Jerusalem, the place that Yahweh had chosen (I Kings 11:13).

The Deuteronomic interpretation of history not only focused on the course of the people's rebellion and Yahweh's word of judgment but it also emphasized the divine forgiveness in history and Yahweh's word of promise. The period of the Judges of premonarchical Israel is presented as a time of a recurring historical pattern in which the people were disobedient, Yahweh oppressed them, the people cried out for deliverance, Yahweh forgave them and raised up a savior figure to deliver them from their distress (see Judg. 2:11–23). Such a scheme carried with it an assurance that judgment need not be Yahweh's last word. The words of the prayer of Solomon similarly hold out a confidence in divine forgiveness:

> If they repent with all their mind and with all their heart in the land of their enemies, who carried them captive, and pray to thee toward their land, . . . then hear thou in heaven . . . and forgive thy people who have sinned against thee, and all their transgressions which they have committed against thee; and grant them compassion. (I Kings 8:48–50.)

The Deuteronomic historian portrayed Yahweh as a God of promise, as one upon whom the people could depend. Moses as the mouthpiece of Yahweh offered to an Israel encamped in the land of Moab promises concerning the exile:

> And when all these things come upon you, the blessing and the curse, which I have set before you, and you call them to mind among all the nations where Yahweh your God has driven you, and return to Yahweh your God, you and your children, and obey his voice in all that I command you this day, with all your heart and with all your soul; then Yahweh your God will restore your fortunes, and have compassion upon you, and he will gather you again from all the peoples where Yahweh your God has scattered you. (Deut. 30:1–3.)

The law and the word of Yahweh had been the fundamental tests of Israel's obedience and the criteria of her judgment. At the same time, they were for the exiles and desolate Jews the vehicles of hope. A constant theme of the Deuteronomic historian revolves around the idea of a "return to Yahweh and his law" always with the assurance of Yahweh's acceptance, for "Yahweh your God is a merciful God; he will not fail you or destroy you or forget the covenant with your fathers which he swore to them" (Deut. 4:31). The summons to return to Yahweh and the law carried with it an assurance that Yahweh would return his people to the land their fathers possessed, even though their exile had carried them to the uttermost parts of heaven, and grant them blessings exceeding those of the fathers (Deut. 30:4–5).

Even the Deuteronomic historian, like the prophets, was concerned with the possibility of a repetition of Israel's rebellious past. He too envisioned a spiritual transformation, an inner change in the Hebrew man.

> Yahweh your God will circumcise your heart and the heart of your offspring, so that you will love Yahweh your God with all your heart and with all your soul, that you may live. (Deut. 30:6.)

For the historian, the judgment of Yahweh in the fall of Jerusalem was not the end of Yahweh's people. Only a refusal to return to Yahweh could slam the door irrevocably.

The hope for the future in the Deuteronomic history was anchored not only in the law of Moses and the covenant blessing and promises but also in the covenant with David, who had been promised a descendant on the throne forever. It is perhaps no accident that the closing episode in this monumental history concerns the release of the exiled Judean king Jehoiachin after thirty-seven years of imprisonment (II Kings 25:27–30). Jehoiachin, the legitimate Davidic heir, the oppressed messiah in a foreign land, was not said to be merely released—he was spoken to kindly, given a place of prominence among his fellow royalty, allowed to lay aside his prison dress, permitted to dine at the king's table, and supplied with a daily allowance.[4] Perhaps in this act the author saw a glimmer of light, a flicker of hope that "Yahweh's messiah, the breath of our nostrils" (Lam. 4:20), could still be a source of Yahweh's blessing.

THE PRIESTLY HISTORY

The second major historical work produced during the exile is the so-called Priestly history which is presently found predominantly in the first four books of the Old Testament.[5] Scholars isolate this material from the Yahwistic history (see above, Chapter 8) on the basis of its theological interests, its rather austere and stylized terminology, and its orientation to matters of cultic practice and worship. Just as in the case of the Deuteronomic history, the Priestly writing incorporates numerous small collections of traditions that are much older than the exile. The majority of these traditions are concerned with cultic matters, such as sacrifices, priestly qualifications and ordination, construction of Yahweh's sanctuary, and regulations related to dietary and cleanliness requirements. Such collections of older traditions and regulations no doubt represent the bringing together of cultic traditions and lore and the writing down of

---

[4] Some cuneiform texts have been discovered in the excavation of Babylon which do mention Jehoiachin and rations allotted him; see W. F. Albright, "King Jehoiachin in Exile," The Biblical Archaeologist, V (1942), pp. 49–55, reprinted in The Biblical Archaeologist Reader, I, pp. 106–112.

[5] For a discussion of the Priestly history, see Ackroyd, Exile and Restoration, pp. 84–102.

descriptions of actual worship procedures in Jerusalem and Judean Yahweh cults. This interest in priestly matters has, of course, been the basis for the name assigned to his work.

As in other Near Eastern cultures, one can assume that there were temple schools, especially at the Jerusalem Temple, where instruction was offered in cultic matters and priestly concerns in order to train candidates for the priesthood and to preserve and organize cultic traditions. The small collections such as the so-called Holiness Code (Lev., chs. 17 to 26) as well as the Priestly history itself probably developed in these temple schools and among the survivors from these schools after the fall of Jerusalem. The conditions after the destruction of the Holy City threatened the life and existence of much of the Jews' historical and cultic traditions, and the desire to preserve these must be seen as one of the basic interests of the Priestly historian.

In the Priestly document, one does not find the lively and engaging type of narrative material that characterized the Yahwistic history. Neither is there in the work the appeal to the heart, the desire to clarify issues, and the attempt to win the reader over to a commitment that runs through the book of Deuteronomy. The language of the Priestly writer is much more matter-of-fact and uninspiring and is occupied with the assertion of perspective and regulations. However, one should not consider the Priestly writer and his sources as being solely concerned with cultic matters and minutiae. Chapter 19 of Leviticus, which forms part of the Holiness Code, contains numerous references and statements that focus on broad moral issues. For example:

> You shall not hate your brother in your heart, but you shall reason with your neighbor, lest you bear sin because of him. You shall not take vengeance or bear any grudge against the sons of your own people, but you shall love your neighbor as yourself: I am Yahweh. (Lev. 19:17–18.)

The Structure of the History. The Priestly history is a narrative work but its primary interest is not to provide a description of historical events as such. Its basic aim is to show the growth and development of cultic institutions and regulations "out of history." The narrative provides the framework for the development of the institutions and laws which in turn justify the narrative.

The material in the Priestly history revolves around four stages or world ages during which the deity concluded two covenants, one with all mankind (represented by Noah) and one with Israel (represented by Abraham). These world ages are: from creation to Noah, from Noah to Abraham, from Abraham to Moses, and the Mosaic era. The writer claims, as did the Yahwist, that Israel was the goal of the creation and evolution of the world. It is in the Mosaic era that history reached its apex and Israel became truly the people of Yahweh. The idea of the division of world history into a number of periods was already present in Israel's earliest confessions which grouped traditions around certain epochs—patriarchs, exodus, wilderness, and settlement.

The narrative structure of the Priestly history is the framework within which the laws and legislation are placed; it is the vehicle to carry the eternal. The narrative material is tied together by a number of threads. One of these threads is a chronological scheme. The reckoning of time begins with creation, and notations are made in reference to the ages of representative figures in each generation. It is this chronology for the early periods of history which allowed the later Jews to develop a calendar with the year 1 as the year of creation (*Anno Mundi* 5730 in the Jewish calendar equals *Anno Domini* 1970 in the Julian calendar). Another thread in the narrative fabric is the genealogical references that trace the ancestral line of the twelve tribes back to Adam, noting also various relationships between the Israelites and neighboring peoples.

A further thread in the narrative is the progressive self-revelation of the deity. The deity in the first two world ages reveals himself and is known under the general name Elohim. In the third era he is known to the patriarchs as El Shaddai and only in the Mosaic period does the deity reveal himself by his intimate name Yahweh. A further connecting link between the world ages is the concept of the covenant. Each of the world ages is characterized by a special covenant relationship between God and man that places man under a relationship of obligation to the deity but that carries with it a promise and a blessing for man. Within the narrative context and the covenant relationship, the deity decrees ordinances which are binding on that particular situation but which then continue to stand as eternal decrees. The history of this covenant relationship displays a constant narrowing of divine election—from the whole of creation in the earliest to the particular people Israel in the latest.

The Priestly Account of Creation. The Priestly account of the origin of the world is found in Gen. 1:1 to 2:4a.[6] Just as in the Yahwistic historian's account of creation (see above, p. 141), the interest of the writer is in the origin of the orders of creation rather than in the origin of "matter" or the earth in general. The focus is more on formation than on creation. This fact can be more clearly seen if the probably more correct translation in the RSV footnote is used in the opening verses: "When God began to create the heavens and the earth, the earth was without form and void."[7] This reading assumes the existence of the earth in a state of watery chaos. Here one has the Biblical "wet" account of creation, whereas the Yahwist account in Gen. 2:4b–25, the "dry account," presupposes the world as a waterless desert chaos.

The creative action of the deity is presented as eight major acts performed over a period of six days. The first creative deed of the deity was the command that light should be. This was then separated from darkness, and the light called day and the darkness named night. It should be noted that the deity spoke and his word commanded the reality "into existence." The creation of the firmament, which was called "heaven," was the content of the second day's activity. We no longer use the term "firmament" in our astronomical vocabulary. The child's sense of the sky as a blue dome carries something of the idea embodied in the reference to the firmament. Most ancient Near Eastern world

---

[6] For a discussion of this account of creation, see Brandon, *Creation Legends of the Ancient Near East*, pp. 146–157.

[7] See Walther Eichrodt, "In the Beginning," in Anderson and Harrelson, eds., *Israel's Prophetic Heritage*, pp. 1–10; and W. R. Lane, "The Initiation of Creation," *Vetus Testamentum*, XIII (1963), pp. 63–73.

views conceived the relatively flat earth as encased in a sphere composed of an upper and lower firmament or dome. The earth was anchored inside the sphere but rested on the subterranean waters. The stars, moon, and sun moved around the "domes" encircling the earth. The firmament held back waters that threatened to flood the sphere. The idea that the earth sat on waters was based on the observance of the seas, springs, and wells whose waters appear to rise from beneath the earth. This picture of the earth and the heavens is the so-called three-story-view of the universe—the atmosphere and the heavens as the upper story; the underworld and the lower firmament, which one might call the basement; and the earth or terra firma (which, sitting on the waters, was not necessarily considered so firma), the ground story.

On the third day, God performed two major acts creating the dry land (earth) and the seas and causing vegetation to grow on the earth. The vegetation the writer divides into two primary classifications: "plants yielding seed" (such as wheat and barley) and "fruit trees bearing fruit in which is their seed" (such as dates and pomegranates).

The creation of the heavenly bodies—the sun, moon, and stars—constituted the deed of the fourth day. The functions of these lights were set: the sun to rule over the day and the moon to rule over the night and both to separate the light from the darkness and also to serve as the indicator for determining the signs, seasons, days, and years, that is, to serve in calculating calendar reckonings and holy days. One cannot help asking the rather obvious question: How did the writer assume that day and night existed on the previous days if there were no sun? It could be argued that this was simply a slip or oversight by the author, but the Priestly account of the creation is so well thought out that this does not seem reasonable. The writer, because of the Mesopotamian astral religion with its worship of the sun, moon, and stars, may have placed their creation on the fourth day to demote them in importance. Or it may have been that the ancients assumed that light had an independent existence apart from the sun. Observation of dawn and twilight and light on cloudy days could have supported a view that saw the sun and the moon as ruling lights but not as the sole source of light.

On the fifth day, God made the fish and the fowl, the swarming things in the waters, even the great sea monsters and the winged birds that fly above the earth. To these creatures, God gave a blessing and a command to be fruitful and multiply.

Two creative events took place on the sixth day: the creation of land animals and of man. The living creatures upon the earth are divided into three groups or species. These are cattle or domesticated animals, such as sheep and goats; creeping things or reptiles and insects; and the beasts of the earth or the wild, undomesticated animals. Man is divided into two classes: male and female. The creation of man is considered the pinnacle of the created order. For the Priestly writer, creation could be described as a pyramid, with man as the apex. (One could describe the Yahwistic account of creation as a wheel with man as the hub.)

In the description of the creation of man, a number of emphases are found. Man is said to be made in the image of God or "in our image." The "us" in

Gen. 1:26 probably has reference to the subordinate heavenly beings, the heavenly council, which appear in later Jewish thought as the angels of God. What did the author mean in his statement that man was made in the image of God? It is almost impossible to answer this question with any certainty, since the writer mentions only the results of man's being so made rather than the content of the image; and furthermore, the Hebrew Scriptures nowhere pick up and expound this idea of man in the image of God. Did it mean that man who walks in an upright position resembles God in this? Or that if one saw God (see Ezek. 1:26), God would look very human? Or that if one were to search for the pattern after which man was made, he would have to search in the heavenly world (see Ps. 8) rather than in the animal world? Or does man stand as a likeness of the deity in the world in a manner similar to the statues set up by rulers in conquered lands in order to express rulership? The writer does say that man, made in the image of God, was to have dominion over all the created orders—"over the fish of the sea, and over the birds of the air, and over the cattle, and over the earth, and over every creeping thing that creeps upon the earth" (Gen. 1:26).

In the Priestly account, male and female in the species "man" are made at the same time, unlike the Yahwist version, which adds the creation of woman as a sort of appendix or afterthought to the creation of Adam. Man and woman were blessed and commanded to reproduce and fill the earth and have dominion over it.

According to this version of creation, man was not initially given the authority to take animal life. Thus man was understood to live for several generations as a vegetarian, being restricted by the deity to eat only from the plants and trees.

After the completion of the creation, the deity is said to have rested on the seventh day and to have set aside the seventh day as hallowed. This was of course the Priestly justification for and understanding of Sabbath observance. It was a commemoration of the deity's day of rest after the week of creation. For the Priestly writer, the Sabbath as a sacred day of rest was written into the structure of the world orders at the time of creation.

There are a number of features in the Priestly account of the creation that deserve comment. When compared with the Babylonian creation story, the *enuma elish*,[8] the Biblical account stands out in its unified, monotheistic presentation. In the Babylonian account, which has many parallels to the Biblical story especially in its world view, creation is the result of a struggle and warfare among the gods, and the narrative lacks the well thought out and balanced perspective. The Biblical account must have been the result of a long process of thought and reflection on the created orders in the light of a monotheistic outlook. In the Priestly account, everything in creation except the original formlessness and darkness is the result of a single creative purposefulness. Such a perspective provided the possibility of a wholistic or unified attitude toward the world. Behind the Priestly portrayal of the creation, there lies an obvious

---

[8] This text is given in translation in Pritchard, ed., *Ancient Near Eastern Texts*, pp. 60–72. A comparison of creation mythologies is given in T. H. Gaster, *Myth, Legend, and Custom in the Old Testament* (Harper & Row, Publishers, Inc., 1969), pp. 3–50.

assumption of the orderly character of heaven and earth. The goodness of creation and its orders also is a constant refrain in the narrative, and this too was dependent upon the creation as the direct result of the divine word and deed and the Hebrew's positive evaluation of natural life.

Another outstanding characteristic of this account of creation is the evolutionary and scientific scheme of its thought. The development of the created order proceeds from the lower to the higher with a deep appreciation for the dependent relationships between higher and lower. This is not to suggest that the writer was anticipating modern evolutionary thought nor that the six days of creation should be compared with some scheme based on six geological phrases. This is merely to point to the fact that the account is the result of sensitive observation and deep reflection. The narrative should certainly be designated religioscientific in that its purpose was not merely to affirm in a religious, confessional sense that God created the heavens and the earth (for this type of affirmation, see Ps. 136). The interest in the types or kinds of vegetation, animals, and so on, reflects a deep desire to describe the actual world, or a scientific interest. This fact should not be ignored simply because our scientific data far excels that which was available to the sixth-century Jew. In the same light, the material has a rather secular cast. Man's appointment to lordship over the world, the command that various species reproduce and according to their kind, and the rather detached relationship of the deity display a divine transcendence toward creation and thus a more secular evaluation of man's function than one finds, for example, in the Babylonian account where man was made "to serve the gods" (i.e., feed them through sacrifices).

The Covenant with Noah. Following the account of the creation, the next episode in the Priestly history revolves around the story of the flood and the covenant with Noah. The span between Adam and Noah is covered only in the genealogy in Gen., ch. 5. The outline of the account of the flood in the Priestly work and its differences from the Yahwistic historian's version can be seen in Chart 4. At this point, we shall focus attention only upon the stipulations of the covenant with Noah. Since Noah was considered the "second father" of mankind, the writer apparently argued that the stipulations of this covenant should be binding upon all men.

Noah and his descendants were granted the right to kill and eat animals and thus break with the previous vegetarian diet that the writer assumed characterized the earliest phase of human history. Flesh, from animals killed for food, had, however, to be thoroughly bled, and the eating of blood, which was considered the seat of life, was prohibited (Gen. 9:1–4). In addition, man was granted the right to execute capital punishment, to avenge the slaughter of a human being: "Whoever sheds the blood of man, by man shall his blood be shed" (Gen. 9:6).

Following the flood, Yahweh promised Noah that never again would such a catastrophic deluge threaten the destruction of all flesh and the earth itself. As a sign of this covenant promise, according to the Priestly writer, the rainbow in the clouds was to remind God of his promise not to destroy again and of his covenant with all flesh (Gen. 9:8–17).

The Abrahamic Covenant. The third epoch in world and Jewish history in the Priestly narrative began with Abraham (Gen., ch. 17), and as in the preceding periods, the writer's interest was on the stream of general human history but by concentrating on Abraham his field of vision is limited to the "chosen" people represented by the patriarch. In the new period, God revealed himself under a new name, "God Almighty" (El Shaddai), and bestowed on the Israelite ancestors a set of new names to characterize the new status (Abram became Abraham and Sarai was changed to Sarah).

The covenant of the Abrahamic age rested on God's assurance that Abraham and his descendants would be the recipients of the everlasting covenant, El Shaddai would be their God, the Land of Canaan would be given to them as an everlasting possession, Abraham's descendants would be a multitude of nations, and kings would be among his offspring (Gen. 17:5–8).[9] The sign of the covenant with Abraham was circumcision, to be performed on every male among his descendants, including both native-born and foreign-purchased slaves (Gen. 17:9–14). Although Abraham was ninety-nine years old and his son Ishmael was thirteen when they were circumcised (Gen. 17:24–25), the covenant stipulation required the males to be circumcised at eight days of age. Circumcision was, of course, not a practice unique to the Hebrews, for all of early Israel's neighbors with the exception of the Philistines observed the practice.[10] However, the Persians and Babylonians, contemporaries of the Jewish exiles, did not practice circumcision and thus the practice came to assume the status of a confession during the exilic age just as did Sabbath observance.

The Mosaic Era. The fourth epoch in the Priestly history was the Mosaic age, which was characterized by God's revelation of himself as Yahweh with the disclosure of this name to Moses.

> God said to Moses, "I am Yahweh. I appeared to Abraham, to Isaac, and to Jacob, as God Almighty (El Shaddai), but by my name Yahweh I did not make myself known to them." (Ex. 6:2–3.)

According to the Priestly historian, it was in the Mosaic era, at Mt. Sinai, that Yahweh revealed to Moses, and that Moses spoke to the people, all the ordinances regulating the form and nature of sanctuary architecture (Ex., chs. 25 to 31; 35 to 40), the sacrificial system (Lev., chs. 1 to 7), the orders of the priesthood (Lev., chs. 8 to 10), the demands for purity (Lev., chs. 11 to 15), the ritual for the Day of Atonement (Lev., ch. 16), the making of vows (Lev., ch. 27), and the organization of the priestly Levites and the camps (Num. 1:1 to 10:10). These are then followed in the Priestly writing by episodes and further legal material associated with the departure from Sinai and the journey toward the Holy Land, perhaps concluding with the reference to the death of Moses now found in Deut. 34:7–9. The sign of this new stage in human and Israelite history was the Sabbath (Ex. 31:12–17) which the people were admonished to

---

[9] See Clements, *Abraham and David,* pp. 61–78.

[10] On the antiquity of circumcision, see Sasson, "Circumcision in the Ancient Near East," *Journal of Biblical Literature,* LXXXV (1966), pp. 473–476.

observe, knowing that just as Yahweh had made heaven and earth in six days and had sanctified the Sabbath, so Yahweh had created his people and sanctified them to himself.

At Sinai, Yahweh had revealed and founded the whole of Israel's cult, and with the consecration of the priests and the offering of the first sacrifice at the tabernacle, this cult had been inaugurated. For the Priestly writer, the Mosaic era, which had begun with the revelation of the name Yahweh, had not come to an end but was the enduring climax to human history. The creation and sanctification of the people Israel and the cult that had entered history at Sinai was for the Priestly historian the goal of the creation and evolution of the world. The reading back into the Mosaic age of the cultic observances and sacral practices that had developed and had been elaborated within the Yahweh cult and, perhaps especially at the Jerusalem Temple and among its priesthood, made an absolute claim for their binding authority on all subsequent generations of Israelites and Judeans. The revelation to Moses and the people at Mt. Sinai was viewed by the Priestly writer as the cultic institutions and regulations that made possible the fulfillment of the promises made to Abraham (Gen. 17:5–8).

The Purposes of the Priestly History. If the Priestly history was composed during the exilic period, then one can imagine and detect multiple reasons for its composition. As was suggested above, one of the obvious motivations must have been the desire to preserve a religious heritage from possible extinction. The turbulent and despondent days following the fall of Jerusalem were a time when Yahwism was gravely threatened and an hour in history when the threads of the past needed to be woven into a fabric if they were to endure.

The Priestly writer was not interested in merely collecting, sifting, categorizing, and preserving this cultic material for purely antiquarian reasons nor for the mere sake of conservation. The Priestly history was addressed to a particular historical situation as both proclamation and program. The writing proclaimed to the Jews in exile an assurance that the whole of world history had been molded by God to culminate in the sons of Abraham, and that the promises to Abraham had not died with any historical calamity but were founded on the divine word as an everlasting covenant throughout the generations (Gen. 17:7). Just as the Deuteronomic history spoke of the scattering of the Jews from the Land of Promise and Yahweh's fidelity to his promise to restore them, so the Priestly history declared that Yahweh would forever remember his covenant with the patriarchs and never completely repudiate the promises (Lev. 26:40–45).

The Torah and cultic legislation incorporated into the Priestly history was presented as a program for the future. "As it had once been in the past, so must it be again." The revealed will of Yahweh must be the foundation of the restored community. It appears that the Priestly historian saw the restored people as a religious and cultic community with the presence of the glory of Yahweh in its midst. The writer doesn't refer to the people as a "nation" but as an "assembly" or "community," and the head of such a community was the high priest. None of the legislation in the Priestly history deals with what might be called political institutions, the state, and the king. Perhaps the writer was advocating the existence of the community as a nonpolitical entity and saw in this the means to exist even under alien power. The people would be the community of God in their obedience to the Torah—when there existed the proper sanctuary, the proper cult, the proper priesthood, and the proper purity—and as a response to their obedience Yahweh would "tabernacle" in their midst. The Priestly writer looked forward to the restored community in the Land of Canaan existing as a cultic, religious community.

THE FINAL FORM OF THE PENTATEUCH

The final form of the Torah that was recognized by the later, postexilic community as authoritative for religious faith and personal conduct incorporated not only the Priestly history but also the Yahwistic history, the book of Deuteronomy, and perhaps a version of earlier Israelite history (referred to as "E" or the Elohistic history) which had developed in the northern state. The combination of these various sources must have taken place over a long period of time and through stages about which we can have no real certainty. The process of compilation is called redaction, and scholars assume that various editors or groups (redactors) participated in this process. The basic structure of the Pentateuch was already reflected in the Yahwistic history and this outline was followed by the Priestly history but with different emphases. The final redactor or editor of the materials may have eliminated duplicate material, added editorial comments and materials still surviving in oral tradition, and combined the materials but he used the Priestly history as a general framework. At times, parallel narratives, as in the case of the creation stories (Gen. 1:1 to 2:4a; 2:4b–25), were retained side by side. At other times, parallel accounts were interwoven, as in the case of the flood story (Gen., chs. 6 to 8; see above, Chart 4).

The Torah in ancient Israel was, of course, a growing and developing entity, and the Pentateuch contains some very old material dating from the people's earliest days and some material probably no older than the exile. Since Moses functioned as the type-figure of the lawgiver and the wilderness was considered a formative type-time when the law was given, chronologically diverse material was given an authoritative sanction by ascription to Mosaic times. The Priestly account of Moses' death perhaps originally stood at the end of Numbers. One of the final acts in the formation of the Pentateuch was the removal of the account of Moses' death from the end of Numbers and its attachment to the end of Deuteronomy. The finale in the Pentateuchal tradition is the death of Moses, the point at which the revelation of the Torah was understood as complete.

The final form of the Pentateuch was to serve Judaism as a handbook on conduct, both ritual and ethical, as a collection of the revealed will and commandments of God. It was a manual to be used as a source book of religious authority. Its general outline shows the predicament of the world (Gen., chs. 1 to 11), the ancestors of Israel and their lives as obedient examples (Gen., ch. 12 to Ex., ch. 19), and the legislation and Torah (Ex., ch. 20 to Num., ch. 36)

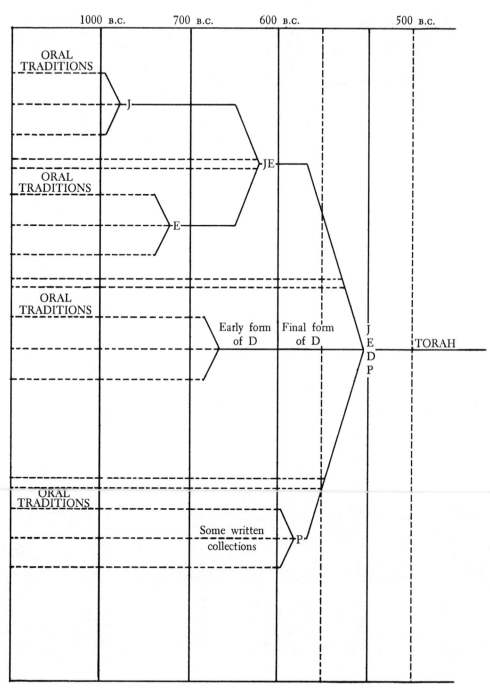

which appear as the climax to the ancestral lives and careers. The reaffirmation of the law by the new generation, the renewal of the covenant before the death of Moses (Deuteronomy), appealed to every subsequent and new generation to enter the divine covenant, to accept the Torah, to share in the past life of the people, and to emulate the life of the ancestors.

Because of the altered cultic situation of the exile, a greater emphasis was focused on the divine word and commandment and thus worship tended toward a word-centered liturgy. It was this emphasis which further opened the way to the liturgical reading of the Torah. It was this Torah which was to serve as the binding thread and the true center in Jewish life and faith. The Temple could be visited, the Torah could be lived with and meditated upon. The Pentateuch was ever with them. The Temple was in Jerusalem but the Torah should be in the heart (Deut. 6:5–9). The Temple and the cult were for special days and occasions, the Torah was for every day and the common occasions.

14 | THE WISDOM LITERATURE

Much of the Old Testament is without parallel in the literature of the ancient Near East. There is, for example, nothing comparable to the ethical, monotheistic, and judgmental literature of the prophets to be found among Israel's neighbors. Although the ancient world was interested in historical matters and in having literary monuments to celebrate its achievements, extended historical writings, such as the Deuteronomic history, were simply not produced outside Israel.

Other Israelite literature has, of course, its more recognizable parallels in the literary deposits of Near Eastern culture. The so-called Book of the Covenant (Ex., chs. 20 to 23) and the Code of Hammurabi contain striking similarities, although there is no need to assume that either was dependent on the other. Again, the opening portions of the Bible that tell of creation, the first man, and the flood have, as has been suggested in earlier chapters, numerous parallels in Near Eastern literature.

The most international in character of all Israel's literary expressions is the class of writing called the wisdom literature.[1] This material is not based particularly on Israel's unique historical experiences and consciousness nor on the nation's cultic and ritual life but is dependent primarily upon what one might call the broad human experience of the ordinary and the everyday. The primary wisdom traditions are found in the books of The Proverbs, Job, and Ecclesiastes, although wisdom concerns are dominant in numerous psalms and in many portions of the Old Testament narrative literature.[2]

A discussion of Israel's wisdom literature is placed at this point in our study not so much because Israelite wisdom literature belongs to the exilic period but

---

Biblical readings: A good example of the older practical wisdom of Israel is found in Prov., chs. 10 to 13. An example of Israel's theological wisdom is Prov., chs. 1 to 9. The book of Ecclesiastes is discussed as an example of Israelite skeptical wisdom.

[1] A collection of non-Biblical wisdom literature is given in Pritchard, ed., *Ancient Near Eastern Texts*, pp. 405–440, 592–604.

[2] See John L. McKenzie, S.J., "Reflections on Wisdom," *Journal of Biblical Literature*, LXXXVI (1967), pp. 1–9; J. L. Crenshaw, "Method in Determining Wisdom Influence Upon 'Historical Literature,'" in the same journal, LXXXVIII (1969), pp. 129–142; and R. E. Murphy, O. Carm., "Assumptions and Problems in Old Testament Wisdom Research," *The Catholic Biblical Quarterly*, XXIX (1967), pp. 407–418.

primarily for the sake of convenience and to reflect a moderate position on the question of literary chronology. Many of the Israelite wisdom traditions are very old; however, the final editing of the wisdom books probably took place during the postexilic period and one book (Ecclesiastes) was almost certainly written after the exile.

THE DEVELOPMENT OF ISRAEL'S WISDOM TRADITIONS

In Israelite culture, the term "wisdom" could refer to a broad spectrum of concerns in which art, expertise, and ability were required elements. It might point in one context to what we would call "skill," in another to "sagacity" or "shrewdness." In its broadest sense, it could refer to a philosophy of life, an attitude toward existence. In this latter sense, wisdom signified an ability to assess life properly, to determine what was practical and advantageous, to act in such a way as to bring one's intention to fulfillment. Involved in the various levels of wisdom were intelligence, sound judgment, moral understanding, and a desire to delve into the profound problems of human existence.

One of the basic requirements of any culture is the socialization of the younger generation by the older members of the socializing group. The socialization process includes introducing the children to and instilling in them a respect for the social mores, the value systems, and the customs of a culture. In Israel, the basic socializing unit was the extended family (the "patriarch" and his descendants to the third or fourth generation). Much of the wisdom tradition had its original situation-in-life usage within the family context as a part of the socialization process. Through the formulation of wise sayings, precepts, and proverbs and through the use of illustrative stories children were taught many of the values of the family, the customs of the people, and a competency in the laws of life or the art of living. The origin of this practice of formulating the wisdom of experience into sayings appealing to the memory and challenging to the will lies deep within the past of human history. The formulation of such precepts and sayings is one of the oldest intellectual activities of man and one that Israel shared with the rest of the cultures of the Near East. The earliest Israelite wisdom was no doubt then fostered in tribal and family situations where the elders sought to pass on to the new generation the insights gained from practical experience and observation and to lay down rules for proper behavior within the life of the community.

With the formation of the monarchy and especially during the Solomonic period, wisdom was cultivated at the royal court as a cultural asset (see above, pp. 123–125). Schools at the royal court, as has been suggested earlier, must have produced scribes trained not only in the field of international diplomacy but also in the field of international wisdom. The wisdom literature, being basically nonreligious in orientation, was capable of being interchanged between cultures without infringing on religious sensitivities and scruples. The portrayal of Solomon as the patron and author of much of the Israelite wisdom traditions is without doubt a reflection of the cultural and wisdom activity and internationalism at the court during his reign. It should not be assumed that this sophisticated and learned wisdom at the court ousted the older folk wisdom. The latter certainly continued to be employed in popular instruction.

Many elements in Israelite wisdom, such as the references to "my son" and some organization structures, suggest that the wisdom traditions were used in

The writing tools of the scribe are illustrated from this reconstructed Egyptian scribal outfit. The items consist of a brush case (center), a pigment pallet for black and red pigments (right), and a water pot for thinning pigments (left). In Egyptian hieroglyphics, these items were drawn to represent "scribe" or "writing."

THE ORIENTAL INSTITUTE, UNIVERSITY OF CHICAGO

instructional situations. This of course presupposed a teacher-pupil relationship of a fairly formal nature. We unfortunately know so little about the process of education and the prehistory of the synagogue schools in ancient Israel that it is difficult to define the "school" context in which the instructor-student relationship functioned. In the excavations at the site of ancient Gezer, a schoolboy's limestone tablet was discovered with an inscription scratched into the surface. The text, probably dating from the time of the United Kingdom and representing a writing exercise, provided a calendar for the year:

> Two months of ingathering.
> Two months of sowing.
> Two months of late sowing.
> Month of pulling flax.
> Month of barley harvest.

> Month when everything [else] is harvested.
> Two months of pruning [vines].
> Month of summer fruit.[3]

Such a tablet as this suggests the existence of schools where writing and reading were taught. In such schools instruction in the cultured qualities and laws of life must have been a part. We can only surmise that schools existed not only at the royal courts in the capital cities but at other important centers where persons were trained to be government officials or scribes who could offer their services and counsel to the community for a fee or simply educated members of the upper classes.

The interest in wisdom developed in certain circles into a speculative or theological pursuit. Wisdom came to be understood as a principle implanted in the world orders at creation or as a schoolmistress to Israel or even as a mediator of revelation. In the postexilic period, wisdom came to be identified with the Torah. The speculative aspect of the wisdom literature is as near as ancient Israel came to the pursuit of what Western man would call philosophy.

ISRAEL'S PRACTICAL WISDOM

For the sake of convenience, it is possible to divide ancient Israelite wisdom into three general categories: practical wisdom, theological and philosophical wisdom, and skeptical wisdom. These three types of wisdom traditions are found in the general literature of the Near East as well.

The extant Biblical examples of Israel's practical wisdom[4] are to be found in the book of The Proverbs. The book is not a carefully thought out literary composition but is an anthology made up of eight distinct collections (see the subscriptions in Prov. 1:1; 10:1; 22:17; 24:23; 25:1; 30:1; 31:1; 31:10). The title to the work attributes the book to Solomon, but this was due to Solomon's function as a "type-person," the legendary patron of the wisdom movement. Some of the collections are even attributed to non-Israelites (Prov. 30:1; 31:1). The central portion of the book (chs. 10:1 to 22:16), which contains 375 individual proverbs, reflects the practical interest of early Israelite wisdom and probably is the oldest of the proverbial collections. Proverbs 22:17 to 24:22 appears to be dependent (in places, word for word) upon the Egyptian wisdom writing entitled The Instruction of Amenemope, which dates between the tenth and sixth centuries.

The practical wisdom traditions revolved around a number of themes: propriety in human behavior, the means to a successful life, the advantages of learning and labor, and the value and meaning of human existence. It strongly emphasized the values of study, hard work, discipline, and moderation—traits that produced or enhanced the successful and well-mannered individual. The

---

[3] Translation is from D. Winton Thomas, ed., *Documents from Old Testament Times* (Harper Torchbooks, 1961), pp. 201–203.
[4] Von Rad, *Old Testament Theology*, Vol. I, pp. 418–441, has an excellent discussion of practical wisdom.

need for man to master himself and his emotions and the environment of which he was a part constantly recurs. Practical wisdom sought to expose the order and regularity in life and to instill in the learner the desire to fit smoothly into the rhythm of life with its recurrent situations.

Generally such wisdom was given expression in succinct, catchy, and assonant form to appeal to the hearer and to aid in memory, just as we say, "Haste makes waste," "Look before you leap," and so on. Each saying stood as an independent unit in itself and expressed a truth that was allowed to stand on its own. Needless to say, contradictory proverbs appear sometimes almost side by side, but this fact even characterizes our own present-day proverbs. (Compare "He who hesitates is lost" with "Haste makes waste.")

Proverbial sayings in ancient Israel took various forms and sought to express their truth in striking fashion. Some were stated in the form of a paradox that pointed to a sort of hidden order in the apparently contradictory world of experience. Such sayings sought to show that what was superficially logical might not be correct.

> One man gives freely, yet grows all the richer;
> another withholds what he should give, and only suffers want.
>> (Prov. 11:24.)

> He who spares the rod hates his son,
> but he who loves him is diligent to discipline him.
>> (Prov. 13:24.)

Other proverbs took the form of riddles in which there was a comparison of phenomena from two totally different planes. One can imagine the teacher providing the first part of the riddle and the student or class offering the corresponding response.

> Like clouds and wind without rain is
> a man who boasts of a gift he does not give.
>> (Prov. 25:14.)

> Like a dog that returns to his vomit
> is a fool that repeats his folly.
>> (Prov. 26:11.)

Some of the sayings merely attempted to give classifications to some persons and behavior. Such classifications were assumed, apparently, to carry an innate authority and thus to demand consent to a certain pattern of behavior.

> A wise son hears his father's instruction,
> but a scoffer does not listen to rebuke.
>> (Prov. 13:1.)

> A good wife is the crown of her husband,
> but she who brings shame is like rottenness in his bones.
>> (Prov. 12:4.)

Some of the proverbs were formulated as legal sayings such as prohibitions or admonitions. This suggests that much of the Biblical wisdom and legal traditions had a common origin in the ancient family folk mores of the Near East.[5]

> Do not rob the poor, because he is poor,
>   or crush the afflicted at the gate. . . .
> Remove not the ancient landmark
>   which your fathers have set.
>   (Prov. 22:22, 28;
>   compare Ex. 23:6; Deut. 19:14.)

Many of the proverbs defy classification and may be referred to simply as moral maxims.

The outlook of most of Israel's practical wisdom rested on a balanced perspective that emphasized both utilitarian and ethical concerns. The acceptance of and obedience to the truth of the proverbial sayings were expected to bring a man happiness, success, culture, and an informed life and opinion. Folly, on the other hand, was the opposite of wisdom and was the source of trouble, unhappiness, loss of friends, and so on. Most of the practical wisdom was very optimistic about man and the world. It assumed that the person capable of being taught could grasp and understand life and that correct action would produce the desired result. The world and the human community were understood as rather rational phenomena that operated primarily on discoverable principles, or at least on enough of these, which allowed man to attune his life to a larger whole that would then reward him. This utilitarian concern is reflected in the fact that even so mundane a fact as correct table manners (Prov. 23:1–3) were given consideration. Such a utilitarian emphasis never really bordered on hedonism or the mere pursuit of pleasure. This was due in no small degree to the widespread emphasis on moderation in the Near Eastern wisdom traditions that tempered the concept of success. All forms of excess fell under the critical eye.[6]

The wisdom traditions extolled the worth of ethical values and implored man to strive for ethical and moral concerns such as honesty, righteousness, humility, charity, and love. However, many of the proverbs that spoke of these virtues did so in terms of an enlightened self-interest.

> He who gets wisdom loves himself;
>   he who keeps understanding will prosper.
>   (Prov. 19:8.)

> A man who is kind benefits himself,
>   but a cruel man hurts himself.
>   (Prov. 11:17.)

> It is better to be of a lowly spirit with the poor
>   than to divide the spoil with the proud.
>   (Prov. 16:19.)

---

[5] See Erhard Gerstenberger, "Covenant and Commandment," *Journal of Biblical Literature*, LXXXIV (1965), pp. 38–51.

[6] See Henri Frankfort, *Ancient Egyptian Religion* (Harper Torchbooks, 1961), pp. 59–87.

He who closes his ear to the cry of the poor
will himself cry out and not be heard.
(Prov. 21:13.)

The present form of the book of The Proverbs emphasizes not only utilitarian
and ethical interests but also religious morality. Although much of Israel's prac-

Scribes recording nonpayment of taxes, shown on the wall of an Egyptian tomb, illustrates the importance of scribes in ancient cultures. The learned man who was educated and could teach was revered in all communities. An Egyptian text, "In Praise of Learned Scribes," declares: "More effective is a book than the house of a builder or tombs in the West. It is better than a well-founded castle or a stela in a temple."

tical wisdom seems to have been almost entirely based on the observation and
experience of everyday life, the world of nature, and the patterns of action and
reaction in the human community, the material frequently speaks with a religious, Yahwistic emphasis. The criterion for human behavior could be the
question of the pleasure or displeasure of Yahweh. False weights were an abomi-
nation to Yahweh, as was arrogance, the justifying of the wicked, or a perverse
mind (Prov. 11:1, 20; 16:5; 17:15; 20:10, 23). In the last analysis, it was Yahweh
who tried the spirit and weighed the heart of man (Prov. 15:3, 11; 16:2; 17:3;
21:2; 24:12). This idea of the weighing of the heart is similar to the Egyptian
concept of the judgment of the dead which involved the weighing of the heart
in scales to see if it balanced with the feather of *maat* (truth). In Israel this
weighing of the heart was not associated with any judgment of the dead, since
the concept of a significant and meaningful existence after death was very late
in developing in "orthodox" Yahwism.[7]

[7] See S. G. F. Brandon, *The Judgment of the Dead* (London: Weidenfeld and Nicolson,
1967), pp. 6–48; 56–75.

The limitations that Yahweh's existence and action imposed upon human understanding and action were pointed out by the wisdom teachers. Man planned in his heart or thought out a course of action or harnessed the horse for battle, but it was Yahweh who guided the purpose and action to completion or granted the victory (Prov. 16:9; 19:21; 20:24; 21:30–31). Such a perspective recognized the incalculable in the midst of human plans and the mysterious in

The weighing of the heart is depicted in this Egyptian drawing. The deceased stands beneath the scales as the god Anubis weighs his heart against the feather of Maat (truth). The result of the judgment is accorded by the god Thoth. A composite figure, called "the devourer," sits at the right to eat the hearts that fail in judgment.

the course of human events. Simultaneously, such a view pointed toward faith and confidence in Yahweh.

> No wisdom, no understanding, no counsel,
> 　can avail against Yahweh.
> 　　　　　　　　　　　　(Prov. 21:30.)

> By loyalty and faithfulness iniquity is atoned for,
> 　and by the fear of Yahweh a man avoids evil.
> 　　　　　　　　　　　　(Prov. 16:6.)

ISRAEL'S THEOLOGICAL WISDOM

In addition to the empirical and practical wisdom, ancient Israel also developed a highly speculative form of wisdom that one might even call philosophic in nature. This type of thought is best represented in the final edited material found in the first nine chapters of the book of The Proverbs.[8] In these chapters, wisdom is no longer primarily understood as an ability to execute a skill or as the understanding that a person possesses which grants him decisive insight into the art of living. Wisdom is presented as an independent entity or as a cosmic principle.

In these chapters, wisdom is portrayed in a personified fashion as a "woman" who beckons and calls man unto herself. She calls in the street and in public places and warns of the calamity awaiting those who unheedingly do not listen to her summons (Prov. 1:20–33). The young man is urged to embrace her (Prov. 4:6–9) and to make her his bride (Prov. 7:4, the term "sister" used to describe the bride is common in Egyptian texts; see S. of Sol. 5:1). Wisdom invites young men to her specially prepared house to feast with her (Prov. 9:1–6).

The presence of wisdom's company is described as of inestimable worth, for she confers wealth, honor, and happiness (Prov. 3:13–18) and even life itself:

> And now, my sons, listen to me:
>   happy are those who keep my ways.
> Hear instruction and be wise,
>   and do not neglect it.
> Happy is the man who listens to me,
>   watching daily at my gates,
>   waiting beside my doors.
> For he who finds me finds life
>   and obtains favor from Yahweh;
> but he who misses me injures himself;
>   all who hate me love death.
>   (Prov. 8:32–36.)

The one giving himself to wisdom was promised her protection (Prov. 2:9–15; 4:6) and a crown of reward (Prov. 4:9). Wisdom promised also to provide man with an understanding of the fear of Yahweh and to grant the knowledge of God (Prov. 2:1–8).

Just as "Lady Wisdom" was depicted as the ideal of one's quest, so "Dame Folly" was portrayed as the seductive deceiver whose embrace was deadly. Frequent reference is made to the "loose woman" or the "adventuress" (Prov. 2: 16–19; 6:20–35). Folly, like wisdom, implored man:

---

[8] See Roger N. Whybray, *Wisdom in Proverbs: The Concept of Wisdom in Proverbs 1–9* (London: SCM Press, Ltd., 1965).

> A foolish woman is noisy;
>> she is wanton and knows no shame.
> She sits at the door of her house,
>> she takes a seat on the high places of the town,
> calling to those who pass by,
>> who are going straight on their way,
> "Whoever is simple, let him turn in here!"
>> And to him who is without sense she says,
> "Stolen water is sweet,
>> and bread eaten in secret is pleasant."
> But he does not know that the dead are there,
>> that her guests are in the depths of Sheol.
>> (Prov. 9:13–18.)

The strange woman, the adulteress, represented both folly, the lack of wisdom and understanding, and the seductive way of life. The latter was associated not only with adultery between the young men and married women (Prov. 2:16–19; 7:19) but also with the offering of themselves by the female devotees of pagan cults, such as the worship of the goddess of love Astarte. The female participants in such a cult were probably required to invite men to share in the sacrifice of their chastity or to join them in sexual rituals at special festival occasions (Prov. 7:6–27; this passage makes reference to the making of sacrifices and vows perhaps of sacred prostitution). The prophetical portrayal of Israel's infidelity as marital unfaithfulness is of course similar in imagery to this wisdom depiction (see Hos., ch. 2; Ezek., chs. 16; 23). The primary accusation leveled against the loose woman or the adulteress was that her way led down to death (early or untimely death?) and her house was the entry gate to Sheol, the realm of the dead.

The imagery of wisdom and folly as wooing women enticing young men preserved a reflection of the worship of the female deity associated with sexuality and sexual rituals. Just as the presentation of Yahweh borrowed from the depictions of El and Baal, so wisdom nurtured the devotion to the feminine archetype, sublimating the portrayal but preserving the erotic undertones and emphasizing the motherly concerns of care, protection, and guidance.

The most adventuresome speculation concerning wisdom in the opening chapters of The Proverbs is in the emphasis placed on wisdom in and at the creation. Yahweh founded the earth and the heavens through wisdom and understanding:

> Yahweh by wisdom founded the earth;
>> by understanding he established the heavens;
> by his knowledge the deeps broke forth,
>> and the clouds drop down the dew.
>> (Prov. 3:19–20.)

This meant that the discovery of the order and law of the universe was a discovery of the thoughts of Yahweh. In a monotheistic system, this of course involved the postulation of a unified order to the whole of existence, an order synonymous with the will and thought of Yahweh.

Wisdom was allowed to praise herself as the first creature of creation who was present with Yahweh before the beginning of the earth (Prov. 8:22–31):

> Yahweh created me at the beginning of his work,
>   the first of his acts of old.
> Ages ago I was set up,
>   at the first, before the beginning of the earth. . . .
> Then I was beside him, like a master workman [or binding together];
> and I was daily his delight,
>   rejoicing before him always,
> rejoicing in his inhabited world
>   and delighting in the sons of men.
>
> (Prov. 8:22–23, 30–31.)

In such a position, wisdom possessed access to and knowledge of creation's secrets and mysteries. Such references to wisdom come very close to the concept of a goddess of wisdom, but they should be seen as the personification of the wisdom of Yahweh in a poetic fashion though dependent on general Near Eastern thought which viewed the creator-deity as the god of wisdom. These concepts of the origin of wisdom before the creation of the world and the creation of the world through wisdom provided the opportunity for the Israelite wise man to integrate the findings of his intellectual curiosity with the belief in the overall lordship of Yahweh.

When one attempts to discover how the wise men defined the content of this wisdom so speculatively conceived, one is confronted with an extremely difficult task since the Biblical traditions give no fully formulated expression of this content. No doubt one should think of this wisdom as the knowledge and understanding gained from observation on and thought about the world of creation and man's place in the universe which were conceived as existing at the time of creation in the mind of God. Such wisdom concepts should be seen not only in the primary wisdom traditions but in such passages as Ps. 8 and the Priestly account of creation (Gen. 1:1 to 2:4a) with their emphasis on the order of creation and man's place in the world.

In addition to relating wisdom to the creation of the world by Yahweh, the most theological portions of The Proverbs affirmed "the fear of Yahweh" as the basic content of and the beginning of wisdom (Prov. 1:7, 29; 2:5; and elsewhere). The "fear of Yahweh," in this context, probably does not refer to the element of awe so much as to the practice of Yahwism in all its aspects. Further developments in the attempt to define the content and function of wisdom are found in the noncanonical books of Ecclesiasticus and The Wisdom of Solomon. In the former, there is a complete identification of wisdom with the Torah (Ecclus. 24:1–23). In the latter, wisdom is designated the creator of the world (Wisd. of Sol. 7:22).

ISRAEL'S SKEPTICAL WISDOM

In Egyptian and Mesopotamian cultures as well as in Israel, there developed a form of skeptical scribal wisdom that challenged many of the traditional assumptions of its day and called into question many of the cherished contemporary religious beliefs. This side of the wisdom traditions is best represented in the Bible by the book of Ecclesiastes but is also found in The Book of Job[9] and certain of the psalms that reflect resignation before the deity.

The book of Ecclesiastes[10] is cast in the form of a royal testament, the farewell reflections of a monarch. This form of instruction, supposedly spoken by the king or prominent official to his son or potential successor, was used in Egypt from the third millennium b.c. The author of Ecclesiastes purports to be a reigning son of David (Eccl. 1:1), presumably Solomon, though the latter's name nowhere appears in the book.

The writer of the book was an intellectual of great individuality. His central thesis is stated in the opening lines: "Vanity of vanities, says the Preacher, vanity of vanities! All is vanity" (Eccl. 1:2). This basic concept is then explored, in autobiographical fashion, by examining and evaluating the customary ways in which man has sought meaning and happiness in life. The author's selection of Solomon as his spokesman was certainly a deliberate choice. As a highly successful ruler who had experienced and tasted life at every level and on so cosmopolitan a plane, who could have spoken better about man's quest for success and happiness and about what life had to offer than he?

The author opens his work with a poem (Eccl. 1:3–11) on the basically hopeless cycle in which man is caught, a cycle in which repetition is the rule of existence and monotony is the only tune to life's song: "What has been is what will be, and what has been done is what will be done; and there is nothing new under the sun." (Eccl. 1:9.) Wisdom and knowledge, the author argues, offer no answer to life and no solution to the problems of existence, since wisdom produces anxiety and sorrow. Even Solomon with all his wisdom did not fully understand (Eccl. 1:12–18). The more one knows, the more questions he confronts:

> For in much wisdom is much vexation,
> and he who increases knowledge increases sorrow.
> (Eccl. 1:18.)

The quest for pleasure is no path to happiness. The writer spoke of Solomon's legendary assemblage of wealth, gardens and parks, slaves and concubines, and

---

[9] On Job, see Robert Gordis, *The Book of God and Man* (The University of Chicago Press, 1965) and Norman H. Snaith, *The Book of Job: Its Origin and Purpose* (London: SCM Press, Ltd., 1968).

[10] A good introduction and exegesis of the book is given by Scott, *Proverbs and Ecclesiastes*, pp. 191–256. See also Robert Gordis, *Koheleth: The Man and His World*, rev. ed. (Schocken Books, Inc., 1967).

even though he sought whatever his eyes desired in unrestrained pleasure-seeking, this too left life without satisfaction although it produced momentary enjoyment (Eccl. 2:1–11). The hope of an enduring fame, the "good name to be chosen rather than great riches" (Prov. 22:1), proved only an illusion, for examination of the evidence showed that the works of the wise are soon forgotten or destroyed by the fool and both the fool and the wise move into oblivion and are subject to the same fate (Eccl. 2:12–17; 9:13–18). Human toil and the desire to amass wealth, the author argues, are also fraught with vanity, for man labors and then is forced to leave his inheritance to those who have not toiled for it, and who knows the inheritor may turn out to be a fool (Eccl. 2:18–23).

Ecclesiastes claims that one cannot find the purpose of life nor an understanding of existence through theological pursuits or through a faith anchored in God. Though he does not argue against the existence and power of God, he does claim that the ways and will of God are unknown and unknowable. Even though man possesses an apparently God-given unquenchable curiosity, he still cannot discover the ways and work of God (Eccl. 3:10–11; 11:5).

> I saw all the work of God, that man cannot find out the work that is done under the sun. However much man may toil in seeking, he will not find it out; even though a wise man claims to know, he cannot find it out. (Eccl. 8:17.)

Man must resign himself to an impassive acceptance of his God-decreed fate and live in the insecurity of uncertainty.

Man cannot assume that God, in some appointed time beyond death, will clarify and rectify matters or eventually set things straight in judgment (Eccl. 3:16–21). For man is only a mortal animal whose fate is the fate of the beasts; as one dies, so dies the other. The author argues that one cannot conclude that the spirit of man ascends to God after death and the spirit of the beast goes to the underworld. The two go to the same place—"all are from the dust, and all turn to dust again" (Eccl. 3:20). Such an argument seems to presuppose the development of a doctrine of life after death or the immortality of the spirit in certain circles of the author's contemporaries.

This unknowability of God and the secretiveness of his works led the author to argue against glib God-talk and vows that had never taken into consideration the problems of theology. Uninformed participation in cultic worship he does not encourage (Eccl. 5:1–6).

The book of Ecclesiastes is in many respects a very polemical book, and its author challenged many of the cherished opinions of his contemporaries. He sought to refute, for example, the assumption that common sense and diligence always produce successful results, insisting instead that human wisdom and activity accomplish nothing significantly new. Man is caught in the ever-recurring times appointed by God (Eccl. 3:1–9), and the little that man accomplishes is negated by death when man leaves the world in the same fashion as he entered it (Eccl. 5:13–17).

The author denies the common belief that retribution inevitably overtakes wickedness and that prosperity follows goodness. Instead, he suggests that there is little or no relationship between act and consequence, between character and reward. The righteous and the wicked, the wise and the fool come to the same end and justice does not prevail in the world. In life, the wicked may prosper and the righteous suffer (Eccl. 7:15):

> There are righteous men to whom it happens according to the deeds of the wicked, and there are wicked men to whom it happens according to the deeds of the righteous. I said that this also is vanity. (Eccl. 8:14.)

The weak may win and the strong lose, the intelligent may be destitute and the foolish rich, since time and chance are the really determinative factors (Eccl. 9:11–12). The good and the wise cannot claim nor depend on the favor of God (Eccl. 9:1–3). Such a view, of course, challenged not only the basic assumptions of the optimistic wisdom but also the foundations of a naïve Yahwism as well.

In spite of his pessimism and despair, the writer stops short of recommending either self-destruction or cynical hedonism. The injustice in the world, the oppression, and the power of the oppressors (Eccl. 4:1) led him at one point to suggest that "to have been" is better than "to be" but perhaps best of all is never "to have been."

> I thought the dead who are already dead more fortunate than the living who are still alive; but better than both is he who has not yet been, and has not seen the evil deeds that are done under the sun. (Eccl. 4:2–3.)

Because he saw the threads of fatalism woven deep into the fabric of life and man's inevitable end in the grave, Ecclesiastes recommended that one accept his fate as a death-oriented creature. Ecclesiastes 12:1–8, whose opening line with only a minor change in the Hebrew text can be read, "In the days of your youth, remember your grave," [11] admonishes the reader to ponder the onset of old age when the vitality of life dwindles away and the sweetness of youth grows sour with age.

In spite of its negative attitudes, Ecclesiastes is far from being completely nihilistic. Throughout the book there rings a positive note on the affirmation of life. Although one lives in a world that cannot be changed and under conditions that require submission to the inevitable, man ought, according to the author, to affirm and cherish life itself as a good thing.

> He who is joined with all the living has hope, for a living dog is better than a dead lion. For the living know that they will die, but the dead know nothing, and they have no more reward. (Eccl. 9:4–5.)

In addition, man must create and cultivate the capacity to enjoy the life he possesses with its work and wisdom and desires (Eccl. 2:24; 3:22; 9:7–10; 11:8).

> What I have seen to be good and to be fitting is to eat and drink and find enjoyment in all the toil with which one toils under the sun the few days of his life which God has given him. (Eccl. 5:18.)

Man should not spend his time in sackcloth and ashes mourning his fate and expending his energies in self-pity. The writer recommends, "Let your garments

---

[11] See Scott, *Proverbs and Ecclesiastes*, pp. 254–255.

be always white [do not look destitute, dress up, be festive]; let not oil be lacking on your head [look groomed], [and] enjoy life with the wife you love" (Eccl. 9:8–9). This emphasis on "eat your bread with enjoyment, and drink your wine with a merry heart" (Eccl. 9:7) is not counsel to the reader to adopt a carousing, orgiastic, gluttonous attitude toward life. Moderation and reserve temper all his recommendations. What the author suggests is that man face the facts and realities of life and, having done so, not react with a restless dissatisfaction or a remorseful retreat. If the inscrutable God grants man the sweetness of enjoyment in life, man should embrace it and drink deeply from its spring in the days of his youth.

One of the immediate questions that arises after reading the book of Ecclesiastes is, How did this book so obviously different in orientation from the rest of the Old Testament ever make it into the canon? The question of its inclusion in the body of authoritative Jewish writings was debated until after the beginning of the Christian era. A number of factors probably contributed to its final acceptance. The foremost of these must have been its assumed Solomonic authorship. In addition, the book does contain numerous proverbial sayings (Eccl. 2:26; 3:17; 7:12–13; 11:9) that reflect traditional wisdom orthodoxy. Some of these may have been included by the author, who considered his subsequent arguments to serve as refutations, while others may have been later additions by a pious copyist. The book has been provided with an appendix (Eccl. 12:9–14), perhaps by someone who circulated or "published" the book. This editor, as he might be called, suggested that the words of Ecclesiastes were worthy of study but he cautioned the reader against some of the content of the writing, noting that "of the making of books there is no end." The appendix concludes with a summary of orthodox piety. After all is said and done, one should "fear God, and keep his commandments; for this is the whole duty of man. For God will bring every deed into judgment, with every secret thing, whether good or evil" (Eccl. 12:13–14). Perhaps a further reason for the acceptance of the book in the Jewish community was its portrayal in excellent literary style of a point of view with which many sympathized and which rang true to their experience.

PART THREE

THE LIFE AND LITERATURE
OF POSTEXILIC JUDAISM

15 | THE PERSIAN
AND HELLENISTIC PERIODS

An old saying declares, "The expectation far exceeds the realization." This was certainly the case with the reconstruction of the Jewish community following the end of the Babylonian exile. The prophetic Zionism in the exile had spoken in glowing terms of the future state awaiting the defeated and exiled people. Jeremiah had referred to the radically new form of the covenant that was to characterize the coming days. Ezekiel had described the new people of Yahweh dwelling in an idealized Land of Canaan. Deutero-Isaiah had exultantly announced the glorious restoration of life in the homeland after an extraordinary new exodus from Babylon. The reality of the return from exile and the restoration of the Jewish community around Jerusalem were far more sober than the prophetic visions. The end of the exile inaugurated a new day for the Jewish people, but it was a time characterized as much by hardship and struggle as by triumph.

THE RETURN FROM EXILE

The domination of the Near East by the neo-Babylonian conquerors of Jerusalem was, as empires go, short-lived. The empire really had only one outstanding dynamic ruler and that was Nebuchadrezzar (604–562 B.C.), whose dynasty was Chaldean, not native Babylonian. Following his death, a gradual but noticeable decline set in and, without the unifying effect of Nebuchadrezzar's personality, economic decay and political disunity eroded the imperial giant.[1] The last Babylonian king was Nabonidus (555–539 B.C.), who was a quaint if not eccentric ruler. He spent time restoring old sanctuaries, especially to the moon-god Sin in Harran, to whom his mother was a devotee and whom the king seems to have advocated as the chief god of the realm.[2] This activity probably

---

Biblical readings: The primary materials discussed in this chapter are the books of Ezra, Nehemiah, and Daniel. The background and early years of the Maccabean revolt are treated in I Macc., chs. 1 to 3. See maps X and XI.

[1] The historical developments are summarized by Saggs, The Greatness That Was Babylon, pp. 140–153.

[2] Among the Dead Sea Scrolls were discovered fragments of a work called The Prayer of Nabonidus in which he appears as a very ill, perhaps deranged, person healed by a Jewish exorcist. For a translation, see André Dupont-Sommer, The Essene Writings from Qumran, tr. by Géza Vermes (Meridian Books, Inc., 1962), pp. 321–325. Nabonidus was a more competent ruler than later historians recognized or propagandists admitted.

brought upon him the displeasure of the Babylonian priesthood of Marduk, the god of the city of Babylon. In addition, Nabonidus was away from Babylon for several years spending his time at the oasis of Teima in northwest Arabia, seeking perhaps to repossess or to strengthen the Babylonian-Egyptian trade routes. His absence from the capital city greatly curtailed the political and religious life of the community.

The Persian ruler Cyrus (559–529 B.C.) took advantage of the international situation and, although having probably once served as an ally of Nabonidus against the Medes, swiftly replaced Nabonidus as the dominant Near Eastern ruler.[3] Cyrus moved to encircle Babylonia by consolidating his rule in the east and by attacking the states of Asia Minor, northern Mesopotamia, and western Arabia. His troops marched into the city of Babylon in October, 539 B.C., after having defeated the Babylonian armies in battle. The city itself offered no resistance to the Persian army, and when Cyrus arrived in Babylon two weeks later he was hailed as a veritable savior.[4] Inscriptions declaring Cyrus to be the ruler of the world, the elect of the god Marduk, and a merciful liberator were set up in Babylon by Cyrus and the Marduk priesthood.[5] This enthusiasm in favor of Cyrus is reflected not only in the literature of other Near Eastern peoples but also in the writings of Deutero-Isaiah (see above, pp. 223–225).

Cyrus followed a policy of toleration toward captive peoples and encouraged the reestablishment of their cultic centers as well as limited cultural autonomy. In the so-called Cyrus Cylinder he made the following claim in regard to captured peoples:

> I returned to the sacred cities on the other side of the Tigris, the sanctuaries of which have been ruins for a long time, the images which used to live therein and established for them permanent sanctuaries. I also gathered all their former inhabitants and returned to them their habitations.[6]

Cyrus took the same attitude toward the Jews, although no reference to them has been preserved in Persian records of the time. The Old Testament refers to Cyrus' edict decreeing the rebuilding of the Temple in Jerusalem and allowing the Jews to return to Palestine from Babylon. The ruler is quoted as tracing his right to rule back to Yahweh, the God of heaven (Ezra 1:2–4). Such an attribution would not have been out of character for Cyrus, for he was depicted as one who could play the part of a worshiper of a people's deity if it proved to be conciliatory and politically advantageous. Such a reference should not, however, be taken as a statement of Cyrus' conversion to Yahwism. Ezra 6:1–5 contains a copy of the edict issued by Cyrus written in Aramaic, the official international language of the time, which authorized the rebuilding of the Jerusalem Temple, the employment of funds from the Persian treasury

---

[3] The rise of Cyrus is discussed by Jacob M. Myers, *The World of the Restoration* (Prentice-Hall, Inc., 1968), pp. 42–54.

[4] See Howard Wohl, "A Note on the Fall of Babylon," *Journal of the Ancient Near Eastern Society of Columbia University*, I (Spring, 1969), pp. 28–38.

[5] See Pritchard, ed., *Ancient Near Eastern Texts*, pp. 315–316. The pro-Cyrus sentiment expressed itself in anti-Nabonidus form; see Pritchard, ed., *ibid.*, pp. 312–315.

[6] Translation is from Pritchard, ed., *Ancient Near Eastern Texts*, p. 315.

for the project, and the return of the Temple vessels taken to Babylon by Nebuchadrezzar. The delivery of the sacred vessels to Jerusalem was delegated by the Persians to Shesh-bazzar, who was called "the prince of Judah" (Ezra 1:5–11) and who may have been a member of the Davidic family (if the

The Cyrus Cylinder speaks of Cyrus' capture of Babylon and of his policy of restoration of exiles. The text claims that it was the Babylonian god Marduk who had selected Cyrus for his task.

THE BRITISH MUSEUM

Shenazzar of I Chron. 3:18 is another form of the same name). After returning the Temple artifacts, Shesh-bazzar is said to have "laid the foundation of the house of God," which suggests that an unsuccessful attempt at restoring or rebuilding the Jerusalem Temple was undertaken (Ezra 5:13–16).

The return of the Jews to Palestine was hardly a major exodus from exile. The response to Cyrus' permission to return to their homeland must initially have been rather meager. This was due to a number of factors. Many of the Jews had comfortably settled in Babylon as Jeremiah (ch. 29:4–9) had recommended and as exilic conditions had allowed. Conditions in Palestine were not overly inviting; the land was sparsely settled, life was agriculturally oriented, Persian control was probably not firmly established, and the trip from Babylon was long and hazardous. The first trickle of returnees was no doubt largely composed of persons interested in reviving the cultic and priestly institutions with perhaps others who had found adjustment to Babylonian life difficult.

Any significant work on the reconstruction of the Temple was delayed until almost two decades after the initial edict of Cyrus. This was due to an apparent apathy on behalf of the Palestinian Jews who had not gone into exile and who may have disliked the claim of the exilic Jews that the hope of the community lay with those who had endured the exile (see Jer., ch. 24). In addition, work was hampered by the citizens of the city of Samaria which was an administrative center for the Persian province Beyond the River (abar nahara) of which Judah was a part. Impetus to rebuild the Temple came from the activities of Zerubbabel, a Davidic descendant, the high priest Joshua, and the two prophets Haggai and Zechariah.

Exactly when Zerubbabel was appointed governor in Jerusalem cannot be determined. It could have been in conjunction with the intense Persian activity in Syria-Palestine by Cambyses (529–522 B.C.), the son of Cyrus, activity that was climaxed by the conquest of Egypt and the Greek island of Cyprus (525 B.C.). Zerubbabel and Joshua restored the altar in Jerusalem and supervised the sacrificial activity (Ezra 3:1–7). When work was begun on the Temple restoration, trouble developed between the Judeans and their neighbors. The latter openly opposed and halted the construction after their initial offer of assistance was shunned by the Jews (Ezra 4:1–5; 5:3–5). Work was not begun again until the second year of Darius I (522–486 B.C.).

Royal Persian tombs at Naqsh-i-Rustam in Iran were cut into the solid rock of a mountainside near the Persian capital at Persepolis. The tombs shown were for Darius I (right), Darius II (center), and Artaxerxes I (left), although source uncertainty exists about the last two identifications. The tomb of Xerxes is to the right outside the picture.
THE ORIENTAL INSTITUTE, UNIVERSITY OF
CHICAGO

The death of Cambyses in 522 B.C. occurred during the time of political turmoil associated with an attempted usurpation of the throne. Revolt broke out throughout the empire, and it was two full years before Darius was firmly in control. This international political unrest is reflected in the prophecy of Haggai, who saw in the turmoil a propitious time and urged his fellow Jews to commence work on the Temple (Hag. 1:1–15). Haggai's preaching shows that the reversal of Judea's fate and the arrival of the "good times" proclaimed by the exilic prophets were still powerful symbols of hope.

Once again, in a little while, I will shake the heavens and the earth and the sea and the dry land; and I will shake all nations, so that the treasures of all nations shall come in, and I will fill this house with splendor, says Yahweh of hosts. . . . The latter splendor of this house shall be greater than the former . . . and in this place I will give prosperity, says Yahweh of hosts. (Hag. 2:6–7, 9.)

The prophet proclaimed the downfall of the Persian imperial power and the reestablishment of the Jewish state, assuring Zerubbabel that he was the servant of Yahweh, the leader designate (Hag. 2:20–23). Haggai's contemporary, the prophet Zechariah, went so far as to declare Zerubbabel and Joshua the two messiahs of Yahweh and he heaped on Zerubbabel accolades reminiscent of such messianic prophecies as Jer. 23:5 and 33:15 (Zech. 3:6–10; 4:1–14; 6:9–14, the latter referring to Zerubbabel as well as Joshua).

Zerubbabel's attitude toward this hope of a restored Davidic state and the downfall of the Persian empire may not have been as enthusiastic as was that of the prophets. Nevertheless, he suddenly disappears from sight, perhaps having been removed or recalled from his post in Darius' consolidation and reorganization of the empire in response to the widespread nationalistic turmoil that had convulsed his far-flung domains. The practice of making a member of the Davidic family the governor of the Jewish community seems to have been too politically risky even for the tolerant Persians. No doubt many Jews lamented this failure of the attempt to revive the old Davidic rule.

The construction of the second Temple was completed and the new edifice dedicated in March, 515 B.C. (Ezra 6:15), some seventy years after the Solomonic Temple had been destroyed by Nebuchadrezzar. The dedication and the renewal of the service of the Temple were celebrated with great joy among the Jewish community who saw it as the symbol of both Yahweh's presence and his blessing upon them (Ezra 6:16–22).

EZRA AND NEHEMIAH

The period from Darius I until the conquest of the Near East by Alexander the Great one and a half centuries later is one of the times of greatest obscurity in the history of pre-Christian Judaism. Two persons dominate the Biblical records concerning this period. They are Ezra and Nehemiah, and it is commonly assumed that the Biblical material has reversed the chronological order of the two men. For our present purpose, the question of whether Ezra worked in Jerusalem prior to, following, or contemporary with Nehemiah can be bypassed.[7]

Nehemiah, even as a Jew, had risen to a position of prominence in the administration of the Persian king whom he served as royal cupbearer. Such a function was one of confidence and importance, and as a functionary in the royal household he was probably a eunuch (see Neh. 6:10–11; eunuchs were not allowed in the Temple precincts, see Deut. 23:1 and compare Isa. 56:3–5).

---

[7] For discussion of this problem, see H. H. Rowley, "The Chronological Order of Ezra and Nehemiah," in his *The Servant of the Lord*, pp. 135–168.

Chart 8: FROM THE EXILE TO THE MACCABEAN REVOLT (586–164 B.C.)

B.C.	EVENTS IN PALESTINE	EVENTS ELSEWHERE
586	Destruction of Jerusalem Palestine governed as Babylonian province Further deportation of Jews after assassination of Gedaliah (582) Priestly history written Deuteronomic history written	Nebuchadrezzar king of Neo-Babylonian empire (604–562) Nebuchadrezzar invades Egypt (568) Jehoiachin released from prison by new Babylonian king Evil-merodach (561) Cyrus becomes king of Anshan (559) Nabonidus, Babylonian king (555–539) Cyrus gains control of Media-Persia (550) Capture of Babylon by Cyrus (539)
	First return of Jews from exile Zerubbabel as governor in Jerusalem	Cambyses, Persian king (529–522) Conquest of Egypt by Persians Darius I king (522–486) after time of revolt
500	Reconstruction of second Temple (520–515)	Persian-Greek wars Battle of Marathon (490) Xerxes I (486–465) Battles of Thermopylae and Salamis (480) Artaxerxes I (465–423) Revolt of Egyptians with aid of Greeks (460); suppressed by Persians (455)
400	Beginning of Ezra's mission (458?) Nehemiah governor (445–?) Rebuilding of Jerusalem walls Ezra (428?) Ezra (398?)	Artaxerxes II (404–358) Unification of Greece by Philip II of Macedonia Reign of Alexander the Great (336–323)
	Alexander gained control of eastern Mediterranean coast (333–332)	Alexander dies in Babylon (323) Seleucus secures Babylon (312)
300 200	Palestine under control of Egyptian Ptolemies (301)	Translation of Hebrew Torah into Greek in Alexandria (ca. 250) Battle of Paneas (200)
	Palestine under the control of the Seleucids (198)	Seleucids defeated by Romans at Magnesia (190) Antiochus IV Epiphanes (175–163)
	Struggle over Jerusalem high priesthood Assassination of Onias III (171) Antiochus' edict outlawing Jewish religion (167); profanation of the Temple Beginning of Maccabean revolt (166) Judas Maccabeus (166–160) Rededication of Temple (164)	Antiochus forced out of Egypt by Romans

In 445 B.C., Nehemiah requested permission of the Persian king to return to Jerusalem and rebuild the city after having heard a report of its plight (Neh. 1:1–3; 2:1–8).[8] Artaxerxes I (465–423 B.C.) granted Nehemiah's request and sent him to Jerusalem as governor. Perhaps one should not view this act as simply an altruistic sentiment on behalf of the Persian monarch. Revolt against the Persians had broken out in Egypt (460–454 B.C.); the governor of the "province Beyond the River" had rebelled in 448 B.C.; the old enemies of the Persians, the Athenian Greeks, had taken a more active role in east Mediterranean affairs; and all of these no doubt convinced Artaxerxes that a fortified and loyal Jerusalem on the eastern flank of the empire would be more desirable than a continuation of the *status quo*.

The refortification of the Holy City, undertaken after a secret nocturnal inspection of the walls (Neh. 2:11–17), was carried out against severe opposition by numerous neighboring powers, but "the people had a mind to work" (Neh., ch. 4). According to the Biblical text, the wall was finished in fifty-two days (Neh. 6:15), which implies more of a repair than complete rebuilding. The later Jewish historian Josephus (ca. A.D. 37–100) states that the rebuilding took two years and four months. After completion of the reconstruction of the fortifications, Nehemiah discovered that "the city was wide and large, but the people within it were few and no houses had been built" (Neh. 7:4). To remedy this situation, one tenth of the population living outside Jerusalem was selected by lot and settled in the city (Neh. 11:1–2).

Several measures were taken by Nehemiah to purge the Jerusalem community of non-Jewish elements and to reform the cultic life and observances of the people. The Ammonite ruler Tobiah, related perhaps by marriage to a Jewish priest, had an "apartment" in one of the Temple courts and he was thrown out (Neh. 13:4–9). The Levites, who had not received proper payment for their services, were looked after through enforcement of the tithe on grain, wine, and oil (Neh. 13:10–14). Nehemiah forbade commerce and traffic on the Sabbath by locking the gates of Jerusalem before the Sabbath sunset and posting guards (Neh. 13:15–22). Male members of the Jewish community had intermarried with foreign women from Ashdod, Ammon, and Moab and had children who no longer spoke the language of Judah. Nehemiah made these men swear an oath that they would not arrange intermarriage between their children and non-Jews (Neh. 13:23–29), admitting that to get them to do so he had "contended with them and cursed them and beat some of them and pulled out their hair" (Neh. 13:25), arguing that they, like Solomon, must expect trouble from foreign women.

Ezra returned to Jerusalem (exactly when is a matter of dispute) bearing the title "scribe of the law of the God of heaven" (Ezra 7:12), which implies that he was a member of the Persian civil service perhaps in charge of Jewish religious matters. He was commissioned by the monarch "to make inquiries about Judah and Jerusalem according to the law of your God" (Ezra 7:14). Such an interest in the laws of the subject nations was nothing new for Persian kings, since

---

[8] See H. H. Rowley, "Nehemiah's Mission and Its Background," in his *Men of God*, pp. 211–245.

Darius had earlier advocated the collection and codification of laws in various areas of the empire.[9] Ezra seems not only to have opposed marriage with aliens but also to have required that men who had married foreign women should divorce them and drive out the offspring of such marriages.[10] Ezra, chs. 9 and 10, contains an account of the enforcement of this requirement along with a list of those who had married foreign women. A special court was instituted with responsibility to judge the people on the basis of the law of God, with power to execute punishment, and with the obligation to teach the law when it was not known (Ezra 7:25–26).

The climax of Ezra's activity was the public reading of the book of the law of Moses before the assembled community on the first day of the seventh month (Neh. 8:1–3). Whether this book of Moses was only the Deuteronomic legislation, the Priestly code, or the entire Pentateuch cannot be determined. The reading was followed by an interpretation of its content by the Levites (Neh. 8:7–8), a process that should possibly be understood as a translation into Aramaic, the general language of the time, with paraphrasing of the content. This public reading of the law was no doubt reflective of the old ceremony of covenant renewal held at the time of the fall festival. The entire Jerusalem community sealed its commitment to obey the law through a covenant ritual that involved self-imprecation with an oath and a curse (Neh. 10:28–31).

It is difficult to overemphasize the importance of the work of Ezra and Nehemiah for the life of Judean Yahwism. The Jerusalem community had been reconstituted, with Ezra's law book recognized as the official constitution. Judah was thus organized as a cultic community, a hierocracy or temple-state and recognized as such by the Persian imperial authority. Internal matters of self-government, such as taxation and law and obedience, were focused in the temple organization with the high priest as the supreme authority and with the civil governor as the appointed representative of the imperial overlord.

Postexilic Judaism in the environs of Jerusalem was strongly oriented toward hierocratic or theocratic concerns. The primary emphasis was on the organization of the Judeans into a religious fellowship and cultic community under the direct control of the will of Yahweh as expressed in the Mosaic Torah. The ethnic and religious purity of the members was a requirement toward this end. A Jew could no longer claim to be a Jew on the basis of membership in an independent political entity. His Jewishness was expressed in his worship of Yahweh, his participation in the Temple cult, and his obedience to the Torah. The great interest in genealogical lists, as in the Priestly code, I Chron., chs. 1 to 9, and throughout Ezra and Nehemiah, must be seen against this background. A good and proper ancestry was a further mark of distinctiveness, especially in a time when foreign marriages were a point of contention.

The exclusivism of the community and the emphasis on strict observance of the law have often been criticized by scholars, but such an attitude is perfectly understandable within the historical needs of the time. In fact, one could argue

---

[9] See Albert T. Olmstead, *History of the Persian Empire* (The University of Chicago Press, Phoenix Books, 1948), pp. 119–134.

[10] In later Jewish tradition, the child of a Jewish mother by a Gentile father was considered Jewish but the child of a Gentile mother by a Jewish father was considered Gentile.

that if such an emphasis on exclusivism had not developed, the Jewish community might have been submerged in the general paganism of its neighbors or in the Zoroastrianism of the Persians. The possibility of conversion to Judaism argues against viewing the Jewish community as a closed society. The following passage comes from a postexilic writer:

> The foreigners who join themselves to Yahweh,
>   to minister to him, to love the name of Yahweh,
>   and to be his servants,
> every one who keeps the sabbath, and does not profane it,
>   and holds fast my covenant—
> these I will bring to my holy mountain,
>   and make them joyful in my house of prayer;
> their burnt offerings and their sacrifices
>   will be accepted on my altar;
> for my house shall be called a house of prayer
>   for all peoples.
>
> (Isa. 56:6–7.)

Two books in the Old Testament—Ruth and Jonah—have generally been ascribed to this period by scholars and considered representative of a more open and universalistic attitude toward foreigners. The former emphasizes the non-Jewish background of David's great-grandmother, the Moabitess Ruth, and the latter emphasizes the pity of Yahweh upon the repentant even if they are citizens of Assyrian Nineveh.

Also current in Judaism at the time were concerns that can be called eschatological (the term is from the Greek word *eschatos*, meaning "last," and refers to teachings or beliefs about the future or end time).[11] Many of the Judeans clung to the belief in a great intervention into history by Yahweh that would fulfill the previous prophetical expectations and predictions. This eschatological perspective with its orientation to the future anticipated the action of Yahweh that would produce historical conditions within which the Jews could live in peace with the nations of the world confined or subdued. At times this expectation could be conceived of in terms of a great catastrophic act with world-shattering effect or in terms of a re-creation of the world and its orders with harsh judgment administered to the opponents of Yahweh.

> Behold, I create new heavens
>   and a new earth;
> and the former things shall not be remembered
>   or come into mind.
> But be glad and rejoice for ever
>   in that which I create;
> for behold, I create Jerusalem a rejoicing,
>   and her people a joy.
>
> (Isa. 65:17–18.)

---

[11] See Otto Plöger, *Theocracy and Eschatology*, tr. by S. Rudman (John Knox Press, 1968).

And it shall come to pass afterward,
    that I will pour out my spirit on all flesh;
your sons and your daughters shall prophesy,
    your old men shall dream dreams,
    and your young men shall see visions.
Even upon the menservants and maidservants,
    in those days, I will pour out my spirit.
                  (Joel 2:28–29;
          see also chs. 2:30 to 3:21.)

These theocratic concerns hoping to create a community governed by divine law, and eschatological concerns looking expectantly to an intervention by Yahweh to fulfill his purpose with his people, may have characterized different groups in Judaism, but certainly many in the community looked on obedience to the law and the service of theocratic concerns as a form of waiting before the eschatological fulfillment.

Descendants of the older Israelite and Judean states existed outside Jerusalem and its environs. Of the "ten lost tribes" of Israel taken into captivity after 722 B.C., little is known, but the Israelites who were left behind continued to exist and as Yahweh worshipers. These northerners shared with Judeans the worship of Yahweh, the Torah, and a Mosaic faith; but hostility between Samaria and Jerusalem grew, eventually to a point where each was declaring the other unorthodox and even illegal.[12] The Samaritans requested and were granted the permission of the Persians to build (or rebuild) a temple on their sacred mountain, Gerizim, and later always referred to Ezra as "Ezra, the accursed." Variant forms of Yahwism and even non-Yahwistic religions were practiced by many Jews outside Judah. At this time a Jewish colony at Elephantine in Egypt had built a temple to Yahweh (recall the Deuteronomic law forbidding this) and apparently worshiped other deities as well.[13] The recent excavation of a post-exilic temple at Lachish illustrates the existence of a multifaceted Judaism outside the environs of Jerusalem.[14] Numerous passages in the so-called Third (or Trito) Isaiah refer to the revival of older non-Yahwistic cults apparently even in Judah (Isa. 57:1–10; 65:1–12). Very little is known of the religious life of the Jews remaining in Babylon at this time but it must have been more similar to the life of Judaism in Jerusalem (without sacrificial worship) than that of either the Samaritan or Elephantine Yahwists.

ALEXANDER THE GREAT AND HIS SUCCESSORS

Before his capture of Babylon, Cyrus had become the master of Asia Minor, and in doing so he had added to his domain a number of Greek settlements

---

[12] See H. H. Rowley, "The Samaritan Schism in Legend and History," in Anderson and Harrelson, eds., *Israel's Prophetic Heritage*, pp. 208–222; and J. D. Purvis, *The Samaritan Pentateuch and the Origin of the Samaritan Sect* (Harvard University Press, 1968).

[13] See Bezalel Porten, *Archives from Elephantine: The Life of an Ancient Jewish Colony* (University of California Press, 1968).

[14] See Yohanan Aharoni, "Trial Excavation in the 'Solar Shrine' at Lachish," *Israel Exploration Journal*, XXVIII (1968), pp. 157–169.

along the Mediterranean. In 494 B.C., a group of these, the Greek cities of Ionia, revolted against the Persians. Darius I, after suppressing the rebellion, decided to bring the city-states of mainland Greece under his control. There followed the famous battle of Marathon (490 B.C.) in which the Persians were worsted, the further clashes in the naval battle of Salamis (480 B.C.), and the land battle of Plataea (479 B.C.) during which the Persians' western ambitions were halted. Greek attempts to invade the Persian east which followed were likewise unsuccessful.

After the middle of the fourth century, the Macedonian ruler Philip II overcame, through force, the endemic disunity of the Greek states and planned a Greco-Macedonian invasion of Asia primarily to free the Greek cities in Asia

Silver coin of Alexander the Great shows the head of the Greek god Heracles on the obverse. The reverse depicts Zeus Aetophoros and bears the inscription: BASILEOS ALEXANDROU, "of King Alexander."

AMERICAN NUMISMATIC ASSOCIATION

Minor. Assassination (in 336 B.C.) cut short his hopes of leading the invasion forces, and the mantle of leadership fell upon the shoulders of Philip's twenty-year-old son, Alexander (336–323 B.C.). In the spring of 334 B.C., the Hellespont was crossed by the young monarch who was never again to set foot on his native land. The Persian colossus proved to be a giant without strength commensurate to its size. The dozen of distinct nationalities within its borders, the diminishing of imperial authority by provincial governors, a defense based on mercenary forces, and two centuries of Persian rule all combined to create an ineffective reaction to the Greeks. In rapid succession, Alexander enjoyed one military triumph after another. By the end of 332 B.C., he had been hailed by the Egyptians as a liberator and in October of the following year, the Persian army was dealt a near fatal blow. Some months later, the Persian monarch was assassinated by his own princes. The way was open for Alexander to move eastward, and he marched his army to the Indus valley but his attempts to force his troops farther met with opposition, and no amount of pleading could push his exhausted and battle-weary men into continuation of the conquest. Alexander returned to Babylon, where he died of a fever in June, 323 B.C., before the beginning of his thirty-third year.

Before his death, Alexander, who had been tutored by Aristotle, had sought to amalgamate his own Greek cultural heritage with that of the conquered peoples. The manner in which this blending of culture and traditions proceeded can be illustrated by Alexander's actions in Egypt. After his conquest of the Nile state, the ruler founded the city of Alexandria (one of over thirty he founded throughout the East) as a center of Greek culture in the midst of an Oriental civilization. Alexander publicly participated in the religious rituals, sacrificing to the gods, and ordered that shrines to the deities be constructed in Alexandria. Simultaneously, Alexander introduced Greek athletic contests into Egypt. One can see in these actions the fusion of Oriental religious and Greek rites and values. Alexander's impact began a new era in the Near East and one that was to be furthered by his successors. This new era, the so-called Hellenistic (from the term *hellēn*, meaning "Greek") Age, saw Greek language, art, customs, and religious and philosophical ideas penetrate the area and in turn fuse with their Oriental counterparts. The establishment of Greek as the international language formed a general basis for the interchange of ideas and practices.[15]

In his rule, Alexander saw himself and was acclaimed as the successor to both the Persian great king and the Egyptian pharaoh; he assumed the titles and splendor of both these offices. After his death, Alexander was proclaimed a god throughout the empire, and cults were set up to his honor in various places. Aristotle had taught that the king was a "god" among men and the Egyptians of course looked on the pharaoh as a deity, and in all likelihood Alexander himself claimed to be divine. This amalgamation of royal ideologies marked the beginning of the Hellenistic ruler cult that was to culminate in the later worship of the Roman emperor.

The possible historical contacts between Alexander the Great and the Jerusalem Jewish community have been shrouded by later legends that spoke of his visit to Jerusalem, his worship in the Temple, and the interpretation to him of Biblical passages predicting his prominence. These legends have little if any historical value whatever. Jerusalem probably offered submission without opposition to Alexander as did much of Syria-Palestine, although he apparently had to dispatch troops to squelch a revolt by the Samaritans, an act that would have ingratiated him to the Jerusalemites.[16]

Alexander died without consolidating his empire and with no plans for succession. His legal heirs were his half-witted half-brother by the name of Philip and an unborn child by his wife Roxana. The latter proved to be a male and

---

[15] On Hellenism and its impact on the Jews, see Victor Tcherikover, *Hellenistic Civilization and the Jews*, tr. by S. Applebaum (The Jewish Publication Society of America, 1959).

[16] A number of Aramaic papyri were recently discovered that probably date from Alexander's destruction of Samaria. See Frank M. Cross, Jr., "The Discovery of the Samaria Papyri," *The Biblical Archaeologist*, XXVI (1963), pp. 110–121.

was named Alexander. Neither of these two, each of whom was subsequently murdered, succeeded Alexander; instead, the empire was divided among his generals, who sought with varying degrees of success to consolidate their holdings and establish their own dominions. The two successors of Alexander who

Alexander the Great making offering to the Egyptian god Amon from a Luxor temple relief illustrates the syncretism of the Hellenistic age. This blending of different cultures is symbolized in the use of both Egyptian hieroglyphic and Greek (at bottom) in the inscription. Alexander, shown presenting a tray of objects to the god, may have been influenced by the Egyptian belief in the divinity of the pharaoh.

THE ORIENTAL INSTITUTE, UNIVERSITY OF CHICAGO

were of great importance insofar as Palestinian and Jewish history was concerned were Ptolemy and Seleucus, both Macedonian aristocrats who had been Alexander's companions in arms. Ptolemy took over Egypt and established a dynasty that was to rule until 31 B.C., while Seleucus was able to establish his rule in Babylon by 312 B.C. Control of Palestine was a matter of dispute for years, being claimed by both the Ptolemaic and the Seleucid states. By about 301 B.C., Ptolemaic control over the area was assured and was to last for a century, although the Seleucid house never gave up its claim to this territory and on occasion fought to acquire it.

The period of Ptolemaic rule over Palestine was one of general political peace and quiet insofar as the Jerusalem community was concerned. The Ptolemies were not aggressive in their effort to spread Greek culture. The Jews were allowed the freedom to govern themselves as a hierocratic community administered by a council of elders under the authority of the high priest just as they had under the Persians. They were, of course, required to pay taxes and to recognize Ptolemaic supremacy over the land. Many prominent Jewish families were strongly in favor of Ptolemaic rule, were attracted to Greek customs and practices, and were allowed to profit from this allegiance. This was especially the case with the Tobiad family who profited from its service to the Ptolemies in tax collection. During this period many Jews migrated to Egypt perhaps because of economic conditions in Palestine. This migration created a large Jewish community in Alexandria which formed the most important non-Greek element in the city's population. These "Egyptian Jews" were treated favorably and were given many privileges approaching self-government.

Palestine came under the control of the Seleucids following the battle of Paneas (200 B.C.) and the expulsion of the Ptolemaic garrison from Jerusalem two years later. Many of the Jews, members of the upper stratum of the priestly class, the Jerusalem aristocracy, and the wealthy, had developed pro-Seleucid sentiments and assisted in Antiochus III's take-over of Jerusalem. The Seleucid forces were welcomed to Jerusalem, and Antiochus reaffirmed the right of the Jews to live "according to their ancestral laws" and did not seek to impose Hellenization but allowed the continuation of the priestly government, with the Mosaic Torah and its applications having binding authoritative power as the city law of Jerusalem. The subsequent course of events may be seen as the background for the Maccabean revolt.

THE MACCABEAN REVOLT

Four factors contributed to the political and religious conditions that precipitated the Maccabean revolt against the Seleucids. In the first place, there developed a growing pro-Hellenistic spirit among segments of the Jewish population.[17] As a rule, this pro-Greek sentiment was confined to the wealthy aristocracy and seems to have been especially characteristic of the Tobiad family. This Hellenistic interest was initially concerned with the externals of Greek culture. Economic and political needs required that one associate intimately with non-Jewish persons, eat unkosher food, and not appear as an exclusivistic character. From this, the adoption of Greek habits in daily life, use of the Greek language, giving Greek names to children, appreciation of Greek art, and so on, became more amicable to Jews and required a certain relaxation in the observance of Jewish customs and laws. Adoption of Greek customs and increased contact with aliens became more the practice not because of philosophical attraction to Hellenism but primarily because of political and economic expediency. Profit and power, not philosophy, were the roots of Jewish Hellenism.

A second contributing factor was the condition of the Seleucid state. The Romans had defeated Antiochus III at the battle of Magnesia in 190 B.C., curtailed Seleucid authority in Asia Minor, taken over much of his fleet and war-elephants, and collected an indemnity. In addition, much of the East had slipped from Seleucid control, leaving only Syria, Palestine, and Northern Mesopotamia firmly under control. This loss of territory created a recurring financial and growing prestige crisis for the Seleucids. Temples, such as the one in Jerusalem, which were often not only quite wealthy in their own right but which also served the functions of banks in ancient times, became far more tempting to Seleucid rulers. Attempts to regain prestige through conquest had to turn toward Egypt and thus toward a greater involvement of the Jews.

---

[17] See Tcherikover, *Hellenistic Civilization and the Jews*, pp. 117–174.

A further element in the developing situation was the struggle for the office of high priest in Jerusalem, a struggle dependent upon the two previously mentioned factors. The high priests, even before the Seleucid period, had been drawn from the Oniad family. Onias III, who had become high priest in about 198 B.C., was accused of being pro-Ptolemaic, a charge backed by the Tobiads. In addition he refused to open the Temple treasures to the Seleucids. While Onias was attempting to rectify matters with the ruler, his brother Joshua, who had changed his Hebrew name to the Greek Jason, was backed by the Tobiads and he bribed the Seleucids into recognizing him as high priest and deposing Onias. Previously, during the Hellenistic period, kings had merely granted or withheld ratification of the candidate, but this move made the office of high priest a position of price and turned the holder into an almost royal official dependent upon the king's favor.

Jason had promised the new Seleucid ruler, Antiochus IV (175–163 B.C.), an additional sum if he could construct a gymnasium in Jerusalem, enlist sons of noble families in an athletic corporation, and "enrol the men of Jerusalem as citizens of Antioch" (II Macc. 4:9; Antioch on the river Orontes was the Seleucid capital). It is uncertain whether the last phrase refers to the establish-

Greek games as represented on a sixth-century B.C. amphora were performed in the nude. Running, wrestling, chariot racing, contests between men and beasts, and other sports were introduced into Judea during the Hellenistic period. Many Jews participated in such games, but the more conservative resisted what they felt were corrupting alien influences.

THE METROPOLITAN MUSEUM OF ART, ROGERS FUND, 1914

ment of Jerusalem as a Greek city with its own constitution or not. At any rate, the move of Jason led to a general Hellenization of Jerusalem. Athletic games in the gymnasium (from a Greek word meaning "naked") were performed in the nude, membership in the athletic corporation was expensive and was limited to the wealthy, games were associated with education and with patron Greek deities, and the creation of the "Antiochenes" (whether as the citizens of Jerusalem as a Greek city or not) produced a distinct body in Jerusalem that enjoyed the privileges of Greek citizenship. The writer of II Maccabees depicts the conditions that developed with Jason's advocacy of "the Greek way of life": young men began to wear the broad-rim Greek hats, priests were no longer intent on their service at the altar but were concerned with athletic events such as wrestling and discus-throwing (II Macc. 4:10–17), and some Jewish youths went so far as to remove the distinctive marks of circumcision that were so obvious in the athletic contests (I Macc. 1:11–15).

Eventually, Jason was outbid for the office of high priest by his representative to the Seleucid court, Menelaus. Jason was forced to flee from Palestine and Onias III, whom many of the orthodox still considered the legitimate high priest, was murdered (II Macc. 4:23–38). Menelaus, "possessing no qualification for the high priesthood" (II Macc. 4:25), began looting the Temple, and riots against such acts broke out in the city.

The fourth development contributing to the immediate background of the Maccabean revolt was the opposition of the Hasidim (spelled Hasideans in its Greek form) to the Hellenization of Jerusalem. The name of this group is derived from the Hebrew term *hasid*, which means "a pious or saintly one." The origin of the Hasidim in the Seleucid period is to be seen in the scribal interpreters of the law and their followers who wished to preserve the law of Moses and its interpretations (the so-called oral law) as the law of the Jewish community. A threat to the law of Moses was a threat to the ancestral way of life, to the whole theocratic ideal, and to the scribal interpreters themselves. The Hasidim were not peaceful and passively pacifistic people, for many of them were certainly willing to fight for their faith. The first reference to the Hasidim in conjunction with the Maccabean revolt refers to them as "mighty warriors of Israel" (I Macc. 2:42). The anti-Hellenistic and antiaristocratic masses in Jerusalem found a point of leadership in the Hasidim.

The immediate background to the Maccabean revolt was the war between the Seleucids and the Ptolemies and the actions of Antiochus IV against the Jerusalem community. In the late '70s of the second century B.C., the Ptolemaic rulers began plotting to retake territory lost to the Seleucids after the battle of Paneas. Antiochus began making plans for the defense of his domain, and as part of this effort he inspected his southern province. This inspection tour brought him to Jerusalem, where he was welcomed by the high priest Jason, was given a torchlight parade, and no doubt left Jerusalem with the impression that he and the Hellenizing cause had the overwhelming support of the city's population.

Antiochus chose to invade Egypt and thus hoped to gain the offensive as well as to add territory to the shrinking Seleucid empire, knowing that the Romans at the time were engaged in the Third Macedonian War. In the course of the war with Egypt, Jerusalem was involved in a number of ways. The Temple in Jerusalem was entered by Antiochus, being offered this prerogative by Menelaus, and he looted some of the Temple treasures (I Macc. 1:20–28; II Macc. 5:15–21). This desecration and pillage of the Temple added fuel to the flames of discontent, for the Jews were already enduring severe taxation as were the other subject people, and more and more of the population assumed a pro-Ptolemaic attitude. On another occasion, a rumor reached Jerusalem that Antiochus had died in Egypt. Jason took this opportunity to leave his hiding place in Transjordan and attack Jerusalem accompanied by some one thousand supporters. Civil war broke out (II Macc. 5:5–10) with perhaps three factions involved: Menelaus and the Hellenizers, Jason and his supporters, and the orthodox or anti-Hellenizers. When news of the Jewish disturbance reached Antiochus, he took the city by storm, put many of its inhabitants to the sword, and sold others into slavery (II Macc. 5:11–14). Having, or so he thought, secured the city and rescued Menelaus and his followers, Antiochus departed, leaving behind troops to control the area. Apparently the uprising was renewed, and a contingent of the Syrian army reentered the city on a Sabbath, pretending to be peaceably disposed, and regained the town executing vengeance (II Macc. 5:22–26) and then refortified the citadel area (Acra) overlooking the Temple area and garrisoned it with troops (I Macc. 1:29–35). II Maccabees notes in passing that Judas Maccabeus and several of his friends escaped from Jerusalem to seek refuge in the wilderness (II Macc. 5:27). In I Macc. 2:66, Judas is described as "a mighty warrior from his youth" and perhaps already he was fighting against the Hellenizers.

Antiochus' efforts to take Egypt had been cut short by the Romans, whose envoy in Egypt was Laenas, an old friend of Antiochus from his days as an exile in Rome. Laenas presented Antiochus with a Senate decree ordering him to abandon his attempted conquest of Egypt, and as legend has it, the envoy drew a circle on the ground around the king and demanded an answer before he stepped out of the circle. Antiochus was forced to accept the dictation of Rome. The Ptolemies had not relinquished their threat to take Palestine, and now the Roman eagle nested on his southern border. Antiochus took extreme measures to consolidate his territory, especially the southern district. The placing of Jerusalem under heavy military control, as mentioned above, was part of this consolidation.

In 167 B.C., Antiochus issued a decree that in his kingdom "all should be one people, and that each should give up his customs" (I Macc. 1:41–42). Such an edict was intended to wipe out the last vestiges of opposition to Antiochus and to create a unified state loyal to himself and the Hellenistic life. I Maccabees says that all the Gentiles accepted the command and even many of the Jews (I Macc. 1:43). However, the exclusivistic and monotheistic faith of the orthodox and Hasidic Jews continued to refuse to buckle in their loyalty to Yahweh and the Mosaic law, so Antiochus moved to eradicate Yahwism. Orders were given to suspend the Temple ritual, possession of a copy of the Torah was punishable, the Sabbath and festival days were outlawed, food laws were to be abolished, and the practice of circumcision was to be discontinued (I Macc. 1:44–61). The observance of Jewish religious practices was made a state crime punishable by death. The Samaritan temple on Mt. Gerizim was constituted a temple to Zeus Xenios ("Zeus the Friend of Strangers") and the Temple in Jerusalem was dedicated to the worship of Olympian Zeus (II Macc. 6:2). A small altar was erected on the altar of burnt offering in the Temple court and swine were sacrificed. Prostitution invaded the Temple area, Jews were forced to eat of the sacrifice on the monthly celebration of the king's birthday, and were forced to participate in celebrations associated with the feast of Dionysus (II Macc. 6:3–7). Such participation in the worship of Zeus could be and probably was understood as the veneration of Antiochus as divine, since he was called Epiphanes ("manifest") and considered to be a manifestation of Zeus and had the coins bearing his image inscribed with the term *theos* ("god"). His subjects who shared a different opinion dubbed him Antiochus Epimanes, Antiochus "the mad dog." II Maccabees describes him as one "thinking in his arrogance that he could sail on the land and walk on the sea" (II Macc. 5:21).

Opposition to Antiochus' policy of Hellenization and his suppression of Yahwism surfaced again in the village of Modein. The order had gone out to construct altars to the Greek gods throughout the land. When the Seleucid troops sought to make Mattathias, a local priest, offer sacrifice, he killed a cooperating Jew and the Syrian officer and tore down the altar (I Macc. 2:1–26). Mattathias then raised the cry of revolt: "Let every one who is zealous for the law and supports the covenant come out with me!" (I Macc. 2:27). He and his five sons fled to the hills and were joined by the Hasidim and others of like sentiment. Mattathias and his followers took action against Jews who had sympathized with the Seleucids. An army was formed and "sinners . . . and lawless men" who had supported the Gentiles were struck down, pagan altars were destroyed, and uncircumcised boys were forcibly circumcised (I Macc. 2:44–48). In many respects, Mattathias' actions were a civil war against apostate Jews, but it brought out the Seleucid army in force to suppress the drive for theocratic independence.

Judas Maccabeus (after whom the movement was named) succeeded his father, Mattathias, who died shortly after the revolt began. Judas was able to defeat a sizable Syrian army and through surprise attack and guerrilla warfare prevented the armies of Antiochus, who was warring in the East against Persia and Media, from suppressing the revolt or from lifting the Jewish blockade of Jerusalem. Judas and his troops were finally able to regain the Temple area from the Seleucid troops, who, however, continued to control the Acra. The Temple was cleansed and repaired and service to Yahweh was restored after a three-year interruption on the twenty-fifth of Kislev, 164 B.C. (I Macc. 4:36–61). This rededication of the Temple became the theme of the yearly festival of Hanukkah (the Feast of Light), an observance decreed by Judas and the assembly as a time of remembrance, perhaps in imitation of the Greek practice of setting aside a day in memory of an event in one's own history but without any basis in the Torah.

At this point, we shall pause in our historical survey and examine the rise of apocalyptic literature and The Book of Daniel which belongs within the context of the Seleucid persecution of the Jews.

THE CHARACTER OF APOCALYPTIC LITERATURE

During the late postexilic period a new literary form developed among the Jews which is commonly referred to as apocalyptic literature (from the Greek word *apokalyptein*, "to uncover," "to reveal") and is represented in the Hebrew Scriptures by The Book of Daniel.[18] The exact motivations behind and the groups responsible for the origin of this type of literature cannot be clearly determined. To a large extent apocalyptic thought can be understood as a development of earlier Jewish interests in the course of history, prophetic predictions concerning the future, and the hopes and expectations of an ideal time to come. On the other hand, apocalyptic thought developed out of a Judaism influenced both overtly and indirectly through the general syncretism of religious thought throughout the Persian era and during the early Hellenistic age. The Zoroastrian religion of the Persians[19] was, like much of Israelite religion, a prophetic faith that possessed its body of sacred writings traced back to revelations made to Zoroaster. Zoroastrianism had its supreme god (Ahura-Mazda) who was the creator and who was worshiped in an imageless cult. The division of its calendar focused on the six great acts of creation. The religion affirmed a resurrection of the dead and a final judgment and it proclaimed the eventual triumph of good over evil and the victory of right over its dualistic counterpart evil. The Hellenistic age was a time of great religious syncretism when deities and cults were identified and amalgamated and often influenced one another unconsciously. Many Hellenistic cults emphasized and were interested in divine mysteries, sharing in the life of the god, cosmology, astrology, and so on, and drew upon various fields of learning.[20] It should be remembered that Judaism shared in the common Persian world for over two centuries and lived rather peacefully for over a century in the Hellenistic world before the eruption of the Hebraism-Hellenism conflict.

A number of interests characterize Jewish apocalyptic literature. It is primarily oriented toward making known the secrets and mysteries of the transcendental world and the course of events leading toward the end time, the fulfillment and annihilation of ordinary history. This emphasis upon the immediate end of the present world order that was to be followed by God's establishment of his rule is a further elaboration of older cultic emphasis on the kingship of Yahweh (see above, pp. 132–134) and the prophets' proclamation of the future acts of God.

As a rule, apocalyptic writers divided history into a number of ages, or epochs, leading up to the climactic movement that would usher in the intervention of God. This division of history into ages was of widespread currency in the Near East and was already reflected in the Priestly narrative. History is, however, no longer merely Israelite or Jewish history but is the larger history of the Near Eastern powers with which Israel had associated during the exilic and postexilic periods. Generally this perspective on history attempted a portrayal, not from within but from a transcendental viewpoint.[21] This apocalyptic interest in his-

[18] On apocalyptic literature in general, see H. H. Rowley, *The Relevance of Apocalyptic*, rev. ed. (London: Lutterworth Press, 1963); and D. S. Russell, *The Method and Message of Jewish Apocalyptic* (The Westminster Press, 1964).

[19] See R. C. Zaehner, *The Dawn and Twilight of Zoroastrianism* (G. P. Putnam's Sons, 1961).

[20] See H. D. Betz, "On the Problem of the Religio-Historical Understanding of Apocalypticism," in *Journal for Theology and the Church, VI: Apocalypticism*, ed. by R. W. Funk (Herder and Herder, 1969), pp. 134–156.

[21] See Martin Noth, "The Understanding of History in Old Testament Apocalyptic," in his *The Laws in the Pentateuch*, pp. 194–214.

tory rested on two assumptions: (1) Israel and the Jews would never be able to live in peace and service to God until the threat of foreign powers and domination was removed; and (2) history itself and the powers involved were incapable of solving the problems of existence, and thus the action of the heavenly realm was required to establish conditions as they ought to be. Thus the apocalyptic writers were generally pessimistic about the historical process.

A further characteristic of Jewish apocalyptic thought was the idea that future events and world history were determined in the distant past and were made known to chosen persons. There were a number of factors that led to this concept. Israelite prophets had come to be accepted as predictors of the future, and history was understood as the working out of Yahweh's word. This perspective was given its greatest expression in the Deuteronomic history (see above, pp. 234–235) but was also canonized in the Torah (see Deut. 18:20–22). There had developed in some circles of postexilic Judaism the idea that revelation and prophecy had ceased with Ezra and the codification of the Torah, thus the future course of history must have been made known before this time and must be contained in the Scriptures or hidden books. Wisdom speculation on cosmological matters and the secrets of the universe[22] were associated with the belief that heavenly figures such as "wisdom," the angels, or humans who had been translated to the heavenly world (Enoch in Gen. 5:21–24 and Elijah in II Kings 2:9–12) possessed access to these matters and could disclose them to the wise and the pious. This explains why apocalyptic works were written pseudonymously, that is, under a name other than that of the actual author, someone who lived during the time preceding Ezra.

Another characteristic of apocalyptic is the extensive use of symbolism which employed cryptic language, numerology, and beastly figures as representative of world powers. The employment of symbolism heightened the element of mystery and secrecy, reflected the developing interest in astral-geographic matters in which zodiac concerns assigned various lands to certain constellations, and allowed the writers to portray and caricature international powers in a far more bizarre fashion than would have been possible in ordinary terminology.

Apocalyptic thought can thus be seen as a highly eclectic speculation dependent upon numerous elements of older traditions that were reformulated in the light of the developing thought and the historical circumstances. Needless to say, apocalyptic thought tended to flourish during times of crises when pessimism and discontent with the *status quo* kindled aflame the embers of hope. The Book of Daniel will allow us to see the form in which these interests expressed themselves.

THE BOOK OF DANIEL

The Book of Daniel is a collection of narratives (chs. 1 to 6) and visions (chs. 7 to 12) associated with Daniel and his friends.[23] In the stories, Daniel is

---

[22] See von Rad, *Old Testament Theology*, Vol. II, pp. 301–315.
[23] On problems in The Book of Daniel, see H. H. Rowley, "The Unity of the Book of Daniel," in his *The Servant of the Lord*, pp. 247–280.

pictured as a Judean in exile in Babylon during the late Babylonian and early Persian periods. The narratives portray Daniel as an extremely pious person who is fastidiously faithful to his Yahwism and as an exceedingly wise man who, like the Chaldean magi, possessed the power of dream interpretation. In the vision accounts, Daniel is pictured as one who had dreams and visions and is granted angelic interpretations of them to be recorded for future generations.

On the basis of the internal historical references, the majority of scholars deny that the book was written during the sixth century, as its chronological statements imply, but instead date the bulk of the book to the period of the Maccabean struggle with Antiochus Epiphanes after the erection of the altar to Zeus in the Jerusalem Temple. In addition, the name Daniel occurs as the name of a legendary figure in numerous texts from antiquity. In Ezek. 14:14, he appears as a hero alongside Noah and Job (see Ezek. 28:3) noted for his righteousness and wisdom. The Ugaritic texts (fourteenth century B.C.) contain a legend about king Danel, and a later Jewish writing called The Book of Jubilees (Jubilees 4:20) mentions a Danel who was the great-great-grandfather of Noah. These references suggest that Daniel was a legendary person common to the folklore of several peoples but who always appeared as a righteous, wise man.

The stories about Daniel and his friends in the first six chapters of The Book of Daniel were intended as exhortations to fidelity to the Jewish religion and to obedience to the commandments offering the faithful the protection and reward of Yahweh. In Dan., ch. 1, Daniel and his friends who were in training as court pages refused to eat the food and drink from the king's table since it was in all probability unkosher and thus would have meant breaking the dietary food laws. Instead, they requested to live on vegetables and water, a diet free of defilement. As the reward for their loyalty they were both physically and mentally superior to their fellow candidates. When Shadrach, Meshach, and Abednego refused to bow down and worship the image set up by Nebuchadnezzar (Dan., ch. 3), they were thrown into a fiery furnace heated seven times hotter than ordinary, but they suffered no harm, being instead accompanied by a heavenly visitor. In ch. 6, Daniel is shown stubbornly refusing to obey the edict of the king that prohibited the worship of Daniel's God. Daniel continued to pray three times daily, facing Jerusalem. For this he was thrown into a den of lions, which, however, had their mouths closed by an angel of God and thus did Daniel no harm.

It is possible that these stories had their origin in times before the Antiochus persecution and were intent on encouraging Jewish obedience to the Mosaic law in the midst of an alien culture. All these stories (Dan., chs. 1; 3; and 6) can be directly related, however, to the persecution of Antiochus. Loyalty to the food laws had become an issue of life and death under Antiochus (see I Macc. 1:62–64). The question of bowing down before an image could certainly be seen in relation to the altar of Zeus set up in the Jerusalem Temple, while the general edict in Dan., ch. 6, prohibiting worship of the Jewish God had its parallel in Antiochus' famous edict. In addition, even the name Nebuchadnezzar contained a veiled reference to Antiochus Epiphanes to those acquainted with numerology. In Hebrew, the letters of the alphabet were assigned a numerical value, so that the first letter had the value of 1, the second 2, and so on.

Nebuchadnezzar's name, which in cuneiform was *nabu-kuddurri-usur* and should have been transliterated as Nebuchadrezzar in Hebrew (as it is in The Book of Jeremiah), has the same numerical value as Antiochus Epiphanes:

$$n + b + w + k + d + n + ' + \d{s} + r$$
$$50 + 2 + 6 + 20 + 4 + 50 + 1 + 90 + 200 = 423$$

$$' + n + \d{t} + y + w + k + w + s + ' + p + y + p + n + s$$
$$1 + 50 + 9 + 10 + 6 + 20 + 6 + 60 + 1 + 70 + 10 + 70 + 50 + 60 = 423$$

This type of correspondence is far too coincidental to be accidental. Behind the figure of Nebuchadnezzar, the apocalypticist could see the face of Antiochus!

Daniel, chs. 2; 4; and 5, were intended to show that God had not forsaken his people to the power of a despotic ruler. In Dan., ch. 2, the king had a dream in which he saw a statue with a gold head, arms and breast of silver, belly and thighs of bronze, legs of iron, and feet of iron and clay mixed. It was shattered by a stone uncut by human hands which then grew to fill the earth. Daniel interpreted this dream to mean that the Babylonian empire would be followed by three others (the final being the divided Hellenistic) which would be destroyed by God, who would then set up his kingdom and reign supreme. For the reader who saw in the post-Alexandrian conditions the feet and toes of clay and iron, the writer was promising an early end to the earthly powers and an act of divine intervention that would establish God's rule.

In Dan., ch. 4, Nebuchadnezzar dreamed of a huge tree that would be hewn down by a heavenly "watcher" with the stump remaining. Daniel interpreted this as the king's temporary fall from power. The account goes on to note that Nebuchadnezzar became "mad" and was driven from among men, ate grass like an ox, grew hair and nails like a bird's feathers and claws, and was covered by the dew of heaven. Only after Nebuchadnezzar praised and honored the Most High (Yahweh) was he returned to his senses and thus regained his kingdom. The God whom the Jews worshiped was he who had the power to depose and reinstate even the emperors themselves!

In Dan., ch. 5, Belshazzar at a great feast went so far as to mock the God of Israel by drinking wine from the holy vessels taken from the Jerusalem Temple. There then appeared a handwriting on the wall which Daniel interpreted as saying that the kingdom had been weighed, found lacking, and would be divided. The message for the reader would be clear: Neither Belshazzar nor Antiochus could mock God and escape his judgment! It was the God of the Jews who was in control of history.

These stories called the readers to an obedience to their deity even to the point of martyrdom. The answer of Shadrach, Meshach, and Abednego to Nebuchadnezzar reflects the author's sentiment: "If it be so, our God whom we serve is able to deliver us from the burning fiery furnace; and he will deliver us out of your hand, O king. But if not, . . . we will not serve your gods or worship the golden image which you have set up" (Dan. 3:16–18). This emphasis of the book on passive suffering for the faith even to the point of death (see II Macc., ch. 7) set the author apart from the Maccabeans and their active resistance and even warfare against the persecuting power.[24] In his one reference to the Maccabean revolt, he described its victories as "a little help" (Dan. 11:34).

In Dan., ch. 7, the author reiterated his understanding of the course of history in the vision of the four beasts that arose out of the sea of chaos. The first was a lion with eagle's wings, the second was a bear with three ribs in its mouth, the third was a leopard with four wings, and the fourth beast was the most terrible, with teeth of iron and with ten horns out of the midst of which arose another, a little horn with a mouth speaking great things. Then Daniel says he saw "the Ancient of Days" (God in his unchangeableness) surrounded by his host. The little horn was slain and its body burned in fire. Then Daniel described "one like a son of man" who appeared before the throne of the Ancient of Days and was given dominion over the world. The phrase "like a son of man" referred to a heavenly subordinate of the deity who was "human and humane" over against the beasts and the bestial. The little horn was none other than Antiochus, who had set himself against the Most High to change the times and the law. The rule of the little horn was to be taken away and he was to be subjected to judgment. The kingdom and the dominion would be turned over to the one like a son of man and the angelic saints ("holy ones") of the Most High. This dominion was to be shared with the "people of the saints" whom the writer no doubt understood as the presently persecuted community of God.[25] In the vision, all the action had its setting in the heavenly world, and the power of the world's empires is ended by a divine act and decree.

In Dan., chs. 8 to 12, the author attempted to pinpoint the actual time of the deity's intervention and predict the end time. He did this by pretending to write a prediction of the events in the Hellenistic age from the vantage point of the Babylonian exile. If the book were accepted as having an exilic origin, then the writer's ability to predict would have given tremendous prestige to the work.

Two passages can be analyzed to illustrate his prediction of the end of the world empires. The first of these is Dan., ch. 9, where the writer began by attempting an exegesis of the prophetic word of Jeremiah about the seventy years of Jerusalem's desolation and service to a foreign ruler (see Jer. 25:11; 29:10). The assumption of the writer was that the prophetic word must be true, and if seventy years passed and Jerusalem was still desolate under a foreign ruler, then the seventy must contain a hidden meaning. Daniel said that he received the true explanation of the reference from the angel Gabriel. The seventy he understood referred to seventy weeks of years or 490 years. In Dan. 9:24–27, he showed how the time would be calculated. From the going forth of the word till the coming of an anointed one was to be seven weeks, or 49 years. The number 586 (the date of the fall of Jerusalem and the beginning

---

[24] On martyrdom in Judaism, see W. H. C. Frend, *Martyrdom and Persecution in the Early Church* (Doubleday Anchor Books, 1967), pp. 22–57.

[25] See Martin Noth, "The Holy Ones of the Most High," in his *The Laws in the Pentateuch,* pp. 215–228.

of its desolation) minus 49 equals 537, the time of the downfall of Babylon and the decree to return and rebuild Jerusalem under Shesh-bazzar (or Zerub-babel?). The next period was to be 62 weeks or 434 years, but here he seems to have used the fixed point of 605 B.C. (the third year of the reign of Jehoiakim mentioned in Dan. 1:1). The number 605 minus 434 equals 171, the time when an anointed one would be cut off; 171 B.C. was the date of Onias III's murder. The last ruler would cause sacrifice and offerings to cease for the last half of the week (from 167; see Dan. 7:25) and then time would run out and the decreed end would be poured out on the desolator (Antiochus Epiphanes). The writer held out an assurance to his readers, whose backs were against the wall, that the sands of time had run out for their oppressor. Keep the faith! Deliverance is coming; God's word will be fulfilled!

In Dan. 11:40–45, the author declared that Antiochus would meet his death encamped between Jerusalem and the Mediterranean. Here the writer drew upon a very old motif in the Zion theology that envisioned the destruction of the enemies in an attack on "the glorious holy mountain" (see above, p. 132). With the death of Antiochus, "all hell would break loose" temporarily but would be put down by the angel Michael, who would rescue those who had remained faithful and whose names had been recorded in the heavenly book on which, no doubt, the course of history was also written (Dan. 12:1).

The author was confronted with one final question: What about those who had remained faithful to the "ancestral ways and faith" and yet did not live to see the ushering in of the ideal kingdom but instead had died a martyr's death? This question was answered by an affirmation of the resurrection from the dead (Dan. 12:2–3). Many of those who sleep in the dust would he awaken, some to everlasting life and others to shame and everlasting contempt. The writer does not envision a resurrection of all the dead but only some, perhaps the martyred faithful and the apostate Jews who had sold out—the former for reward, the latter for punishment. The idea of a resurrection from the dead was very late then in gaining a foothold in Judaism. The need to reconcile faith, justice, and the actualities of life in a time of martyrdom had forced the issue.[26]

---

[26] The original book of Daniel probably ended with Dan. 12:4, where he was commanded to write his words in a sealed book. Daniel 12:5–13 may have been added when the predicted end did not occur.

16 | THE HASMONEAN
AND ROMAN PERIODS

The Maccabean revolt begun by Mattathias provided the Jewish people with leadership in their struggles against the Seleucids. Eventually it led to the last period of religious and political independence for the Jewish people in ancient times. This independent rule of the family of Mattathias came to an end with the incorporation of Palestine into the Roman Empire.

Events and developments within Judaism during the period of independence and during the early days of Roman control were of tremendous import for Jewish life and faith. In many respects, the tone for later Jewish life was set during the first two centuries of Roman rule. The Judaism of this period was the womb within which Christianity was conceived and nurtured. A summary of the historical, literary, and theological developments within Judaism during the Hasmonean (named after Hasmoneus, the legendary great-grandfather of Mattathias) and early Roman periods not only will allow us to see the progress of Jewish life but also will serve as background to the origin and growth of early Christianity.

HISTORICAL DEVELOPMENTS [1]

The Triumph of the Maccabeans (*166–142* B.C.). In a number of strategic battles, Judas Maccabeus was able to defend his movement against Seleucid forces. He excelled in guerrilla warfare, fighting "like a lion in his deeds, like a lion's cub roaring for prey" (I Macc. 3:4). Judas was able to retake the Temple precincts and to restore Yahwistic worship. He was unable to capture the citadel with its garrison of Syrian troops overlooking the Temple grounds. Judas collected copies of the Torah, which had been outlawed by Antiochus Epiphanes

---

Biblical readings: The history of the Maccabean rule to 134 B.C. is given in I Macc., chs. 4 to 16. II Maccabees, which is a less reliable history, discusses the Jewish struggle only through the time of Judas Maccabeus. The basic sources for the history of the Hasmonean and Roman periods are the writings of Josephus. See maps XII–XIV.

[1] The political, social, and religious history of the Hasmonean and Roman periods (up to A.D. 65) is discussed in Solomon Zeitlin, *The Rise and Fall of the Judaean State*, Vols. I and II (The Jewish Publication Society of America, 1962–1967). A third volume is projected. Unfortunately Zeitlin does not date the Dead Sea Scrolls to either of these periods.

(II Macc. 2:14), and no doubt sought to restore the ancestral code as the law of the land, which meant the practical annulment of the decree of Antiochus. He conducted offensive religious war against the Syrian cults (I Macc. 5:44, 68) and the Hellenizers among the Jews (I Macc. 3:8), at times completely exterminating the male population of a town (I Macc. 5:51). After the death of Antiochus, the Syrian rulers consented "that their [the Jews'] temple be restored to them and that they live according to the customs of their ancestors" (II Macc. 11:25), which meant an officially recognized abolition of the Hellenistic reform. The high priest Menelaus was treated as a scapegoat by the Syrians and was executed. Alcimus, a Hellenizer but a member of the priestly Oniad family, was appointed to succeed him. The Hasidim sought a compromise with the new high priest, but Alcimus seized sixty and had them killed (I Macc. 7:5–18). The civil war which had quieted for a time resumed, and the Seleucid army was called in to support Alcimus. After winning a major victory in which the Syrian general was killed, Judas died in battle (I Macc. 9:1–22).

Leadership of the nationalist movement fell to Judas' younger brother Jonathan (160–142 B.C.), who carried on the struggle with spasmodic attacks on the enemy. The Hellenizers under Alcimus' leadership were able to stay in power only through massive Syrian support. After Alcimus' death not one of the Hellenizers was able to hold power, and the office of high priest was left vacant for seven years. Internal dissension in the Seleucid house and the cost of the military operations against the Maccabeans forced the Seleucids to a settlement with Jonathan, who "began to judge the people, and he destroyed the ungodly out of Israel" (I Macc. 9:65–73). He was subsequently granted the "authority to recruit troops, to equip them with arms" and he secured the release of hostages held in the citadel (I Macc. 10:6). In the course of a struggle over the Seleucid throne, Jonathan was appointed high priest and at the Feast of Tabernacles in 152 B.C. he appeared in public garbed in the robes of his office (I Macc. 11:20–27). The Seleucids conceded part of Samaria to Jonathan and greatly reduced the Jewish taxation (I Macc. 11:28–37). As general and governor of Judea (I Macc. 10:65) and as high priest, Jonathan was a loyal vassal to the king of Syria and participated in the life and struggles of the Seleucid rule. Involvement in the dynastic struggle of the Seleucids led to Jonathan's being seized and killed by a pretender to the throne (I Macc. 12:39–48; 13:23).

With the rule of Jonathan, the Maccabean cause had triumphed and in its victory it had drastically changed the complexity of Jewish life. In their struggles against the Seleucids, the Jews had once again become a military and political power with an army capable of strongly asserting itself in Syro-Palestinian affairs. In addition, it was no longer a state incapable of independent action nor a Greek city subject to the Seleucids but a body politic with its own national interests and rights. In addition, the needs of the hour and the response of the Maccabeans had created a ruling family that had rallied the masses against the aristocracy, the wealthy, and the priestly hierarchy. Some of the power and glory of the old Judean state had been rewon but under the leadership of men who could not stand nor rule in the line of David.

The Rule of the Hasmoneans (142–63 b.c.). Simon (141–134 b.c.), the last surviving son of Mattathias, succeeded Jonathan and was recognized by the ruling Seleucid king. In 141 b.c. the citadel was conquered and the last vestige of Syrian control was removed from Jerusalem (I Macc. 13:31–42, 49–53). Then, by decision of the general Jewish assembly of elders and priests, Simon was elected by his own people as high priest, military commander, and governor in perpetuity (I Macc. 14:41–49) which allowed him to bequeath his authority to his offspring. Simon thus became the primary possessor of political, military, and religious authority. Before Simon's death, further conflict with Syrians developed over Simon's take-over of the towns of Jaffa and Gezer. Simon and two of his sons were murdered by a son-in-law who hoped to acquire leadership (I Macc. 16:11–24), and it was left to Simon's son John Hyrcanus (134–104 b.c.) to battle the Syrians, who were soon to place Jerusalem under siege.

John Hyrcanus' rule began inauspiciously when he was forced to submit to disarming of his troops and to pay indemnity to the Syrians. But this humiliation was short-lived when once again internal struggles among the Seleucids freed Judea for independent action. Hyrcanus embarked on a policy of territorial expansion and extended the state's borders to include land east of the Jordan Valley, the district of Samaria to the north, and the land of Idumea (the name comes from the old state of Edom, which had occupied southern Judah during and after the struggle with the Babylonians in the sixth century) to the south. The Yahwistic temple of the Samaritans on Mt. Gerizim was destroyed and the Idumeans were forcibly circumcised, converted to Judaism, and compelled to keep the law. Most of the Greek cities in Palestine were taken over, a factor that contributed greatly to the economic life of the Hasmonean state.

It was during the rule of Hyrcanus that the real beginning occurred of one of the unique contributions made by the Hasmoneans, namely, the introduction of Hellenistic ways into Jewry without the abandonment of Judaism.[2] Hyrcanus was more sympathetic toward the noble and more politically-minded families in Jerusalem than toward the orthodox and Hasidic masses on which Maccabean strength had depended. He employed foreign mercenaries who created a personal force independent of the general population committed only to the ruler. Josephus reports that Hyrcanus even looted the tomb of King David of its treasure. The names of his three sons were changed from Judas, Mattathias, and Jonathan to Aristobulus, Antigonus, and Alexander Janneus. The life of the Hasmonean court began to rival the splendor of that of other Hellenistic rulers, and references to banqueting and drinking parties appear. The movement that had begun as a theocratic struggle was becoming a secular establishment. The movement that had been instituted by the people was becoming institutionalized in a dynasty independent of the people. The movement that had begun to defend and ensure theocratic concerns was becoming a movement of conquest and offense.

The first detailed references to a group called the Pharisees appear in

---

[2] See Elias Bickermann, *From Ezra to the Last of Maccabees* (Schocken Books, Inc., 1962), pp. 153–165.

Chart 9: FROM THE MACCABEAN REVOLT TO DESTRUCTION OF THE TEMPLE (166 B.C. to A.D. 70)

B.C	EVENTS IN PALESTINE	EVENTS ELSEWHERE
166	Beginning of Maccabean revolt	Antiochus IV Epiphanes, Seleucid ruler
	Rededication of Temple (164)	
	High priest Menelaus executed by Seleucids (163)	Death of Antiochus IV (163)
	Continued struggles between Jewish Hellenizers and Hasidim	
	Jonathan, leader of revolt (160–142)	
	Jonathan appointed high priest (152)	Alexander Balas, Seleucid ruler (150–145)
		Struggle over Seleucid throne
		Demetrius II Nicator (145–139)
	Jonathan killed by pretender to Seleucid throne (142)	Antiochus VI Epiphanes (145–142)
	Simon (141–134)	Trypho, claimant to Seleucid throne (142–138)
	Creation of Independent Judah (141)	
	Acra taken; Simon elected high priest	
	Simon murdered (134)	
	John Hyrcanus, Judean ruler (134–104)	
	Annexation of much surrounding territory	
	Beginning of Qumran community?	
	Samaritan temple destroyed	
	Aristobulus (104–103)	
	Claimed title of "King of the Jews"	
	Galilee annexed	
100	Alexander Janneus (103–76)	
	Pharisees persecuted	
	Height of Hasmonean power	
	Salome Alexandra (76–67)	
	Aristobulus II, king and high priest (67–63)	
	Civil war	
	Pompey captures Jerusalem (63)	
	Hyrcanus II appointed high priest	
	Antipater, the real power	
	Civil struggles led by Aristobulus and his followers	Pompey defeated by Julius Caesar at Pharalus (48)
	Herod appointed governor of Galilee (47)	
		Julius Caesar assassinated (44)
		Struggle for Roman power
	Invasion of Parthians (41)	
	Herod made "King of the Jews" (40)	
	Herod captures Jerusalem (37)	
		Octavian defeats Antony, at Actium (31)
		Augustus (Octavian) emperor (27 B.C. to A.D. 14)
	Rebuilding of Jerusalem Temple (20 B.C.–?)	
	Birth of Jesus (8–6 B.C.?)	

Death of Herod (4)
Sons of Herod
   Archelaus (4. b.c. to a.d. 6)
   Philip (4 b.c. to a.d. 34)
   Herod Antipas (4 b.c. to a.d. 39)

0
a.d.

Judea placed under procuratorship (6)
  Census of Quirinius
  Revolt led by Judas
	Tiberius (14–37)

Pontius Pilate (26–36)
  Preaching of John the Baptist
  Ministry of Jesus
  Crucifixion (30 ?)
Conversion of Paul (32 ?)	

	Caligula (37–41)
Herod Agrippa I (41–44)	Claudius (41–54)
Herod Agrippa II (king of parts of Palestine, 50– ?)	Expulsion of Jews from Rome (49) Nero (54–68)

Jewish revolt against Rome (66–73)
  Destruction of Qumran community
  (68)
	Struggle for rule (68–69)

Capture of Jerusalem; Destruction of Temple (70)	Vespasian (69–79)
Fall of Masada (73)	

Josephus' discussion of John Hyrcanus' rule. The Pharisees, about whose origins we are only dimly aware, appear to have been the successors to the earlier Hasidim and scribes who were experts in the interpretation and application of the Torah on which the government of the theocratic or hierocratic state depended. Apparently some of the Pharisees objected to the policies of Hyrcanus and claimed that he was a usurper, perhaps with no claim to the high priesthood, implying that he was conceived while his mother was a prisoner of Antiochus. Hyrcanus then broke with the Pharisees and relied heavily on the aristocratic priestly families, the Sadducees, whom, it should be recalled, had been the primary supporters of the earlier attempts at Hellenization.

Hyrcanus died at a ripe old age and left behind a kingdom that was powerful and prosperous, at least for the aristocracy of priests, military officers, landowners, and merchants. His successor, Aristobulus (104–103 b.c.), was a ruthless, ambitious man who conquered the district of Galilee to the north and forced the residents, many of whom were Syrian and Greek, to convert to Judaism. Aristobulus was the first Hasmonean to proclaim himself "King of the Jews." Something of his character can be seen in the fact that he allowed his mother to die of hunger while she was imprisoned and permitted his bodyguard to kill his brother. His remorse over his brother's murder was said, however, to have hastened his own death.

Aristobulus' widow, Salome Alexandra, released her late husband's brother, Alexander Janneus (103–76 b.c.), from prison. She married him and had him proclaimed high priest and king. Under Janneus, the territorial holdings of the Hasmoneans reached their apogee. He added most of the territory along the Mediterranean coast as well as the highlands of Transjordan. "From Dan to Beer-sheba" was again in Jewish hands. Aristobulus' constant warfare and the fact that he was not overly competent in military affairs left Palestine torn by the scars of battle and interfered with its commercial and economic interests.

Janneus' rule was torn by severe dissension at home. Hostility toward him emerged during a celebration of the Feast of Tabernacles when the assembled crowd pelted him with citrons while he officiated in the Temple. The Pharisees charged him with being the descendant of a captive and therefore unfit for the high priesthood. Janneus, enraged and insulted, turned his mercenaries loose on the population, and Josephus says that over six thousand were killed. He had the Temple barricaded and permitted only the priests to enter. Civil war broke out and lasted for six years. The "rebels" eventually appealed for help from the Seleucid king (a descendant of Antiochus Epiphanes!) who invaded the country. The rebels gave their support to Janneus when it appeared that Jerusalem was about to be captured and the tide of battle turned. Janneus, however, was not noted for his great mercy and he proceeded with his actions against the leaders of the revolt. Josephus described the king as drinking at a banquet surrounded by his concubines and looking out at eight hundred crosses on which his opponents were crucified, many of whom watched their wives and children being cut to death.

Janneus was succeeded by his wife Salome Alexandra (76–67 B.C.), who ruled as queen, and her son Hyrcanus II received the office of high priest. Alexandra sided with the Pharisaic element rather than with the aristocratic and Sadducean elements and brought to the land a generally peaceful respite of seven years. Hyrcanus was an unillustrious, effeminate, and peace-loving character, but his younger brother Aristobulus II was exactly the opposite and organized the Sadducean and military factions and seized power in a show of force at the time of his mother's death.

The years of Aristobulus' rule (67–63 B.C.) were torn by civil strife and warfare. Hyrcanus II, who had little ambition of his own, fell under the influence of Antipater, the governor over Idumea, whose ambition was sufficient for the two. Hyrcanus was nudged into an attempt to oust Aristobulus and perhaps could have succeeded had it not been for the influence of Rome, which had taken over Syria from the Seleucids. Both of the brothers appealed to Rome for support. The Roman general Pompey arrived in Damascus in 63 B.C. and was met by three Jewish deputations—one from Hyrcanus and another from Aristobulus, both requesting Roman help, and a third claiming to represent the Jewish people, perhaps backed by the Pharisees, who advocated that neither prince should be supported but suggested that the monarchy should be abolished, that Pompey should assume political power, and that Judea should be reconstituted as a theocratic state under the office of high priest.

The Early Period of Roman Rule (63 B.C. to A.D. 73). Pompey was forced to lay siege to the city of Jerusalem in order to subdue Aristobulus and his followers. The Hasmonean sought peace with the Romans but his ardent followers, after the imprisonment of their leader, barricaded themselves on the fortified Temple mount. It was necessary for the Romans to build ramps and siege towers and this they did by working primarily on the Sabbath, when they were free from Jewish harassment. Three months passed before the walls of the

Temple fortress were breached by the Roman battering rams. Roman soldiers slew, according to Josephus, twelve thousand, many of them priests quietly continuing with their officiation at the altar. Pompey himself entered the Temple and despite the protestations of the priests walked into the sacred Holy of Holies, the innermost shrine of the Temple, which was entered only once a year and then only by the high priest on the Day of Atonement. Pompey discovered the shrine empty in spite of the Gentile tales that spoke of enormous treasures and grotesque objects kept there. Although he withdrew from the Temple empty-handed and commanded the resumption of worship, this act in Jewish eyes was one of horrendous sacrilege. Aristobulus and his family, along with other Jews, were carried as exiles to Rome and were forced to march as captives in Pompey's triumphal procession in 61 B.C.

Judea was turned into a tributary of Rome with its territory limited to Judea proper, part of Idumea, Perea east of the Jordan, and Galilee. An indemnity of ten thousand talents (a talent would be equivalent to several thousand dollars) was imposed on Judea, and a Roman garrison was stationed in Jeru-

The forum at Gerasa (modern Jerash), enclosed within fifty-six towering columns, illustrates the impressive ruins of this ancient city of the Decapolis. Largely rebuilt by the Romans, this city was a major center in Transjordan and possessed numerous temples to Roman gods.

salem. Many former Greek cities were "liberated" and ten, nine of them east of the Jordan, were organized into a league (Decapolis). Hyrcanus was appointed high priest before Pompey left Judea, but it was Antipater who was the real power.

Civil strife among the Jews and opposition to the Romans were far from over; in fact, they were only beginning. Aristobulus' following, later his two sons, and finally he himself (after fleeing from Rome), led several uprisings in opposition to Hyrcanus and Antipater and thus the Romans. On numerous occasions, Roman troops were required to squelch a revolt or to storm a fortress in order to suppress the followers of the ever-hopeful Hasmonean who could portray his position as one of "patriotism." Aristobulus and his son Alexander were later involved in the Roman conflicts between Pompey and Julius Caesar, but both were killed; one was poisoned, the other beheaded. The struggle, however, was carried on by Aristobulus' son Antigonus.

Antipater was a skilled diplomat and politician. He was capable of evaluating the Roman scene, and in the struggles for power, he was able to support the winning side or to change his allegiance at the proper time and to offer valuable assistance at strategic moments. He switched his allegiance from Pompey to Caesar, and with the triumph of the latter, Hyrcanus and Antipater were rewarded by being declared ethnarch ("ruler of the people") and governor respectively. Antipater sought to convince the Judeans of the value of quiet acceptance of the Romans and compliance with their rule. Josephus says that "he took the country into his own hand, finding Hyrcanus indolent and without the energy necessary to a king," but to the latter "his affection and loyalty underwent no change." The Jewish historian praised him as "a man distinguished for piety, justice, and devotion to his country." Antipater appointed his son Phasael governor of Jerusalem and another son, Herod, governor of Galilee perhaps in an effort to bring tranquillity to the land.

Herod proved to be the rising star in the political constellation of Palestine.[3] Roman political life for several years after the murder of Julius Caesar on March 15, 44 B.C., was characterized by open warfare between would-be masters of the Roman world. During this period, the Parthians, eastern enemies of Rome, invaded Syria and Palestine. Antigonus, who had stubbornly refused to give up his lust to rule, joined forces with the Parthians. Civil war broke out once again in Judea. Phasael and Herod proved to be no match for the invading Parthians, and Herod barely escaped with his life to Rome. Antigonus with Parthian assistance took Jerusalem and was proclaimed king and high priest. Hyrcanus was mutilated by Antigonus and thus was disqualified from the priesthood (see Lev. 21:16–23). Herod was well received in Rome and was named by Antony and Octavius (later known as Augustus) with senate confirmation as "king of Judea" (40 B.C.), but he was a king without a throne and without a country. Even with Roman help, Herod had to fight his way back to Jerusalem. Antigonus tried to rally complete Judean support against Herod, claiming that the latter was "a commoner and an Idumean, a half-Jew." Herod took Jerusalem in 37 B.C., and Antigonus was subsequently killed by the Romans.

The reign of Herod (37–4 B.C.) was generally peaceful and prosperous on the surface. Successive land grants from Antony and Augustus expanded the boundaries of his kingdom, so that it eventually included Idumea, Judea, Samaria, Galilee, Perea, and the territory north and east of the Sea of Galilee—

---

[3] On Herod's life and rule, see Samuel Sandmel, *Herod: Profile of a Tyrant* (J. B. Lippincott Company, 1967).

an area almost equivalent to that of the ancient kingdom of Solomon. Herod inaugurated many building programs, founding and rebuilding many cities and adorning them with the beauty of Hellenistic architecture and often Gentile temples. On the seacoast, he built a magnificent harbor which he named

The port of Caesarea was built by Herod the Great and named in honor of Caesar Augustus. Requiring over a decade to construct, the city, with its artificially built harbor, was the capital of Judea under the procurators. Roman and Crusader ruins today mark the site of the ancient town.

ROBERT B. WRIGHT

Caesarea. Palatial retreats and fortresses were constructed on the periphery of the settled areas, the most extravagant and unusual being Masada.[4] Much of Jerusalem was reconstructed, including the restoration of the Temple, about which later Jewish writers declared that "one who has not seen Herod's temple has never seen a beautiful building."[5] From the standpoint of the Romans, Herod ruled wisely and generously.

---

[4] See Yigael Yadin, *Masada: Herod's Fortress and the Zealots' Last Stand* (Random House, Inc., 1966).
[5] See Kenyon, *Jerusalem*, pp. 138–154.

In many respects Herod was no better or worse than any number of provincial kings throughout the Empire, though perhaps more competent and ambitious than the average. By ruling when he did, he was destined to be remembered and sometimes maligned by Jews and Christians, both of whom outlived the Roman Empire which Herod served so obediently. Having attained the kingship of Judea, Herod retained it, through suspicion and insecurity, with acts that were merciless and ruthless. He was husband to ten different wives and father to at least fifteen children. In palace and court, Herod's suspicion and jealousy made it difficult if not impossible for him to distinguish slander and gossip from truth. A list of his immediate family and friends whose deaths were Herod's responsibility is impressive for its extent: Aristobulus, his Hasmonean brother-in-law, whose popularity as high priest Herod could not endure; the aged Hyrcanus II, whose very presence seemed to threaten Herod's absolute rule; Mariamne, the Hasmonean wife of the king, who was known and famous for her beauty but whose fidelity Herod doubted; Alexandra, his Hasmonean mother-in-law; Castobar, his brother-in-law; Alexander, Aristobulus, and Antipater, his sons, whose real or imagined ambitions to their father's throne Herod disdained.

Herod was king of the Jews but he was no Jewish king. Neither Jewish religion nor Jewish ethics found a supporter in him. He was more Greek than Jew, but necessity perhaps demanded it. An ardent Judaism would have meant inevitable clash with Rome. Herod was Jewish when it was convenient, but he could ignore or suppress Judaism when it was personally profitable to do so. He was certainly unloved by the Jewish people, and his rule and life were ensured by an elaborate espionage system, police state tactics, and general and brutal suppression of opposition.

Herod had made three wills in rapid succession, and the Roman emperor Augustus (27 B.C. to A.D. 14), after some hesitation, carried out the main features of the third will made only days before his death. His son Archelaus (4 B.C. to A.D. 6) became ethnarch of Idumea, Judea, and Samaria, although Herod had stipulated that he be made king. Dissatisfaction was so widespread and he so alienated his subjects that after ten years of rule he was deposed and banished by the Romans. His territory became a Roman province with a procurator as the chief official directly responsible to the emperor but to some extent under the jurisdiction of the procurator of Syria. Armed conflict broke out between the Romans and a crowd of Jewish pilgrims in Jerusalem for the Festival of Pentecost in 4 B.C. and at the time Archelaus was deposed a far more serious rebellion occurred in Galilee. This was led by a man named Judas who was assisted by a Pharisee named Saddok.[6] The revolt was precipitated by the emperor's orders that a census be taken by Quirinius, the legate of Syria, to assess the economic resources of the territory being placed under direct

---

[6] This Judas was the son of a certain Hezekiah who had led a patriotic guerrilla campaign in Galilee against the Romans and Roman sympathizers while Herod was governor of Galilee. Herod had Hezekiah and many of his followers killed; for this Herod was forced to appear before the Jerusalem Sanhedrin.

Roman control.[7] Judas upbraided his countrymen for being willing to pay tribute to Rome and for tolerating any mortal master, since God was their lord. This was the first time in almost a century and a half that the Jews had been directly ruled over by foreigners. Josephus says the rebellion was so severe that over two thousand of the captured rebels were crucified by the Romans. The high priest Joazar took a leading role in the revolt of A.D. 6, siding with the Romans and seeking to persuade the people to submit to the census. This Judas the Galilean was the founder of a sect in Judaism (apparently the Zealots) which, again according to Josephus, was associated in general with the doctrine of the Pharisees. The sect, stressing the absolute sovereignty of Yahweh over his people and the freedom of the Jews, was to influence Jewish life for years to come.

Another son of Herod, Philip (4 B.C. to A.D. 34), was made tetrarch of the districts north and east of the Sea of Galilee. Little is known of his life, though he evidently ruled his predominantly Gentile territory wisely and well. A third son, Herod Antipas (4 B.C. to A.D. 39), became tetrarch of Galilee and Perea. He was noted primarily for his building projects, his marriage to Herodias, the wife of his half-brother (which scandalized the pious Jews), his execution of John the Baptist, and the fact that he was ruler in Galilee during the lifetime of Jesus. Antipas was charged with conspiracy against Rome and was banished to Gaul in A.D. 39.

Judea continued to be ruled until A.D. 41 by Roman procurators whose primary duties were to function as chief tax collectors and to ensure peace by curbing any attempts at sedition or insurrection. These Roman rulers, especially with their power to depose and appoint high priests, were a constant reminder of Jewish subservience to a foreign power. The most famous of these procurators was the fifth, Pontius Pilate (A.D. 26–36), who is remembered as the Roman officer who gave the order to crucify Jesus (this will be discussed later). Pilate had several altercations with the general Jewish population. He allowed Roman soldiers to bring images that were used in worship into Jerusalem on their standards. He later hung golden shields, bearing the name of the emperor and used in the royal cult, on the walls of Herod's old palace in Jerusalem and used Temple funds to construct a new aqueduct to supply water for the city. Reactions of the people were put down with force and bloodshed. Pilate was dismissed from his office in A.D. 36 after he had hastily sent his troops against a group of Samaritans and a substantial massacre had resulted. The Samaritans had gathered at the bidding of a prophet who had promised to show them the sacred vessels that Moses had supposedly buried on Mt. Gerizim.

For a time, Palestine, or parts thereof, was again under the rule of Herod's descendants. Agrippa I (A.D. 37–44) came to rule over virtually the same territory as that of his grandfather, and his son Agrippa II ruled over various parts of the country from A.D. 53 until his death at the end of the century. Agrippa I received his appointment from the emperor Gaius Caligula, whom to call

---

[7] Luke 2:1–2 refers to this census as the time of Jesus' birth, but if Herod was king at the time Jesus was born, then his birth must be placed around 6 B.C.

mentally unbalanced may be an understatement. The latter ordered, in A.D. 39, that a statue of Zeus (or Caligula?) be set up in the Jerusalem Temple as a reprimand for the Jewish destruction of an altar constructed by the Gentiles in Jamnia. When the Roman legate entered Palestine to carry out the edict, the entire country was at the point of rebellion. The legate and Agrippa stalled for time and argued for recension of the order. Caligula's sudden and violent death by assassination, a fate which the Jews saw as ordained by God, removed the threat but not the fact that Judeans were ruled by heathen foreigners who might impose any form of impious demand upon them.

Anti-Roman activity continued.[8] A certain Theudas (see Acts 5:36), who claimed to be a prophet, led several hundred of his followers down to the Jordan only to be captured and decapitated (ca. A.D. 45). The procurator Tiberius Alexander (A.D. 46–48), the scion of a Jewish patrician family who had forsaken his religion, crucified two of the sons of Judas the Galilean apparently for insurrection. Josephus says that twenty to thirty thousand Jews were slaughtered in a fracas during the procuratorship of Comanus (A.D. 48–52). Relationships continued to deteriorate. Would-be saviors and miracle-workers promising deliverance to the Jews became more numerous, and a new group called the Sicarii (from *sica*, "dagger") began the practice of clandestine assassination of pro-Roman Jews using concealed daggers. Their first victim was the high priest. The Temple priesthood became embroiled in controversy with the lower order of priests in opposition to the clerical aristocracy which was mostly pro-Roman.

The "Great Rebellion" of the Jews against Rome in A.D. 66–73 was the culmination of multiple clashes between Jewish religion and local Roman government, the latter amply seasoned with misgovernment. The immediate catalysts were a clash between the Gentile and Jewish residents of Caesarea and the raiding of the Temple treasury by the procurator Florus. The lines were drawn when Eleazar, the son of the high priest, with support from the lower clergy and many of the people, but against the wishes of the hierarchy, stopped the daily sacrifice offered in the Jerusalem Temple on behalf of the emperor and the Roman people. Menahem, the son of Judas the Galilean, and his Zealot followers seized the fortress of Masada, slew the Roman garrison stationed there, and captured a supply of arms. Menahem made it to Jerusalem, arriving, according to Josephus, as a king, but for some reason he was killed by Eleazar or his followers. The city of Jerusalem was taken, the high priest and many pro-Romans were killed, and the revolt spread throughout the country. The Roman Twelfth Legion Fulminata ("the Thundering One") was sent to Jerusalem to squelch the revolt but was driven from the field (summer, A.D. 66). Roman defeat was interpreted as Yahweh's blessing: the insurrection became a holy war. The rebels set up a government in Jerusalem, divided the country into military districts, and struck its own silver coins. Three legions, under the command of Vespasian, were dispatched to Judea by the emperor Nero, but fighting did not resume until A.D. 68. During this short respite from

---

[8] For a discussion of anti-Roman activity, A.D. 6–73, see S. G. F. Brandon, *Jesus and the Zealots* (Charles Scribner's Sons, 1967), pp. 65–145.

battle, internecine struggles broke out between the sacerdotal aristocracy and the Zealots and among the Zealots themselves. Only in the last days of the revolt were these differences overcome.

Masada is a rocky outcrop rising 1,300 feet above the western shore of the Dead Sea. Early in his reign, King Herod built himself a palatial, three-tiered retreat whose ruins are visible in the left center. Fortifications, defense towers, storehouses, barracks, and other facilities were constructed on top of the mountain. The Zealots seized the site at the outbreak of the Great Rebellion in A.D. 66. The last of these—960 men, women, and children—committed suicide in A.D. 73 rather than surrender to the Romans.

CONSULATE GENERAL OF ISRAEL, HOUSTON

The siege of Jerusalem came in the summer of A.D. 70. In late August the Roman legionnaires stormed the Temple and burned it. The expected and prophesied miracle of divine intervention, referred to by Josephus, did not occur. The Romans erected their standards in the sacred precincts and offered sacrifice to them. Josephus says, in numbers that are certainly exaggerated, that 1,100,000

Jews perished during the siege of Jerusalem. Thousands of prisoners and great bounty were taken by the victorious general Titus. The mighty fortress of Masada did not fall until A.D. 73 when the defenders led by Eleazar ben Jair, a descendant of Judas the Galilean, chose to commit mass suicide rather than to surrender.

The victory of Vespasian and Titus over the Jews was celebrated in Rome. Josephus says that the purple curtains from the Temple, the ceremonial copy of the Torah used in the Temple, and other spoils of war were carried in a

The Arch of Titus, erected in Rome, depicts part of the triumphal procession of A.D. 71 which celebrated Titus' suppression of the Jewish revolt. One scene on the arch shows the victorious Roman legionnaries carrying spoils from the Jerusalem Temple.

triumphal procession through the streets of Rome. The Arch of Titus portrays part of this procession and shows Roman legionnaires carrying the massive seven-branched candlestick (the *menorah*), the silver trumpets, and altar of shewbread. Coins were struck for both Vespasian (A.D. 69–79) and Titus (A.D. 79–81), showing a mourning Judea sitting beneath a palm tree and inscribed with the words *Judaea Capta*.

The Great Rebellion against the Romans was a tragic event that left a deep scar in the subsequent life of Judaism. The Holy City was ravished; the Temple

Jewish and Roman coins from the time of the Great Rebellion reflect the hopes associated with the Jewish cause and the triumph of the Romans. (Left) A Hebrew shekel from A.D. 67 shows a pomegranate with three buds and carries an inscription: "Jerusalem the Holy." Other Jewish coins of the revolt were inscribed "For the Freedom of Zion." (Right) A denarius of Vespasian commemorates the fall of Jerusalem in A.D. 70. A Jewess is pictured seated in mourning beneath a trophy of arms.

AMERICAN NUMISMATIC ASSOCIATION

destroyed, never to be rebuilt; the sacrificial cult and worship ended; and the messianic hope and the belief in divine intervention had suffered a severe blow. But Jewish nationalism and apocalyptic hope flamed again during the reign of the emperor Hadrian (A.D. 117–138). The ruler let it be known that he planned to found a Roman colony in Jerusalem and to build pagan temples there. Such news stirred anew the Jewish spirit. Revolt was planned, this time with well-laid and centralized preparations. The spiritual or religious leader was Rabbi Akiba, who declared Simeon bar Cochba (or Kosibah) the messiah. The latter was known as the "Prince of Israel" and was apparently descended from the Davidic family line. The revolt broke out in A.D. 131 and was not eradicated until four years later and after the Roman army had suffered great losses. After the desperate effort of the Jewish rebels had been quelled, a new city, Roman Jerusalem, called Aelia Capitolina, was built on the ancient site.

LITERARY DEVELOPMENTS

The Hasmonean and Roman periods were times of intense literary activity in Judaism. We have examined The Book of Daniel in detail and utilized the books of I and II Maccabees in reconstructing the history of Maccabean and Hasmonean times. A knowledge of only the Biblical materials does not acquaint one with the bulk of these writings, since the overwhelming majority of them never made it into any authorized canon.

The Wailing Wall in Jerusalem is sacred to Jews throughout the world. A portion of the west wall of the Temple of Herod, this area was left undestroyed after the fall of Jerusalem.

CONSULATE GENERAL OF ISRAEL, HOUSTON.

The Septuagint.[9] From the time of the Babylonian exile and especially during the Hellenistic period, Jews had migrated to Egypt in great numbers. In Alexandria, which became, next to Rome, the largest and most splendid city in the Greco-Roman world, the Jews comprised a considerable portion of the population. With the widespread adoption of Greek as the vernacular language, the Jews in Egypt knew Hebrew only as a second language, if at all. It was in Alexandria that the Hebrew Scriptures were first translated into Greek. This process perhaps began as a free translation of the Hebrew passages read in worship services. A sort of official translation of the Pentateuch was made or developed. This translation came to be known as the Septuagint (from the Latin word for "seventy"). A pseudonymous writing of the late second century, The Letter of Aristeas, tells the story that lies behind this name. According to it, seventy (or seventy-two) elders were brought from Jerusalem to Egypt in the third century B.C. at the command of the Ptolemaic ruler, and working there for seventy days, they produced seventy identical copies. This account is largely legendary, intended to give authority and to claim inspiration for the Greek translation. Without doubt, the Pentateuch was translated into Greek in Alexandria during the third century. Eventually, over the next two or three centuries, all the books of the Hebrew Bible were translated and collected in a Greek version. In addition, the Septuagint (the name was later applied to the entire collection) contained a number of books that were later excluded from the Hebrew canon. This Greek translation was used more widely by Jews outside Palestine but was certainly known to Palestinian Jews, and it became the Bible of early Hellenistic Christianity and was subsequently repudiated by the Jews who produced other Greek translations of their Scriptures.

Those writings which were included in the Septuagint but which are not found in the Hebrew Scriptures are often referred to as the Apocrypha in Protestant circles and as deuterocanonical among Catholics.[10] The former term originally meant "hidden" and was applied to works in some way kept from public usage. The term took on the connotation "spurious" or "heretical" in some Christian circles but is now used in the sense of noncanonical.

The Pseudepigrapha.[11] A large number of Jewish writings that have never been part of any officially recognized canon were produced during the period from the second century B.C. to the second century A.D. These are often referred to as Pseudepigrapha (by Catholics as Apocrypha), a term that means "false or spurious writings." The name applied to these works was occasioned by the fact that many of the writings were fictitiously attributed to Adam, Enoch, Moses, Isaiah, and other great and ancient characters. These books were

---

[9] See Sidney Jellicoe, *The Septuagint and Modern Study* (Oxford University Press, Inc., 1968).

[10] Introductions to the apocryphal literature are given in Robert H. Pfeiffer, *History of New Testament Times with an Introduction to the Apocrypha* (Harper & Brothers, 1949) and Bruce M. Metzger, *An Introduction to the Apocrypha* (Oxford University Press, Inc., 1957).

[11] Translations of and introductions to the pseudepigraphal materials are given in Robert H. Charles, ed., *The Apocrypha and Pseudepigrapha of the Old Testament in English*, Vol. II (Oxford University Press, Inc., 1913, reprinted 1963).

composed in various languages (Hebrew, Greek, and Aramaic), and some have survived only in versions in other languages and often in a form reflecting the influence of Christian thought and perhaps Christian editing. Some of these works are legendary histories (such as The Lives of the Prophets, The Book of Jubilees, and The Martyrdom of Isaiah), others are collections of psalms (The Psalms of Solomon), and some are a form of wisdom literature (IV Maccabees). Some of these writings are apocalyptic works (Enoch and Apocalypse of Baruch) concerned with the final course of history and the establishment of the rule of God. Such books must have been fairly popular among many Jews around the beginning of the Christian era and among many early Christians. Their use by Jews was later discouraged because their apocalyptic character had helped stimulate false hopes which led to the calamities of A.D. 70 and 135 and their use and revision by Christians placed them under suspicion of containing heretical teachings.

The Dead Sea Scrolls.[12] An important collection of writings, widely and popularly known as the Dead Sea Scrolls, has been discovered through the work of archaeologists and the clandestine digging of Arab bedouin. The initial discovery of these scrolls was made in 1947 (or 1945?) by an Arabic shepherd boy searching for a lost goat in the mountain chain that encircles the west side

Cave IV at Qumran, whose openings are visible in the cliff face, was about one hundred yards from the settlement buildings. The cave was one of eleven in the vicinity which have yielded scrolls. The gorge, or stream bed, called Wadi Qumran, from which the ruins are named, can be seen in the background.

ROBERT B. WRIGHT

of the Dead Sea. Subsequent finds of manuscripts and other material were made in caves in the vicinity, and a systematic excavation of the nearby ruins over-

---

[12] Translations of most of these texts can be found in Dupont-Sommer, *The Essene Writings from Qumran*; and Géza Vermes, *The Dead Sea Scrolls in English* (Penguin Books, 1963).

looking the rugged valley called Wadi Qumran revealed the headquarters of the community that produced the scrolls. The scrolls include copies or fragments of every book of the Old Testament, with the exception of Esther, parts of some of the apocryphal and pseudepigraphical writings, selections of texts, paraphrases, and commentaries on various Old Testament books, and a number of writings distinctive to the Qumran community. Some of the copies of Old Testament writings provided scholars with manuscripts older by a thousand years than any known at the time.

The most important of the Qumran texts are the writings distinctive to the community, providing us with a glimpse of the beliefs and faith of a pre-Christian Jewish sect. These include a document called The Rule of the Community (or The Manual of Discipline), which furnishes a description of the organizational life of the Qumran community and some of the rules by which its members were governed. Another work, The Damascus Document, which was first discovered in the genizah (a storage place for used sacred manuscripts) of a Cairo synagogue, probably had its origin in the same community, since fragments of the work have been found in the Dead Sea caves.[13] It too outlines the rules of life for the community. Another document, The Rule for the Final War (called by its publisher The Scroll of the War of the Sons of Light Against the Sons of Darkness),[14] describes the final holy war to be fought before the establishment of the reign of God. In addition, other writings were a scroll of psalms unique to the community, commentaries on Biblical books that interpreted Biblical passages in relation to the history of the community, a scroll inscribed on copper listing the hiding places of treasures, a document describing the heavenly Jerusalem, and a scroll concerned with the new temple.[15]

The origin of the Qumran community is still a matter of dispute.[16] In all likelihood, the community was founded during the Hasmonean rule of the second century B.C. The founder of the community was a person called the Teacher of Righteousness (or the Rightful Teacher), who was later killed and his followers persecuted by "the Wicked Priest." The community considered itself to be the elect of God and members of the new covenant.[17] The members believed that the Temple cult and priesthood in Jerusalem were apostate and they utilized a calendar differing from that of the Jerusalem community. The community was governed by a council (of twelve or fifteen members) and an overseer. Admission policy required a probationary period of two years and a

[13] See Chaim Rabin, The Zadokite Documents, 2d ed. (Oxford University Press, Inc., 1958).

[14] For a discussion of the text and translation, see Yigael Yadin, The Scroll of the War of the Sons of Light Against the Sons of Darkness (Oxford University Press, Inc., 1962).

[15] The latter, as well as other scrolls and fragments, has not yet been published. See Yigael Yadin, "The Temple Scroll," The Biblical Archaeologist, XXX (1967), pp. 135–139.

[16] For a discussion of various theories, see Jósef T. Milik, Ten Years of Discovery in the Wilderness of Judaea, tr. by J. Strugnell (London: SCM Press, Ltd., 1959), pp. 44–98.

[17] See Helmer Ringgren, The Faith of Qumran, tr. by E. T. Sander (Fortress Press, 1963). The literature on the Qumran community, its life, and its practices is legend. The best elementary work on the subject is Menahem Mansoor, The Dead Sea Scrolls (Wm. B. Eerdmans Publishing Company, 1964); and the most ambitious, but with an interpretation that puts the origin of the sect in the Christian era, is Godfrey R. Driver, The Judaean Scrolls (Oxford: Basil Blackwell, 1965).

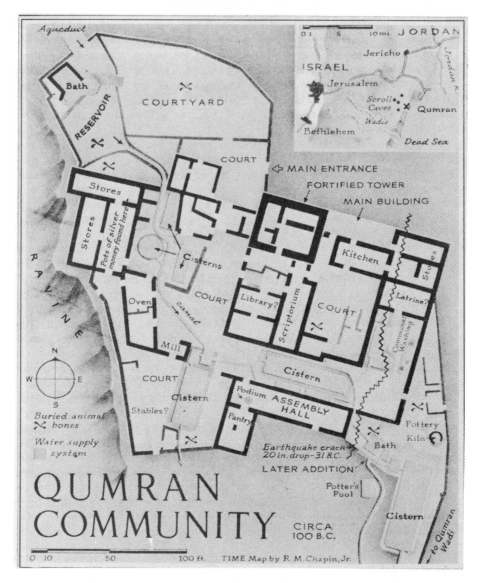

The building complex at Qumran served as the headquarters for the Dead Sea Scrolls community. This particular site, whose general location is shown in the inset map, was chosen because of the isolation, its proximity to the area spoken of in the eschatology of Ezek., ch. 47, and the prior existence of a cistern and ruins at the spot dating from the seventh century. The members of the community did not live in the main buildings but occupied caves and insubstantial dwellings in the area.

TIME MAP BY R. M. CHAPIN, JR.

vote by the membership. The rules governing the community were very strict, as was its discipline of members, especially in regard to revealing the secrets of the community. Purification baths (or baptisms) were an important, apparently daily, part of the members' ritual. This monastic community believed itself to be the eschatological community awaiting the final intervention of God and it looked to the coming of a prophet and two messiahs (a priestly one from the line of Aaron and a royal one from Israel, perhaps Davidic) to inaugurate the end time. A ritual meal of bread and wine was shared by the community in anticipation of the messianic banquet to come. The Qumran community was apparently destroyed by the Roman Tenth Legion advancing toward Jerusalem in A.D. 68.

Apologetic and Missionary Literature. The geographer Strabo (64 B.C. to A.D. 24) once wrote that "Jews are already gotten in all cities, and it is hard to find a place in the habitable earth that has not admitted this tribe of men, and is not possessed by them." This is certainly an overstatement of the situation, but it does point to a fact that is of tremendous importance to the history of Judaism and the development of Christianity, namely, that the majority of the Jews at the beginning of the Christian era lived outside Palestine in what is called the Diaspora, or the Dispersion.[18] As such, the Jews were an alien and minority element in the general Hellenistic world of Greco-Roman times. The treatment of the Jews by their contemporaries varied from place to place, but various forms of anti-Judaism were common. The Jews in the Dispersion were bound by religious ties and sentiments to the Jewish community in Jerusalem and Judea. A half-shekel tax was paid to the Temple every year, and pilgrimages to Jerusalem expressed the Jewish tie to the mother community. The life and worship of the Jews in synagogues throughout the Roman Empire and their dietary practices and religious observances set the Jews apart from the local communities. The Romans had made a number of concessions to the Jewish population of the Empire. The Maccabean Simon had reached an agreement with Rome that granted the Jews freedom of worship throughout the Empire. Julius Caesar and the Roman senate guaranteed and expanded this agreement, which was respected by most of the later emperors. The Jews were not required to worship Roman gods and were allowed to modify their participation in the emperor cult and worship. They could offer sacrifices and prayers on behalf of rather than to the emperor, oaths and references to the emperor's divinity were avoided, and synagogues were not required to display imperial images. The Jews were granted the right of assembly to worship, to contribute money to the Temple, to observe the Sabbath, and other religious privileges as well as some special civil privileges.

Anti-Judaism was prevalent in the Empire. Jews were accused of being atheists in that they worshiped only one god. Sabbath and dietary laws were often considered fanatical by the general population. The general suspicion of Eastern cults and groups was applied to the Jews, who could easily be used as

---

[18] On the status and life of the Jews in the Dispersion, see Victor Tcherikover, *Hellenistic Civilization and the Jews,* pp. 269–377.

scapegoats. Multiple slanderous stories circulated about what the Jews "really" did in worship and in their sacrificial ritual. The dominant anti-Judaism was more a cultural than an official state attitude.

Much of the Jewish literature produced in the Diaspora was apologetic and missionary in intent, that is, it was designed to defend and propagate Judaism in the Hellenistic world. The literature sought, perhaps in addition to winning converts, to create a favorable attitude toward Judaism that would improve the lot of Jews living in a non-Jewish environment and to encourage Jews not to forsake their own religious traditions in favor of Hellenistic culture and learning.

Two of the most famous apologetic Jewish writers were Flavius Josephus (ca. A.D. 37–100) and Philo Judeus (ca. 20 B.C. to A.D. 50). The former[19] was a commanding officer of the Galilean Jewish forces during the first revolt before his surrender to the Romans. After the war he was settled in Rome and given an imperial pension with the rights of Roman citizenship and spent the rest of his life in literary pursuits. He wrote a history of the Jewish war with Rome, a book titled *The Antiquities of the Jews*, an autobiography, and an apology for Judaism called *Contra Apion*. Josephus tried to show, perhaps falsely, that the first Jewish revolt did not represent the true sentiments of the Jews toward the Romans but was a rebellion fomented by brigands and troublemakers. Philo was an Alexandrian Jew,[20] a contemporary of Jesus, who was well trained in both Hellenistic philosophy and the Hebrew Scriptures. He attempted in his writings to demonstrate that the two, when properly understood, say essentially the same thing. He expounded the Scriptures through the use of a method called "allegorical interpretation" which looked for hidden esoteric and philosophical meanings behind the literal sense of the Scriptures. Philo's greatest influence was on subsequent Christian writers and theologians who adopted his allegorical method of Biblical interpretation.

Rabbinic Literature.[21] The acceptance of a body of literature or a document as a binding authoritative rule of life leads to the development of persons who interpret the document's stipulations and these interpretations in turn are often assigned an authoritative status. In Judaism the written Torah was interpreted in order to explain its contents and to define its scope as well as to adopt its ordinances to changing social, economic, and cultural conditions. This interpretation was done by scribes, teachers, and learned laymen, many of whom were addressed as "rabbi," a term expressing honor and respect. An example will

---

[19] See H. St. John Thackeray, *Josephus: The Man and the Historian*, reissued with an introduction by Samuel Sandmel (KTAV Publishing House, Inc., 1968).

[20] See Samuel Sandmel, *Philo's Place in Judaism* (The Hebrew Union College Press, 1956).

[21] The classic work on rabbinic literature and thought is G. F. Moore, *Judaism in the First Centuries of the Christian Era*, 2 vols. (Harvard University Press, 1927). This work, however, ignored the apocalyptic elements in Judaism. On the problems involved in describing Judaism at the beginning of the Christian era, see Samuel Sandmel, *The First Christian Century in Judaism and Christianity: Certainties and Uncertainties* (Oxford University Press, Inc., 1969), pp. 58–142. A sampling of rabbinic literature can be found in Charles K. Barrett, *The New Testament Background: Selected Documents* (Harper Torchbooks, 1961), pp. 139–172; and R. Travers Herford, ed., *The Ethics of the Talmud: Sayings of the Fathers* (Schocken Books, Inc., 1962).

illustrate the necessity for this type of interpretation. The Torah prohibited working on the Sabbath. Such a prohibition, however, raised a host of questions requiring clarification. What constituted work? What was not work? When did the Sabbath begin and end? Was this statute universally binding, or could it be circumvented under extenuating circumstances? And so on. The oral laws that grew up around the written law served, according to the rabbis, as a "fence around the law."

The earliest method of teaching the oral Torah was by means of a running commentary or *midrash* ("interpretation") on the Biblical text. If the exposition yielded a legal teaching, the result was called *halakah* ("rule"); if it yielded a nonlegal, ethical, or devotional result, it was called *haggadah*. A further method of teaching oral law developed and was known as *mishnah* ("repetition"), which involved teaching without direct reference to specific texts of written torah. The two methods of instruction continued side by side, though the latter became increasingly popular. A great mass of interpretative material came into existence during the Hasmonean and Roman periods and much of this may have been written down before the beginning of the Christian era. There developed in the pre-Christian period the conviction that this oral law had binding authority just as did the written law, and many argued that both the oral and the written law had been revealed to Moses on Mt. Sinai and that the oral laws had simply been passed down by word of mouth from generation to generation. This oral Torah was eventually codified and reduced to writing in what is known as the Talmud. There are two forms of the Talmudic material: the "Palestinian Talmud," whose final form was produced in the fifth century A.D., and the much larger "Babylonian Talmud," which was finished in the following century.

An additional type of rabbinic literature is known as *targum* ("translation"). Targums were translations of the Hebrew texts of the Scripture into Aramaic, often with explanations and interpretations. These translations became necessary when Hebrew ceased to be the general spoken language and Aramaic was the more generally used language. Some Aramaic translations were in existence in written form at the beginning of the Christian era.

THE RELIGIOUS INSTITUTIONS OF JUDAISM

Three institutions in Judaism in the pre-Christian and early Christian period were of primary significance: the Temple, the Sanhedrin, and the synagogue. The Temple, located in Jerusalem, was the symbolic center of Jewish piety and the actual center of important facets of Jewish religious life, for daily sacrifices as well as the sacrifices associated with the great annual festivals were offered there. The Deuteronomic reformation had outlawed the offering of sacrifice at any temple other than the Jerusalem Temple; however, there were exceptional examples of Jewish sacrificial ritual being set up in temples built elsewhere. One of these was the temple built by Onias IV (ca. 170 B.C.), a claimant to the high priesthood under Antiochus Epiphanes, at Leontopolis in Egypt to which he had fled. This temple was destroyed by Vespasian after over two centuries of usage. Pilgrimages were made to the temple at the time of the three annual festivals: Passover, Weeks (Pentecost), and Tabernacles. Most Jews in the Diaspora were unable to afford the financial cost involved in a pilgrimage to Jerusalem and thus had to be content with the wish to visit the Temple rather than with the visit itself. The high priest was the chief officer of the Jerusalem Temple and officiated at special services of worship. Other priests served in the Temple on a rotating basis, for one week at a time, twice during the year.

The Herodian Temple was divided into a number of courts. The outer "court of the Gentiles" could be visited by non-Jews and was surrounded with a low stone wall on which there was an inscribed warning: "No man of another nation to enter within the fence and enclosure round the temple. And whoever is caught will have himself to blame that his death ensues." [22] Beyond this court was an area ("the women's court") into which Jews might take their wives. The next area, into which women could not go, was "the court of Israel," and beyond this was "the court of the priests" which only the clergy could enter. The Temple was not only a religious center, it was a powerful economic institution. In addition to its regular income (gifts and a half-shekel per year tax on every Jew), private and public money and treasures were kept there and the Temple functioned as a bank. Foreign money had to be exchanged by pilgrims, and money-changers functioned within the Temple, receiving a percentage for their services.

The Sanhedrin (from the Greek word *synedrion*, meaning "council"), composed of seventy-one members, was centered in Jerusalem and was presided over by the high priest. The body developed out of the earlier courts of the theocratic community. The Sanhedrin exercised both legislative and judicial power in religious and, to some extent, civil matters. Its authority tended to vary considerably under different political regimes and in different historical situations. In addition to the supreme Sanhedrin, other courts existed and apparently there were subordinate Sanhedrins in several Jewish cities.

The third major institution in Judaism and the only one to survive the destruction of Jerusalem in A.D. 70 was the synagogue. This institution, which came into existence as a result of the Deuteronomic reformation, was very significant and influential in the life of Judaism. While the essence of temple worship was animal sacrifice and the leaders were hereditary priests, the essence of synagogue worship was the study of the law, religious instruction, and prayer and its leaders were commoners or laymen. Synagogues were found throughout Palestine and in all the lands of the Diaspora, where they proved to be the centers around which Jewish life revolved. Worship services were held on festival days and on the Sabbath and in Palestine on Mondays and Thursdays as well. Generally schools for religious instruction for boys were attached to the synagogue. The scribes and the rabbis, who were the professional students and teachers of the Torah, although they held no official or ecclesiastical position, centered their teaching activity around the synagogues.

---

[22] The translation is that of a Greek inscription stone, once part of the Temple, recovered from a Jerusalem cemetery in 1871.

THEOLOGICAL DEVELOPMENTS AND SECTS IN JUDAISM

Theological development in Judaism during the postexilic period was far from uniform. Significant differences arose not only between Palestinian and Diaspora Jews but also between various groups in Palestine itself. At the beginning of the Christian era, almost all groups of Jews, however, seemed to have agreed upon certain fundamental beliefs, all of which had their roots in the Old Testament.

Basic to all Judaism of the period was monotheism, the belief in the existence of one living, personal, holy, and just God, who was not only the creator and sustainer of all the universe but who was also intimately and actively involved in the affairs of human history and required obedience to his will. Closely related to this was the idea of election. Jews believed that this God had chosen the nation Israel out of all the peoples of the world to be the special recipients of his grace and the instruments of his will. A third basic feature of Jewish faith was the belief that the Torah was the revelation of God's will for his people and that obedience to its precepts was the mark of true faithfulness. Sin was understood essentially as disobedience to the Torah and, as such, an act of rebellion against God. The necessity of repentance was stressed, and although God was proclaimed as a righteous God of judgment, he was also depicted as gracious and eager to forgive. Furthermore, virtually all Jews seemed to believe that somehow, sometime in the future, God would intervene in human affairs in such a way as to make it possible for Israel to live peacefully and securely as the elect people in full obedience to the requirements of the Torah.

The major differences within Jewish theology centered around three points: the content of the Torah, the proper relationship between the obedient community and the rest of mankind, and the nearness and nature of the future time of fulfillment. On the first point, the content of the Torah, some accepted only the written Torah and the explicit ordinances as found in the Pentateuch, while others accepted as binding various other written and oral traditions and ordinances that had grown up around the Biblical Torah.

On the second point, the proper relationship between the obedient community and the rest of mankind, a twofold problem existed: the relationship between faithful and unfaithful Jews and the relationship between Jews and Gentiles. In attempting to deal with the first problem, some withdrew almost completely from the society of their fellow Jews because of what they regarded as the unfaithfulness of the nation as a whole and lived rigidly disciplined lives in monastic communities. Others merely refused to associate intimately with those whose zeal for the law fell short of their own, without, however, withdrawing from the society and the culture of the time. Some, of course, saw no problem here. In attempting to deal with the second problem, certain groups advocated the violent overthrow of foreign oppressors and looked for the eventual destruction or subjugation of the Gentiles to the Jews. Others simply avoided close contact and association with foreigners as much as possible. Some sought various means of accommodation and association with the non-Jewish world.

On the third question, that of God's intervention in the future, numerous differing and often conflicting viewpoints existed. Some believed that God himself would intervene and establish his Kingdom, fulfilling the promises of the prophets. Others expected him to send some agent or representative to accomplish this. Some believed that the agent who would inaugurate the Kingdom was to be a superhuman figure from heaven. Others thought of the future messiah as a human savior from the line of David or Aaron who would rule over the Jews in peace and prosperity. Some Jews insisted that human activity (i.e., armed rebellion against foreign rulers) was a necessary prelude to the Kingdom's advent. Others advocated a passive acceptance of present conditions with the conviction that God would intervene in his own time and way. Some looked for a kingdom of God on earth that would be essentially a reestablishment on a much grander scale of the ancient Davidic empire, while others expected a heavenly kingdom that would mean the end of worldly existence. Many perhaps hoped for no more than the opportunity to live obediently as a theocratic community under earthly conditions. The role and relationship of the Gentiles to the coming Kingdom were given varied expressions. According to some, Gentiles would share in the "good time" coming, while others excluded them altogether or relegated them to an inferior status. Accompanying such eschatological speculation was much discussion and debate on related topics, such as the possibility and nature of life after death, future judgment, and everlasting reward and punishment.

Most of these differences within Judaism were matters of degree and not of kind. The manner of interpreting the Scriptures was of great significance in the way in which answers were given to these questions. Sharing in the life and worship of the Temple and the synagogue tended to bind together most of the Jews of differing beliefs. It should not be assumed that every Jew was a professional nor even an amateur theologian who had worked out a system of thought and belief!

As a result of these theological differences and emphases, as well as the influence of cultural and economic concerns, there were a number of groups, parties, or sects in Judaism (outside the Samaritan sect, which in a way was Jewish).[23] Prior to the first revolt, Judaism was far from being a monolithic community of faith. It was instead a fairly variegated phenomenon. Archaeological discoveries, such as that of the Dead Sea Scrolls and the Qumran community, have tended to confirm the varied currents in Judaism. The Jewish historian Josephus described what he called the four philosophical sects in Judaism, namely, the Pharisees, Sadducees, Essenes, and "the fourth philosophy" (apparently the Zealots). Josephus desired to show in these categorizations the parallels between Jewish parties and current Hellenistic philosophical groups, and to this extent his descriptions probably represent oversimplifications.

The Pharisees (the name is assumed to have derived from the Hebrew term *parash*, "to separate," i.e., from impurity and transgression) have unfortunately

---

[23] On Jewish sects, see Roland K. Harrison, *The Dead Sea Scrolls* (Harper Torchbooks, 1961), pp. 72–101; Godfrey R. Driver, *The Judaean Scrolls*, pp. 51–125; and Marcel Simon, *Jewish Sects at the Time of Jesus*, tr. by J. H. Farley (Fortress Press, 1967).

been viewed in terms of the New Testament description of them where they were interpreted as either genuine hypocrites or else as concerned only with the externals of religion. This description, which is largely derived from the time after Jews and Christians went their separate ways, is very polemic and hostile and has been the source of a great injustice to a movement founded on a sincere striving for virtue and righteousness. The Pharisees are first mentioned in literature discussing the second century B.C., and their origins are to be sought in the activity of the Hasidim, who opposed the developing Hellenization of the Jews. A basic ambition of the Pharisees who were laymen or "lay lawyers" was the desire to make the Bible and its laws relevant and applicable to changing and contemporaneous situations. Advocating the validity and necessity of the oral law, they were in this regard progressives or modernists. The Pharisees were open to the development of new ideas that could not be supported by explicit statements in the Torah but that could be deduced through exegesis. Thus they accepted and advocated the ideas of the resurrection of the dead, perhaps also the immortality of the soul, a future world where men would be rewarded or punished, and angels as guardians of persons and nations as well as mediators between man and God. Many of the Pharisees were supporters of messianism, the expectation of a future ruler from the house of David who would usher in a new era and a transformation of the conditions of existence, and thus were eschatologically oriented.

Whereas the Pharisees were the party of the Bible and the synagogue, the Sadducees (the name seems to be derived from Zadokite, the line of priests traced back to Zadok, high priest under Solomon) were the party of the Temple, the priesthood, and the court. As a rule they were associated with or were members of the Jerusalem aristocracy and nobility. They rejected the necessity of the oral law or midrashic exposition of Scripture that was developed by the Pharisees. For them, only the written Torah (the Pentateuch) had explicit ordinances and binding authority. They did not accept the doctrine of resurrection from the dead, adhering instead to the old idea of Sheol, nor did they believe in angelology. In addition, the Sadducees were much more willing than others to accommodate Hellenistic ideas and to take a "live and let live" attitude in regard to Jewish nationalism. The Sadducees disappeared from history after the first revolt.

Josephus refers to the Essenes and provides a discussion of their beliefs. They were a monastic-type sect separate from the ordinary human relations and they required of their members a strict obedience (more strict even than the Pharisees) to the law and its applications. Persons joining this group went through a probationary period of two or three years. Much of a member's time was spent in work, studying and reading the law, and prayer. According to some of the Essenes, the priestly order and cult in Jerusalem were apostate and thus they did not share in the Temple services. Property was held in common and communal meals were eaten and some understood as a substitute for the Temple service. The similarity between the Essenes and the Covenanters of the Qumran community suggests a very close kinship if not identity.

Josephus' fourth philosophy is generally referred to as the Zealots, who were the "Home Rule Party." This group advocated the absolute sovereignty of Yahweh over Israel and they were spokesmen for Jewish freedom. Josephus traces their origin back to Judas the Galilean, and as we have seen, Judas' descendants were leaders in various actions against the Romans and Jewish sympathizers and took a leading role in the first revolt. The Zealots were a militant party willing and capable of fighting for freedom from Rome.

Numerous other groups within Judaism are mentioned in ancient literature but of most of these little is known. No doubt the majority of the Jews were not consciously members of any sect but fell into what was known as the *ame ha-aretz* ("the peoples of the land"). Many of these must have respected the leadership of the Pharisees, the piety of the ascetic groups, and the patriotism of the Zealots.

PART FOUR

THE LIFE AND LITERATURE
OF EARLY CHRISTIANITY

17 | IN QUEST OF
THE HISTORICAL JESUS

In the fourth decade of the first century A.D., a new sect arose in Judaism. Beginning as a small group of Palestinian Jews, it had, within a few years, spread its faith to the major cities of the eastern Mediterranean world. The faith of this community was centered around Jesus of Nazareth, whom it proclaimed as the Messiah. It claimed that in him God had fulfilled the prophetic promises of the Old Testament and the eschatological hopes of contemporary Judaism.

In attempting an examination of the origins of the Christian movement and the development of the New Testament within the early church, we immediately see a number of questions. Who was this Jesus? What can we know about him? What led the early church to center its faith around him? What relationship did he have to the movement that proclaimed him as its founder? Or, to condense the questions into one: What can be known about the historical Jesus? This question leads initially, like all historical questions, to an examination of the extent, content, and nature of the source materials available that might elucidate his life and career.

THE SOURCES

Source materials for the study of the historical Jesus are those writings which mention Jesus and were produced at a time contemporary with the rise and development of the early church. Jesus himself left no written documents or autobiographical reflections, nor are there in existence any sources concerning him that were composed before his death. One can approach the sources that do exist as if they comprised a series of concentric circles with those circles nearest the center being the writings that were produced by members of the early community.

Roman Authors. At the outer periphery of the sources from the first and early second centuries that refer to Jesus are the writings of some Roman historians who do provide some knowledge about Jesus. The Roman writers who made reference to Jesus were Suetonius and Tacitus. Neither of these, however, set out to discuss Jesus directly but referred to him within the context of discussions

319

of other matters. It comes as something of a disappointment to modern Christians (and historians!) that the life and career of Jesus did not ripple the waters of the contemporary Roman world of his day.

In his work on the life of Claudius, Suetonius (ca. A.D. 75–160) writes that "since the Jews were continually making disturbances at the instigation of Chrestus, he expelled them from Rome" (*Vita Claudii*, XXV. 5). This passage refers to the emperor Claudius' expulsion of the Jews from Rome in A.D. 49. It is commonly assumed that Chrestus was a misunderstanding of Christus (= Christ, which is the Greek term used to translate the Hebrew word "messiah") and that the disturbances which broke out in the Jewish community were caused by Christians preaching about Jesus. In his writing on Nero, Suetonius mentions the Neronian persecution of A.D. 64 and says that "punishment was inflicted on the Christians, a sect of men adhering to a novel and mischievous superstition" (*Vita Neronis*, XVI). This last reference offers only one evidence for the existence of the Christian community and provides an assessment of the movement by a learned Roman, and the first is so dubious as to be of no real value insofar as the historical Jesus is concerned.

Tacitus (ca. A.D. 60–120), in his *Annales*, also described the persecution of Christians under Nero and the fact that when the Romans began to suspect that the emperor had ordered the burning of the city, he seized upon the Christians as a scapegoat. Tacitus then writes:

> And so, to get rid of this rumor, Nero set up as the culprits and punished with the utmost refinement of cruelty a class hated for their abominations, who are commonly called Christians. Christus, from whom their name is derived, was executed at the hands of the procurator Pontius Pilate in the reign of Tiberius. Checked for the moment, this pernicious superstition again broke out, not only in Judea, the source of the evil, but even in Rome, that receptacle for everything that is sordid and degrading from every quarter of the globe, which there finds a following (*Annales*, XV. 44).

This passage not only provides an early opinion about the nature of Christianity but also offers information about the existence of Jesus and the place and approximate date of his activity and death.

Jewish Sources. One would have anticipated that Josephus, who wrote a rather detailed history of Jewish affairs during the first seven decades of the first century, would have had quite a lot to say about Jesus and the origins of Christianity as a Jewish sect. However, this is not the case, for Josephus makes reference to Jesus in only two places and one of these passages seems to contain a number of Christian additions. The latter passage occurs in the *Antiquities* following Josephus' discussion of Pilate's suppression of a disturbance caused by his having used Temple money to construct an aqueduct.

> At this time appeared Jesus, a wise man, *if one may call him a man at all*. For he was a doer of wonderful works, a teacher of men, who received the truth with gladness. And he attracted Jews as also people of the Greek sort in great number. *This was the Christ*. And when on the denunciation of our leading men Pilate had punished him with crucifixion, those who had loved him

formerly did not cease therefrom. *He appeared to them alive again on the third day, for the godly prophets had foretold this and innumerable other wonderful things concerning him.* And even now the race of men called after him Christians has not died out (*Antiquities*, XVIII. 3.3).

The words italicized in the above quotation are generally considered inauthentic, and even the entire passage is missing from some of the Greek manuscripts, none of which are earlier than the eleventh century. Only a Christian could have written such a description of Jesus, and Josephus was no Christian. A second reference to Jesus is made by Josephus in conjunction with a statement about the death of James. The passage reads: "Ananus summoned the council to judgment and brought before it the brother of Jesus, the so-called Christ, James by name" (*Antiquities*, XX. 9. 1). The most that could be gleaned from Josephus about Jesus is the fact that he was acknowledged by some as the Messiah, was crucified by Pilate, and had followers called after him.

In addition to Josephus, numerous references to Jesus occur in the Talmud. Many of these are quite polemical, coming from a period after the open break between Judaism and Christianity, and thus are of no historical value. Others have a greater claim to reliability and have been summarized as follows by a modern Jewish scholar:

There are reliable statements to the effect that his name was Yeshu'a (Yeshu) of Nazareth; that he "practiced sorcery" (i.e., performed miracles, as was usual in those days) and beguiled and led Israel astray; that he mocked at the words of the Wise; that he expounded Scripture in the same manner as the Pharisees; that he had five disciples; that he said that he was not come to take aught away from the Law or to add to it; that he was hanged (crucified) as a false teacher and beguiler on the eve of the Passover which happened on a Sabbath; and that his disciples healed the sick in his name.[1]

In spite of the fact that most of the Talmudic and classical Jewish references are value judgments about Jesus and the early church, they do provide a nucleus of material about the historical man himself.

Non-Biblical Christian Sources. The twenty-seven books that now make up the New Testament (four Gospels, one narrative about the spread of Christianity, twenty-one letters, and an apocalypse) do not represent the totality of Christian writings about Jesus and the early church that were produced in the first century and a half of the present era. There were a number of other writings and gospels produced that did not make it into the Christian Scriptures of the canon. These writings are referred to as the New Testament Apocrypha.[2] Many

---

[1] Joseph Klausner, *Jesus of Nazareth: His Life, Times, and Teaching*, tr. by H. Danby (Beacon Press, Inc., 1964, paperback reprint of 1929 edition), p. 46. Klausner's work is an excellent discussion of Jesus from a Jewish perspective. A more recent Jewish treatment from a slightly different perspective is Samuel Sandmel, *We Jews and Jesus* (Oxford University Press, Inc., 1965).

[2] Much of the apocryphal gospel material probably dates from after the second century. The gospel material is available in Edgar Hennecke, *New Testament Apocrypha*, Volume One: *Gospels and Related Writings*, ed. by Wilhelm Schneemelcher, English translation ed. by R. McL. Wilson (The Westminster Press, 1963).

of these have been known and used for years, while others have only recently been discovered. One such work that falls into the latter category is the Gospel of Thomas discovered in Egypt in 1946 along with a dozen or so other early Christian documents.[3] This writing consists of 114 sayings of Jesus, many identical or closely akin to sayings found in the New Testament, but is devoid of a description of the life and acts of Jesus. Other gospels, and in the apocryphal material everyone from Mary to Pontius Pilate has a "gospel" or writing attributed to him, attempted to supplement the canonical writings by describing Jesus' early childhood, the details of his trial, and even his experiences during his descent into hell! Unfortunately practically none of these pseudononymous writings can be dated with any degree of certainty. Some examples from the gospel by "Thomas the Israelite" will illustrate their content.

> When this boy Jesus was five years old he was playing at the ford of a brook, and he gathered together into pools the water that flowed by, and made it at once clean and commanded it by his word alone. He made soft clay and fashioned from it twelve sparrows. And it was the sabbath when he did this. And there were also many other children playing with him. Now when a certain Jew saw what Jesus was doing in his play on the sabbath, he at once went and told his father Joseph: "See, your child is at the brook, and he has taken clay and fashioned twelve birds and has profaned the sabbath." And when Joseph came to the place and saw it, he cried out to him, saying: "Why do you do on the sabbath what ought not to be done?" But Jesus clapped his hands and cried to the sparrows: "Off with you!" And the sparrows took flight and went away chirping. The Jews were amazed when they saw this, and went away and told their elders what they had seen Jesus do.

> His father was a carpenter and made at that time ploughs and yokes. And he received an order from a rich man to make a bed for him. But when one beam was shorter than its corresponding one and they did not know what to do, the child Jesus said to his father Joseph: "Put down the two pieces of wood and make them even from the middle to one end." And Joseph did as the child told him. And Jesus stood at the other end and took hold of the shorter piece of wood, and stretching it made it equal with the other. And his father Joseph saw it and was amazed, and he embraced the child and kissed him, saying: "Happy am I that a God has given me this child." [4]

This material is obviously the product of a pious and devout Christian imagination, but it contains no semblance of historical actuality and can thus be dismissed as a valid source of information on the historical Jesus. The apocryphal material, however, does show that Christians continued to devise stories, episodes, and sayings that they attributed to Jesus as well as to offer interpretations and embellishments of the Biblical material after the writing of the canonical

---

[3] Translated in the work mentioned in footnote 2 above, pp. 511–522. For a discussion of these so-called Nag Hammadi texts, see W. C. van Unnik, *Newly Discovered Gnostic Writings* (London: SCM Press, Ltd., 1960).

[4] Translations are from Hennecke, *New Testament Apocrypha*, Volume One, pp. 392–393, 396–397.

Gospels.[5] Such a process certainly did not begin with the apocryphal writings but has its prehistory within the New Testment traditions themselves.

The Canonical Writings Outside the Gospels. The letters of the New Testament make surprisingly little reference to what could be called the historical Jesus, and, in fact, little notice is given to the traditions found in the Gospels. From Paul, for example, one would only learn that Jesus was born of a woman (Gal. 4:4), was a descendant of David (Rom. 1:3), had brothers (I Cor. 9:5) one of whom was named James (Gal. 1:19), that he broke bread and shared a cup with his followers on the night he was betrayed (I Cor. 11:23–26), was crucified, dead, buried, and on the third day was raised from the dead and appeared to various followers (I Cor. 15:4–8). In addition, Paul quotes sayings of Jesus about divorce (I Cor. 7:10–11), the meaning of the last supper (I Cor. 11:23–26), and alludes to a saying that those proclaiming the gospel should get their living by the gospel (I Cor. 9:14). This amazing paucity of material could mean that Paul was not overly interested in the traditions about Jesus, which many scholars consider unlikely (but see II Cor. 5:16). It could have been that his letters were addressed to groups whose knowledge of these traditions he presupposed or to situations that did not demand their usage.

The non-Pauline letters provide even fewer references to traditions about the historical Jesus. There is, however, a perspective found in the book of Revelation that should be noted. John, the writer of this book, was imprisoned on the isle of Patmos. While "in the Spirit on the Lord's day" (Rev. 1:10)—that is, in an ecstatic state in the context of a worship service—he was spoken to by the exalted Christ (Rev. 1:10–20), who dictated to him letters to be sent to seven churches (Rev., chs. 2 and 3). These letters were written as the direct word of the exalted Lord. The fact that revelations from the "heavenly Christ" could be understood as sayings of the Lord should be kept in mind in examining the question of the "teachings of Jesus."

This survey of the non-Biblical and non-Gospel material mentioning Jesus shows that, in the last analysis, an attempted portrayal of the Jesus of history must be dependent upon the New Testament Gospels. When one turns to these writings, however, one is immediately confronted with a rather unusual phenomenon, namely, the existence of four Gospels: Matthew, Mark, Luke, and John. How did four collections of traditions about Jesus develop? Why were there four attempts to portray Jesus? Why did not the church pick only one? Or at least combine the traditions?

WHY FOUR GOSPELS?

Already in the latter half of the second century, some church leaders were concerned about the existence of four Gospels, although this concern was not

---

[5] The apocryphal gospel material is very similar in many respects to the Jewish *midrash* and *haggadah* on the Torah. See Sandmel, *The First Christian Century*, pp. 180–181.

felt in all the churches.[6] In some churches and areas only one Gospel seems to have been used, and in other churches all four were accepted as authoritative without the existence of four accounts of the life and teachings of Jesus occasioning any great discussion. The bishop of Lyons, Irenaeus (died ca. A.D. 200), argued that God had decreed and entrusted four Gospels to the church just as there were four covenants in history (Noah, Abraham, Moses, and Christ), four points to the compass, and four winds of the heavens. Such a rationalization obviously represents either a desire to overcome a certain uneasiness or an attempt to theologize in favor of the *status quo*.

Attempts were made to remove the offense of the existence of multiple Gospels. One such effort was made by a churchman from Asia Minor by the name of Marcion. He came to Rome shortly before A.D. 150 and, in addition to advocating the rejection of the Old Testament as Christian Scripture, proposed that the Gospel of Luke (with slight alterations) be recognized as the one authoritative Gospel. Marcion's position was not accepted by any group other than his own church (he had been excluded from the church at Rome for heretical ideas and founded his own Christian movement).

Another second-century Christian, Tatian (ca. A.D. 170), utilizing all four Gospels, omitted the parallels and harmonized the differences and thus produced a single "Gospel harmony." His work was widely used in his native Syrian church, but was not accepted universally and in fact was hostilely opposed in many places.

What was disturbing to those early church leaders who were troubled about the matter was the fact that Christianity possessed four Gospels that offered differing portrayals of Jesus and his teachings.[7] Early churchmen, then, were aware of the differences between the Gospels and the fact that the different writers possessed different emphases. The acceptance and canonization of four Gospels in the early church was perhaps dependent upon both practical and theological reasons. All four of the canonical Gospels were in wide use during the second century, and usage tended to ensure authoritative acceptance. There is some evidence to suggest that different Gospels were utilized and strongly favored in different geographical areas within the early church, and thus the acceptance of four Gospels was a sort of "ecumenical compromise." Also, the theological emphases of the various writers, who were considered to have been apostles or disciples of apostles, were considered orthodox and the acceptance of the four allowed a greater opportunity for freedom of interpretation. In addition, the differences between the Gospels were considered as supplementary and thus complementary to one another.

Any attempt to reconstruct a life of Jesus or to paint a portrait of the historical Jesus discovers the multiplicity of the Gospels as something of an offense or at least a hindrance. Differences between the Gospels must be evaluated and analyzed. The existence of such differences (the nature and significance of

---

[6] See Oscar Cullmann, "The Plurality of the Gospels as a Theological Problem in Antiquity," in his *The Early Church*, ed. by A. J. B. Higgins (The Westminster Press, 1956), pp. 39–54.

[7] Some of the early church fathers were concerned with what might be called historical-critical problems. See Robert M. Grant, *The Earliest Lives of Jesus* (Harper & Brothers, 1961).

these will be discussed later) demands that one explain the similarities as well. The comparative study of the Gospels and their differences has led to three main conclusions. (1) None of the Gospels is a biography in any meaningful sense of the word. They do not attempt to present a history of Jesus that places him within the general cultural, historical, and social world of his time. (2) The Gospels are primarily theological and religious tracts. They are impressionistic portraits, not a picture of Jesus, and are more interested in preaching and confessing faith in Jesus than in presenting objective history. (3) The authors of the Gospels were creative writers and theologians who stamped their individuality and concerns on their presentations of Jesus. Each writer offered his own distinctive interpretation of Jesus. The study of the Gospels is not, in the first place, a study of the historical Jesus, but a study of four theological writings and their creative authors. Any attempt to reconstruct the historical Jesus must penetrate this creativity and individuality of the Gospel writers.[8]

THE SYNOPTIC PROBLEM

A cursory examination of the four Gospels reveals, on the one hand, the striking similarity that exists between Matthew, Mark, and Luke and on the other hand, the differences between these three and the Gospel of John. John differs from the first three Gospels in the geographical framework given to the ministry of Jesus, in the manner in which the teachings of Jesus are presented, and in the episodes that are narrated. John has Jesus carrying on a simultaneous ministry with John the Baptist, while the other three Gospels date the beginning of Jesus' ministry from the imprisonment of the Baptist. John has Jesus making three visits to Jerusalem and remaining there on one occasion for more than half a year, whereas the first three Gospels speak only of Jesus' journey to Jerusalem during the week of his crucifixion. John pictures a ministry of about three years for Jesus, while the other three suggest a time of less than a year. In John, Jesus preaches in long discourses, focusing on specific topics, while Matthew, Mark, and Luke give the teachings of Jesus in the form of short disconnected sayings and parables. Only a few narratives that appear in the first three Gospels occur in John, whereas the latter Gospel contains a number of episodes not referred to in the others. It is obvious from these differences that the first three Gospels are the result of a different perspective and interest than is the fourth Gospel.

Since the first three Gospels are so much alike in general perspective, plan, content, and wording, they have been considered literarily dependent upon one another. For this reason, they are referred to as "the Synoptic Gospels." (The term "synoptic" is from the Greek word *synopsis*, which means "common perspective.") In the preface to his Gospel, the author of Luke mentions that "many have undertaken to compile a narrative" of Jesus' life and ministry and

---

[8] The study of the theological influence and motivation of the Gospel writers is called "redaction criticism." See Norman Perrin, *What Is Redaction Criticism?* (Fortress Press, 1969); Joachim Rohde, *Rediscovering the Teaching of the Evangelists*, tr. by D. M. Barton (The Westminster Press, 1968); and R. H. Stein, "What Is Redaktionsgeschichte?" *Journal of Biblical Literature*, LXXXVIII (1969), pp. 45–56.

that he was attempting "to write an orderly account" (Luke 1:1–4). Such a statement implies a knowledge of other Gospels and a dependency upon them.

The points of similarity between the Synoptic Gospels are so numerous and striking that they cannot be coincidental. The course of Jesus' activity is represented in a similar manner in all three. Jesus' public appearance is associated with the activity of John the Baptist. In each Synoptic, the references to John are then followed by narratives of Jesus' baptism and temptation. Upon John's imprisonment, Jesus begins a preaching career in Galilee, and the events narrated about his ministry follow a strikingly similar sequence. The representation of his career consists of a multitude of individual units, some narrative and some preaching and teaching, which are frequently brought together without much chronological or geographical setting. Jesus journeys to Jerusalem, conducts a short ministry there, is arrested, tried, and crucified. The similarity between the Synoptic Gospels is not limited to the outline of the narratives and the nature and content of the teaching but extends even to style, language, and vocabulary. The accompanying chart shows one example that illustrates the parallelism between the Gospels.

This similarity between the Synoptics should not be taken to mean that they are, for all practical purposes, identical. There are differences of perspective, content, arrangement, and wording between the three. Matthew and Luke are much fuller accounts than is Mark, possessing infancy narratives, genealogies, extended sermons, and so on, which are not found in Mark but which also differ from one another. At points, Matthew and Luke have similar material which, however, is not found in Mark.

In the history of Biblical study, beginning with the ancient church fathers, numerous attempts have been made to explain this commingling of similarities and differences, dependency and independency, agreements and disagreements between the three Gospels—in other words to solve what is called the "Synoptic problem." The most widely accepted solution to this problem[9] rests on the following assumptions: (1) Mark's Gospel was the first one and was used by the authors of Matthew and Luke; (2) the authors of Matthew and Luke had a second source of materials common to both of them but not employed by Mark; and (3) the authors of Matthew and Luke utilized materials (or created materials) that were unique to each of their Gospels.

The Priority of Mark.[10] The assumption that Mark's Gospel was the first one and was used by the other Synoptics is based on a number of arguments. With the exception of six short passages, totaling only about twenty verses, the entire content of the Gospel of Mark is reproduced in Matthew and Luke. Mark contains 661 verses; Matthew reproduces about 600 of these, Luke about 300. If one assumes that Mark was dependent upon Matthew and Luke, it would be almost impossible to explain why Mark omitted so much material. The sequence of the

---

[9] A classic discussion of this solution to the Synoptic problem is B. H. Streeter, *The Four Gospels: A Study of Origins* (The Macmillan Company, 1924, rev. ed., 1951).

[10] The priority of Mark has been challenged by W. R. Farmer and others. See W. R. Farmer. *The Synoptic Problem* (The Macmillan Company, 1964).

MATT. 19:16–26	MARK 10:17–27	LUKE 18:18–27

And behold, one came up to him, saying, "Teacher, what good deed must I do, to have eternal life?" And he said to him, "Why do you ask me about what is good? One there is who is good. If you would enter life, keep the commandments." He said to him, "Which?" And Jesus said, "You shall not kill, You shall not commit adultery, You shall not steal, You shall not bear false witness, Honor your father and mother, and, You shall love your neighbor as yourself." The young man said to him, "All these I have observed; what do I still lack?"

Jesus said to him, "If you would be perfect, go, sell what you possess and give to the poor, and you will have treasure in heaven; and come, follow me." When the young man heard this he went away sorrowful; for he had great possessions.

And Jesus said to his disciples, "Truly, I say to you, it will be hard for a rich man to enter the kingdom of heaven.

Again I tell you,

it is easier for a camel to go through the eye of a needle than for a rich man to enter the kingdom of God." When the disciples heard this they were greatly astonished, saying, "Who then can be saved?" But Jesus looked at them and said to them, "With men this is impossible, but with God all things are possible."

And as he was setting out on his journey, a man ran up and knelt before him, and asked him, "Good Teacher, what must I do to inherit eternal life?" And Jesus said to him, "Why do you call me good? No one is good but God alone. You know the commandments:

'Do not kill, Do not commit adultery, Do not steal, Do not bear false witness, Do not defraud, Honor your father and mother.' "

And he said to him, "Teacher, all these I have observed from my youth." And Jesus looking upon him loved him, and said to him, "You lack one thing; go, sell what you have, and give to the poor, and you will have treasure in heaven; and come, follow me." At that saying his countenance fell, and he went away sorrowful; for he had great possessions.

And Jesus looked around and said to his disciples, "How hard it will be for those who have riches to enter the kingdom of God!" And the disciples were amazed at his words. But Jesus said to them again, "Children, how hard it is to enter the kingdom of God! It is easier for a camel to go through the eye of a needle than for a rich man to enter the kingdom of God." And they were exceedingly astonished, and said to him, "Then who can be saved?" Jesus looked at them and said, "With men it is impossible, but not with God; for all things are possible with God."

And a ruler asked him, "Good Teacher, what shall I do to inherit eternal life?" And Jesus said to him, "Why do you call me good? No one is good but God alone. You know the commandments:

'Do not commit adultery, Do not kill, Do not steal, Do not bear false witness, Honor your father and mother.' "

And he said, "All these I have observed from my youth." And when Jesus heard it, he said to him, "One thing you still lack. Sell all that you have and distribute to the poor, and you will have treasure in heaven; and come, follow me." But when he heard this he became sad, for he was very rich. Jesus looking at him said, "How hard it is for those who have riches to enter the kingdom of God!

For it is easier for a camel to go through the eye of a needle than for a rich man to enter the kingdom of God." Those who heard it said, "Then who can be saved?"

But he said, "what is impossible with men is possible with God."

narratives in the three Gospels suggests a dependence on Mark. In the material common to all three Gospels, Matthew and Luke agree in sequence with Mark, but when they diverge from Mark, each goes his separate way. Matthew and Luke never agree when they depart from Mark's ordering. Even in language and word choice, Matthew and Luke appear dependent on Mark, though at times they correct his Greek to produce a smoother text and a better reading.

The Material Common to Matthew and Luke. Only about one half of Matthew and of Luke is taken from or is dependent upon Mark. Matthew and Luke have over 200 verses that they share in common but that do not occur in Mark. This material is often almost identical in form and content as the following example shows:

<table>
<tr><td align="center">Matt. 24:45–51</td><td align="center">Luke 12:42–46</td></tr>
<tr>
<td>Who then is the faithful and wise servant, whom his master has set over his household, to give them their food at the proper time? Blessed is that servant whom his master when he comes will find so doing. Truly, I say to you, he will set him over all his possessions. But if that wicked servant says to himself, "My master is delayed," and begins to beat his fellow servants,

and eats and drinks with the drunken, the master of that servant will come on a day when he does not expect him and at an hour he does not know, and will punish him, and put him with the hypocrites; there men will weep and gnash their teeth."</td>
<td>Who then is the faithful and wise steward, whom his master will set over his household, to give them their portion of food at the proper time? Blessed is that servant whom his master when he comes will find so doing. Truly I tell you, he will set him over all his possessions. But if that servant says to himself, "My master is delayed in coming," and begins to beat the menservants and the maidservants, and to eat and drink and get drunk, the master of that servant will come on a day when he does not expect him and at an hour he does not know, and will punish him, and put him with the unfaithful.</td>
</tr>
</table>

This commonalty of material in Matthew and Luke could be explained by assuming that Luke was dependent on Matthew or vice versa. The most commonly accepted explanation, however, is the assumption that the two Gospels were dependent upon a third source. This non-Marcan material shared by Matthew and Luke is generally referred to as Q (from the German word *Quelle*, meaning "source"). This material appears to have contained references to the preaching of John the Baptist, multiple sayings attributed to Jesus, and some stories about Jesus focusing on his controversies and miracles. No source such as this is known as an independent document, nor is it referred to by early church writers. Q may never have existed as a written document.[11] Instead, the non-Marcan mate-

---

[11] See A. M. Farrer, "On Dispensing with Q," in D. E. Nineham, ed., *Studies in the Gospels* (Oxford: Basil Blackwell, 1955), pp. 55–88. On the supposed content of Q, see Vincent Taylor, "The Original Order of Q," in A. J. B. Higgins, ed., *New Testament Essays* (Manchester: Manchester University Press, 1959), pp. 246–269.

rials common to Matthew and Luke may have been derived from rather fixed oral traditions current in the early church.

Material Unique to Matthew and Luke. When one removes the Marcan and Q traditions from Matthew and Luke, a residue of material remains that is unique to each of these Gospels. Some scholars have assumed that these two bodies of traditions once existed as written documents and designated them M and L. It is doubtful, however, if such writings ever existed. It is more likely that the authors were simply dependent upon oral traditions circulating in the early church and may even have created some of this material.

The classical, or so-called four-source, solution to the Synoptic problem is illustrated in the following diagram:

CHART 11: DIAGRAM OF THE FOUR-SOURCE SOLUTION
TO THE SYNOPTIC PROBLEM

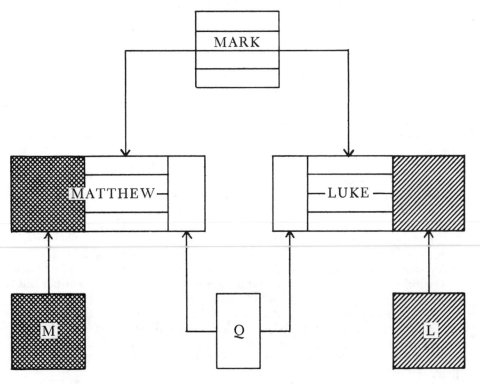

THE TRADITIONS OF JESUS IN THE EARLY CHURCH

Behind the sources used by the Gospels, whether written or oral, stood the church. Before sources were collected, the church congregations had used the traditions about Jesus in their evangelism to win converts, in their worship, in their instruction of new members, in their controversies with opponents, in their desire to affirm a self-awareness as a community, and in their efforts to express this self-awareness to outsiders. Traditions that the churches could employ in these various areas are the traditions that have been preserved. The New Testament writers refer to the existence and use of the traditions about Jesus in a number of places. Paul speaks of passing on to the church in Corinth the traditions that he had received (I Cor. 15:3). The writer of the Gospel of John notes that he was aware of other traditions about Jesus that he did not include in his writing (John 20:30–31), while the introduction to Luke speaks of "the narrative of the things which have been accomplished among us" as these were transmitted by "eyewitnesses and ministers of the word" (Luke 1:1–2).

The traditions about Jesus, which now make up the four Gospels and their sources, had a long and involved history of usage before they reached their final literary form. Scholars have attempted to get behind the literary form of these traditions and discover the manner in which these were transmitted in their pre-literary or oral stage. Such an attempt seeks to ascertain the life situations in the early church in which these were used. The assumption behind such an investigation is the legitimate belief that the needs and interests of the early churches determined the selection, form, and content of the traditions.

An example of a tradition that was transmitted in a form for use in the church's worship will illustrate the argument. The story of the last supper of Jesus (Mark 14:17–26; Matt. 26:20–30; Luke 22:14–39) in all three of the Synoptic Gospels speaks of the meal as a Passover celebration. According to the Biblical Torah and later Jewish tradition, a number of features were part of the Passover, or *paschal*, celebration. Among these were the asking of questions about the meaning and significance of the observance, the recitation of the exodus narrative and the *haggadah* (interpretative material) associated with it, the eating of the roast lamb, unleavened bread, and bitter herbs, the use of *haroset* (a dip of fruit and wine mixture), the drinking of three (perhaps four) cups of wine, and the singing of the *hallel* (Ps. 113 to 118). The Gospels in their account of Jesus' Passover meal refer only to the breaking of bread, the passing of the cup (both accompanied by a saying of Jesus), and the singing of a hymn. If this were a Passover meal, why were practically all the elements omitted from the tradition? The answer appears rather obvious: later Christian worship only made use of the cup, the bread, and the sayings of Jesus in its celebration of this event. This is clear from Paul's discussion of the Lord's Supper in I Cor. 11:17–32, where only the eating of the bread and the drinking of the cup are mentioned. It was then the celebration of the Lord's Supper (or Eucharist) in the early churches that has molded the form and content of the tradition about Jesus' last supper.

Scholars have attempted to analyze all the Gospel traditions, in a manner comparable to the above analysis of the last supper tradition, in order to determine how these traditions were employed by the early church and the form which these traditions had in their oral stage. This type of study is referred to as "form criticism." [12] The first effort of form criticism is directed toward ascertaining the

---

[12] See Edgar V. McKnight, *What Is Form Criticism?* (Fortress Press, 1969).

independent units in which the Gospel traditions circulated and classifying these according to form.[13]

One such form or type of tradition is "the pronouncement story." These are brief episodes about Jesus that give a particular setting, generally refer to some action in Jesus' encounter with other people, and are climaxed by a significant saying or pronouncement of Jesus. One of the best examples of this type of form is Mark 12:13–17 (Matt. 22:15–22; Luke 20:20–26):

> And they sent to him some of the Pharisees and some of the Herodians, to entrap him in his talk. And they came and said to him, "Teacher, we know that you are true, and care for no man; for you do not regard the position of men, but truly teach the way of God. Is it lawful to pay taxes to Caesar, or not? Should we pay them, or should we not?" But knowing their hypocrisy, he said to them, "Why put me to the test? Bring me a coin, and let me look at it." And they brought one. And he said to them, "Whose likeness and inscription is this?" They said to him, "Caesar's." Jesus said to them, "Render to Caesar the things that are Caesar's, and to God the things that are God's." And they were amazed at him. (Mark 12:13–17.)

Pronouncement stories were used by the early church in teaching its members about particular subjects using the saying or action of Jesus in the story as the authoritative point, in preaching the faith of the early church, and in controversy with opponents where the action or saying of Jesus served as the church's justification or authority. The setting for many of these stories must be viewed as a typical or ideal setting rather than as an actual historical setting in the life of Jesus. Many of the references in the Gospels, such as "on the sabbath," "in the synagogue," "early in the morning," and so on, illustrate this typical quality.

A second form is "the miracle story," which consists of a description of the circumstances, the cure or miraculous act worked by Jesus, and a reaction by those involved in or witnesses to the miracle. The report of Jesus' healing of Bartimaeus in Mark 10:46–52 (Matt. 20:29–34; Luke 18:35–43) provides an example of this type of tradition:

> And they came to Jericho; and as he was leaving Jericho with his disciples and a great multitude, Bartimaeus, a blind beggar, the son of Timaeus, was sitting by the roadside. And when he heard that it was Jesus of Nazareth, he began to cry out and say, "Jesus, Son of David, have mercy on me!" And many rebuked him, telling him to be silent; but he cried out all the more, "Son of David, have mercy on me!" And Jesus stopped and said, "Call him." And they called the blind man, saying to him, "Take heart; rise, he is calling you." And throwing off his mantle he sprang up and came to Jesus. And Jesus said to him, "What do you want me to do for you?" And the blind man said to him, "Master, let me receive my sight." And Jesus said to him, "Go your way; your faith has made you well." And immediately he received his sight and followed him on the way. (Mark 10:46–52.)

---

[13] The most important and influential work on New Testament form criticism has been Rudolf Bultmann, *History of the Synoptic Tradition*, 2d ed., tr. by John Marsh (Harper & Row, 1968), which was originally published in 1921. A pioneering and still valuable work originally published in English is Vincent Taylor, *The Formation of the Gospel Tradition* (St. Martin's Press, Inc., 1933, 2d ed. 1935).

A third form of tradition is "the parable." The term "parable" and its Hebrew counterpart *mashal* were applied to a wide variety of picturesque forms of expression, such as illustrative story, metaphor, simile, riddle, and so on. It is one of the most frequent forms of tradition in the Gospels. Mark 4:30–32 (Matt. 13:31–32; Luke 13:18–19) is an example of this form of tradition.

> And he said, "With what can we compare the kingdom of God, or what parable shall we use for it? It is like a grain of mustard seed, which, when sown upon the ground, is the smallest of all the seeds on earth; yet when it is sown it grows up and becomes the greatest of all shrubs, and puts forth large branches, so that the birds of the air can make nests in its shade." (Mark 4:30–32.)

Parables were used in a number of contexts and for a number of reasons in the early church—to proclaim a call to Christian commitment, to illustrate the nature of Christian behavior, and to interpret the content of Christian faith.

Another form in the teaching traditions is what might be broadly called "sayings," or "aphorisms." These tend to be very similar to parabolic teaching except that the elements of illustration and narrative are omitted. An example of a saying tradition is found in Mark 4:21–25 (Luke 8:16–18), where several sayings have been brought together.

> And he said to them, "Is a lamp brought in to be put under a bushel, or under a bed, and not on a stand? For there is nothing hid, except to be made manifest; nor is anything secret, except to come to light. If any man has ears to hear, let him hear." And he said to them, "Take heed what you hear; the measure you give will be the measure you get, and still more will be given you. For to him who has will more be given; and from him who has not, even what he has will be taken away." (Mark 4:21–25.)

The sayings of Jesus are very similar to the wisdom proverbs of the Old Testament but oftentimes with obvious Christian perspectives. Parallels to many of the sayings of Jesus can be found in the literature of Judaism from a time contemporary with the development of the early church.

The sayings of Jesus were used by the early church in its teaching and preaching and perhaps were circulated in independent form. The sermon of Paul given in Acts 20:18–35 illustrates the usage of these sayings. The apostle's sermon concludes with a quote attributed to Jesus: "Remembering the words of the Lord Jesus, how he said, 'It is more blessed to give than to receive' " (Acts 20:35)—a saying of Jesus not found in the Gospels. Evidence of collections of such sayings appears in the Gospels. For example, Luke 6:27–38 contains a number of sayings in which love is a central consideration and possibly a theme providing an organizational principle.

Other forms of Gospel tradition are more difficult to categorize. Several units or pericopes are stories about Jesus, such as the account of the baptism, the temptation, the entry into Jerusalem, the resurrection, and so on. These may have been used in various contexts in the early church and served as vehicles for the church's declaration of its faith in Jesus. The longest of this type of material is the passion narrative concerning Jesus' betrayal, trial, crucifixion, and burial. This seems to have existed as an extended and connected narrative from the earliest days of the church, although in the Synoptics, Matthew and Luke are fuller accounts and refer to sayings and episodes not found in Mark. The passion narrative was most likely used by early Christians as their Passover (or Lord's Supper) *haggadah* and would have thus been most frequently used in the context of worship (just as this material is still read during Holy Week).[14]

Form criticism has contributed greatly to an understanding of the Gospel traditions in their preliterary form. It has shown that the majority of these traditions circulated as independent units before being brought together to form small collections. At every stage in the transmission, the selection and the form of the traditions were influenced by the practical needs of the church, such as preaching, teaching, worship, controversy, and so on. The study of the Synoptic problem revealed how little the Gospels were attempts to produce a biography of Jesus. Form criticism has shown that even behind the sources, biographical concerns were subordinate to the theological and practical needs of the church.

One of the questions that arises out of form critical study is: Did the early Christians create traditions and sayings that were then attributed to Jesus? And if so, to what extent was this done? It is of course much easier to pose the question than to offer an answer. Our survey of the sources available for a knowledge of the historical Jesus has shown that the apocryphal literature is filled with such created traditions. One can assume that the beginning of this process was already present in the early church, but how far this had developed before the writing of the Gospels cannot be determined.

There were three possible sources on which the early church could draw for traditions that could be ascribed to Jesus. One of these was the teachings and sayings current in the culture of the time. Ideas and quotations in use in contemporary Judaism could easily have been attributed to Jesus. As was noted above, many of the Gospel traditions have parallels in rabbinic literature. Another possible source was the Christian exegesis of Old Testament passages. In eschatologically oriented Jewish sects, such as the Qumran community, practically all Old Testament passages were read as prophecies about the life of the sect. The early church also employed such an exegetical treatment of the Hebrew Scriptures. A possible example of this type of usage of the Old Testament is found in the pericope of the descent of the holy family into Egypt (Matt. 2:13–21). The origin of this episode, which is not found elsewhere, seems to be dependent upon an exegesis of Hos. 11:1, Jer. 31:15, and the narrative of the pharaoh's slaughter of infants at the time of the birth of Moses (Ex. 1:15 to 2:10). Thus the narrative of the event is an outgrowth of exegesis. A third source of traditions ascribed to Jesus may be seen in the activity of early Christian prophets and leaders who claimed revelations from the risen and exalted Lord whose authority was equal to the church-transmitted words of Jesus. Paul contended (in Gal. 1:12) that he had not received his gospel from men nor had he been taught it; instead, he had acquired it "through a revelation of Jesus Christ." The writer of Revelation sent to churches letters that contained the words of "the exalted Christ" revealed to him.

---

[14] See Reginald H. Fuller, "The Double Origin of the Eucharist," *Biblical Research*, VIII (1963), pp. 60–72.

Form critical studies have been more successful in analyzing the forms of early Christian tradition about Jesus than in discovering the actual life situations in which these were used and the impact the situation had on the traditions. Two further examples will illustrate that many of the traditions about Jesus were molded and interpreted to meet the developing needs of the church and to reflect its growing faith. In the parable of the marriage feast (Matt. 22:1–14; Luke 14:16–24; what appears to be an earlier form is preserved in the Gospel of Thomas, saying 69), what was originally a parable to compare the Kingdom of God with a great feast and to show that response to the invitation is a prerequisite to attendance has become an allegory. Those who refused the invitation are the Jews and those—the poor and maimed and blind and lame—who responded are the Gentiles. Matthew even mentions that the king sent his troops against those who refused the invitation and burned their city, an obvious reference to and an explanation of the Roman destruction of Jerusalem in A.D. 70. Matthew's version of the baptism of Jesus by John the Baptist shows how the church sought to explain this episode. John's baptism was associated with a confession of sin (Matt. 3:6), but there developed in the church the idea of Jesus' sinlessness (see I Peter 2:22). If Jesus were sinless, why did he submit to a baptism associated with repentance from sin? Matthew 3:13–17 answers this question by saying that John recognized that Jesus should not be baptized (adding a statement about John's recognition of Jesus' superiority). Jesus' baptism is explained not as an act of repentance but as an act to "fulfill all righteousness."

REDISCOVERING THE HISTORICAL JESUS

Out of nineteenth- and twentieth-century research on the Gospels and the early church has come the firm conclusion that it is impossible to write a biography of Jesus.[15] The Gospels themselves are not attempts at historical biography; they are theological writings preaching and confessing Christian faith in Jesus. Scholars, however, have not given up on their attempts to discover and reconstruct at least an outline and the contours of the activity, message, and fate of Jesus.[16] To some extent, the attempt to rediscover the historical Jesus is not unlike the effort to excavate an ancient site. The archaeologist attempts to

---

[15] See Albert Schweitzer, The Quest of the Historical Jesus, tr. by W. Montgomery (The Macmillan Company, Macmillan Paperbacks, published with a new introduction by James M. Robinson, 1968; originally published in German in 1906, in English in 1910); and H. K. McArthur, The Quest Through the Centuries (Fortress Press, 1966).

[16] The literature on the quest for the historical Jesus is enormous. The issues involved and examples of the discussions of Jesus are given in Hugh Anderson, ed., Jesus (Prentice-Hall, Inc., 1967); and H. K. McArthur, In Search of the Historical Jesus (Charles Scribner's Sons, 1969). On the so-called new quest, see Ernst Käsemann, "The Problem of the Historical Jesus," in his Essays on New Testament Themes, tr. by W. J. Montague (London: SCM Press, Ltd., 1964), pp. 15–47; and James M. Robinson, A New Quest of the Historical Jesus (London: SCM Press, Ltd., 1959). Two relatively recent treatments of Jesus are Ethelbert Stauffer, Jesus and His Story, tr. by R. and C. Winston (Alfred A. Knopf, 1960); and Günther Bornkamm, Jesus of Nazareth, tr. by I. and F. McLuskey with James M. Robinson (Harper & Brothers, 1960). The latter two works are worlds apart in viewpoint and illustrate the diversity of approaches to the quest.

remove the superimposed later strata in order to uncover the original remains. In the Gospels, however, the later strata are interwoven with the original materials. One such stratum is the redaction and interpretation of the Gospel writers who contributed their theological insights in the selection, organization, and editing of the traditions. These authors must be viewed as creative writers whose works and the literary frameworks that they provided for the traditions are important elements in the developing theology of early Christianity. The Gospel writers were not merely collectors of tradition. They were far more than the last sieve through which the traditions of Jesus passed; each offered a distinctive interpretation of the traditions. A second stratum is the developing church's interpretation of the traditions in terms of the church's needs and beliefs. Perhaps one should speak here in terms of strata instead of stratum, for the early church, as we shall see, was no monolithic institution. There were Jewish and Gentile, Palestinian and Hellenistic, and Pauline and non-Pauline churches in existence before the writing of the Gospels and the traditions were used and understood in differing ways in the various churches. A third stratum is the earliest Christians' interpretation of the traditions in the light of the Easter faith when the acts and deeds of Jesus were understood from the perspective of the resurrection. The final stratum would be the original acts and words of Jesus prior to any influence by the Christian faith.

There is, of course, no easy way in which the various strata can be peeled away to reveal the *ipsissima verba* (the exact words) of Jesus and to expose the original activity of Jesus. Many scholars would argue that such an attempt is not only impossible but even unnecessary, if not outrightly illegitimate. For them, it is the "Christ of faith," not the "Jesus of history," that is of significance for the life and faith of the church and believers.

The majority of scholars attempt to work with a "set of criteria" which permits the determination of the earliest stratum of the traditions that go back to Jesus. These criteria vary from scholar to scholar, but all are used in an attempt to discover the authentic words of Jesus.[17] One such criterion is "the criterion of dissimilarity." A saying of Jesus is assumed to be authentic if it is distinctively different from contemporary Judaism and from the post-Easter faith of the church. If a saying of Jesus has no parallel in the Judaism of his day and cannot be shown to be a belief developed in the early church, such a saying, it is assumed, must go back to Jesus. Such a criterion obviously only attributes a minimum of material to Jesus. This criterion has a number of possible weaknesses. Why would not Jesus often have used sayings and points of view current in Judaism? Could not Jesus and the early church have said the same thing on many points? It could be assumed that only those statements which show a clear Palestinian background and an Aramaic (which is assumed to be the language spoken by Jesus) coloring could be authentic.

A second criterion that is used is "the criterion of coherence."[18] Once a

---

[17] For a discussion of these criteria, see H. K. McArthur, "Basic Issues: A Survey of Recent Gospel Research," *Interpretation*, XVII (1964), pp. 39–55; and Norman Perrin, *Rediscovering the Teaching of Jesus* (Harper & Row, Publishers, Inc., 1967), pp. 38–49.

[18] See C. E. Carlson, "A *Positive* Criterion of Authenticity," *Biblical Research*, VII (1962), pp. 33–44.

number of sayings have been accepted as authentic on the basis of dissimilarity, then additional material that coheres with this can be accepted. Such an establishment of authentic material rests on the assumption of the correctness of the previous criterion. A further criterion is "the criterion of multiple attestations." If a tradition or theme appears in several Gospels (or the sources behind the Gospels), then the material is considered authentic; or at least, it has a greater chance of being authentic than material found in only one Gospel. The use of such criteria obviously seems to be arguing in a circle; nonetheless, some such approach has to be employed in attempting to determine the mission and message of Jesus behind the layers of church traditions.

How much of the Gospel material will be considered authentic depends in a large degree upon the presuppositions on which one works. Some scholars assume that any given statement in the Gospels is authentic unless there are compelling reasons for believing otherwise. Others work from the opposite perspective and assume that the burden of proof rests upon the claim of authenticity; i.e., only those traditions which can be proven authentic are to be used in discussing the mission and message of Jesus.

Any attempted reconstruction of the historical Jesus and his preaching must satisfactorily fulfill three basic goals.[19] (1) It must understand Jesus within the context of first-century Palestinian Judaism. Many reconstructions have portrayed Jesus in terms of eighteenth-century Romanticism, nineteenth-century liberalism, or twentieth-century existentialism. Jesus was a first-century Jew, and attempts at portrayal must understand him within this context. (2) Any reconstruction must explain the reasons for his death. What, in his life and teachings, led to his crucifixion? In many ways, the answer to this question is determinative for one's depiction of Jesus. (3) Any attempt to reconstruct a picture of the historical Jesus and his teaching must explain why he attracted a following during his ministry and why this following took root in the form of the early church.

In our next chapter we shall attempt to look at the mission and message of Jesus, but will do so within the context of a study of the Gospel of Mark and some of the parallel Gospel material.

---

[19] See N. A. Dahl, "The Problem of the Historical Jesus," in Carl E. Braaten and Roy A. Harrisville, eds., *Kerygma and History* (Abingdon Press, 1962), pp. 138–171.

18 | JESUS IN THE GOSPELS

"The portrait of Jesus in the Gospels is kindred to an oil painting, and one had best stand at a distance, and not move up too close, or one will see only the brush lines and the accumulated oil—not Jesus himself." [1] Such a verdict is based on sound reasoning. Thus, in this chapter we shall look at the portrait of Jesus given in the Gospel of Mark, examining not only the finished painting but also the brushstrokes of the artist. Hopefully such an examination will meet the three goals mentioned at the end of the preceding chapter.

THE GOSPEL ACCORDING TO MARK [2]

Early church tradition ascribed The Gospel According to Mark to John Mark, who was a traveling companion of Paul (Philemon 24; Col. 4:10; Acts 12:12, 25; 15:36–40). All the Gospels were written anonymously in that none of them contains reference to the name of the author within the body of the writing. The original title to Mark is found in the first verse of the book; the superscription ("The Gospel According to Mark") is a later church addition. The earliest reference about the writing of the Gospel is a statement from Papias, bishop of Hierapolis, ca. A.D. 140:

> Mark became the interpreter of Peter and he wrote down accurately, but not in order, as much as he remembered of the sayings and doings of Christ. For he was not a hearer or a follower of the Lord, but afterward, as I said, of Peter, who adapted his teachings to the needs of the moment and did not make an ordered exposition of the sayings of the Lord. And so Mark made no mistake when he thus wrote down some things as he remembered them; for he made

---

Biblical readings: The discussion of Jesus in this chapter is based primarily on The Gospel According to Mark. The use of such a work as B. H. Throckmorton, Jr., ed., Gospel Parallels: A Synopsis of the First Three Gospels, 3d ed. (Thomas Nelson & Sons, 1967), is helpful in comparing Mark's material with the other Synoptics. See maps XIV and XVI.
[1] Sandmel, The First Christian Century, p. 191.
[2] On The Gospel According to Mark, see R. H. Lightfoot, The Gospel Message of St. Mark (Oxford University Press, Inc., paperback ed., 1962); James M. Robinson, The Problem of History in Mark (London: SCM Press, Ltd., 1957); and Willi Marxsen, Mark the Evangelist, tr. by James Boyce et al. (Abingdon Press, 1969).

it his especial care to omit nothing of what he heard, and to make no false statement therein.[3]

A further reference (by Irenaeus, ca. A.D. 130–200) stated that the Gospel was written in Rome after the death of Peter and Paul in A.D. 64. Papias (and the source he quoted) recognized that Mark's Gospel was no biography and that it was composed of somewhat disconnected episodes (he may have been using the organization of Matthew and Luke as standards for his evaluation of Mark's Gospel). The fact that the second-century church sought to ascribe writings to apostles or to disciples of apostles may be the basis for Mark's association with Peter (but see I Peter 5:13). As we shall see, Rome as the place of origin has much to commend it.

If the literary-historical study of the Synoptic Gospels is correct, then Mark was the first to bring together the various collections[4] (and independent units) of the deeds and words of Jesus and the extended passion narrative to form "a gospel." In many respects, the path toward this development had already been laid in the confessional statements and preaching of the early church. Short confessions of faith, eventually represented in the Apostles' Creed, had summarized the church's faith in Jesus, emphasizing in a special way the passion, death, resurrection, and lordship of Christ (see, for example, I Cor. 15:3–7).[5] In the New Testament, both the act of preaching and the content of the preaching are referred to as kerygma (from the Greek word *keryssein*, "to herald," "to proclaim"). The kerygma had emphasized the mighty acts of God in Jesus, proclaimed his suffering, his resurrection, and offered salvation to the believer.[6] In form, Mark was composed as a literary expansion of the kerygma, as a literary proclamation of the message of salvation.

The outline of The Gospel According to Mark is rather simple: a prelude, or introduction (Mark 1:1–13); a ministry in and around Galilee (Mark 1:14 to 9:50); the journey to Jerusalem (Mark, ch. 10); Jesus in Jerusalem (Mark 11:1 to 16:8). The writer obviously wished to produce a geographical polarity between Galilee, where Jesus' ministry met with some success, and Jerusalem, where Jesus' ministry encountered hostility and ended in crucifixion. Such a geographical division must reflect the theological interest of the writer rather than the historical course of events. This scheme was taken over from Mark by the other Synoptics, but the Gospel of John provides a picture radically different from this geographical orientation.

A person with an inquisitive mind reading Mark for the first time but already familiar with Christian beliefs would probably sense immediately many of the issues that arise out of the Gospel. In the story of Jesus' baptism, the writer lets

---

[3] Papias was quoted by the early church historian Eusebius (ca. A.D. 260–340). Translation is from Henry Bettenson, ed., *Documents of the Christian Church* (Oxford University Press, Inc., 1943), p. 39.

[4] Some of the larger units in Mark may have already existed as collections. For example, Mark 2:1 to 3:35 (conflict stories); 4:1–34 (parables); and 4:35 to 5:43 (miracles).

[5] See V. H. Neufeld, *The Earliest Christian Confessions* (Wm. B. Eerdmans Publishing Company, 1963).

[6] See C. H. Dodd, *The Apostolic Preaching and Its Development* (London: Hodder & Stoughton, 1936).

the reader in on a clue to Jesus' identity when he declares that a voice from heaven spoke to him saying, "Thou art my beloved Son; with thee I am well pleased" (Mark 1:11). Yet when one continues to read, one comes upon episode after episode in which silence is enjoined upon any who recognize Jesus' identity. The demons recognize him but he commands them not to make him known (Mark 1:23–24, 34; 3:11–12). Persons are cured by Jesus and then forbidden to make known the source of their cure (Mark 1:44; 5:43; 7:36; 8:26). When his intimate disciples confess that they know who he is (Mark 8:27–30) or are allowed to behold his glory momentarily (Mark 9:2–9), they are sharply admonished not to make this public. This consistent injunction to silence is commonly referred to as "the messianic secret" in Mark.[7] The fact that the references to this mystery appear primarily in the editorial remarks of the author rather than in the traditions he used suggests that this was a deliberate emphasis of the writer.

A second major theme in Mark is the continual misunderstanding of Jesus by his disciples and followers.[8] Time after time events occur, and the writer mentions the failure of the disciples to understand what is taking place; Jesus teaches, and his followers do not comprehend his teaching. After the stilling of the storm, the disciples are filled with awe but not comprehension (Mark 4:35–41). After the feeding of the multitudes, the disciples "did not understand about the loaves" (Mark 6:52; also ch. 8:14–21). When Jesus spoke of suffering, even Peter rebuked him (Mark 8:31–33). They questioned "what the rising from the dead meant" (Mark 9:9–10) as if they had never heard of the idea of resurrection. They sought to prevent children from approaching Jesus (Mark 10:13) and misunderstood the nature of sharing in Jesus' glory (Mark 10:35–41). Jesus' mother and brothers did not understand him; they were unresponsive and suspicious, and his friends thought he was "beside himself" (Mark 3:21, 31–35). The disciples and Jesus' family are portrayed as blind to the truth, misunderstanding even when "he explained everything" (Mark 4:33–34). Before the crucifixion they deserted him (Mark 14:50), and Peter, the chief of the disciples, on three occasions denied his affiliation with Jesus (Mark 14:66–72). Why did the disciples, who had enjoyed an intimate association with Jesus as well as private instruction, not understand and yet the Roman soldier who only witnessed the crucifixion could exclaim: "Truly this man was the Son of God!" (Mark 15:39)?

Further, according to Mark, Jesus spoke to the multitudes in parables, not so that they might understand but in order that they would not comprehend his teaching:

> To you has been given the secret of the kingdom of God, but for those outside everything is in parables; so that they may indeed see but not perceive, and

---

[7] See G. H. Boobyer, "The Secrecy Motif in St. Mark's Gospel," *New Testament Studies,* VI (1960), pp. 225–235; T. A. Burkill, *Mysterious Revelation: An Examination of the Philosophy of St. Mark's Gospel* (Cornell University Press, 1963); and Lewis S. Hay, "Mark's Use of the Messianic Secret," *Journal of the American Academy of Religion,* XXXV (1967), pp. 16–27.

[8] See J. B. Tyson, "The Blindness of the Disciples in Mark," *Journal of Biblical Literature,* LXXX (1961), pp. 261–268.

may indeed hear but not understand; lest they should turn again, and be forgiven. (Mark 4:11–12.)

To the reader, this is of course one of the most shocking statements in the entire Gospel.

Another emphasis in the Gospel of Mark is the hostility toward Jesus shown by the Jewish leaders and vast elements of the population. The Jewish leaders —the scribes and the Pharisees especially—are shown not merely reacting to Jesus but plotting and scheming to destroy him. The scribes questioned his presumption (Mark 2:6), the Pharisees denounced him for association with tax collectors and sinners (Mark 2:16), the Pharisees and the Herodians consulted on a common course to destroy him (Mark 3:6; 12:13), attempts were made to trap him (Mark 8:11; 10:2; 12:13), the chief priests and scribes plotted to have him arrested and killed (Mark 14:1–2), false witnesses were secured to testify against him (Mark 14:55–59), the Jewish leaders "delivered him to Pilate" (Mark 15:1) and finally incited the Jewish masses to demand his death (Mark 15:11), and the chief priests and scribes mocked him upon the cross (Mark 15:31–32). In his own country the people's unbelieving reaction to him led Jesus to declare that "a prophet is not without honor, except in his own country, and among his own kin, and in his own house" (Mark 6:4). The questioning of his "sanity" by friends and family led Jesus to declare that "whoever does the will of God is my brother, and sister, and mother" (Mark 3:21, 31–35). Some of the pre-Marcan traditions may have already possessed an element of hostility toward the Jews and a desire to blame them for Jesus' death. Nonetheless, Mark heightened this emphasis considerably and in his editorial comments portrayed the Jewish leaders as scheming to destroy him.

Numerous attempts have been made to explain these special emphases in Mark but none has been overly successful. The motives behind the writing of the Gospels were probably multiple and complex and any attempt to find a single purpose behind any Gospel is suspect of oversimplification. An earlier attempt to explain "the messianic secret" argued that Jesus had carried out a ministry in which he made no messianic claims about himself and that Mark first introduced the claims into the material under the guise of the secrecy. However, Mark did not have to introduce this messianic claim into the material, for most of the pericopes he took over were already permeated with a messianic interpretation of Jesus. Perhaps the emphasis on secrecy may go back to Jesus' refusal to accept or claim messianic titles and authority that the later church claimed for him, but it was probably Mark's way of pointing to a certain understanding of Jesus. For the writer, the revelation of Jesus was a concealed revelation that could be grasped only in the light of the resurrection faith. At the same time, the secrecy motif emphasized that the historical Jesus was the same as the resurrected Christ. There was a depth of mystery and a meaning to Jesus and his teachings, and especially his suffering, but only to the eye of faith.

It has recently been argued that the emphasis on the misunderstanding of the disciples and Jesus' hostility toward his family was the writer's way of denying the authority of both the Palestinian Jewish church and Jesus' family.[9] Jesus'

---

[9] See Sandmel, *The First Christian Century*, pp. 185–187; and Brandon, *Jesus and the Zealots*, pp. 273–280.

brother James later emerged as head of the Jerusalem church, and blood relationship to Jesus continued to be influential in the Jerusalem church after James's death. Mark claimed that obedience, not kinship, was the test of discipleship. As we have seen, a "dynastic" principle was a factor in the leadership of the Jewish Zealots, and Mark may have opposed any such emphasis on the family of Jesus. The Gospel of Mark does not reflect the concerns of Palestinian Jewish Christianity and does not appear to have been written to appeal to a Jewish audience. Numerous references that explain Jewish practices and beliefs and Aramaic phrases would be necessary only to a non-Jewish readership (see Mark 1:9; 3:17; 5:41; 7:3-4, 11, 34; 12:18; 14:12; 15:22, 42). The fact that the Gospel was addressed to Gentiles and the denigration of the Jews, the disciples, and Jesus' family have led to the assumption that Mark was a polemic against Jewish Christianity and an attempt to authenticate Gentile Christianity.

A number of factors suggest that the Gospel of Mark may have been written as an apologetic defense of Christianity addressed to the Romans.[10] We have already mentioned the early church tradition which associated the Gospel with Rome. The apocalyptic discourse in Mark, ch. 13, seems to presuppose the fall of Jerusalem and the destruction of the Temple, as well as the expanding Gentile mission. Although one cannot be certain, it is possible that the emphasis on Jesus' repudiation by the Jews, especially those in Jerusalem, and the blame placed upon them for his crucifixion were a way of disassociating Jesus from the Jewish people and cause. The Jewish revolt and the Roman celebration of the fall of Jerusalem (see above, pp. 300–303) would not have enhanced the cause of a movement that preached a Jewish messiah executed at the hands of the Romans. The most overt confession of faith in Jesus in the entire Gospel is attributed to the Roman centurion who stood guard at the cross. He recognized and affirmed what the disciples had not understood and what the Jews did not comprehend (Mark 15:39).

JESUS AND JOHN THE BAPTIST

There seems to be no question but that the initial public ministry of Jesus was associated with the activity of John the Baptist.[11] The Gospels are unanimous in this regard. In Mark (ch. 1:2–11), four factors are emphasized about John. (1) He was the fulfillment of Old Testament prophecy, the promised messenger who would prepare the way (Mal. 3:1 but which Mark attributes to Isaiah) and the voice crying in the wilderness (see Isa. 40:3). (2) John was a preacher of repentance, proclaiming a "baptism of repentance for the forgiveness of sins" (Mark 1:4). He functioned as an ascetic figure on the periphery of society, wore camel's hair clothing, and lived off the land. (3) John the Baptist was the forerunner of Jesus who proclaimed Jesus (although Mark does not

---

[10] For the arguments supporting such an apologetic interest, perhaps overstated, see Brandon, *Jesus and the Zealots*, pp. 221–282.

[11] See C. H. H. Scobie, *John the Baptist* (Fortress Press, 1967); and Walter Wink, *John the Baptist in the Gospel Tradition* (Cambridge University Press, 1968).

make the fact explicit, it is obvious) as one mightier than he who would baptize with the Holy Spirit. (4) John was the baptizer of Jesus, who received in his baptism a divine assurance of his status.

Caesar Augustus (27 B.C. to A.D. 14) was the ruler of the Roman Empire at the time of Jesus' birth. This silver medallion shows Augustus, with the inscription: "Emperor Caesar." The reverse portrays a capricorn bearing a cornucopia within a wreath of laurel, the birth sign of Augustus.

AMERICAN NUMISMATIC ASSOCIATION

It is obvious that Mark has presented a Christian interpretation of John the Baptist but an interpretation that has not developed to the extent found in the other Gospels. In Matthew, John recognized Jesus, hesitated about the lesser baptizing the greater, and received a divine assurance that Jesus was the beloved son (Matt. 3:13–17). In Luke, John and Jesus are described as kinsmen and even before their birth John is subordinated to Jesus (Luke 1:36–45). In the Gospel of John, the Baptist is merely a voice who heralded Jesus as the Son of God, and no reference to the baptism of Jesus is given (John 1:29–34).

The Christian interpretation of John the Baptist was based on a desire to depict him as the prophetic forerunner of Jesus who fulfilled the Old Testament predictions of "the return of Elijah" before the end of time (see Mal. 4:5–6; Mark 9:9–13; Matt. 17:9–13) and thus to show John in a subordinate role to Jesus (see John 6:25–30; Matt. 11:11). The Baptist attracted a following of disciples (Mark 2:18) that continued to exist as a community long after his death (Acts 18:24 to 19:7).[12] He was revered by this Baptist community as one

---

[12] In the Mesopotamian region, there still exists a small Baptist sect, called the Mandeans, which claims to perpetuate the movement initiated by John the Baptist.

Modern Bethlehem encircles the sixth-century church which marks the series of caves designated in the fourth century by Constantine's mother as the place of Jesus' birth. Although the Gospels of Mark and John do not refer to Bethlehem, Matthew and Luke speak of Jesus' birth at Bethlehem, the ancient home of the Davidic family.

ROBERT B. WRIGHT

superior to Jesus (using the argument that the superior baptizes the inferior) and was believed by some to be the Messiah. Controversy and competition between Jesus and his followers and the John the Baptist sect are referred to in the Gospels (Mark 2:18–22; John 4:1) and continued after the rise of the early church. The early church sought, however, to turn the founder of a rival sect into an ally by aligning him with the Christian cause.

Historically, John the Baptist was a prophetic spokesman of the imminent eschatological day of the Lord which he proclaimed as a day of judgment and wrath. John seems to have shared in the evaluation of Jewish life found among various sects which held that many of the people were apostate and had thus ceased to be God's people. In the ordeal to come, being "a son of Abraham" would not be sufficient. John demanded that his hearers repent from their sins, be baptized, and display appropriate ethical conduct. According to the Gospel of Luke (ch. 3:10–14), John preached a radical form of ethics, enjoining his hearers to share their food and clothing. Such seems to imply participation in an eschatological brotherhood, somewhat similar to the community at Qumran. The similarities between John's preaching and the teachings of the Dead Sea community as well as John's preaching in such close geographical proximity to the Qumran settlement have led to the assumption that John was either a member of the sect or was influenced by its teachings.[13] He may have once been a member of the community or he may have been reared in its midst (see Luke 1:80). However, John differed from the Qumran community in a number of ways. (1) He was an open preacher of the coming judgment, not, like the Qumran covenanters, a guardian of eschatological secrets. (2) John's baptism was a unique, once-for-all act of repentance, not a repeatable act of purification. (3) The military orientation of the Qumran community and their expectation of the "final war" found no place in the recorded preaching of John.

John was eventually put to death by Herod Antipas, after a ministry of uncertain duration. According to the New Testament, John's death was occasioned by his criticism of Herod's marriage to his own sister-in-law (Mark 6:17–29). In Josephus' description of John's death, however, there is no mention of the question of Herod's nuptial life (which, nonetheless, may have been an issue), but instead John is said to have been executed because Herod feared that John's "extensive influence over the people might lead to an uprising. . . . Herod thought it much better, under the circumstances, to get John out of the way in advance, before any insurrection might develop, than for himself to get into trouble and be sorry not to have acted, once an insurrection had begun" (Antiquities XVIII. 5.2). John thus died a martyr's death, and his memory was honored by many Jews long after he was buried by his disciples. The New Testament writers, and maybe the disciples of John also, were hesitant to acknowledge that he was executed as a possible leader of an insurrection and thus as a threat to the state.

What was the possible historical relationship between the Baptist and Jesus? The latter seems to have responded to John's preaching of the imminent eschatological judgment and his urgent demand to be baptized in preparation for the coming ordeal. It is entirely possible that Jesus was for a time a disciple of the Baptist. The Synoptics state that Jesus came to John from Galilee, that he was baptized in the Jordan, stayed for a time in the wilderness, and came into

---

[13] See W. H. Brownlee, "John the Baptist in the New Light of Ancient Scrolls," in Krister Stendahl, ed., The Scrolls and the New Testament (Harper & Brothers, 1957), pp. 33–53.

Galilee again after the arrest of John. According to the Fourth Gospel, Jesus was associated with John for some time (John 1:35–42), carried on a Judean ministry before the arrest of the Baptist (John 3:22–24), rivaled John in attracting followers (John 4:1–3), drew some of his disciples from John's following (John 1:35–42), and was recognized by many as the successor to John (John 10:40–41). The Fourth Gospel claims that John did not limit his ministry to the wilderness area around the southern Jordan but worked also in the district of Samaria (John 3:23).

Any attempt to reconstruct the mission and message of the historical Jesus must take with utmost seriousness the possible relationship between Jesus and John the Baptist, the consequence of John's arrest on Jesus' ministry, and the impact of John's execution on Jesus, even if these are given only surface treatment in the Gospels. Jesus may have served as a disciple of John for a period, carrying on an associated or simultaneous ministry in Judea. The arrest of the Baptist must have profoundly affected his followers. Jesus returned to Galilee and there began his open preaching career, in many respects a continuation of the ministry of John the Baptist.

The prelude to Mark's Gospel concluded with two significant elements: the dove and the voice at the baptism and the reference to the temptation in the wilderness. The first informed the reader of Jesus' true identity and assured him of Jesus' awareness of that identity. The second stressed the fact that Jesus' career was to be no mere human struggle but a conflict with the powers of evil, the outcome of which was already certain. These episodes are reflections of the author's affirmations of faith rather than objective events or insights into the self-understanding of Jesus.

JESUS' GALILEAN MINISTRY

Mark's account of Jesus' Galilean ministry consists of a number of independent units that he has drawn together, occasionally providing them with rather general geographical settings ("by the Sea of Galilee," "a lonely place," "at table in his house," "in the synagogue," "up into the hills," and so on) and at times with more specific settings ("in the synagogue at Capernaum," "at Gennesaret," "the village of Caesarea Philippi," and so on). Mark has tended to emphasize the mighty acts of Jesus rather than his teaching. The material on the Galilean ministry can be treated thematically around the following subjects: Jesus' preaching of the Kingdom of God, his call to discipleship, Jesus' activity and conflicts, miracles and exorcisms, the question of messiahship, and Jesus and the Son of Man.

Jesus and the Kingdom of God.[14] Mark introduced Jesus' public ministry by referring to his proclamation of the coming of God's Kingdom and his consequent call for repentance and faith.

---

[14] See Norman Perrin, *The Kingdom of God in the Teaching of Jesus* (The Westminster Press, 1963); and Rudolf Schnackenburg, *God's Rule and Kingdom*, tr. by J. Murray (Herder & Herder, 1963).

Now after John was arrested, Jesus came into Galilee, preaching the gospel of God, and saying, "The time is fulfilled, and the kingdom of God is at hand; repent, and believe in the gospel." (Mark 1:14–15.)

The idea of the Kingdom of God was the central element in the preaching of Jesus. But having said this, one must determine what was meant by the concept

The traditional mount of the Beatitudes is located along the shores of the Sea of Galilee. Jesus' northern activity and preaching centered around the Sea of Galilee. From fishermen plying their trade on this inland lake came his first followers, according to the Synoptic traditions.

ROBERT B. WRIGHT

"Kingdom of God" and how Jesus employed the idea in his preaching. An important element in the Old Testament and earlier Israelite religion was the divine kingship of Yahweh. Israel had celebrated in the cult the kingship and rule of Yahweh, the nation had praised the rule of God, and prophets had preached of Yahweh the king. The idea of the rule of God in human affairs was deeply rooted in Old Testament thought, and for the Jews, God had always been and always would be king, for his was an everlasting Kingdom. In apocalyptic literature and thought, the idea of the Kingdom of God had taken on new nuances. Apocalyptic thought, which had surfaced during times of hardship and persecution, had emphasized the eschatological kingship of God. According to this view, God would at some time in the future intervene decisively in human history in such a way as to punish the wicked, reward the good, and establish forever a realm of righteousness, peace, and security for his people.

This apocalyptic thought about the Kingdom of God as the final and deci-

A synagogue at Capernaum from the third century A.D. has been partially restored. Jesus is said to have worshiped and taught in a synagogue at Capernaum (Mark 1:21). This third-century house of worship may have been constructed on the site of the synagogue of Jesus' day.

ROBERT B. WRIGHT

sive act of God is best illustrated in The Book of Daniel (chs. 2:44; 4:3; 7:13–14, 23–27). In these passages, the Kingdom and rule of God stand as the antithesis to all the earthly kingdoms that had ruled over Israel. The setting up of the Kingdom of God is portrayed as ending the earthly rule of these powers, as transforming the status of the world, as ending history as such, and as ushering in the new day for the people of the saints of the most high. The establishment of God's Kingdom would involve a cataclysmic act of God that would produce a state of blessing and joy for the redeemed.

This expectation of the Kingdom of God found expression in synagogue prayers, just as in the Lord's prayer.

> Magnified and sanctified be his great name in the world which he has created according to his will. May he establish his kingdom in your lifetime and in your days and in the lifetime of all the house of Israel even speedily and at a near time.[15]

The apocalyptic orientation of Jesus' proclamation of the Kingdom is suggested by the phrase, "The time is fulfilled." According to such apocalyptic writers as the author of Daniel, history's course was moving toward its allotted end, and when the time had been fulfilled, God would inaugurate his rule. It should be recalled that the author of Daniel tried to predict the exact course of history and to pinpoint the time of the end. The content of Mark's summary (Mark 1:14–15) of Jesus' preaching stressed the imminence of the Kingdom, not only in the statement that the time is fulfilled but also in the statement that the Kingdom "is at hand" and that men should take immediate action in the light of this: "repent, and believe in the gospel [or good news]."

How did Jesus understand the nature of the Kingdom, the time of its arrival, and his relationship to both of these? In several passages in Mark, Jesus appears as the prophet who proclaims the "coming" of the Kingdom. This emphasis on the coming of the Kingdom (Mark 9:1) stressed that the Kingdom was not some creation of man, some culmination of human effort but was rather the inbreaking from the beyond. In the parable[16] of the seed growing of itself (Mark 4:26–29), Jesus described a farmer who scattered seed and then went on with his routine. The seed sprouted and grew and eventually the harvest came. Such is the Kingdom of God which comes "of itself," and, like the farmer, one "knows not how." The Kingdom and its mystery (or secret, Mark 4:11) are not immediately obvious and the extent of its greatness defies comprehension. The parable of the mustard seed (Mark 4:30–32) speaks of the Kingdom as a mustard seed ("the smallest of all the seeds on earth") which when it matures is the greatest of shrubs, so large that birds can build nests in its shade. Who would have comprehended the greatness of the mustard plant from merely observing the tiny seed? Such is the incomprehensibility of the Kingdom!

Jesus proclaimed the Kingdom of God as the supreme value for which man

---

[15] Translation is from Perrin, *Rediscovering the Teaching of Jesus*, p. 57.

[16] The parables of Jesus have as a rule been interpreted in the light of his Kingdom proclamation in recent literature. See C. H. Dodd, *The Parables of the Kingdom*, rev. ed. (Charles Scribner's Sons, 1961); and Joachim Jeremias, *Rediscovering the Parables* (Charles Scribner's Sons, 1966).

should be willing to surrender all. If one's hand, foot, or eye causes one to stumble, it is better to cut it off or pluck it out rather than to miss the Kingdom (Mark 9:42–48). In Mark 9:45–47, the Kingdom is equated with "life," so that to enter the Kingdom is to enter life, to lose the Kingdom is torment and hell. The value of the Kingdom and the joy associated with it are described in Matthew (ch. 13:44–46; without Marcan parallel) as a treasure hidden in a field or as a pearl of great value for which one should sell all that he has in order to buy it.

The Kingdom confronts man as a gift which he, like a child, must receive (Mark 10:15). The prerequisites for entry into the Kingdom or for receiving it as a gift are repentance and faith (Mark 1:15), this childlikeness, and a willingness to sacrifice material possessions and all ordinary responsibilities and relationships (Mark 9:47; 10:23–25).

Did Jesus proclaim the Kingdom as present or future? This question has been the subject of some of the most heated discussion in twentieth-century New Testament research. Did Jesus proclaim the coming Kingdom as an event completely in the future along the lines of the apocalyptic thought of his day ("thoroughgoing eschatology")? [17] Or did he reinterpret and spiritualize the Jewish concept of the Kingdom, believing that it had entered human history through his own activity and message ("realized eschatology")? [18] Or did he proclaim both the futurity and the presence of the Kingdom ("self-realizing eschatology")? [19] Biblical passages can be quoted that seem to support all three positions, and it is this ambiguity which has fed the debate.

A number of passages in Mark support the idea of a futuristic eschatology—the Kingdom is yet to come. Mark 1:15 states that the Kingdom "is at hand," where the verb employed means "to approach." In Mark 9:1, Jesus is quoted as saying, "There are some standing here who will not taste death before they see the kingdom of God come with power." Both of the passages still consider the coming of the Kingdom to be in the future, although both imply a very imminent advent.

Greater difficulty is encountered in attempting to find statements in Mark that unambiguously support the idea of the Kingdom as present. One such passage is Mark 3:22–27, but here the exegete must depend upon the parallels to this passage in Matt. 12:22–29 and Luke 11:17–23. This pericope is a controversy story in which Jesus is accused by the scribes of being possessed by Beelzebul (a term synonomous with "Satan"), through whom he works his exorcisms. Jesus argues that if Satan is casting out Satan, then his Kingdom is divided and thus is coming to an end. The story leads up to a proclamation of Jesus which stipulates that one cannot enter a strong man's house and plunder his possessions unless the strong man (= Satan) is bound. The saying implies that in the activity of Jesus, Satan has been bound, which would be a manifestation of the arrival of the Kingdom. Matthew and Luke have added a state-

---

[17] See Schweitzer, *The Quest of the Historical Jesus*, pp. 330–397.

[18] The primary exponent of realized eschatology in the English-speaking world has been C. H. Dodd; see his work cited in footnote 16 above.

[19] See W. G. Kümmel, *Promise and Fulfilment: The Eschatological Message of Jesus*, tr. by D. M. Barton (London: SCM Press, Ltd., 1957).

ment that makes this explicit: "If it is by the Spirit (or finger) of God that I cast out demons, then the kingdom of God has come upon you" (Matt. 12:28; Luke 11:20). If the last text is authentic, and very few scholars have questioned its attribution to Jesus, then Jesus seems to have understood the Kingdom of God as operative in his ministry. (The fact that exorcisms could be attributed to Satan shows that the presence of the Kingdom was not a manifest conclusion to be drawn from the evidence.) The similes found in Mark 2:18–22 with their references to the presence of the bridegroom (= Jesus), new cloth on old garments, and new wine in old wineskins affirm the aspect of newness and joyousness that one might associate with the Kingdom but the idea itself is absent.

It would seem reasonable to conclude that Jesus thought of the Kingdom of God as still in the future, but so near that its impending advent should become the decisive factor in man's present attitudes, decisions, and conduct. Jesus may have interpreted his own career as a manifestation of the Kingdom's imminence. Jesus' teaching, and especially the parables, argued that the decisions, attitudes, and acts of a man must be made and done in the light of the imminent Kingdom.

The Call to Discipleship. Jesus not only preached the advent of the Kingdom and the demand of repentance and conversion, he also associated with himself a number of intimate followers—disciples—who shared in his preaching and "missionary" activity. Stories of the call of some of these are given in the Gospel of Mark. In Mark 1:16–20, Jesus is said to have been passing by the Sea of Galilee and saw Simon and Andrew, whom he called to follow him. The two immediately left their fishing nets and followed Jesus. Farther on, James and John, sons of Zebedee, likewise forsook their fishing and followed Jesus. Mark 2:13–14 describes the call of Levi, a tax official, who left his business to accompany Jesus. In the present form in Mark, these stories assume that upon their first encounter with Jesus, the disciples responded to the call of discipleship. It is doubtful if such was the actual case, since these stories seem to have been influenced by early Christian evangelism which called for immediate response to the kerygma and which emphasized the power of the word of Jesus to call men into his service. The Fourth Gospel reports that Andrew and Simon had been disciples of John first and then followed Jesus (John 1:35–42). If such were the case, then they no doubt were already familiar with Jesus. Behind the call of the disciples, one must assume far more familiarity with Jesus and his preaching than the Gospels report.

The association of a rabbi and his followers or pupils ("disciples") was common in the Judaism of the time. Reference is made in the Gospels to the disciples of John the Baptist (Mark 2:18) and the disciples of the Pharisees (Matt. 22:16). In the rabbi-pupil relation, the teacher instructed his followers, who then in turn could instruct others. Some teachers, such as the Teacher of Righteousness at Qumran and John the Baptist, founded a community of followers that continued after the death of the teacher. Such was the case with Jesus.

Jesus is said to have selected twelve disciples for a close association with himself and to be sent out to preach (Mark 3:14). According to Mark 3:16–19, the following were the names of the twelve:

(1) Simon Peter
(2) James, son of Zebedee
(3) John, son of Zebedee
(4) Andrew
(5) Philip
(6) Bartholomew

(7) Matthew
(8) Thomas
(9) James, son of Alphaeus
(10) Thaddaeus
(11) Simon the Cananaean
(12) Judas Iscariot

Three other lists of the twelve appear in the New Testament (Matt. 10:1–4; Luke 6:12–16; Acts 1:13), and minor variations between the lists do exist. The number "twelve" was of course a symbolical figure reflecting the idea of the twelve tribes of early Israel. There seems to have been a greater emphasis on "the twelve" in the early church than in the career of Jesus. The reference to these disciples as apostles (Mark 6:30; Luke 6:13) reflects the usage of an early church title read back into the ministry of Jesus. There seems to be no doubt that Jesus did call into a special relationship with himself a small circle of disciples that must be distinguished from the followers of Jesus in the wider sense.

The twelve disciples were said to have been sent on a preaching mission by Jesus (Mark 6:7–13, 30). The disciples, in groups of two, presumably proclaimed a message similar to that of Jesus (Mark 6:12; see Luke 9:2). In addition, they were said to have cast out many demons and to have anointed the sick with oil and healed them. The disciples traveled without provisions, depending upon the support of those responding to the proclamation.

Very little is known about these disciples of Jesus. They certainly were not from the aristocracy of Jewish society, but to argue that they were uneducated and ignorant men is certainly an oversimplification. Very little can be said about their political sentiments. Many of them were described as Galileans and Galilee was one of the hotbeds of anti-Roman, Jewish nationalism. Simon the Cananaean was apparently a member of a revolutionary group since Cananaean is the Hebrew equivalent of the Greek term "Zealot." James and John, the sons of Zebedee, were nicknamed Boanerges, "sons of thunder" (= thunderbolts), but the reason for this designation is not known.

Jesus' Activity and Conflicts. The activity of Jesus in carrying out his ministry differed in a number of ways from that of John the Baptist. The latter was at home in the wilderness, at the fringes of society, he was an ascetic in dress and food, and he was a proclaimer of the coming judgment. Jesus, on the other hand, seems to have followed a nonascetic approach to life, was more open in his relationships with people, and, in his preaching as well as his activity, emphasized the great joy and blessings of the Kingdom rather than its judgment. Jesus was not "a voice crying in the wilderness." Matt. 11:18–19 says that John came neither eating nor drinking (i.e., living ascetically) but the Son of Man (= Jesus) came eating and drinking and he was dubbed a glutton and a drunkard. Jesus is said to have associated with the moral and religious "outcasts" of his day. He ate with tax collectors and sinners (Mark 2:15), some of his disciples were fishermen and one was a tax collector, and his followers were drawn from the *ame ha-aretz.*

An important question, in this regard, concerns Jesus' attitude toward Jewish law and the "tradition of the elders." Mark contains a number of conflict or controversy stories in which Jesus clashes with the Jewish religious leaders over eating companions and habits (Mark 2:15–17; 7:1–8, 14–23), fasting (Mark 2:18–22), and Sabbath observance (Mark 2:23–28; 3:1–6). Jesus' eating with tax collectors and sinners was condemned by the Pharisees, to whom Jesus replied, "Those who are well have no need of a physician, but those who are sick; I came not to call the righteous, but sinners" (Mark 2:17). When Jesus' disciples ate with unwashed hands, they were accused by the Pharisees of failure to live according to the tradition of the elders (= the oral law). Jesus' response was an accusation that the Pharisees were hypocrites, holding fast to the tradition of men but forsaking the commandment of God (Mark 7:6–8). Mark 7:14–23 contains a quotation of Jesus which argues that it is not what goes into a person that defiles but what comes from within, from out of the heart. What a man eats goes to his stomach; out of the human heart flow men's actions. Mark comments that such a statement was equivalent to declaring all foods clean (Mark 7:19). Jesus and his disciples (according to Mark 2:18–22) did not observe the Jewish fast days as did the disciples of John and the Pharisees. The failure of his disciples to fast was justified, according to Mark, by Jesus' declaration that when the new arrives, you do not stitch it to the old and while the bridegroom is present the wedding merriment must go on (Mark 2:19–22).

A number of conflict stories focus on the question of the observance of the Sabbath. On a Sabbath, Jesus and his disciples were said to have been going through a grainfield and the disciples began to pull some of the heads of the grain and to eat them (Mark 2:23). This plucking of the grain could be interpreted as harvesting, and harvesting as labor was an act prohibited on the Sabbath. According to the present form of the pericope in Mark (ch. 2:23–28), Jesus justified such an act by appealing to David's eating of special temple bread loaves although it was not lawful for him to do so. This justification seems to be dependent on early church practices. If the old David could bypass the law and allow his disciples to do so, then surely could not the new and greater David (= Jesus) do the same? This breaking of the Sabbath law is actually given two additional justifications: "The sabbath was made for man, not man for the sabbath" and "The Son of man is lord even of the sabbath" (the latter is probably an early church interpretation). The justification that "the sabbath was made for man" has its counterpart in the rabbinic saying: "The sabbath is given over to you, not you to the sabbath." [20] Mark 3:1–6 is a narrative of Jesus' healing on the Sabbath, which is justified by Jesus' question, "Is it lawful on the sabbath to do good or to do harm, to save life or to kill?"

All these stories show Jesus taking a rather relaxed attitude toward the observance of the law and the traditions of the elders. The New Testament evidence, however, is somewhat ambiguous on the question of Jesus' interpretation of the Torah. Throughout the Gospel of Mark, Jesus tends to ignore the requirements of the oral law and to reinterpret some of the stipulations of the Torah.

---

[20] See Barrett, *The New Testament Background*, pp. 153–155, for this quote and other rabbinical teachings on Sabbath observance.

In the latter category belongs Jesus' statement that one should not only obey the commandments but should also sell what one has, give the returns to the poor, and follow him (Mark 10:17–22). In Mark 10:2–9, Jesus appears to cast doubt on the divine origin of some of the laws saying that the law granting a man the right of divorce was merely a concession to the human condition while the will of God required that two become one and remain permanently in that state. Texts in the other Synoptics, especially Matthew, have Jesus emphasize the binding character of the law and warn against "whoever relaxes one of the least of these commandments" (Matt. 5:17–20). In addition, Jesus appears as a new law-giver who intensifies and spiritualizes the old commandments of the Torah (Matt. 5:21–48).

Much of the conflicting evidence probably reflects differing viewpoints in the first-century church rather than contradiction inherent in the teaching of Jesus. The Gentile church tended to proclaim an end to the law and its observance while Jewish Christianity continued to emphasize the value of the law. It is possible that Jesus as a Jew had no desire to see the Torah annulled or abolished but at the same time he did repudiate many of the oral laws that had developed to safeguard the original commandments and did reinterpret the spirit of the Torah with a much greater freedom than was customary. Jesus' teaching, in its Gospel form, never seems to have appealed to the weight of authority and tradition for support as was customary among the rabbis.

Many Synoptic passages represent Jesus as stressing the immediacy of God's power and will, demanding ethical behavior in the light of the Kingdom's imminence, and insisting that every encounter of a man's life is in reality an encounter with God and a demand for decision and ethical response. For Jesus, these factors may have been as determinative as the Torah.

Miracles and Exorcisms.[21] A large percentage of the Marcan material on the Galilean ministry is concerned with the "mighty acts" performed by Jesus. For convenience in discussions, these mighty works can be divided into exorcisms, healings, and nature miracles. It shall be noted that such a division is purely arbitrary. Exorcism is the practice of expelling demons and evil spirits from persons and places, often through the use of incantations or the performance of certain occult acts. The exorcism of demons, who were considered the cause of disease, physical abnormalities, and mental disorders among other things, is an ancient custom dating back to the time of the Sumerians. There is no case of exorcism in the Old Testament, although there are laws forbidding magical practices which suggest that such things as exorcism were a part of the Israelite culture but were not officially condoned. The practice of exorcism is attested in Judaism in the post-Biblical period. The Prayer of Nabonidus among the Qumran Scrolls mentions the cure of Nabonidus by a Jewish exorcist. In the apocryphal book of Tobit, the angel Raphael reveals to Tobit the power to exorcize demons through the burning of a special fish's liver and heart and the ability to cure blindness by using the fish's gall (Tobit 6:1–8). The New Testament writ-

---

[21] See Reginald H. Fuller, *Interpreting the Miracles* (The Westminster Press, 1963); and H. van der Loos, *The Miracles of Jesus* (Leiden: E. J. Brill, 1965).

ers assumed the existence of exorcism among the Jews (Matt. 12:27), and exorcists were known in the Greco-Roman culture.

The exorcisms of Jesus found in the Gospel of Mark involved the casting out of demons from a man in the synagogue at Capernaum (Mark 1:21–28), from the Gerasene demoniac (Mark 5:1–13), from the daughter of a Syrophoenician woman (Mark 7:24–30), and from a boy (Mark 9:14–29). Mark considered the casting out of demons to be one of the characteristic forms of Jesus' ministry (Mark 1:34, 39). Reference is made to the fact that Jesus' disciples practiced exorcism (Mark 3:15; 6:13) and that even strangers cast out demons in the name of Jesus, a practice that Jesus did not repudiate (Mark 9:38–41).

Numerous examples of healing are attributed to Jesus in Mark. He cured Simon's mother-in-law of a fever (Mark 1:29–31), a leper (Mark 1:40–45), a paralytic (Mark 2:1–12), a man with a withered hand (Mark 3:1–6), the daughter of Jairus (Mark 5:21–23, 35–43), a blind man of Bethsaida (Mark 8:22–25), and blind Bartimaeus (Mark 10:46–52). Frequent reference is made by Mark in his editorial comments about Jesus' healing (Mark 1:32–34; 3:7–12; 6:53–56). In some of these healings, reference is made to the use of spittle by Jesus. He placed his fingers in the ears of the deaf mute, put spit on the man's tongue, and sighed (Mark 7:33–34). In one instance, he is said to have spit on a blind man's eyes (Mark 8:23). Most of the episodes record only the fact that Jesus touched the persons and that the recipients possessed faith in Jesus' curative powers. One of the healings (actually an exorcism), however, was said to have been performed without Jesus' seeing the person cured. Jesus was said to have been unable to work mighty acts (except for some healings) in his own country because of the people's unbelief (Mark 6:5–6) and no healings or exorcisms are reported from his Jerusalem ministry. It was Galilee and the surrounding areas that were the lands of special wonders wrought by Jesus.

A number of Jesus' mighty works may be referred to as "nature miracles." The miracles belonging to this group in Mark are the stilling of the storm (Mark 4:35–41), the feeding of the five thousand (Mark 6:35–44), the walking on the water (Mark 6:45–52), the feeding of the four thousand (Mark 8:1–10), and the cursing of the fig tree (Mark 11:12–14, 20–21). In these, Jesus is shown calming the turbulent waters of the Sea of Galilee, multiplying a few fish and loaves to satisfy the hunger of thousands, walking across the lake to enter a boat with his disciples, and cursing a fig tree causing it to wither.

Students of the Bible have sought in various ways to "explain" the nature miracles of Jesus. Were they originally only parables and stories which he told but which his later followers turned into events? Were they ordinary events which the disciples misunderstood? Were these stories originally told about someone else (such as Greek gods) and then applied to Jesus? Were the stories the creations of the early church? Did the writers record these without any desire that they be understood as anything more than symbols? How one interprets the miracles will depend in no small measure upon two factors: the role assigned to the early Christians in the formation of the Gospel traditions and the world view held by the interpreter.

Within the Gospels, the stories of the miracles and exorcisms functioned in several ways. (1) They bore testimony to the belief that Jesus was no ordinary person. The power of God was present and active in his work. (2) They sought to offer to the reader, and, in their oral form, the hearer, a way of faith in him whose whole life had been a miracle. The exalted Lord was none other than the wonder-worker Jesus of Nazareth. (3) The miracles of Jesus were seen as the fulfillment and transcendence of Old Testament prophecy. Just as Moses and the Hebrews in the wilderness and Elijah and Elisha in their service had witnessed the miraculous and had been granted the power to perform the unusual, so also Jesus. (4) The miracles were declared to be evidence of the coming of the Kingdom, the dawning of the new age, the arrival of the eschatological time. Matthew (ch. 11:2–6) and Luke (ch. 7:18–23) have preserved a tradition that appears as an answer to John the Baptist's query concerning whether Jesus was the one to come. The answer declares that "the blind receive their sight and the lame walk, lepers are cleansed and the deaf hear, and the dead are raised up, and the poor have good news preached to them" (Matt. 11:5). In other words, the miracles were signs that the Messiah had come, the new day had dawned. In the healings and casting out of demons, the evil powers ("the strong man") were being bound and their kingdom invaded. (5) The Gospel writers sought to depict the time of origin, the beginning of the Christian movement, as a unique period, as a "type-time." The events from which the subsequent Christian movement flowed were events whose origin was transcendental not terrestrial.

Can one ascertain the historical Jesus and the events behind the miracles and exorcism stories? Jesus must have functioned as an exorcist and a healer. He may have understood his own work in this regard as evidence that his proclamation of the Kingdom's imminence was correct. Even the most reliable Jewish evidence concerning Jesus considered him a "miracle-worker." Jesus' ascription of this work to "the spirit of God" must mean that he saw the exorcisms as signs of "the kingdom's coming." What events lie behind the nature miracles must remain an open question. The difference between the work of an exorcist and walking upon the water is not only a difference in degree but in kind as well.

The Question of Messiahship.[22] Did Jesus in his public career and/or in his private teachings and discussions with the disciples claim to be the expected Jewish Messiah? The Hebrew term "messiah" (which means "anointed" and was originally used in reference to the Hebrew kings) or its Greek equivalent "Christos" (which is anglicized as "Christ") was applied by the early church to Jesus. All the New Testament Gospels presuppose that Jesus regarded himself as the Messiah. In order to attempt an answer concerning the question of Jesus' self-understanding about messiahship, we must first look at the ideas of messianic expectation in contemporary Judaism and then examine more closely the Gospel evidence about Jesus' messiahship.

The basic content of the Jewish messianic expectations developed out of the Judean theory of Davidic kingship (see above, pp. 125–130). Alongside the royal theory of kingship with its claims about the current ruler, there was developed

---

[22] A recent survey on Messianism and the Messiah is given in Ferdinand Hahn, *The Titles of Jesus in Christology*, tr. by H. Knight and G. Ogg (The World Publishing Company, 1969), pp. 136–239.

by Judean prophets the idea of the ideal Davidic ruler whose reign would fulfill the claims and promises of Davidic kingship. This was then used as the means for judgment of the reigning monarch as well as for the projection of hopes concerning the future. With the end of the Davidic rule in Jerusalem, both the claims of the Davidic royal ideology and the hopes of the ideal ruler were projected into a future expectation. Such expectations can be termed "messianism." In these expectations and hopes, the ideal ruler (only occasionally actually referred to as the Messiah) was primarily a political, nationalistic redeemer-ruler figure. With the expanded role of the office of high priest in postexilic Judaism, the function of the high priest, who was also an "anointed one," opened the way for futuristic expectations about the ideal, expected anointed (messiah) of priestly lineage. In some circles of pre-Christian Judaism, such as the Qumran community, there existed the expectation of two messiahs.[23] Jewish messianism was then not a completely unified element. Apocalyptic thought did not utilize the idea of a messiah very much if at all. Many Jews may not have shared in any form of messianism, due perhaps to a satisfaction with the *status quo*, to disillusionment with these hopes (Jewish expectations had been dashed on a number of occasions), or to pessimism about the historical process (what one might call "the secularization of history"). The dominant messianism at the time of Jesus seems, however, to have been the expectation of a human savior, the bringer of salvation, along the lines of the Davidic royal theology.

Although all the Gospels presuppose that Jesus regarded himself as the awaited Messiah, the statements about this are ambiguous. In the Fourth Gospel, Jesus is recognized as the Messiah from the very beginning of his public ministry (John 1:35–51) and explicitly claims the title for himself (ch. 4:25–26). In the Synoptic Gospels, Jesus never openly and explicitly claims to be the Messiah. The one exception to this is Mark 14:61–62 where Jesus answers the question of the high priest—"Are you the Christ?"—with an affirmation. The parallels to this passage in Matt. 26:63–64 and Luke 22:67–70, however, are equivocal and Jesus circumvents the question which would suggest that Mark's answer is redactional. The title "messiah" does not occur in Q. Such evidence suggests that Jesus never publicly claimed to be the Messiah; if he had, the Synoptics would surely have been less equivocal on the point.

Attempts to explain this problem of Jesus' messiahship have generally followed three lines of approach. (1) One line of argument suggests that Jesus did not use the term because its military, political, and materialistic overtones would have been misleading to the Jews of the day, creating in them false hopes of the restoration of the kingdom of David. Such a claim would also have led to his speedy elimination by the Romans, who feared the threat of revolution. (2) Other scholars insist that Jesus did not refer to himself as Messiah because he saw his messianic role as still in the future, to be realized when the Kingdom of God should come, or because he felt the need to interpret the role of the Messiah through his own activity before allowing the title to be applied to himself. (3) Others argue that neither Jesus nor anyone else during his lifetime

---

[23] See K. G. Kuhn, "The Two Messiahs of Aaron and Israel," in Stendahl, ed., *The Scrolls and the New Testament*, pp. 54–64.

regarded him as the Messiah and that this identification first occurred in the early Christian church.

Of these theories, the third, with some modifications, seems to be the most historically plausible. Jesus seems to have regarded himself as the forerunner, the herald, or the prophet of the coming Kingdom of God. If Jesus' preaching was primarily oriented toward apocalyptic concerns, then the concept of messiahship may not have been very integral to his thought since messianism with its worldly, political orientation was not a necessary constituent feature of apocalypticism with its otherworldly, transcendental orientation. However, one must not preclude the possibility that followers of Jesus did look upon him as the Messiah and desired to proclaim him as such. It is possible that some such action lies behind Jesus' rebuke of Simon Peter in the Caesarea Philippi story (Mark 8:27–33; see John 6:15).

Jesus and the Son of Man.[24] If the term "messiah" is of infrequent occurrence in the Gospels, this is not the case with the designation "son of man." This phrase occurs only in contexts within the Gospels where Jesus is the speaker and occurs very seldom outside the Gospels. "Son of man," as a phrase, appears in the Old Testament with two usages. It is used frequently in The Book of Ezekiel where the prophet describes himself being addressed by the deity as son of man. Here the usage is a periphrasis for "me, I, or you," a sort of indirect reference to oneself. The term also appears in the Old Testament as a synonym for "man or mankind." Such a usage is found in Ps. 8:4. The term used in this latter manner is also found in the apocalyptic Book of Daniel where a heavenly figure is described as one "like a son of man" (Dan. 7:13), that is, "one like a human being." The term is not a title in either of these usages.[25]

In the Gospel of Mark (and the other Synoptics as well), the phrase "Son of man" is used by Jesus in three contexts.[26] (1) Some sayings refer to the activity of the Son of Man on earth. In Mark 2:10, Jesus says that "the Son of man has authority on earth to forgive sins" and associates this with his healing of a paralytic. Mark 2:28 declares that "the Son of man is lord even of the sabbath." Both of these passages refer to the authority of the Son of Man on earth. To the reader, it is obvious that in these two cases the person referred to as "Son of man" is Jesus. It could be that the usage here merely reflects the use of the term as a self-designation employed instead of the pronoun "I." However, a special

---

[24] The literature on the problem of the Son of Man is voluminous. The most recent comprehensive and significant studies are Heinz E. Tödt, *The Son of Man in the Synoptic Tradition*, tr. by D. M. Barton (The Westminster Press, 1965); A. J. B. Higgins, *Jesus and the Son of Man* (Fortress Press, 1965); and Norman Perrin, "The Son of Man in the Synoptic Tradition," *Biblical Research*, XIII (1968), pp. 3–25.

[25] The phrase "son of man" appears in the pseudepigraphical book of Enoch, especially in chs. 70–71. This material has often been used to elucidate the New Testament passages, but whether this should be done is doubtful. See Norman Perrin, "The Son of Man in Ancient Judaism and Primitive Christianity: A Suggestion," *Biblical Research*, XI (1966), pp. 17–28.

[26] See the article of Perrin mentioned in footnote 24 above; and Hans Conzelmann, *An Outline of the Theology of the New Testament*, tr. by John Bowden (Harper & Row, Publishers, Inc., 1969), pp. 131–137.

emphasis in Mark's Gospel is on the authority of Jesus (see Mark 1:22, 27), a theme that may have influenced the author's use of the sayings in this category. (2) A second group of passages speak of the Son of Man and his necessary suffering. These are Mark 8:31; 9:9–13, 31; 10:33–34, 45; 14:21, 41. These passages all speak of the suffering, death, and resurrection of the Son of Man (= Jesus) and thus seem clearly to represent a reading back into Jesus' sayings the faith of the early church. Therefore they cannot be an authentic recollection of the teaching of the historical Jesus. (3) A third group of sayings refers to the exalted heavenly figure who will come in glory from heaven. These are found in Mark 8:38; 13:26; 14:62. In all these references, Jesus speaks of the Son of Man as though he were another person. This group of passages suggests that if Jesus did use the term "Son of man" as a title, he did so to refer not to himself but to a coming figure who would descend from heaven to inaugurate the new age. To the reader of the Gospels it would be obvious, however, that Jesus was to be understood as referring to himself wherever the title "Son of man" appears, but this represents the perspective of the early church.

Our survey of the Marcan material on the Son of Man suggests that if Jesus used the phrase, he did so only in reference to a figure other than himself or merely, as was current in Judaism, as a periphrasis for "I." The line of development that led to the interpretation of Jesus as the heavenly Son of Man will be discussed in the next chapter.

JOURNEY TO JERUSALEM

Jesus' ministry in Galilee came to an end when he set out for Jerusalem.[27] As an itinerant preacher, he had proclaimed the coming Kingdom of God and the requirements of God the king laid upon those who responded. He had functioned as an exorcist and a healer. His preaching and activity had attracted both attention and followers. There were, perhaps, many reasons why people listened to and followed him. His prophetic attitude, which ascribed an authority to his words equal to the Torah, his sympathy toward and association with publicans and sinners, his mighty acts, his proclamations of the apocalyptic expectations, which implied an anti-Roman-Herodian attitude, and his invitation to share in the benefit and blessings of the Kingdom were all possibly significant factors. The enthusiasm of the followers had at times perhaps pushed the movement toward messianic tendencies.

In his description of Jesus' pre-Jerusalem ministry, Mark had incorporated sufficient material to suggest that his Gospel was intended not just for Jews but also for Gentiles. Jesus, according to Mark, had taken forays into Phoenicia (Mark 7:24–30) and to the Greek cities of the Decapolis (Mark 7:31–37). In both places, he had been met with immediate and favorable response. Whether these stories of excursions into non-Jewish territory are based on authentic recollections about Jesus or are reflections of Mark's interest in Hellenistic Christianity cannot be determined.

---

[27] On Jerusalem at the time of Jesus, see Joachim Jeremias, *Jerusalem in the Time of Jesus*, tr. by F. H. and C. H. Cave (Fortress Press, 1969).

Mark, ch. 10, discusses the journey of Jesus to Jerusalem. All three Synoptics assume only one visit to Jerusalem (with the exception of his visit at the age of twelve, see Luke 2:41–51), which ended in Jesus' crucifixion. The Fourth Gospel, as was noted above, claims that much of Jesus' ministry was carried out in the Holy City with several visits being made. How one evaluates these two differing perspectives depends largely on one's assessment of the historicity of the Johannine traditions.

The Marcan narrative of Jesus' journey from Galilee to Jerusalem uses the journey primarily as the skeleton around which to collect a number of traditions. The content of the narrative does, however, suggest two things: (1) Jesus' journey to Jerusalem was not direct. A ministry in Judea and beyond the Jordan took place (Mark 10:1) with a favorable reaction to Jesus. Thus the Gospel of Mark depicts Jesus as carrying out a ministry in all districts of Palestine with the exception of Samaria (which the Fourth Gospel later develops). (2) The ministry of Jesus on the way to Jerusalem, therefore outside Galilee, was characterized by the same interests as the Galilean ministry. Jesus engaged in controversy with the Pharisees (Mark 10:2–9), offered to his disciples teachings that transcended the Torah (Mark 10:10–12), expounded on the theme of the Kingdom and the nature of discipleship (Mark 10:13–31), instructed the Twelve concerning his true ministry and the role of the earthly, suffering Son of Man (Mark 10:32–45), and healed a blind man who possessed the necessary insight to recognize Jesus' true identity (Mark 10:46–52).

Why did Jesus choose to go to Jerusalem? According to Mark, Jesus had to fulfill the role of the Son of Man: "The Son of man will be delivered into the hands of men, and they will kill him; and when he is killed, after three days he will rise" (Mark 9:31; see also ch. 9:12). But this contention represents interpretation after the fact and displays the Marcan idea that it was as the suffering Son of Man that Jesus showed himself as the true Son of God.

What catalyst triggered Jesus' journey to Jerusalem cannot be determined with certainty. Was the execution of John the Baptist a major influence (Mark 6:14–29)? It is impossible to determine, but it should be recalled that the arrest of John was a significant influence on the beginning of Jesus' Galilean ministry. Two factors have been suggested as the possible reasons for Jesus' journey to Jerusalem other than the fact that he was participating in the Passover pilgrimage. Both may have played a role. In the first place, he probably went to Jerusalem to deliver the message of the coming Kingdom to the leaders of the city and the Jewish faith and to the pilgrims assembling for the Passover celebrations. Jerusalem was, after all, the sacred center, the spiritual capital of Judaism, and was the symbol of Jewish hopes and dreams. Not to have delivered the message of the Kingdom to Jerusalem would have been unthinkable. Secondly, Jesus probably went to Jerusalem expecting the advent of the Kingdom. The Gospel of Luke notes that as Jesus and his disciples neared Jerusalem "they supposed that the kingdom of God was to appear immediately" (Luke 19:11). This statement regarding the expectation concerns only the disciples, but Jesus seems to have shared their sentiments (see Mark 14:25).

JERUSALEM MINISTRY AND CRUCIFIXION

The Marcan traditions concerning Jesus' ministry in Jerusalem and the events associated therewith may be broken down in the following daily sequence:[28]

Sunday: "Triumphal Entry" (Mark 11:1–11)
Monday: "Cleansing of the Temple" (Mark 11:12–19)
Tuesday: (a) Teaching in the Temple (Mark 11:20 to 12:44)
              (b) Private Instruction of Peter, James, John, and Andrew (Mark, ch. 13)
Wednesday: At Bethany (Mark 14:1–11)
Thursday: The Last Supper, Betrayal, and Hearing Before the High Priest and Sanhedrin (Mark 14:12–72)
Friday: Trial Before Pilate, Crucifixion, and Burial (Mark, ch. 15)
Saturday: Sabbath
Sunday: Visit to the Tomb by the Women (Mark 16:1–8)

Several emphases are present in Mark's account of Jesus' entry into Jerusalem (Mark 11:1–11).[29] There is, first of all, the deliberateness of Jesus' entry. A colt was fetched from a nearby village with the owner having apparently been contacted previously about its usage. It has been customary to see in Jesus' entry on a colt the enactment of the prophecy of Zech. 9:9. Mark, however, does not allude to this; it is the Gospel of Matthew that develops this theme. Secondly, Jesus rode into Jerusalem accompanied by a crowd, no doubt many of his followers and disciples from Galilee. The crowd made Jesus' entry a noted event, spreading their garments and branches along the roadway. Such an entry could not have gone unnoticed by the Jerusalem population. Thirdly, the crowd proclaimed the coming of the Kingdom; although in its present form in Mark, the kingdom referred to is the kingdom of David, not of God. The shout "Hosanna" ("Save us") was a commonly used shout of prayer employed as an acclamation of praise. Jesus, and presumably his followers, "went into the temple; and looked round at everything" and withdrew from the city.[30] Such a survey of the Temple precincts must have been preparatory to the events in the Temple on the following day.

The Gospel of Mark records two events on the following day: Jesus' cursing of the fig tree (Mark 11:12–14) and his "cleansing" of the Temple (Mark 11:15–19). It is the latter that is of most consequence. Jesus entered the Temple precincts, overturned the tables of the money-changers and the pigeon sellers, prevented anyone from carrying anything through the Temple, taught concern-

---

[28] This scheme of course does not correspond to the Jewish day-reckoning, since the Jewish day was calculated from sunset to sunset not from midnight to midnight.

[29] On the influence of The Book of Zechariah on the Synoptic description of Jesus' entry, see Robert M. Grant, *Historical Introduction to the New Testament* (Harper & Row, Publishers, Inc., 1963), pp. 350–351.

[30] Matthew and Luke differ from Mark on the day of the "cleansing of the temple" by placing this event on the day of the "triumphal entry."

ing the true nature of the Temple, raised fear among the priests because of the multitude accompanying him, and withdrew from the city only at the coming of evening. This complex of actions by Jesus is almost universally referred to as the "cleansing of the temple" but this is a far too innocuous desig-

The southeast corner of the Herodian Temple platform illustrates the impressive masonry of Herod's rebuild and calls to mind Jesus' statement that of the Temple, there would "not be left . . . one stone upon another" (Mark 13:2). From its foundation deep underground, the Temple platform was over 140 feet in height.

ROBERT B. WRIGHT

nation.[31] The acts of Jesus and his followers constituted what might better be called an attack or assault on the Temple. Jesus and his followers seem to have seized control of the Temple, for a time, and to have withdrawn only at the close of the day. Such a movement by Jesus and his followers would have been an immediate threat to the priestly aristocracy and to the high priest who held his office and exercised his authority with Roman permission. In this regard, the attack on the Temple was an attack on Roman authority. Why the Temple police and the Roman soldiers stationed in the Fortress of Antonia did not move in and immediately arrest Jesus is hinted at in the statement that the chief priests and the scribes feared him because all the multitude was astonished at his teaching. The description of the Temple as a den of robbers (see Jer. 7:11) was certainly not calculated to win friends among the priestly aristocracy who profited financially and politically from the Temple operations. Without any doubt, it was this attack on the Temple more than anything else that eventually resulted in the execution of Jesus (Mark 11:18).

According to Mark, the last public ministry of Jesus in Jerusalem took place on the day following the "cleansing of the temple" (Mark 11:20 to 12:44). Jesus

---

[31] See Victor Eppstein, "The Historicity of the Gospel Account of the Cleansing of the Temple," *Zeitschrift für die neutestamentliche Wissenschaft*, LV (1964), pp. 42–58; and N. Q. Hamilton, "Temple Cleansing and Temple Bank," *Journal of Biblical Literature*, LXXXIII (1964), pp. 365–372.

returned to the Temple precincts, again accompanied by a sympathetic multitude (Mark 12:12). Practically all the material in this section is intent on emphasizing the conflict between Jesus and the Jewish religious leaders. He discussed the question of his authority using the example of John the Baptist to support his claim to do "these things" (teach? stir up the multitude? cleanse the Temple?) with an authority, like the prophets, from God (Mark 11:27–33). Jesus is said to have told a parable which asserted in a symbolic way, but which the leaders understood, that the unfaithful and murderous tenants (the Jewish leaders) must give an accounting to the landlord (God) for their actions in the vineyard. The reference to the destruction of the tenants and the giving of the vineyard to others appears to be a Marcan comment on the destruction of Jerusalem and the development of Hellenistic Christianity (Mark 12:1–11).

The Pharisees and some Herodians, endeavoring to entrap him (Mark 12:13–17), were said to have posed a question to Jesus: "Is it lawful to pay taxes to Caesar or not?" Jesus responded after asking for a Roman coin: "Render unto Caesar the things that are Caesar's, and to God the things that are God's." The answer of Jesus, which on the surface appears so straightforward, was a masterpiece of ambiguity. To a Roman reader of the Gospel, Jesus' statement could be taken as supporting the Jewish payment of tribute to Rome. To any Zealot who might have heard Jesus, giving tribute to Rome was rendering to Rome what belonged to God, i.e., the land of Palestine and its resources. Further discussions and teachings of Jesus are noted by Mark: with the Sadducees on the resurrection (Mark 12:18–27), with the scribes over the chief commandment and the interpretation of Ps. 110:1 (Mark 12:28–40), and with his disciples over a widow's gift of a penny (Mark 12:41–44).

The thirteenth chapter of Mark is a collection of eschatological predictions that is commonly called "the little apocalypse." The first two verses of this chapter contain Jesus' prediction of the destruction of the Temple—"There will not be left here one stone upon another." In the light of the evidence presented against Jesus at his hearing before the high priest (Mark 14:58), it is entirely possible that Jesus did speak of the destruction of the Temple as part of the coming of the eschatological Kingdom (see also Acts 6:14). The rest of this chapter is a compilation of various types of material, some of it seems to have circulated in a pre-Marcan written form ("let the reader understand," Mark 13:14). Part of the material may represent a reworking of some Jewish apocalyptic texts while other traditions presuppose the life and faith of developing Christianity. The "desolating sacrilege" (see Dan. 11:31) may have originally been a reference to the statue ordered set up in the Temple by the emperor Caligula in A.D. 40 or to the Roman standards placed there after the fall of Jerusalem in A.D. 70. The entire chapter assumes a fairly lengthy interval between the time of Jesus and the coming of the Kingdom, an element not characteristic of the preaching of Jesus.

According to Mark, Jesus spent Wednesday of "Holy Week" in Bethany (Mark 14:1–11), a village on the eastern slopes of the Mount of Olives. Three concerns are reflected in the Marcan material. (1) The Jewish leaders plotted about how to arrest Jesus by stealth in order to kill him without triggering a tumult. (2) Judas Iscariot consulted with these leaders about plans to carry out the arrest. (3) Jesus was anointed with a precious ointment by a woman, which Mark says Jesus interpreted as anointment preparatory to his burial. However, Mark 14:8–9 seems clearly reflective of later Christian faith.

On Thursday evening, Jesus and his disciples shared the last supper in a private house in Jerusalem. According to the Synoptics, this last meal of Jesus with his intimate circle of disciples was a celebration of the Passover which was observed in the evening on the fourteenth day of the Jewish month Nisan. The Gospel of John places the last supper a day earlier (John 13:1–2; 18:28) and Mark 14:2 hints at this as well. Various attempts have been made to solve this discrepancy, among which are the following: (1) John is correct: the supper was a fellowship meal perhaps anticipating the Passover; no crucifixion would have taken place on the day of the feast for fear of the crowd; and the Synoptics reflect the faith of the early church which saw in the Christian Eucharist a replacement of the Jewish Passover; (2) the Synoptics are correct, and John has placed the meal a day earlier in order to synchronize the crucifixion of Jesus with the slaughter of the Passover lambs; and (3) both are correct [32] and consider the meal a Passover observance; but two different calendar reckonings were used, with John being dependent on the Essene (or Qumran) calendar which differed from the calendar in use in Jerusalem. Of these solutions, number two is to be preferred.

The narrative of the last supper has been told, as noted earlier, in a form influenced by the Eucharistic observances of the early church. According to Mark, Jesus declared that he would "not drink again of the fruit of the vine until that day when I drink it new in the kingdom of God" (Mark 14:25), i.e., Jesus understood the meal in an eschatological sense anticipating the coming of the Kingdom. Following the meal, Jesus and his disciples, less Judas, left the upper room, withdrawing to the Garden of Gethsemane (= "the garden of the oil press") across the brook Kidron at the foot of the Mount of Olives. Here Jesus agonized in prayer, distressed and troubled. He prayed that the Father's will would be done. For the Gospel writers, the "cup" mentioned by Jesus was his forthcoming death. Did Jesus express his anxiety about the future fearful of what was to happen to him? Or was his distress one of disillusionment and perplexity about the coming Kingdom and the course his ministry had taken in Jerusalem?

Jesus was arrested in Gethsemane when Judas gave the signal by kissing him. The fact that Judas knew where to find Jesus suggests that Gethsemane had been a prearranged meeting place. Going there had broken with Jesus' pattern of returning to Bethany nightly. Why Jesus and his disciples met in the Garden cannot be determined, but the Mount of Olives was expected to play a significant role in the eschatological "last days" according to Zech. 14:4. Had Jesus and his followers met there to await the Kingdom? To plot strategy? Or out of custom as John 18:2 suggests? Mark refers to those who accosted Jesus as a crowd sent by the Jewish officials, armed with swords and clubs. One of

---

[32] See M. H. Shepherd, Jr., "Are Both the Synoptics and John Correct About the Date of Jesus' Death?" *Journal of Biblical Literature*, LXXX (1961), pp. 123–132. A discussion of Jewish calendars and the date of the crucifixion is given in Godfrey R. Driver, *The Judaean Scrolls*, pp. 316–335.

Jesus' disciples (the Fourth Gospel says Peter) drew his sword and lashed out at the crowd cutting off the ear of the high priest's slave. The fact that one of Jesus' disciples was armed suggests that many of his followers may not have been passively oriented. One of his disciples was designated "the Zealot" and others bore names that have been taken as reflective of Zealot tendencies.[33] Luke 22:38 has preserved a reference to the fact that the disciples had said to Jesus at the last supper, "Look, here are two swords," to which Jesus had replied, "It is enough." The crowd that had come to take Jesus had expected trouble. Jesus' response to them—"Have you come out as against a robber?"— uses the Greek word *lestes*, which is employed in Josephus with the meaning "revolutionary." Jesus is shown in the story as not leading resistance but preventing it. With Jesus' arrest his followers dispersed, one naked leaving behind his linen wrapping.

The Marcan narrative, which is followed rather closely in Matthew and Luke, proceeds to report Jesus' hearing before the assembled Jewish leaders.[34] In Mark 14:55, explicit reference is made to a meeting of the Jewish council, the Sanhedrin, before whom witnesses were called to testify and Jesus was interrogated. For a number of reasons scholars have questioned the historicity of this nighttime meeting of the Sanhedrin (Luke omits any reference to it), since the second century A.D. tractate on the Sanhedrin in the Mishnah forbids holding trial in capital cases during the night.[35] In addition, a verdict of conviction in a capital case could not be made on the day the hearing began (the two meetings of the Sanhedrin mentioned in Mark 14:55 and 15:1 would have fallen on the same Jewish day which extended from sunset to sunset). Capital punishment could be executed on a feast day, however. It is uncertain whether the procedures stipulated in the Mishnah were already being practiced in Jesus' day or not. Since the Sanhedrin did not carry out the conviction, perhaps the council simply met to draw up charges against Jesus that could then be presented to the Romans. The council probably did not have the authority to carry out a crucifixion of one charged with what amounted to sedition.

The charges brought against Jesus involved his threat to destroy the Temple (Mark 14:58) and his messianic pretensions (Mark 14:60–64). Mark's narrative of the trial is characterized by a number of emphases that may not necessarily be historical. (1) The author was anxious to show that Jesus was innocent of all charges except one—the allegation that he was the Messiah. (2) The testimony against Jesus is pictured as being based on trumped-up charges and on false witnesses whose testimony did not agree. (3) The effort is made to blame the Jewish leaders, almost entirely, for the death of Jesus and thus to exonerate Pilate and the Romans. After the second hearing before the Sanhedrin on Fri-

---

[33] See Oscar Cullmann, *The State in the New Testament*, rev. ed. (London: SCM Press, Ltd., paperback edition, 1963), pp. 14–22.

[34] The trial of Jesus has been widely discussed by both Christian and Jewish scholars. See most recently: Paul Winter, *On the Trial of Jesus* (Berlin: Walter de Gruyter & Co., 1961); and S. G. F. Brandon, *The Trial of Jesus of Nazareth* (Stein & Day, 1968).

[35] On Jewish judicial procedure, see the texts in Barrett, *The New Testament Background*, pp. 169–172.

day morning, Jesus was turned over to the Romans, but Mark does not mention what charges were brought against him other than Pilate's question, "Are you the King of the Jews?" (Mark 15:2). Luke 23:2 says the charges were that he had perverted the nation, forbidden the payment of tribute to Caesar, and claimed to be the messianic king. There seems to be no reason to doubt that the charges against Jesus were based on three factors. (1) He had, like John the Baptist, attracted a sizable and enthusiastic following that Jewish authorities and the Romans viewed as a threat to Palestinian peace. (2) Jesus' preaching of the coming Kingdom of God and the claims made by Jesus and his followers were obviously viewed as anti-Roman, antiestablishment. Any proclamation of the coming Kingdom carried with it at least an implicit claim about the destruction of the *status quo*. Although Jesus may not have made messianic claims for himself some of his followers certainly seem to have done so. (3) Jesus' acts in cleansing the Temple must have, as the Gospels report, caused fear among the priestly aristocracy, for the act was close to, if not outright, sedition. It is possible that the activity of Jesus and his followers in the Temple was accompanied by outbreaks elsewhere in the city of Jerusalem. Mark mentions the fact that Barabbas was a rebel "who had committed murder in the insurrection" (Mark 15:7). The reference to "the insurrection" is not further defined, but it is entirely possible that this uprising had occurred earlier in the week and may have coincided with the Temple cleansing (see Luke 23:19: "an insurrection started in the city").

The depiction of the trial before Pilate, whose headquarters were in Caesarea but who was in Jerusalem to oversee the Passover celebrations, seems to go out of its way to blame the Jewish population for the execution of Jesus. Pilate is shown as being convinced of Jesus' innocence (Mark 15:10). According to Mark, it was customary for the procurator to release a prisoner at the time of the festival (Mark 15:6), but such a practice is not mentioned in any literature other than the Gospels. Mark employs this supposed practice of Pilate in order to allow the Jews to render the final verdict regarding Jesus. When presented with the choice of releasing Barabbas or Jesus, the crowd, stirred up by the chief priests, demanded the crucifixion of Jesus (Mark 15:11–14). If such an episode is historical, one wonders what had happened to the multitudes who had supported Jesus earlier and whom the priests had feared might create a tumult if Jesus were even arrested. It is most likely that the episode about the release of Barabbas had its origin in polemic against the Jews, in apologetic attitudes toward the Romans, and other than in historical actuality.

Pilate had Jesus scourged and then delivered to the troops to be crucified. Jesus was so weakened by the events of the trial and the scourging that he was unable to carry the crossbeam used in his own crucifixion; the upright post, generally of a height sufficient only to elevate the victim above the ground, was not carried. The charge for which a man was crucified was often attached to the crossbeam. According to Mark, the inscription of the charge against Jesus read: "The King of the Jews" (Mark 15:26). The Gospel writers, who do not agree on the wording, have used the written charge as an affirmation (John 19:20 mentions that it was written in Hebrew, Latin, and Greek). The original form must have been written expressing a claim to royal authority rather than an affirmation of Jesus' kingship. Before the crucifixion Jesus was offered wine mixed with myrrh as a mild narcotic, but he refused the drink.

The Caesarean inscription mentioning Pilate, which was uncovered in recent archaeological excavations, provides a contemporary reference to the Roman procurator but designates him as a "prefect." The Latin text reads [   ] TIBERIEUM/[PON]TIUS PILATUS/[PRAEF]ECTUS IUDA [EAE].

ISRAEL DEPARTMENT OF ANTIQUITIES AND MUSEUMS

Crucifixion was an Asiatic practice in origin, which had been employed by the Jewish Hasmonean rulers and had been adopted by the Romans from the people of the eastern Mediterranean world. Crucifixion was a humiliating and slow means of execution. The victim was crucified in public view, generally after being stripped naked. No vital part of the body was damaged, and often victims could live for days on the cross. The cause of death was not the act of crucifixion itself but the fatigue, hunger, thirst, and possibly asphyxiation associated with it. According to Mark, Jesus was crucified at nine o'clock in the morning and, after a rather brief interval, died at three o'clock in the afternoon. Jesus was crucified between two robbers (*lestes* = revolutionary?). The bystanders, onlookers, and priests were said to have mocked him while he hung upon the cross. Jesus' last words from the cross, according to Mark, were, "My

God, my God, why hast thou forsaken me?" (Mark 15:34), which are the opening words of Ps. 22. Was Jesus repeating the psalm on the cross? Or expressing his despair? Or lamenting the failure of God to intervene? Or does the reference reflect the early church's interpretation of Ps. 22 in the light of Jesus' death?

The pavement of the Antonia Tower courtyard dates from the time of Herod the Great. This tower, which overlooked the Temple compound, was the center of Roman authority in Jerusalem. Procurators delivered their legal decisions here and it is logical to assume that Jesus stood trial before Pilate at this spot.

ROBERT B. WRIGHT

One cannot be certain. Mark reports that the bystanders thought he was calling Elijah (Mark 15:35).

Mark 15:38–39 states that, concurrent with the death of Jesus, the curtain of the Temple was ripped from top to bottom and the Roman centurion who stood facing Jesus confessed: "Truly this man was the Son of God." The first of these statements reflects the developing church's belief that in Jesus, God

had repudiated the Jewish religion. In the second, Mark provided testimony to
the Gentile recognition of Jesus and reaffirmed his own belief in Jesus as the
Son of God.

Jesus was removed from the cross and his corpse placed in a rock-cut tomb
by Joseph of Arimathea, whom Mark describes as "a respected member of the
council, who was also himself looking for the kingdom of God" (Mark 15:43;

The sepulcher of Herod's family shows
the entrance to the tomb which could
be blocked by a massive circular stone
rolled across the passageway. The
Gospel traditions assume that such a
tomb as this was used for Jesus' burial.
ISRAEL DEPARTMENT OF ANTIQUITIES AND
MUSEUMS

Matt. 27:57 refers to him as a disciple of Jesus). Because of the approach of
the Sabbath, Jesus' body was simply laid in the tomb wrapped in a linen shroud;
there was no time before the evening to carry out the acts associated with burial.
The tomb was closed with a stone.[36]

THE RESURRECTION

After the account of the burial of Jesus, the Marcan narrative contains only

[36] Not even the year of Jesus' death can be established with certainty. Suggestions range from
A.D. 27 to 33. The most likely date is April 6 or 7, A.D. 30. On the question of the burial
place of Jesus, see R. H. Smith, "The Tomb of Jesus," *The Biblical Archaeologist*, XXX
(1967), pp. 74–90; and André Parrot, *Golgotha and the Church of the Holy Sepulchre*,
tr. by Edwin Hudson (Philosophical Library, 1957).

one further episode (Mark 16:1–8). Mary Magdalene, Mary the mother of James, and Salome (see Mark 15:40–41, 47) are said to have come to the tomb when the Sabbath was past (early on Sunday morning) and discovered the stone rolled away from the opening of the tomb. Inside the tomb they encountered a young man clothed in a white robe (an angel?) who assured them that Jesus had risen. The women were commanded to go and tell his disciples and Peter that Jesus "is going before you to Galilee; there you will see him, as he told you." The women, overcome with trembling and astonishment, left the tomb, but "they said nothing to any one, for they were afraid."

The oldest manuscripts of Mark end at this point. There are copies of Mark dating from the fifth century and later that do not end with verse eight. Some of these contain twelve additional verses; others only a short addition. Did Mark's Gospel end with ch. 16:8? Apparently the form of the Gospel used by Matthew and Luke broke off at this point, for the two do not use a common source from this point on. The supplements to the Gospel from the fifth century have no really strong manuscript claim to authenticity. The Gospel of Mark then originally ended at ch. 16:8 or was mutilated, and the end from this point on was lost. That the author stopped his writing at this point seems most likely.

The early church claimed that death had not finished Jesus, that God had raised him. Mark apparently rested his belief in the resurrection, or asked his readers to do so, on the women's testimony of the empty tomb and the assurance of the messenger in the tomb. Mark recorded no appearances of the risen Christ.[37] The other Gospels, however, do contain traditions about the appearance but there is "no part of the Gospel story that shows less fixity than the accounts of the appearance of the risen Jesus." [38] Various forms of witness to the resurrection were existent in early Christianity. These will be examined in the next chapter on the life and faith of the early church.

[37] See N. Q. Hamilton, "Resurrection Tradition and the Composition of Mark," *Journal of Biblical Literature*, LXXXIV (1965), pp. 415–421.
[38] Frank W. Beare, *The Earliest Record of Jesus* (Abingdon Press, 1962), p. 220.

19 | THE LIFE AND FAITH
OF THE EARLY CHURCH

The movement begun by Jesus did not end with his death. Shortly after his crucifixion, Jesus' followers appeared in Jerusalem openly proclaiming that God had raised him from the dead and calling upon their fellow Jews to accept him as the Messiah. God's purpose with his people Israel, they declared, had reached a new stage of development, a stage predicted by the prophets and anticipated by the whole of the Hebrew Scriptures. The new age dreamed of and longed for by the apocalypticists had finally dawned. Converts were won to the new faith. Out of these followers of Jesus and the new converts to the faith, the Christian church emerged. For a time, the church existed as a sect within Judaism. The movement of the church into the Gentile world was a secondary development.

THE NATURE OF THE SOURCE MATERIAL

Unfortunately our knowledge of the earliest phase of Christianity is severely limited. This is due to a lack of sufficient source material. The only historical narrative about the first twenty years or so of the primitive Christian church is found in the first twelve chapters of the book of Acts. This book, however, was not written by the mother church of Jerusalem nor by a member of that community. Neither was it written during the earliest years of the church's development.

The book of Acts is actually the second part of a two-volume work.[1] The first half of this writing is the Gospel of Luke; the second part is a history of the church from its beginning until the arrival of Paul in Rome. The author was a third-generation Christian, which would place the writing of Luke-Acts near the end of the first century. In the prologue to his work (Luke 1:1–4), the author of Luke mentions "the eyewitnesses and ministers of the word" (the first and second generation) as well as the "many" who "have undertaken to compile a narrative of the things which have been accomplished among us"

Biblical readings: The basic material discussed in this chapter is found in Acts, chs. 1 to 12.
[1] See Charles K. Barrett, *Luke the Historian in Recent Study* (London: The Epworth Press, 1961) and Leander E. Keck and J. Louis Martyn, eds., *Studies in Luke-Acts* (Abingdon Press, 1966), for surveys of the problems and research on Luke-Acts.

(second generation and later). The purpose of the author was "to write an orderly account" which he apparently hoped would be better than that of his predecessors (and perhaps replace them?).

The author of Luke-Acts divided the history of salvation into three main epochs.[2] The first was the time of Israel and the Jews, which came to an end with John the Baptist. This epoch was characterized by the use of the Law and the Prophets (see Luke 16:16). The second period was the time of Jesus, the midpoint of history when Jesus worked through the power of the Spirit (Luke 4:14). The third epoch was the time of the church when the activity of the Spirit worked through the Christian community and its leaders.

Of all the Gospel writers, the author of Luke-Acts was most interested in placing Christian origins within the broader context of world history. The birth of Jesus in Bethlehem is correlated with the decree of Caesar Augustus and the subsequent census under Quirinius (Luke 2:1–2). The beginning of John the Baptist's ministry is chronologically tagged by references to several Roman and Jewish rulers (Luke 3:1–2). Only Luke mentions the Roman emperors (Acts 11:28; 18:2, as well as the passages noted above). For the author, the origins of Christianity were not "done in a corner" (Acts 26:26). This historical interest of the writer is reflected in the fact that the history of Jesus and of the early church is part of world history. The treatment of Jesus in the Gospel of Luke comes nearer to being a "life of Jesus" than in any of the other Gospels. The life of Jesus is considered as the beginning of a still-continuing church history in the midst of the world.

The interest of the author of Luke-Acts in the church led him to show how the church orbited outward from the mother community in Jerusalem until it reached Rome, the capital of the Empire, in the form of Paul. Or in the terminology of the writer, to show how the word of God increased and disciples multiplied (Acts 6:7; 12:24; 19:20) and how the followers of Jesus were his "witnesses in Jerusalem and in all Judea and Samaria and to the end of the earth" (Acts 1:8). This development of the church is presented in Acts, however, in a very idealized way. Differences that existed in the early church are occasionally noted (in Acts, ch. 15, for example), but these are presented as being settled by appropriate actions of the church. Nothing comparable to the differences and the struggles reflected in the letters of Paul appears in Acts. The first epoch in the history of the church is presented as a "type-time," an idealized era when the church was pure and uncorrupted, blameless before men and God.

In some respects, Luke-Acts, dedicated to someone called Theophilus (a patron?), is more apologetic toward the Romans than is even Mark. The work in this respect reminds one of the writings of Josephus composed at the Roman court as apologies for the Jews. In Luke-Acts, it is the men of Israel who crucified and killed Jesus (Acts 2:22–23; 3:13–15). In the account of the crucifixion of Jesus, Pilate is almost completely exonerated; he appears almost as an innocent bystander at the trial. Pilate, on two occasions (Luke 23:4, 13–16), de-

---

[2] See Hans Conzelmann, *The Theology of St. Luke*, tr. by Geoffrey Buswell (Harper & Brothers, 1960).

clares Jesus innocent of the charges brought against him by the Jewish leaders and finally simply delivers Jesus "up to their will" (Luke 23:25).

There is much about the early church that one would like to know which the author of Luke-Acts does not mention. What, for example, were the origins of the church in Alexandria in Egypt? How was the church in Rome begun and who was responsible? What eventually happened to the mother church in Jerusalem and to Jewish Christianity in general? What happened to Galilean Christianity? How did the members of Jesus' family rise to prominence in the Jerusalem church? Insofar as the evidence of the book of Acts is concerned, and that of the rest of the New Testament as well, these questions must remain, enticing but unanswerable.

The book of Acts is thus not a full history of the early church. It is, in fact, not even a record of the acts of the early apostles, for it is only Peter and some of the early Jerusalemites and Paul whose acts are described. The book of Acts in spite of its shortcomings remains, however, the basic source for any discussion of the life and faith of the early church.

Additional information about the early church can be gleaned from the Gospels and from other New Testament writings, especially the letters of Paul. The Gospels too contain traditions about and sayings of Jesus that reflect the faith and life of the early Christian communities. Form criticism is of help in distinguishing the stratum in the Gospel traditions which goes back to the early church. The letters of the New Testament occasionally point behind the time of their own composition to practices and traditions of earlier times. The writings of Paul are, after all, the earliest written documents in the New Testament. In these letters excerpts from hymns and early Christian confessions are often quoted in the form in which they were transmitted in the early church. Non-Biblical sources, such as Josephus, tell us very little about the life of the early church. Many features and contours of the early church must therefore remain rather obscure.

THE RESURRECTION FAITH

At the very center of the early church's faith, preaching, and life stood the conviction of the resurrection of Jesus.[3] Without this conviction, there would have been no Christian faith or church. In spite of this importance of the resurrection faith, the traditions about and the interpretations of the resurrection in the early church were not homogeneous. This fact was noted at the end of the previous chapter, and at this point we must examine these interpretations and traditions more closely.

The basic traditions concerning the resurrection in the New Testament are found in the speeches in the first part of the book of Acts, in the letters of Paul

[3] A survey of the faith and preaching of the early church with references to recent literature is given in Conzelmann, *An Outline of the Theology of the New Testament*, pp. 28–93. On the resurrection, see C. F. D. Moule, ed., *The Significance of the Message of the Resurrection for Faith in Jesus Christ*, tr. by D. M. Barton and R. A. Wilson (London: SCM Press, Ltd., 1968).

where he quotes traditions passed on to him, and in the Gospels which report the story of the empty tomb and narratives about the resurrection appearances of Jesus. In the speeches of Acts,[4] there are remnants of an interpretation of the resurrection that considered the resurrection in terms of Jesus' exaltation to the heavenly world. Acts 2:36 states "that God has made him both Lord and Christ, this Jesus whom you crucified." This statement argues that it was in the resurrection that Jesus became the Lord and the enthroned Messiah (recall that enthronement and anointing were closely tied together in the royal coronation ritual). Jesus, however, was not enthroned as Messiah in an "earthly realm." Acts 2:32–35 interprets Jesus' "raising up" (= resurrection) by God as his exaltation at the "right hand of God." In other words, exaltation, resurrection, and ascension are all terms describing the same event. This interpretation was based, as Acts 2:34–35 suggests, on an exegesis of Ps. 110:1 which in its original usage had been part of the coronation ritual of the Davidic kings. The text, however, had come to be understood in an eschatological sense as a reference to the exaltation and status of the coming Messiah (see Mark 12:35–37). This interpretation of the resurrection of Jesus as enthronement is reflected in a few other passages in the New Testament (see Acts 13:33; Rom. 1:3–4).

How and why did the early Christians come to believe in the resurrection-exaltation of Jesus? The clue to this question is provided by Paul's summary of the resurrection appearances. The early church believed in the resurrection because the resurrected Christ had appeared to his followers. In I Cor. 15:3–7, Paul quotes what he had passed on to the Corinthian church about the resurrection of Jesus and contended that this tradition was what he had received from the early church.[5] Paul declares that Jesus was "raised on the third day in accordance with the scriptures" (I Cor. 15:4). What Scriptures he was talking about is not certain (Hos. 6:2; Jonah 1:17; or perhaps some reference in a writing considered sacred but not found in the canon?). Paul continues by saying that Jesus appeared to Cephas (= Peter), to the Twelve (counting Judas or not?), to five hundred brethren at once, to James (the noncanonical Gospel of the Hebrews tells of Jesus' appearance to his brother James),[6] and to all the apostles (I Cor. 15:5–7). Finally, Paul says that Jesus last of all appeared to him (I Cor. 15:8). Here Paul places the appearance of Jesus to him on an equal footing with the appearances to others and considers it to have been the same type of appearance. The evidence supplied by Paul is very similar to that found in the speeches in Acts and referred to above (except that no appearances are mentioned in the early speeches in Acts[7]), namely, that Jesus was raised up by God to the heavenly world and that he appeared to various followers from there, among whom was Paul.

---

[4] These speeches are the general creation of the author but do seem to utilize fragments of very early traditions. See Eduard Schweizer, "Concerning the Speeches in Acts," in Keck and Martyn, eds., *Studies in Luke-Acts*, pp. 208–216.

[5] See Hans Conzelmann, "On the Analysis of the Confessional Formula in I Corinthians 15:3–5," *Interpretation*, XX (1966), pp. 15–25.

[6] For a translation of the account, see Hennecke, *New Testament Apocrypha*, Vol. I, p. 165.

[7] See W. O. Walker, Jr., "Postcrucifixion Appearances and Christian Origins," *Journal of Biblical Literature*, LXXXVIII (1969), pp. 157–165.

In the New Testament Gospels, the resurrection of Jesus and the appearances are treated in a different manner. According to the Gospel accounts, Jesus was raised by God from the dead, the empty tomb was discovered, Jesus then appeared to and conversed with his disciples, and, after a time, he ascended to heaven (in Luke 24:51; after forty days in Acts 1:3–11), after which there were no more appearances comparable to those to his earliest disciples and followers.

The divergencies between the Gospel accounts are numerous and rather striking. Mark recorded no resurrection appearances. In Matt. 28:9–10, 16–20, Jesus appears to the women at the tomb and then to his eleven disciples on a mountain in Galilee. In Luke 24:13–53, Jesus is said to have appeared to two of his followers on the road to Emmaus and to his disciples in Jerusalem (see also Acts 1:3–11). The Gospel of John, chs. 20 and 21, has preserved traditions about Jesus' appearances to Mary Magdalene at the tomb, to his disciples in Jerusalem, and again to his disciples beside the Sea of Galilee.

In addition, the Gospels differ from one another on the details concerning the discovery of the empty tomb. In Matt. 28:1–10, Mary Magdalene and the other Mary go to the tomb, an earthquake occurs, and an angel descends from heaven and rolls away the stone. According to Mark 16:1–8, it was Mary Magdalene, Mary the mother of James, and Salome who came to the tomb only to discover the stone rolled away from the opening and a young man inside the tomb. In Luke 24:1–12, the women who went to the tomb were Mary Magdalene, Joanna, Mary the mother of James, and other women; the stone was discovered rolled away; and two men in dazzling apparel stood by the tomb. In John 20:1–10, Mary Magdalene is said to have come to the tomb alone and to have discovered the stone rolled away, after which she ran and told Simon Peter and the disciple whom Jesus loved, who then came to the tomb and discovered that it was empty.

These differences between the Gospel accounts of the discovery of the empty tomb and the resurrection appearances and between the appearance stories in the Gospels and the references in I Cor. 15:4–8 have never been satisfactorily explained by scholars. It is obvious that the Gospel writers were not dependent upon a common source for their accounts of the resurrection appearances. The diversity is too great for an assumption of dependency. The tradition that Paul has preserved was obviously not identical with any set of traditions presently found in the Gospels. It must be assumed that there were numerous accounts of revelations of the risen Christ in circulation in the early church, and these were drawn upon by the various writers in a manner dependent upon what traditions they were familiar with and the purposes of the appearances in their works. Many scholars assume, perhaps correctly, that the Gospel traditions are later than the traditions quoted by Paul and show legendary expansions. It is also generally assumed that the appearance traditions (though not necessarily in the form we now possess) are earlier than the empty-tomb traditions.

Paul used the resurrection traditions in I Cor., ch. 15, for two purposes: (1) The resurrection traditions served to authenticate his claims to apostleship; the risen Lord had revealed himself to Paul. (2) The traditions of the resurrection of Jesus supported his arguments to the Corinthians concerning the resurrection of Christians from the dead.

A number of emphases can be seen in the Gospel accounts of the resurrection: (1) The resurrection stories affirmed the continuity and identity of the earthly Jesus and the risen Christ. The exalted Lord in the church was none other than the resurrected Jesus, not some otherworldly redeemer. (2) The resurrection appearance stories were used to affirm the humanity or corporeality of the Christ. Jesus was shown after the resurrection bearing not only the marks of the crucifixion (Luke 24:39–40; John 20:24–29) but also eating and sharing food with his followers (Luke 24:42–43). (3) The appearance traditions contain an emphasis on the commissioning of his disciples for the work of the church in the world. The only appearance recounted in Matthew concludes with Jesus' command that the disciples go into all the world, make disciples of all nations, baptizing the believers and teaching converts to observe all that Jesus had commanded (Matt. 28:16–20). Luke-Acts placed the final commission of the disciples to be witnesses in the period between the resurrection and the ascension. The Fourth Gospel states that the resurrected Jesus commanded his disciples to go into the world just as Jesus had been sent into the world and breathed upon them the Holy Spirit (John 20:19–23; see also ch. 21:15–17). According to the Gospels, it was not only the earthly Jesus but the risen Christ who had sent his followers into the world to preach the gospel and win converts.[8] Christians could not therefore claim that Christianity was a secret non-missionary cult possessing its mysteries and secrets to be guarded and preserved only for the initiated like the Qumran community, for example. (4) The scheme of resurrection appearances–ascension in Luke-Acts served to mark off as unique the period of the appearances of the risen Christ. After the ascension, there could be no more appearances similar to those granted the original church. In Acts, not even Paul experienced a true resurrection appearance but only a revelation—a blazing light and a voice from heaven (Acts 9:1–9; 22:6–11; 26:12–18). This emphasis on the uniqueness of the resurrection appearances and their cessation with the ascension tended to differentiate them from all subsequent revelations of the exalted Christ and imbued their recipients with a special sanctity as witnesses.[9]

THE KERYGMA OF THE EARLY CHURCH

The early Christian church was a preaching and confessing community. It was in its preaching that the primary faith of the early church came to expression. Unfortunately, no fully developed sermons had been preserved in the New Testament. However, the speeches recorded in the book of Acts do contain what

[8] The commissioning of the disciples by the risen Christ may have carried a greater authority in the church than a report of his commissioning of them before the crucifixion. The words of the risen Christ are given an authority at least equal to those attributed to the "historical" Jesus. See Frank W. Beare, "Sayings of the Risen Jesus in the Gospel Tradition: An Inquiry into Their Origin and Significance," in W. R. Farmer et al., eds., Christian History and Interpretation (Cambridge University Press, 1967), pp. 161–181.

[9] On the importance of the "witness" in Luke-Acts, see Charles H. Talbert, Luke and the Gnostics (Abingdon Press, 1966), pp. 17–32.

are obviously sketches and summaries of early preaching (they are too short to be classified as full-blown sermons). These speeches emphasize the dominant themes that characterized the early kerygma.[10] In addition, many of the letters of the New Testament reflect the structure of early preaching, namely, the proclamation of the faith of the community followed by exhortation to conversion or to a type of ethical action and behavior. The content of the early preaching can be treated thematically.

According to the Scriptures. The early Christian church shared a common body of sacred writings with contemporary Judaism (on the canonical status of the various writings at the beginning of the Christian era, see above, pp. 19–23). These Scriptures were used by the Christians in understanding the life and work of Jesus as well as in their preaching to their contemporaries.[11] The early Christian use of the Hebrew Scriptures was more dependent upon an eschatological than upon a "legalistic" interpretation. In this regard, the Christian exegesis of the Old Testament writings was more similar to that of the Qumran community and the apocalypticists than to rabbinical Judaism. This eschatological understanding of the Scriptures, especially the Prophets and The Psalms, viewed the Biblical materials as predictions and prophecies about the future and especially about the messiah and the new age. This meant that the early Christians understood and preached the Old Testament in the light of their understanding of Jesus and they understood and preached Jesus in the light of their understanding of the Scriptures. We have already seen an example of this in the early church's understanding of the resurrection as Jesus' exaltation to the right hand of God in the light of Ps. 110:1. The most frequently used Old Testament Scriptures were the Prophets and The Psalms because the prophets were considered, especially by apocalyptic circles, as predictors of the future, and since the psalms were attributed to David, then his writings must certainly, it was reasoned, have predicted the coming messiah of the Davidic line.

The early church claimed that the goal of God's history with his people Israel had reached a new stage with Jesus. Time after time, the speeches in Acts (but also the Gospels and Paul's letters) declare that the promises of the Old Testament Scriptures have been fulfilled:

Acts 2:16—This is what was spoken by the prophet Joel . . .
[followed by a quotation of Joel 2:28–32].

Acts 2:25—For David says concerning him . . .
[followed by a quotation of Ps. 16:8–11].

Acts 13:32—We bring you the good news that what God
promised to the fathers, this he has fulfilled
to us their children by raising Jesus; as also
it is written in the second psalm . . .
[followed by a quotation of Ps. 2:7].

---

[10] See Dodd, *The Apostolic Preaching and Its Development.*
[11] On the early Christian use of the Old Testament, see Barnabas Lindars, *New Testament Apologetic* (The Westminster Press, 1961).

Jesus in the Church's Kerygma. As one would expect, proclamation about Jesus was a central element in the preaching of the early church. The Kingdom of God had been dominant in the preaching of Jesus; in the early church's preaching, Jesus was dominant. The proclaimer of the Kingdom had become the center of the church's proclamation. In the proclamation about Jesus, the resurrection-exaltation served as the fulcrum upon which the past and the future work of Jesus rested. Having already looked at the resurrection faith, we can now examine the church's proclamation of the significance of the "life" of Jesus and its preaching of Jesus as the "coming one."

According to Acts 2:22, part of the church's kerygma emphasized the mighty acts of God in Jesus:

> Jesus of Nazareth, a man attested to you by God with mighty works and wonders and signs which God did through him in your midst. (Acts 2:22.)

The career of Jesus was proclaimed as the work of God, and Jesus' mighty acts were declared as testimony to the presence of God in Jesus. It was this theological interest in the mighty acts of Jesus which led to the use of the traditions about Jesus in the preaching of the church and eventually to the production of the Gospel form.

A major factor in the life of Jesus that had to be interpreted in the church's preaching was his death. In some respects, the idea of a suffering and dying Messiah was a problem to the church and a hindrance in the church's proclamation to the Jews, for the Messiah was traditionally a triumphant not a humiliated figure.

One explanation of Jesus' death attributed it to the will and work of man. In the period immediately after the resurrection and perhaps for some time following, the church did not blame the Jewish people as a whole for the death of Jesus. Responsibility was primarily laid at the feet of the Romans and the Jewish sacerdotal aristocracy—collaborators with Rome. By many of the Jewish people, even those not accepting him as the Messiah, Jesus must have been viewed as a Jewish martyr who died at the hands of the Roman oppressors. There were perhaps many parallels between the Jewish evaluation of John the Baptist and Jesus. (The Gospels have preserved references about the belief that Jesus was John the Baptist raised from the dead; see Mark 6:14–16; 8:28). The Gospels (see Mark 11:29–33) and Josephus both noted the high esteem in which John was held by large segments of the Jewish population. Jesus had been betrayed and murdered like the prophets of old (Acts 7:51–53). Jesus was a prophet martyred for God's cause and for his people.

Jesus' death not only was understood in terms of his martyrdom "by the hands of lawless men" but it was also interpreted as the will of God. In Acts 2:23, side by side with the description of the death of Jesus as the result of the will of men, stands a statement which declares that Jesus was "delivered up according to the definite plan and foreknowledge of God." The death of Jesus was a manifestation of God's plan. Acts 3:18 says: "What God foretold by the mouth of all the prophets, that his Christ should suffer, he thus fulfilled." In Paul's summary of the early tradition of the church he reports that Jesus died for our sins "in accordance with the scriptures" (I Cor. 15:3). The early Christians saw in the Old Testament passages concerning suffering the predictions of the eschatological sufferings of the Messiah, interpreting these of course in the light of the passion and death of Jesus. The reference to the "prophets" in Acts 3:18 does not mean that passages viewed as predictions of the suffering of Jesus were limited to the prophetical books. Any of the supposed Old Testament writers could be understood as "prophets." The Psalms Scroll from Qumran, for example, states, in a description of the psalms written by David, that "all these he composed through prophecy." [12] The early church seems to have been greatly dependent upon the descriptions of suffering in the psalms of lamentation, interpreted eschatologically, for their understanding of the suffering and death of Jesus as the fulfillment of the will of God and the predictions of the prophets.[13]

When and how the death of Jesus came to be understood as a saving act cannot be precisely determined. Paul's statement "that Christ died for our sins" (I Cor. 15:3) presupposes an interpretation of the death of Jesus as a saving event. However, none of the early speeches in Acts proclaims the death of Jesus as a redeeming event. Nonetheless, an understanding of the death of Jesus as a saving and a redeeming act must have developed quite early. A number of factors seem to have contributed to such an understanding. (1) Jesus' death coincided closely with the observance of the Jewish Passover, which celebrated the Hebrew redemption: God's saving of his people from Egyptian slavery. The association of Jesus' death with the Passover would have led to an interpretation of his death as a redemptive event.[14] (2) Implicit in the concept of martyrdom is the idea that the martyr dies for a cause and thus on behalf of those who share in the cause.[15] (3) The cultic system of Judaism in its expression in the Jerusalem Temple was oriented to the idea of sacrifice—the death of animals as part of the worship of God and as a means of redemption. The death of Jesus in its association with the Passover was open to an interpretation not only in terms of the slaughter of the Passover lamb but also in terms of the entire Jewish sacrificial system. (4) The vicarious character of the Suffering Servant in Deutero-Isaiah—his suffering as the means of salvation for others— was also utilized by the developing church.[16] When the Suffering Servant passages came to be used in interpreting the life and death of Jesus is an open question. The story of the Ethiopian eunuch in Acts 8:26–39 identified Jesus with the person spoken of in Isa. 53:7–8. However, the influence of the Suffering Servant figure is not nearly so dominant in the New Testament as one might have suspected.[17]

Not only did the early church proclaim Jesus as the Messiah raised up to the

---

[12] 11QPs[a] XXVII:11. See J. A. Sanders, *The Psalms Scroll of Qumran Cave XI* (Oxford University Press, 1965), pp. 91–93.

[13] See Lindars, *New Testament Apologetic*, pp. 75–137.

[14] See Fuller, "The Double Origin of the Eucharist," *Biblical Research*, VIII (1963), pp. 60–72.

[15] See Eduard Schweizer, *Lordship and Discipleship* (London: SCM Press, Ltd., 1960), pp. 22–41.

[16] See Jeremias and Zimmerli, *The Servant of God*, pp. 80–106.

[17] See M. D. Hooker, *Jesus and the Servant* (London: S.P.C.K., 1959).

exalted position at the right hand of God; it also proclaimed him as the one who would come on the clouds of glory. The early Christians expected the imminent return of Jesus from heaven (his Parousia) and the final establishment of the Kingdom of God. How had the church come to believe in the triumphant return of Jesus? The early church not only preached about Jesus, it continued to preach what Jesus had preached. There was a continuity in many respects between the kerygma of Jesus and the kerygma of the early Christians.[18] The early church no doubt continued the proclamation of the coming Kingdom, otherwise this element would not have found such a prominent place in the Gospel traditions. The church continued the proclamation begun by Jesus but proclaimed, in addition to this, that Jesus' message had been vindicated in that God had raised him from the dead. Thus the idea of the imminence of the Kingdom was kept alive in the church's preaching.

The idea of Jesus enthroned at the right hand of God and the belief in the coming of the Kingdom were combined with a Christian interpretation of "the one like a son of man" in Dan. 7:13–14. The seventh chapter of Daniel is the fullest statement in the Old Testament on the establishment of the Kingdom, and the "one like a son of man" plays a central role in the text. This figure is shown coming to the Ancient of Days (= God) with the clouds of heaven and is presented to him. In the Christian use of this passage, Jesus was identified with the Son of Man.[19] The account of the stoning of Stephen in Acts, ch. 7, shows that the exalted Jesus was identified with the Son of Man. Stephen is said to have gazed into heaven and saw "Jesus standing at the right hand of God; and he said, 'Behold, I see the heavens opened, and the Son of man standing at the right hand of God'" (Acts 7:55–56). Since Jesus was already exalted before God in the resurrection, the coming on the clouds and the final establishment of the Kingdom were understood in terms of Jesus' return as the Son of Man. All the futuristic Son of Man sayings in the Synoptic Gospels (see above, pp. 357–358) reflect this understanding of the coming of the Son of Man as a coming to earth in glory and judgment. "You will see the Son of man sitting at the right hand of Power, and coming with the clouds of heaven" (Mark 14:62).

The early church could and did express its faith in the return of Jesus in concepts other than those of the apocalyptic Son of Man. In a speech attributed to Peter in Acts, ch. 3, reference is made to an appeal to repentance

> that times of refreshing may come from the presence of the Lord, and that he may send the Christ appointed for you, Jesus, whom heaven must receive until the time for establishing all that God spoke by the mouth of his holy prophets from of old.[20] (Acts 3:19–21.)

---

[18] This continuity has been stressed in the so-called new quest of the historical Jesus. See James M. Robinson, *A New Quest of the Historical Jesus*, pp. 93–125.

[19] For discussions of this subject but with a slightly different emphasis from that of the present work, see Reginald H. Fuller, *The Foundations of New Testament Christology* (Charles Scribner's Sons, 1965), pp. 142–151; and Perrin, *Rediscovering the Teaching of Jesus*, pp. 164–173.

[20] On this description of Jesus, see John A. T. Robinson, "The Most Primitive Christology of All?" in his *Twelve New Testament Studies* (London: SCM Press, Ltd., 1962), pp. 139–153.

THE LIFE AND WORSHIP OF THE PRIMITIVE CHURCH

The Christian church first moved onto the stage of recorded history in Jerusalem. It is quite possible that there was a formation of a Christian community in Galilee concurrent with the beginnings of the church in Jerusalem; however, there are no records of such a development.[21] The early church in Jerusalem evidently had no thought of breaking away from Judaism to form a new religion. Rather, they seem to have regarded themselves as an eschatological community within Judaism for whom Jesus had been and was the Messiah who would return shortly in triumph. The fact that they recognized and proclaimed Jesus as the Messiah did not exclude them from Judaism, either in their own estimation or in that of the Jewish leaders. Many of the latter no doubt believed that the early disciples proclaiming Jesus were deluded. The Christians, however, felt that they had a superior understanding of Judaism than that of the Jewish leaders and believed that it was they who properly read and understood the Hebrew Scriptures.

The opening chapters of Acts show the early Christians continuing their participation in temple and synagogue worship (Acts 2:46; 3:1; 5:42). Evidence also suggests that the Christians limited their preaching and missionary work to an appeal to only the Jews.[22] The proclamation of the kerygma was followed by an exhortation to the hearers to "repent, and be baptized" (Acts 2:38). Baptism was the rite of initiation and acceptance into the fellowship of the community that was also associated with the remission of sins. The origin of the practice of Christian baptism has been much disputed.[23] Baptism was practiced at the time as an initiatory rite: proselytes into Judaism were baptized, respondents to the preaching of John were baptized, and the Qumran community practiced a form of baptism. Christian baptism appears to have more closely resembled the baptisms performed by John the Baptist and his disciples—it was an act of repentance from sins in preparation for the coming eschatological event. Baptism was performed in the name of Jesus and was associated with the receipt of the gift of the Holy Spirit (Acts 2:38).

The early Christian community was a "spirit possessed" community. Part of the eschatological expectations in Judaism was the anticipation of the renewed outpouring of the Spirit (see Joel 2:28–32). The early church proclaimed itself as the eschatological community to whom the spirit had been given. The presence of the spirit manifested itself in the community in the form of ecstatic speaking in tongues (glossolalia), revelatory experiences, and healing.

Acts, ch. 2, contains a narrative of the events associated with the Feast of Pentecost (seven weeks after the Passover) in which reference is made to speaking in tongues. The followers of Jesus, according to Acts 1:15 about 120 people,

---

[21] See L. E. Elliott-Binns, *Galilean Christianity* (London: SCM Press, Ltd., 1956).

[22] See S. G. F. Brandon, *The Fall of Jerusalem and the Christian Church*, 2d ed. (London: S.P.C.K., 1957), pp. 15–53.

[23] See H. H. Rowley, "Jewish Proselyte Baptism and the Baptism of John," in his *From Moses to Qumran*, pp. 211–235; and Conzelmann, *An Outline of the Theology of the New Testament*, pp. 47–50.

assembled in Jerusalem at the time of the Feast, were all filled with the Holy Spirit and began to speak in other tongues. The followers exhibited unusual behavior which was taken, by outsiders, as evidence of overindulgence in drink but Peter assured them this was not the case since it was only the third hour of the day (nine in the morning). Instead, he argued that this strange behavior was evidence of possession of the Spirit (Acts 2:14–16). The author of Luke-Acts interpreted the phenomenon of glossolalia as the ability to speak in other languages. Jews from various countries were said to have been assembled in Jerusalem for the Feast and each heard "them telling in our own tongues the mighty acts of God" (Acts 2:11). According to Paul, whose writings predate Luke-Acts, glossolalia was a nonhuman form of speech unintelligible to the hearers except when there was some person present who possessed the gift of interpretation and could "translate" the ecstatic utterances.[24] (Paul discusses this spiritual gift in I Cor., chs. 12 to 14.) Paul's description of the phenomenon is probably more accurate than that found in Acts. Glossolalia reminds one of the unusual ecstatic experiences of the early Hebrew prophets while under the influence of the Spirit and there seems no reason to doubt that the early church was on occasion characterized by ecstatic behavior.

The early Christians also underwent revelatory experiences. Stephen at his stoning, full of the Holy Spirit, was said to have seen the heavens open and Jesus standing at the right hand of God (Acts 7:55–56). Peter fell into a trance and received revelations concerning the eating of unclean food (Acts 10:9–16). Paul wrote of a man (himself?) who had been caught up to the third heaven (II Cor. 12:2). John on the isle of Patmos produced the book of Revelation on the basis of a revelation of the exalted Lord. The early Christians certainly claimed to have received revelatory experiences through the Spirit. Such working of the Spirit was taken as assurance that the prophecies had been fulfilled and the new age had dawned. Some of these revelatory experiences perhaps stand behind some of the resurrection appearances of Jesus to his followers.

According to Acts, as well as other New Testament writings, the early disciples, like Jesus, possessed the power of exorcism and healing (Acts 3:1–10; 5:12–16; 8:5–8; 9:32–42). The early Christians are said to have been able to cure the sick, cast out demons, and raise the dead. The sick were said to have been placed on the streets "that as Peter came by at least his shadow might fall on some of them" (Acts 5:15). Some of the early church members must have functioned as healers and exorcists. However, in Luke-Acts, one can see the tendency toward "hero-worship" of the early church leaders and the glorification of the days of Christianity's origins. Paul is presented in Acts as a healer and a miracle-worker (Acts 14:8–10; 19:11–17; 20:9–12; 28:1–9); however, in his own writings Paul never refers to these events, although he did note healing and miracles as gifts of the Spirit (I Cor. 12:9–10).

In addition to participation in regular Jewish worship, the early Christians also held special worship services and fellowship gatherings in homes. They de-

---

[24] See Frank W. Beare, "Speaking with Tongues," *Journal of Biblical Literature*, LXXXIII (1964), pp. 229–246; and S. D. Currie, " 'Speaking in Tongues,' " *Interpretation*, XIX (1965), pp. 274–294.

voted themselves to prayer (Acts 1:14), to teaching and fellowship (Acts 2:42), and to testimony to the resurrection of Jesus (Acts 4:33). The teaching and instruction of new members and the exposition of the meaning of the Christian faith must have been major elements in this Christian worship in the homes. Frequent reference is also made to "the breaking of bread" and the fact that they "partook of food with glad and generous hearts" (Acts 2:42, 46). These seem to suggest the observance of communal meals shared by the early community. It is entirely possible that in some of these there was a celebration of the Last Supper of Jesus as well as the continuation of the practice of eating together shared by Jesus and his original followers. The writings of Paul suggest that the original celebration of the Last Supper or Eucharist took place within the context of a general meal or a love (agape) feast (see I Cor., ch. 11).[25] The sharing of a special meal together was a characteristic of the Qumran community, which ate the meal of bread and wine in anticipation of the messianic banquet in the new age.[26] This emphasis may have been a factor in the Christians' eating together with glad and generous hearts.

A feature of the early Jerusalem community was its common sharing of property and goods. "All who believed were together and had all things in common; and they sold their possessions and goods and distributed them to all, as any had need" (Acts 2:44–45; see also ch. 4:32–37). In Acts 5:1–11, a story is told of a man named Ananias and his wife Sapphira, who sold a piece of property to contribute the proceeds to the Christian community. Acting deceptively about the actual money involved, the couple kept part of the pledged proceeds, only to be struck dead when confronted by Peter with the facts. Such an emphasis on the mutual sharing of worldly goods was not unique to Christianity, it being a characteristic of several Jewish sects at the time.[27] Several reasons probably lay behind this communality of possessions. (1) There was a strong sense of a common bond and destiny that bound the early Christians together being reenforced by the idea that the Christians were the new elect people of God. (2) Christianity, and here apparently based on ideas going back to Jesus, had an attitude that depreciated wealth. (3) The hope of the coming Kingdom and the Parousia of Jesus dominated the life of the community, and such an eschatological perspective meant that the life and goods of the community must be expended to preach the gospel while there was still time.

The leadership of the early Jerusalem church seems to have been in the hands of the original followers of Jesus. Luke referred to the primary leadership group as the twelve apostles, but judging from the rest of the New Testament, especially the letters of Paul, the "apostle" category was never limited to

---

[25] See Conzelmann, An Outline of the Theology of the New Testament, pp. 50–59, for a discussion of the origin and nature of the Christian observance. A good general discussion of early Christian worship is given in C. F. D. Moule, Worship in the New Testament (John Knox Press, 1961).

[26] See K. G. Kuhn, "The Lord's Supper and the Communal Mean at Qumran," in Stendahl, ed., The Scrolls and the New Testament, pp. 65–93.

[27] See Joseph A. Fitzmyer, S.J., "Jewish Christianity in Acts in Light of the Qumran Scrolls," in Keck and Martyn, eds., Studies in Luke-Acts, pp. 233–257.

twelve. The "twelve" was no doubt an existent group that reflected the concept of the church as the true Israel. The original disciples of Jesus comprised the original twelve. If Luke has preserved an accurate historical tradition, the early church sought to preserve this nucleus of twelve and elected, by lot, Matthias to replace Judas (Acts 1:15–26). Peter appears in the early part of Acts as the most influential member of the Jerusalem church. Sometime later, and exactly when and how is not known, James the brother of Jesus became the head of the Jerusalem church. Even after the death of James, kinship to Jesus seems to have played a role in the leadership of the Jerusalem community.[28]

THE DEVELOPMENT OF A MISSION TO THE GENTILES

Developments within the Christian community in Jerusalem soon led to radical changes in the nature and life of the Christian church. The first of these was associated with the appearance and growth within the Jerusalem Christian community of a group of Greek-speaking Jewish believers. These are called the Hellenists (Luke also uses this term merely to refer to Greeks). In origin, they were probably members of a Greek-speaking synagogue in Jerusalem who had accepted the preaching of the crucified and resurrected Jesus as the Messiah. Eventually tension developed between the Hellenists and the Hebrews (= Aramaic-speaking Jews). According to Acts 6:1–6, this tension developed over the distribution of food, and the Hellenists claimed that partiality was shown to the Hebrews. A group of seven, apparently from the Hellenist community although the Acts account is not explicit, was selected to provide for a proper distribution and to serve as leaders (deacons?) along with the twelve. The seven were set aside to their tasks by prayer and the laying on of hands.

Stephen, one of the seven, was soon involved in controversy with the Jews over his interpretation of Jewish history.[29] In addition, he seems to have taken a more critical attitude toward the Temple cult and the law than had been common among the other Jewish Christians (Acts 6:8–15). Stephen was brought before the Sanhedrin charged with preaching that the Temple would be destroyed and the laws of Moses changed. In his defense before the council, Stephen delivered a blistering speech charging the Jews with a constant history of disobedience (Acts 7:1–50). This history of disobedience to God (resisting the Holy Spirit), according to Stephen, had reached its apogee in the refusal of the Jews to accept Jesus as the Promised One and Stephen charged them with murder in the death of Jesus (Acts 7:51–53). As a result of his speech, Stephen was stoned to death (Acts 7:54 to 8:1).

The rise of the Hellenist Christians had created not only tension within the Christian community but also tension between the Christians and the non-Christian Jews. The Hellenists were, of course, Jewish but they saw a greater difference between themselves and the non-Christian Jews than was the case

---

[28] See Brandon, *The Fall of Jerusalem and the Christian Church*, pp. 45–53.
[29] See M. H. Scharlemann, *Stephen: A Singular Saint* (Rome: Biblical Institute Press, 1968).

with the "Hebrew" Christians. It was with the Hellenists that the conflict between Christianity and Judaism began. There are references to the fact that the
earlier Christians had been ordered by the Jewish leaders not to preach Jesus
(Acts 4:1–22; 5:27–42) but this was more a form of harassment than of open
conflict.

The Hellenist Christians and perhaps others had to leave Jerusalem; the
original apostles remained (Acts 8:1–3). The scattering of the Hellenists meant
that the Christian message was carried from Jerusalem to adjacent areas. Philip
preached in Samaria and won followers to the Christian cause (Acts 8:4–13).
Soon churches appeared as far away as Damascus (Acts 9:10–22) and Antioch
(Acts 11:20–26). The supremacy of the Jerusalem church and of Peter over
these new Christian communities seems, however, to have been recognized
(Acts 8:14–24; 9:32).

Almost inevitably, this spread of the Christian faith meant that non-Jews
were brought into the church. Apparently these earliest Gentile converts were
persons known as "God-fearers" who were attracted but not converted to
Judaism (see Acts 10:1–2). According to Acts, ch. 10, it was Peter who was
partially responsible for the inclusion of Gentiles in the church.[30] A Roman
centurion named Cornelius sought out Peter, as the result of a vision, and the
latter preached to Cornelius and his Gentile friends. These not only responded
favorably to the preaching but began to manifest the gift of the Holy Spirit,
speaking in tongues (Acts 10:44–46). This conversion of Gentiles to Christianity was greeted by an attitude of caution, if not suspicion, by the Jerusalem
Jewish Christian community (Acts 11:1–18). But faith, conversion, and the gift
of the Spirit had to be recognized.

The incorporation of Gentiles into the church opened the way for Christianity to develop in two different directions: Palestinian-Jewish Christianity
under the leadership of the original disciples and then of James and Hellenistic
Christianity (both Jewish and Gentile) in the larger Mediterranean world. This
development brings us to Paul, the one who called himself "the apostle to the
uncircumcised."

---

[30] One wonders whether the Lucan emphasis on Peter as the "founder of the Gentile mission"
(see also Acts 15:6–11) is historical in the light of Gal. 2:11–14.

20 | PAUL AND THE CHURCH
IN THE GRECO-ROMAN WORLD

The rapid spread of Christianity beyond the geographical boundaries of Palestine and outside the structures and thought of Judaism was of tremendous consequence for the developing faith and life of the church. New centers in the church rose to prominence. Hellenistic Christianity had to define itself in dialogue, on the one hand, with Judaism and Jewish Christianity and, on the other hand, with the religions and thought of the Greco-Roman world. The most important and creative figure both in the expansion of Hellenistic Christianity and in its theological expression was Paul, to whom more than one third of the New Testament was attributed.

THE ENVIRONMENT OF HELLENISTIC CHRISTIANITY

The non-Jewish world into which Paul and others first carried the Christian gospel around the middle of the first century A.D. was characterized by three primary features, primary, that is, insofar as their significance for Christianity was concerned.

The first of these was the power and stability of the Roman Empire. The architect of the Empire was Augustus (27 B.C. to A.D. 14), who came to power following the death of Julius Caesar and the civil wars and struggles that preceded and followed his death. Augustus ruled over an empire that incorporated virtually the whole of the Mediterranean world. The years of his rule and that of his successors have been rightly dubbed the Pax Romana, or Roman Peace. It was a time of political unity and military stability insofar as the empire as a whole was concerned. Commercial activities in the Empire could depend upon an elaborate network of well-built roads and highly developed maritime trade. Roman supervision of the trade routes had almost eliminated piracy and banditry, so that travel was generally easy and safe. The common language of the Empire was Greek, although Latin was widely used in the Western provinces, and this provided a base for communication. Native languages were employed in everyday use.

Biblical readings: The material discussed in this chapter is found in Acts, chs. 13 to 28, Galatians, I and II Thessalonians, I Corinthians, Romans, Philippians, and Philemon. See map XV.

The social structure of the Empire was not overly rigid. At the top of the system were the members of Roman senatorial families and the equestrian order. Below these were the free men, freedmen, and slaves. Membership in the highest ranks was based primarily on property qualifications. A slave could purchase his freedom. Roman citizenship was granted to many inhabitants of the provinces. Non-citizens could purchase citizenship or acquire it through service in the auxiliary military forces. Citizenship carried with it the right of trial before Roman judges, instead of local ones, the privilege of appeal to the imperial court at Rome, and sometimes the exemption from certain local taxes.

Education was stressed in the Empire, and during the Pax Romana the level of literacy was rather high. Throughout the Empire, the material conditions of life were characterized by prosperity. The distribution of wealth was, of course, very uneven and the income of common laborers was very low, probably due in no small measure to the inexpensive competition of slave labor.

The unifying bond of the Empire was the emperor.[1] An imperial cult existed as the means by which loyalty was expressed. The practices in the imperial cult varied greatly from province to province. At the official level it was controlled, but unofficially it often displayed itself in extravagant form. In Rome and Italy, sacrifices could be offered to the "genius" of the living emperor but not to him. In the provinces, sacrifices were made to "Rome and Augustus." Altars and, later, temples were set up for the imperial cult and were staffed with priests. All over the Empire, sacrifices and games took place on festival occasions, especially on the birthday of the emperor. The Roman senate was accustomed to voting the deification of dead emperors, following Julius Caesar, who had served well. It was argued, and "witnesses" testified, that the soul of the dead emperor winged heavenward from the funeral pyre. In the provinces, deification was often ascribed before death by the more enthusiastic of the loyalists. Some emperors (Caligula, Nero, and Domitian) claimed divinity during their lifetimes and demanded compulsory veneration. In the imperial cult, religion and patriotism were combined.

A second feature of the Greco-Roman world was the multiplicity and intermingling of religions.[2] The older religions of Rome and Greece had been civic religions in which the gods were those recognized by the state or the city-state. The incorporation of areas outside Greece and Rome led to the amalgamation of cults and the identification of gods. The Greek Zeus, for example, was identified with the Roman Jupiter and with the Syrian Baal Shamem ("Lord of the heavens"). In this fashion, previously national religions acquired universality. Many of the older civic religions had been undermined somewhat by philosophical criticism and the decline of the importance of the city-state. The religions of the subject peoples were often attractive to the Greco-Romans.

---

[1] See Ethelbert Stauffer, *Christ and the Caesars*, tr. by K. and R. Gregor Smith (The Westminster Press, 1955).

[2] See Frederick C. Grant, ed., *Hellenistic Religions: The Age of Syncretism* (The Liberal Arts Press, 1953), and his *Ancient Roman Religion* (The Liberal Arts Press, 1957), as well as his *Roman Hellenism and the New Testament* (Charles Scribner's Sons, 1962); and Arthur Darby Nock, *Early Gentile Christianity and Its Hellenistic Background* (Harper Torchbooks, 1964).

Such religions were not bound to the state and generally they preserved an exotic and flamboyant ritual and priesthood.

The ancient fertility rituals and religions were preserved and continued in the form of "mystery cults." [3] These religions, which had originally sought the renewal of the life of the community as a whole, became much more oriented to the needs of the individual. They provided spiritual experiences that offered the worshiper a transcendence of his human condition, the hope of rebirth and immortality, and a sense of sharing in the life of the divine. Deities in the mystery cults were dying and rising gods, a remnant of their origin in vegetation religions. Following appropriate purification, in a secret ceremony the initiant was admitted into the cult and its mysteries. The adherents of the cult formed a corporation or community that provided its members with a sense of belonging. The mystery cults attracted some who were more interested in the fad of fashionability than in the desire for a profound religious experience.

This syncretism, or mixing of originally diverse religious traditions and practices, offered an almost unlimited number of religious alternatives to the people of the Greco-Roman world. It was a time of great religious toleration but also a time of religious relativism. Intolerant and antisyncretistic faiths such as Judaism and Christianity did not harmonize well with the general spirit of the Greco-Roman attitude toward religion. Their failure to adopt a syncretistic attitude proved to be not only a stigma of distinctiveness; it was also a source of internal strength as well as an attractive feature in an age when absolute religious certainty was the exception rather than the rule.

A third feature of the Greco-Roman world was the union of philosophy and religion in some quarters.[4] For many, especially among the well educated, the philosophical criticisms of religious beliefs and practices had undermined interest in the traditional religions but not in theology as such. Various systems of philosophical, theological, and ethical interests existed with fairly decided religious overtones. The most popular of these were Stoicism and Epicureanism.

Stoicism, whose name comes from the *Stoa*, or "porch," where Zeno (ca. 340–265 B.C.) its founder taught, was perhaps the dominant philosophy in the Greco-Roman world. For the Stoics, virtue was the only good and vice the only evil. Virtue was understood as living in conformity with nature. The real world was the world of material beings. The universe was animated and directed by a creative fire or germinative reason that was not conceived of in personal terms. The universe was determined and directed toward an ultimate purpose and was pervaded by providence. Man possessed "a spark" of the universal soul and found his real purpose when he lived contented and attuned to the natural. Lists of ethical qualities were drawn up, enumerating the duties of man in his various relationships and stressing social responsibility. Stoicism appealed to man as man and expressed the hope of universal brotherhood.

Epicureanism, which took its origin from Epicurus (ca. 341–270 B.C.), held that the goal of life was happiness. Happiness required that man be delivered

---

[3] See Samuel Angus, *The Mystery-Religions and Christianity*, with an introduction by T. H. Gaster (University Books, 1966); and F. C. Grant, *Hellenistic Religions*, pp. 105–149.

[4] See Barrett, *The New Testament Background*, pp. 54–90.

from the fear of gods and men, pain and death, and be capable of the full enjoyment of pleasure. For Epicurus, religion with its ritual and theology was a great enemy to happiness. Gods existed but they were far removed and uninterested in man and the world. The Epicurean world view was based on the "atomic theory," which argued that all things are made of atoms in constant movement but without a constant purpose, design, or divine guidance. With death, the individual's atomic structure dissolved. Belief in immortality was an absurdity. Throughout history, Epicureanism has had a bad press. Epicurus' concept of happiness did not advocate an orgiastic, self-indulgent attitude toward life. Happiness was tranquillity, the ability to be unshaken by any calamity or ill in life, the capacity to think of pleasant things even in the midst of pain and in the face of death.

Dependent upon religion, philsophy, and superstition was astralism, the belief that the world and men's lives were controlled by the heavenly bodies. To some extent, Stoicism encouraged astrological concerns in its argument that nothing happens without purpose. If the planets and constellations exist and demonstrate regularity, then there must be a reason for this. Astrology was, of course, very old, having occupied an important place in Mesopotamian religion alongside the national cults. In many cultures, the stars and planets were assumed to be gods. The combination of the older astrology and of the more recently discovered findings of Greek science and mathematics about the universe gave astralism an intellectual as well as a magical appeal. If man's fate and fortune were determined by the stars, then one must attempt to discover and live by the secrets of these "powers and principalities" and do all he can to placate and control them.

The most wide-ranging syncretism of philosophical and religious elements in the Greco-Roman world was Gnosticism.[5] This term, which is derived from the Greek word *gnōsis*, meaning "knowledge," is used to refer to a variety of religious and philosophical phenomena. Gnosticism as a fully developed system of religious thought was widespread in the ancient world during the second century of the Christian era. The exact origins of Gnosticism are, however, unknown, although many elements in Gnosticism are much older than the second century. Gnostic thought drew upon ideas from Iranian, Babylonian, Egyptian, Greek, Jewish, and, in its most developed form, Christian thought. A number of beliefs characterized Gnostic speculation. (1) The world was considered evil, a creation by one of the lesser powers of the universe, and true man's prison. The world was believed separated from the true god by a series of extraterrestrial realms under the control of various powers. (2) Man possessed a divine spark with an innate immortality. This spark was distinguished from both body and soul. (3) Salvation consisted in the escape of this divine, immortal element from the world (which was under the control of hostile powers and was characterized by death, defeat, and decay) and its return to its origin.

---

[5] See Robert M. Grant, ed., *Gnosticism: A Sourcebook of Heretical Writings from the Early Christian Period* (Harper & Brothers, 1961); Hans Jonas, *The Gnostic Religion*, 2d ed. (Beacon Press, Inc., 1963); Robert M. Grant, *Gnosticism and Early Christianity*, rev. ed. (Harper Torchbooks, 1966); and R. McL. Wilson, *Gnosis and the New Testament* (Fortress Press, 1968).

(4) Salvation came through revealed knowledge (*gnōsis*) brought to man by a redeemer from the heavenly world of light. This knowledge informed man of the true, unknown god, of the divine element in man, and of the means of return. The redeemer was one who descended to the world and then returned above after proclaiming this knowledge. According to the second-century Gnostic group called the Valentinians, Gnosticism was about:

> who we were, what we have become;
> where we were, whither we have been thrown;
> whither we are hastening, whence we have been redeemed;
> what birth is, what rebirth is.[6]

When the Christian faith moved into the larger Greco-Roman world, it had to compete with other movements. Some of these offered salvation through elaborate, secret ritual (the mystery cults), others through revealed knowledge (Gnostic groups), or philosophy and ethics (Stoicism and Epicureanism), or through astrology and magic (astralism). In the long run, Christianity was to some extent influenced by these movements and adopted from their vocubulary, thought-world, and perhaps ritual. Christianity presented itself, not as offering another set of problems, but as offering solutions to problems and, above all, religious certainty.

PAUL: BIOGRAPHICAL AND CHRONOLOGICAL MATTERS

In terms of long-range influence, Saul of Tarsus, better known by his Roman name Paul, was far and away the most important of the early Christian leaders.[7] His activities as a missionary preacher and teacher, together with his authorship of numerous New Testament letters, adequately guaranteed his place among the most significant figures in Christian history. Paul was not the first nor the only missionary to the Gentiles, but certainly he was the most important and the best known one. His creative interpretation of the Christian faith marked an important juncture in the developing theology of the early church. His own letters give eloquent testimony to the controversies and disputes in which he and his theology were engaged—not only with non-Christians but with fellow believers as well. Paul's activities and writings provide numerous insights not only into his theological thought but also into the problems, concerns, and interests of Christian communities around the middle of the first century.

Sources for Knowledge of Paul. There are two kinds of New Testament evidence available for an understanding and interpretation of Paul's life and work: about two thirds of the book of Acts, which provides an account of Paul's conversion and his missionary work, and the letters actually written by Paul. Certain of the apocryphal writings contain information about his life and

---

[6] Translation is from Conzelmann, *An Outline of the Theology of the New Testament*, p. 12.
[7] A general textbook introduction on Paul and the problems associated with Pauline studies is Donald J. Selby, *Toward the Understanding of St. Paul* (Prentice-Hall, Inc., 1962).

personality but the historicity of these is very uncertain. One such writing does provide the following description of Paul: "A man small of stature, with a bald head and crooked legs, in a good state of body, with eyebrows meeting and nose somewhat hooked, full of friendliness; for now he appeared like a man, and now he had the face of an angel." [8] The material in the book of Acts presents a rather idealized view of Paul and his activities and at times seems to conflict with Paul's own letters at certain significant points.

The letters ascribed to Paul in the New Testament are fourteen in number. Several of these, however, are no longer considered to have been written by Paul. Practically no one today believes that Paul wrote The Letter to the Hebrews. (Even in the early church, the work was not attributed to Paul and its authorship was discussed as an open question.) The majority of scholars do not consider Paul to have been the author of the so-called pastoral letters (I and II Timothy and Titus). These are widely, and perhaps correctly, understood as pseudonymous writings, that is, written by someone other than Paul but claiming Pauline authorship. Scholars are virtually unanimous in assuming that Paul wrote Romans, I and II Corinthians, Galatians, Philippians, I Thessalonians, and Philemon. Scholarly opinion is divided over the question of Paul's authorship of II Thessalonians, Colossians, and Ephesians.

The letters of Paul contain only a few references and suggestions about his life and activity. However, they provide insights into his mind and his understanding of his ministry and offer a rich picture of his views and thought. The book of Acts tells us little about Paul's mind and thought but it does tell us much about what he did.

In any attempt to understand Paul and his theology, the fact must be recognized that his letters are exactly what the designation suggests, namely, letters. These are not well-thought-out theological writings (with the possible exception being Romans), nor are they systematic attempts on the part of Paul to expound his version of Christianity. He certainly did not set out to compose Scripture! The letters of Paul are instead "occasional writings," which followed the customary letter-writing style of the time. His letters were dictated to scribes, with some being signed personally. They were addressed to specific church situations in which Paul had worked and to congregations with which he was personally familiar (with the exception of Romans). His letters dealt with particular issues and problems that were immediate matters of concern. Biographical matters were discussed by Paul only when they could be employed to illustrate or buttress an argument. The needs of the particular situation determined the theological issues discussed.

Paul's Background and Early Activity. Very little is known about the background and early life of Paul. He was a Jew of the tribe of Benjamin (Rom. 11:1; II Cor. 11:22; Phil. 3:5). According to The Acts,[9] he was born and reared

---

[8] This appears in a work called "Acts of Paul and Thecla." Translation is from Edgar Hennecke, *New Testament Apocrypha: Volume Two: Writings Relating to the Apostles; Apocalypses and Related Subjects* (The Westminster Press, 1964), p. 354.

[9] The Acts account of Paul has been severely criticized by John Knox, *Chapters in a Life of Paul* (Abingdon Press, 1950).

in Tarsus, a Hellenistic city of Cilicia in Asia Minor (Acts 21:39). He was born a Roman citizen of Tarsus (Acts 21:39). Paul was evidently his Roman name; Saul was his Jewish name. Only the former is used in his letters.

Paul's education seems to have been both Hellenistic and Jewish. He knew the Greek language well and had at least some acquaintance with Hellenistic literary, philosophical, and religious traditions. He referred to himself as a zealous Pharisee (Phil. 3:5–6), and Acts 22:3 indicates that he had studied in Jerusalem with Gamaliel, one of the leading rabbis of the day. His interpretation of the Old Testament shows a familiarity with the rabbinic method of Scriptural exegesis. Paul followed a trade (I Thess. 2:9) which, according to Acts 18:3, was that of a tentmaker.

Paul first appears in the New Testament as a persecutor of the Christians (Acts 7:58 to 8:3; 9:1–2; Gal. 1:13, 23; Phil. 3:6). He is said to have witnessed the martyrdom of Stephen in Jerusalem, standing watch over the garments of those who cast the stones (Acts 7:58). The motives for Paul's original opposition to the Christian movement are never clearly spelled out, although in Gal. 1:13–14 Paul associates his persecution of Christianity with his zeal for Judaism and "the traditions of my fathers." This implies an opposition based on the new movement's attitude toward the law and suggests a persecution directed against Hellenistic-Jewish Christianity.

Paul himself has very little to say about his conversion to Christianity. He speaks about an appearance to him of the resurrected Christ (I Cor. 9:1; 15:8) and also that God "was pleased to reveal his Son to me" (Gal. 1:15–16). The author of Acts reports on three occasions (Acts 9:1–19; 22:4–16; 26:9–18; with minor variations between the accounts) the story of Paul's conversion on the road to Damascus.[10] These accounts have been embellished somewhat with legendary details. Paul implies (Gal. 1:17) but never states that his conversion to Christianity took place in the region of Damascus. Neither Paul nor the writer of Acts supplies us with details sufficient to reconstruct the psychological processes that preceded and accompanied his conversion. Paul's statement that after his vision of Christ he "went away into Arabia" (Gal. 1:17) has been taken as a suggestion that his conversion was a radical experience whose implications took some time for Paul to assimilate personally. As a result of his conversion experience, Paul acknowledged the truth of the Christian claim that Jesus was the Messiah and that God had acted in him in such a way as to open up a new way of salvation—the way of faith apart from the law. Paul accepted and gloried in what he understood to be God's appointment of him as an apostle or missionary to carry the Christian message to the Gentiles.

The Chronology of Paul's Life. Scholars attempting to work out an absolute chronology for Paul's life have very little data with which to work.[11] Church tradition placed his death in the persecution of Christians by Nero in A.D. 64.

---

[10] See H. G. Wood, "The Conversion of St. Paul: Its Nature, Antecedents and Consequences," *New Testament Studies*, I (1954/5), pp. 276–282.

[11] On the chronology, see Reginald H. Fuller, *A Critical Introduction to the New Testament* (London: Gerald Duckworth & Co., Ltd., 1966), pp. 6–15; and Willi Marxsen, *Introduction to the New Testament*, tr. by Geoffrey Buswell (Fortress Press, 1968), pp. 17–23.

His conversion seems to have taken place shortly after the beginning of the church in Jerusalem, which is probably to be dated to the first third of the fourth decade (A.D. 30–33). His conversion had to take place before A.D. 40, since Paul refers to his escape from Damascus while the Nabatean Aretas (IV) was king and in control of the Damascus area (II Cor. 11:32–33; see Acts 9:23–25 where, typically, the Jews are blamed). Aretas died in A.D. 40. The Jerusalem council held "to settle" the problem of Gentile Christians (Acts, ch. 15) probably occurred about A.D. 49. If the references of Paul in Gal. 1:18; 2:1 to seventeen years (any part of a year could be reckoned as a whole) refer to the period before the Jerusalem council, then Paul apparently was converted about A.D. 32–34. One could presumably place his birth about the beginning of the Christian era. According to Acts 18:12, Paul was in Corinth while Gallio was proconsul of Achaia. An inscription found at Delphi in 1905 correlates Gallio's proconsulship with "Claudius being Imperator for the twenty-sixth time." [12] This would place Paul in Corinth about A.D. 51 or 52, assuming that Gallio held office for only one year. Correlation of this material with the later references in Acts would date Paul's arrest in Jerusalem and his arrival in Rome sometime during the last half of the sixth decade (A.D. 55–60).

PAUL'S MISSIONARY TRAVELS

After Paul's conversion to Christianity, he stayed in Arabia Nabatea for a time and then returned to Damascus (Gal. 1:17). After what Paul calls three years (which could have been one full year and parts of two others), he went up to Jerusalem, where he says he saw Cephas (Peter) and James the Lord's brother (Gal. 1:18–19). This trip to Jerusalem is probably referred to in Acts 9:26–30, although Paul and the author of Acts do not describe the visit in identical terms.[13] Paul then departed for Syria and Cilicia, where he stayed for several years (Gal. 1:21). Nothing is known of Paul's activity during this period. After fourteen years, Paul returned to Jerusalem accompanied by Barnabas and Titus (Gal. 2:1). Acts 11:27–30; 12:25 probably refers to this trip. The Acts account says that Barnabas and Paul were sent to Jerusalem by the church in Antioch to carry relief to the brethren who lived in Judea. Paul does not mention this relief in his Galatians account but his intent in referring to this second trip was not to narrate the chain of events but to argue a point that we shall examine later (see Gal. 2:10).

The Acts account of Paul's missionary work recounts three journeys which he made for the purpose of propagating the gospel (Acts 13: 1 to 14:28; 15:36 to 18:22; 18:23 to 21:16). Acts does not enumerate these journeys but does definitely separate them into three itineraries. On the first journey (Acts 13:1 to 14:28), he and Barnabas sailed to Cyprus, then crossed over to the mainland of southern Asia Minor, and after partially retracing their steps they returned

---

[12] See Barrett, *The New Testament Background*, pp. 48–49.

[13] On the visits of Paul to Jerusalem, see Charles H. Talbert, "Again: Paul's Visits to Jerusalem," *Novum Testamentum*, IX (1967), pp. 26–40.

to Antioch. The second journey took Paul, accompanied by Silas (Silvanus) and Timothy, back to some of the churches in southern Asia Minor and then into Macedonia, where he visited many of the Greek cities around the Aegean Sea (Philippi, Thessalonica, Beroea, Athens, and Corinth). He then journeyed to Ephesus from where he sailed to Caesarea in Palestine. The third journey started again from Antioch, and Paul revisited churches in eastern Asia Minor and the European mainland, after which he returned to Jerusalem by way of Tyre and Caesarea. Paul, in his letters, does not speak of his journeys in the form of these itineraries, but many of the details in Acts are confirmed by statements in his writings. It is entirely possible that the author of Acts has schematized the travels of Paul by dividing them into three distinct journeys, all of which end with Paul returning to Jerusalem (Acts 15:4; 18:22; 21:15). The author of Acts played down the tension that existed between the Jewish Christian church in Jerusalem and the Gentile churches. One of the ways he did this was by emphasizing Paul's relationship to the "mother" church (which Paul however de-emphasized for a different reason).

Regardless of how one evaluates the three-journey scheme of Acts, it is obvious that Paul traveled extensively for several years in the eastern Mediterranean area. During these travels, Paul preached the Christian message and established churches. He stayed for rather lengthy periods in Corinth (Acts 18:1–17) and in Ephesus (Acts 19:1–41). The existence of Jewish synagogues in most of the cities he visited facilitated his preaching of the gospel. The synagogues were used as a place to preach to the Jews and to the "God-fearers" (Gentiles attracted to Judaism but not converts). In many places, Paul was met by strong opposition from both Jews and Gentiles. Paul remained in contact with many of the churches he founded by revisiting the congregations or through correspondence. It is the latter which provides us with insight into the thought of the apostle. Instead of attempting a systematic description of Paul's thought [14] (assuming this as a possibility is a weighty assumption!), we shall examine the content, problems, and issues discussed in some of his letters.

THE LETTER TO THE GALATIANS

Little is known about the churches of Galatia to which Paul addressed his letter. The Acts contains no record of the founding of the Galatian churches and only mentions the land of Galatia twice (Acts 16:6; 18:23). Uncertainty about the location and nature of these congregations is furthered by the ambiguous usage of the term "Galatia" in antiquity. The territory of Galatia in central Asia Minor had been created in the third century B.C. when several tribes of Celts from Europe settled in the area. The name Galatia is derived from the word "Celt." During the Roman period, the territory was made into a province but its extent was greatly increased. Whether Paul and Acts used the term in its narrower or broader sense is not certain.

---

[14] For the most recent attempt, see Conzelmann, An Outline of the Theology of the New Testament, pp. 155–286.

The Letter to the Galatians was written by Paul in a state of great agitation and is the most defensive of all his writings. Galatians contains no complimentary paragraph; it is combat material, with Paul at once both the aggressor and the defender. The following is an outline of the book: (1) Introduction (Gal. 1:1–5); (2) Censure of the churches for their desertion of Paul's gospel (Gal. 1:6–10); (3) Paul's defense of his gospel and apostolic office (Gal. 1:11 to 2:21); (4) The gospel of justification through faith and its relationship to the law (Gal. 3:1 to 4:31); (5) A summary of the issues (Gal. 5:1–12); (6) Christian freedom and ethical conduct (Gal. 5:13 to 6:10); and (7) Conclusion (Gal. 6:11–18).

This epistle was Paul's attempt to defend himself and his interpretation of the Christian gospel and to rescue the Galatian Christians from what Paul understood as a false gospel. When this has been said, several questions automatically arise. Who was attacking Paul, necessitating his heated defense? What were their charges against him? How did this false gospel differ from Paul's? What was the origin of this "other" gospel? Only some of these questions can be answered, for we only have Paul's defense which does not even name the opponents.

A number of themes appear in the letter that Paul used in his defense and in hopes of convincing the Galatians to return to his gospel. An examination of these will illustrate Paul's thought and perhaps that of his opponents. (1) Paul argues that his gospel was the result of a revelation of Jesus and that it was therefore of divine not human origin (Gal. 1:11–17).[15] In the opening words of the letter, Paul had described himself as "an apostle—not from men nor through man, but through Jesus Christ and God the Father." He claimed that God had set him apart before he was born in order to call him to his task. After his conversion, Paul claims that he "did not confer with flesh and blood" (contrast Acts 9:10–22) nor did he go up to Jerusalem. Paul's arguments here must have been directed against some charge that claimed he preached only a human gospel and not a gospel of heavenly or divine origin.

(2) Paul further contends that he was in no way dependent upon the leaders of the Jerusalem church for his gospel although the Jerusalem apostles had approved the content of his preaching and recognized his mission to the Gentiles (Gal. 1:18 to 2:10). Paul supports this argument by discussing his visits to Jerusalem. On the first visit he says he saw only Cephas and James the Lord's brother; in fact, he was not even known by sight to the Judean Christians (contrast Acts 9:26–29). Paul's passion on this issue led him to swear that he was not lying! Later, Paul says, he was again in Jerusalem and on this occasion encountered some opposition "because of false brethren secretly brought in" but after not relenting his position, the three reputed pillars of the church (James, Cephas, and John) recognized his mission to the uncircumcised and gave him the right hand of fellowship. Not only had he never subjected himself to the authority of the Jerusalem apostles, Paul argued that he had on

---

[15] See D. M. Hay, "Paul's Indifference to Authority," *Journal of Biblical Literature*, LXXXVIII (1969), pp. 36–44.

one occasion actually opposed Cephas publicly when Cephas had ceased eating with the Gentiles in Antioch, after "certain men came from James," for fear of the "circumcision party" (Gal 2:11–21). Paul's arguments on this theme defended his independence from the mother church in Jerusalem and the apostolic leaders there. His opponents must have charged that Paul was a subordinate to the Jerusalem Christian community.

(3) Paul argued that he did not preach circumcision (Gal. 2:3–5; 5:11). His statement, "But if I, brethren, still preach circumcision, why am I still persecuted?" suggests that Paul's opponents in Galatia were using Paul to support the practice of circumcision, i.e., the necessity of Christians to observe the Jewish laws. It also suggests that Paul had met severe criticism (persecution?) either from Jews or Jewish Christians for preaching a Christian faith that did not require circumcision. Paul claimed that he had once taken the Greek Titus to Jerusalem with him and had staunchly refused to yield to those who insisted that he be circumcised.

A survey of these three themes in the book has allowed us to see some of the charges brought against Paul and to view his defense. Is it possible to discover what might have been the occasion that allowed the exponents of these charges to attack Paul? The only possible circumstances narrated in the book of Acts that might have served this purpose are found in Acts 16:1–4 with their background in ch. 15. Acts, ch. 15, is the Lucan account of an apostolic council held in Jerusalem to discuss whether Gentile Christians should be circumcised as was advocated by the more orthodox Christian Jews. The council decided that circumcision should not be required but that Christian converts should "abstain from what has been sacrificed to idols and from blood and from what is strangled and from unchastity" (Acts 15:29). Later, Paul, who had attended the Jerusalem council and argued against the requirement of Gentile circumcision, set out on his travels again. Acts reports that he wanted Timothy to accompany him and, since Timothy was Greek and in their travels they would be encountering many Jews, Paul circumcised him (Acts 16:1–3). Then as the small band traveled north, they are said to have delivered the decision reached by the Jerusalem council to the churches in the cities they passed through (Acts 16:4). If Paul passed on the decision to the Galatian churches when he went through that region (Acts 16:6) and the knowledge of Timothy's circumcision by Paul became known, then one can see how Paul's opponents could have quickly (Gal. 1:6) used this evidence against him (Gal. 1:10).[16] His opponents could have easily pictured him as a subordinate to the Jerusalem church, as preaching a message derived from men, and as advocating circumcision in practice if not in theory.

Now to return to the themes of the letter to the Galatians. (4) A fourth emphasis of Paul, and in many ways the very heart of the letter, was his argument that there is only one authentic gospel. This was the gospel that Paul himself preached, a gospel that proclaimed salvation by faith not by works of

---

[16] See Talbert, "Again: Paul's Visits to Jerusalem," *Novum Testamentum*, IX (1967), pp. 32–40.

law (Gal. 1:6–9; 3:1 to 4:31). Paul declared that even if an angel from heaven should preach a gospel contrary to that which he had preached, he should be accursed. "Let him be *anathema!*"

In supporting his argument "that a man is not justified by works of the law but through faith in Jesus Christ" (Gal. 2:16), the apostle appealed first to the personal experience of the Galatians and then to the Old Testament. His appeal to experience was in the form of a number of questions (Gal. 3:1–5), all of which were intended to force the Galatians to answer, "By faith not by works!" His appeal to the Old Testament was to show that Abraham was a man of faith (as are his true offspring) and not a man who acquired salvation through obedience to the law (Gal. 3:6 to 4:31). Paul's use of Abraham as his example of faith displays a number of lines of reasoning.[17] Abraham believed the promise of God and it was reckoned to him as righteousness. This shows that man is saved by faith. Abraham was not saved by the law, for the law was not given until the time of Moses, four hundred and thirty years after Abraham, and then it was ordained by angels through an intermediary, not given directly by God. Since the promise accepted by faith preceded the law, the law could not nullify the promise. Whoever would try to acquire salvation through the law must recognize that the Old Testament declares that the man who fails to keep the law completely is cursed. The man of faith knows that Jesus has been cursed for him.

The promise that the nations (= Gentiles) would be blessed through Abraham and his offspring has been fulfilled in Jesus; for in Christ, there is no longer the division of people into Jew and Greek, slave and free, male and female. Being in Christ through faith means being a son of Abraham; it is faith that makes one a son of Abraham, not keeping the law or being circumcised.

"Why then did God give the law?" must have been sensed by Paul as a logical response by the Galatians. Paul's answer was that the law was a guardian or a custodian to bring home the reality of sin until the fullness of time should come. But with Jesus, faith had come and man, the believer, was redeemed from even the law. Paul then argues that the example of the sons of Abraham also proves his argument. Abraham had two sons, one by Hagar who was Abraham's slave, but the other son Isaac (by Sarah) was a child of promise, a son of the free woman.[18] Hagar, according to Paul, was an allegorical representation of Mt. Sinai and Jerusalem, and her offspring were the Jews striving to please God by the law (or flesh). Isaac, the son of promise, the child of the heavenly Jerusalem, was a fellow brother of the Christians, who were children of promise persecuted like Isaac of old by their fellow brothers, the sons of the slave. Paul argued that indeed the Jews were sons of Abraham but unlike the Christians they were the offspring of a slave, not the children of promise and faith, the true sons of Abraham and even of God. The fact that through faith

---

[17] The question of Abraham's obedience to the law was a concern of contemporary Judaism that argued that the laws were present in a preexistent form from the time of creation, and so Abraham was a pre-Mosaic observer of the Mosaic laws.

[18] Philo also interpreted the stories of Hagar and Sarah as allegories in which Hagar stood for the elementary "encyclical studies" while Sarah represented "virtue." See Sandmel, *The First Christian Century*, pp. 118–121.

in Christ the Gentiles were being blessed and the promise to Abraham fulfilled shows that it is Christ and the Christians who are Isaac's counterpart and the recipients of the promise's fulfillment.

Before moving on to discuss the ethical implications of being "children . . . of the free woman," Paul summarizes his argument on the nature of the gospel and its relationship to the question of circumcision (Gal. 5:1–12). He warns the Galatians that those who submit to circumcision in the hope of being saved or justified will be bound to keep the whole law and will have cut themselves off from grace, faith, and Christ. For the Christian, the one in Christ, what matters is faith working through love, not circumcision nor uncircumcision. Paul displays his exasperation at the Galatians and those who had unsettled them. He wishes that those who were trying to force circumcision on his converts would castrate themselves.

(5) A final theme in the letter is Paul's discussion of the nature of ethical action in the light of Christian freedom (Gal. 5:13 to 6:10). He argues that Christian liberty must not be understood as freedom from moral and ethical behavior. Paul appeals in a number of ways to support his claim for a Christian style of life. He quotes from Lev. 19:18 that one should love his neighbor as himself and that in so doing man has fulfilled the whole law. The Christian is one who is led by the Spirit and whose life should be dominated by the desires of the Spirit and should show the fruit of the Spirit. The works of the flesh are the opposite of the works of the Spirit. By "being led by the Spirit," Paul meant what he had earlier referred to as freedom, the service of love, the life of faith, and no doubt the personal experience of contact and communion with the divine (see Gal. 3:1–5). The Christian has crucified the flesh (in baptism?), his disobedient state. Paul not only appealed to the Old Testament and the life of the Spirit as the bases for a certain life-style; he also exhorts the Galatians to fulfill "the law [or principle] of Christ." By this he means the bearing of another's burdens, the willingness to suffer for the other's good after the example of Jesus. Finally he warns that at the future judgment man will be held accountable to God and only he who has sown well will reap a good harvest.

Having examined the contents of The Letter to the Galatians, can we identify Paul's opponents who upset the church? Paul's references to "some who trouble you" (Gal. 1:7), "they" (Gal. 4:17; 6:13), "who hindered you" (Gal. 5:7), "he who is troubling you, whoever he is" (Gal. 5:10), "those who unsettle you" (Gal. 5:12), offer little help and even suggest that Paul's familiarity with his opponents was not overly precise. The evidence suggests that they were a group familiar with Judaism and that they may have been Jews or Jewish Christians.[19] The members of the Galatian church were, however, Gentile in origin, having been influenced, before conversion, by astralism (Gal. 4:8–9).[20]

---

[19] See J. B. Tyson, "Paul's Opponents in Galatia," *Novum Testamentum*, X (1969), pp. 241–254. For an attempt to understand the Galatian problem in terms of secular history, see D. B. Bronson, "Paul, Galatians, and Jerusalem," *Journal of the American Academy of Religion*, XXXV (1967), pp. 119–128.

[20] A recent trend has been to view Paul's opponents as "Syncretists"; see Talbert, "Again: Paul's Visits to Jerusalem," *Novum Testamentum*, IX (1967), pp. 29–31, with bibliographical references. One could, however, view the astral concerns in the letter as a reflection of Paul's rather than his opponents' theology.

The opponents apparently were not Jewish Christians sent from Jerusalem, or Paul would have condemned them for breach of the agreement reached at the Jerusalem council. If Jewish in background, they seem to have also been influenced by astral concerns (Gal. 4:3, 9–10), but this was not unheard of in Judaism.[21]

THE THESSALONIAN CORRESPONDENCE

Thessalonica, the capital of the Roman province of Macedonia, was located on the Via Egnatia, the great military road that connected Rome with the East. The founding of the church at Thessalonica is discussed in Acts 17:1–10. Paul is said to have preached in the Jewish synagogue there on three Sabbaths and to have argued with the Jews over the messiahship of Jesus. The converts to Christianity are described as some of the Jews, a great many of the devout Greeks, and not a few of the leading ladies. The Jews then stirred up a riot, and Paul was forced out of town; some of his converts were dragged before the city authorities.

In I Thessalonians, Paul discusses the occasion of the letter's writing. Paul, in Athens and anxious about the church's welfare, had sent Timothy back to Thessalonica to aid and instruct the congregation and upon his return Paul had written the letter. Paul seems to refer to a rather lengthy stay in Thessalonica (I Thess. 2:7–12) as opposed to the Acts reference to three sabbaths. Philippians 4:16 mentions two gifts of assistance that Paul received from Philippi while he was staying in Thessalonica. This would imply a reasonably long stay. Paul does not refer to any Jewish opposition to the church but mentions the persecution of the Christians by their "own countrymen" (I Thess. 2:14). The Acts account should be modified in the light of these considerations. The scheme that has Paul preach in a synagogue, make some converts, encounter Jewish opposition, and then leave under duress, seems to represent another example of Lucan schematization.

The following outline is a broad summary of I Thessalonians: (1) Introduction (I Thess. 1:1); (2) Thanksgivings and reminiscences about the founding of the church (I Thess. 1:2 to 2:16); (3) Paul's thoughts about the church since he left Thessalonica (I Thess. 2:17 to 3:13); (4) Exhortation to proper ethical behavior (I Thess. 4:1–12); (5) Discussion of the Parousia and the fate of Christians who have died (I Thess. 4:13 to 5:11); (6) Additional ethical injunctions (I Thess. 5:12–22); and (7) Concluding benedictions and remarks (I Thess. 5:23–28).

According to Paul's recollections, the Thessalonian converts had eagerly responded to his preaching and Paul had been overjoyed at this response claiming that the congregation there had become an example throughout Macedonia and Achaia (I Thess. 1:2–8). The reference to the fact that the people had "turned to God from idols, to serve a living and true God" (I Thess. 1:9) suggests that

---

[21] Astrological concerns were current at Qumran. See Dupont-Sommer, *The Essene Writings from Qumran*, p. 52.

the Thessalonian congregation must have been predominantly Gentile. It also suggests that Paul not only had preached the distinctive Christian kerygma but that he had also preached theology in its narrower sense, i.e., the correct doctrine of God. Such preaching based on Jewish monotheism must have been an important element in the proclamation of Christianity to non-Jewish people.

Ancient Athens was dominated by the presence of the Acropolis with its Parthenon dedicated to Athene, the city's patron goddess, and the Areopagus ("Mars' Hill"), where a court of justice met. Paul's visit to Athens and his sermon on Mars' Hill are reported in Acts 17:12–34.

ALISON FRANTZ

In the more or less personal material in I Thessalonians, one of Paul's basic concerns is the persecution of the young church. The gospel had been preached and received in Thessalonica with "much affliction" and "great opposition" (I Thess. 1:6; 2:2). The Christians had been subjected to suffering just as had Jesus and the early church (I Thess. 2:14–16). Paul's anxiety after leaving and going on to Athens had been his fear of the congregation's afflictions and whether or not the Christians would buckle under the persecution (I Thess. 2:17 to 3:5) or, as Paul put it: "for fear that somehow the tempter had tempted you and that our labor would be in vain" (I Thess. 3:5). Had they failed to remain loyal to their faith, their failure could have been interpreted by Paul as the work of the tempter (or Satan; I Thess. 2:18) just as their response to the gospel was interpreted as their being chosen by God (I Thess. 1:4–5). The exact nature of this persecution cannot be determined. Acts 17:6–7 speaks of the Christians being dragged before the city authorities and charged with having "turned the world upside down" (disturbing the peace?) and "acting against the decrees of Caesar, saying that there is another king, Jesus." At this time in the development of the church there was no official Roman policy of Christian persecution. The opposition must have been general harassment that perhaps triggered riots of some sort. When this disturbed the peace, the "Christian question" did become an issue for the city authorities, who were entrusted with preserving law and order and accountable to higher authority for failure to do so.

Paul's reaction to the persecution and the suffering of the Thessalonians was first of all to declare that they stood in a good tradition! Paul stated that he, the early church, and, indeed, Jesus had suffered affliction (I Thess. 1:6; 2:14–16), and thus the Thessalonians are imitators, for which they can be proud. Secondly, Paul encouraged the Christians to continue living as they had, enduring the affliction and opposition.

Paul's ethical admonitions and instructions (I Thess. 4:1–12; 5:8–22) represented the type of teaching in the Christian way of life or ethical behavior which he had previously taught the congregation. He wanted these written statements to serve in a way as a substitute for his teaching in person (I Thess. 2:17–18). The ethical instructions of Paul in I Thessalonians are concerned with a number of issues and are often stated in quite general terms. The listing of admonitions in I Thess. 5:12–22 reminds one of the lists of ethical rules drawn up by the Stoics. Paul warns against sexual immorality (I Thess. 4:3–8), encourages love of the brethren (I Thess. 4:9–10a), and exhorts the members to live quietly, minding their own affairs, and to work (I Thess. 4:10b–12). Later in the letter he emphasizes the necessity of the Christians to encourage one another (I Thess. 5:11) and to respect those who minister in the church (I Thess. 5:12–13). His ethical admonitions conclude with a series of ethical clichés (I Thess. 5:14–22).

The rationale that Paul used as the motivation for his ethical admonitions rested on three arguments. (1) He argued that the Thessalonians ought to follow a certain pattern of life in order "to please God" (I Thess. 4:1). His instruction he called "the will of God." Elsewhere in the book, Paul spoke about his desire to please God in his ministry and charged the congregation "to lead a life worthy of God" (I Thess. 2:4, 12; see also I Thess. 3:13, "unblamable in holiness before our God"). Such references suggest that Paul understood certain ethical behavior as the will of God, obedience to which was demanded if one were to please God. (2) In one section, Paul exhorted his readers to follow certain ethical behavior so that they might "command the respect of outsiders" (I Thess. 4:12). Here the basis for ethical behavior seems to be public opinion or the desire to win public approval for the new Christian movement. (3) A final ethical motivation used by Paul is what might be called eschatological. Paul argues that the Christians are the sons of the day and are already destined "to obtain salvation through our Lord Jesus Christ," therefore they should live as sons of the day and as ones who know that their salvation is assured (I Thess. 5:5–11).

Paul discussed one major doctrinal question in I Thessalonians, a question apparently brought back from the church by Timothy. The problem resulted from the fact that some of the people who had converted to Christianity had died. The question was: What would happen to those believers who died be-

fore the Parousia of Jesus? Whether this was the first time Paul had encountered this question or not cannot be determined. He answered it, however,
as if he had never discussed the question previously with the Thessalonians (I
Thess. 4:13–18). Paul's answer was that one should not let this problem be a
source of doubt, for there was no real problem involved. The dead would be
resurrected. Just as Jesus had died and had risen again, even so God would
raise up those who have fallen asleep (= died). Paul declared that the Lord
(Jesus) would descend from heaven with a cry, the archangel's call, and the
sound of the trumpet of God. With his appearance, the dead would be raised
and then those still alive ("we") would be "caught up together with them in the
clouds to meet the Lord in the air." The last expression refers to the early
Christian proclamation that Jesus would come on the clouds of glory.

Following his discussion of the fate of those who died before the Parousia,
Paul reminds the church that the day of the Lord, his Parousia, cannot be
calculated but will come like a "thief in the night" (I Thess. 5:1–5). But Paul
assures them that they are sons of the day, not sons of the night, and, remaining that way, the day will not be a surprise like a thief. It is obvious that Paul
had preached and still held to an imminent Parousia.

The second letter to the Thessalonians raises a number of problems of interpretation, and this whether one takes it as a genuine letter of Paul or not.[22] The
problems arise out of the fact that parts of II Thessalonians are so similar to
parts of I Thessalonians that they appear to have been copied, while at the
same time other parts of the two books in their description of the Parousia
appear worlds apart. For these and other reasons, many scholars doubt that Paul
actually wrote the epistle. It shall be assumed in the following discussion that
Paul wrote the letter, not long after having composed I Thessalonians but after
some significant changes had taken place in the Thessalonian congregation.

The following is an outline of the contents of II Thessalonians: (1) Introductory greeting (II Thess. 1:1–2); (2) Thanksgiving for the church's growth
and the promise of punishment at Jesus' Parousia for those who are not
Christians (II Thess. 1:3–12); (3) The apocalyptic plan and the Parousia (II
Thess. 2:1–12); (4) Further thanksgiving and request for the church to remain
loyal to the teachings of Paul (II Thess. 2:13 to 3:5); (5) The problem of
idleness in the church (II Thess. 3:6–15); and (6) Conclusion (II Thess. 3:16–
18).

There are two primary problems discussed in II Thessalonians. These are the
manner of the arrival of the Parousia and the idleness of many of the Thessalonian church members. Excitement over the coming of the Lord centered
around the fact that someone in the Thessalonian community was teaching
"that the day of the Lord has come" (or "is at hand") and had apparently
supported such an argument by circulating a supposed letter of Paul to that
effect (II Thess. 2:2). The Thessalonians, or some at least, were caught up in
this teaching and became possessed by an overheated expectation of the immi-

---

[22] For arguments against Paul's authorship, see Marxsen, *Introduction to the New Testament*,
pp. 37–44; and for the arguments in favor of Paul's authorship, see Paul Feine, Johannes
Behm, and W. G. Kümmel, *Introduction to the New Testament*, tr. by A. J. Mattill, Jr.
(Abingdon Press, 1966), pp. 187–190.

nent Parousia that may have been the cause of the idleness among some of the community. To combat this attitude, the writer argues that before the end something like an apocalyptic timetable must unfold. This scheme or apocalyptic plan contained a number of steps (II Thess. 2:3–12): rebellion, the revelation of the man of lawlessness, who will exalt himself as God and seat himself in the temple of God but who is presently being held back by "the restraining one," and following the revelation of the lawless one, who will be supported by Satan, Jesus will appear and slay him. When one compares this apocalyptic timetable with Paul's description of the Parousia in I Thess. 4:13 to 5:4, the differences are striking. II Thessalonians 2:1–12 sounds like the type of apocalypticism current in some circles of Judaism (see Dan., ch. 11; Mark, ch. 13) with a Christian coating. This, however, does not mean it is non-Pauline. The idea that signs must precede the end and yet the end comes unexpectedly was not inconsistent in apocalypticism. However, the existence of two different emphases so chronologically close and from the same author does assume a drastic change in the Thessalonian church. But, after all, the early church congregations were pretty volatile!

The idleness in the church (II Thess. 3:6–13) may have been a by-product of the expectation of the immediate end. If tomorrow may never arrive, why work today? However, the expectation of the end and the idleness are never brought together as cause and effect in the letter. I Thessalonians 4:10b–12 suggests that encouragement to work may have been a constant need in the Thessalonian community and that such an attitude would have been reinforced by an imminent expectation. Paul expounded two reactions to this failure to work. (1) He argued that "if any one will not work, let him not eat." Paul used the example of his own labors in their midst to encourage a working attitude. (2) Paul suggested that the church discipline its slothful members ("keep away from any brother . . ."; II Thess. 3:6), but he warned the congregation to look on such a member "not as an enemy, but warn him as a brother" (II Thess. 3:15).

FIRST CORINTHIANS

The narrative of Paul's founding of the church in Corinth is given in Acts 18:1–18. His stay in the city was quite lengthy, extending over a year and a half. According to the Acts account, the church was made up of both Greeks and Jews; among some of the latter were important members of the Corinthian synagogue.

Corinth had a long history as a cosmopolitan, wealthy, and magnificent city. It had been destroyed in 146 B.C. and rebuilt by the Romans in 44 B.C. and later served as the capital city of the province of Achaia. Corinth was a great commercial center located on two seas. Its existence as a major world city gave the town a heterogeneous population. Religious syncretism flourished and the city was famous for its wickedness. "To Corinthianize" was a slang expression meaning "to live an immoral life." In the famed Corinthian temple of the goddess Aphrodite, according to Strabo, more than one thousand sacred prostitutes offered their services in devotion to the glory of the goddess.

Paul carried on an extensive correspondence with the Corinthian church. Although the New Testament appears to contain only two letters to the church, there are a number of reasons that suggest II Corinthians is actually a collection of several letters.[23] In I Cor. 5:9–11, Paul refers to a previous letter he had

Corinth was perhaps the most important city in Greece in Roman times. Excavations at the site of the ancient city have exposed the agora, or central market and meeting place. The bema, where Paul was brought before Gallio, is at left center. The imposing citadel, Acrocorinth, towers over the ruins.

written that was obviously not I Corinthians. It has been assumed that II Cor. 6:14 to 7:1, which breaks the line of argument in II Corinthians, represents a fragment of this earlier letter. II Corinthians 2:3 and 7:8 refer to a very severe letter written by Paul which cannot be I Corinthians either. II Corinthians, chs. 10 to 13, whose tone is very harsh, may represent part or all of this letter. It can be taken for granted then that Paul wrote at least four letters to the Corinthians of which what is called First Corinthians would have been the second. Our discussion of the correspondence will be limited to First Corinthians.[24]

The following is an outline of the contents of I Corinthians: (1) Greetings

[23] See Feine-Behm-Kümmel, *Introduction to the New Testament*, pp. 211–215, for arguments for and against this theory.
[24] See J. C. Hurd, Jr., *The Origin of I Corinthians* (The Seabury Press, Inc., 1965).

and thanksgivings (I Cor. 1:1–9); (2) Paul's discussion of several abuses reported to him (I Cor. 1:10 to 6:20), i.e., internal strife (I Cor. 1:10 to 4:21), immorality (I Cor. 5:1–13; 6:12–20), and appearances before pagan courts (I Cor. 6:1–11); (3) Paul's answers to questions raised in a letter sent to him by the Corinthians (I Cor. 7:1 to 15:58), i.e., questions on sexual matters (I Cor. 7:1–40), the eating of sacrificial food (I Cor. 8:1 to 11:1), women in public worship (I Cor. 11:2–16), the observance of the Lord's supper (I Cor. 11:17–34), spiritual gifts and glossolalia (I Cor. 12:1 to 14:40), and the problem of the resurrection (I Cor. 15:1–58); (4) The collection for the Jerusalem church (I Cor. 16:1–4); and (5) Personal matters and conclusion (I Cor. 16:5–24).

Paul's knowledge of the problems and discussions within the Corinthian church which precipitated his writing I Corinthians came to him in several ways. Reports of dissension in the church had been passed along to Paul, who at the time was in Ephesus (I Cor. 16:8), by "Chloe's people" (I Cor. 1:11), about whom nothing further is known. The church at Corinth may have met in her home. The church had written a letter to Paul requesting his response to some problems and questions (I Cor. 7:1). This letter had apparently been delivered to Paul by the three men mentioned in I Cor. 16:17, who perhaps supplemented the letter with oral information. Such communication as this shows how the churches kept in contact with Paul and perhaps with one another.

In the opening chapters of the epistle (I Cor., chs. 1 to 4), Paul discusses the dissensions and quarreling in the church. There were four cliques in the church which characterized themselves as belonging to Paul, Apollos, Cephas, or Christ (I Cor. 1:12). Each of these groups seemed to have claimed a superiority to the others. Paul had founded the church, and Apollos, who was an Alexandrian Jew noted for his eloquence and who had converted to Christianity (see Acts 18:24–28), had ministered in the church at Corinth. Nothing is known about any visit of Cephas to the church, but such a visit was certainly possible. The groups in the church seem to have developed as a result of the peoples' devotion, attachment, and overestimation of their teachers and baptizers. The "Christ group" probably claimed a superiority but one not founded on some Christian missionary. Behind the groups' claim of belonging to some leader there was also, no doubt, a claim to possess some knowledge (gnōsis) not shared by the other groups.

Paul's arguments against this dissension stressed several points. In the first place (I Cor. 1:10 to 2:16), he contended that the Christian faith does not rest on lofty words or eloquent wisdom. Rather the gospel rests on what is a stumbling block to Jews and folly to the Greeks, namely, the crucifixion of Jesus. There is a mystery to the gospel but it is the mystery of God's purpose in the crucifixion, a hidden wisdom of God which those who crucified him did not recognize. Secondly, Paul argues that he and Apollos are only servants and stewards of God assigned to their tasks and should be understood in this light (I Cor. 3:1 to 4:21).

Beginning with I Cor. 5:1, Paul discusses the immorality in the Corinthian church. A Christian was living with his father's wife, his own stepmother, and the church had not interfered in this practice condemned even by pagans. Paul recommends that the man be excluded from the Christian fellowship, turned over to Satan (excommunicated?) in the hope that he might be saved on the day of the Lord. Paul says this is the course of action he would take if he were present and since he was "present in the spirit" the church should go ahead and take this action. Apparently some in the church were arrogant and boastful about this expression of Christian freedom (I Cor. 5:2, 6) but for Paul it was "bad yeast in the dough" (cf. I Cor. 5:6–8). Paul warns against intercourse with (temple?) prostitutes (I Cor. 6:12–20). Basing his argument on the Hebrew idea that in the sexual relationship two people become one, he declares that sexual relations with a prostitute unites the man with her into one body. The body is meant for the Lord, is a member of Christ, and is the temple of the Holy Spirit. Immorality has no place in such a scheme. Using the body to glorify God is one way of remonstrating for the price of salvation.

In their legal disputes with one another, the Corinthian Christians had taken their lawsuits into the Roman courts (I Cor. 6:1–11). Paul was strongly opposed to such a practice. "Can it be that there is no man among you wise enough to decide between members of the brotherhood?" he asked. One could not expect a Christian decision in a pagan court. Surely, he argued, Christians, who are one day going to judge the world and even the angels, ought to be able to decide ordinary disputes. At any rate, the very existence of lawsuits between Christians was evidence of failure. As a Christian one should suffer wrong rather than take an issue to court; certainly no one should profit at his brother's expense.

Beginning with I Cor., ch. 7, Paul discusses the questions sent to him by the Corinthians. I Corinthians, ch. 7, concerns problems of marriage and sexual behavior. What question about sexual practices was submitted to Paul is not given, but the opening statements suggest that some Corinthians advocated asceticism in sexual matters and regarded intercouse as wrong. This would be exactly the opposite of the attitude countered in I Cor. 5:1–2; 6:12–20. How could Christians have developed opposite attitudes toward sexual practices, some advocating a libertine ("anything goes") and others an ascetic interpretation of sexuality? The answer to this question is to be found in the Gnostic interpretation of the world (see pp. 388–389). Gnostic ideas seem to have been incorporated into the interpretation of Christianity by the Corinthians (note Paul's frequent reference to gnosis; I Cor. 1:5; 8:1, 7, 10, 11; 12:8; 13:2, 8; 14:6). According to the Gnostics, this world is evil, and the real world is the world above. In acquiring "true knowledge" man is saved from this world and raised above it to the real world. The Gnostic's relation to this evil world may take one of two approaches. This world may be considered totally evil and inferior, and thus the goal is to avoid contact with the world; so asceticism is the life posture. Or the Gnostic may consider this world of no consequence to the saved; the real world is above, so that nothing one does can contaminate the redeemed soul. This attitude produces a libertine approach to life.

Paul was overwhelmingly in favor of the ascetic approach to sexuality, though probably not for the same reasons as would have been advanced by a Gnostic. Paul offered three arguments for an ascetic approach to sexuality, or why people should remain unmarried. In the first place, he advocated a general principle: it is best for a man not to touch a woman (I Cor. 7:1). Secondly, he argued that a person ought to stay in whatever state he was in when God called him (I Cor. 7:17–31). If married, stay married; if a slave, never mind, though it is permissible to acquire one's freedom; if uncircumcised, stay that way; and if unmarried, stay unmarried. The reason for remaining in the state in which one was called is that the impending crisis (the end of history, the Parousia) is near and this fact must be the principle governing life and dictating behavior. "The form of this world is passing away." Thirdly, Paul argued that marriage hinders one's interest in the Lord's work and attracts him to worldly affairs, such as pleasing his mate, and thus the married can only offer a divided devotion to the Lord.

Paul possessed enough common sense, however, not to try to impose a celibate state on everybody. For him, marriage was a sort of concession (I Cor. 7:6) to human weakness. The ideal state was being unmarried like Paul. If tempted to immorality, people should marry. It was better to marry than to be aflame with sexual passion. If one's "passions are strong, and it has to be, let him do as he wishes: let them marry—it is no sin" (I Cor. 7:36). Even living betrothed, but unmarried and without sexual intercourse, was better than marriage (I Cor. 7:36–38).[25]

Paul argued that divorce was wrong, saying that such an attitude was not just his but also the Lord's (I Cor. 7:10–11; see Mark 10:10–12). The divorced should remain unmarried or be reconciled to the former spouse. Paul did argue that one could divorce if married to an unbeliever who demanded a divorce; divorce was a lesser evil than living unpeaceably (I Cor. 7:12–16). He recommended staying married to an unbeliever if the latter consented to being married to a Christian. Paul argued that the unbelieving partner and the children were consecrated through the believing partner. But he does not mention what the content of this consecration was.

The question of eating food offered to idols is the theme of I Cor., chs. 8 to 10.[26] Chapter 9 appears as almost an insertion, for it is only loosely related to what precedes and follows. One could assume that Paul took a break (for a meal or a night's sleep) in his dictation of the letter after ch. 8:13, and when he began dictating again, the question of the apostle's remuneration and the nature of his service were on his mind and this was where he started. The problem of eating meat sacrificed to idols had apparently arisen because some of the Corinthians claimed that after possessing Christian gnōsis a person realized that the gods receiving such sacrifices were nonexistent. Thus a "knowing" Christian could visit the temple and eat at the sacrificial banquet without any qualms of conscience. The problem arose when the weaker members saw these stronger (or more Gnostic) Christians eating in pagan temples and because of their weak consciences stumbled in the faith (by reverting to paganism? by eating but also believing in the existence of the idol gods?). Paul's answer to this problem was to argue that if eating meat caused a brother Christian to fall, then

---

[25] On the question of Paul's having possibly been married and the interpretation of I Cor., ch. 7, see J. M. Ford, "Levirate Marriage in St. Paul (I Cor. VII)," *New Testament Studies*, X (1963/4), pp. 361–365.

[26] See Charles K. Barrett, "Things Sacrificed to Idols," *New Testament Studies*, XI (1964/5), pp. 138–153.

he would be a vegetarian forever. In wounding the conscience of the weak, one was sinning against Christ. Of course, Paul argued, there was nothing wrong with eating meat bought in the marketplace (slaughterhouses were frequently attached to temples) or even in sharing a meal with unbelievers unless the conscience of a weaker brother objected (I Cor. 10:23–30). Paul, however, does reason that Christians should not share in the pagan worship services (I Cor. 10:14–22). When pagans sacrifice, they make their offerings to what are in actuality demons. To share in the worship of demons will jeopardize the worship of the Lord since, Paul argues, this will arouse the jealousy of the Lord. By eating in the worship service, one becomes a "partner" (sharing in union) with the demon, just as by sharing in the Lord's cup one becomes a "partner" of the Lord.

In his discussion of eating meat sacrificed to idols, Paul makes several references to the fact that the situation often determines how the Christian should act and what he should declare right and wrong. There is nothing wrong with eating meat consecrated to heathen deities unless it takes place in a situation where some Christian brother might be harmed. Paul contended that he always tried to fit the situation in order to serve God. "To the Jews I became as a Jew. . . . To those outside the law I became as one outside the law. . . . To the weak I became weak. . . . I have become all things to all men, that I might by all means save some. I do it all for the sake of the gospel, that I may share in its blessings" (I Cor. 9:19–23). In the situations of service to God, one should not seek his own advantage nor the expression of his own conscience but do all to the glory of God, trying to cause no offense to Jews, Greeks, or the church of God (I Cor. 10:31 to 11:1).

Women in Corinth were worshiping in the church services with uncovered heads. Paul comments on this practice though he apparently was not requested to do so (I Cor. 11:2–16; this passage does not begin with the "now concerning" introduction which Paul used in taking up the matters raised in the letter sent to him). Christian men had developed the practice of worshiping bareheaded and the women were following this trend. Paul employed a number of arguments to support his opinion that women should cover their heads while "praying and prophesying [preaching?]" but I Cor. 11:13 suggests that he may not have considered his arguments overly strong. In the first place, the veil that covered the hair, ears, and forehead was a sign that the woman was under authority. Paul shared the general belief that woman was inferior to man. The hierarchical ordering was God, Christ, man, then woman since woman was made from man (see Gen. 2:21–22). How Paul would have squared such an argument with his statement that in Christ "there is neither male nor female" (Gal. 3:28) we do not know. (As Paul says, he could be all things to all men, depending on the needs of the situation—or of his argument?) Secondly, Paul argues that by nature women should have covered heads, for long hair is a woman's pride. Covering the head in worship is an extension of this. If a woman will not cover her head, she should simply shave off her hair, but this was of course a sign of prostitution. Thirdly, Paul contended that women should cover their heads in worship "because of the angels." Perhaps Paul had the idea that women with uncovered heads would be a temptation to the angels (see Gen. 6:1–4). In the

Qumran Scrolls, reference is made to the presence of angels in the worship service.[27]

The proper observance of the Lord's supper and the agape meal (see above, pp. 381–382) is discussed by Paul in I Cor. 11:17–34. At the celebrations in the Corinthian church, the meal and Eucharist were observed with church factions evidencing themselves; some members were overeating and overdrinking, and there was a lack of common sharing in the meals. Paul tried to correct this condition by first quoting the church tradition concerning Jesus' actions at the Last Supper and the church's practice of using the bread and the cup in its services. Paul then proceeds to comment on the manner and attitude of observance. Unworthy observance was a profanation of the body and blood of the Lord. The identification of the bread and wine with the body and blood of Jesus shows that the early church had come to look upon the observance as a Sacrament similar to the meals of the mystery religions in which the flesh and body of the deity were eaten. One must examine himself and his motives before eating and drinking. Paul warns against observance of the ritual without proper recognition of the "body," that is, its context within the church as the body of Christ (see I Cor. 12:12–13). The communal character of the observance, its function within the life of the church, was being neglected by the Corinthians who overstressed the individual. This incorrect observation Paul saw as a source of divine judgment and concluded that this judgment was why some of the Corinthians were "weak and ill, and some had died."

A major concern in the Corinthian church, and apparently an item of controversy, was the value and use of "spiritual gifts." Paul discussed this question in I Cor., chs. 12 to 14. Some in the church felt that they had reached such a "spiritual or gnostic level" that they could declare, "Jesus be cursed!" (I Cor. 12:3). Such a declaration could only have derived from Gnostic thought where the emphasis was placed on the spiritual world, not on the physical world, and on the heavenly Christ as the ascending-descending spiritual redeemer rather than on the life of the human Jesus. The counterpart to the Gnostic "Jesus be cursed" would have been "Blessed be the heavenly Christ." Paul denounced such a Gnostic-influenced attitude and declared "Jesus is Lord" as the confession inspired by the Spirit of God.

Paul argued that there were varieties of spiritual gifts, service, and working in the church, but these were not granted to people so that one might claim a superiority. The gifts of healing, working miracles, prophesying, speaking in tongues, teaching, and so on, were given to the various Christians for the common good (I Cor. 12:4–11). The church was the body of Christ and like any body the parts had to function together and no part could declare itself superior to another (I Cor. 12:12–31). For Paul, all these gifts must work together with love as the aim. As almost an aside to the main argument, Paul wrote a description of love (I Cor., ch. 13).[28] This "Poem on Love" has, of course, become one of the best-

---

[27] See Joseph A. Fitzmyer, S.J., "A Feature of Qumran Angelology and the Angels of I Cor. XI.10," *New Testament Studies*, IV (1957/8), pp. 48–58.

[28] The fact that I Cor., ch. 13, breaks into the main argument has been taken as evidence that the chapter is an interpolation. See E. L. Titus, "Did Paul Write I Corinthians 13?" *Journal of Bible and Religion*, XXVII (1959), pp. 299–302.

known passages from ancient literature. For Paul, the poem was only an element in his argument. One can only wonder what Paul might have written had he deliberately set out to compose material such as I Cor., ch. 13.

Speaking in tongues was one of the more cherished spiritual gifts among the Corinthians and Paul devoted a long discussion to the practice (I Cor. 14:1–40). Paul did not oppose glossolalia (I Cor. 14:5). He claimed that his possession of the gift exceeded that of any Corinthian (I Cor. 14:18). He interpreted speaking in tongues as a form of prayer to God (I Cor. 14:2), the means of personal edification (I Cor. 14:4), as a sign of the Spirit's presence to unbelievers (I Cor. 14:22), and as a means of edifying and instructing the believers provided someone was present who could interpret (I Cor. 14:27–28). He considered glossolalia of less value to the church than prophesying (I Cor. 14:5). It is obvious that speaking in tongues was the utterance of unintelligible speech, the speaking in a spiritual tongue (I Cor. 14:9). Paul warned against overemphasis on this phenomenon. One must strive for understanding, the ability to communicate, not enthusiastic spiritualism. Five words, understandable and instructive, are better than ten thousand words of glossolalia. If the entire congregation engaged in speaking in tongues, outsiders present would think the place mad and would hardly be converted to a worship of God (I Cor. 14:23–25). God is no God of confusion (I Cor. 14:33).

Paul's comments on glossolalia allowed him to refer indirectly to the ministries within the church (I Cor. 12:27–31) and to some elements in early Christian worship (I Cor. 14:26–32). It is obvious from both of these passages that there was no officially recognized governmental structure nor regulated or regular order of worship in the Pauline churches. In his discussion of functions within the church, he mentions "first apostles, second prophets, third teachers [in modern terminology one would have said "missionaries, preachers, and teachers"], then workers of miracles, then healers, helpers, administrators, speakers in various kinds of tongues" (I Cor. 12:28). There were, therefore, in the church various tasks and offices but no clearly arranged lines of authority. Paul does seem to have assumed that he possessed special authority in the churches he had started because of his missionary role in their founding. In his comments on worship ("when you come together"), Paul mentions a hymn, a lesson (from Scripture?), a revelation (interpretation?), a tongue, and an interpretation. These could be offered in various orders, and the whole congregation could participate. Paul insisted on only two things: preserve some semblance of order, and no more than three speaking in tongues and these one at a time and only when an interpreter was present. Paul's statement that "as in all the churches of the saints, the women should keep silence in the churches" (I Cor. 14:33b–34) seems to clash with his earlier reference to women praying and prophesying (I Cor. 11:5). Some scholars have considered this admonition to female silence as a non-Pauline addition. "For a woman to speak in church" (I Cor. 14:35), which Paul considered shameful, may only refer to her participation in church discussions and disputations.

The final major topic that Paul discussed in I Corinthians was the subject of the resurrection of Christians (I Cor., ch. 15).[29] Some in the Corinthian church

---

[29] See Conzelmann, *An Outline of the Theology of the New Testament*, pp. 184–191.

had come to believe that "there is no resurrection of the dead" (I Cor. 15:12).
Why they had come to such a belief and what they taught in place of the resurrection of the dead are not known. Did they accept death as the end? This seems
unlikely, for belief in life after death was widespread in the ancient world and
the resurrection of Jesus was a central element in the kerygma. Did they argue
that "the resurrection" merely refers to an added spiritual dimension to this life?
Perhaps. Did they advocate a faith in the immortality of the soul that denied
the necessity for the resurrection of the body? This is possible. Or did they understand the resurrection of both Jesus and the Christians in a Gnostic sense,
i.e., in terms of the redeemer and the redeemed's return to the heavenly world?
This also is possible; we simply do not know.

Paul affirmed the belief in the future resurrection of Christians by appealing
to the kerygma with its emphasis on the resurrection and the appearances (I
Cor. 15:1–11). If Christ be not raised, he argued, then the Christian faith is in
vain. If Christ has not been resurrected, then the Christians have misrepresented
God, Christians are still in their sins, and those who have died have perished (I
Cor. 15:12–19). But, in fact, Paul declares, Christ has been raised and just as
death struck the human race in Adam, so with Christ there has come the resurrection from the dead. Christ is the first ("first fruits") to be raised, but at his
coming those who belong to Christ ("the rest of the crop") will be raised. All
things will be subjected to Christ, but the last enemy to be destroyed will be
death (I Cor. 15:20–28). If the dead are not to be raised, Paul asks, why are
people baptized on behalf of the dead? Such substitutionary baptism presupposes hope in the resurrection (I Cor. 15:29–34). This practice, here not criticized by Paul, is not mentioned elsewhere in the New Testament and how widespread it was is not known.

Paul anticipates the arguments of his readers and discusses what he believes
about the nature of the future resurrection (I Cor. 15:35–57). The resurrection
will not be the mere reanimation of the body; the body will undergo a radical
change. The resurrected body will be a spiritual, a heavenly body. Paul used
the analogy of planting grain: the kernels that are planted are what comes up,
but how different the plant from the seed. There will be continuity, but radical
transformation as well. (On the relationship of the resurrection to the Parousia,
see I Cor. 15:51–53 and above pp. 400–402).

One of the interests of Paul in expressing the unity of the Christians was the
collection of gifts he was making in the Gentile churches to be sent to the
Christians in Jerusalem.[30] Paul reminded the Corinthian church of the contribution and asked the members to put aside something, according to their ability,
every Sunday until Paul could come and pick it up.

THE LETTER TO THE ROMANS

Of all Paul's writings, Romans is by far the best organized, the most reflective
and detached, and the most comprehensive statement of his theological

[30] See K. F. Nickle, *The Collection: A Study in Paul's Strategy* (London: SCM Press, Ltd., 1966).

thought.[31] In many respects, Galatians and Romans are very similar because both expound Paul's understanding of the gospel as the proclamation of salvation through faith apart from obedience to the law. Galatians, however, was produced in the heat of a controversial situation; the tone of the letter was both aggressive and defensive. Romans is a calm exposition of the central content of Paul's understanding of the Christian faith.

The occasion for the writing of Romans is discussed in the body of the letter. Paul had not founded the church at Rome, in fact, he had never visited the city with its Christian congregation.[32] His knowledge of the church there was second-hand. Paul wrote his letter to the Roman church as part of his plans to begin missionary work in the eastern part of the Empire. He considered his missionary work in the eastern Mediterranean as finished. The writing of Romans was one of the initial steps in what Paul hoped would be a new phase in his Christian ministry. Spain was his ultimate goal (Rom. 15:24). Paul's ambition was, as he states, "to preach the gospel, not where Christ has already been named, lest I build on another man's foundation" (Rom. 15:20). The Christian work in the East was well on its way, and in Paul's understanding of his task there was "no longer any room for work in these regions" (Rom. 15:23). But Spain was virgin territory. The Letter to the Romans was Paul's introduction of himself and his gospel to the Roman church in hopes that the church there would welcome him and aid in his Spanish mission.

Romans was probably written from the city of Corinth near the end of Paul's last missionary journey in the East. He had one task to perform before he could sail for Rome. He had to journey to Jerusalem to deliver the contributions he had collected from the Gentile churches for the Christians in Jerusalem (Rom. 15:25–29). Paul openly expressed his fears about the upcoming trip to Jerusalem (Rom. 15:30–33). These were not fears without foundation, for Paul's trip to Jerusalem, as we shall see in the next section, was to affect in a drastic fashion the manner in which he was to arrive in Rome.

The following is an outline of the letter to the Romans: (1) General greetings and introduction (Rom 1:1–15); (2) The theme of the letter (Rom. 1:16–17); (3) Man without the gospel (Rom. 1:18 to 3:20); (4) The nature of the gospel (Rom. 3:21 to 4:25); (5) The Christian life under the gospel (Rom. 5:1 to 8:39); (6) The failure of the Jews to respond to the gospel (Rom. 9:1 to 11:36); (7) The ethical life of the Christian (Rom. 12:1 to 15:13); and (8) Concluding matters (Rom. 15:14 to 16:27).

"Both Jews and Greeks Are Under the Power of Sin." In the first main section of the letter (Rom. 1:18 to 3:20) Paul discussed the nature of the human predicament which created the universal need of the gospel. The Greek and the Jew, of course, did not stand in the same relationship to God but both were accountable

---

[31] It has been argued that Romans was used by Paul as a circular letter to a number of churches. See T. W. Manson, "St. Paul's Letter to the Romans—and Others," in his *Studies in the Gospels and Epistles*, ed. by Matthew Black (The Westminster Press, 1962), pp. 225–241.

[32] The origins of the Roman church are unknown, but there must have been a Christian community in Rome before A.D. 50.

for their condition and both stood under the wrath of God. According to Paul, there is a universal knowledge of God that has manifested itself in the creation (Rom. 1:19–20). The nature of God as Creator makes itself known in the things that are made, or in creation. The world of creation testifies about the nature of the Creator. This is what one could call a general or natural knowledge of God. Man also possesses a knowledge of God's decree concerning human behavior (Rom. 1:32), namely, that those who do perform certain acts and possess certain attitudes deserve to die. Paul seems to be referring to this same idea when he declared that the Gentiles who do not possess the law (the Torah) do by nature what the law requires—they are a law to themselves (Rom. 2:14–16). What the law requires is written on their hearts, and both their conscience and their thought bear witness to this unwritten law.

If God and the law are known by man, could man find salvation and acceptance by God if he lived by this knowledge? Paul hints that this question could be answered in the affirmative. He says that "to those who by patience in well-doing seek for glory and honor and immortality, he [God] will give eternal life," for God will render to every man according to his works (Rom. 2:6–7). Elsewhere he argues that if man is a doer of the law, he is righteous before God and since the Gentiles may do by nature what the law requires, it is possible that his conscience and thoughts will excuse him "on that day when, according to my gospel, God judges the secrets of men by Christ Jesus" (Rom. 2:14–16; but see Rom. 3:20).

Paul's interest lay in showing why the Greeks stood under the wrath of God. His argument is twofold. In the first place, the Greeks who have a knowledge of God as Creator do not worship him. Instead they worship the creature and the creation, serving images resembling mortal man or birds or animals or reptiles rather than the immortal God (Rom. 1:21–25). They are thus without excuse. Secondly, he argues that their actions are unnatural (see Rom. 2:14–16), for in their dishonorable passions they have exchanged natural relations for unnatural (i.e., the use of homosexual practices[33]) and thus God has given them up and their lives are characterized by all manners of wickedness (Rom. 1:26–32). Those who do such things stand under the wrath and judgment of God (Rom. 2:6, 9–11).

In his discussion of the need of the Jews for salvation through faith (Rom. 2:17 to 3:20), Paul reiterates some of the arguments that we encountered in Galatians. The Jews have advantages over the Gentiles, for they possess the law, the oracles of God, and these contain references to the need for salvation through faith. If one is to be saved by works of the law, then he must obey the law completely. But even the Scriptures declare that no one is righteous before God (Rom. 3:9–18). The Jews possess advantages over the Greeks but they are no better off so long as they strive for righteousness through the law.

"Now the Righteousness of God Has Been Manifested." Paul's exposition of the nature of the gospel (Rom. 3:21 to 4:25) is primarily a declaration that,

---

[33] Homosexuality was not officially condemned in the Greco-Roman world: in fact, it was frequently condoned and encouraged, unlike in the Jewish tradition, where homosexual practices were officially taboo.

with the coming of Jesus Christ, the ultimate measure of a man's standing before God is not based upon his success or failure in measuring up to any code of behavior intended to bring him righteousness before God. With Jesus, a new age, the new aeon, in the history of salvation has arrived. Salvation and righteousness have come as a gift, not only to the Jews but to the Greeks as well. This leaves no possibility of boasting, for the principle of faith excludes any claim whatsoever to a work-righteousness (Rom. 3:21–31). Paul attempts to argue from Scripture that righteousness through faith was God's intent all along and again he does this by using Abraham as an example (Rom. 4:1–25).

"Since We Are Justified by Faith." The actuality of the Christian life and the freedom it brings to man under the gospel are discussed by Paul in Rom. 5:1 to 8:39. Through faith in Christ, the acceptance of righteousness as a gift, the Christian has been delivered from the wrath of God with whom he now has peace (Rom. 5:1–11). Paul speaks of this peace with God in terms of reconciliation, the restoration of a relationship after alienation and estrangement. This reconciliation is associated with the event of Christ's death. Christ died for the ungodly and for the enemies of God. Since Paul relates the reconciliation with being justified by Christ's blood, it is obvious that he understood Jesus' death as a sacrifice, as redemption understood in sacrificial terms. Emphasis is also placed on the fact that "much more, now that we are reconciled, shall we be saved by his life" (Rom. 5:10). Here the reference to "his life" seems to apply to the present life of the resurrected Christ. Paul and most of the New Testament writers often spoke of salvation, reconciliation, and so on in three tenses. Man was reconciled and saved in the death and resurrection of Jesus (Rom. 5:10); man is saved by his faith, in the present, in Christ; and the Christian looks forward to the final salvation at the Parousia and the resurrection (Rom. 5:2). Man in faith knows salvation as a past event, as a present possession, and as a future hope.

The idea of the two ages or the first man and the new man is discussed by Paul in terms of an Adam-Christ parallel or contrast (Rom. 5:12–21).[34] As sin and death entered the world through Adam, so the grace of God and life entered the world through Christ.

The Christian, according to Paul, is not only free from the wrath of God, he is also free from sin (Rom., ch. 6). Paul introduces this topic after having said that "in Adam" sin abounded and increased but that where sin increased grace abounded even more. He continues: "Are we to continue in sin that grace may abound?" (Rom. 6:1). He anticipates the argument that if God's graciousness corresponds to human sinfulness, why not be really sinful so God could be really gracious? Paul argued against such an attitude (which obviously was adopted by some in the early church, especially those with strong libertine Gnostic tendencies) by using two illustrations. Firstly, the Christian should not continue to sin since he had died to the old life of sin in baptism (Rom. 6:1–14).[35] Paul interprets baptism as a sharing in the death of Christ. In baptism, the ini-

---

[34] See Robin Scroggs, *The Last Adam* (Fortress Press, 1967).
[35] See Eduard Schweizer, "Dying and Rising with Christ," *New Testament Studies*, XIV (1967/8), pp. 1–14; and Oscar Cullmann, *Baptism in the New Testament*, tr. by J .K. S. Reid (London: SCM Press, Ltd., 1950).

tiate was buried with Christ and raised to walk in newness of life. If one has died to sin, then he should no longer let sin reign over him. Secondly, he argues that the Christian has been freed from slavery to sin but he is now a slave of righteousness (Rom. 6:15–23). As a slave to God, man must live in obedience to him and this means that one can no longer be a slave to sin.

The Christian is also free from the law (Rom. 7:1–25). Like a woman whose husband has died and who is is free to marry again, so the Christian who belongs to Christ has of necessity witnessed the death of the law. The Christian no longer serves under the old written code; he now serves in the "new life of the Spirit" (Rom. 7:1–6). Again Paul confronts the question of the function of the law (Rom. 7:7–25). Law itself is not sin but law does increase sin. Paul argues that if it had not been for the law, he would not have known sin, for sin (here conceived of as almost a power) used the law. The commandment not to covet only increased covetousness. Man can know what he ought to do and he can will to do it but he cannot do it. The law tells him that he has not done what he should. The reason he cannot do what he wills and wants is that the power of sin is working in his life. One may delight in the law and its commands, but the power of sin turns the delight into wretchedness. With the mind and intent one serves the law of God, but with the actuality and the flesh he serves the law of sin for "I do not do the good I want, but the evil I do not want is what I do" (Rom. 7:19).[36]

The freedom of the Christian is the freedom of the Spirit, a freedom from sin and death (Rom. 8:1–11). What the law could not do God has done. Paul argues that these "who walk not according to the flesh but according to the Spirit" actually fulfill "the just requirement of the law" (Rom. 8:4). According to Paul, the possession of the Spirit was a guarantee of the certainty of ultimate salvation (Rom. 8:12–17). The Christian, like Jesus, was a son of God and could pray like Jesus "Abba! Father!" [37] in the Spirit. As a child of God, the believer in the Spirit can be confident that he will be an heir with Jesus.

In Rom. 8:18–25, Paul speaks of the cosmic redemption awaiting the whole of creation. Creation which has been groaning in travail, subjected to futility, and in bondage to decay is portrayed as waiting to be set free. Paul does not develop this idea of the redemption of creation either here in Romans or elsewhere. Apparently, he anticipated a future transformation of creation, a redemption of the world which had been subjected by the deity but subjected in hope. The hope of this final salvation, involving not only creation but "the redemption of our bodies" (Rom. 8:23), Paul proclaimed with an absolute assurance (Rom. 8:26–39). Both the Spirit and Christ raised to the right hand of God intercede on behalf of the Christian (Rom. 8:26–27, 34). Paul declares that nothing can challenge the hope of those whom God "predestined to be conformed to the image of his Son" (Rom. 8:29).

---

[36] Whether Paul is describing man under the law or man under grace in Rom. 7:14–25 has been often debated. See Conzelmann, *An Outline of the Theology of the New Testament*, pp. 228–235.

[37] See Joachim Jeremias, "Abba," in his *The Prayers of Jesus* (London: SCM Press, Ltd., 1967), pp. 11–65.

For I am sure that neither death, nor life, nor angels, nor principalities, nor things present, nor things to come, nor powers, nor height, nor depth, nor anything else in all creation, will be able to separate us from the love of God in Christ Jesus our Lord. (Rom. 8:38–39.)

"My Brethren, My Kinsmen by Race." The fact that the Jewish people as a whole did not respond favorably to the Christian kerygma was a matter of great concern to Paul. In Rom., chs. 9 to 11, the apostle gives his fullest attempt at a theological explanation of the unbelief of the Jews. Paul expressed a willingness to be cut off from Christ if this could be offset by the acceptance of Christ by the Jews. The Jews, with the law, the promise, the glory, the patriarchs, and even Christ himself, have not become Christians (Rom. 9:1–5). With the Gentiles' becoming Christians, God seems to be creating for himself a new people, a new children of promise. For Paul, this was to some extent analogous to the rejection of Esau the son of Isaac in favor of Jacob. Not all the descendants of Abraham then are sons of promise. God's freedom allows him to be merciful to whomever he wills and like a potter he can mold his work as he wills (Rom. 9:6–29). The reason, according to Paul, for the fact that the Gentiles have been declared righteous, but not the Jews, is that the Jews have not pursued righteousness through faith but through works, but they did not succeed in fulfilling the law. It is the hearing of faith that makes one righteous. Even Moses and the prophets spoke of the others and the Gentiles who would come to God and to whom he would turn. But Israel was "a disobedient and contrary people" (Rom. 9:30 to 10:21).

Paul held out hope for the eventual conversion of the Jews to Christianity. In fact, he points out, a remnant of Israel has been saved already, for some Jews did respond in faith (Rom. 11:1–10). The rejection of Christ by the Jews has been the means of bringing salvation to the Gentiles. This incorporation of the Gentiles is sort of an expedient of grace, for it is intended to make the Jews jealous "until the full number of the Gentiles come in," after which Israel will be saved (Rom. 11:11–12, 25–32). Paul warned his Gentile audience that they must remember they are only a branch grafted into the original tree (Rom. 11:13–24). His hope is that the branch of Israel may again be grafted onto the tree so that the natural branch (Israel) may grow together with the grafted branch from the wild olive tree (the Gentiles).

"What Is Good and Acceptable and Perfect." As in practically all the letters written by him, Paul moves from the discussion of theological issues to a consideration of ethics or specific ethical problems. Following a general statement that Christians should present their "bodies as a living sacrifice, holy and acceptable to God, which is your spiritual worship," Paul proceeds to comment on various aspects of Christian behavior. Christian service should express and advance the unity of the church as the body of Christ (Rom. 12:3–8); love should be genuine (Rom. 12:9–13); and the Christian should never seek vengeance but should strive to "overcome evil with good" (Rom. 12:14–21).

In Rom. 13:1–7, Paul comments on the Christian's relationship to governmental authority or the state.[38] Paul recommends that one be subject to the governing authorities, pay taxes, and honor and respect the authorities. His positive attitude toward the state is based on his contention that all authority comes from God and governmental authority is willed by God in order "to execute his wrath on the wrongdoer." The authorities are ministers of God. The state serves as a terror to bad and evil action through the use of the power of the sword but to those who are good, the state is "God's servant for your good." The Christian therefore should not resist the authorities nor fear them, for behind the authorities stand God and his wrath.

According to Paul, the Christian could fulfill the law (Rom. 13:8–10). Not when he tried to do so in order to secure righteousness but when he loved his neighbor as himself, for the whole law was summed up in one sentence: "You shall love your neighbor as yourself." As in most of his letters, Paul makes reference to the eschatological character of Christian behavior (Rom. 13:11–14); the "night is far gone, the day is at hand," therefore the Christian must live as he would live on that day.

Paul's lack of direct familiarity with the Roman church probably explains why there is so little discussion of specific problems in the letter. His only specific application of his ethical thought concerned the problem of the strong and the weak in the Roman congregation (Rom. 14:1 to 15:6). Apparently, some of the Roman Christians ("the weak") were following a vegetarian diet and observing special days. Others in the church ("the strong") ate anything and possessed no qualms about special days. Paul makes it clear that he personally has no sympathy with vegetarianism or "sabbatarianism." However, he argues that Christians must have great sympathy with those who do. The Christians must respect one another's scruples provided these are based on genuine convictions and the special observances are done in honor of God. Above all, one must not pass judgment on his brother because of his scruples of faith. God is the final judge. The Christian must show a sense of individual responsibility to God and respect for the other man's convictions, knowing that he will stand before the judgment seat. If the scrupulous ("the weak"), however, feels that his conscience is affronted by the strong, then Paul argues that this requires a bit more than tolerance (Rom. 14:15–23). Convinced that "nothing is unclean in itself" (Rom. 14:14), Paul contends that the strong must base his action not merely on his conviction but on a desire to pursue peace and love and this may mean, for the sake of the Kingdom of God, that one will avoid what makes his brother stumble. The Christian, like the example of Christ, must not try to please himself but must be willing to bear reproach.

PAUL'S LAST YEARS AND THE PRISON EPISTLES

Several times in his letters, Paul spoke of a contribution of money which he was gathering from the Gentile churches to take back to the Christians in Jeru-

---

[38] Doubts have been raised about the authenticity of this passage. See James Kallas, "Romans XIII.1–7: An Interpolation," *New Testament Studies*, XI (1964/5), pp. 365–374.

salem (I Cor. 16:1–4; II Cor. 8:1 to 9:15; Rom. 15:25–33). He seems to have hoped that this contribution would help to heal the tension existing between the church in Jerusalem and the Gentile churches founded by Paul. There was obviously still a great deal of suspicion of Paul in the Jerusalem church about his preaching of a gospel of freedom from the Torah, and he expressed a hope that his "service for Jerusalem may be acceptable to the saints" (Rom. 15:31).

Paul returned to Jerusalem bearing his gift from the Greeks (Acts 21:15–16). According to the Acts account, Paul was warned that many of the Jewish Chris-

An inscription in the Herodian Temple warning Gentiles was part of a stone balustrade that marked the limits beyond which Gentiles could not go. The inscription noted that the intruder would have himself to blame for his death which might ensue. Paul was accused of bringing Gentiles into the precincts open only to Hebrew men (Acts 21:28).

ISRAEL DEPARTMENT OF ANTIQUITIES AND
MUSEUMS

tians who were zealous for the law were strongly opposed to Paul (Acts 21:17–21). Following the advice of James and the elders, Paul went out of his way to show his adherence to the law (Acts 21:22–26). Paul's presence in the Temple and the suspicion that he had brought uncircumcised Greeks into the Temple precinct precipitated a riot. Paul was rescued from the crowd and taken into protective custody by a Roman official (Acts 21:27–36). According to Acts, Paul tried to defend his position by speaking to the Jews in Hebrew but again was met with hostility (Acts 21:37 to 22:29). A hearing was held before the Sanhedrin and when a plot against Paul's life was discovered, he was removed from Jerusalem to Caesarea (Acts 22:30 to 23:35). There were further hearings before two successive Roman procurators, Antonius Felix (A.D. 52–59) and Por-

The Roman theater at Caesarea, which could seat several thousands, testifies to the greatness of the city built by Herod. Caesarea was an early center in the developing church. Paul was imprisoned in the town for two years, and some have suggested that the prison letters were written during his Caesarean imprisonment.

cius Festus (A.D. 59–62), and one before the puppet Jewish king Herod Agrippa II (Acts 24:1 to 26:32). After the second hearing before the Roman procurator, Paul had appealed to Caesar, a privilege he enjoyed as a Roman citizen. After being imprisoned in Caesarea for over two years, Paul was sent to Rome to stand trial (Acts 27:1 to 28:28). The book of Acts ends with Paul still awaiting trial in Rome after a two-year stay in the city (Acts 28:30–31). Early Christian tradition claims that Paul was released after two years, traveled extensively in either Spain or the eastern Mediterranean area or both, and was again arrested, tried, and finally executed. But how much of the material about Paul that attempts to fill in the time after the conclusion of Acts is pure legend cannot be determined. About all one can say is that Paul was probably put to death in Rome during the reign of the emperor Nero (A.D. 54–68) and most likely during the emperor's persecution of Christianity in A.D. 64.

There are four letters attributed to Paul that are called "the prison epistles." These are Ephesians, Philippians, Colossians, and Philemon. The title for these letters comes from the fact that the letters make reference to being written from prison (Eph. 3:1; 4:1; 6:20; Phil. 1:7, 13, 16–17; Col. 4:10, 18; Philemon 10, 13, 23). If Paul wrote these letters from prison, what prison? In II Cor. 11:23–29, Paul provides an extensive list of his "trials and tribulations" and among these he mentions being imprisoned often. The book of Acts speaks of three imprisonments of Paul: overnight in Philippi (Acts 16:23–34), for two years in Caesarea (Acts 24:27), and for two years in Rome (Acts 28:30). Since the prison epistles do not mention the location of the imprisonment, one could assume that they were written from either Caesarea or Rome (overnight in Philippi hardly seems a possibility) or perhaps from some imprisonment not mentioned in Acts. The traditional view has assigned these letters to the time of Paul's Roman imprison-

Arcadian Way at Ephesus led from the main part of the city down to the harbor town. The city was famous for its temple to Artemis, the Greek goddess of the hunt and fertility and childbearing. Paul spent over two years in Ephesus, and this fact along with Ephesus' geographical location has led to the assumption of an Ephesian imprisonment as the occasion for the writing of the letters from prison.

ment. In recent years, many scholars have argued that Paul was perhaps imprisoned in Ephesus and that some of the letters were written from there.[39] Such an assumption would solve some of the problems inherent in the idea of Rome as the place of origin. In the letters, Paul refers to visits (not his but other persons') between the places to which the letters are being sent and the place from which Paul is writing. Also, he speaks of plans to visit the churches as soon as possible. These two factors do not fit well with a Roman origin, since Rome and the churches addressed were separated by hundreds of miles and Paul's plans called for him to visit Spain at the next opportunity, not to return to the eastern Mediterranean. No theory of origin can be proven conclusively.

Many scholars doubt whether Paul wrote Colossians and Ephesians.[40] Because of the problem of authenticity and the lack of space, the present discussion will be limited to Philippians and Philemon from among the "letters of captivity" (the pastoral letters, which are also attributed to Paul, will be discussed in the final chapter). The following is an outline of the letter to the Philippians: (1) Introduction (Phil. 1:1–2); (2) Thanksgiving for the Philippians (Phil. 1:3–11); (3) Comments by Paul on his situation (Phil. 1:12–26); (4) Exhortations to the congregation (Phil. 1:27 to 2:18); (5) Comments on Timothy and Epaphroditus (Phil. 2:19–30); (6) Warnings against false teachers (Phil. 3:1–21); (7) Specific admonitions and thanks for a gift (Phil. 4:1–20); and (8) Conclusion (Phil. 4: 21–23).

Judging from this letter, it is obvious that Paul cherished his relationship with the Philippians and that this sentiment was reciprocated. Philippi was the first town visited by Paul in Europe; however, Acts does not report any overwhelmingly favorable initial reaction to Paul (Acts 16:11–40). The Philippians were generous and grateful toward Paul. While in Thessalonica, he had received two gifts from the Philippian church (Phil. 4:16; see II Cor. 11:8–9) and the letter addressed to them was a "thank you" note for a further "CARE package" (Phil. 4:18).

Much of the letter to the Philippians is taken up in Paul's discussion of his present situation. He was imprisoned but he saw his imprisonment as the means for advancement of the gospel. Paul's reputation and his influence were known throughout the whole praetorian guard and apparently many in Caesar's household had become or were believers (Phil. 1:12–14; 4:22; these references are best understood if addressed from Rome). Paul discusses the question of his trial and its outcome. He anticipates deliverance but there are times, he admits, when he is tempted to think of death as an advantage and a gain. Nonetheless, his commitment to his missionary task and to his Christian friends leads him to express the hope of deliverance (Phil. 1:19–26).

Paul's exhortations to the Philippians (Phil. 1:27 to 2:18) deal with a number of rather general issues which we have seen in other of his letters. He mentions living worthy of the gospel even in times of opposition and suffering (Phil. 1:27–30), the need to seek the interests of others and the unity of the community

---

[39] See G. S. Duncan, *St. Paul's Ephesian Ministry* (Charles Scribner's Sons, 1930).

[40] Marxsen, *Introduction to the New Testament*, pp. 177–198, sums up the evidence against Pauline authorship.

(Phil. 2:1–11), and the hope that in the day of Christ (the Parousia) he will be able to show his pride in them (Phil. 2:12–18). These exhortations provided Paul with the opportunity to incorporate "a Christ hymn" (Phil. 2:6–11)[41] into his letter to illustrate what it means to have a self-renunciating disposition. This hymn, probably not written by Paul but borrowed from the current Christian tradition, presents Jesus as one who took the form of a servant though he was in the form of God. He humbled himself and became obedient unto death but was then exalted by God. Jesus, according to the hymn, has been given a name above every name, and at his name everyone will bow and confess that Christ is Lord. This hymn depicts the developing doctrine of Christ (Christology) which emphasized his incarnation ("in the likeness of men"), his suffering obedience, his exaltation, and his final triumph.

In Phil. 2:19–30, Paul discussed his desire to send Timothy to the church in Philippi and the fact that he is sending the Philippian Epaphroditus back. The latter had suffered a severe illness and almost died while acting as emissary to carry the church's gift to Paul. Such personal comments as these allow us to see more vividly the actual conditions under which the early churches operated.

In ch. 3, the tone of the letter changes drastically. Previously, Paul had written in a friendly mood and only referred in rather general terms to the existence

A Roman milestone on the Appian Way which would have been passed by Paul on his way to Rome and his anticipated appearance before the Caesar. Such mileposts marked distances along the route. The Appian Way was the most important highway leading into Rome from the south.

FOREIGN MISSION BOARD, SBC

of problems in the Philippian church (Phil. 1:28), but beginning with Phil. 3:2, Paul warns against "the dogs, . . . the evil workers, . . . those who mutilate

---

[41] For a discussion of the hymn and the argument that the passage speaks only of Jesus' earthly life, see Charles H. Talbert. "The Problem of Pre-existence in Philippians 2:6–11," *Journal of Biblical Literature*, LXXXVI (1967), pp. 141–153.

the flesh." This radical increase in severity could be explained by assuming that Paul received some additional information about the church while dictating the letter or that Philippians, like II Corinthians, is a collection of two or more letters or parts thereof.[42] Whoever these "dogs" were, they seem to have emphasized circumcision and to have boasted in their "Jewishness," for Paul counters them by quoting his own Judaic heritage but points out how gladly he gave it all up in order to know Christ Jesus and righteousness through faith. These false teachers also seem to have claimed that they had acquired perfection, "arrived," perhaps in some Gnostic sense of perfection. To this Paul argues that he is still pushing on, forgetting those things which lie behind and straining forward to what lies ahead. Again he admonishes the Christians to be imitators of him.

One of the most interestingly human episodes in early church history forms the background for one of the shortest writings in the Bible—the prison epistle to Philemon. The letter concerns a runaway slave named Onesimus and is addressed to his owner Philemon. This is the only letter of Paul addressed to an individual and even this letter adds a reference to two more people "and the church [that meets] in your house." (There were, of course, no church buildings as such in the first century.) Onesimus had apparently stolen from his owner and absconded (Philemon, v. 18) and eventually landed in the same jail with Paul. While imprisoned, Paul had converted him to Christianity (Philemon, v. 10) and upon Onesimus' release, Paul sent him home carrying a letter to his master. In it Paul expresses a confidence that Onesimus, formerly useless, will now be useful to his owner (Philemon, v. 10; the word Onesimus meant "useful"). Paul does not request that Philemon grant Onesimus his freedom nor does he attack the, at the time, almost universal practice of slavery. Paul recommends that he be accepted back "as a brother" both to Paul and Philemon (Philemon, v. 16). In other words, Paul asks that their union in Christ as brothers be recognized as transcending their human relationship as master and slave. Paul then promises that whatever Onesimus owes he, Paul, will pay (Philemon, v. 18). Though a prisoner for Christ, Paul's hope was indomitable—"prepare a guest room for me," he wrote, looking forward to a get-together of slave, master, and apostle, brothers in Christ.

---

[42] See Fuller, A Critical Introduction to the New Testament, pp. 34–37.

21 | REFORMULATIONS
OF THE GOSPEL TRADITIONS

The transmission, elaboration, and editing of the traditions about Jesus were elements in an ongoing process in the early church. By the end of the first century, four Gospels, at least, had been written and were in use by the churches. In addition to these written Gospels, oral traditions about Jesus continued in use. Papias (ca. A.D. 130), who was acquainted with the gospel in written form, said that he continued to consult with persons who had been followers of the elders about the sayings attributed to the disciples of the Lord. The reason for this inquiry he gave as follows: "For I did not consider that I get so much profit from the contents of books as from the utterances of a living and abiding voice." [1]

Only the author of Luke tells us why he wrote his Gospel: to present an orderly account. There must have been many motives involved in the writing of Gospels even after Mark was written. One of these, as Luke implies, was to present the career and teachings of Jesus in a more satisfactory form. The needs of the church were certainly of importance. The letters of Paul clearly reflect the diversity that existed in the church. The Gospels as statements of Jesus' life and teachings may be seen as attempts to establish a line of authority, namely, the authority of the written word of Jesus. Papias spoke of "those who record strange precepts," which implies that, even in written form as well as in oral tradition, the teachings of Jesus were being developed in forms that diverted widely from the oral traditions in their earliest stages. The Gospels, whether intentionally or not, helped to crystallize the traditions at a certain stage and could serve as standards for determining the valid tradition.

The form and content of the Gospels were determined not only by the internal life of the church but also by the background and interests of the writer. In addition, the audience envisioned for the Gospel was a determinative factor in the form of presentation.

The last quarter of the first century was a time of consolidation in both Judaism and Christianity. For the Jews, the destruction of the Temple and the city of Jerusalem meant a reorientation of Jewish religion. Although the Phari-

---

Biblical readings: The Biblical traditions discussed in this chapter are found in the Gospels of Matthew and John.

[1] Translation is from Bettenson, *Documents of the Christian Church*, p. 38.

saic element was to dominate, the period following the fall of Jerusalem saw a time of internal struggle and reorganization within Judaism. By the time of the Council of Jamnia (ca. A.D. 90), Judaism was well on its way to its classic Pharisaic and rabbinical form.

> The Age of Jamnia marks the change from the temple-oriented Judaism comprising a variety of sects which characterized the pre-Destruction era to a Judaism structured around the decentralized synagogue, yet in other areas moving toward centralization, canonization, and uniformity.[2]

During this period, too, Christianity began a real movement toward consolidation and uniformity that was to reach its apogee before the middle of the second century. We will examine this phenomenon more closely in the next chapter but it should be kept in mind in our examination of Matthew and John, for the production of written gospels was a significant movement in that direction. Christianity was moving into the time of the third and fourth generations, the original eyewitnesses and apostles were moving off the scene, the Parousia and the establishment of the Kingdom were delayed, Judaism separate from Christianity was going through a process of consolidation, and Christianity was losing its historical and theological rootage in Judaism and was finding substitutes elsewhere.

THE GOSPEL ACCORDING TO MATTHEW

The Gospel of Matthew contains no explicit references to its authorship nor to the place of origin. The earliest church testimony to a work composed by a Matthew is a tradition quoted by Papias:

> Now concerning Matthew it was stated: "So then Matthew recorded the oracles (*logia*) in the Hebrew tongue, and each interpreted them to the best of his ability." [3]

There is practically no evidence to suggest that the present Gospel of Matthew was written in Hebrew. In fact, just the reverse, for Matthew used the Gospel of Mark, which was written in Greek. Assuming that the reference of Papias does not refer to our Gospel of Matthew, scholars have sought in various ways to explain his statement.[4] (1) Some assume that the document referred to was an early collection of the sayings of Jesus, perhaps Q. (2) The reference to oracles has been interpreted as a collection of Old Testament prophecies now found incorporated in the Gospel. (3) The writing mentioned has been taken as a reference to a pre-Marcan form of Matthew which was translated into Greek at the time that it was expanded by the addition of the Marcan materials. (4) Others argue that Papias' statement reflects the early second-

---

[2] Martin A. Cohen, "The First Christian Century: As Jewish History," in Hyatt, ed., *The Bible in Modern Scholarship*, p. 242.

[3] Translation is from Bettenson, *Documents of the Christian Church*, p. 39.

[4] See C. S. Petrie, "The Authorship of 'The Gospel According to Matthew': A Reconsideration of the External Evidence," *New Testament Studies*, XIV (1967/8), pp. 15–32.

century effort to authenticate the Gospels by a guarantee of apostolic authorship. Such a view as the last leaves unexplained why a reference should have
been made to a composition in the Hebrew language if Papias knew the present
form of the Gospel in Greek. We simply are unable to explain Papias' reference
other than to deny that he was talking about the present form of the Gospel.[5]

The assumption that Matthew was the author of the book may have depended upon the fact that Matt. 9:9 gives the name of the tax collector who
became a disciple as Matthew (Levi in Mark 2:14). One of the twelve disciples
bore this name. (Levi is never mentioned as one of the twelve disciples, but
"Matthew" may have been a second name given to Levi just as "Peter" was
to Simon.) Scholars have generally assumed that Matthew was written after
A.D. 70, perhaps in the 80's, in Syria, perhaps at Antioch. These are hypotheses
which may be correct, although they cannot be proven.[6]

The following is a general outline of The Gospel According to Matthew:
(1) The infancy narratives (Matt., chs. 1; 2); (2) The early ministry of Jesus
(Matt., chs. 3; 4); (3) The Sermon on the Mount (Matt., chs. 5 to 7); (4)
The mighty acts of Jesus (Matt., chs. 8; 9); (5) Discourse on the disciples'
mission and martyrdom (Matt. 10:1 to 11:1); (6) Responses to Jesus' ministry
(Matt., chs 11; 12); (7) Discussion on the parables of the Kingdom (Matt.
13:1–52); (8) Rejections and withdrawals with the disciples (Matt. 13:53 to
17:27); (9) Discourse on life in the Christian community (Matt., ch. 18);
(10) The Jerusalem ministry (Matt., chs. 19 to 22); (11) Woes on the scribes
and Pharisees and eschatological discourse (Matt. 23:1 to 26:2); and (12) The
passion narrative and the resurrection appearances (Matt. 26:3 to 28:20).

A comparison of this outline with that of the Gospel of Mark reveals a
number of differences. Matthew has expanded the content of the Gospel traditions: at the beginning with the infancy narratives, at the end by the addition
of the account of the resurrection appearances, and internally by the addition
of traditions, especially in the form of teaching, not found in Mark. It is also
obvious that the author of Matthew has produced a much more organized
Gospel than did Mark by compiling a number of collections of narrative material followed by collections of teaching materials. In examining the Gospel
more closely, we shall focus on several of the special features of the book both
in content and structure.

The Fulfillment of Scripture. The life and career of Jesus are interpreted as
the fulfillment of Old Testament Scriptures that are understood as predictions.
The fact that events in the life of Jesus could be shown as fulfillment of Old
Testament "prophecies" constituted for Matthew proof that Jesus was what
the early church claimed him to be. Twelve times, Matthew refers to an event

---

[5] The existence of Jewish-Christian "Gospels" or of a *targum* on Matthew in Aramaic may
have been the source of Papias' description. For a discussion of these Jewish Gospels, see
P. Vielhauer, "Jewish-Christian Gospels," in Hennecke, *New Testament Apocrypha: Volume
One*, pp. 117–165.

[6] S. G. F. Brandon has challenged this view and argues that Matthew is the product of a
Jewish Christianity in Alexandria. See his *The Fall of Jerusalem and the Christian Church*,
pp. 217–248.

and then introduces an Old Testament Scripture to which the event is correlated with an almost stereotyped formula: "This was to fulfill what was spoken by . . ." These are the twelve quotations:

(1) Matt. 1:22–23. The virginal conception of Jesus by the Holy Spirit was a fulfillment of Isa. 7:14.

(2) Matt. 2:5–6. Jesus' birth at Bethlehem fulfills the prediction of Micah 5:2.

(3) Matt. 2:15. The flight into and the exodus from Egypt was spoken of in Hos. 11:1.

(4) Matt. 2:17–18. The massacre of the innocent children fulfills Jer. 31:15.

(5) Matt. 2:23. Jesus' residence at Nazareth fulfills the prediction that "he shall be called a Nazarene." The exact source of this quote is unknown. It may have been based on Isaiah's reference to the "branch" (*nezer*) in Isa. 11:1 or in Zech. 6:12 (though a different word for branch occurs in the latter).

(6) Matt. 4:14–16. Jesus' Galilean ministry is a fulfillment of Isa. 9:1–2.

(7) Matt. 8:17. Jesus' healing ministry fulfills Isa. 53:4.

(8) Matt. 12:17–21. Jesus' silence about his status fulfills Isa. 42:1–4.

(9) Matt. 13:14–15, 34–35. Teaching in parables and the people's failure to understand are a fulfillment of Isa. 6:9–10 and Ps. 78:2.

(10) Matt. 21:4–5. The triumphal entry is a fulfillment of Zech. 9:9.

(11) Matt. 26:56. The arrest of Jesus fulfills "the Scriptures of the prophets" (unspecified; see Mark 14:49).

(12) Matt. 27:9–10. The purchase of the field with the thirty pieces of silver given to Judas fulfills "what has been spoken by the prophet Jeremiah" (see Jer. 32:6–15; the reference to thirty pieces of silver seems to come from Zech. 11:12).

The use of Old Testament texts to interpret the person and work of Jesus was a very early Christian practice (see above, p. 376), and is thus pre-Matthean. The interpretation of texts as messianic and eschatological was, of course, pre-Christian and is already present in the Old Testament where the later authors reinterpret earlier writings. Matthew's use of these quotations suggests a use of the Old Testament not merely by the church for its own understanding but as a method of proof-texting in Christian dialogue and argument with the Jews.[7]

Matthew's use of the Biblical quotations raises the following question: Did he find the incidents in the traditions and then simply correlate these with the Old Testament texts? or did he begin with the texts and create the events to

---

[7] The use of these quotations has been studied by Krister Stendahl, *The School of St. Matthew* (Fortress Press, 1968). He traced their usage back to the exegetical activity of a Christian "school." For a comparison of these quotations and their usage with the exegesis of the Dead Sea community at Qumran, see Bertil Gärtner, "The Habakkuk Commentary (DSH) and the Gospel of Matthew," *Studia Theologica*, VIII (1954), pp. 1–24.

correspond? Since most of the events that Matthew saw as fulfillments of the Old Testament prophecies were already present in Mark, this suggests that as a rule he fitted the texts to the incidents. In at least one case, it is obvious that Matthew has altered the tradition to fit the text. In Zech. 9:9, the passage speaks of the king coming to Zion, "humble and riding on an ass, on a colt the foal of an ass." This is a good example of Hebrew parallelism in which the second line of a saying restates the preceding line or a part thereof without attempting to add anything new. The author of Matthew took this passage as a reference to two animals, an ass and a colt, and has Jesus riding into town astride two animals (Matt. 21:6–7). How he may have envisioned such a feat is not mentioned. The other Gospels speak of a single animal (Mark 11:7) but this was not considered a complete fulfillment by Matthew.

There may have been cases in which Matthew created episodes as fulfillment of the prophecy. The most likely examples of this are the story of the flight into Egypt (see above, p. 333) and the account of Judas' death and the purchase of the field (compare Acts 1:18–20 with Matt. 27:3–10).

The Infancy Narratives.[8] The Gospel of Mark opens with the account of the preaching of John the Baptist and his baptism of Jesus. Matthew and Luke contain "prologues" concerning the birth and infancy of Jesus. (Luke also contains material about the birth of John and the relationship between the mothers of John and Jesus.) The combination of the Lucan and Matthean infancy material in our "Christmas stories" often overlooks the differences between the birth narratives of the two Gospels. For example, Matthew's account assumes that Bethlehem was the home of Mary and Joseph; Luke's account places their home in Nazareth. In Matthew the annunciation is made to Joseph in a dream but in Luke it is made to Mary, who is awake. In Matthew, Joseph appears as a central character but in Luke it is Mary who is the central person. Only Matthew tells the story of the visit of the Magi and only Luke tells of the shepherds.

Matthew's infancy cycle opens with a genealogy of Jesus (Matt. 1:1–17) which traces his lineage back to David (see Rom. 1:3) and Abraham and thus associates him with the two most prominent figures in Hebrew history. Such a genealogy claimed authentic Davidic descent for Jesus the Messiah. The ancestral line is traced back through Joseph's family, not Mary's. Matthew divides the ancestral line into three sections (Abraham to David, David to deportation, and from the deportation to Christ) with fourteen generations in each division. The origin of the schema of fourteen generations is probably based on the numerical value of David's name $(d + w + d = 4 + 6 + 4 = 14)$. Four women appear in the listings: Tamar, Rahab, Ruth, and the wife of Uriah (Bathsheba). All four of these women were somewhat irregular participants in the line of descent. References to them may have been included as a defense against the Jewish charges concerning the circumstances of Jesus' birth.

The story of Jesus' birth (Matt. 1:18–25) emphasizes the virginity of Mary

---

[8] See C. H. Cave, "St. Matthew's Infancy Narrative," *New Testament Studies,* IX (1962/3), pp. 382–390.

and the conception of Jesus by the Holy Spirit. This would suggest that the genealogy of Jesus traced through Joseph (also in Luke 3:23–38) was in circulation and in use in the early church prior to the developing emphasis on the virgin birth. Matthew does not seem to have created the story of the virgin birth solely on the basis of Isa. 7:14 since Luke was familiar with the emphasis on the virgin birth but without any explicit reference to the passage from Isaiah (but see Luke 1:31). In the Hebrew of Isa. 7:14, the reference to the young woman is not the usual term for "virgin," however, the Greek term for "virgin" is used in the Septuagint translation, which Matthew quotes here. The genealogy of Jesus stresses a "son of David" Christology, while the story of the virgin birth stresses a "son of God" Christology.[9] The virgin birth, like the stories of the miraculous birth of Old Testament heroes (such as Isaac and Samuel), emphasized the direct intervention of God into the affairs of man and stressed the radical departure that resulted from this.

The account of the visit of the Wise Men (Matt. 2:1–12) stresses the celestial corroboration of the significance of Jesus' birth and illustrates the type of homage due Jesus. The Wise Men (or Magi, originally a term designating a class of Median priests) were Easterners acquainted with astrological and astronomic knowledge and lore. Legends of the visit of the Magi and the association of special stars with the birth of rulers were widespread in the ancient world. It is interesting that Matthew does not quote Num. 24:17, which states "a star shall come forth out of Jacob," a passage quoted in the messianic texts from Qumran and used as the title of the Jewish leader, Bar-Cochba ("son of the star"), at the time of the second revolt against Rome (A.D. 132–135). Later Christian tradition spoke of three Wise Men, assigned them names, and developed further legends about their origin.

The remainder of the stories in the infancy circle of Matthew are used to illustrate the fulfillment of Old Testament Scriptures.

The Five Discourses. The Gospel of Matthew contains five blocks or collections of teaching material (Matt., chs. 5 to 7; 10; 13; 18; 23 to 25).[10] Each of these is followed by a stereotyped statement: "And when Jesus finished these sayings . . ." (Matt. 7:28; 11:1; 13:53; 19:1; 26:1). These statements serve as conclusions to the preceding teaching material and as introductions to the following blocks of narrative material.

The first of these discourses is the so-called Sermon on the Mount (Matt., chs. 5 to 7).[11] This sermon has no counterpart in Mark. Luke does contain a similar discourse by Jesus, "the sermon on the plain" (Luke 6:17–49), which

---

[9] See Fuller, *The Foundations of New Testament Christology*, pp. 195–197, 202.

[10] B. W. Bacon, *Studies in Matthew* (Henry Holt & Co., 1930), argued that the collection of material into five blocks was a deliberate attempt by Matthew to present the Christian torah as a new pentateuch. For a recent discussion of this, see W. D. Davies, *The Setting of the Sermon on the Mount* (Cambridge: Cambridge University Press, 1964), pp. 14–25.

[11] The most comprehensive study of the Sermon on the Mount is the work by Davies referred to in footnote 10 above. The main arguments of the work are now presented in a condensed, paperbound form: Davies, *The Sermon on the Mount* (Cambridge: Cambridge University Press, 1966).

has several parallels to the material in Matt., chs. 5 to 7. Some of the sayings in the Sermon on the Mount are found in different contexts in Luke. The parallel material in Matthew and Luke is generally assumed to have come from Q. However, there is much material in this section of Matthew that is without parallel in any other Gospel. These factors suggest that the sermon is an editorial collection of sayings that as a compilation goes back to the author of Matthew.

The Sermon on the Mount is presented in the Gospel as the Christian counterpart to the Hebrew Torah, and Jesus is depicted as the new Moses. Like Moses, who gave the law from Mt. Sinai, Jesus taught his disciples "on the mountain" (Matt. 5:1). The content of the sermon comprised for Matthew the new law of the Christian faith. The motif of Jesus as a new Moses and the Christian faith as a new exodus are also found in the infancy narratives of Matthew. There Jesus, like Moses, is a threatened child protected by God and like Moses he comes out of Egypt.

The sermon opens with the Beatitudes (Matt. 5:3–12), which pronounce blessedness upon certain classes (the poor in spirit, those who mourn, the meek, those who hunger and thirst for righteousness, the merciful, the pure in heart, the peacemakers, and those persecuted for righteousness' sake). The Beatitude as a saying form is found in the Old Testament and was a feature of Jewish teaching (see Ecclus. 25:7–10).[12] The Beatitudes in Matthew may be taken as rather characteristic expressions of the Jewish piety of the time. The Gospel material does present the Beatitudes with more of an eschatological orientation than was common in Judaism (especially in their Lucan form; see Luke 6:20–23).

Following the Beatitudes, the sermon contains statements on the disciples (= early Christians, for Matthew) as the salt of the earth and the light of the world (Matt. 5:13–16). In Matt. 5:17–20, Matthew has Jesus declare the perpetual validity of the law. "Till heaven and earth pass away, not an iota, not a dot, will pass from the law until all is accomplished" (Matt. 5:18). For the writer, Jesus firmly placed himself in support of the Jewish Torah. But the writer's purpose here is not to have Jesus merely proclaim the binding nature of the Mosaic law, although he does declare that whoever relaxes even the least of the commandments and teaches others to do so will be the least in the Kingdom of heaven (Matt. 5:19). The writer's primary purpose is to affirm the binding character of the law of Jesus. Jesus is said to have come not to set aside the Law and the Prophets but to fulfill them, i.e., to proclaim a way that transcends the Jewish law (Matt. 5:17). The new law demands a righteousness exceeding that of the scribes and Pharisees (Matt. 5:20).

The new righteousness exceeding that of the old Torah and the new requirements of the Christian torah are then spelled out in six antitheses that contrast the new with the old (Matt. 5:21–48). The old law forbids murder; the new Christian morality condemns the internal anger against a brother and requires reconciliation before worship (Matt. 5:21–26). The old law prohibited adultery; the new one condemns even the lustful desire as a transgression

---

[12] Practically all the Beatitudes as well as the Golden Rule can be found in rabbinic literature.

equivalent to actual adultery and recommends that one pluck out the eye or cut off the hand if this would prevent one from sinning (Matt. 5:27–30). The old law permitted divorce; in the Christian ethic, divorce is prohibited except on grounds of adultery (Matt. 5:31–32). (Mark 10:11–12 and I Cor. 7:10–11 have Jesus absolutely forbidding divorce.) Oaths were allowed under the old law; but in the new, oaths are forbidden, since a simple yes or no should guarantee honesty (Matt. 5:33–37). Retaliation was granted in the old law, but the new demands of the Christian way require nonresistance to evil and express themselves in acts of good toward the bad (Matt. 5:38–42). According to Matthew, the old law required love for the neighbor and hatred for the enemy (there is no commandment in the Torah saying "hate your enemy"; contrast Prov. 25:21–22) but the disciple must love his enemies and pray for his persecutors so that he may be a son of the Father and perfect as the Father is perfect (Matt. 5:43–48). Matthew presents the new Christian torah as exceeding the Jewish Torah and in doing so also offers a criticism of Jewish law.[13]

Christians are warned that they must not practice their piety before men in order to be seen, for, if this is the objective, then the Father in heaven will not reward the practitioner of piety (Matt. 6:1). This principle is then applied to three specific types of piety. (1) Almsgiving must be done in such a manner that not even the left hand knows what the right hand is doing (Matt. 6:2–4). (2) Prayer must not be performed in public for the honor of being seen, as the hypocrites (Jews?) pray, nor with the heaping up of words to bombard the deity like the Gentiles. Instead, prayer must be offered in secret (Matt. 6:5–8) and in the manner of the Lord's Prayer (Matt. 6:9–13). He who is unwilling to forgive those trespassing against him cannot expect forgiveness from the Father (Matt. 6:14–15). (3) One must not fast with a disheveled appearance, intent on showing one's agony for the cause. One should fast but should avoid drawing attention to the fact. Instead of disfiguring the face, one should wash up and use a little hair tonic (Matt. 6:16–19). All of these examples conclude with the promise that "your Father who sees in secret will reward you."

The devotion of the disciples must be absolute, their commitment to the faith complete. Matthew uses three examples to illustrate this uncompromising call to discipleship. Man must lay up treasures in heaven, not on earth, for earthly treasures are subject to diverse threats. Where a man's treasure is, there is his heart and commitment also (Matt. 6:19–21). The eye is the lamp of the body and if the eye is sound, the body will be full of light. If the disciple does not possess a singleness of vision, his body and life will be filled with darkness (Matt. 6:22–23). No man can serve two masters, since there is no such thing as a double loyalty. The believer cannot serve mammon ("riches") and God at the same time (Matt. 6:24).

Although the disciple cannot lay up treasures on earth or do homage to mammon, he still should not be anxious about the necessities of life. In Matt.

---

[13] See Gerhard Barth, "Matthew's Understanding of the Law," in G. Bornkamm, G. Barth, Heinz J. Held, eds., *Tradition and Interpretation in Matthew*, tr. by Percy Scott (The Westminster Press, 1963), pp. 58–164.

6:25–34, Matthew discusses the question of anxiety. The Christian should not be anxious about his food, drink, clothing, or about tomorrow. If he seeks first the Kingdom of the Father and his righteousness, then he can rest assured that the necessities of life will be provided (Matt. 6:33). To illustrate the care and concern of the Father, the writer draws upon examples from the world of nature. The birds of the air and the lilies and the grass in the fields neither plant nor sow, toil nor spin, and yet God cares for them. If the Father cares for these, he surely will care for the citizens of his Kingdom.

A number of admonitions and warnings (Matt. 7:1–12) precede the conclusion to the sermon. One should not judge his brother. What is holy should not be given to dogs, nor pearls to swine (a saying whose allusions are not clear). The Christian is assured that those who ask receive; those who seek find; and to those who knock, it will be opened. Such an assurance rests on the confidence that God the Father will give good gifts to his children. The writer sums up the Law and the Prophets with the statement that has come to be known as the Golden Rule: "So whatever you wish that men would do to you, do so to them."

The conclusion to the sermon (Matt. 7:13–27) reiterates the challenge to Christian obedience and the radical character of discipleship. Entrance to the Kingdom is a narrow gate, the way that leads to life is a difficult road, and those finding it are few (Matt. 7:13–14). This saying on the narrow and the broad ways of life expounds the theme of life as "the two ways" (see Deut. 30:15–20; Jer. 21:8). It serves both as an encouragement to choose and perhaps as an explanation for the despondency in men's response to the Christian proclamation. The writer warns of false prophets who appear in sheep's clothing but inwardly are ravenous wolves (Matt. 7:15–20). Prophets and the works of prophecy are to be judged by their fruit. This reference to false prophets without doubt reflects the internal struggles within the Christian church, a product of its diversity and perhaps also the desire of some to profit from the "powers of the new age" (see Acts 8:14–24; 19:11–20; Phil. 3:17–21). Immediately following this warning, there appears a reaffirmation of the requirement of obedience (Matt. 7:21–23). It is not the one who says "Lord, Lord," nor even those who are able to prophesy and cast out demons who will enter the Kingdom of heaven and escape the judgment "on that day." Only he who does the will of the Father is the true disciple. For the writer of Matthew, there is no question about the source of the will of the Father; it is not the Mosaic Torah but the teachings of Jesus, the Christian torah. For the author, there is no place in the Christian faith for a libertine attitude toward life or a Christian proclamation that does not stress radical obedience.

The Sermon on the Mount is rounded off with a parable (Matt. 7:24–27) that stresses the security of the one "who hears these words of mine and does them" and illustrates the fate of those who hear the words but do not obey them.

The second major discourse in Matthew is in ch. 10. In the Gospel, this sermon functions as a "manual for missionary activity," containing rules and encouragement for the missionaries of the developing church. The Sermon is set within the context of Jesus' sending out his twelve disciples to proclaim the imminence of the Kingdom. The charge of Jesus to his disciples—"Go nowhere among the Gentiles, and enter no town of the Samaritans, but go rather to the lost sheep of the house of Israel" (Matt. 10:5–6)—may represent an authentic element from the preaching of Jesus. The same can be said for Matt. 10:23 —"You will not have gone through all the towns of Israel, before the Son of man comes." However, for the writer, the first charge serves to show that the Jews were given the first chance to accept the gospel. The writer has no intent to argue that the gospel should be restricted to the Jews (see Matt. 28:16–20). The second statement about the coming of the Son of Man before the gospel had been preached to all the towns of Israel is used by the writer to express his belief in the confirmed obdurate character of the Jews. The end will come before the Jews have converted and "it shall be more tolerable on the day of judgment for the land of Sodom and Gomorrah" (Matt. 10:15) than for them.

The character of the missionary task involved the proclaiming of the nearness of the Kingdom, the healing of the sick, the raising of the dead, the cleaning of lepers, and the casting out of demons (Matt. 10:7–8a). The Christian disciple was to carry on his missionary tasks without providing for his own support, being sustained instead by those who responded to the proclamation (Matt. 10:8b–15). The disciple could expect to be brought before synagogue authorities and flogged and then dragged before Gentile governors and kings (Matt. 10:16–18). If one takes Paul as an example, these are, of course, the experiences that were encountered. This presence before the authorities would offer to the Christians the opportunity to witness for the faith. Christians should not worry about their testimony before officialdom but should merely allow the spirit to bear witness through them (Matt. 10:19–20). The disciples were promised that family relations would be stretched to the breaking point and those among their own kin might be the ones to deliver them up (Matt. 10:21–22). Strained and trying relationships must have developed within early family circles that were only "part Christian" and most especially in those families that were part Christian, part Jewish.

The latter part of this sermon on missionary service offers a rationale and a framework within which persecution for the sake of the gospel could be understood and endured. (1) The servant (= the Christian) is not above his master (= the Christ). If Jesus' activity was designated as the work of Beelzebul, how much more can Jesus' followers expect their work to be maligned (Matt. 10:24–25). The Christians, in their suffering for the proclamation, can realize their solidarity with the Master, their membership in his household. (2) The disciples are assured of the special providence and care of God (Matt. 10:26–33; see Matt. 6:25–34). The disciples should not fear to proclaim the gospel openly, for the Father who oversees the sparrow and numbers the hairs of the head will surely care for those who acknowledge him before men. The Christian missionary must not fear man, who can only destroy the body; he must fear God, who can destroy body and soul in hell. (3) Persecution and suffering must be expected as the Christian's lot, for Jesus did not come to bring peace on earth but a sword. He came to set a man against the members of his own family (Matt. 10:34–36). Commitment to Jesus is the overriding requirement of faith; it is the factor that requires absolute loyalty; it transcends all human relationships and commitments (Matt. 10:37). The man who would follow Jesus must be willing to "take up his cross," face death squarely, but knowing that to lose one's life for him is to find one's own life (Matt. 10:38–39).

The sermon on missionary service concludes with the assurance that to receive a missionary or a prophet is to receive Jesus, and the least of deeds done for a disciple will never go unrewarded (Matt. 10:40–42).

The third discourse in the Gospel is a collection of sermon parables on the Kingdom (Matt. 13:1–52). The first of these is the parable of the sower (Matt. 13:3–23, 36–43), which has its parallel in Mark 4:1–20. The author of Matthew took over Mark's idea that the parables were taught to instruct the disciples in the secrets of the Kingdom and that to the outsiders they were a source of misunderstanding but he modifies this to some extent, substituting "because" (Matt. 13:13) in place of Mark's "so that" (Mark 4:12) and by quoting Ps. 78:2, which speaks of parables as the means to "utter what has been hidden since the foundation of the world" (Matt. 13:34–35). The use of the parable of the sower shows that there developed in the early church a way of understanding the parables in the light of the situation of the church rather than of leaving the parables as Jesus' proclamation of the coming Kingdom. In fact, Matthew seems to argue that "every scribe who has been trained for the kingdom of heaven" (Matt. 13:52) possesses the ability to interpret "the treasure" so as to bring out new insights. Elsewhere (Matt. 10:27), the writer suggests that the church possesses esoteric knowledge based on Jesus' teachings. The church is somewhat like a sect that possesses its special knowledge, but it is a sect whose "secrets" are openly proclaimed. The manner in which Jesus' parables were further understood is illustrated in the "second secret explanation" of the parable of the sower (Matt. 13:36–43). The Marcan material already contained one explanation (Matt. 13:10–23 = Mark 4:10–20). This second explanation of the parable is used to elucidate the presence of the church ("the sons of the kingdom") in the midst of the world alongside "the sons of the evil one." The harvest is the end, the time of judgment when the weeds will be burned and even the Kingdom purged. This interpretation of the parable does, however, suggest an interval before the final end.

The parable of the wheat and tares (Matt. 13:24–30, unique to Matthew) emphasizes the judgment and the separation to come at the time of harvest. The parable of the net (Matt. 13:47–50), which is also peculiar to Matthew, has a similar interest. The separation of the good fish from the bad cannot occur until the close of the age. Both of these parables, like the second interpretation of the parable of the sower, stress the punishment to come upon the evil and the bad, the weeds and the tares. This aspect of judgment, which falls even on some "within" the Kingdom should be compared with its counterpart, the emphasis on reward stressed in the Sermon on the Mount.

Two of the parables stress the secret presence of the Kingdom and encourage the awareness of the Kingdom's beginning with Jesus, even though in a small way and in an inconspicuous manner. These are the parables of the mustard seed (Matt. 13:31–32) and the leaven (Matt. 13:33). Two parables stress the absolute worth of the Kingdom, for which a man should be willing to sell all that he has (Matt. 13:44–45).

The fourth Matthean discourse is concerned with the question of the internal relationship between Christians and discipline within the church (Matt., ch. 18). Matthew has brought together material that has parallels in the other Synoptics (Matt. 18:1–14), uniting this around the idea of the members of the Kingdom as the "little ones," and supplementing this with traditions unique to the Gospel (Matt. 18:15–35). The first four pericopes (Matt. 18:1–14) stress the importance of even the least in the Kingdom. This section is introduced by a question about the greatest in the Kingdom, i.e., the question of rank. In the Qumran sect, for example, rank was a matter of serious concern both in the life of the actual community and in the concepts of the eschatological future. According to the Synoptics, Jesus taught that whoever humbled himself as a little child was the greatest in the Kingdom, and the early church avoided any internal esoteric hierarchy. Matthew warns that it would be better to be at the bottom of the sea weighted down with a millstone than to cause a little one to sin (Matt. 18:5–6). Temptation is necessary, but woe to the man by whom it comes (Matt. 18:7–9). The parable of the lost sheep is used to illustrate the concern of the Father for the little ones (Matt. 18:10–14).

The procedure for handling disputes in the church is laid down in Matt. 18:15–20. Only Matthew among the Gospels speaks of the church (here and in Matt. 16:18). This pericope on brotherly relations in the church presupposes a developing Christian community. Matthew stipulates that it is the brother sinned against who must take the initiative in settling disputes. The first step must be a face-to-face encounter between the parties in the dispute. If this does not settle matters, witnesses may be used to confirm the issues. After these two steps have been taken and have failed, the matter must be presented to the church, and if the offender refuses to listen to the church, he is to be excluded (excommunicated). The church is here given the power "to loose and to bind"; that is, it has the power to permit and prohibit with the assurance that what is agreed upon by the church on earth is confirmed in heaven. Elsewhere, this power to loose and to bind is given to Peter (Matt. 16:19). The Matthean material stresses the primacy of Peter and contains the saying of Jesus that declares Peter to be the rock upon which the church will be built and emphasizes him as the possessor of the keys of the Kingdom of heaven (Matt. 16:18–19).[14] The Gospel of Matthew must have had its origin in a circle of early Christianity in which Peter was held in high esteem. Peter's prominence during the lifetime of Jesus and in the life of the early church is however recognized by all the Synoptics and Acts; Matthew merely anchors this prominence in a direct promise of Jesus. This recognized regard for Peter, if Gal. 2:11–14 is any indication, would probably not have been characteristic of Pauline congregations.

Forgiveness for the offender must be unlimited—"seventy times seven" (Matt. 18:21–22). Matthew illustrates this last point with the parable of a king who

---

[14] On the importance and nature of Peter and the Matthean passages, see Oscar Cullmann, *Peter: Disciple—Apostle—Martyr*, 2d ed., tr. by Floyd V. Filson (The Westminster Press, 1962). On Peter and the church at Rome in the light of recent Vatican excavations, see D. W. O'Connor, *Peter in Rome: The Literary, Liturgical, and Archaeological Evidence* (Columbia University Press, 1969).

forgave a debtor who in turn was unwilling to forgive a fellow servant. The merciful king reacted in anger and withdrew his forgiveness of the debt and cast the debtor in prison (Matt. 18:23–35). As the king acted, so will God. The Christian who has been forgiven much must also forgive. He who does not forgive will not be forgiven.

The fifth major block of discourse material contains seven woes against the scribes and Pharisees (Matt., ch. 23), the Matthean version of Mark's little apocalypse (Matt., ch. 24), and three parables of the eschatological end and the judgment (Matt., ch. 25). The seven woes against the scribes and Pharisees represent some of the harshest and bitterest anti-Jewish polemic in the New Testament, which is after all a rather sharply anti-Jewish book. The developing antagonism between church and synagogue (note the absence of the Sadducees in this chapter) and the caricatures that evolved are clearly evidenced in much of the Matthean material. The scribes and Pharisees are condemned for preaching, not practicing, the burden of the law. They are described as hypocrites through and through, who do their religion to be seen by men and for their own honor and glory. This caricature serves as the occasion to repudiate the titles of rabbi and father and to proclaim that whoever exalts himself shall be humbled and whoever humbles himself shall be exalted (Matt. 23:1–12).

The first woe (Matt. 23:13) charges that the scribes and Pharisees will not enter the Kingdom nor will they allow others to enter. Perhaps behind this woe is to be seen the efforts of the Jewish leaders to prevent would-be converts from joining the Christian community. The second woe (Matt. 23:15) accuses the scribes and Pharisees of traversing sea and land to win a single proselyte and then turning him into twice the child of hell as they themselves. The third woe (Matt. 23:16–22) condemns them for respecting the gold of the Temple more than the Temple itself. The fourth woe (Matt. 23:23–24) declares that the Pharisees in their religion have an eye for the insignificant and the inconsequential but have a complete blindness for such weighty matters as justice, mercy, and faith. The original humor behind the saying about "straining out a gnat and swallowing a camel" fails to shine through in the context. The fifth woe (Matt. 23:25–26) describes them as observing an outward ceremonial cleanliness but neglecting the inner purity. The sixth woe (Matt. 23:27–28) declares the outward beauty of the Pharisaic practices to be the beauty of whitewashed sepulchers, a coating covering the bones and uncleanliness of the dead. The final woe (Matt. 23:29–36) condemns the scribes and Pharisees for adorning the monuments of the righteous (the prophets) while they (the Pharisees) are the descendants of the men who murdered the prophets. On their heads rests the blood of all the slain righteous, from the first, Abel, to the last, Zechariah the son of Barachiah.[15] It is predicted that the blood of the righteous will be required of the present (Matthew's own) generation.

This chapter concludes with Jesus' lament over Jerusalem (Matt. 23:37–39). "How often would I have gathered your children . . . and you would not."

---

[15] The identification of this figure is not certain. His death in A.D. 68 may be referred to in Josephus, Wars (IV. 5. 4).

Matthew here clearly has in mind the early church's proclamation to the Jews, for the Gospel records only one visit of Jesus to Jerusalem. The Jews are declared to be an obstinate people destined for desolation.

The apocalyptic material in Matt. 24:3–51 is a discussion of the "signs of the times" preceding the end (see II Thess. 2:1–12). Much of this material is exactly paralleled in Mark., ch. 13, but in its presynoptic form it is of diverse origin.[16] The church is warned that before the end many pretenders will come claiming to be the Messiah, and tribulations (wars, famines, and earthquakes) will be rampant in the world, but these are the suffering prelude to the final time (Matt. 24:3–8). Christians will be delivered up, hated among the nations, martyred for the cause, and be subjected to internal strife and heresy within the church. The gospel will be preached throughout the world before the end will come (Matt. 24:9–14). The great desecration of the Temple will take place in conjunction with an extravagant outburst of tribulation (Matt. 24:15–28). The reference to the "desolating sacrilege" was probably an apocalyptic interpretation of Caligula's action ordering an image to be set up in the Temple. The Gospel writers seem to have incorporated part of this material from a written (Jewish?) source. The Gospel of Luke (Luke 21:20–24) speaks, not of a sacrilege in the Temple, but of armies surrounding Jerusalem (A.D. 68–70?). Before the end of time, calamities in the world of nature will occur and cosmic disturbances will take place (see Amos 8:9–10 and Joel 2:30–32 for earlier use of the same imagery). Such cosmic disturbances will herald the coming of the Son of Man (Matt. 24:29–31).

Christians are warned to read the signs of the times and know that the end is near (Matt. 24:32–35). Just as the early leaves on the fig tree signal the onset of summer, so the signs of the time warn of the nearness of the end. Matthew believed that the time of the end was to come in his generation (Matt. 24:34). Although the end is near at hand, its actual arrival cannot be specifically pinpointed (Matt. 24:36–44). The end time will be like the days of Noah when the world was caught by the Flood. The hope of the Christian is preparedness, "for the Son of man is coming at an hour you do not expect" (Matt. 24:44). The day of the end will be a time of judgment not only for the world but also for Christians and the church (Matt. 24:45–51). The faithful and wise servant will be rewarded, but the wicked servant will be judged and punished along with the hypocrites.

Matthew's idea that at the end time Christians and the church will be judged by their obedience to the Christian torah[17] is further developed in Matt., ch. 25, through the use of three parables. (In a way, Matt. 25:31–46 is more of a prophetic vision than a parable. Only Matt. 25:14–30 has a parallel in the other Gospels—in Luke 19:11–27.) The parable of the ten virgins (Matt. 25:1–13) compares the end to a wedding party associated with the arrival of the bridegroom.

---

[16] See Lars Hartman, *Prophecy Interpreted: The Formation of Some Jewish Eschatological Texts and of the Eschatological Discourse Mark 13 Par.*, tr. by N. Tomkinson (Lund: C. W. K. Gleerup, 1966).

[17] Many scholars have attempted to explain away Matthew's emphasis on this point and the "legalistic" attitude of the Sermon on the Mount. See Sandmel, *The First Christian Century*, pp. 209–210.

The foolish virgins made no preparation for a delay in his arrival and thus they were caught without oil for their lamps. These foolish virgins (= unprepared members of the church) were excluded from the feast just as the unfaithful and unprepared Christians at the end time. The parable of the talents (or of the money left in trust) further develops the theme of the judgment of the church (Matt. 25:14–30). The parable told of a master who went on a trip but who, before departing, left money with his servants. Upon his return, the servants were required to account for their use of the entrusted funds. The faithful servants were rewarded, but the one servant who had not increased his trust was condemned and cast into outer darkness. For Matthew, this parable is an allegory. The master is Jesus; his departure is his resurrection; the funds are the responsibilities and requirements of the Kingdom; the return of the master is Jesus' Parousia; and the reckoning of accounts is the judgment of the church and Christians.

The collection of material around the theme of the end time and the judgment is concluded with the portrayal of the last judgment at the Parousia of the Son of Man (Matt. 25:31–46). At the coming of the Son of Man all the nations shall be judged and the sheep (righteous) and the goats (unrighteous) shall be separated, one to the right hand and the other to the left hand of his throne. The emphasis in the passage, however, falls not upon the judgment of the world but upon the judgment of the Christians or disciples about their obedience to the demands and needs of Jesus while the church awaits the Parousia. The needs of the rank-and-file brothers in the church (the hungry, the thirsty, the stranger, the naked, the sick, and the imprisoned) are the needs of the exalted Son of Man, for they are his representatives (see Matt. 10:40–42; 18:5–14). The absence of the Lord is the time of service, and the time of service will end with the time of judgment. For the Christian, there is no refuge in the sense or feeling of having served or of being righteous. The only refuge is obedient service to the representatives of Christ, to the commands of the teachings of Jesus.

Summary. The Gospel of Matthew portrays Jesus as the Messiah, the Son of David, the Son of God, the fulfiller of Old Testament prophecy, but above all as the Teacher. Jesus is the teacher who proclaims to his disciples a way of righteousness exceeding that of the scribes and Pharisees (Matt., chs. 5 to 7). This righteousness manifests itself in the Christian mission (Matt., ch. 10), is an integral part of the Kingdom (Matt., ch. 13), is the basis for life in the church (Matt., ch. 18), and at the coming of the Son of Man, the church and the disciples will be judged by their loyalty and obedience to this new torah, the way of righteousness (Matt., chs. 23 to 25).

The Gospel of Matthew appears to have been written as a summary of the Christian faith but with an emphasis on the instruction of Christians for life in the community, in the Kingdom of God.[18] It was more of course than a manual of discipline; it was a handbook on Christian theology but with an emphasis on the way of righteousness in the church, the new Israel of God.

---

[18] See Günther Bornkamm, "End-Expectation and Church in Matthew," in Bornkamm-Barth-Held, eds., *Tradition and Interpretation in Matthew*, pp. 15–51.

THE GOSPEL ACCORDING TO JOHN

In spite of decades of scholarly research and study,[19] the Fourth Gospel remains the most enigmatic writing in the New Testament. The enigma of the Gospel arises from our present inability to see it within the developing historical and theological mainstreams of early Christianity. It displays an independence from both the Pauline exposition of the Gospel and from the perspectives represented in the Synoptics. On the one hand, Paul emphasized the kerygma of Christ's death and resurrection as the unique redemptive act of God in history, looked forward to the Parousia as the culmination of the divine purpose, but largely disregarded the traditions about Jesus' life and their importance for Christian faith. The important thing for Paul was what God had done and would do in and through Jesus and not so much what Jesus himself had done. The Synoptics, on the other hand, emphasized and developed the traditions about the life of Jesus as a miracle-worker, divine teacher, suffering righteous one, as the Messiah who during his lifetime had demonstrated his messiahship. For Paul, the essence of the Christian faith must be accepting the deliverance wrought by God in Christ. For the Synoptics, emphasis was placed on the acceptance of the life and teachings of Jesus as the life and teachings of God's chosen one, to be followed by the believer and to serve as the pattern for Christian living. The Gospel of John was more interested in who Jesus was and in the new life he brought to his followers, but John chose to present this by an emphasis on the revelation of Jesus' true identity through the acts and teachings of his life.

The Fourth Gospel, then, belonged to the "periphery" of early church history and thought insofar as our present knowledge is concerned, although its periphery may turn out to have been far more widespread than has been previously recognized. Recent discoveries have brought to light the literature of two periphery movements associated with the mainstreams of early Judaism and Christianity. These are the Qumran Scrolls from the Dead Sea area of Palestine and early Christian Gnostic writings from Egypt. Among the latter are the Gospel of Thomas, the Gospel of Truth, and other as yet unpublished works.[20] The Gospel of John has its nearest parallels in the dualistic theology of Qumran, in the Gnostic literature from Egypt, and in the Syrian Mandean texts with their interests in John the Baptist. The origin of the Gospel is to be seen in a syncretistic environment where Christianity was in dialogue with and dependent upon a gnosticizing heterodox Judaism.

The earliest church reference to the origin and authorship of the Gospel comes from Irenaeus near the end of the second century. According to this church father, "John, the disciple of the Lord, who also leaned on his breast,

---

[19] See W. F. Howard, *The Fourth Gospel in Recent Criticism and Interpretation*, rev. by Charles K. Barrett (London: The Epworth Press, 1955); and the survey in Feine-Behm-Kümmel, *Introduction to the New Testament*, pp. 134–175.

[20] See James M. Robinson, "The Coptic Gnostic Library Today," *New Testament Studies*, XIV (1967/8), pp. 356–401.

himself produced his gospel, while he was living in Ephesus in Asia." [21] John here refers to John the son of Zebedee. The differences between the Synoptics and John (see above, p. 325) raise serious questions about the Gospel's authorship by an original disciple. Irenaeus' statement merely reflects the second-century church's desire to authenticate the Gospels by tracing their origin back to an apostle. Authorship must be left an open question, although Ephesus, especially with the presence there of a circle of the followers of John the Baptist (Acts 19:1–7), appears as likely a place of origin as any other. The purpose of the Gospel is summarized in the statement that "these are written that you may believe that Jesus is the Christ, the Son of God, and that believing you may have life in his name" (John 20:31).

The following is a very broad outline of the Gospel of John: (1) Prologue (John 1:1–18); (2) The revelation of Jesus to the world through sign and discourse (John 1:19–51; chs. 2 to 12); (3) Jesus' special revelation to his disciples and his return to the Father (John, chs. 13 to 20); and (4) Epilogue (John, ch. 21).

The Incarnation of the Divine Logos (John 1:1–18). The prologue to John is dominated by the idea of the Word (*logos*) become flesh.[22] The idea of the word, or *logos*, was widespread in the ancient world in both Jewish and Greek thought. The word of God in the Old Testament was what "came to" the prophets. In Greek thought, and especially in Stoicism, the *logos* was eternal, the universal reason. The idea of the word as the universal reason is not found in Judaism. The nearest idea to this in Hebrew literature is the description of "wisdom" as an eternal entity found in the book of The Proverbs (see above, pp. 255–258). For the Gospel writer, the concept of the *logos* is the means to express the status of the preincarnate Christ. The Word was in the beginning before creation. This is stressed in the fact that the two opening words of the Gospel are identical to the opening words of the book of Genesis. The Word was with God and was God. Not only was the *logos* divine; it was the agent of creation. Through him was light and life that permeated the darkness of the world. The world, however, did not know him and even his own received him not. The uniqueness of the Gospel's view of the *logos* is the writer's identification of Jesus with the eternal, divine Word, the stress on the incarnation ("became flesh") of the Word.

The early Christian emphasis on the exalted status of Jesus reached its apogee in the prologue to the Fourth Gospel. We have seen that in the early church there was one interpretation that stressed Jesus' sonship, his messiahship, as having begun at the resurrection-exaltation. For Mark, this sonship began at the baptism. In Matthew and Luke, the sonship was from birth. In John, the sonship is eternal. The life of Jesus represents a temporary incarnation of the only Son, the Logos. Jesus is the heavenly redeemer, the heavenly messenger,

---

[21] Translation is from Bettenson, *Documents of the Christian Church*, p. 40.
[22] See Ernst Käsemann, "The Structure and Purpose of the Prologue to John's Gospel," in his *New Testament Questions of Today*, tr. by W. J. Montagne (Fortress Press, 1969), pp. 138–167.

who fulfills his work on earth to return to that glory which he had with God the Father before the world was made (John 17:5).

The Revelation to the World (John 1:19–51; chs. 2 to 12). Jesus, the incarnation of the divine Son, revealed his status to the world through signs and sermons. This was a status witnessed to by John the Baptist but recognized only by those who become children of God (John 1:12–13).

The manner in which the Gospel writer portrays the acts of Jesus and the fashion in which he presents the teachings of Jesus raises questions about his knowledge of the Synoptic traditions.[23] The differences between John and the Synoptics suggest that he was not dependent upon these in a literary form or at least did not feel himself bound to them. The sermons or discourses of Jesus are more the author's meditations than the actual words of Jesus. The writer was certainly familiar with the general outline of Jesus' ministry, for he begins it with Jesus' relation to John the Baptist and ends it with the crucifixion-resurrection account, which is similar in broad detail to that of the Synoptics. As was suggested earlier (see above, p. 345), his broad picture of Jesus' relationship with the Baptist may be more historical than that of the Synoptics. He may have been dependent in this regard upon the Baptist circles in Ephesus.[24] The writer was not so much interested in the actual events of the life of Jesus as he was in the symbolic character of those traditions he has recorded. Even the actual historical relation between John and Jesus is not really a concern of the writer. John merely functions as a pointer "to bear witness to the light" (John 1:6–8).

In the Gospel's discussion of John (John 1:19–51; 3:22–36), the latter displays no doubt about Jesus' true identity, nor do his disciples. John appears as a Christian preacher who recognizes and proclaims the truth about Jesus. John, like his disciples, is the ideal Jew, "an Israelite indeed, in whom is no guile" (John 1:47), one who unlike the other Jews recognized Jesus as equal with God (John 5:18).

The Gospel presents Jesus' revelation of himself to the world by narrating seven mighty acts of Jesus that the author calls signs and by giving discourses of Jesus that explain his person and function. In addition to the signs and sermons, there are other acts of Jesus that show Jesus and Christianity as the fulfillment and replacement of the "symbols" of Judaism. The organization of material into narrative and discourses is not unique to the Fourth Gospel. Matthew also employed this tactic with an even more rigidly structured scheme than John but of course with a greatly different interest and set of traditions.

The first sign of Jesus was the turning of water into wine at a marriage feast in Cana of Galilee (John 2:1–12). At the wedding, the supply of wine was depleted and Jesus ordered that six stone jars used "for the Jewish rites of purification" (John 2:6) be filled with water. This was then miraculously changed into wine that far exceeded the quality of the previous wine. The act is depicted

---

[23] See C. H. Dodd, *Historical Tradition in the Fourth Gospel* (Cambridge: Cambridge University Press, 1963).

[24] See Ernst Käsemann, "The Disciples of John the Baptist in Ephesus," in his *Essays on New Testament Themes*, pp. 136–148.

as a sign that the way of Jesus, symbolized by the marvelous wine, transforms and exceeds the way of the Jews, symbolized by the water and the stone jars. Jesus reveals himself as the "bringer of the new."

The newness of the way is further illustrated by John's placement of the story of the cleansing of the Temple after the marriage episode (John 2:13–25). This tradition is similar to that found in the Synoptics, but the latter have obviously preserved its original historical context. Jesus, at the Feast of Passover, announces the replacement of the Temple with "his body." "Destroy this temple, and in three days I will raise it up" (John 2:19) is an allusion to his resurrection (John 2:22) but perhaps also to be understood in terms of the church as the replacement of Judaism.

Two dialogues serve as counterparts to the two acts and further develop the concept of the newness. The dialogues are really discourses in which the person other than Jesus serves merely as the means for developing the theme. The first of these is with the Pharisee Nicodemus, a ruler of the Jews (John 3:1–21). The discourse method of the writer can be clearly seen in this section. Unlike the preaching of Jesus in the Synoptics, Jesus in the Fourth Gospel gives long speeches developing a single theme. (This tendency one can also see in Matthew's use of compilations around a single theme.) The theme is developed not by a collection of sayings or parables but through a meditative monologue that explores the various aspects of the theme. In this regard, it is almost impossible to tell where the discourse of Jesus ends and the meditative explanation of the writer begins. (Note the RSV footnotes to this passage). The participant in the dialogue raises an issue or is confronted with a statement by Jesus. The answer of Jesus is misunderstood, and further dialogue and discourse follow pursuing the central theme. In the discourse with Nicodemus, the theme is the question of the new birth and its necessity to enter the Kingdom. Water can be transformed into wine, people must be born "anew" (or "from above": the word can be translated either way and was no doubt chosen deliberately because of this possibility). Nicodemus misunderstands the reference to being born again, taking it literally. Jesus explains that it is a spiritual thing. Nicodemus replies, "How can this be?" Jesus' answer is that only he, who has descended from heaven, can bear witness and that coming to and believing in him who has been sent is the way to escape judgment and to see the light. Jesus' coming into the world is judgment; belief in him means that the judgment is past. In Jesus' speech to Nicodemus, one can see the writer's love of expressing his belief in symbols by using words with double meanings (again/above, spirit/wind) and by symbolical and dualistic contrasts (earthly/heavenly, world/heaven, light/darkness, spirit/flesh).

The conversation with the woman at the well also emphasizes the aspect of newness (John 4:1–42). Jesus requests water from the woman, who is surprised that a Jew would ask a drink from a Samaritan. Jesus responds with a discussion of the living water which is free to anyone who will drink and which grants eternal life (John 4:7–15). Then follows a discussion of worship in which Jesus declares the worship in Jerusalem and on Mt. Gerizim (the sacred mountain for the Samaritans) is superseded by the worship of God in spirit (John 4:16–26). Emphasis is placed on "the hour is coming, and now is" for Jesus is the

Messiah, the bringer of the spirit, and the one who will show all things. In other words, with the coming of Jesus, the true worship is Christian worship under the power of the Spirit. The conversation with the Samaritan woman then leads many others to belief because of her testimony (John 4:27–30, 39–42) and allows the writer to emphasize that with Jesus the hour of harvest has arrived (John 4:31–38).

The second sign of Jesus was the healing of an official's son (John 4:46–54). This is immediately followed by the account of the healing of an invalid man at the Pool of Bethzatha in Jerusalem on a Sabbath during a Jewish festival (John 5:1–18). The child in the former account was healed without Jesus even seeing the lad, and the man at the pool was cured after an illness of thirty-eight years but without knowing who Jesus was. The fact that the healing took place on the Sabbath and Jesus' statement that "my Father is working still, and I am working" (John 5:17) raises the question of Jesus' authority. This question is then answered in Jesus' speech on the nature of his authority (John 5:19–47). Jesus claims that his authority is the authority of the Father granted to the Son. This authority is the authority to execute judgment as the Son of Man. He who responds to Jesus in belief does not come into judgment, for he has passed already into life. There are three witnesses who testify that Jesus has been sent by the Father and is thus the Son of Man, the executor of judgment. These are John the Baptist (John 5:31–35), the works which Jesus accomplishes (John 5:36), and the Father who has sent him, who bears witness through the writings of the Scriptures (John 5:37–47).

The fourth and fifth signs are given in the account of the multiplication of the loaves and fish to feed five thousand (John 6:1–14) and the walking on the sea (John 6:15–21). These are then followed by Jesus' discourse and dialogue with the Jews and his disciples on himself as being the bread of life (John 6:22–71) and by further discourse and dialogue in Jerusalem at the Feast of Tabernacles in Jerusalem concerning Jesus as the one from above sent by God (John, chs. 7; 8).

The miracles of the fourth and fifth signs are very similar to the parallel accounts in Mark 6:31–52. The response of the people following the feeding was an effort to "take him by force to make him king" (John 6:15), a reference not found in the Synoptics but which may reflect an authentic recollection of efforts to rally a nationalistic movement around Jesus. The unique factor in the Fourth Gospel is Jesus' discourse on himself as the "bread of life," "the food which endures to eternal life." Jesus discourses on himself as the bread which comes down from heaven and gives life to the world. Jesus is the new manna from heaven but unlike the old manna in the wilderness, the new manna offers life, for "if any one eats of this bread, he will live for ever; and the bread which I shall give for the life of the world is my flesh" (John 6:51). The sacramental interpretation of the Eucharist in which the bread and wine are understood as the flesh and blood of Jesus, which grants eternal life, is clearly reflected in Jesus' statement that "he who eats my flesh and drinks my blood has eternal life" (John 6:54).

The second dialogue and discussion following the fourth and fifth signs is placed in Jerusalem (John, chs. 7; 8). In this, Jesus speaks of himself as the one doing the will of God unlike the Jews who do not even obey the law (John 7:16–24). He proclaims himself as the one sent by God (John 7:25–36), as the source of living water (John 7:37–39), as the light of the world and the one from above to which he would return (John 8:12–59).[25] These sayings are interspersed with a condemnation of "the Jews" (not scribes, Pharisees, and Sadducees as in the Synoptics) for their failure to keep the law (John 7:19) and to accept two witnesses (the Father and Jesus) as true, as their law required (John 8:15–18) and for their departure from Abraham, who rejoiced to see "the day" that the contemporary Jews were dishonoring (John 8:31–59).

The sixth sign is found in the account of Jesus' healing of a man blind from birth at the pool of Siloam in Jerusalem (John 9:1–17). This is then followed by dialogue between the healed man and the Jews (here occasionally referred to as Pharisees) in which the healed bears witness to Jesus (John 9:18–34). This is then followed by a discourse of Jesus on himself as door of the sheepfold and the good shepherd (John 10:1–38). The interrelationship between the sign, the dialogue, and the discourse is centered in the question of discipleship to Jesus. The healed man was banned from the synagogue because of his confession that Jesus was the Christ (John 9:22, 34). This presupposes a condition in which the church and the synagogue were squared off against each other. Jesus assures the excommunicated of the validity of his decision (John 9:35–41) and in the discourse assures the Christians and would-be converts that Jesus is the true shepherd, the door to the sheepfold, and that his followers are the true sheep possessing eternal life and security. The status of Jesus as the true shepherd is founded on his action of laying down his life for his sheep like a real shepherd (John 10:11–18) and on his relationship to the Father: "I and the Father are one" (John 10:30); "The Father is in me and I am in the Father" (John 10:38).

The seventh and final sign in the revelation of Jesus to the world is found in the account of the raising of Lazarus (John 11:1–44). This sign of the resurrection of Lazarus, who had been dead for four days, forms the point of departure for the remainder of Jesus' revelation to the world (John 11:45 to 12:36a). The chief priests and the Pharisees react to the sign by seeking means of putting Jesus to death in order to preserve peace (John 11:47–53). But even these bore hidden witness to Jesus, for the high priest realized that "it is expedient for you that one man should die for the people" (John 11:50). Many others believed because of this sign (John 11:45). Six days before the Passover, Jesus was again with Lazarus (John 12:1–8), and crowds gathered because of the sign of Lazarus (John 12:9–11). The crowds who greeted Jesus at the triumphal entry (John 12:12–19) were a continuation of the people's response to the raising of Lazarus (John 12:17–18). The theme of the resurrection is the topic of Jesus' conversation with the Greeks who had come to Jerusalem for the festival (John 12:20–26). It is also the point of departure for Jesus' comment on his glorification (John 12:23–26) and his exposition of his death and resurrection as the lifting up of the Son of Man (John 12:27–36a).

---

[25] The pericope of the woman taken in adultery (given in older translation as John 7:53 to 8:11) appears in some early texts of John at this point; in other texts at the end of the Gospel; not at all in some; and one text places it after Luke 21:38.

The conclusion to the section on Jesus' revelation to the world is given in John 12:36b–50. The conclusion is twofold. There is first a summary statement (John 12:36b–43) which explains that "though he had done so many signs before them, yet they did not believe in him" (John 12:37) in terms of the words of Isaiah (Isa. 53:1; 6:10) about the revealing of the arm of the Lord and the hardening of the heart and the blinding of the eyes. The people's general failure to believe is understood as the fulfillment of prophecy. The second part of the conclusion is presented as a speech of Jesus (John 12:44–50) in which he declares that he has come as light into the world being sent by the Father and that whoever believes in him believes in the One who sent him. The emphasis in the speech falls on those who hear his sayings and fail to obey, rejecting both Jesus and his sayings. For these, there is reserved a day of judgment when Jesus' word will serve as the instrument of judgment.

Jesus' Revelation to His Own and the Return to the Father (John, chs. 13 to 20). The last major section in the Gospel contains Jesus' special revelation and teachings to his disciples and the account of the trial, crucifixion, and resurrection. In the narrative portion of this material, John adheres fairly closely to the account of the traditions of the passion as these seem to have been developed in the early church. The major differences between the Fourth Gospel and the Synoptics are the former's interpretation of the last supper and the omission of any reference to the Eucharistic words of Jesus, the different date of the crucifixion (see above, p. 363), and the insertion of a lengthy discourse of Jesus into the context of the farewell meal.

In John, the last supper of Jesus is presented without any reference to Jesus' breaking of bread and the drinking of the cup (John 13:1–30). The meal is not presented as a Passover celebration. The Fourth Gospel does not anchor the observance of the Eucharist to the last supper but instead places Jesus' teaching in the context of the discourse on the feeding of the five thousand (John 6:22–58). That John knew of a sacramental interpretation of the observance there can be no doubt (John 6:53). The Fourth Gospel emphasizes Jesus' washing of the disciples' feet, an act illustrating the humble service of the Teacher and Lord, a service to be imitated in the church (John 13:12–20). Jesus' response to his disciples, Simon Peter in particular, and their reaction to the foot washing stresses the form of obedient service to one another within the Christian community.

Judas Iscariot is shown leaving the meal before Jesus begins his discourses to the disciples and his prayer to the Father (John 13:21–30). One wonders if the writer did not avoid mention of the Eucharist words in the context of the meal because of the presence of Judas (and Satan in him; John 13:2, 27) at the supper. After the departure of Judas, Jesus begins his dialogue and discourse with his disciples. As in many of the other discourses, the writer uses the misunderstanding of the disciples to further the discourse of Jesus. Jesus describes the approaching hour as the time of the glorification of the Son of Man (John 13:31–32) and stresses the new commandment to love one another (John 13:33–35). The misunderstanding of Peter concerning Jesus' reference to his "going" (John 13:36–38) introduces Jesus' speech in ch. 14 and the dialogue progresses with questions from Thomas, Philip, and Judas (not Iscariot). The speech stresses Jesus' return to the Father (John 14:1–7) and his identity with the Father (John 14:8–11). The disciples are assured of the greater works they will do (John 14:12–14). Jesus promises the disciples that when he goes away the Father will send the counselor, the Holy Spirit, who will teach them all things and make manifest all that Jesus has taught them (John 14:15–31). Throughout there is an emphasis on Jesus' love of the Father, the command-ment to love one another and Jesus, and the promise that those who love the Son will be loved by the Father.

John, chs. 15 to 16, reiterates many of the themes of the preceding chapter but introduces two new elements. In John 15:1–11, the relationship between Jesus and his followers is described as the relationship of the branches to a vine. As the branches remain on the vine, they bear fruit; branches that do not bear fruit are to be cut off and thrown into the fire and burned. One could say that this figure of the vine and the branches reflects the Fourth Gospel's doctrine of the church in a manner comparable to Paul's idea of the church as the body of Christ. The second new element is the hatred of the world for the Christians who are to be hated as was Jesus and persecuted like him (John 15:18 to 16:11). The return of Jesus to the Father, a motif found throughout the Gospel, is dealt with again in John 16:16–33. "I came from the Father and have come into the world; again, I am leaving the world and going to the Father" (John 16:28).

Jesus' prayer to the Father in John, ch. 17,[26] on behalf of the disciples requests that they may be kept in the Father's name, that they may be preserved from the evil one, that they may be one as the Son and the Father are one, and that they may be in his presence to behold his glory given before the foundation of the world.

One or two features in the resurrection appearances of John call for special notice. One of these is the emphasis on the giving of the spirit before the ascen-sion. Jesus is said to have appeared to the disciples after the resurrection and to have commissioned them to go into the world even as Jesus had come into the world (John 20:19–21). For their special task, Jesus breathes upon them the Holy Spirit and grants them the power to forgive sin (John 20:22–23). Per-haps the original conclusion of the Gospel, excluding the statement of purpose in John 20:30–31, is to be found in Thomas' confession of faith, "My Lord and my God!" (John 20:28), and Jesus' response: "Have you believed because you have seen me? Blessed are those who have not seen and yet believe" (John 20:29).

Epilogue. Chapter 21 of the Gospel appears to be an addendum added to the work after the original conclusion at John 20:30–31. Whether by the original author or by someone else is difficult to tell. This appendix contains the account of an appearance to the disciples beside the Sea of Tiberias (Galilee) and the associated miraculous catch of fish (John 21:1–14; see Luke 5:1–11). The chapter also contains a special concern with Simon Peter and the "disciple whom

---

[26] See Ernst Käsemann, *The Testament of Jesus: According to John 17,* tr. by G. Krodel (Fortress Press, 1968). He discusses not only this chapter but the whole of Johannine thought.

Jesus loved" who appears elsewhere in the Gospel (John 13:23; 19:26; 20:2) but is never identified. John 21:24 claims that the Gospel was written by this disciple, which tends to suggest that all of ch. 21 was added to the original Gospel after the death of Peter and "the disciple whom Jesus loved."

Summary. If it can be said that the historical Jesus proclaimed the Kingdom of God and the early church proclaimed Jesus, then in the Gospel of John, Jesus proclaims himself. Jesus is presented in the Fourth Gospel as the worker of signs which declared him as the one "equal to God, the incarnate *logos*." Jesus is the one from the heavenly world, who knows all things, who descends to the world, who reveals his glory before men and to his disciples, and who returns to the heavenly world from which he came. For the writer, it is the significance of the Christ that matters, not the details about Jesus. For the author, Jesus was, before the creation of the world and during his ministry, what the early church claimed he was following the resurrection: the divine Son of God.

22 | CONFLICT AND CONSOLIDATION IN THE DEVELOPING CHURCH

The Christian movement which began as a small eschatological sect in Judaism had spread, by the end of the first century, to practically all the major urban centers of the Mediterranean world. There were many factors that contributed to the rapid expansion of the Christian faith in its earliest days. Foremost among these was the understanding of the gospel as public proclamation. The early Christians saw themselves as the possessors of a unique message, with only a limited time before the end in which to proclaim it. This aspect was no doubt a characteristic taken over by the church from the ministry of Jesus. A second factor was the nature of the Christian "ministry." In the church and the world, any Christian could proclaim the faith. Many of the chief agents in the expansion of Christianity were men and women who were engaged in "secular" professions but who could bear witness to the faith. It is indeed surprising how little a role the original disciples associated with Jesus played in the spread of Christianity. Only Peter stands out, in the material of the New Testament, as a major missionary personality. A third factor of consequence was the network of synagogues in the Jewish Diaspora. These offered a ready audience both among the Jews and the half-proselytized "God-fearing" Greeks who had been attracted to Judaism. Paul's gospel of a law-free Christianity must have been very appealing to the latter, for it offered them the attractive elements of Judaism without the necessity of obedience to the law. The Jewish revolt against Rome (A.D. 66–70) perhaps tarnished the luster of Judaism in the Greco-Roman world and weakened its cause. As a result, Jewish missionary work among the Gentiles was hindered, from which the church's activity probably profited. A final factor in the spread of Christianity was the existence of the church, especially in its Hellenistic form, as a cult. In spite of the church's aggressive proclamation of the gospel, it also possessed its initiation ritual (baptism), closed meals (the agape meal and the Eucharist), and a strong sense of communal fellowship. In addition, like the cults, the church was not a national or state religion but a fellowship, a society, transcending the boundaries of local allegiances and cutting across the levels of the social strata.

Biblical readings: The primary material discussed in this chapter is found in Hebrews, Colossians, Revelation, the pastoral epistles (I and II Timothy; Titus), and the Johannine letters (I, II, and III John).

The initial phase of the church's expansion is called the apostolic age. The idea of the age of the apostles as distinct from later periods is already reflected in the New Testament writers, especially in Luke-Acts. To a limited extent, the idea that a new stage of church history began during the 60's has validity. With the death of Peter and Paul in the persecution of Nero (A.D. 64), the death of James in Jerusalem (A.D. 62), and the Jewish revolt against the Romans (A.D. 66–70), a new situation did develop in the church that can be appropriately called the post-apostolic age. This was a time of conflict and consolidation for the developing church which lasted until the middle of the second century. In this final chapter, we shall survey the reflection of this conflict and consolidation as it found expression in the New Testament.

THE FATE OF JEWISH CHRISTIANITY

The center of early Jewish Christianity was the mother church in Jerusalem. Unfortunately, our knowledge of the life and fate of Palestinian Jewish Christianity is severely limited, for the source material is so sparse and laconic.[1] The material is limited to the New Testament (mainly the book of Acts), an occasional reference by Josephus, and the rather legendary statements found in Christian sources from the second and fourth centuries. Leadership of the Jerusalem church quickly passed from Peter and the other apostles to James the brother of Jesus. By the time of Paul's first visit to the Jerusalem church (Gal. 1:18–20), James was already a leader of the community.

Jewish Christians formed a sect within the larger Jewish community in Jerusalem. Unlike the members of the Qumran community, Christian Jews did not withdraw from their fellow countrymen, nor did they repudiate the life and faith of contemporary Judaism. This relationship between Christian and non-Christian Jews was obviously fraught with a potential for tension, and the ability of the two groups to live together speaks well of Jewish-Christian relations in those early days and suggests both toleration and restraint.

With the development of a greater self-awareness by the Christian community, tension became inevitable and passed beyond the level of harassment. Open hostility developed with the Hellenist Stephen's frontal attack on Judaism (Acts, ch. 7). It should be recalled, however, that the Hellenists had been a source of tension within the Jewish-Christian community (Acts 6:1) prior to the altercation between Stephen and the Jewish leaders that resulted in his being stoned. Unfortunately, the nature and reasons behind the persecution of Christians carried out by Saul are not known. But the way was opened for a general deterioration between the two communities. Roman authority and the fear of disturbing the *status quo* may have been factors in reducing open confrontations.

When Herod Agrippa I was king in Jerusalem (A.D. 41–44), he openly persecuted the Christian community and "laid violent hands upon some who be-

---

[1] See Hans-Joachim Schoeps, *Jewish Christianity: Factional Disputes in the Early Church*, tr. by D. R. A. Hare (Fortress Press, 1969).

longed to the church" (Acts 12:1). James the son of Zebedee was executed, and Peter imprisoned (Acts 12:2–5). According to Acts, this pleased the Jews. There are no references to this persecution by Herod in the writings of Josephus. Presumably the persecution of the Christians, if the tradition is authentic, was a way Herod used in seeking to gain the general support of the Jewish population. Herod's sudden death, which Josephus reports came as the result of abdominal ills that seized him while at the theater in Caesarea, was interpreted by the Christians as punishment from God (Acts 12:20–23).

James was martyred in Jerusalem in ca. A.D. 62. According to Josephus, he was stoned along with "certain others" at the instigation of the high priest Ananus. The high priest was able to carry out this execution because of a

Chart 12: EARLY CHRISTIANITY (A.D. 30–135)

A.D.	EVENTS IN THE CHURCH	EVENTS IN THE ROMAN EMPIRE
	Stoning of Stephen (32?)	
	Conversion of Paul (32?)	
		Caligula (37–41)
		Order to erect statue in Jerusalem Temple
		Claudius (41–54)
	Execution of James, son of Zebedee (44)	Herod Agrippa I, king of parts of Palestine (41–44)
	Jerusalem conference (49?)	Expulsion of Jews from Rome (49)
50	Paul in Corinth (51–52)	
		Nero (54–68)
	Paul arrested in Jerusalem	
	Martyrdom of James, the brother of Jesus, in Jerusalem (62)	
	Martyrdom of Paul and Peter in Rome (64?)	Persecution of Christians (64)
		Jewish revolt against Rome (66–73)
		Destruction of Qumran (68)
		Destruction of Temple (70)
		Fall of Masada (73)
		Struggle over Roman rule, (Galba, Otho, Vitellius, 68–69)
		Vespasian (69–79)
75		
		Titus (79–81)
	Some persecution of Christians	Domitian (81–96)
		Jewish Council at Jamnia (90?)
100		Nerva (96–98)
	Martyrdom of Ignatius (107?)	Trajan (98–116)
	Persecution of church	Jewish uprisings in Cyrene, Egypt, and Cyprus (115–117)
125	Papias, bishop of Hierapolis	Hadrian (117–138)
		Jewish revolt led by Bar-Cochba (132–135)
		Capture of Jerusalem

temporary vacancy in the Roman procuratorship. According to a second-century Christian account, James was killed by a Jerusalem mob. At the Passover, he was asked to give his judgment concerning Jesus and when he proclaimed him as the Son of Man, he was thrown down from the pinnacle of the Temple, stoned, and clubbed to death. There seems no reason to doubt that he suffered a martyr's death in the early 60's. Why James was put to death cannot be determined. Were the Jews merely waiting for an opportunity to assault the Christians and did they take advantage of the absence of a procurator to act? Or did the Jews oppose the Christians for their unwillingness to take part in the opposition toward Rome which was building to a climax? James was succeeded by Symeon, a cousin of Jesus.

What part the Jewish Christians played in the revolt against Rome is an open question. A Christian tradition from the early third century says that, just before the Romans lay siege to Jerusalem, the Christians fled the city in a group and migrated to the Gentile city of Pella, east of the Jordan.[2] This tradition is difficult to accept. How could the Christians have fled the city which was threatened or already under siege and cross miles of territory held by the Roman armies, which could scarcely be counted on to differentiate between Christian Jews and any other sort? Early in the revolt, Jewish nationalists had attacked Pella, one of the cities of the Decapolis, and the town could hardly be expected to be overly friendly to a newly arriving Jewish group. There may have been some migration to Pella before the open revolt, and the legend of the general flight may be a "foundation story" to explain the existence of the later extensive Christian community there. It has recently been argued that the Jewish Christians in Jerusalem and elsewhere in Palestine retained their fidelity to the nationalism of the Jews and fought and died alongside their fellow countrymen in the siege of the Holy City.[3] There may be an element of truth in such a view.

For the subsequent history of Jewish Christianity, we are dependent upon references from the second- and fourth-century writers. Mention is made in these to Jewish Christians called Ebionites ("the poor ones") and Nazarenes (or Nazorenes). The latter is used as a name for Christians in Acts 24:5 (see Matt. 2:23) and the former may have been already applied to Jerusalem Christians (see Gal. 2:10; Rom. 15:26; Luke 6:20). The Ebionites stressed the observance of the Jewish law and tradition.[4] They denied the virgin birth of Jesus, rejected the Gentile mission, and were vegetarians. Among these Jewish Christians, James was highly venerated and was presented as a man of outstanding Jewish piety. He is said to have been a Nazirite (one devoted to the deity) from his mother's womb, abstaining from strong drink and animal food and from cutting his hair. According to tradition he spent so much time on his knees in intercessory prayer that his knees were calloused like those of a camel.

---

[2] On this tradition and the possibility of the flight, see Elliott-Binns, *Galilean Christianity*, pp. 65–70; and for a different evaluation of the evidence, see Brandon, *The Fall of Jerusalem*, pp. 167–177.

[3] See Brandon, *Jesus and the Zealots*, pp. 198–220.

[4] See Joseph A. Fitzmyer, S. J., "The Qumran Scrolls, the Ebionites, and Their Literature," in Stendahl, ed., *The Scrolls and the New Testament*, pp. 208–231.

The Jewish Christian sects, a sad shadow of the original Jerusalem church, faded from the pages of history. With the separation of Judaism and Christianity into two antagonistic groups, there was little place for a community with one foot in each camp.

There is no writing in the New Testament whose origin can with any certainty be attributed to Palestinian Jewish Christianity. The book that seems to have the closest affinity to Jewish Christian thought is The Letter of James.[5] This writing, which is addressed "to the twelve tribes in the Dispersion" (James 1:1) or the church as the New Israel in the Greco-Roman world (see I Peter 1:1), is attributed to "James, a servant of God and of the Lord Jesus Christ" (James 1:1). Although there are five different Jameses mentioned in the New Testament, the reference here is undoubtedly to James the brother of Jesus. Serious doubt has been raised about whether he was the author, however. This doubt rests on the following arguments: (1) The letter's authority was disputed in the early church; (2) the first reference to the letter's authorship by the brother of the Lord comes from the early fourth century; (3) one with James' position would probably have made mention of his position; and (4) the writing is composed in excellent Greek style, which would not seem to have been the manner in which James might have written. Most scholars view the book as the composition (or adaption of an original Jewish writing) of a Hellenistic Jewish Christian who did give expression to a form of Jewish Christianity.

The book is not so much an epistle (note the absence of any farewell or benediction) as it is an essay on ethics. Like much of the proverbial wisdom of the Old Testament, the work has no methodical train of thought that binds the whole together. The writing is a collection of aphorisms and precepts interspersed with occasional brief discussions.

The primary focus of James is the emphasis on the necessity of works. Men must "be doers of the word, and not hearers only" (James 1:22). A person who is only a hearer and not a doer is like a person who sees himself in a mirror but quickly forgets what he is like. The Christian must look into "the perfect law, the law of liberty" and, having seen its demands, must become a performer of what the law requires (James 1:23–25). Religion for the writer is, at heart, a matter of ethics.

> Religion that is pure and undefiled before God and the Father is this: to visit orphans and widows in their affliction, and to keep oneself unstained from the world. (James 1:27.)

The law of liberty is the standard of both behavior and judgment (James 1:25; 2:12). Adherence to the law requires complete obedience. "For whoever keeps the whole law but fails in one point has become guilty of all of it" (James 2:10). The writer, however, disavows any boasting about obedience to the law or good works. Man cannot boast even about tomorrow, for life is only "a mist that appears for a little time and then vanishes" (James 4:14). Obedience to the law is merely doing what is right and "whoever knows what is right to do and fails to do it, for him it is sin" (James 4:17).

---

[5] See Feine-Behm-Kümmel, *Introduction to the New Testament*, pp. 284–292.

In its ethical admonitions, the book encourages the members to endure temptation through self-control, realizing that their temptations come from desire rather than from God (James 1:2–15). Steadfastness and patience in good will be rewarded, and the Christian must display the patience of Job (James 1:12; 5:7–11). Relationships among the Christians must be based on impartiality; one must not show favoritism toward the rich (James 2:1–7), for wealth is, after all, a fleeting and impermanent thing (James 5:1–6) generally acquired through dishonorable means (James 2:6–7). The tongue is one of man's supreme problems, for it reacts so quickly to lack of self-control and yet is so destructive (James 3:1–12). Speaking evil against another is to usurp the role of God as judge and is to be strongly condemned (James 4:11–12). Instead of judging, one should seek to return the sinner to the truth (James 5:19–20). The writer recommends prayer and the anointment with oil for the sick (James 5:13–15) and states that prayer and mutual confession to one another are means to forgiveness and healing (James 5:16–18).

Perhaps the most prominent element in the book, from the viewpoint of the development of theology, is the writer's rebuttal of the idea of salvation apart from works (James 2:14–26). According to him, faith without works is dead. The demons believe in God and shudder from their belief—but they are still demons. A hungry and ill-clad man receives no help if he is merely told to "go in peace, be warmed and filled" without having had his needs met. Abraham was "justified by works and not by faith alone," for he believed but he was also willing to offer up his son Isaac as a sacrifice. Rahab, the prostitute, was saved because she was willing to aid the messengers sent to her—she took action. "So faith apart from works is dead" just as the body without the spirit is lifeless (James 2:26).

Was the writer here deliberately attacking Paul's teaching on salvation through faith apart from works? His description of the position he is attacking ("faith apart from your works"), the quotation from Gen. 15:6 ("Abraham believed God, and it was reckoned to him as righteousness"), and the use of Abraham throughout the argument strongly suggest that he was directly familiar with Paul's writings (especially Galatians) or with persons who espoused Paul's point of view. That the writer of James believed the proclamation of salvation by faith apart from works was detrimental seems obvious. His work must be seen as an attempt to counterbalance this aspect of the Pauline gospel. The inclusion of the book in the New Testament canon, along with Matthew, went a long way toward neutralizing Paul's special emphasis on justification by faith.

THE CHURCH AND THE ROMAN EMPIRE

Conflict between the Roman Empire and Christianity was slow in developing.[6] For a time, Christians were such a minute minority in the Empire that they caused no major stir. In addition, as long as Christianity was considered and

---

[6] See Frend, *Martyrdom and Persecution in the Early Church*, pp. 113–172; and Cullmann, *The State in the New Testament*.

considered itself a part of the Jewish community, the Christians were not very visible. Judaism's position as a legally acceptable religion in the Empire was well established in spite of the anti-Jewish sentiment that occasionally surfaced. With Christianity's developing separation from Judaism and its numerical growth, tension and eventual conflict were almost inevitable.

The non-Jewish hostile treatment of Christians, which appears occasionally in the book of Acts, was the local action of those intent on preserving the peace or else consisted of general harassment by the population at large. The earliest persecution of Christians stemmed from general social pressures rather than from official imperial policy.

The first open persecution of Christians by Roman authority of which we have knowledge occurred in association with the great Roman fire in A.D. 64 during the reign of Nero. This extensive conflagration which severely damaged

Nero and Vespasian were oppressors of Christians and Jews. Nero (A.D. 54–68), at left, blamed the Christians for the Roman fire which began July 19, 64, and subjected them to humiliating and atrocious treatment. Vespasian (A.D. 69–79), on the right, was appointed to command the Roman forces against the Jews in the Great Rebellion. He left the field before the fall of Jerusalem to assume the office of emperor.

AMERICAN NUMISMATIC ASSOCIATION

ten of the fourteen districts of the city was rumored to have been started by Nero, who wished to enlarge his palace complex and gardens. Nero sought to shift the blame to the Christians and inflicted on them a multitude of "exquisite tortures." Some were, according to Tacitus' account,[7] wrapped in animal skins and torn apart by dogs; others were crucified and set aflame after being soaked in oil. Nero threw open his gardens for the spectacle and drove about in his chariot.

[7] Given in Bettenson, *Documents of the Christian Church*, pp. 1–2.

The fact that Christians could be blamed for the fire suggests that they were recognized as a distinct element among the citizenry of Rome and were held in suspicion by the general population. Tacitus calls the Christian movement "a deadly superstition" and designates the Christians as "criminals." Christians were arrested and convicted, "not so much of the crime of arson, as of hatred of the human race." This latter reference perhaps points to the charges of infanticide and cannibalism that were leveled against Christians on the basis of a misunderstanding (or slander?) of the Eucharist. The church as a cultic community with closed meetings and an exclusivistic theology that declared Christians as the sole possessors of the truth was open for public misunderstanding and ridicule. Tacitus reports that the persecution created sympathy for the sect, since it was carried out "to gratify the cruelty of an individual."

Nero's actions appear to have been the extravagant expressions of a desperate man, a massacre executed through the arbitrary exercise of police action. The persecution was not widespread, and no legal change in the status of Christianity resulted. After Nero's death, the senate nullified all his decrees and condemned his memory—but on the basis of his general rule, not for his slaughter of the Christians.

During the years of Domitian's rule (A.D. 81–96), the lot of the Christians worsened considerably. Under him, the emperor-cult flourished. To most of the Greco-Romans, the public veneration of the emperor, the ascription to him of titles such as "lord" and "savior" and addressing him as "Master and God" were probably little more than expressions of political loyalty. To the Christians, with their faith in Jesus as lord and savior, participation in the imperial cult was pure blasphemy. Their refusal to share in this "emperor-worship" could be interpreted by the officials only as a clear indication of treason. In addition to fostering imperial worship, Domitian banned astrologers and philosophers from Rome in an official edict. Included in this group were apparently oriental cults, among them Christianity. He accused the consul Flavius Clemens and his wife Flavia Domitilla of godlessness. Flavius along with others was executed and his wife was exiled. It has been assumed that they were Christians, but for this there is no absolute evidence. Under Domitian, persecution on religious grounds occurred for the first time in the Roman Empire.

Under Trajan (A.D. 98–117), Christianity seems to have become, for the first time, an officially illegal religion. Apparently there was legislation in this regard. The clearest evidence for the persecution of Christians during this period is contained in correspondence between Pliny, imperial legate in Bithynia and Pontus, and Trajan.[8] Pliny wrote to the emperor (ca. A.D. 112) requesting a statement of policy in regard to Christians and their persecution. He asked such questions as the following: Is there any differentiation to be made on the basis of age? Is a person to be granted pardon if he repents (recants Christianity)? Does merely the possession of the name "Christian" constitute a crime or does one have to persecute on the basis of crimes connected with the name? According to Pliny's correspondence, a defendant who pleaded guilty was cus-

---

[8] Pliny and Trajan exchanged dozens of letters, some of these referring to Christian persecution. For a selection of these, see Bettenson, *Documents of the Christian Church*, pp. 3–6.

The Roman Forum was the center of civic activities in Rome. It contained numerous temples to Roman gods, basilicas for the transaction of banking and law, and triumphal arches and imperial buildings. Rome was lauded by the poets as "the home of the gods," "the queen of the cities," and "the epitome of the world."

FOREIGN MISSION BOARD, SBC

tomarily condemned without witnesses. Before being executed, the defendant was questioned three times about his confession and was offered the chance to recant. Christians who were Roman citizens were sent to Rome to stand trial. One could recant by cursing Christ and offering a libation before the imperial statue. Pliny's investigations had not produced, to his own satisfaction, evidence about the secret crimes committed by Christians. Pliny's uneasiness about the situation had been aggravated by the appearance of an anonymous pamphlet containing the names of supposed Christians. Some people on the list denied being Christians, though some confessed to having once been Christians. (Apparently someone may have seen the persecution as an opportunity to rid the community of some of its citizens; perhaps his debtors or enemies?)

Trajan responded by saying that there was no general rule to be followed universally. Christians, however, should not be sought out; they must be accused and convicted. Liberation and full pardons should be granted if a Christian denied his faith and made this plain by worshiping the gods. Persons accused, convicted, and unwilling to recant were to be punished. Unsigned lists should not be admitted as evidence in trials of Christians.

Ignatius, the bishop of Antioch, was martyred during Trajan's reign. On his way to Rome, he wrote to the Roman church and spoke of his coming death and of his expectation to be devoured by wild beasts. With Ignatius, one can see the interpretation of martyrdom as the supreme and noblest form of witness. He spoke of being ground by the teeth of the animals like "the wheat of God" in order to become "the pure bread of Christ."

The relationship between the Christians and the Empire is discussed in several of the New Testament writings. The attitude of Christians toward the state varied from time to time depending on the circumstances. Paul had recommended obedience to the governing authorities as representatives of the

The Colosseum was begun by Vespasian and finished by his son Titus as a public arena. Capable of seating 50,000, the colosseum was often used for gladiatorial contests, and many Christians went to their death as part of the entertainment offered to spectators in the later years of the Empire.

power and will of God (Rom. 13:1–7; see above, pp. 415–416). The Gospel of Mark contains traditions which argue that persecution is inevitable for the Christian and he must endure it with faith and fortitude (Mark 8:34–38; 13:9–13; both these passages in their present form reflect a developed, perhaps post-Neronian, situation).

The First Letter of Peter insists that Christians must honor and obey the state even in times of tension and urges them to live in such a way that no possible charge of wrongdoing can be sustained against them.

Maintain good conduct among the Gentiles, so that in case they speak against you as wrongdoers, they may see your good deeds and glorify God on the day of visitation. Be subject for the Lord's sake to every human institution, whether it be to the emperor as supreme, or to governors as sent by him to punish those who do wrong and to praise those who do right. For it is God's will that by doing right you should put to silence the ignorance of foolish men. Live as free men, yet without using your freedom as a pretext for evil; but live as servants of God. Honor all men. Love the brotherhood. Fear God. Honor the emperor. (I Peter 2:12–17.)

The letter assumes that Christians will suffer for the sake of righteousness but it recommends that persecution be accepted with patience, forgiveness, and love (I Peter 3:9–17). The Christian is to endure suffering and "the fiery ordeal," looking upon these as a participation in the suffering of Christ (I Peter 4:12–19). I Peter speaks of being "reproached for the name of Christ" and recommends that "if one suffers as a Christian, let him not be ashamed, but under that name let him glorify God" (I Peter 4:14, 16). This suggests the development of a persecution or at least public harassment merely for bearing the name "Christian."

One of the purposes of Luke-Acts seems to have been to dispel any fear of Christianity as a subversive element in Roman society. The nonrevolutionary nature of the activities of both Jesus and the early Christians as well as the protective role that Roman officials had sometimes played toward Christians are emphasized. Roman authorities are shown frequently rendering a verdict that declares Jesus and the Christians to be innocent, not guilty of being lawbreakers (see Luke 23:1–25; Acts 16:35–39; 18:12–17; 21:27–40; 25:1–12). Such evidence was intended to show that Christian faith and loyalty to the Roman Empire are not necessarily contradictory.

The persecution of the Christian faith, either officially or unofficially, presented the Christians with the possibility of renouncing the faith as the means to escape suffering and hostility. One of the purposes of The Letter to the Hebrews was to deal with exactly this problem. The letter was written in a time of actual or threatened persecution.[9] The writer refers to the fact that the recipients of his letter had not yet had to face fierce persecution. "In your struggle against sin you have not yet resisted to the point of shedding your blood" (Heb. 12:4). The Christians had already passed through one serious trial, the description of which sounded somewhat reminiscent of Nero's persecution.

Recall the former days when, after you were enlightened, you endured a hard struggle with sufferings, sometimes being publicly exposed to abuse and affliction, and sometimes being partners with those so treated. For you had compassion on the prisoners, and you joyfully accepted the plundering of your prop-

---

[9] The date, origin, and authorship of Hebrews are all unknown. The discovery of a writing from Qumran that portrays Melchizedek as a heavenly redeemer figure similar to the one in Hebrews would suggest an origin in an area familiar with Essene thought (Alexandria perhaps?). On the Qumran text, see Joseph A. Fitzmyer, S.J., "Further Light on Melchizedek from Qumran Cave 11," *Journal of Biblical Literature*, LXXXVI (1967), pp. 25–41.

erty, since you knew that you yourselves had a better possession and an abiding one. (Heb. 10:32–34.)

They were now confronted with the possibility of renewed and open hostility. Judging from the content of the letter, some Christians were giving up their faith to return to Judaism. The writer presents the Christian church in terms of Israel in the wilderness where times and conditions were difficult and many "murmured" wishing to give up the march to the Promised Land and return to Egypt. His readers would have seen the parallelism. The author then proceeds to show the superiority of the church on the way to the Israel in the wilderness.

The Letter to the Hebrews is throughout an exhortation to Christians to remain in the faith and not to give up the common life (Heb. 10:23–25). The author warns his readers that to give up the faith is to separate oneself from salvation; a renunciation of Christianity opens the way to judgment and closes the door of repentance (Heb. 10:26–39; 12:1–17).

> For it is impossible to restore again to repentance those who have once been enlightened, who have tasted the heavenly gift, and have become partakers of the Holy Spirit, and have tasted the goodness of the word of God and the powers of the age to come, if they then commit apostasy, since they crucify the Son of God on their own account and hold him up to contempt. For land which has drunk the rain that often falls upon it, and brings forth vegetation useful to those for whose sake it is cultivated, receives a blessing from God. But if it bears thorns and thistles, it is worthless and near to being cursed; its end is to be burned. (Heb. 6:4–8.)

A unique attitude toward the Roman Empire is found in the book of Revelation. This writing has had a controversial history of interpretation within the life of the Christian church. It has often been interpreted, as has most apocalyptic literature, as a document containing, in a veiled manner, predictions concerning the course of history until the final consummation. The book is widely and properly understood today within the context of early Christianity. Written in exile on the isle of Patmos (Rev. 1:9), the book is probably to be dated to the reign of Domitian. During the latter's rule, a new temple to the emperor was constructed in Ephesus. Apparently the desire of Domitian to purge the Empire of unpatriotic religions was taken in great earnestness in parts of Asia Minor, and the persecution of Christianity was carried out with a vengeance. In Revelation, Rome is presented as the very embodiment of the demonic forces of evil, the new Babylon to the people of God. The writer looks forward with eager anticipation to the imminent divine judgment and vengeance against those who persecute the chosen (Rev. 6:9–11; 7:13–14; 13:1–18; 14:8–12; 17:1–18). This picture of an all-out conflict between Rome backed by Satan and the church supported by Christ was of course never an actuality. Like the apocalyptic Book of Daniel in the Old Testament, the apocalyptic book of Revelation envisioned the struggles of the times as a cosmic battle between God and evil and in both of these, the final victory was just beyond the horizon, but already dawning.

THE DELAY OF THE PAROUSIA

Jesus had proclaimed the imminence of the Kingdom of God. The early church had preached that Jesus would soon return as the Son of Man in judgment. Paul shared this same hope, assuming that the Parousia would occur during his own lifetime. In the postapostolic age, the delay of the Parousia brought about a serious crisis in the life and faith of the church. In one way or another, most of the New Testament writings from this period attempt to deal with this problem. Four viewpoints seem to have been current.

Some Christians clung persistently to the eschatological fervor of the apostolic age, insisting that the Lord's coming was near at hand. This view is expressed throughout the apocalyptic book of Revelation, where the persecution in Asia Minor during the days of Domitian was taken as the prelude to the end. The great and final battle of Armageddon (Rev. 16:16) was just around the corner. Rev., ch. 17, shows how the writer of this book viewed the unfolding of history moving toward its end. This chapter concerns the judgment of Rome, which is described as "the great whore," "the woman sitting upon the scarlet beast" that had seven heads and ten horns. The seven heads represented the seven hills (of Rome) and the seven emperors. These seven emperors are described as follows: "five of whom have fallen" (Augustus, Tiberius, Caligula, Claudius, and Nero), "one is" (Vespasian), "the other has not yet come, and when he comes he must remain only a little while" (Titus, who ruled only two years). There is an eighth beast "that was and is not" for "it belongs to the seven." The last reference denotes that the writer produced his work under the eighth king (Domitian) but pretended to be writing during the time of the sixth (Vespasian). His description of the eighth as one of the seven implies that he considered Domitian in his persecution of the Christians to be "Nero returned." The idea that Nero had not died (he had committed suicide during a period of revolt and anarchy) but would return to Rome at the head of a Parthian army was current in the Empire and actual pretenders ("pseudo Neros") did put in appearances. The writer of Revelation took up this idea and interpreted Domitian as the returned Nero. In Rev. 13:18, the number of the beast is said to be six hundred, sixty-six. Nero Caesar spelled in Hebrew has this numerical value (n + r + o + n + q + s + r = 50 + 200 + 6 + 50 + 100 + 60 + 200 = 666). The eighth emperor was to appear with the ten horns (the ten Parthian provincial kings) and wage war upon the Lamb (Christ) but would be defeated. After this, Babylon (Rome) would fall and the New Jerusalem would be established on earth and the apocalyptic scheme played out (Rev., chs. 18 to 22).

Others in the church, instead of retaining confidence in the apocalyptic end, seem to have given up their faith in the Parousia and concluded that the belief of the first Christians had been erroneous. Evidence for this position is found in II Peter, which contains a rebuttal of this attitude.

First of all you must understand this, that scoffers will come in the last days with scoffing, following their own passions and saying, "Where is the promise of his coming? For ever since the fathers fell asleep, all things have continued as they were from the beginning of creation." (II Peter 3:3–4.)

The writer reaffirms the idea of the coming end but argues that it must be seen in a proper perspective.

But do not ignore this one fact, beloved, that with the Lord one day is as a thousand years, and a thousand years as one day. The Lord is not slow about his promise as some count slowness, but is forbearing toward you, not wishing that any should perish, but that all should reach repentance. But the day of the Lord will come like a thief, and then the heavens will pass away like a loud noise, and the elements will be dissolved with fire, and the earth and the works that are upon it will be burned up. (II Peter 3:8–10.)

A third viewpoint in regard to the Parousia is represented by those who reinterpreted the church's eschatological hope. This is most clearly seen in the Gospel of John, where the emphasis was placed not on the future coming of the Kingdom but on the significance of Jesus' first coming. The real hope of the Christian, escape from judgment and the possession of eternal life, is presented as a present reality, as a present possession (John 3:16–21, 36; 5:24; 6:47, 53–54; 12:31–32; 17:3). One might call this a "realized eschatology," but even in the Gospel of John there is still an element of a future eschatology (John 5:25–29; 6:54). However, with the first appearance of Jesus, his resurrection, and the coming of the Holy Spirit, the essentials of the eschatological age have been already realized.

The viewpoint that finally prevailed in most quarters, however, was the belief that Jesus himself would return sometime in the future, but that this event might be farther away than the first Christians had believed (II Thess. 2:1–12; II Peter 3:3–15; Luke 12:35–40; 17:22–37). The delay of the Parousia meant that the early church had to adjust to a continuing, even if temporary, existence in the world as it was. The church had to formulate its faith and develop structures that would ensure its continuity and survival.

THE PROBLEM OF FALSE TEACHINGS

The letters of Paul provide clear evidence not only of the great diversity but also of the theological tensions that existed in the early church. All Paul's writings, except for Romans and Philemon, are addressed to situations in which there were either misunderstandings about Paul's gospel or there were opponents who sought to discredit his preaching and to proclaim a "more excellent way."

One of the first problems that developed within the early church revolved around the question of the observance of the Jewish Torah. Even within the church at Jerusalem, there seems to have been tension over the question of Christianity's relationship to Jewish history, life, and institutions (Hellenists versus Hebrews). On the one hand, Hellenistic Christianity with Paul as its most eloquent spokesman advocated a Christianity free from the Jewish law. The major faction in the church in Jerusalem and no doubt many Hellenistic

Jews advocated Christianity "as a form of Judaism" that did not abrogate the law. Churches that were under the influence of both Gentile and Jewish Christianity were involved in tensions over this question. This is clearly evidenced by Paul's discussion of his confrontation with Peter at the church in Antioch after Peter ceased sharing meals with the Gentiles when "certain men came from James" (Gal. 2:11–14). One can wonder how typical this case may have been but it was certainly far from being an isolated "unfortunate incident." [10] "Judaized" Christianity and Gentile Christianity, apart from the law, existed within the church for at least a generation. However, the picture of the early church as torn between these two struggling elements with each attempting to sabotage the other is completely unhistorical. Evidence in Paul's letters and in the apostolic council illustrates the efforts made to preserve peace and good relations between the mother church in Jerusalem (and Jewish Christianity) and the rapidly expanding Gentile church. The collection that Paul took up in Gentile churches for the Christians in Jerusalem was an effort to symbolize the unity of Christians just as the annual half-shekel tax paid to the Jerusalem Temple symbolized the unity of Judaism.[11]

The church's first real theological problem then was to work out the question of Christianity's continuity and discontinuity with Judaism, its observance or nonobservance of the Jewish Torah.[12] Jewish Christianity accepted the total continuity of Christianity and Judaism. Paul's answer to this problem was to affirm the continuity between Judaism and Christianity through his use of Abraham but to deny the continuity of the law. For the writer of Hebrews, Judaism was simply a lower form of Christianity, or to put it differently, Christianity was a higher form of Judaism. The problem was soon partially submerged because Christianity became more and more a Gentile religion and Jewish Christianity became an isolated sect. The problem resurfaced in a new form in the early second century over the issue of the Old Testament as Christian Scripture.

The major problem of "false teaching" in the church came not from the influence of Judaism but from the world of Greco-Roman syncretism. Disputes growing out of the amalgamation of Christianity with syncretistic thought and variant interpretations of the faith had already developed during Paul's lifetime. These gained momentum in the late first and early second centuries and eventually forced the church in the third and fourth centuries to make some rather final and binding decisions regarding what was and what was not "orthodox" or acceptable to Christian teaching. During the postapostolic age, however, the church possessed neither the structure nor the criteria for making such binding decisions. Much of what we know about these "false teachings" is to be found

---

[10] Walther Schmithals, *Paul and James*, tr. by D. M. Barton (London: SCM Press, Ltd., 1965), uses this as the title of one of his chapters. This work is an important contribution to the study of the early church and especially of the question of Paul's opponents. It is a far more reasonable attack of the older so-called "Tübingen School" approach to this problem than Johannes Munck's *Paul and the Salvation of Mankind*, tr. by Frank Clarke (John Knox Press, 1959).

[11] See Nickle, *The Collection*, pp. 74–99.

[12] See Sandmel, *The First Christian Century*, pp. 172–174.

in the New Testament in writings that opposed them. Often, then, we are acquainted with only the arguments used against the "false teachers" and not with a full description of their thought.

The kinds of teachings that seem to have presented the most serious challenge to what later triumphed as the orthodox or "catholic" Christianity can be treated together under the general heading of Gnosticism. As was noted earlier Gnosticism as a fully developed system does not appear until the second century A.D. Many of its features however can be recognized in various syncretistic movements even before the beginning of Christianity.

> There is one element which binds all the various systems together. This is the doctrine, to a considerable extent shared with Jewish apocalyptic writers of the period, that the world is bad; it is under the control of evil or ignorance or nothingness. It cannot be redeemed; indeed, for some Gnostics the world is the equivalent of hell. Only the divine spark, which somehow is imprisoned in some men, is capable of salvation.[13]

This Gnostic attitude toward the world and salvation, or ideas similar to it, was the main source of theological conflict in the postapostolic church.

The theological disputes associated with "Gnostic tendencies" are reflected in the letter to the Colossians,[14] the pastoral epistles (I and II Timothy, Titus),[15] and the Johannine letters (I, II, and III John). These writings refer to "the philosophy and empty deceit" (Col. 2:8), "the doctrines of demons" (I Tim. 4:1), and "the godless chatter and contradictions of what is falsely called knowledge" (I Tim. 6:20) that were espoused by the "antichrists" (I John 2:18), "the false prophets" (I John 4:1), "many deceivers" (II John 7), and "liars whose consciences are seared" (I Tim. 4:2).

The false teachers are attacked in these writings on three primary issues: their understanding of Christ (Christology), their misunderstanding of the nature of Christian ethics, and their overemphasis on realized eschatology. All of these can be viewed as rooted in Gnostic concepts.

The Christological arguments opposed in these letters seem to have either identified Christ as one of the elemental spirits of the universe and/or denied his real incarnation, the fact that Jesus was human. According to second-century Gnostic thought, the heavenly world was separated into a number of spheres ruled over by elemental powers. A similar idea appears to be the back-

---

[13] Robert M. Grant, ed., *Gnosticism: A Sourcebook of Heretical Writings*, p. 15.

[14] Paul's authorship of Colossians is generally accepted throughout the English-speaking world and denied by most German scholars. Whoever the author was, the writing shows the development of false teachings based on a fairly developed form of syncretism or gnosticism. This of course does not mean that Paul could not have written it, for Paul had encountered and argued against similar false teachings at Corinth. See Robert M. Grant, *Historical Introduction to the New Testament*, pp. 204–206.

[15] More and more scholars are advocating the non-Pauline origin of the pastorals. The basic work in English on the problem is P. N. Harrison, *The Problem of the Pastoral Epistles* (Oxford: Humphrey Milford, 1921). Objections to Paul's authorship rest on (1) arguments of language and style; (2) the assumed historical situation; (3) the character of the false teachings; and (4) the theology and church development reflected in the letters. It is possible that the letters (especially II Timothy) do incorporate fragments of genuine farewell letters of Paul.

ground of the heresy attacked in Colossians. The writer, himself using Gnostic thought and terminology, points out that Christ is "the image of the invisible God, the first-born of all creation" and "in him all the fulness of God was pleased to dwell" (Col. 1:15, 19). In other words, Christ is no subordinate power among others; in everything he is "pre-eminent" (Col. 1:18). In Christ is "hid all the treasures of wisdom and knowledge" (Col. 2:3). Not only is Christ not to be considered some elementary universal power but he is actually the victor over the principalities and powers, for in the crucifixion he disarmed and triumphed over these, freeing man from their powers (Col. 2:8–15). The Christian is no longer in servitude "to the elemental spirits of the universe" nor should he worship these angelic powers or consider Christ to be one of them (Col. 2:16–20).

In the Johannine letters, the Christological fallacy appears to have been what is called "docetism," the view that Christ was purely a spiritual being who had descended from heaven to earth but had only appeared (docetism is from the Greek word meaning "to seem" or "to appear") to assume human existence. A quotation giving a description of a second-century Gnostic view of Jesus will make clear this type of thought.

> Jesus was born not of a virgin but of Joseph and Mary, like all other men, and he became more righteous, more prudent, and more wise than all. After his baptism, from the Absolute Sovereignty above all the Christ descended upon him in the form of a dove; then he proclaimed the unknown Father and worked miracles. At the end, the Christ withdrew from Jesus; Jesus suffered and was raised, but the Christ remained impassible, since he was spiritual.[16]

In such thought, a radical differentiation is made between the human Jesus and the heavenly Christ, who merely "used" the real Jesus. The heavenly Christ is not human, does not become flesh, is impassible, and does not suffer.

I John was addressed to a situation that had apparently experienced a schism in the church and a withdrawal from the congregation of some of its members (I John 2:19). The question at issue, seemingly, was the interpretation of Jesus as the incarnate Christ. "Who is the liar but he who denies that Jesus is the Christ? This is the antichrist, he who denies the Father and the Son" (I John 2:22). The writer assures his audience that it is only a false prophet who would deny that Jesus has come in the flesh (I John 4:1–6). "Every spirit which confesses that Jesus Christ has come in the flesh is of God" (I John 4:2; see II John 7). Some members of the congregation being addressed had claimed a superior *gnōsis* about Jesus (I John 2:4) which led to a denial of his humanity. Against these the author argues that the true *gnōsis* is the orthodox view: Jesus was Christ in the flesh.

In addition to the Christological false teaching, the pastorals and the Johannine writings condemn the ethical theories of their opponents. Gnosticism, with its idea of the absolute evil of the world, could lead to two extreme forms of ethical life. On the one hand, "asceticism" could be advocated which, because the world and flesh were bad, stressed the renunciation of all things associated

---

[16] From Robert M. Grant, ed., *Gnosticism: A Sourcebook of Heretical Writings*, p. 41.

with the flesh. On the other hand, the idea that the Gnostic had already been saved from the world could lead to "antinomianism" which advocated no moral restrictions at all since nothing in this evil world could taint him who possessed the heavenly gnōsis. Both of these positions are attacked.

The ascetic attitude is noted in Colossians and I Timothy. The former refers to those who "pass judgment on you in questions of food and drink or with regard to a festival or a new moon or a sabbath" (Col. 2:16). There were those who advocated "self-abasement" and defined what one could handle, touch, or taste (Col. 2:18–23). I Timothy mentions those who advocated celibacy and vegetarianism (I Tim. 4:1–3). Against such attitudes, the writers stressed the freedom of the Christian from the elemental spirituals and special regulations (Col. 2:16–22), the ineffectiveness of asceticism controlling the flesh (Col. 2:23), and the goodness of creation which declared that everything created by God is good and nothing is to be rejected if taken in a spirit of thanksgiving and consecration (I Tim. 4:4–5).

Antinomian attitudes (already encountered by Paul at Corinth) are attacked in I John and Titus. The former argues that the "one who knows him" will obey his commandments and abide by the commandment to love one another. He who disobeys the commandments and claims to know God is a liar (I John 2:1–17). Love of God is to be shown through love of one another (I John 4:7–21). Titus reprimands the false teachers for a failure to profess God through their deeds (Titus 1:10–16) and advocates a Christian life that is sober, upright, and godly, a model of good deeds (Titus, ch. 2).

Some Christians claimed that the hopes of the faith, the eschatological blessings, were a reality in the present and thus denied the future resurrection (II Tim. 2:18). The emphasis in this form of teaching stressed "realized eschatology" to the point of declaring that the resurrection was past already, that resurrection was identical to their time of faith and enlightenment.

Throughout the literature dealing with false teachings, the writers emphasize the "orthodox faith," or correct belief, and argue that this faith has been passed down through proper tradition and that its authenticity has been guaranteed by a succession of witnesses who testify to its truthfulness. With these two emphases, the church was moving toward preserving and ensuring an orthodox faith. The emphasis on tradition would lead to the acceptance of authentic and trustworthy written expressions of the faith. This would eventually lead to the creation of a New Testament canon. The second emphasis on authentic witnesses to the faith would lead to the development of an institutional church whose official ministers would oversee the authentic faith.[17]

THE DEVELOPMENT OF THE INSTITUTIONAL CHURCH

The delay of the Parousia, the expansion of the Christian faith, the death of the first and second generations of Christians, and the development of false teachings within the church all contributed to the development of a more

---

[17] On these elements, see Talbert, *Luke and the Gnostics*, pp. 57–70.

institutionalized church or "early catholicism." In this early catholicism, interest focused not only on the content of faith and the proper ethical life but also on the structures of leadership that would ensure their orthodoxy. In some respect, practically every New Testament writing is concerned with this issue. Even Paul, in his attacks on his opponents and in his exposition of the "true gospel," was arguing for a correct belief (orthodoxy) and opposing "false gospels" (heresy).[18] His quotations of early church tradition as in I Cor. 11:23-26 and I Cor. 15:3-7, his appeal to himself as an apostle of authority as in the letter to the Galatians, and his appeal to the content of his previous letters as in II Corinthians and Philippians contain many of the elements that were to characterize early catholicism—church tradition, authoritative leaders, and written expressions of faith (as well as credos).

The various stages in the development of an established church leadership or hierarchy of ministry cannot be clearly defined.[19] The development in Gentile Christianity differed from that of the mother church in Jerusalem, where kinship to Jesus was a dominant, if not the overriding, qualification. The Gospels were already concerned with the question of authority although Mark less so than the others.[20] Matthew placed the life of the church under the authority of Christian torah and Peter. Luke-Acts stressed the importance of authorized men who were authentic witnesses to the tradition. John emphasized the divine guidance of the community by the Holy Spirit that would lead the church into all truth. (I John is concerned with the testing of the spirit.)

By the time the pastoral letters were written, a fairly structured system of church officials had developed or was being advocated. These letters refer to the office of bishop and to deacons and stipulate the qualifications of each (I Tim. 3:1-13; Titus 1:7-9). Reference is also made to elders (I Tim. 5:1, 17-19; Titus 1:5-6) but the relationship between deacon and elder is not certain. The greeting in Phil. 1:1 had also referred to bishops and deacons. I Tim. also describes the "widow" and the qualifications of that office (I Tim. 5:3-16). The "status of widow" was apparently a church office and may have been equivalent to deaconess, a title that occurs only in Rom. 16:1. (Pliny's correspondence with Trajan mentions two deaconesses.)

References to ordination by the "laying on of hands" appear not only in the Acts account of the setting aside of the seven (Acts 6:1-6) but also in II Tim. 1:6.

These officers and ministers in the church are charged with passing on the traditions that have been received (II Tim. 2:1-7), with handling the "word of truth" (II Tim. 2:15), with correcting the opponents (heretics, vs. 24-25), and with the appointment of "elders in every town" (Titus 1:5-6).

---

[18] See Ernst Käsemann, "Paul and Early Catholicism," in his *New Testament Questions of Today*, pp. 236–251.

[19] See Eduard Schweizer, *Church Order in the New Testament*, tr. by Frank Clarke (London: SCM Press, Ltd., 1961) for the best discussion.

[20] See Sandmel, *The First Christian Century*, pp. 183–185.

BIBLIOGRAPHY

Books marked with an asterisk (*) are available in paperback editions either as originals or as special reprints.

A. History of the Bible and Biblical Studies

Blackman, E. C., *Biblical Interpretation*. The Westminster Press, 1959.

Bruce, F. F., *The English Bible*. Oxford University Press, Inc., 1961.

*Fuller, Reginald H., *The New Testament in Current Study*. Charles Scribner's Sons, 1962.

*Grant, Robert M., *A Short History of the Interpretation of the Bible*, rev. ed. The Macmillan Company, 1963.

Greenslade, S. L., *et al.*, eds., *The Cambridge History of the Bible*, Vols. I–III. Cambridge: Cambridge University Press, 1963–1970.

*Hahn, Herbert F., *The Old Testament in Modern Research*, expanded ed., with a survey of recent literature by Horace D. Hummel. Fortress Press, 1966.

Hunter, A. M., *Interpreting the New Testament 1900–1950*. London: SCM Press, Ltd., 1951.

Hyatt, J. Philip, ed., *The Bible in Modern Scholarship*. Abingdon Press, 1965.

MacGregor, Geddes, *A Literary History of the Bible: From the Middle Ages to the Present Day*. Abingdon Press, 1968.

*Neill, Stephen, *The Interpretation of the New Testament, 1861–1961*. Oxford University Press, Inc., 1964.

*Rowley, H. H., *The Old Testament and Modern Study*. Oxford University Press, Inc., 1951.

Wood, James D., *The Interpretation of the Bible: A Historical Introduction*. London: Gerald Duckworth & Co., Ltd., 1958.

B. General Introductions to the Bible

Black, Matthew, and Rowley, H. H., eds., *Peake's Commentary on the Bible*, 2d ed. Thomas Nelson & Sons, 1962.

Brown, R. E., S.S.; Fitzmyer, Joseph A., S.J.; and Murphy, R. E., O. Carm.; eds., *The Jerome Biblical Commentary*. Prentice-Hall, Inc., 1968.

467

*Grant, F. C., and Rowley, H. H., eds., *Hastings Dictionary of the Bible*, 2d ed. Charles Scribner's Sons, 1963.

*Koch, Klaus, *The Book of Books: The Growth of the Bible*, tr. by Margaret Kohl. The Westminster Press, 1969.

*―― *The Growth of the Biblical Tradition: The Form-Critical Method*, tr. by S. M. Cupitt. Charles Scribner's Sons, 1969.

McCasland, S. Vernon, *The Religion of the Bible*. Thomas Y. Crowell Company, 1960.

McKenzie, John L., S.J., *Dictionary of the Bible*. The Bruce Publishing Company, 1965.

Rowley, H. H., ed., *A Companion to the Bible*, 2d ed. Edinburgh: T. & T. Clark, 1963.

*Wright, G. Ernest, and Fuller, Reginald H., *The Book of the Acts of God*. Doubleday & Company, Inc., 1960.

C. Geographies and Atlases

Aharoni, Yohanan, *The Land of the Bible*, tr. by A. F. Rainey. The Westminster Press, 1967.

*―― and Avi-Yonah, Michael, *The Macmillan Bible Atlas*. The Macmillan Company, 1968.

Baly, Denis, *Geographical Companion to the Bible*. McGraw-Hill Book Company, Inc., 1963.

*―― *The Geography of the Bible*. Harper & Brothers, 1957.

Grollenberg, L. H., *Atlas of the Bible*, tr. by J. M. H. Reid and H. H. Rowley. Thomas Nelson & Sons, 1956.

*May, Herbert G., ed., *Oxford Bible Atlas*. Oxford University Press, Inc., 1962.

Rowley, H. H., *The Modern Reader's Bible Atlas*. Association Press, 1961.

*Smith, George Adam, *The Historical Geography of the Holy Land*. Harper Torchbooks, 1966.

Wright, G. Ernest, and Filson, Floyd V., *The Westminster Atlas to the Bible*, rev. ed. The Westminster Press, 1956.

D. Non-Biblical Source Materials

*Barrett, Charles K., *The New Testament Background: Selected Documents*. Harper Torchbooks, 1961.

*Charles, Robert H., ed., *The Apocrypha and Pseudepigrapha of the Old Testament in English*, 2 vols. Oxford University Press, Inc., 1913.

*Danby, Herbert, *The Mishnah: Translated from the Hebrew with Introduction and Brief Explanatory Notes*. Oxford University Press, Inc., 1933.

Grant, F. C., *Ancient Roman Religion*. The Liberal Arts Press, 1957.

―― *Hellenistic Religions: The Age of Syncretism*. The Liberal Arts Press, 1953.

Grant, Robert M., *Gnosticism: A Sourcebook of Heretical Writings from the Early Christian Period*. Harper & Brothers, 1961.

Hennecke, Edgar, *New Testament Apocrypha*, 2 vols., ed. by Wilhelm Schnee-melcher, English tr. ed. by R. McL. Wilson. The Westminster Press, 1963–1964.

*Herford, R. Travers, ed., *The Ethics of the Talmud: Sayings of the Fathers*. Schocken Books, Inc., 1962.

*Montefiore, C. G., and Loewe, H., eds., *A Rabbinic Anthology*. Meridian Books, 1963.

Pritchard, James B., ed., *Ancient Near Eastern Texts*, 3d ed. Princeton University Press, 1969.

*Thomas, D. Winton, *Documents from Old Testament Times*. Harper Torchbooks, 1958.

E. Introductions to the Old Testament

Anderson, Bernhard W., *Understanding the Old Testament*, 2d ed. Prentice-Hall, Inc., 1966.

Anderson, George W., *A Critical Introduction to the Old Testament*. London: Gerald Duckworth & Co., Ltd., 1959.

Bentzen, Aage, *Introduction to the Old Testament*, 2d ed. Copenhagen: G. E. C. Gad Publisher, 1952.

Buck, Harry M., *People of the Lord*. The Macmillan Company, 1965.

Eissfeldt, Otto, *The Old Testament: An Introduction*, tr. by Peter R. Ackroyd. Harper & Row, Publishers, Inc., 1965.

Flanders, Henry Jackson, Jr.; Crapps, Robert Wilson; and Smith, David Anthony; *People of the Covenant: An Introduction to the Old Testament*. The Ronald Press Company, 1963.

Fohrer, Georg, *Introduction to the Old Testament*, tr. by David E. Green. Abingdon Press, 1968.

Gottwald, Norman K., *A Light to the Nations*. Harper & Brothers, 1959.

Harrelson, Walter, *Interpreting the Old Testament*. Holt, Rinehart and Winston, Inc., 1964.

Harrison, Roland K., *Introduction to the Old Testament*. Wm. B. Eerdmans Publishing Company, 1969.

Jensen, Joseph, O.S.B., *God's Word to Israel*. Allyn and Bacon, Inc., 1968.

Larue, Gerald A., *Old Testament Life and Literature*. Allyn and Bacon, Inc., 1969.

Moriarty, Frederick L., *Introducing the Old Testament*. The Bruce Publishing Company, 1960.

Pfeiffer, Robert H., *Introduction to the Old Testament*. Harper & Brothers, 1948.

*Robert, A., and Feuillet, A., eds., *Introduction to the Old Testament*, tr. by P. W. Skehan, *et al.* Doubleday & Company, Inc., 1970.

Sandmel, Samuel, *The Hebrew Scriptures: An Introduction to Their Literature and Religious Ideas*. Alfred A. Knopf, Inc., 1963.

Weiser, Artur, *The Old Testament: Its Formation and Development*, tr. by D. M. Barton. Association Press, 1961.

F. Israelite History and Archaeology

*Albright, W. F., *Archaeology and the Religion of Israel*. Doubleday & Company, Inc., 1970.

*—— *The Archaeology of Palestine*, rev. ed. Penguin Books, 1960.

*—— *The Biblical Period from Abraham to Ezra*. Harper Torchbooks, 1963.

*Alt, Albrecht, *Essays on Old Testament History and Religion*, tr. by R. A. Wilson. Doubleday & Company, Inc., 1967.

Bright, John, *A History of Israel*. The Westminster Press, 1959.

Bruce, F. F., *Israel and the Nations: From the Exodus to the Fall of the Second Temple*. Wm. B. Eerdmans Publishing Company, 1963.

*Campbell, Edward F., Jr., and Freedman, David N., eds., *The Biblical Archaeologist Reader*, II. Doubleday & Company, Inc., 1964.

*Ehrlich, Ernst Ludwig, *A Concise History of Israel*, tr. by James Barr. Harper Torchbooks, 1965.

Freedman, David N., and Greenfield, J. C., eds., *New Directions in Biblical Archaeology*. Doubleday & Company, Inc., 1969.

*Harrison, Roland K., *The Archaeology of the Old Testament*. Harper Torchbooks, 1967.

*Kenyon, Kathleen M., *Archaeology in the Holy Land*, 2d ed. Frederick A. Praeger, Inc., Publisher, 1965.

—— *Jerusalem: Excavating 3000 Years of History*. McGraw-Hill Book Company, Inc., 1967.

Maly, Eugene H., *The World of David and Solomon*. Prentice-Hall, Inc., 1966.

McKenzie, John L., S.J., *The World of the Judges*. Prentice-Hall, Inc., 1966.

Myers, Jacob M., *The World of the Restoration*. Prentice-Hall, Inc., 1968.

Newman, Murray, *The People of the Covenant*. Abingdon Press, 1962.

Noth, Martin, *The History of Israel*, 2d ed., tr. rev. by Peter R. Ackroyd. Harper & Brothers, 1960.

—— *The World of the Old Testament*, tr. by V. I. Gruhn. Fortress Press, 1966.

Rowley, H. H., *From Joseph to Joshua*. Oxford University Press, Inc., 1950.

Thomas, D. Winton, ed., *Archaeology and Old Testament Study*. Oxford University Press, Inc., 1967.

*Weber, Max, *Ancient Judaism*, tr. and ed. by Hans H. Gerth and Don Martindale. The Free Press of Glencoe, 1952.

*Wright, G. Ernest, ed., *The Bible and the Ancient Near East*. Doubleday & Company, Inc., 1961.

*—— and Freedman, D. N., eds., *The Bible Archaeologist Reader*, I. Doubleday & Company, Inc., 1961.

*—— *Biblical Archaeology*, abridged ed. The Westminster Press, 1962.

G. Israelite Religion and Theology

Ackroyd, Peter R., *Exile and Restoration: A Study of Hebrew Thought of the Sixth Century B.C.* The Westminster Press, 1968.

*Albrektson, Bertil, *History and the Gods: An Essay on the Idea of Historical*

Events as Divine Manifestations in the Ancient Near East and in Israel. Lund: CWK Gleerup, 1967.

Albright, W. F., *From the Stone Age to Christianity: Monotheism and the Historical Process,* 2d ed. Doubleday & Company, Inc., 1957.

*—— *Yahweh and the Gods of Canaan.* Doubleday & Company, Inc., 1968.

*Buber, Martin, *The Prophetic Faith.* Harper Torchbooks, 1960.

*Clements, Ronald E., *God and Temple: The Idea of the Divine Presence in Ancient Israel.* Fortress Press, 1965.

*Eichrodt, Walther, *Theology of the Old Testament,* 2 vols., tr. by J. A. Baker. The Westminster Press, 1961–1967.

*Hillers, D. R., *Covenant: The History of a Biblical Idea.* The Johns Hopkins Press, 1969.

*Johnson, Aubrey R., *Sacral Kingship in Ancient Israel,* 2d ed. Cardiff: University of Wales Press, 1967.

*Kraus, Hans-Joachim, *Worship in Israel,* tr. by Geoffrey Buswell. John Knox Press, 1966.

*Mowinckel, Sigmund, *He That Cometh: The Messiah Concept in the Old Testament and Later Judaism.* Abingdon Press, 1956.

Muilenburg, James, *The Way of Israel: Biblical Faith and Ethics.* Harper Torchbooks, 1966.

Noth, Martin, *The Laws in the Pentateuch and Other Essays,* tr. by D. R. Ap-Thomas. Fortress Press, 1967.

*Pedersen, Johannes, *Israel: Its Life and Culture,* Vols. I–IV. Oxford University Press, Inc., 1926–1940.

*von Rad, Gerhard, *Old Testament Theology,* 2 vols., tr. by D. M. G. Stalker. Harper & Row, Publishers, Inc., 1962–1965.

*—— *The Problem of the Hexateuch and Other Essays,* tr. by E. W. Trueman Dicken. McGraw-Hill Book Company, Inc., 1966.

Rowley, H. H., *The Relevance of Apocalyptic,* rev. ed. London: Lutterworth Press, 1963.

*—— *Worship in Ancient Israel.* Fortress Press, 1967.

Russell, D. S., *The Method and Message of Jewish Apocalyptic.* The Westminster Press, 1964.

*de Vaux, Roland, O.P., *Ancient Israel: Its Life and Institutions,* tr. by John McHugh. McGraw-Hill Book Company, Inc., 1961.

—— *Studies in Old Testament Sacrifice.* Cardiff: University of Wales Press, 1964.

*Vriezen, Th. C., *An Outline of Old Testament Theology,* tr. by S. Neuijen. Oxford: Basil Blackwell, 1958.

—— *The Religion of Ancient Israel,* tr. by Hubert Hoskins. The Westminster Press, 1967.

*Wright, G. Ernest, *God Who Acts: Biblical Theology as Recital.* London: SCM Press, Ltd., 1952.

*Zimmerli, Walther, *The Law and the Prophets: A Study of the Meaning of the Old Testament,* tr. by Ronald E. Clements. Harper Torchbooks, 1967.

H. The Prophets

*Clements, Ronald E., *Prophecy and Covenant*. London: SCM Press, Ltd., 1965.

Gottwald, Norman K., *All the Kingdoms of the Earth: Israelite Prophecy and International Relations in the Ancient Near East*. Harper & Row, Publishers, Inc., 1964.

Heschel, Abraham J., *The Prophets*. Harper & Row, Publishers, Inc., 1962. Available in an abridged paperback (Harper Torchbooks, 1969).

Hyatt, J. Philip, *Prophetic Religion*. Abingdon Press, 1957.

Johnson, Aubrey R., *The Cultic Prophet in Ancient Israel*, 2d ed. Cardiff: University of Wales Press, 1962.

Lindblom, Johannes, *Prophecy in Ancient Israel*. Fortress Press, 1962.

*McKane, William, *Prophets and Wise Men*. London: SCM Press, Ltd., 1965.

*von Rad, Gerhard, *The Message of the Prophets*, tr. by D. M. G. Stalker. London: SCM Press, Ltd., 1968.

*Scott, R. B. Y., *The Relevance of the Prophets*, rev. ed. The Macmillan Company, 1968.

Vawter, Bruce, C. M., *The Conscience of Israel: Pre-exilic Prophets and Prophecy*. Sheed & Ward, Inc., 1961.

Westermann, Claus, *Basic Forms of Prophetic Speech*, tr. by H. C. White. The Westminster Press, 1967.

I. Intertestamental History and Theology

*Bickermann, Elias, *From Ezra to the Last of Maccabees*. Schocken Books, Inc., 1962.

Black, Matthew, *The Scrolls and Christian Origins*. Charles Scribner's Sons, 1961.

*Charles, Robert H., *Eschatology: The Doctrine of a Future Life in Israel, Judaism and Christianity*, with an introduction by G. W. Buchanan. Schocken Books, Inc., 1963.

*Cross, Frank M., Jr., *The Ancient Library of Qumran*, rev. ed. Doubleday & Company, Inc., 1961.

Driver, Godfrey R., *The Judaean Scrolls*. Oxford: Basil Blackwell, 1965.

*Dupont-Sommer, André, *The Essene Writings from Qumran*, tr. by Géza Vermes. Meridian Books, Inc., 1962.

Farmer, W. R., *Maccabees, Zealots, and Josephus*. Columbia University Press, 1956.

Foerster, Werner, *From the Exile to Christ*, tr. by Gordon E. Harris. Fortress Press, 1964.

Guignebert, Charles, *The Jewish World in the Time of Jesus*. University Books, 1959.

Mansoor, Menahem, *The Dead Sea Scrolls*. Wm. B. Eerdmans Publishing Company, 1964.

Metzger, Bruce M., *An Introduction to the Apocrypha*. Oxford University Press, Inc., 1957.

Milik, Jósef T., *Ten Years of Discovery in the Wilderness of Judaea*, tr. by J. Strugnell. London: SCM Press, Ltd., 1959.

*Moore, G. F., *Judaism in the First Centuries of the Christian Era*, 2 vols. Harvard University Press, 1927.

Pfeiffer, Robert H., *History of New Testament Times with an Introduction to the Apocrypha*. Harper & Brothers, 1949.

*Plöger, Otto, *Theocracy and Eschatology*, tr. by S. Rudman. John Knox Press, 1968.

*Reicke, Bo, *The New Testament Era: The World of the Bible from 500 B.C. to A.D. 100*, tr. by David E. Green. Fortress Press, 1968.

Ringgren, Helmer, *The Faith of Qumran*, tr. by E. T. Sander. Fortress Press, 1963.

Sandmel, Samuel, *Herod: Profile of a Tyrant*. J. B. Lippincott Company, 1967.

Stendahl, Krister, ed., *The Scrolls and the New Testament*. Harper & Brothers, 1957.

*Tarn, W. W., *Hellenistic Civilisation*, 2d ed. Meridian Books, Inc., 1964.

Tcherikover, Victor, *Hellenistic Civilization and the Jews*, tr. by S. Applebaum. The Jewish Publication Society of America, 1959.

*Vermes, Géza, *The Dead Sea Scrolls in English*. Penguin Books, 1962.

Zeitlin, Solomon, *The Rise and Fall of the Judaean State*, 2 vols. The Jewish Publication Society of America, 1962–1967. A third volume is to be published.

J. Introductions to the New Testament

Crapps, Robert Wilson; McKnight, Edgar V.; and Smith, David Anthony; *Introduction to the New Testament*. The Ronald Press Company, 1969.

*Davies, W. D., *Invitation to the New Testament*. Doubleday & Company, Inc., 1966.

*Enslin, Morton Scott, *The Literature of the Christian Movement*. Harper Torchbooks, 1956.

Feine, Paul; Behm, Johannes; and Kümmel, W. G.; *Introduction to the New Testament*, tr. by A. J. Mattill, Jr. Abingdon Press, 1966.

*Fuller, Reginald H., *A Critical Introduction to the New Testament*. London: Gerald Duckworth & Co., Ltd., 1966.

*Grant, Robert M., *The Formation of the New Testament*. Harper & Row, Publishers, Inc., 1965.

———— *Historical Introduction to the New Testament*. Harper & Row, Publishers, Inc., 1963.

Kee, Howard Clark; Young, Franklin W.; and Froehlich, Karlfried; *Understanding the New Testament*, 2d ed. Prentice-Hall, Inc., 1965.

*Marxsen, Willi, *Introduction to the New Testament*, tr. by Geoffrey Buswell. Fortress Press, 1968.

*Moule, C. F. D., *The Birth of the New Testament*, 2d ed. Harper & Row, Publishers, Inc., 1966.

Price, James L., *Interpreting the New Testament*. Holt, Rinehart and Winston, Inc., 1961.

Robert, A., and Feuillet, A., eds., *Introduction to the New Testament*, tr. by P. W. Seehan, *et al.* Desclee Company, 1965.

*Sandmel, Samuel, *A Jewish Understanding of the New Testament*. University Publishers, Inc., 1960.

Spivey, Robert A., and Smith, Dwight Moody, Jr., *Anatomy of the New Testament*. The Macmillan Company, 1969.

Tenney, Merrill C., *New Testament Survey*, rev. ed. Wm. B. Eerdmans Publishing Company, 1961.

*Wikenhauser, Alfred, *New Testament Introduction*. Herder & Herder, 1963.

K. The Early Church

Brandon, S. G. F., *The Fall of Jerusalem and the Christian Church*, 2d ed. London: S.P.C.K., 1957.

*Bultmann, Rudolf, *Primitive Christianity in its Contemporary Setting*, tr. by Reginald H. Fuller. Meridian Books, 1956.

Caird, G. B., *The Apostolic Age*. London: Gerald Duckworth & Co., Ltd., 1955.

*Cullmann, Oscar, *Early Christian Worship*, tr. by A. S. Todd and J. B. Torrance. London: SCM Press, Ltd., 1953.

————— *The Early Church*, ed. by A. J. B. Higgins. The Westminster Press, 1956.

*————— *The State in the New Testament*, rev. ed. Charles Scribner's Sons, 1963.

*Elliott-Binns, L. E., *Galilean Christianity*. London: SCM Press, Ltd., 1956.

Filson, Floyd V., *A New Testament History*. The Westminster Press, 1964.

*Frend, W. H. C., *Martyrdom and Persecution in the Early Church*. Doubleday & Company, Inc., 1967.

*Funk, Robert W., ed., *Apocalypticism:* Vol. 6 of *Journal for Theology and the Church*. Herder & Herder, 1969.

Grant, Robert M., *The Sword and the Cross*. The Macmillan Company, 1955.

*Hahn, Ferdinand, *Mission in the New Testament*, tr. by Frank Clarke. London: SCM Press, Ltd., 1965.

*Lietzmann, Hans, *The Beginnings of the Christian Church*, 3d ed., tr. by B. L. Woolf. London: Lutterworth Press, 1953.

*Moule, C. F. D., *Worship in the New Testament*. John Knox Press, 1961.

Sandmel, Samuel, *The First Christian Century in Judaism and Christianity: Certainties and Uncertainties*. Oxford University Press, Inc., 1969.

Schoeps, Hans-Joachim, *Jewish Christianity: Factional Disputes in the Early Church*, tr. by D. R. A. Hare. Fortress Press, 1969.

*Weiss, Johannes, *Earliest Christianity*, 2 vols., tr. by F. C. Grant. Harper Torchbooks, 1959.

L. New Testament Theology

*Bultmann, Rudolf, *Theology of the New Testament*, 2 vols., tr. by Kendrick Grobel. Charles Scribner's Sons, 1951–1955.

*Conzelmann, Hans, *An Outline of the Theology of the New Testament*, tr. by John Bowden. Harper & Row, Publishers, Inc., 1969.

*Cullmann, Oscar, *The Christology of the New Testament*, rev. ed., tr. by S. C. Guthrie and C. A. M. Hall. The Westminster Press, 1963.

—— *Salvation in History*, tr. by S. G. Sowers. Harper & Row, Publishers, Inc., 1965.

Fuller, Reginald H., *The Foundations of New Testament Christology*. Charles Scribner's Sons, 1965.

*Hahn, Ferdinand, *The Titles of Jesus in Christology*, tr. by H. Knight and George Ogg. The World Publishing Company, 1969.

*Kramer, Werner, *Christ, Lord, Son of God*, tr. by Brian Hardy. London: SCM Press, Ltd., 1966.

Lindars, Barnabas, *New Testament Apologetic*. The Westminster Press, 1961.

*Moule, C. F. D., *The Significance of the Message of the Resurrection for Faith in Jesus Christ*, tr. by D. M. Barton and R. A. Wilson. London: SCM Press, Ltd., 1968.

*Richardson, Alan, *An Introduction to the Theology of the New Testament*. Harper & Row, Publishers, Inc., 1958.

Schnackenburg, Rudolf, *New Testament Theology Today*, tr. by David Askew. Herder & Herder, 1963.

Schweizer, Eduard, *Lordship and Discipleship*. London: SCM Press, Ltd., 1960.

M. The Synoptic Gospels

Bacon, B. W., *Studies in Matthew*. Henry Holt & Co., 1930.

Barrett, Charles K., *Luke the Historian in Recent Study*. London: The Epworth Press, 1961.

*Beare, Frank W., *The Earliest Records of Jesus*. Abingdon Press, 1962.

Bornkamm, Günther; Barth, Gerhard; and Held, Heinz J.; *Tradition and Interpretation in Matthew*, tr. by Percy Scott. The Westminster Press, 1963.

Briggs, R. C., *Interpreting the Gospels*. Abingdon Press, 1969.

Bultmann, Rudolf, and Kundsin, Karl, *Form Criticism*, tr. by F. C. Grant. Harper Torchbooks, 1962.

*—— *History of the Synoptic Tradition*, 2d ed., tr. by John Marsh. Harper & Row, Publishers, Inc., 1968.

*Conzelmann, Hans, *The Theology of St. Luke*, tr. by Geoffrey Buswell. Harper & Row, Publishers, Inc., 1961.

*Dodd, C. H., *The Parables of the Kingdom*, rev. ed. Charles Scribner's Sons, 1961.

Farmer, W. R., *The Synoptic Problem*. The Macmillan Company, 1964.

*Fuller, Reginald H., *Interpreting the Miracles*. The Westminster Press, 1963.

Grant, Frederick C., *The Gospels: Their Origin and Growth*. Harper & Brothers, 1957.

Gundry, R. H., *The Use of the Old Testament in St. Matthew's Gospel*. Leiden: E. J. Brill, 1967.

*Higgins, A. J. B., *Jesus and the Son of Man*. Fortress Press, 1965.

Jeremias, Joachim, *The Parables of Jesus*, rev. ed., tr. by S. H. Hooke. Charles Scribner's Sons, 1963. Available in an abridged paperback edition as *Rediscovering the Parables*. Charles Scribner's Sons, 1966.

Keck, Leander E., and Martyn, J. Louis, eds., *Studies in Luke-Acts*. Abingdon Press, 1966.

Manson, T. W., *The Sayings of Jesus*. London: SCM Press, Ltd., 1949.

———— *Studies in the Gospels and Epistles*, ed. by Matthew Black. The Westminster Press, 1962.

*———— *What Is Redaction Criticism?* Fortress Press, 1969.
1948.

Marxsen, Willi, *Mark the Evangelist*, tr. by James Boyce *et al.* Abingdon Press, 1969.

Perrin, Norman, *The Kingdom of God in the Teaching of Jesus*. The Westminster Press, 1963.

———— *Rediscovering the Teaching of Jesus*. Harper & Row, Publishers, Inc., 1967.

*———— *What Is Redaction Criticism?* Fortress Press, 1969.

*Robinson, James M., *The Problem of History in Mark*. London: SCM Press, Ltd., 1957.

Rohde, Joachim, *Rediscovering the Teaching of the Evangelists*, tr. by D. M. Barton. The Westminster Press, 1968.

Schnackenburg, Rudolf, *God's Rule and Kingdom*, tr. by J. Murray. Herder & Herder, 1963.

Stendahl, Krister, *The School of Saint Matthew*. Fortress Press, 1968.

Streeter, B. H., *The Four Gospels: A Study of Origins*, rev. ed. Macmillan & Co., Ltd., 1930.

Talbert, Charles H., *Luke and the Gnostics*. Abingdon Press, 1966.

Tödt, Heinz E., *The Son of Man in the Synoptic Tradition*, tr. by D. M. Barton. The Westminster Press, 1965.

N. The Quest for the Historical Jesus

*Anderson, Hugh, ed., *Jesus*. Prentice-Hall, Inc., 1967.

———— *Jesus and Christian Origins*. Oxford University Press, Inc., 1964.

Braaten, Carl E., and Harrisville, Roy A., trs. and eds., *The Historical Jesus and the Kerygmatic Christ: Essays on the New Quest of the Historical Jesus*. Abingdon Press, 1964.

*Fuchs, Ernst, *Studies on the Historical Jesus*, tr. by Andrew Scobie. London: SCM Press, Ltd., 1964.

*Kümmel, W. G., *Promise and Fulfilment: The Eschatological Message of Jesus*, tr. by D. M. Barton. London: SCM Press, Ltd., 1957.

McArthur, H. K., *The Quest Through the Centuries*. Fortress Press, 1964.

*———— ed., *In Search of the Historical Jesus*. Charles Scribner's Sons, 1969.

Reuman, John, *Jesus in the Church's Gospels*. Fortress Press, 1968.

*Robinson, James M., *A New Quest of the Historical Jesus*. London: SCM Press, Ltd., 1959.

Saunders, Ernest W., *Jesus in the Gospels*. Prentice-Hall, Inc., 1967.

*Schweitzer, Albert, *The Quest of the Historical Jesus*, tr. by W. Montgomery with an introduction by James M. Robinson. The Macmillan Company, 1968.

O. Portrayals of the Historical Jesus

*Bornkamm, Günther, *Jesus of Nazareth*, tr. by I. and F. McLuskey with James M. Robinson. Harper & Brothers, 1960.
*Brandon, S. G. F., *Jesus and the Zealots*. Charles Scribner's Sons, 1967.
Bultmann, Rudolf, *Jesus and the Word*, tr. by L. P. Smith and E. H. Lantero. Charles Scribner's Sons, 1958.
Enslin, Morton Scott, *The Prophet from Nazareth*. Schocken Books, Inc., 1967.
Guignebert, Charles, *Jesus*, tr. by S. H. Hooke. University Books, 1956.
Klausner, Joseph, *Jesus of Nazareth: His Life, Times, and Teaching*, tr. by H. Danby. Beacon Press, Inc., 1964.
Stauffer, Ethelbert, *Jesus and His Story*, tr. by R. and C. Winston. Alfred A. Knopf, Inc., 1960.
Taylor, Vincent, *The Life and Ministry of Jesus*. Abingdon Press, 1955.

P. Paul and the Pauline Epistles

Beardslee, W. A., *Human Achievement and Divine Vocation in the Message of Paul*. London: SCM Press, Ltd., 1961.
Bouttier, Michel, *Christianity According to Paul*, tr. by Frank Clarke. London: SCM Press, Ltd., 1966.
*Davies, W. D., *Paul and Rabbinic Judaism*, 2d ed. Harper Torchbooks, 1967.
*Dibelius, Martin, *Paul*, ed. by W. G. Kümmel, tr. by Frank Clarke. The Westminster Press, 1953.
*Dodd, C. H., *The Meaning of Paul for Today*. Meridian Books, Inc., 1957.
Furnish, Victor Paul, *Theology and Ethics in Paul*. Abingdon Press, 1968.
*Hunter, A. M., *The Gospel According to St. Paul*. The Westminster Press, 1967.
———— *Paul and His Predecessors*, rev. ed. The Westminster Press, 1961.
Klausner, Joseph, *From Jesus to Paul*, tr. by W. F. Stinespring. Beacon Press, Inc., 1961.
Munck, Johannes, *Paul and the Salvation of Mankind*, tr. by Frank Clarke. John Knox Press, 1959.
*Nock, Arthur Darby, *St. Paul*. Harper Torchbooks, 1963.
*Sandmel, Samuel, *The Genius of Paul*. Schocken Books, Inc., 1970.
*Schmithals, Walther, *Paul and James*, tr. by D. M. Barton. London: SCM Press, Ltd., 1965.
Schoeps, Hans-Joachim, *Paul: The Theology of the Apostle in the Light of Jewish Religious History*, tr. by H. Knight. The Westminster Press, 1961.
*Schweitzer, Albert, *Paul and His Interpreters*, tr. by W. Montgomery. Schocken Books, Inc., 1964.
Selby, Donald J., *Toward the Understanding of St. Paul*. Prentice-Hall, Inc., 1962.

Q. The Gospel of John

Brown, R. E., S.S., *The Gospel According to John (i–xii)*. Doubleday & Company, Inc., 1966. An additional volume to be published.

Dodd, C. H., *Historical Tradition in the Fourth Gospel*. Cambridge: Cambridge University Press, 1963.

*———— *The Interpretation of the Fourth Gospel*. Cambridge: Cambridge University Press, 1953.

Howard, W. F., *The Fourth Gospel in Recent Criticism and Interpretation*, rev. by Charles K. Barrett. London: The Epworth Press, 1955.

Käsemann, Ernst, *The Testament of Jesus: According to John 17*, tr. by G. Krodel. Fortress Press, 1968.

Martyn, J. Louis, *History and Theology in the Fourth Gospel*. Harper & Row, Publishers, Inc., 1968.

Sidebottom, E. M., *The Christ of the Fourth Gospel*. London: S.P.C.K., 1961.

Smith, Dwight Moody, Jr., *The Composition and Order of the Fourth Gospel*. Yale University Press, 1965.

INDEXES TO TEXT

INDEXES TO TEXT

SUBJECT INDEX

AUTHOR INDEX

Ackroyd, Peter R., 154, 160, 215, 223, 230, 236, 470
Aharoni, Yohanan, 75, 76, 77, 80, 120, 153, 196, 206, 274, 468
Albrektson, Bertil, 136, 470
Albright, W. F., 55, 58, 84, 85, 99, 102, 103, 200, 236, 470, 471
Alt, Albrecht, 61, 75, 97, 470
Altmann, A., 60
Anderson, Bernhard W., 76, 141, 220, 225, 238, 274, 469
Anderson, George W., 469
Anderson, Hugh, 334, 476
Anderson, R. T., 178
Angus, Samuel, 387
Ap-Thomas, D. R., 12
Astour, Michael C., 31, 60, 171
Avi-Yonah, Michael, 468

Bacon, B. W., 428, 475
Baly, Denis, 35, 468
Barrett, Charles K., 310, 352, 364, 370, 387, 392, 406, 438, 468, 475
Barth, Gerhard, 430, 437, 475
Beardslee, W. A., 477
Beare, Frank W., 369, 375, 381, 475
Behm, Johannes, 401, 403, 438, 451, 473
Bentzen, Aage, 51, 469
Bettenson, Henry, 338, 423, 424, 439, 453, 454
Betz, H. D., 283
Bevan, Edwyn R., 7
Bickermann, Elias, 291, 472
Black, Matthew, 411, 467, 472, 476
Blackman, E. C., 467
Blank, Sheldon H., 181, 207
Bodenheimer, F. S., 70
Boobyer, G. H., 339
Bornkamm, Günther, 334, 430, 437, 475, 477
Bouttier, Michel, 477

Braaten, Carl E., 336, 476
Brandon, S. G. F., 141, 238, 254, 300, 341, 364, 380, 383, 425, 450, 474, 477
Braun, H., 69
Briggs, R. C., 475
Bright, John, 55, 188, 470
Bronson, D. B., 397
Brown, R. E., S.S., 467, 478
Brownlee, W. H., 344
Bruce, F. F., 56, 467, 470
Brueggemann, Walter, 173, 231
Buber, Martin, 471
Buchanan, G. W., 472
Buck, Harry M., 469
Bultmann, Rudolf, 331, 474, 475, 477
Burkill, T. A., 339
Buss, M. J., 88, 168

Caird, G. B., 474
Callaway, Joseph A., 74
Campbell, Edward F., Jr., 58, 74, 470
Carlson, C. E., 335
Case, Shirley Jackson, 9
Cave, C. H., 427
Charles, Robert H., 305, 468, 472
Chase, Mary Ellen, 10
Childs, Brevard S., 65, 188, 205
Clements, Ronald E., 93, 95, 131, 139, 197, 242, 471, 472
Coats, George W., 68, 69
Cohen, Martin A., 424
Conzelmann, Hans, 357, 371, 372, 373, 380, 382, 389, 393, 409, 414, 475
Cooke, Gerald, 128
Crapps, Robert Wilson, 469, 473
Crenshaw, J. L., 247
Cross, Frank M., Jr., 61, 69, 89, 180, 276, 472
Cullmann, Oscar, 9, 324, 364, 413, 434, 452, 474, 475
Currie, S. D., 381

494

BIBLICAL PASSAGES INDEX

WESTMINSTER

Historical Maps of Bible Lands

EDITED BY

G. ERNEST WRIGHT

Parkman Professor of Divinity
The Divinity School, Harvard University

FLOYD V. FILSON

Professor Emeritus of New Testament Literature and History
McCormick Theological Seminary

TABLE OF MAPS

MAP INDEX

3